FINANCIAL INSTITUTIONS, MARKETS, AND ECONOMIC ACTIVITY

McGRAW-HILL SERIES IN FINANCE

McGRAW-HILL FINANCE GUIDE SERIES

Tim S. Campbell

PROFESSOR OF FINANCE
UNIVERSITY OF UTAH

FINANCIAL INSTITUTIONS, MARKETS, AND ECONOMIC ACTIVITY

McGraw-Hill Book Company

New York St. Louis San Francisco Auckland Bogotá
Hamburg Johannesburg London Madrid Mexico
Montreal New Delhi Panama Paris São Paulo
Singapore Sydney Tokyo Toronto

This book was set in Melior by Better Graphics.
The editors were Bonnie E. Lieberman and Edwin Hanson;
the designer was Joan E. O'Connor;
the production supervisor was Charles Hess.
The drawings were done by Fine Line Illustrations, Inc.
R. R. Donnelley & Sons Company was printer and binder.

FINANCIAL
INSTITUTIONS, MARKETS,
AND ECONOMIC
ACTIVITY

5 6 7 8 9 0 DODO 8 9 8 7 6 5

ISBN 0-07-009691-0

Library of Congress Cataloging in Publication Data

Campbell, Tim S.
Financial institutions, markets, and economic activity.

(McGraw-Hill series in finance)
Includes index.
1. Finance. 2. Financial institutions.
3. Finance—United States. 4. Financial institutions—United States. I. Title. II. Series.
HG173.C27   332   81-8237
ISBN 0-07-009691-0   AACR2

CONTENTS

v

PREFACE

In recent years a course in financial markets has not often been a key part of the finance curriculum. There seem to be at least two reasons for this. One reason is that until relatively recently the explosive progress in developing an analytical theory of finance largely left behind financial institutions and, therefore, much of the material of a financial markets course. In the minds of many, the financial institutions area became a weak sister to portfolio theory and corporate finance. At the same time, a territorial dispute between "finance" and "money and banking" has persisted which has often left financial markets classes at loose ends. The task of developing the background material on markets which is important for financial and investment decision making has often been left to the money and banking class, but this material has often been only tangentially related to the more traditional of these classes.

The tide may now be turning for the financial markets course. There is growing appreciation of the idea that if the individual decision-making skills emphasized in corporate finance are to be fully developed, the student needs a more thorough understanding of the operation and structure of financial markets than has often been available in the past. Moreover, in the past few years there has been a substantial increase in academic research which approaches the issues pertaining to financial institutions from the vantage point of financial theory. This complements the traditional literature on financial institutions which is grounded in macroeconomics. In fact, there has been a considerable integration of macroeconomics and finance in the literature. However, these contributions have not yet been presented in a way that is easily accessible to the student or to the professor who is not intimately familiar with this literature but who is interested in restructuring his or her course. At the same time, an increasing number of those who teach courses in money and banking have become dissatisfied with the almost exclusive preoccupation of that course with commerical banks and the Federal Reserve System. They are gradually beginning to think of the issues addressed in money and banking as logically fitting into a broader outline which treats a more diversified package of issues concerning the operation of financial markets.

This book is directed toward filling this gap. The analysis developed here has clear foundations in neoclassical price theory, the theory of finance, and macroeconomics. The book is intended to serve for a course in financial markets which easily integrates with courses in corporate finance, investments, and capital market theory or for a course in money and banking which is not too narrowly focused on macroeconomic issues and monetary policy. The course and the book might be used in almost any sequence with these other courses. The book may be best suited for hybrid course labeled "Financial Markets and Economic Activity" which draws from the theory of finance, traditional money and banking, and the economics of regulation. Hopefully, the logical appeal of this organization and approach will make the hybrid course the course of the future.

The principal purpose of the book is to bring modern economic and financial theory to bear on the organization and behavior of financial markets and institutions. Its purpose is institutional, but it draws heavily on theory. Every effort is made to present theory which is useful in terms of the insight it offers and to develop it in a concise and direct manner. The only prerequisite for the student to understand the material is an introductory-level treatment of economics, particularly microeconomics. The book is oriented toward teaching the student to understand applied price theory and to be able to examine the financial world with the tools it affords.

This book is divided into five parts. The first develops the microeconomic foundations of financial markets and explains the determination of the value of real and financial assets in capital markets. After an introductory chapter which explains some basic price-theoretic concepts about value and markets, there is a chapter which develops the impact of time on the value of assets. This chapter contains much traditional material on present value. The emphasis in the present value material is not on computational skill but on the conceptual problem of valuing returns distributed over time. The next two chapters deal with uncertainty and the value of assets. The first of these chapters examines how investment decisions should be made under uncertainty. Initially, the discussion concentrates on choices between mutually exclusive investments. Then it shows how diversification affects the risk and return on a portfolio of assets. The next chapter explains the rudiments of the capital asset pricing model. The chapter also contains a critique and appraisal of the usefulness of this model which is designed to prepare the reader for an encounter (from some other source) with alternative models, such as the arbitrage pricing model. This division of the material makes it possible to introduce the reader to the valuation of risky investment and the role of diversification, without having to deal with the capital asset pricing model. The final chapter in Part I deals with value determination when information abouts returns is costly. Recent insights into the role of heterogeneous expectations and asymmetric information in financial markets are explained here. In addition, the topic of market efficiency is introduced. This chapter provides a foundation for some of the later material on the behavior and regulation of financial markets and intermediaries.

Part II develops the theory of the determination of market yields. It begins with a chapter which explains the determinants of the real interest rate and the flow of funds in the economy. The chapter integrates flow of funds analysis with a development of the Fisherian theory of real and nominal interest rates. After this foundation in the theory of interest, attention is directed toward the determination of specific nominal interest rates in the next chapter. The emphasis here is on explaining the distinctions between observed nominal rates and the underlying real rate. This chapter also distinguishes between the segmentation and substitution views of interest-rate determination. Specific determinants of yield spreads are examined and some empirical evidence is reviewed. The segmentation as opposed to substitution theme is carried into the next chapter on the term structure of interest rates. This chapter explains and illustrates the computation of forward rates and then develops the expectations (perfect substitution), as opposed to the segmentation and preferred habitat theories of the term structure of interest rates. The segmentation-substitution approach provides an integrated explanation of the differences in prices of assets which differ by maturity, as well as by other distinguishing characteristics. In addition this section emphasizes rational expectations in explaining the forecasts of inflation rates incorporated in nominal interest rates and forecasts of short-term rates incorporated in long-term rates. It also explains the role of futures markets.

Part III provides a survey of the major types of financial markets and securities in the U.S. economy and develops material on alternative ways in which financial markets are organized. The first chapter analyzes the operation of auction and over-the-counter markets, while the second chapter focuses on the functions of financial intermediaries. The chapter on intermediaries emphasizes the reasons why financial intermediaries play such an important role in our contemporary economy. The final three chapters in this section provide a survey of the markets for consumer, corporate and government borrowing and lending, and the securities issued in these markets. The emphasis here is on explaining the institutional environment and some of the basic trends observable from recent data on these markets. In addition, this section applies the theoretical material developed in the preceding two sections.

Part IV deals with government regulation of financial markets. The first chapter lays the foundation for the detailed analysis of regulation of financial intermediaries as well as auction and over-the-counter markets which is presented in the subsequent four chapters. This chapter explores rationales for regulation based on the desire to promote competition and avoid problems stemming from an imperfect distribution of information. The second chapter of Part IV deals with the regulation of securities markets, with particular emphasis on price competition on the New York Stock Exchange, the evolution of a national market system, and disclosure regulation. The third chapter analyzes the regulation of commercial banks. This chapter seeks to explain why commercial banks have historically been subject to instability and shows how regulation, beginning in the mid-nineteenth century, changed the fundamental nature of the financial contract between a bank and its depositors. In the next chapter the regulatory system governing non-bank financial intermediaries is examined. This chapter covers depository thrift institutions as well as insurance companies and pension funds. Finally, the last chapter analyzes Federal Reserve control of the money supply as an integral part of the regulatory system for financial markets. Part IV seeks to place the recent changes in the regulation of depository institutions in context with the historical evolution of regulation in the United States. It also seeks to explain a theory of regulation, or a logical basis for regulation, as a response to problems in the operation of a competitive market. This makes it possible to evaluate why regulation may or may not be necessary.

Part V deals with financial markets and aggregate economic activity. The first chapter develops the monetarist or the portfolio-adjustment approach to explaining the impact of financial markets on the real economy. This chapter relies heavily on Milton Friedman's arguments about monetary policy and the economy. The next chapter characterizes what has been labeled the post-Keynesian view of the impact of financial markets on the economy as essentially reflecting the cost of credit. The distinctions between the competing theories of financial markets and economic activity are synthesized as depending largely on the degree of efficiency and segmentation in markets. The last chapter of this section examines financial markets and monetary policy in an inflationary economy. Competing theories of inflation and the impact of monetary policy are examined and the role of inflation as a tax is developed. Finally, the performance of debt and equity markets in an inflationary economy is examined. The selectivity of topics exercised in designing this section reflects the view that many of the topics covered in the traditional money and banking course are more logically developed in a macroeconomics class, but that the links between financial markets and aggregate economic activity logically belong to a course in financial markets.

ACKNOWLEDGMENTS

Writing a first book is a painful experience. And while any number of people told me this would be the case before I started, I chose not to listen. With hindsight I have come to believe that those who are inclined to take such warnings seriously are surely the ones who choose not to write their first book. A certain amount of naive self-confidence is essential for a first-time author. But I also discovered that writing a book was a tremendously enlightening and even pleasant experience. Above all else, you acquire a new perspective and insight into your subject matter. But you also learn a tremendous amount about yourself—you find out whether you like the role of commentator but not necessarily whether you are good at it. If you do like it, the pain is probably worthwhile. If you do not, you will not write your second book. I suppose I have learned that I like the role of commentator— after all I am referring to this as my first book.

I want to thank all those people who warned me about the pain, though I will not list all their names. I also want to thank those people who helped me with the manuscript and provided support in other ways once I decided to ignore the words of caution. The first person who shared any of my thoughts about this book was Paul Boltz. His early encouragement was especially valuable. My student at that time, and more recently coauthor, William Kracaw also provided very valuable early encouragement as well as numerous helpful suggestions as the manuscript emerged. A number of other individuals read early chapters, provided stiff criticism, but encouraged me to proceed. They include Richard Bookstaber, David Glenn, Ronald Lease, and John McConnell. It was at this point that I actually swallowed the hook.

As the project got underway a number of reviewers began to carefully appraise the entire manuscript. One individual in particular, who was not known to me at the outset, became an invaluable critic. His comments and suggestions were always helpful and insightful. As time went on I learned his identity and have been able to thank him personally. His name is Kim Dietrich. A number of other individuals provided additional valuable commentary. They include Robert Edmister, University of Maryland; Owen Gregory, University of Illinois Chicago Circle Campus; Robert Johnston, George Mason University; Paul Nadler, Rutgers University; Arnold Sametz, New York University; Charlene Sullivan, Purdue University; and Raymond Torto, University of Massachusetts.

The editorial staff at McGraw-Hill deserves special thanks. Bonnie Lieberman, the finance editor, has been exceptionally helpful since our first introduction. Chuck D'Ambrosio also read the entire manuscript and provided invaluable comments and suggestions. I also benefited immeasurably from an editorial critique of some early chapters by Mike Elia. It has been exceptionally pleasant to work with the entire McGraw-Hill staff.

A special thanks goes to the College of Business of the University of Utah, which supported me throughout this effort. I especially appreciate the typing job done by Liz Baer over a year and one-half. There are also a sizable number of students who were compelled to use a partially complete manuscript. They deserve my thanks as well as my apology.

Finally, my wife Kathy deserves a public thank you, not only for accepting the ill temper this project sometimes generated but for carefully reading and reviewing every page that I wrote. She was and is simply invaluable.

Tim S. Campbell

FINANCIAL INSTITUTIONS, MARKETS, AND ECONOMIC ACTIVITY

Chapter One

INTRODUCTION

This book is about financial markets—how they work, how they might work better, and, in some instances, how they don't work at all. Of all the markets we might think of in the world, financial markets are one of the most interesting and the most important. They are interesting because they are complicated. It therefore becomes a challenge to figure out how they work. They are also interesting because they seem to hold out the possibility to each of us of making or losing a great fortune. In this sense, they have most (though certainly not all) of the attractions of Las Vegas.

Financial markets are important because they are intimately linked to every other market and every individual in the economy. They provide the mechanism by which every business firm raises funds to carry out its operations. As consumers we all use financial markets in order to improve our personal well-being. Financial markets also provide the mechanism by which we can store our wealth. In other words, the returns we earn in other markets can be stored in the financial markets for future use. The importance of financial markets therefore lies in their linkage with all our spending decisions, both in our personal lives and in the business world.

1

As consumers and personal investors or as business people, we can take either an active or a passive role in financial markets. In fact, this flexibility is one of the beauties of competitive financial markets. If we are passive, we simply consult market prices or rates of return and borrow or invest at the most attractive rates. A well-functioning competitive financial market will assure us that this is an efficient investment. On the other hand, if we want to get more actively involved in the market, we can seek to learn more about the prospective returns on various investments and, in the process, improve the odds a little. In a competitive market we should also expect a fair return on our investment of extra time and effort in learning about investments. The time and energy you spend reading and studying this book is a part of this learning process. From your effort you should expect to acquire sufficient background information so that you can understand how financial markets work.

In this chapter we will have a limited objective. We simply want to get oriented to the major topics we will address and the methodology which will be employed throughout the book. The methodology used in the field of financial economics, of which this subject matter is a part, has exploded in complexity and sophistication in the decade of the 1970s. Relative to the tools and theories used today, those in use more than a decade ago seem extremely crude. This growth in technology has increased our understanding of financial markets and it has also made us more acutely aware of what we still do not understand. In this chapter we will seek to construct a secure enough foundation in the methodology of finance and orientation toward the subject matter of the remaining chapters that you will be able to maximize the return on your investment in information as we proceed through the book.

THE ROLE OF FINANCIAL ASSETS AND MARKETS

A financial asset is a claim on some future income. The asset might be as simple as a Treasury bill which represents a promise by the U.S. Treasury to pay a certain amount, say $10,000, at a specified future date. It might be as complicated as a share of stock in a corporation. This is a promise to pay the holder a portion of the profits earned by the company and not retained for its own investments. A financial market is the place or mechanism whereby financial assets are exchanged and prices of these assets are set.

Throughout this book we will deal with both financial assets and markets. Therefore, it is beneficial if we start out with a clear understanding of the functions served by both the assets and the markets. We have some notion of what assets and markets can do for us as individuals. Probably the most obvious thing is that, if we are lucky, they can make us rich, and, if we are unlucky, they can make us poor. But our interest here is to understand what they can do for the economy. What useful economic functions do financial assets and financial markets serve?

The Two Principal Functions of Financial Assets

Financial assets provide the economy with two services. First, they provide a means by which funds can be transferred from those who have a surplus to those who have profitable investments for those funds. Second, they provide the means to transfer risk from those who seek to undertake investments to those who provide funds for those investments. Therefore, financial assets are the record or the claim which facilitates an exchange of funds and a shift of risk. These two functions are summarized in Figure 1-1.

The first function of financial assets is probably the most obvious. A competitive economy is composed of a number of businesses and individuals which have productive uses for more financial resources than they have on hand at any one time. The variety of these uses is enormous, ranging from high-technology investments undertaken by large corporations to investments in homes by individuals. In all of these investments, if there were no way to obtain funds from other sources, the investment would be impossible to undertake. Hence, the availability of outside resources is crucial to the level of investments and therefore to the level of employment and income in the economy.

These funds are supplied by those in the economy who have fewer profitable investments than they do resources. These entities can profitably lend to those with productive investments if they can receive a reliable promise to share in the returns from those investments. The financial asset represents that promise. It is issued by the user or borrower of funds to the supplier of funds and it represents a claim on that user or on the investment he or she is undertaking. The fact that such assets exist and are exchanged raises the level of income and wealth of the economy as a whole because it means that more productive investment may be undertaken.

Unfortunately, the return on most productive investments cannot be predicted with certainty. As a result, such investments are risky. The incentive to undertake risky investments hinges on how the returns will be distributed or who bears the risk of the investment project. If the party who

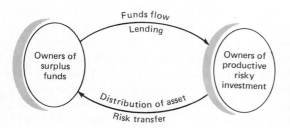

FIGURE 1-1
Principal functions of financial assets. Funds flow from those with a surplus to those who can make productive investments. Those who undertake risky investments transfer risk to those who supply funds.

undertakes the investment bears all the risk, then his or her incentive to engage in the investment may be limited. But if that risk can be redistributed or shared with the suppliers of funds, that is, those who are not actually involved in undertaking the investment, then the incentive to go through with the investment will be enhanced. Financial assets provide the mechanism through which this sharing of risk takes place. Those with excess supplies of funds lend them to those with productive but risky investments. In exchange they receive a financial asset which entitles them to a share of the future return of the investment, but also distributes part of the risk of the investment to them.

The Two Principal Functions of Financial Markets

Financial assets can be created and exchanged between a supplier and user of funds without ever utilizing an organized financial market. But in a developed economy, this is more the exception than the norm. Most assets are exchanged through some kind of financial market. These markets assume widely diverse forms, from public auction markets like the New York Stock Exchange to highly diffused markets like the market for savings deposits from financial intermediaries. But both of these are financial markets where financial assets are exchanged. The markets serve two useful functions above and beyond those served by the assets exchanged in those markets. The first function is that a market provides the holder of an asset with liquidity. The second is that the market reduces the cost of executing transactions.

A market provides liquidity by offering a place or mechanism through which financial assets can be resold or liquidated. Liquidity is an extremely valuable feature for an asset. If an asset is not liquid and cannot be resold, then the only way to receive the value of the asset is to wait to receive the future income promised by the asset. That future income is what makes the asset valuable. But there can often be contingencies when a particular owner of an asset would find it advantageous to pass title to that future income on to someone else in order to collect and make use, today, of the value of that future income. The existence of a market where assets can readily be bought and sold increases the options and flexibility of all market participants. They can either sell or wait, depending upon which promises the greater personal benefit.

In all such exchanges of assets there are costs. These are generally called costs of transacting and costs of contracting. One example of such costs is best understood if you consider the difficulties which would be involved in trying to hunt for the right exchange were there no organized market. Suppose you owned shares of stock in General Motors and you wanted to sell these and buy Exxon. If there were no organized market you would have to go hunting for someone who owned Exxon. Moreover, that person would have to be willing to take General Motors stock in exchange. You might have to resort to placing an ad in the barter column of the newspaper in order to find such a person. The financial market, however, performs this service for you. It reduces your cost of transacting by eliminating the need for you to engage in a costly search for someone who wants to trade what you want for what you have. The market can also reduce the cost of collecting information about the future returns on financial assets and about the activities of those who are undertaking productive investments to ensure that they are acting in your interests. It can also assist in enforcement of the terms of contracts if it is discovered that breaches of contract have occurred.

These two principal functions of a financial market are summarized in Figure 1-2. The figure depicts the same sort of exchange process which was illustrated in Figure 1-1. But now the exchange passes through an organized market. The figure summarizes the fact that the financial market is valuable to those who want to purchase and sell financial assets because it increases the liquidity of assets and reduces the cost of exchanging them.

THE METHODOLOGY OF FINANCIAL ECONOMICS

Financial economics is or tries to be like any science. Its purpose is to understand what is, or to learn what makes the world operate the way it does. This understanding is then used as a basis to improve the world. That is, it leads to prescriptions about how things ought to be done. But unlike the physical sciences, financial economics as well as other branches of economics, deals with the behavior of people in a market economy. This introduces complexities and difficulties in the methodology which other traditional scientific disciplines have not had to deal with. Before we can examine the various theories which will be presented in this book and the available evidence on them, we need to have a firm grasp of the methodology of financial economics.

Positive and Normative Economic Theory

Any theory, particularly an economic theory, can be designed to serve one of two purposes. As a result, there have come to be virtually two types of economic theories, or two types of economics: positive and normative. We

FIGURE 1-2
Principal functions of a financial market: liquidity and reduction of transactions costs.

will cover both positive and normative financial economics in this book and it is important to understand what the difference is.

A normative theory is a procedure or set of rules for accomplishing a stated objective. It is an explanation of what ought to be. For example, one might propose a normative theory of how to play bridge, or bet on the horses, or invest in the stock market. Such a theory would essentially be a strategy for winning or investing successfully. In the case of investing in the stock market the objective might be to maximize your wealth. The theory would then be a set of rules which should lead you to the objective of maximizing wealth. It is a theory as long as it cannot be established that the set of rules in the theory will always lead to the desired objective with perfect certainty. There may, therefore, be competing theories about how to reach a given objective. In bridge, horse racing, and the stock market there are numerous theories of how to prosper. None can be verified with certainty, though some may be rejected more easily than others.

A positive theory is a statement of what is, rather than what ought to be. It is a description of how some part of the observable world works. For example, a positive theory pertaining to the stock market might offer an hypothesis as to how the prices of assets in the market are actually determined. The positive theory in and of itself would not necessarily offer any guidelines for action. Of course, the ultimate usefulness of any positive theory lies in the improvements we can make in the world. That is, we construct positive theories to improve our understanding of how the world works. And we use that understanding to guide our actions and decisions. Therefore, the purpose of positive theory is not purely to improve our understanding. Instead, it is to provide us with a background of information so that we can make better decisions.

It is fairly simple to imagine what a normative theory might look like. It is essentially a "How-to . . ." book with a forecast of a desired result. But it is not always obvious what a positive theory should look like. First of all, a positive theory should serve as a filing system or an outline. That is, a good theory should allow us to organize and classify the things which we observe in the world. In this way it serves to reduce the complexity of the world around us and helps us to divide the world up into manageable parts. But a positive theory must do more. It must make some prediction about observable phenomena. And the prediction must be one that is at least potentially testable. For example, one theory which we will explore in this book is known as Fisherian interest rate theory. In its simplest form the theory says that the interest rates which we observe in the world can be broken into two components. The first is known as the real rate of interest and the second is a premium which is equal to the rate of inflation which the market expects. This is a useful classification or filing system. It helps us decompose what we observe into understandable components. But it is not in itself a prediction of observable phenomena. However, we can add an additional proposition which makes it at least potentially testable. The additional proposition is that the real interest rate is constant through time. This implies that observed changes in interest rates can be accounted for by changes in the anticipated rate of inflation. If we could simply measure the anticipated rate of inflation, then we could test this hypothesis.

Another common feature of positive theories is that they are based on assumptions which are highly unrealistic. Students often find this very troublesome. But it is important to realize that any theory is a simplification of reality, and any simplification must, by its very nature, be unrealistic. The lack of realism of the foundations or assumptions of any theory should not be troublesome in itself. The relevant question is whether the theory makes useful predictions about behavior which is important and observable in the world. Any theory must offer such predictions on the basis of assumptions which are, to some degree, unrealistic. It is best to judge a theory by its predictions rather than by the realism of assumptions. However, good theories, that is, ones which make good predictions, are not often based on assumptions which ignore major ingredients of the real world. A theory with good predictions usually is based on assumptions which incorporate the key features of reality. Such theories still must be simplifications and will therefore appear unrealistic. The trick involved in constructing a good theory is to simplify reality in a way that does not ignore the important elements of the observable world. But the only test of what is important lies in the predictive power of the theory.

In this book we will utilize both positive and normative financial economics. We will lean more heavily on the normative side than many economics texts, but we will lean more heavily on the positive than many business texts. The reason is that our ultimate objective is normative, as is the purpose of any business training. But the immediate focus of this book is on how financial markets work, that is, on positive theories of financial markets.

Empirical Methodology

We have learned that any positive theory must have predictive power. It must include some testable hypothesis. Therefore, the tasks involved in financial economics can be divided into two main categories, constructing the theories and testing them. In this book we will not be doing any actual testing ourselves, but we will review empirical evidence produced by financial economists on a number of hypotheses about financial markets.

As in the physical sciences, the concern with testability has created a need for precision in formulating and stating positive theories. This demand for precision has led to a heavy reliance on mathematics. The benefit of mathematics is that it allows us to be sure that a theory does not suffer from logical faults. All good theories should be able to be stated in words, but it is often beneficial to state the more complicated ones in mathematics as well. The precision of the mathematical expression often makes it possible to come to understand relationships which are too complicated if expressed only in words.

Once an hypothesis is formulated and stated precisely, then it is necessary to attempt to test the hypothesis or verify its prediction. It is important to see that in constructing such tests it is virtually impossible to ever conclusively prove a theory. All we can hope to do is confront the theory with more and more demanding tests and attempt to disprove it. If we discover that a theory survives a number of such tests, then we can begin to have confidence in it. But we can never really establish the *truth* of a theory. The most we can hope for is to fail to disprove it.

Most empirical testing in financial economics is based on classical statistics. This means that the test is designed to discriminate between two competing hypotheses based on the assumptions about probability distributions. For example, returning to our theory about the determinants of observed interest rates, the Fisherian hypothesis says that we can use changes in anticipated inflation to explain changes in observed interest rates. If we could directly measure the anticipated rate of inflation, then we might seek to test this hypothesis by writing an equation which says that the interest rate is determined by the anticipated inflation rate. Such an equation might be written as follows:

$$\text{Interest rate} = a + b \text{ (anticipated inflation rate)}$$

This equation says that we take the anticipated inflation rate, multiply it by the value of b, add this to the value of a, and we should have the interest rate. If we could conduct a controlled experiment, we would allow the inflation rate to increase and observe the resulting interest rate. From our observations we would be able to measure a and b. If we found that b was zero, then we would reject the Fisherian hypothesis. But if it were equal to $+1$, then we would conclude that the Fisherian hypothesis was correct, for the Fisherian hypothesis says that the interest rate is equal to the anticipated rate of inflation plus the real interest rate.

A problem which is common to almost all testing in financial economics is that we cannot conduct controlled experiments. This means that we cannot cause the nation's inflation rate to increase just to see if interest rates will rise by the same amount. Rather, we have to use the evidence which the world offers us and draw what conclusions we can from it. This limitation introduces a host of problems into our empirical testing. It by no means makes most empirical testing impossible, but it does mean we have to use some ingenuity to be able to draw reliable conclusions from the evidence we can get. When we deal with empirical evidence in this book we will discuss some of the limitations on how it should be interpreted.

Many of the theories we will examine in this book are potentially testable and some have been subjected to many tests. But the tests are not completely conclusive. No single theory has been left unscathed by all the tests. This means that there are often competing explanations for observed behavior. This is particularly true regarding the competing theories of how financial markets influence spending decisions in the rest of the economy, and regarding the effects of regulation on financial markets. On both of these issues there are strong schools of thought or advocates of competing theories which often have little in common. When we discuss these topics and others where there are disagreements, we will be particularly interested in isolating the key factors which account for the different theories and assessing the evidence which supports each side. In most cases, it will be impossible to say which school of thought is correct. Our purpose will be to understand both sides of these arguments.

TOPICS COVERED IN THIS BOOK

This book addresses four major topic areas. They can be stated most succinctly as simple questions. These questions are:

1 How are financial assets priced?
2 What are the basic characteristics of the financial markets and institutions operating in the United States today?
3 Why and how are these markets and institutions regulated by the government?
4 How do these financial markets influence the remainder of the economy?

The first question is the subject of the first two parts of the book. In Part One we will examine individual financial assets to determine how they are priced. Then, in Part Two we will examine the determinants of aggregate interest rates or yields in the economy.

Part One is concerned with two principal concepts. The first is how time influences the value of assets. Time is important because every asset is a claim on future income. Therefore, we have to take account of how the time distribution of future income influences the value or price of an asset. The second concept is uncertainty. All of the returns to assets are uncertain. We need to understand how uncertainty influences value.

In Part Two we will examine market interest rates or interest rates on different types of securities. Thus, we will deal with more aggregate assets than in Part One. The central issues which we will examine are essentially the same as in Part One. We will examine the various determinants of market interest rates.

In Part Three we will address the second of the four questions. First, we will examine the possible ways that financial markets can be organized and we will consider some examples of each form of organization. Then we will explore the reasons for the emergence of financial intermediaries as a tremendously important part of our financial system. Finally, we will survey the three major sectors of financial markets: the markets for consumer, business, and government financing. Our emphasis here will be on understanding the institutional details of these markets as well as gaining an appreciation of the major issues in the operation of each market.

In Part Four we will explore the regulatory system for financial markets. We will first concentrate on the economic rationale for regulating financial markets. Then we will analyze the major features of our regulatory system. The regulatory system can be broken into three major parts pertaining to securities markets, commercial banks, and nonbank financial intermediaries. The late 1970s and the 1980s are a time when there is considerable sentiment to deregulate the American economy. This has led to a resurgence of controversy over regulation of financial markets. In the case of financial markets, the current regulatory system has emerged gradually over a century. And it has been easy to lose track of the central reasons for this regulatory system. In this part we carefully examine the evolution and motives for regulation and assess the performance of the system which existed during the 1970s.

Part Five deals with the final question. The three chapters in Part Five seek to explain both sides of a long-standing debate about how financial markets influence spending decisions, national income, inflation, and the level of employment in the economy. The first chapter summarizes what has come to be known as the monetarist view of this subject. The second chapter summarizes the Keynesian view and compares the two. The final chapter concentrates on the central contemporary problem in this debate: the links between financial markets and inflation.

SUMMARY

More than anything else, this book is intended to give the student of finance a sufficient background to be a sophisticated participant in the marketplace. This book is not a practical guide to investing. Nor is it a route map through the complex decisions which a practicing financial manager must make. This book is about the marketplace in which both the investor and the financial manager must operate. It is intended to provide the theory, evidence, and institutional detail that a market participant needs in order to be successful. There are two other factors, skill and luck. You will not learn those from this or any other book.

REFERENCES

Friedman, Milton: "On the Methodology of Positive Economics," *Essays in Positive Economics*, University of Chicago Press, Chicago, 1953.

THE VALUE OF ASSETS

The first part of this book explains how individual assets are valued. The value of an asset is determined by the stream of income which will accrue to that asset in the future. There are two important characteristics of the income stream which determine the value of that asset. The first is the time distribution of income—whether that income will be received in the near or the distant future. The second is the uncertainty surrounding that future in-—or the risk pertaining to the magnitude of that income. These are the concepts which occupy Part One of the book. The first chapter in Part One provides an introduction to the whole issue of value determination. It explains the functions of assets and markets in a competitive economy and it presents an intuitive orientation to the way time and uncertainty influence value. The second chapter in Part One, Chapter Three, deals with time. This chapter presents the concepts of present value and internal rate of return and shows how these concepts are used to value specific financial claims. Chapters Four and Five deal with uncertainty. Chapter Four shows how individual investment decisions are made under uncertainty and how to construct a diversified portfolio of assets. Chapter Five shows how risky assets are valued in a competitive marketplace when investors hold diversified portfolios of assets. Chapter Six looks deeper into the way value is determined by exploring how information about future returns to an asset is generated. This chapter shows how a financial market produces and aggregates information about individual assets. It also introduces the concept of an efficient use of information. Throughout Part One the emphasis is on how *individual* assets are priced in the market. Part Two jumps to a higher level of aggregation and explores the determinants of the value or rate of return on groups of assets such as corporate bonds or municipal bonds.

Chapter Two

INTRODUCTION TO THE
CONCEPT OF VALUE

Value is an arcane concept. The mystery surrounding the concept of value is somewhat similar to the mystery surrounding concepts like truth or honesty or virtue. It is not so much that it is difficult to provide reasonable definitions of these words—we will shortly give value a relatively precise definition— rather, it is that the value of most everything is hard to determine, just as truth, honesty, and virtue are hard to determine. Whenever we buy something—a home, a car, or a tube of toothpaste—we are often left wondering whether we paid a "fair" price. We never seem to satisfactorily answer the question: What is this item really worth? There seems to always remain a mystery to be solved. The search for an answer to this kind of question is like the search for truth. The search has no logical stopping point. The search itself may be fascinating, but practical people are inclined to say: Enough is enough! Yet despite its elusiveness, we must have a way to establish value.

Economists have an ingenious way of coping with this problem, as they do with many others. They invoke an assumption to render it harmless. The assumption is relatively simple. It merely sidesteps the mystery of value by saying that when given a choice between different products at different prices, people are able to choose which they prefer. They do not pause indefinitely, pondering the true value of the assets between which they must choose. When a number of people meet to express these choices, we have what we term a market. The market then determines value. The market merely aggregates the choices of the individual participants. The most useful concept of value is therefore one of "market value." That is, the value of an asset is what the market says it is. Some may feel that the market has improperly valued an asset, that the true value of the asset is not what the market says it is. But, in a very fundamental sense, this misses the point. The true value of an asset is a will-o'-the-wisp. It is no more knowable than truth or virtue. The useful questions are: How do individuals estimate the value of assets and how does the market aggregate their estimates into a market value?

This section of this book is directed toward answering these questions. This chapter explains and illustrates some of the basic concepts which must be understood before individual estimates of value and the operation of the market can be successfully explained. In particular, this chapter is concerned with explaining the difference between the concepts of income, value, and wealth. The intuition of how time and uncertainty affect income, value, and wealth is developed. The remaining chapters of Part One contain a more systematic and analytical treatment of these topics.

INCOME, VALUE, AND WEALTH

Income, value, and wealth are words that are sometimes rather loosely used in everyday conversation. But for the purposes of this book some reasonably precise definitions of the words will prove tremendously useful. It is not so much that it is important to be overly preoccupied with the precision of the definitions, but the distinctions between the meanings of these words are the basis for some of the most important concepts that will be developed in this chapter and used throughout the book.

The two concepts which distinguish these words are the period of *time* and the *claim* or *title* involved. Wealth and *value* refer to a specific point in time and measure what is termed a "stock." Income covers a period of time and measures what is therefore termed a "flow." Of the two stock concepts of wealth and value, value refers to the worth of a particular asset while wealth refers to an individual's or a group of individuals' claim to assets. Value implies nothing about title to an asset, whereas wealth refers to possession. The purpose of a financial market and of financial contracts is to establish and provide for the exchange of claims to the assets and the income which they will generate, and to determine the value of those claims. That is, markets and contracts determine value and title to that value, or wealth.

To understand these concepts more thoroughly it is important to consider more elaborate definitions and some examples for each of the three words: income, value, and wealth.

Income

Income can be defined as compensation received during a period of time. The most important part of this definition is the reference to a period of time, such as an hour, a week, a month, or a year, rather than a point in time, such as December 31, 1982. Because income is a flow and covers a period rather than a point in time, it is measured in dollars per unit of time. When it is necessary to speak of the income for more than one period, then reference is made to a stream of income. For example, a good basketball player may expect to have a useful (i.e., playing) life of 10 years and an expected income of say, $250,000 per year. This would then be called the income stream he or she generates from playing basketball.

It is useful to think of income streams and assets as having a one-to-one relationship. This means that each asset has an income stream, as in the case of the basketball player. And each income stream must be generated by, or belong to, some asset. The income stream therefore provides a compensation to the owner of the asset. It is in this sense that income is defined as a compensation.

The most obvious example of the income which accrues to an asset is the income that a person receives by owning a share of stock in a corporation. That income takes two forms: dividends and capital gains or losses. Dividends are the profits of the firm which are distributed to shareholders at regular intervals. Capital gains and losses are the gains or losses experienced due to increases or decreases in the price of the stock. For example, actual dividends and capital gains or losses for 10 years for IBM are shown in Table 2-1. The final two columns of this table show the income stream for a share of stock expressed in the standard manner of dollars per share and expressed as

TABLE 2-1

IBM Stock Performance Per Share

YEAR	CAPITAL GAINS* ($)	DIVIDEND ($)	TOTAL INCOME ($)	PERCENT RETURN†
1969	.55	.72	1.27	1.94
1970	−5.47	.96	−4.51	−6.84
1971	4.32	1.04	5.36	8.86
1972	10.95	1.08	12.03	18.53
1973	−.80	1.11	.30	.40
1974	−24.40	1.38	−23.10	−30.70
1975	−2.48	1.68	−.86	−1.70
1976	15.90	2.00	17.90	37.24
1977	2.34	3.24	5.58	8.73
1978	1.76	3.02	4.78	7.22

*Capital gain is the change in price of the stock per year. For example, if the stock went from $50 to $55 per share, then the capital gain is $5.
†The percent return is the total income dividend by the price of the stock at the beginning of the period.

a percent of the price of the share of stock or in a rate of return. This kind of income stream can easily be computed for any company such as IBM which is publicly owned and traded.

Another example of compensation to an owner of an asset is the income paid to an individual for services he or she provides. This is the most common usage of the word income. While income is often thought of as a payment for labor services, it is usually only in economic circles that this labor income is thought of as a return on an asset. But, in fact, it is, and the asset is usually called human capital. Human capital is an extremely important part of the entire stock of wealth in the United States.

The income received by human capital often takes a nonpecuniary as well as pecuniary form. This is referred to as a psychic income. It means that the service provided is itself pleasurable and hence, part of the income is the sense of satisfaction or pleasure of doing the job. Forest rangers, artists, and university professors are often thought to have a sizable psychic income. While they are not always included in this group, entrepreneurs may also often receive a sizable psychic as well as pecuniary income.

It may not be reasonable to limit psychic income only to human capital. For example, the value of gold is sometimes thought to include a psychic component. In a world such as the one which exists today where governments do not tie the value of their currencies to gold, some argue that gold should be valued according to its use in jewelry and dental work. But in the latter half of the 1970s the value of gold went well above its use in these types of activities. One explanation for this is that people felt secure holding gold, secure in the sense that if there were a sizable depression, gold would once again be used as a medium of exchange which would not greatly depreciate in value. The price they were therefore willing to pay for gold reflected not only the protection against loss if the economy had a serious collapse but also the ease of mind they acquired by knowing they had this protection, and maybe even some "fad" value.

Another nonpecuniary form of income is often referred to as the service flow from an asset, or "income in kind." For example, an owner-occupied house provides a service flow. But the house pays no cash dividends. Still, the income stream from owning a house can be thought of in the same manner as the income stream from owning a share of common stock in IBM. Both, houses and stocks, however, can provide capital gains and losses. Therefore, the income stream from the house is the service flow plus the capital gain or loss in each period.

Value

The *value* of an asset is the price that the market is willing to pay for title to the income stream which that asset is expected to generate. This definition of value implicitly refers to "market value," which asserts that the only relevant value of an asset is the one which the market determines.

The most straightforward example of the determination of value is the value of a share of common stock. The value of a share is determined by the stream of income which the share is expected to generate. That is, the price of a share represents the capitalized value of the income stream which will accrue to the owner of the asset in the future. By "capitalized" value it is meant that a "stock" rather than a "flow" concept is involved. The capitalized value is the worth of the income stream at a point in time.

The basic idea behind capitalizing an income stream is simply to add up the "discounted" individual flows of income in each period. The word discounted covers a lot of ground. Simply put, each period's income is discounted for time and risk. The problems involved in actually accomplishing this occupy the rest of this section of the book. But the basic principle behind these procedures is simple. When income is uncertain, as is definitely the case with dividends and capital gains, and when it is to be received in the future, then the value of that income today will generally be less than the amount which is actually expected in the future. The difference between the amount expected in the future and its value today represents the amount the income has been discounted. The price of a share of common stock in IBM is essentially determined by what the market expects the income stream from holding that stock will be and the discount the market applies to that stream of income for time and risk.

The definition of value employed here raises some interesting problems for some types of assets, particularly human capital. For very good reasons, which will be explored later, some assets are essentially nonmarketable. That is, no market exists for them and it is impossible to sell them. This is really an extreme example of what we call a "thin" market, one in which assets are traded very infrequently. As the market for an asset becomes thin, it becomes difficult to determine the precise value of that asset at any given point in time. In the extreme case where no trades take place at all, the market provides no quantification of value. The most obvious example of a nonmarketable asset is human capital, or the assets which generate a labor income, or simply, people. People can sell their labor services and receive income. But, with a few exceptions, they cannot sell title to their services over their useful life. At one time in the United States, and in other parts of the world, some people could sell title to the income from another individual's services. This is a market for slaves. But, by and large, individuals cannot sell title to their own services in a market for human capital and never have been able to do so.

One of the interesting questions this raises is: How do you determine the value of human capital? Or even more fundamentally: If value is defined as essentially "market" value and some assets have very thin markets or are nonmarketable, does that mean they have no value? If a person expects to receive a sizable stream of labor income, then his or her human capital is not without value. But the value may not be precisely quantified because there are problems which prevent the market from ever effectively valuing this type of asset. Throughout the book reference will be made to the value of human capital or to human wealth. It should be understood that the procedure for assessing value is still essentially one of discounting the income stream which the asset generates. But the nonmarketability of the asset means that the precise magnitude of this value will be difficult to assess.

Markets are quite capable of capitalizing pecuniary as well as non-pecuniary income. For example, there is a well-organized market which capitalizes the stream of service income provided by residential houses. The price of a house in a real estate market represents this capitalized value. The assets traded in a real estate market are highly nonstandard. That is, each house is a distinct asset which commands a separate price. In some other markets where the income stream from the asset may be partially non-pecuniary, the asset is highly standardized, for example, gold. All gold of the same quality commands the same price.

There is another way to think about value. The distinction is that thus far we have considered what can be called "intrinsic" value. That is, value is defined by the income stream generated by an asset. The alternative can be labeled "relative" value. That is, assets which are identical should have the same value. Another way of putting this is to say that the value of an asset is determined by the value of close substitutes. If close substitutes diverge in value, then there will be an opportunity for any market participant to profitably buy up the undervalued asset until the prices of the two are driven into equilibrium. In this way *relative* prices or values of assets are determined by the incentive of all market participants to seek profitable opportunities to trade.

Wealth

Wealth represents the total value of assets to which an individual or group of individuals has title. The principal distinction between wealth and value is that wealth indicates title or claim to assets and the income streams they generate. It is therefore an aggregate measure of the value of assets. The level of aggregation may be very modest, as in the wealth of a single individual, or it may be substantial, as in the wealth of a city, a state, or a nation.

The concept of income and even of value is largely an economic notion. This means that the generation of income is essentially determined by the economics of production decisions, and the determination of value is a matter of the economics of how a market capitalizes an income stream. But the forces which influence wealth are as much legal factors as they are economic ones. The law essentially determines title and therefore the wealth of individuals, or the distribution of claims to assets across individuals. The law defines the nature of enforceable contracts and contracts define the nature of an individual's claims to assets.

Because contracts have such an important impact on the distribution of wealth, it will prove important to have an understanding of some of the implications of alternative financial contracts. There are two aspects of financial contracting that will be important topics in this book. The first pertains to the types of assets which exist in the economy. The second pertains to the types of markets in which these assets are traded. A market is essentially a mechanism for the exchange of title and the execution of contracts. We examine the costs involved in using different types of markets and the characteristics of the assets traded in these markets. For example, some markets are dominated by financial intermediaries and some are not. When an intermediary is involved in the market, particularly one which is insured by the government, it dramatically changes the nature of the financial contracts between suppliers and users of funds and it introduces new assets into the market. We will try to develop an understanding of how these contracts differ and how various markets operate.

An interesting and important example of the effect on individuals of the way financial contracts are written pertains to inflation. Changes in the aggregate price level affect borrowers and lenders of funds quite differently, depending upon the type of financial contract to which they have agreed. Some types of contracts can index the terms of the contract to the price level. This applies both to contracts between private parties and contracts between private parties and the government. Other types of contracts will lead to redistributions of wealth if the price level changes. For example, one type of contract is the agreement to pay federal income taxes. Personal income tax schedules in the United States are progressive so that the tax rate increases with the level of income. Moreover, they are based on a specific nominal level of income, that is, income which is not adjusted with inflation. But as inflation rates increase so that the nominal level of personal and taxable income increases, tax liability increases at a higher rate than the rate of inflation. When a family's nominal income increases just enough to cover inflation it effectively breaks even, before taxes. But if this throws the family into a higher tax bracket its real income is decreased. An example of this effect, based on the 1975 tax law, is presented in Table 2-2.[1] The table shows the effect of a 10 percent inflation on individuals with various levels of income in the case where the tax brackets change with inflation and in the case where they do not, that is, where they are indexed. For example, a family of four which had a 1975 taxable income of $20,000 would have had an effective tax rate of 13 percent before inflation. But if that income were inflated by 10 percent and the tax brackets were not adjusted for inflation, or indexed, then the effective rate would jump to 13.7 percent. With tax schedules which are indexed to inflation, there would be no change in the effective tax rate. This example shows how individuals and the government are affected by the terms of the contract which determines income tax liability.

---

[1] See Emil M. Sunley, Jr., and Joseph A. Pechman, "Inflation Adjustment for the Individual Income Tax," in *Inflation and the Income Tax*, The Brookings Institution, Washington, D.C. (1976), p. 156. Copyright © 1976 by the Brookings Institution.

TABLE 2-2

Effect of 10 Percent Inflation on the Tax Liabilities of a Family of Four at Selected Income Levels, 1975

INCOME BEFORE INFLATION ($)	TAX BEFORE INFLATION		TAX AFTER 10 PERCENT INFLATION			
			NO INDEXING		WITH INDEXING	
	AMOUNT ($)	EFFECTIVE RATE (%)	AMOUNT ($)	EFFECTIVE RATE (%)	AMOUNT ($)	EFFECTIVE RATE (%)
30,000	4,964	16.5	5,799	17.6	5,460	16.5
50,000	11,570	23.1	13,556	24.6	12,727	23.1
100,000	33,800	33.8	38,700	35.2	37,180	33.8
250,000	115,760	46.3	130,460	47.4	127,336	46.3
500,000	262,760	52.6	292,160	53.1	289,036	52.6
1,000,000	556,760	55.7	615,560	56.0	612,436	55.7

TYPES OF WEALTH

It is useful to have a classification system for types of wealth or claims to assets. The classification scheme presented here is extremely brief and simple. It is very close to one that was originally used by Milton Friedman as a framework in which to examine the demand for money which we will examine in Part Five of this book.[2] The value of this simple framework for categorizing types of wealth is like the value of any filing system. If the large number of assets which exist in the real world can be organized into a few simple categories, then it becomes easier to understand the operation of the real world. In particular, when attention is turned toward understanding the demand for different types of assets, as it will be later in the book, then it is extremely useful to have a simple framework and clear definitions of different types of assets. The types of wealth can be classified into five broad categories: debt, equities, tangible assets, human capital, and money. The characteristics of each of these will be considered in turn.

Debt

Debt is a claim on a prespecified portion of the income stream accruing to an asset. Debt claims, or bonds, are often referred to as *fixed income* securities in that they promise to pay a fixed amount each period for a number of time periods. For example, a bond may be a claim on an individual or a firm where that individual has promised to pay $1,000 per year for 10 years and $10,000 in the tenth year, or it might simply be $1,000 per year for 10 years.

[2]See Milton Friedman, "The Quantity Theory, A Restatement," in *Studies in the Quantity Theory of Money*, University of Chicago Press, Chicago, 1956.

The promised payments can take on any conceivable form as long as there is a prior commitment to that pattern of payment. For example, the actual amount of payment might be tied or indexed to the aggregate price level, so that as prices go up, the amount of the payment increases as well. This is referred to as an indexed bond and though the income stream is not fixed, it is still very much a debt claim. The fact that a commitment is made for a certain payment does not mean that bonds are free of risk, for a commitment may be broken. The value of a bond depends upon the value of the underlying asset on which it is a claim. If the income from the asset on which the bond is a claim is insufficient to make the committed payment, then the payment is said to be in default. The income stream accruing to a bond is therefore risky and the value of the bond is determined by capitalizing that income stream.

Equities

Equities are "residual" claims on the income stream accruing to an asset. By residual we mean that all other claims against the income stream of the asset are deducted first. This includes payments to all the suppliers of goods and services to a company as well as the claims of bondholders and the government's tax claims against the firm. The residual nature of the equity claim has some extremely important implications. When people derive their compensation from an equity or residual claim, they have a strong incentive to take actions which increase the value of that residual. In general, actions which promote efficient use of the asset and which minimize costs will lead to a larger residual stream of income. The residual claim can be viewed as one type of contract which provides a distinct set of incentives for the people who control the use of the asset. We will have more to say about such incentive effects later.

The principal reason for the existence of the equity or stock form of security is the feature of limited liability which it carries. This means that stockholders can lose only the price they have paid for their common stock. They have no further liability for the actions of the corporation or its managers. Hence, the stock's value is totally independent of who holds it. This has made common stock a highly transferrable type of asset. If liability were not limited in this way, then the value of the security would change if a rich person sold it to a poor person, simply because the personal assets which stood behind the security would be reduced. Therefore, limited liability has made the equity security an impersonal asset and, in a sense, the corporation on which it is a claim impersonal as well.

Tangible Assets

Tangible assets are those assets which primarily provide a stream of services rather than pecuniary income. We can divide tangible assets into six primary categories. The categories themselves provide examples of tangible assets. They include residential structures, nonresidential structures, land, producer durables (such as tools and machines), consumer durables, and inventories. There is clearly some ambiguity as to whether each of these assets provides a service flow or a pecuniary income stream. For example, a house may be rented so that it creates a cash flow, but this is really a direct payment for the service flow on a period-by-period basis. It does not fundamentally change the nature of the asset.

Human Capital

The nation's *human capital* is the stock of future labor services which can be produced by the nation's population. It should be clear that this is exceptionally difficult to value. Nonetheless, it is an important part of the economy's total stock of wealth. Some argue that the strength of the United States economy has traditionally been a product of its large stock of human capital.

Money

Money is that item used by an economy as a medium of exchange and unit of account. The income stream which money generates has long been thought by many to be a service flow or return in kind. But part of the return on money could be a pecuniary return. Substantial attention will be devoted to this issue in Chapters Nineteen to Twenty-one. There has been considerable debate about exactly how to define money, or more precisely, exactly what constitutes money in the U.S. economy. We won't resolve that here. But the criterion that will be used for choosing a workable definition of what constitutes money is those items which best fit the definition stated above, that is, those which serve as a medium of exchange and unit of account.

EXPECTATIONS, MARKETS, AND VALUE

A common characteristic of all the examples of assets discussed above is that the income streams they generate are uncertain. That uncertainty is most apparent in the case of the income stream accruing to a shareholder of common stock. There is no guarantee about the magnitude of dividend payments or about capital gains for shareholders in any company. The same is true of debt securities such as corporate or municipal bonds. While these securities carry a promised interest payment, there is still uncertainty about whether the promise will be kept. Those who once thought that the bonds issued by New York City or by the Penn Central Railroad were "safe" investments can certainly attest to this fact.

One of the principal contributions of financial economics has been the development of systematic ways of dealing with this uncertainty. At the simplest level, the market bases its estimate of the value of an asset on what it *expects* will be the income or return generated by that asset. The market also demands a premium to bear the *risk* that it perceives in that income stream. Chapters Four and Five focus on an analytical treatment of how the market uses these concepts of expected return and risk. But at this juncture it is important to acquire an intuitive grasp of the issues that underlie that more analytical treatment. To keep this discussion relatively simple we will concentrate on the role of expectations and postpone the treatment of risk.

The market value of a company's shares of stock represents the market's best guess of what the capitalized income stream accruing to those shares will equal. This is exceptionally difficult to estimate. Invariably, it depends on what the market thinks the firm's future earnings and investment opportunities will be. This, in turn, depends upon the market's assessment of the skills of management, the intensity of competition from other firms in the company's markets, the pace of technological advance, the rate of inflation, and so forth. While it seems virtually impossible to take all these things into account in pricing the firm's shares, in a sense, the market does just that. Every bit of knowledge the market has becomes incorporated into the price. But this is not as strong a statement as it may sound at first. For example, suppose the market as a whole knew something about the income stream which was expected to accrue to shareholders but failed to take account of it in the price of the stock. Were this the case, everyone in the market would know that the stock was undervalued and try to buy more of it. Their attempts to buy more would drive up the price until they all felt that the price they had paid for the stock was just worth what they expected to receive in the future by holding title to the income stream. The nature of the market is therefore to incorporate its best guess of future events into the price of an asset.

A host of interesting questions arises about how the market formulates this best guess of the value of an asset and incorporates it into the price. A number of these questions will be dealt with in the chapters ahead, but a few will be taken up briefly here.

Anticipated and Unanticipated Information

What will happen to the price of a company's stock if a new management team is announced? One answer might be that if the new management team is perceived as being an improvement over the old team, then the price of the company's stock will go up. The increase will reflect the capitalized value of the additional profits that the market expects will be generated by the new managers, less the compensation paid to the managers for generating those profits. But this is not quite correct because it ignores the distinction between *anticipated* and *unanticipated* events. Suppose the market had already anticipated that a new management team was needed and that a new one would be chosen by the firm's board of directors. Then the price of the firm's stock prior to the announcement of the new management would reflect the anticipated value of their contribution to the firm. If the announcement that a new team had actually been chosen and the revelation of its identity incorporated no surprises, then the price of the firm's shares would be unaffected by the announcement. On the other hand, if a surprise were contained in the announcement, the value of the firm's shares would adjust to reflect that *unanticipated* information. It is therefore critical to distinguish between anticipated and unanticipated events or information. The market is always trying to guess the future and it incorporates all the information it can in the process. Only something that is truly new to the market will lead to changes in prices.

The same distinction can be applied to the effect of inflation on the economy. When inflation rates are high and volatile, as they were perceived to be in the late 1970s, there is a strong incentive to try to accurately estimate the future rate of inflation and include that estimate in the terms of financial contracts. For example, interest rates generally reflect the market's anticipation or best guess of the future inflation rate. To see how this is accomplished suppose that people who have funds to lend demand a 5 percent interest rate when they expect the inflation rate to be zero. In order to come out the same, these people would have to demand 15 percent if they expected the inflation rate to be 10 percent. Only then would they expect to receive the same return after inflation of 10 percent as they would on a 5 percent loan with no expected inflation. But suppose some event takes place after the terms of the loan contract are agreed to, but before it is paid off, which changes the lender's expectations of inflation. That event might be something like the formation of an oil cartel or the election of a new administration in Washington or the appointment of a new Chairman of the Board of Governors of the Federal Reserve. The point is that the value of the loan contract will be materially affected only to the extent that the event, whatever it might be, was unanticipated. If the market had anticipated it, the effect would already be a part of the inflation estimate and therefore of the loan terms.

Capital markets perform the function of aggregating information about the future income stream accruing to an asset. The market's *anticipations* of future events are therefore incorporated in the prices of assets. It is only *unanticipated* information which causes prices to change. The distinction between anticipated and unanticipated events is important. Failure to make this distinction has led to much misunderstanding about the way markets operate. The significance of this distinction will become apparent in later chapters.

Intrinsic and Speculative Value

As has already been explained in the sections above, the value of an asset is determined by the stream of income it will generate. There are generally two components to that income stream. It is easiest to think about these in the case of common stock. Income accrues to common stockholders in the form of dividends or capital gains or losses. The same sort of division may be applied to other types of assets, such as houses. Houses yield a flow of services and there may be capital gains or losses on the price of a house. For most all assets, both of these components of income are uncertain. This uncertainty can sometimes lead to what some people call "speculative" prices of assets.

History is packed with examples of what people have called speculative booms. The name generally conveys the impression of wild and irrational behavior. The basic idea behind speculative pricing of an asset is that people bid up the price of an asset because they believe its price will go up in the future. The anticipation of future capital gains leads to a current increase in price, but there is nothing really speculative in this behavior. It merely recognizes that capital gains are an important part of the future income stream accruing to an asset. The supposedly wild and irrational nature of this behavior lies in the belief that the anticipated capital gains cannot be justified by future dividend payments. To see what this means it is necessary to examine the two components of income a little more closely than has been done thus far.

There is something a little bit circular in saying that the price of a share of stock is determined by future dividends and capital gains. For if the price today is determined by dividends and capital gains, then the price tomorrow will be determined by future dividends and capital gains. And this will be true for all future prices. But expected future prices are today's anticipated capital gains and losses; they also determine today's prices. The implication is that it is the perception of changing future dividends which accounts for capital gains and losses. In turn, it is the expectation of future dividends which really accounts for today's price. Or, as some choose to say, the "intrinsic" value of the asset is determined by the expected future stream of dividends. The interesting question, which is much easier to pose than to answer, is: Are there really speculative booms where the value of assets deviates from their intrinsic value?

Burton Malkiel recounts some of the details of a so-called speculative boom over tulip bulbs which took place in Holland in the sixteenth century. A brief excerpt from Malkiel's vivid account very effectively explains what happened:

> It all began rather unspectacularly around the middle of the sixteenth century. It was at the time that the tulip made its European debut, having been imported from Constantinople, where it had long been a favorite. The Dutch took to the flower, and it became a sign of good taste for any man of means to have a collection. While the prices of bulbs were high relative to those of other flowers, the tulip's first eighty years in Holland were marked by a prosperous tranquility. But then a slowly creeping bulbomania set in. By the early 1630's, the tulip had become a much sought after fad. One year a certain color was "in"; the next, a particular species. Since the "in" tulip commanded the highest prices, it seemed perfectly natural for merchants to try predicting what varieties would be popular

in the coming year—just as department store buyers try to gauge the public fancy in color and hemlines for the next season. The next step in the tulip-bulb craze was for several smart Dutchmen to ask: Why stop at simply trying to obtain a normal inventory of saleable merchandise? Why not buy up an extra-large stockpile before the prices go up? That's how you beat others to the gun. And that's how speculative crazes are born!

So many people tried to beat the gun that it finally went off. Tulip-bulb prices began to rise wildly. As people saw that big profits were being made, they rushed into the market like lemmings into the sea. Charles Mackay, who chronicled these events in his book Extraordinary Popular Delusions, *noted that the ordinary industry of the country was dropped in favor of speculation in tulip bulbs. Nobles, citizens, farmers, mechanics, seamen, footmen, maid-servants, even chimney sweeps and old clotheswomen dabbled in tulips. Everyone imagined that the passion for tulips would last forever, and buyers from all over the world would come to Holland and pay whatever prices were asked for them. Prices of bulbs rose to unbelievable heights. A single bulb of the Harlem species was exchanged for twelve acres of building ground. After all, it's easier to build a castle in the air than on the ground. Another variety fetched 4,600 florins, a new carriage, and two gray horses, plus a complete set of harnesses. A bulb of the Viceroy species commanded the sum of all the following items in exchange: seventeen bushels of wheat, thirty-four bushels of rye, four fat oxen, eight fat swine, twelve fat sheep, two hogsheads of wine, four tons of beer, two tons of butter, 1,000 pounds of cheese, a complete bed, a suit of clothes, and a silver drinking cup thrown in for good measure.*

At last some of the smart Dutchmen who had earlier decided to build up inventories started to wonder what tulip bulbs were actually "worth" and ultimately began to ask more questions. They wondered if public enthusiasm could last forever. Could tulip prices really go any higher, or even stay at current inflated levels? Should they get out now while they were ahead? The answers to such questions usually convinced the owner of tulip bulbs to sell. Prices plummeted and panic reigned. Government ministers stated officially that there was no reason for tulip bulbs to fall in price—but no one listened. Dealers went bankrupt and refused to honor their commitments to buy tulip bulbs. A government plan to settle all contracts at 10 percent of their face value was frustrated when bulbs fell even below this mark. And prices continued to decline. Down and down they went until the tulip became almost worthless.[3]

Stories about speculative booms are interesting and exciting because they hold out the prospect of large and quickly made profits. But if they really are *speculative* booms, they hinge on somebody incurring a quickly made large loss. Speculative booms are also interesting to think about in times of inflation, as people try to move into assets that they believe will not deteriorate in value. The basic question these events pose is whether it is *rational* for people to buy assets at a price which they do not believe is justified by the anticipated stream of dividends accruing to that asset. You

[3] Selection is reprinted from *A Random Walk Down Wall Street* by Burton G. Malkiel, with permission of W. W. Norton & Company, Inc. Copyright © 1975, 1973 by W. W. Norton & Company, Inc.

can be sure that in the long run, the market acts in a rational manner. But in any given situation it is not always easy to determine exactly what the rational action may be.

No answer is going to be given to the question that is raised about the real nature of so-called speculative booms. In this case, the question is controversial and there may or may not exist a clear answer to it. But the question itself is useful because it begins to focus attention on how markets work and what is rational behavior.

VALUE CREATION AND WEALTH TRANSFER

Value Creation and Destruction

The economic system in any country is basically engaged in producing goods and services. The dollar value of the goods and services produced in any given time period is the gross national product. It is a measure of the national flow of income during a period of time which is designed to eliminate all double counting. For example, steel is used in the production of automobiles. Therefore, when you measure the value of cars produced, you have measured the value of the steel used in their production. It would then be double counting to add the value of steel produced to the value of automobiles in order to measure income.

We can also view the productive activities of a country from the vantage point of a stock measure of the economy's output as well as a flow measure. Here we can speak of the total wealth of the economy or the aggregate value of all the society's assets. This is really the value of the economy's capital stock, including such things as human capital. It is useful to think of this as the capitalized value of the expected stream of income which accrues to all of the country's assets. Again, it is important to avoid double counting. It would be inappropriate to add up the value of all the assets on everyone's balance sheets to determine total wealth. This would involve double counting in that one person's liability is the asset of another person. Rather, the total value of society's assets is the sum of every individual's net worth. It should be apparent that while the concept is unambiguous, there are immense practical problems involved in actually trying to measure the *total* wealth of a society. For example, how do you value human capital?

Despite problems of measurement, it is apparent that the society's total stock of wealth is constantly changing. It almost never changes by very much, relative to the total, in any one year. But it does change. When we, as an entire economy, produce more than we consume, or forgo consumption, we save and add to the stock of wealth. We might say that we create value. On the other hand, when we consume more than we produce we dissave and the stock of wealth declines. We therefore destroy value. Whether a country's wealth increases or decreases is largely a result of its own choice. Some purely technological factors influence the ability to produce goods and services from a given stock of capital. But decisions about saving or dissaving, the extent of labor productivity, and the types of incentives to produce built into the culture and included in contractual arrangements, are important determinants of the development of a country's wealth. The degree to which a society creates or destroys value is therefore due to a combination of technological factors and conscious choice.

Wealth Transfers and Property Rights

We have used the words "value" and "wealth" virtually interchangeably when speaking of society as a whole. At this highest level of aggregation the fact that wealth refers to the claim or title of an individual or group becomes irrelevant. But the actions of economic agents in society and the external events over which we have little control can shift the distribution of wealth as well as create or destroy value. It is important to see the distinction. Value creation means that the aggregate wealth of society has changed. A wealth redistribution means a shift of individual claims on assets, but no change in aggregate wealth. It is just as important to understand the kind of wealth transfers that can take place as it is to understand how value may be created or destroyed.

It is useful to again consider the significance of the definition of wealth. Wealth defines title or claim to an asset. Or, to use a phrase which has become popular in economic circles, wealth conveys a "property right." Wealth conveys a right to the income stream which an asset is expected to generate. The wealth of individuals and the wealth of the society hinge on the strength of property rights. That is, wealth depends upon the certainty with which title is enforceable. For example, suppose a country's legal system is not highly developed. This may mean that judges are not well trained, or that the bench is not highly regarded in society and therefore does not attract able individuals. As a result, judicial decisions are capricious and one cannot make economic decisions with a clear understanding of the property rights that will be enforced by the courts. The same conditions may result if a country is subject to frequent political instability, where decisions of the courts and the title to property are subject to the control of changing governments.

Property rights are essentially defined by contracts. Contracts can be enforced in a variety of ways. Sometimes it is necessary to enforce them through the courts, but such enforcement can be costly. Often times informal business sanctions are more effective than enforcement through the courts. For example, if two parties to a contract expect to have future business relations they expect will be profitable, then this will limit the incentive to break an existing contract, because a breach of contract by one party may jeopardize the profitable long-run relationship. In general, the strength of both formal and informal mechanisms for enforcing contracts will determine the strength of property rights.

If we were able to perfectly and costlessly enforce property rights, then only those events that are truly outside the control of society would lead to wealth transfers. For example, suppose people's tastes in recreation shift from downhill skiing to cross-country skiing. The effect would be that the owners of companies which produce downhill skiing equipment would lose wealth and the owners of companies which produce cross-country skiing equipment would gain. This essentially random event causes a wealth transfer. Moreover, no change in the extent to which property rights are enforced would change this.

But there are a number of interesting and relevant examples of wealth transfers where the root issue is the extent to which property rights will be enforced. Some of these examples are fundamental problems concerning the operation of capital markets and will receive considerable attention throughout this book. The purpose of the discussion at this juncture is to focus attention on the common underlying issue, the enforceability of property rights.

Inflation is probably the most important contemporary example of a phenomenon that leads to wealth transfers. To be more precise, it is *unanticipated* inflation which creates wealth transfers. This is a problem which will be dealt with in some detail later, particularly in Chapters Eight and Twenty-two. But the basic property rights issue can be laid out here without giving away the rest of the story. As explained in the earlier section titled "Anticipated and Unanticipated Information," when the terms of a bond are agreed to, they reflect the market's *expectation* of inflation. If lenders demand 5 percent when they expect zero inflation, then they would demand 15 percent with an expectation of 10 percent inflation. Now suppose that they expect a zero inflation rate and the actual inflation rate turns out to be 10 percent. In this situation the lenders lose. (A more detailed treatment of how they lose is presented in Chapter Twenty-two.) Moreover, the lender's loss is the borrower's gain. The point of the story is that if inflation exceeds expectations, it pays to have borrowed. In effect, you will have bought something yesterday and paid for it today with devalued money. It will therefore cost you less. But it is important to see that for this to work, inflation must be above expectations. It is *unanticipated inflation* which creates wealth transfers. This is because the terms of debt contracts incorporate the market's expectations of the future. Borrowing or lending to beat inflation is therefore a game that you *cannot expect to win, unless* you believe you have better information than the market.

The idea that this kind of wealth transfer is really an issue of property rights is not obvious. To fully appreciate the connection it is necessary to understand the underlying causes of inflation. An initial perspective on this problem can be acquired by comparing the inflation of the 1970s with the deflation experienced by the United States in the late nineteenth century. In the late nineteenth century the supply of money in the United States was determined largely by the available supply of gold. And as it turned out, there was a relative scarcity of gold in the world until the gold discoveries in various parts of the globe in the late 1890s. This relative scarcity of gold led to a slow rate of growth in the U.S. supply of money, which, in turn, led to a relatively prolonged period of deflation. One apparent effect of that deflation was to cause a redistribution of wealth from western farmers who were in debt to eastern financiers who extended them credit, or at least so those farmers alleged. The terms of that credit reflected an expectation of a particular path for the level of prices. But the apparently unanticipated and persistent deflation led to a transfer of wealth. It is difficult now to precisely specify what the expected inflation rate was and what the magnitude of the actual wealth transfer may have been. But the western farmers may certainly have believed that the deflation was impoverishing them; at least they claimed it was. The most famous political outcome of this deflationary period was the presidential candidacy of William Jennings Bryan, who campaigned for coinage of silver. His famous "Cross of Gold" speech contended that his constituency was being "crucified on a cross of gold."

By contrast, in the 1970s, the United States experienced a period where inflation rates were seemingly above, sometimes quite a bit above, the market's expectations. This led to redistributions of wealth from those who lent funds at terms that turned out to be too low, to those who borrowed and paid off their debts with cheaper dollars. But in both cases the underlying problem is that it is difficult either to construct or enforce contracts which protect the property rights of individual citizens against the forces that cause inflations and deflations. In the late nineteenth century the problem was that the supply of gold was under no one's control and was fundamentally a result of the incentives for production and search for gold supplies. In the mid-twentieth century the problem is that the supply of money and credit is under the control of the United States and other national governments. And, thus far, it has been difficult for the U.S. government to write contracts with itself that protect the citizen's property rights against changes in the price level.

There are other interesting examples of wealth transfers which result from conflicts in the enforcement of property rights. For many years individuals from throughout the world purchased property on the California coastline. Some intended to develop it intensely; others intended to leave it largely unchanged. Then in the early 1970s the State of California passed Proposition 10, which established the California Coastal Commission. This commission has the authority to restrict development on all property within so many feet of the mean high tide line. The property owners contended that the effect of this proposition was to expropriate their wealth. And so it did. The proponents of the proposition contended that it protected the state's wealth, which was the capitalized value of the scenic beauty and recreational use people gained from an uncluttered coastline (though they certainly didn't say it this way). The question is: Whose property rights should be protected? No attempt will be made here to answer this question. But the example illustrates the complexity and pervasiveness of the property rights issue.

A final example returns the focus of attention to organized capital markets rather than economic issues with large social implications. For some time during the early 1970s, Westinghouse Corporation negotiated contracts to provide uranium to public utilities for use in nuclear power plants. The interesting aspect of the contracts which Westinghouse agreed to was their stipulation that they would provide uranium at fixed prices. This meant that the utilities that signed such contracts were going to have a safe source of uranium at a prearranged price. By 1977 Westinghouse had contracted to supply utilities with approximately 80 million pounds of uranium through the 1990s. At that time they were reported to have approximately 15 million pounds available through their own sources, which were independent of the worldwide market price of uranium. It has been estimated that the average price of uranium during the period when most of these contracts were signed was in the range of $9 per pound. By January 1977 the price had risen to $41 per pound. This exposed Westinghouse shareholders to an estimated liability of $2 billion if all of these contracts were honored at the market price. It should be clear that the terms of the contract created the opportunities for large wealth transfers.

Westinghouse took the issue to court and argued that they should be excused from honoring the contracts. Their argument was that a cartel had formed and pushed the price of uranium to artificially high levels. This was allegedly an eventuality that they could not have foreseen and they argued that they should not be penalized for it.[4] The point of raising this issue is not to evaluate the merits of the argument used by Westinghouse; rather it is to vividly illustrate the types of wealth transfers that result from alternative types of contracts. The issue at stake is who should bear the cost of the increased price of uranium, and should the reason for that increase be a legitimate determinant of the resulting redistribution of wealth? The strength of property rights is critically determined by the way such disputes are resolved.

SUMMARY

The purpose of this chapter has been to set the stage for the following, more analytical treatment of the way markets determine value and wealth. There have been three important concepts which have been the focus of attention throughout the chapter. They are the role of time and uncertainty in deter-

---

[4]See "$1 Billion Test of Contract Law," *Business Week* (December 22, 1975), p. 15.

mining value and the role of contracts in determining wealth. The intent of this chapter has been to develop an intuitive understanding of these concepts. In a sense, this chapter has been occupied with the big picture. In the next chapters of Part One we will turn our attention toward filling in the details and to introducing some rigor into the analysis.

QUESTIONS TO IMPROVE UNDERSTANDING

1 Explain the difference between wealth and value. Why does wealth have a legal aspect to it that value does not?
2 Discuss the various forms which income may take. Can the market value all these different types of income streams?
3 What is human capital? Why is it argued that the market has difficulty valuing human capital? Can you imagine that there are exceptions to the statement that human capital cannot be valued? How about a case where someone is injured and goes to court to claim damages? Does this court have to decide the value of lost human capital? How does this differ from the idea of a regular market for human capital?
4 Explain the difference between a debt claim and an equity claim. What feature of an equity security has made it so successful in modern societies?
5 Suppose a company which produces automobiles announces a revolutionary method for assembling automobiles that will reduce production costs by an estimated 20 percent. How do you think this announcement will affect the price of that firm's securities?
6 What does the phrase "property right" mean? How does the enforceability of contracts influence property rights?
7 Explain the difference between anticipated and unanticipated inflation. What does it mean to say that unanticipated inflation creates a wealth transfer?

REFERENCES

"Opposites: GE Grows While Westinghouse Shrinks," *Business Week* (January 31, 1977), pp. 60–64.

"$1 Billion Test of Contract Law," *Business Week* (December 22, 1975), p. 15.

Alchian, Armen, and Harold Demsetz: "Production, Information Costs and Economic Organization," *American Economic Review* (December 1972), pp. 777–795.

Friedman, Milton: "The Quantity Theory, A Restatement," in *Studies in the Quantity Theory of Money*, University of Chicago Press, Chicago, 1956.

Malkiel, Burton: *A Random Walk Down Wall Street*, Norton, New York, 1973.

Sunley, Emil M., Jr., and Joseph A. Pechman: "Inflation Adjustment for the Individual Income Tax, in *Inflation and the Income Tax*, The Brookings Institution, Washington, D.C., 1976.

Chapter Three

TIME AND THE VALUE
OF ASSETS

In this chapter we will examine the importance for the value of assets of the time distribution of future income. In other words, we'll examine the role of time in determining the value of assets. Time is the simpler to deal with of the two principal factors which influence asset values. The other important determinant of value, uncertainty about the magnitude of future income, will be the subject of the next three chapters.

As explained in Chapter Two, the basic strategy involved in dealing with both time and uncertainty is to devise a procedure for converting the stream of income which will accrue to an asset in the future into a single value for that asset today. We refer to this as capitalizing the income stream of the asset and often refer (somewhat redundantly) to the value of the asset as the capitalized value. The problem of uncertainty aside, it would be a trivial task to capitalize the income stream of an asset if market participants were unconcerned about the differences between equal amounts of income paid at different points in time, or if market participants considered a dollar paid 1 year from now to be worth the same today as a dollar paid 2 years from now (adjusted for inflation). The value of the asset would simply be defined as the sum of the income flows that will accrue in each future period. This can be expressed algebraically as (assuming no change in the price level)

$$\text{Value} = \sum_{t=1}^{N} I_t \tag{3-1}$$

where I_t is the income which accrues in period t and Σ means to add up all the values of I_t, allowing t to assume the values 1 through N. For example if $N = 3$ and $I_1 = 15$, $I_2 = 12$, and $I_3 = 7$, then the value equals 34. But the process of capitalizing income streams is not as simple as Eq. (3-1) suggests. The reason is that there is a positive interest rate in the world. The fact that such a positive interest rate exists means that the market as a whole is not unconcerned with differences between equivalent amounts of money received in distinct time periods.

In this chapter we will be concerned with exploring the implications for the valuation of assets of the fact that there is a positive interest rate. We won't be concerned, at this juncture, with the determinants of the interest rate. That is the subject of Part II. Instead we will develop the meaning and interpretation of the rate of interest. Then we will examine the concepts of present value and internal rate of return. Finally, we will use these concepts to explore some examples of prices and yields of different types of assets observed in the market.

THE CONCEPT OF THE INTEREST RATE

The Interest Rate as a Price

The financial markets are replete with numerous different interest rates, each of which pertains to a particular type of financial asset or liability. The complexity of the marketplace itself sometimes obscures the meaning of these interest rates and the role they play in the market. It is therefore important to abstract from the complications of the real-world market to acquire a precise understanding of the interest rate.

The simple single-period interest rate defines the price that is paid for postponing payment of $1 for one period. For example, if the interest rate is 8 percent per year, then the cost of paying the market $1 one year from now instead of paying that dollar today is $0.08. Similarly, if the amount in question were $100 rather than $1, then the cost of the 1 year postponement would be $8 rather than $0.08. The total cost of the postponement can therefore be expressed as the product of the price per dollar of a one-period postponement multiplied by the amount of payment:

$$\text{Cost of postponement} = iA \tag{3-2}$$

where i is the single-period rate of interest and A is the amount of payment in question.

The interest rate can be thought of in the same way as any other price in the marketplace. There is nothing particularly unique about the function of the interest rate as a price. The only distinction between this price and others in other markets is that the product involved is a little more abstract. We must therefore attempt to define, as precisely as possible, the product which is priced by the interest rate. We have already indicated that the interest rate is the price of postponing payment. But this is still somewhat ambiguous because it is not the timeliness of the payment itself which is valuable; rather, it is what the payment can be used for, or it is the opportunity cost of not having the funds available. When an individual to whom a payment is due agrees to postpone that payment, he or she has forgone the opportunity to consume. The interest rate can therefore be viewed as the price of forgone consumption, for the opportunity cost of delayed access to the funds is the postponement of consumption. More often we think of the interest rate as the price of borrowing or the price of credit. In effect, this is simply the more typical way of saying that the interest rate is the price of postponing payment or of forgone consumption.

The interest rate is also often said to be the "price of money." This is an unfortunate phrase which causes much confusion. Money and credit are not interchangeable terms. As was explained in Chapter Two, money is one form of wealth, as distinct from, say, equity or bonds. Money therefore refers to a particular type of claim or wealth, while credit refers to the total stock of liabilities in a particular market or in the economy as a whole. Credit is not a measure of wealth in that it is the sum of all balance sheet liabilities, without any netting out of double counting. Therefore, the price of credit, or of deferred payment, cannot be the price of money. The usual retort to the assertion that the interest rate is the price of money is: No, the inverse of the price level is the price of money. The logic behind this argument is the subject of Part V of this book.

Historical Perspective on the Interest Rate

Credit has been a valuable commodity, and therefore the interest rate an important price, for centuries. As far back as 1500 B.C. the Assyrians used credit instruments. Somewhat more recently interest rates became a focal point for special regulation by the central authority. In medieval and Renaissance Europe that authority was the Catholic church. The church's position on charging a price for credit was not based on any kind of notion of what was a fair or conscionable price, but rather on the objectionable nature of the credit contract itself. The church objected to the intertemporal nature of the contract, the fact that it bridged time. From the standpoint of the church, what transpired tomorrow was the domain of God, not man. Hence, for man to profit on God's domain was considered sinful. And the church held that interest of any amount was a sin against God. This created some difficulty in that a zero interest rate was a disequilibrium, albeit, a divinely inspired one. At a zero rate of interest, there was an excess demand for credit; more people wanted to borrow than wanted to lend.

The marketplace evolved a number of ways to resolve this disequilibrium. One way to circumvent the church's prohibition on the extraction of interest was for a class of specialists to emerge as lenders for whom the eternal penalties of the church were of little consequence. This role was filled by the Jews of medieval Europe. As long as the church relied upon the divine for punishment of the sin of charging interest, then Jewish lenders felt immune from punishment. However, if the church opted to impose worldly penalties, as it periodically did, then the cost to the lender became substantially greater. In effect, the real return to lenders declined and they were compelled to raise their prices to bring their real returns back to an equilibrium level.

But during this period, one did not necessarily have to go outside the ranks of those who professed an allegiance to the church to find lenders who charged interest for credit. They simply had to be more discreet about their pricing than did the Jews. One method practiced by the Medici of Renaissance Italy was to include an implicit charge for interest in the pricing of currency exchanges between different cities, which at that time issued their own currencies. For example, the rate of exchange between the currencies of Barcelona and Florence for a merchant traveling between the cities would depend upon the travel time involved and include a premium for the interest covering that time period. Raymond de Roover, in his book on the Medici, concluded from the terms of exchange for such a contract in 1438 that the annual interest rate was 10.2 percent.[1]

Ever since medieval times the interest rate has been singled out for special treatment by governmental authorities. It is impossible to say with certainty whether this is in part a holdover from the restrictions of the Catholic church against interest in the Middle Ages. But it may be that these ancient restrictions created a climate which allowed other restrictions on interest rates to persist into modern times. One type of restriction is the law which regulates what constitutes a usurious rate of interest. Unlike the medieval church, usury laws do not condemn interest rates per se. They condemn interest rates which are perceived to be too high, that is, usurious. Many states have had usury laws until recently and some states still do, particularly regarding mortgage interest rates. These laws stem from the belief that lenders have the ability, if not restricted by the state, to take unfair advantage of unwitting borrowers.[2]

---

[1]See Raymond de Roover, *The Rise and Decline of the Medici Bank, 1397-1494*, W. W. Norton, New York, 1966. Also see Martin Mayer, *The Bankers*, Ballantine, New York, 1974, for an excellent discussion of banking in the Middle Ages and a synthesis of Roover's treatment of the Medici bank.
[2]For a recent study of one type of usury law, see George J. Benston, "Rate Ceiling Implications of the Cost Structure of Consumer Finance Companies," *Journal of Finance*, 32 (September 1977), pp. 1169-1194.

Another form of interest rate restriction is the one placed on rates of interest that financial institutions, specifically commercial banks and savings and loans, are allowed to pay to savers. This restriction, which has been imposed by the federal government, is motivated by quite different considerations than those which have led to usury laws. These ceilings have been imposed to limit the ability of financial institutions to compete against each other in the apparent belief that if left unrestricted, such competition would drive large numbers of institutions into bankruptcy. We will look more closely at both of these types of restrictions on interest rates in Part IV of this book.

Some Difficulties in Computing the Interest Rate

The interest rate can be defined in a number of different ways. At this juncture we will examine a few of these various incarnations of the interest rate. Most of the distinctions between various interest rates which we will examine here provide foundations for more extensive treatments of particular aspects of financial contracts which are taken up in later chapters. Throughout this discussion we will deal with single-period interest rates. Multiple-period rates will be analyzed in Chapter Nine. We will consider six specific types of interest rates.

THE SIMPLE INTEREST RATE   The simple interest rate is so named because it is the simplest to define. It is defined with reference to a bond or a loan contract. Suppose the amount of the loan or the initial value of the bond is represented by P_1 and the amount or the value of the bond due at the end of one period by P_2. Then the interest rate, represented by i and measured as a decimal is defined as

$$1 + i = \frac{P_2}{P_1} \tag{3-3}$$

The equation can be manipulated in either of two ways: If we know the initial value of the loan and the interest rate, then we can solve for the amount due; or, if we know the amount due and the interest rate, then we can solve for the current value of the loan. If, for example, the interest rate is 9 percent and the amount due at the end of the period is $1,200 then $P_1 =$ $1,200/1.09 = $1,100.92.

COMPOUND INTEREST   When we deal with bonds or loans that are longer than one period, then we must be careful to distinguish between simple and compound interest. To see the distinction suppose we examine a bond with an initial value of P_1 as above, and a value of P_5, four rather than one period later. What is the single-period interest rate earned by this bond or the yield per period on this bond? One way to determine this rate might be to simply divide the percentage price increase by the number of periods involved, in this case four periods. We will define this as the average simple interest rate:

$$\frac{((P_5/P_1) - 1)}{4} = i \qquad (3\text{-}4)$$

For example, if P_1 and P_5 assumed the values of 100 and 220, respectively, then the average simple interest rate would be $((220/100) - 1)4 = 30$ percent.

This method does not provide an accurate measure of the interest actually earned by the asset in each period. The shortcoming of the procedure is that it ignores the fact that interest earned in early periods increases the base on which interest is paid in later periods. In effect, it ignores the fact that interest compounds. We therefore refer to the appropriate measure of the interest rate as the compound rather than the simple interest rate. To see how to define the compound interest rate we will trace through the growth of the value of the asset each period from 1 to 5. If we buy a bond which increases in value at an interest rate of i per period, then the relationship between its value in period 2 and its value in period 1 is defined as in Eq. (3-3):

$$P_2 = P_1 (1 + i) \qquad (3\text{-}5)$$

The relationship between the values in periods 3 and 2 can be defined in the same way:

$$P_3 = P_2 (1 + i) \qquad (3\text{-}6)$$

But by substituting from Eq. (3-5) for the value of P_2 this yields

$$P_3 = P_1 (1 + i)(1 + i) = P_1 (1 + i)^2 \qquad (3\text{-}7)$$

This substitution process can be continued until we derive an expression for P_5:

$$P_5 = P_1 (1 + i)^4 \qquad (3\text{-}8)$$

We can now easily use this expression to solve for the compound as opposed to the average simple interest rate. We merely divide through both sides of Eq. (3-8) by P_1 and take the fourth root:

$$i = \sqrt[4]{\frac{P_5}{P_1}} - 1 \qquad (3\text{-}9)$$

In the example used above where P_5 and P_1 are 220 and 100, respectively, the compound interest rate is 22 percent as compared to 30 percent for the average simple interest rate. Whenever the interest rate is referred to henceforth in this book and other places, it should be understood that it is the compound rather than the simple interest rate.

THE INTEREST RATE ON A DISCOUNT LOAN   The typical loan contract is usually stated with the following terms. For a single-period loan the initial amount of the loan is P_1 and the interest rate is equal to i. This means that at the end of the period the amount owed to the lender is $P_2 = (1 + i) P_1$. This is identical to the statement of simple interest above. However, the loan may also be made on a discount basis. The amount of the discount loan is stated in terms of the amount to be repaid rather than the amount which is lent, that is, in terms of P_2 rather than P_1. In addition, the quoted interest payment is based on P_2 rather than P_1; that is, P_1 is determined as follows: $P_1 = (1 - i_d) P_2$, where i_d is the stated interest rate on a discount basis. This has the effect of understating the true interest rate that is paid, for one minus the true interest rate is still equal to $P_2/P_1 = 1/(1 - i)$. If, for example, the amount that is owed at the end of the period is \$1,000 and the stated interest rate for the discount loan is 10 percent, then the amount that is actually lent is \$900 and the actual interest rate on this loan is (\$1,000/\$900) $- 1 = 11$ percent.

THE COUPON AND THE MARKET INTEREST RATES   Many bonds have both a coupon and a market interest rate. In order to distinguish between these two interest rates it is necessary to explain the terms of a coupon bond. Most coupon bonds have maturities longer than one period and we'll examine examples of these later in the chapter. But at this point we will deal with a very simple coupon bond that has only one period to maturity. A coupon bond has what is termed a "face value" and the face value along with the coupon rate determines the amount that will be paid to the lender at the bond's maturity. For example, a single-period bond with a \$1,000 face value and 6 percent coupon interest rate will pay \$1,060 at maturity. That is,

$$P_2 = (1 + i_c)F \tag{3-10}$$

where i_c is the coupon interest rate and F is the face value of the bond. Now that we know how P_2 is determined we still can return to Eq. (3-3) for the determinants of either the market value of the bond, P_1, or the market interest rate on the bond, i. If we know the market interest rate, then we can solve for the market value of the bond as follows:

$$P_1 = \frac{P_2}{1 + i} \tag{3-11}$$

Conversely, if we know the market value of the bond, we can solve for the market interest rate:

$$i = \frac{P_2}{P_1} - 1 \tag{3-12}$$

For example, for the bond with a face value of $1,000 and a coupon interest rate of 6 percent, if the market interest rate is 10 percent, then the price of the bond must be $1,060/1.1 = $963. Only at this price will the bond have a yield which is the same as the one prevailing in the market. Therefore, the coupon rate merely defines the payment that will be made to the lender. It need not be the same as the interest rate which the market demands for lending funds.

REAL AND NOMINAL INTEREST RATES   In our discussion of interest rates thus far we have not mentioned the possibility that the price level will change during the period covered by a bond or a loan. If the price level changes, then the real return received by the lender and the real cost paid by the borrower will change. This is because the values of financial contracts are denominated in terms of money, dollars in the United States. This is clear from an examination of the value of the contract at its beginning and termination, that is, the values of P_1 and P_2. Both of these values are expressed in dollars. But if the general level of prices changes from time period 1 to time period 2, then the real interest rate, the interest rate net of inflation, is altered. To make this statement more specific we will define the real interest rate that is actually received by the lender, i_R, as

$$i_R = \left(\frac{P_2}{P_1} - 1\right) - \text{inflation rate} = i_N - \text{inflation rate} \qquad (3\text{-}13)$$

where i_N is the nominal interest rate of i used in the equations above. For example, if the nominal interest rate is 10 percent, and the inflation rate is 6 percent, then the real rate is 4 percent.

When inflation rates are high and volatile, it is real rather than nominal interest rates which are of concern to investors. As a result, investors will adjust the nominal interest rates they demand so that the real returns they expect to receive are viewed as an appropriate compensation for lending funds. We will examine this process of adjusting the nominal rate in more detail in Chapter Eight.

BEFORE-TAX AND AFTER-TAX INTEREST RATES   Most types of interest income are subject to income tax from both federal and state governments. Therefore it is important to distinguish between interest rates before taxes and after taxes. For any individual the distinction depends upon his or her marginal tax rate, that is, the tax rate that is paid on the marginal amount of income that the interest payment represents. Effective marginal tax rates from federal income taxes are illustrated in Table 2-2. With this marginal tax rate represented by l, the relationship between the before-tax and after-tax nominal interest rates for a particular individual can be expressed as

$$i_A = i_N(1 - l) \qquad (3\text{-}14)$$

where i_A is the after-tax nominal interest rate. Equation (3-14) indicates that the after-tax interest rate is equal to the before-tax interest rate reduced by the marginal tax rate of the individual in question. For example, if the nominal interest rate is 16 percent, then the after-tax nominal rate for a person in the 50 percent tax bracket is 8 percent.

We can combine the adjustments we have made for taxes and inflation rates to arrive at the after-tax real interest rate for an individual in the market. If we represent the after-tax real interest rate by i_{RA}, then its relationship to the nominal interest can be defined as follows:

$$i_{RA} = i_N(1 - l) - \text{inflation rate} \tag{3-15}$$

For example, for an individual with a 30 percent marginal tax rate who receives a nominal interest rate of 16 percent and experiences inflation of 10 percent, the real after-tax return will be $.16 \times .7 - .10 = 1.2$ percent. The discrepancy between the real after-tax rate and the nominal interest rate is substantial. It highlights how misleading it can be to examine nominal interest rates without careful consideration of taxes and inflation. As the example shows, a 16 percent interest rate is not particularly high with 10 percent inflation and a 30 percent tax rate.

INTRODUCTION TO PRESENT VALUE

In this section we will examine the concept of present value. The material we have examined so far in this chapter has really been a prelude for the analysis that is presented in this section. In the previous section, when we determined the value of a bond at the beginning of period 1, P_1, we dealt with present value. But now we will examine the concept of present value in a more general framework. In the next section we will extend these ideas and introduce the internal rate of return.

Four Present Value Problems

We will examine four types of problems dealing with present and future value. We will then use these problems to consider the concept of internal rate of return. The problems are set up so that they become progressively more complicated. In addition, when they are first presented they are in a simpler and less general form than need be the case. We will consider the simpler form first and then consider the complications after we have dealt with the basic structure of the four problems.

PROBLEM 1   Suppose we place $1 in the bank at an interest rate of i and leave it there for N years. What will the value of that dollar be at the end of the N years? First of all we will consider the very simple case where N is equal to one. In this instance, the value of the dollar at the end of the year, which we will refer to as the future value (FV), is

$$FV = 1(1 + i) \tag{3-16}$$

This is simply the expression for simple interest defined above. If the dollar is left on deposit for more than one period earning the interest rate of i per period, then we must simply compound the interest to arrive at the future value. At the end of N years the future value is

$$FV = 1(1 + i)(1 + i) \cdots (1 + i) \tag{3-17}$$

This can be rewritten as

$$FV = 1(1 + i)^N \tag{3-18}$$

For example, if the interest rate is 10 percent and N is equal to 10 years, then $FV = \$1.00(1.10)^{10} = \$2.59$.

PROBLEM 2 Suppose we place $1 in the bank every year for N years. What will be the value of that stream of deposits at the end of the N years? This problem can be viewed as the sum of a sequence of problems identical to problem 1. At the end of N years the value of the first dollar deposited is $1(1 + i)^N$; the value of the second dollar deposited is $1(1 + i)^{N-1}$, and so forth. The future value of the stream of dollars can therefore be expressed as

$$FV = 1(1 + i) + 1(1 + i)^2 + 1(1 + i)^3 + \cdots + 1(1 + i)^N \tag{3-19}$$

which can be simplified to read:

$$FV = \sum_{t=1}^{N} 1(1 + i)^t \tag{3-20}$$

For example, if $N = 5$ and $i = 5$ percent, then

$$
\begin{aligned}
FV &= \$1.05 + (\$1.05)^2 + (\$1.05)^3 + (\$1.05)^4 + (\$1.05)^5 \\
&= \$1.05 + \$1.103 + \$1.158 + \$1.216 + \$1.276 \\
&= \$5.80
\end{aligned}
$$

PROBLEM 3 In problems 3 and 4 we will reverse the questions posed in problems 1 and 2. That is, we will be concerned with the present value (PV) rather than the future value. If we reverse question 1, then we can ask the following: What is the value, today, of $1 received N periods from now? To answer the question we merely reverse the answer to question 1.

The present value of the dollar is equal to the "discounted value" of the dollar:

$$PV = \frac{1}{(1 + i)^N} \qquad (3\text{-}21)$$

This is merely another way of saying that there is an amount, PV, which if invested for N years at i percent, will have a value of $1 at the end of N years. For example, if N is equal to 10 and i is equal to 5 percent, then the present value of the dollar is $1/(1.05)^{10} = .61$.

PROBLEM 4   The reverse to question 2 is the following: What is the value, today, of a stream of income of $1 received at the end of each period for N periods? It is important to note whether the dollar is received at the beginning or the end of the period. In problem 2 we implicitly assumed the deposit was made at the beginning of the period. In this problem we assume that the dollar is received at the end of each period. Note that this is the same assumption that was made in problem 3. This distinction may seem a little awkward at first, but it is standard practice in present value calculations. This problem is merely a sequence of problems like problem 3. The value of the first dollar received is $1/(1 + i)$; the value of a second dollar received is $1/(1 + i)^2$; and so on until the value of the last dollar received is $1/(1 + i)^N$. The present value of the stream of income can therefore be expressed as

$$PV = \sum_{t=1}^{N} \frac{1}{(1 + i)^t} \qquad (3\text{-}22)$$

For example, if i is equal to 5 percent and N is equal to 5, then

$$PV = \frac{1}{(\$1.05)} + \frac{1}{(\$1.05)^2} + \frac{1}{(\$1.05)^3} + \frac{1}{(\$1.05)^4} + \frac{1}{(\$1.05)^5}$$
$$= \$.952 + \$.907 + \$.864 + \$.823 + \$.783$$
$$= \$4.33$$

These four questions and the formulas which accompany them are summarized in Table 3-1.

Generalizing the Four Problems and the Concept of Annuity

The computational burden involved in computing either the present value or the future value of a stream of income is apparent from the example in problem 4 above. If N is relatively large, then the computations involved are burdensome. Fortunately, there is a relatively simple procedure which can

TABLE 3-1

Summary of the Four Basic Questions of Present and Future Value

QUESTION	FORMULA FOR THE ANSWER
FUTURE VALUE QUESTIONS	
1 What is the future value of \$1 invested for N years at $i\%$?	$FV = 1(1 + i)^N$
2 What is the future value of \$1 invested every year for N years?	$FV = \sum_{t=1}^{N} 1(1 + i)^t$
PRESENT VALUE QUESTIONS	
3 What is the present value of \$1 received N years from now?	$PV = \dfrac{1}{(1 + i)^N}$
4 What is the present value of \$1 received every year for N years?	$PV = \sum_{t=1}^{N} \dfrac{1}{(1 + i)^t}$

be used to avoid these difficulties when the problem has the simplifying feature of problems 2 and 4 as described above, that the amount received each period is the same. In these problems the amount received each period was \$1. But it could be any amount. As long as the amount each period is the same, the stream of income is referred to as an "annuity." In this instance the computational burden can be reduced substantially. To see how this reduction can be accomplished we will first generalize the solutions of the four problems presented above and then we will explain the procedure for dealing with annuities.

A limiting feature of these four problems, as they have been described, is that the amount of income in each period is restricted to \$1. This simplifies the initial statement in the present value equations. But the actual income per period can be any amount. Therefore we can generalize each of the solutions to the four problems for an arbitrary amount of income. In problems 1 and 3, where there is only one payment, we can symbolize the payment with A, and in problems 2 and 4, where there are N payments, each of which may be different, each will be represented by A_t in time period t. Each of the solutions may now be rewritten for this more general income stream by substituting A and A_t in the earlier equations.

Problem 1:

$$FV = A(1 + i)^N \tag{3-23}$$

Problem 2:

$$FV = \sum_{t=1}^{N} A_t(1 + i)^t \tag{3-24}$$

Problem 3:

$$PV = \frac{A}{(1 + i)^N} \tag{3-25}$$

Problem 4:

$$PV = \sum_{t=1}^{N} \frac{A_t}{(1+ i)^t} \tag{3-26}$$

Equations (3-24) and (3-26) will be referred to as the future and present value equations throughout the remainder of this book. They indicate the basic procedure for valuing an income stream when problems involving uncertainty about the income stream are ignored. Notice that Eqs. (3-23) and (3-25) are simply a special case of Eqs. (3-24) and (3-26) where $A_t = 0$ for all values of t except $t = N$. In these special cases the subscript can be dropped altogether.

In order to use Eqs. (3-24) and (3-26) for the future and present value of an income stream, it is important to be familiar with some of the procedures available which greatly simplify the burden involved in computing these values. Most of these computations are most easily performed on electronic calculators. But they may also be performed using tables of simple present values and annuities. Abbreviated forms of these tables are provided in an appendix to this book. Here we will explain the nature of an annuity and the reduced computational burden that is accomplished by use of the tables or a calculator.

Equations (3-24) and (3-26) describe annuities if one simplifying restriction holds. This restriction is that the income stream is a constant so that the subscript of t on A may be dropped. The restriction can be written algebraically as $A_j = A_k$, for all values of j and k from 1 to N. For example, a constant income stream would be $1,000 per year for 10 years, while a nonconstant stream would be $1,000; $2,000; $2,500; $212. When the income stream is constant, it is referred to as an annuity. In this case, it is possible to use an annuity procedure on a calculator or an annuity table to determine either the present or future value of the annuity. The advantage in computation which is gained with an annuity can be seen from Eq. (3-26) as follows. When A_t is constant for all t, and the subscript is omitted, then the equation can be rewritten as

$$PV = \sum_{t=1}^{N} \frac{A}{(1 + i)^t} \tag{3-27}$$

But this can be simplified by extracting A from the summation:

$$PV = A \left[\sum_{t=1}^{N} \frac{1}{(1 + i)^t} \right] \tag{3-28}$$

It is now possible to compute the value of the second part of the right-hand term, $\sum_{t=1}^{N} [1/(1 + i)^t]$, for *any* values of i and N.

The advantage of the annuity is that these terms can be computed ahead of time and are then available to be used with *any* value of A. This is why an annuity table or a calculator is useful. Tables contain the values of $\sum_{t=1}^{N} [1/(1 + i)^t]$ for a selection of i and N. One can therefore simply look up the relevant entry in the table and multiply it by the value of the periodic payment A. The annuity table in the Appendix contains these terms, indexed by i and N. For example, an annuity of $1,000 per year for 10 years at 10 percent has a present value of $6,145, where the annuity factor, 6.145, is found in the appropriate position in the table, as illustrated in Figure 3-1.

The same simplifying procedure can be used for the present value of a single future payment. In this case, the table of present value factors simply contains values for $1/(1 + i)^N$, again indexed by i and N. For example, the present value of $1,000 received 10 years from now at 10 percent interest is equal to $385.50.

ADDITIONAL FEATURES OF PRESENT VALUE

Net Present Value

The concept of present value is used in setting almost all prices in financial markets. In fact, the prices of financial assets *are* the discounted values of expected future earnings, adjusted for risk. In addition, the present value procedure is the principal technique which can be used to evaluate an investment. However, when used in this context, we need to amend the procedure slightly. The amendment that we need to add changes nothing we have done so far. We merely need to distinguish between the *total* or gross present value of an asset and the *net* present value of an asset. What we have discussed so far is actually the gross present value. To see the distinction it is best to consider an example.

Suppose we are considering whether to undertake an investment which promises to pay $10,000 per year each year for 10 years. Also suppose that the interest rate which we perceive represents our opportunity cost is 12 percent. Finally, suppose that the asset which yields this future stream of income can be purchased for $50,000. The question we have to ask ourselves is what the asset is worth to us. We can determine this by computing the gross present value (GPV). The value is determined as indicated in Eq. (3-26).

Annuity table: Present value of $1 *per year* for each of *t* years $= 1/r - 1/[r(1 + r)^t]$

Interest rate per year

Number of years	1%	2%	3%	4%	5%	6%	7%	8%	9%	10%	11%	12%	13%	14%	15%
1	.990	.980	.971	.962	.952	.943	.935	.926	.917	.909	.901	.893	.885	.877	.870
2	1.970	1.942	1.913	1.886	1.859	1.833	1.808	1.783	1.759	1.736	1.713	1.690	1.668	1.647	1.626
3	2.941	2.884	2.829	2.775	2.723	2.673	2.624	2.577	2.531	2.487	2.444	2.402	2.361	2.322	2.283
4	3.902	3.808	3.717	3.630	3.546	3.465	3.387	3.312	3.240	3.170	3.102	3.037	2.974	2.914	2.855
5	4.853	4.713	4.580	4.452	4.329	4.212	4.100	3.993	3.890	3.791	3.696	3.605	3.517	3.433	3.352
6	5.795	5.601	5.417	5.242	5.076	4.917	4.767	4.623	4.486	4.355	4.231	4.111	3.998	3.889	3.784
7	6.728	6.472	6.230	6.002	5.786	5.582	5.389	5.206	5.033	4.868	4.712	4.564	4.423	4.288	4.160
8	7.652	7.325	7.020	6.733	6.463	6.210	5.971	5.747	5.535	5.335	5.146	4.968	4.799	4.639	4.487
9	8.566	8.162	7.786	7.435	7.108	6.802	6.515	6.247	5.995	5.759	5.537	5.328	5.132	4.946	4.772
10	9.471	8.983	8.530	8.111	7.722	7.360	7.024	6.710	6.418	6.145	5.889	5.650	5.426	5.216	5.019
11	10.37	9.787	9.253	8.760	8.306	7.887	7.499	7.139	6.805	6.495	6.207	5.938	5.687	5.453	5.234
12	11.26	10.58	9.954	9.385	8.863	8.384	7.943	7.536	7.161	6.814	6.492	6.194	5.918	5.660	5.421
13	12.13	11.35	10.63	9.986	9.394	8.853	8.358	7.904	7.487	7.103	6.750	6.424	6.122	5.842	5.583
14	13.00	12.11	11.30	10.56	9.899	9.295	8.745	8.244	7.786	7.367	6.982	6.628	6.302	6.002	5.724
15	13.87	12.85	11.94	11.12	10.38	9.712	9.108	8.559	8.061	7.606	7.191	6.811	6.462	6.142	5.847
16	14.72	13.58	12.56	11.65	10.84	10.11	9.447	8.851	8.313	7.824	7.379	6.974	6.604	6.265	5.954
17	15.56	14.29	13.17	12.17	11.27	10.48	9.763	9.122	8.544	8.022	7.549	7.120	6.729	6.373	6.047
18	16.40	14.99	13.75	12.66	11.69	10.83	10.06	9.372	8.756	8.201	7.702	7.250	6.840	6.467	6.128
19	17.23	15.68	14.32	13.13	12.09	11.16	10.34	9.604	8.950	8.365	7.839	7.366	6.938	6.550	6.198
20	18.05	16.35	14.88	13.59	12.46	11.47	10.59	9.818	9.129	8.514	7.963	7.469	7.025	6.623	6.259
25	22.02	19.52	17.41	15.62	14.09	12.78	11.65	10.67	9.823	9.077	8.422	7.843	7.330	6.873	6.464
30	25.81	22.40	19.60	17.29	15.37	13.76	12.41	11.26	10.27	9.427	8.694	8.055	7.496	7.003	6.566

FIGURE 3-1

This figure illustrates how to find the correct present value for a stream of income 10 years long discounted at 10 percent. The factor is 6.145.

$$\text{GPV} = \sum_{t=1}^{10} \frac{\$10,000}{(1.12)^t}$$
$$= \$56,502$$

We cannot tell from the gross present value alone whether we should pur-chase this asset. We have to take one more step and compare the gross present value with the purchase price or the cost of the asset. We will label this cost C. Now we can define the difference between these two as the net present value (NPV).

$$\text{NPV} = \text{GPV} - C \qquad (3\text{-}29)$$

In the example, the NPV is

$$\text{NPV} = \$56,502 - \$50,000 = \$6,502$$

The net present value simply measures the difference between the present value of the future revenues and the cost of the investment. It is therefore a measure of "economic" value.

The advantage of net present value is that it can be used to define a simple rule for evaluating investments. An investment is worthwhile if it has positive economic value or a positive net present value when evaluated at an appropriate discount rate. If the discount rate utilized reflects the opportu-nity cost to the investor, then all investments with positive net present value will make a positive contribution to that investor's total worth.

The Internal Rate of Return

There is another way to view the relationship between the income stream an asset generates and the present value of that asset. Instead of taking an interest rate as given and using it to discount the future income to arrive at a present value, we can use the value of an asset and its future income stream to derive its rate of return. This is virtually what we did earlier in this chapter to explain the simple and compound rates of interest. For example, one plus the simple interest rate was defined as the payoff from an asset one period hence, divided by its current or present value: $P_2/P_1 = 1 + i$. Equa-tions (3-23) and (3-25) simply generalize this expression to the case where there are N periods of time involved. In either case, we can define the interest rate in these equations as the internal rate of return when we take the present and future values as given and solve for the interest rate which satisfies the equation. In the case of the present value equation for a single payment, Eq. (3-25), if we are given the payment to be received N periods hence, A, and the value of that payment today, PV, then we can solve for an interest rate which we will label i^*. This is the interest rate earned on this asset and is defined as the internal rate of return. By solving for i^* in Eq. (3-25) we conclude that

$$i^* = \sqrt[N]{\frac{A}{PV}} - 1 \qquad (3\text{-}30)$$

This is virtually the same as Eq. (3-9) where $N = 4$, $A = P_5$, and $PV = P_1$. We can also use net present value to provide an equivalent definition of the internal rate of return. The interest rate which yields a zero net present value for an investment is the internal rate of return. This is the same as saying that it is the interest rate which yields a present value of future income which is equal to the cost of an asset.

To understand this definition of the internal rate of return it is useful to return to the example about net present value discussed in the preceding section. The example involved an investment with a stream of $10,000 per year for 10 years and a cost of $50,000. In the discussion of net present value we learned that the net present value of this investment, when discounted at 12 percent, was $6,502. We could also compute the net present value for this investment at a selection of alternative discount rates. If we did so, we could then plot these combinations of net present value and discount rate in a diagram. Such a diagram is presented in Figure 3-2. The vertical axis in the figure measures net present value in dollars and the horizontal axis measures the discount rate. The downward-sloping line in the figure illustrates that the net present value declines as the discount rate increases. Now we can illustrate the internal rate of return. The internal rate of return is the discount rate which yields a net present value of zero. In this example, that internal rate of return is approximately 15 percent. This is the point where the downward-sloping line crosses the vertical axis. This is the same thing as saying that the internal rate of return is the discount rate which yields a present value for the future income on the investment of $50,000.

It is important to observe that the only substantive difference between the concepts of present value and internal rate of return is the choice about what is taken as given and what must be derived. When we solve for the present value, the interest rate is taken as given. This interest rate is often called a discount rate but it is not referred to as an internal rate of return. Conversely, when the present value is taken as given, we can solve for the implied interest rate according to Eq. (3-30), and we label this the internal rate of return. The present value and the internal rate of return may therefore be thought of as flip sides of the same coin. If we know the interest rate or yield that the market demands, then we can determine an asset's value in dollars. Conversely, if we know the value placed on an asset by the market, we can determine the yield the market is demanding. We cannot determine one without the other.

The internal rate of return is relatively easy to define analytically and compute when there is a single future payment involved, as is the case in

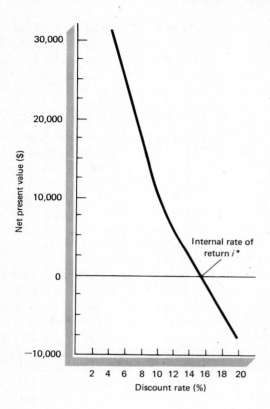

FIGURE 3-2
Net present value of an investment which pays $10,000 per year for 10 years and costs $50,000. The figure shows that the internal rate of return is approximately 15 percent.

Eq. (3-30). It is not nearly as straightforward when there is a stream of future income, as is the case for the present value equation, Eq. (3-26). In this instance we must resort to more complicated procedures to derive the value of the internal rate of return. To define the internal rate of return in this instance we merely state that if we know the current value of the asset, PV, and we know the cash-flow stream, A_t, then there will exist an interest rate, i^*, which satisfies Eq. (3-26).

$$PV = \sum_{t=1}^{N} \frac{A_t}{(1 + i^*)^t} \tag{3-31}$$

But to say that such an interest rate exists is not to show how to determine what its value is. Analytically, that is a rather complicated task. Fortunately, there is a relatively simple procedure for estimating the internal rate of return. This procedure is essentially a method of hunt and peck. Basically the procedure is as follows. Arbitrarily choose an interest rate and determine the present value of the income stream A_t based on that interest rate. If the present value you compute is higher than the actual value of the asset, then increase the interest rate and repeat the calculations. Generally, this converges on the accurate internal rate of return. One way to accomplish this is by using the present value tables. Or, if the cash-flow stream is an annuity, most financial calculators will perform the calculations automatically. For example, if the present value of an asset is $10,000 and the income stream is $1,200 per year for 10 years, then the internal rate of return can be found to be 3.5 percent.

For assets with income in more than one future period, the internal rate of return is not always well defined. There may be more than one internal rate of return and there may be no internal rate of return. For example, suppose you are considering an investment project with the following cash flows: year 1, −$4,000; year 2, +$25,000; and year 3, −$25,000. This project has two internal rates of return, 25 percent and 400 percent. The problem is that Eq. (3-31) is a polynomial of order N. The task of solving for i^* requires the identification of the roots of the polynomial.[3] If there are multiple roots of the polynomial, then, in effect, there are multiple internal rates of return. In these cases the multiple roots obscure the meaning of the results. Fortunately, it is easy to tell by inspecting the income stream when multiple roots are a possibility. They are possible only when in some future periods, there is negative income. If all future values of A_t are positive, then there will be a single internal rate of return. The implication is that it is best to avoid the internal rate of return altogether if future income in some periods is negative.

Finally, it is important to reemphasize that present value and internal rate of return are merely reverse sides of the same coin. The concept that lies behind them is that each asset has a value. This value can be expressed directly in dollars if we know the yield demanded by the market. Conversely, it can be expressed in the form of an interest rate if we know the dollar value placed on it. We simply cannot have one without the other.

Taking Account of the Frequency of Compounding

There is one final complication which can be introduced into the procedure for determining present and future values. The complication is that interest may be compounded more than once per period. The real complication here is that we have a common unit for comparison. But the compounding may be more frequent than annually and when it is, we do not generally change the interest rate to express it on a quarterly, monthly, or daily basis. Changes in the frequency of compounding alter the present and future values and the effective annual interest rate that is earned.

To see what happens as the frequency of compounding is increased we will modify the present and future value equations for the case of a single payment to accommodate an arbitrary frequency. But the same modifications apply to the more general cases of multiple payments as described in

[3]See Eugene F. Fama and Merton H. Miller, *The Theory of Finance*, Holt, Rinehart and Winston, New York, 1972, pp. 137–143, for a more detailed discussion of difficulties surrounding the internal rate of return.

Eqs. (3-24) and (3-26). Suppose that compounding takes place m times per year at an annual interest rate of i, or an interest rate of i/m per compounding. The present value of A dollars received N periods from now would be

$$PV = \frac{A}{(1 + i/m)^{mN}} \tag{3-32}$$

For example, if the annual interest rate is 12 percent and compounding is done once per quarter, then the present value of $1,000 received one year hence is PV $= \$1,000/(\$1.03)^4 = \$888.49$.

It is quite possible to imagine compounding so frequently that it virtually becomes continuous or that the frequency of compounding approaches infinity. In this case, it is necessary to examine what happens as m approaches infinity in Eq. (3-32). While we will eschew dealing with all the mathematics involved in evaluating this equation as m approaches infinity, we can neatly summarize the form of the equation which results.[4] The present value of A dollars received in N years when compounding is continuous at an annual interest rate of i, can be expressed

$$PV = \frac{\$1,000}{e^{iN}} = \$1,000(e^{-iN}) \tag{3-33}$$

where e is called the natural logarithm and has the value 2.718. Similarly, the future value of $1,000 invested today on the same terms would be

$$FV = \$1,000(e^{iN}) \tag{3-34}$$

If, for example, i is 10 percent, N is 2 years, and A is $1,000, then the present value is $\$1,000/(2.718^{.2}) = \$818.74$. Had the compounding been annual, the present value would be $826.44. Therefore, in this example, increasing the frequency of compounding from annual to continuous decreased the present value by $7.70.

Perpetuities

The process of capitalizing an income stream into a present value is applicable to virtually all assets in the market. For example, the present value equation provides the basic framework for valuing equity securities. But particularly in the case of equities, and with some other assets as well, the time horizon over which the income stream will be generated is not precisely defined. That is, many assets do not have a specific maturity which defines the point at which the income stream terminates. Instead, the asset generates income for an indefinite future. One way to deal with assets which

---

[4]For a more complete treatment of the case of continuous compounding, see J. Hirshleifer, *Investment, Interest, and Capital*, Prentice-Hall, Englewood Cliffs, N.J., 1970.

have no specific termination point is to assume that they will go on forever. Such assets are usually referred to as perpetuities. While few if any things actually go on forever, the assumption is not really that troublesome. The reason is that in any present value equation with a positive interest rate, events, that is, inflow of dollars, become increasingly less significant today, the farther in the future they take place. The fact that dollars received in the future are discounted by one plus the interest rate raised to the power of the time interval involved, means that the significance, today, of future income will decline rapidly as the time interval increases. Only if the income stream itself is growing can this perpetuity assumption lead to real difficulties.

In order to examine how the value of assets is determined when those assets are assumed to go on forever, we will ignore the prospect for growth in the income stream accruing to an asset, and examine the present value of a perpetual but constant income stream. That is, we will examine an annuity with an infinite maturity. There is at least one real-world example of such an annuity. For many years the British Treasury has sold bonds called "Consols." These are promises to pay a constant stream of income literally forever. The prices and yields of these securities are determined using the basic present value equation, but now the maturity, N, equals infinity. The price of the Consol is therefore defined as

$$PV = \sum_{t=1}^{\infty} \frac{A}{(1 + i)^t} \tag{3-35}$$

where i is the market yield on a Consol and A is received at the end of each period. To simplify this equation we can multiply both sides by $(1 + i)$, which yields

$$PV(1 + i) = A + \frac{A}{(1 + i)} + \frac{A}{(1 + i)^2} + \cdots + \frac{A}{(1 + i)^{N-1}} \tag{3-36}$$

Subtracting Eq. (3-35) from Eq. (3-36), we obtain

$$PV(1 + i) - PV = A - \frac{A}{(1 + i)^N}$$

As N approaches infinity, as in the case of the perpetuity, $A/(1 + i)^N$ approaches zero. As a result PV can be simplified to

$$PV = \frac{A}{i} \tag{3-37}$$

or the yield can be expressed as

$$i = \frac{A}{PV} \tag{3-38}$$

This simply says that the yield on a perpetuity is equal to the ratio of the periodic payment to the asset's current value. If, for example, $A = \$600$ and $PV = \$12,000$, then $i = 5$ percent.

PRESENT VALUE OF BONDS AND STOCKS

Now we can use the concept of present value to deal with the two principal types of securities which are traded in the financial markets: bonds and stocks. We will take up bonds first and then stocks.

The Value of a Coupon Bond

There are a wide variety of different types of debt instruments traded in financial markets. Each such debt instrument has a price and a market interest rate, or yield. The price is simply the present value of the future income stream accruing to the bond if it is held to maturity and discounted at the market yield for that bond. Similarly, the market yield is simply the internal rate of return for the same income stream, given the market price of the bond. These prices and yields are quoted in the financial press on a regular basis and it is important to see more precisely how they are computed.

One quite common type of debt instrument is referred to as the coupon bond. We discussed the distinction between a coupon and market interest rate early in the chapter. Coupon interest is the promised interest payment to be paid periodically on a bond. It is generally stated as some percentage of the face or maturity value of the bond. For example, a 5 percent coupon bond with a face value of $10,000 would pay $500 every year to the owner of the bond until the bond matured. At maturity the bondholder would receive the face value of $10,000.

To see how the market prices a coupon bond we will consider an example with the following characteristics. The bond has a maturity value of $100,000 with a 5 percent coupon interest rate, paid semiannually. The bond was originally issued with a maturity of 20 years, but there are now exactly 10 years remaining to maturity and the current date is January 1, 1982. We want to ask two questions about this bond. First, we want to know what the market price of this bond would be, given the yield on 10-year bonds. Then we want to know what the yield would be, if we knew the price of the bond. The market computes the value of a bond both in terms of a dollar price and in terms of a market yield. Given one, we can determine the other and we want to see how this is done in our example.

The first thing we need to do in order to determine the price or the yield for the bond is carefully define the income stream that will accrue to the bond. With a 5 percent coupon rate the bondholder will receive $5,000 per year in interest. But because this bond stipulates semiannual payment, $2,500 will be received every 6 months. In addition, at the end of 10 years, or on January 1, 1992 the bondholder will receive the $100,000 maturity value. The cash flows that will be received on each future date are shown in the table below:

	JULY	JAN.	JULY	JAN.	. . .	JULY	JAN.
Date	82	83	83	84		91	92
Cash flow	$2,500	$2,500	$2,500	$2,500		$2,500	$102,500

In order to determine either the market price or yield we need to set up the present value equation for this bond. From the time path of future payments to the bondholder we know that there are 19 periods, each 6 months long, when the bondholder will receive $2,500 per period. In the twentieth period the bondholder will receive $102,500. The present value equation can therefore be written as

$$PV = \sum_{t=1}^{19} \frac{\$2,500}{\left(1 + \frac{i}{2}\right)^t} + \frac{\$102,500}{\left(1 + \frac{i}{2}\right)^{20}}$$

We have to discount by half the annual interest rate because we are compounding every 6 months rather than annually, due to the fact that coupon payments are made every 6 months.

We can use this equation to solve for either the market price of the bond or the yield, given the other value. If the market yield on this type of bond is 7 percent, then the price of the bond is determined as follows:

$$PV = \frac{\$2,500}{1.035} + \frac{\$2,500}{(1.035)^2} + \frac{\$2,500}{(1.035)^3} + \cdots + \frac{\$2,500}{(1.035)^{19}} + \frac{\$102,500}{(1.035)^{20}}$$
$$= \$85,787$$

On the other hand, if the price of the bond is $95,000, then the market yield must be determined through the hunt-and-peck procedure described above. It turns out to be approximately 5.7 percent. There is no shortcut except to use trial and error, unless you have a calculator which will do it for you.

Valuing Equity Securities

The value of a perpetuity discussed at the end of the last section provides the basis for valuing any income stream which is presumed to last forever, but which is not expected to be constant. The equity security is an example of this situation. As was discussed in Chapter Two, the stream of income which accrues to an equity security is composed of the dividend payment and the capital gain or loss on the price of the stock. As a result, the current price is the capitalized value of future dividends and capital gains and losses. But the price at any point in the future is, in turn, dependent on dividends or capital gains or losses even further in the future. The implication is that the current price is really the capitalized value of future dividends as long as the firm continues to exist, plus the value of the firm at termination if it should be sold. If we assume that the firm goes on forever, then the current value is virtually the capitalized value of future dividends. The general present value equation for the equity value of the firm, ignoring uncertainty about the magnitude of future dividends, can then be written as

$$PV = \sum_{t=1}^{N} \frac{D_t}{(1 + i)^t} \tag{3-39}$$

where D_t is the dividend payment anticipated in time period t. The only distinction between this case and the perpetuity considered earlier is that the dividend payments are subscripted for time, indicating that they will be distinct values each period.

If we can say nothing more about the way future dividends will evolve over time, then Eq. (3-39) is essentially the end of the story about time and the value of assets. But if we can postulate a regular pattern about the evolution of dividends, then we can simplify the equation considerably. One way to do this is to assume that dividends grow at some constant rate, say g. Then if dividends are initially at a level of D_0, the dividend payment in any future period t can be written:

$$D_t = D_0(1 + g)^t \tag{3-40}$$

Substituting this into Eq. (3-39) yields

$$PV = \sum_{t=1}^{N} \frac{D_0(1 + g)^t}{(1 + i)^t} \tag{3-41}$$

This equation for the value of an equity security can now be simplified, just as could Eq. (3-35) for the value of a British Consol, if i is greater than g. That is, we can simplify the equation if the discount rate is greater than the rate of growth of dividends. If this were not the case, then the value of the asset would be infinite because the numerator grows at a faster rate than the denominator. But if i exceeds g, then the denominators in Eq. (3-41) will increase faster than will the numerators, and PV will have a finite value.

To see this, consider an example where dividends are growing at 10 percent from an initial amount of $10 and i is only 5 percent. We only need to write out a few terms of Eq. (3-41) to see the effect:

$$PV = \frac{10(1.1)}{1.05} + \frac{10(1.1)^2}{(1.05)^2} + \frac{10(1.1)^3}{(1.05)^3} + \cdots$$

$$= \frac{11}{1.05} + \frac{12.10}{1.1025} + \frac{13.31}{1.1576} + \cdots$$

$$= 10.48 + 10.98 + 11.50$$

As we add more terms, they keep getting larger. This means there will be no finite value for PV if the firm goes on forever.

The simplification yields the following result for the value of the asset as N approaches infinity:[5]

$$PV = \frac{D_1}{(i - g)} \qquad\qquad (3\text{-}42)$$

or for its rate of return

$$i = \frac{D_1}{PV} + g \qquad\qquad (3\text{-}43)$$

These are directly analogous to Eqs. (3-37) and (3-38). For example, the price of the equity is equal to the dividends in the next period discounted as if they would be perpetual, at a rate which is equal to the discount rate, net of the rate of growth in dividends. This approach to valuation, which is known as the Gordon growth model, is one of the principal tools used for valuing equity securities in the market.

To illustrate the use of Eq. (3-42) for the value of equity securities, let's suppose we are examining a company with a fairly long history of dividend payments. From this history we can formulate an estimate of the future growth rate in dividends. There are a number of ways we might do this. But probably the simplest is to compute the growth rate in each past year and then utilize the average of those past growth rates. This assumes that the

---

[5] Multiply both sides of Eq. (3-41) by $(1 + i)/(1 + g)$ and subtract Eq. (3-41) from the result. This yields

$$\frac{PV(1 + i)}{(1 + g)} - PV = D_0 - \frac{D_0(1 + g)^N}{(1 + i)^N}$$

As long as i exceeds g, then as N approaches infinity, $D_0(1 + g)^N/(1 + i)^N$ approaches zero. As a result, we can write:

$$PV\left[\frac{1 + i}{1 + g} - 1\right] = D_0$$

$$PV\left[\frac{(1 + i) - (1 + g)}{1 + g}\right] = D_0$$

$$PV\frac{(i - g)}{(1 + g)} = D_0$$

$$PV = \frac{D_1}{i - g}$$

future will be like the past, which it may not be. If we have good evidence about how the future will differ, then we should use it. But without such evidence, the average probably represents a reasonable estimate of the future. Suppose that after performing these computations we find that the average growth rate for dividends has been 6 percent. Next suppose that the discount rate which represents our opportunity cost is 10 percent. Finally, suppose that the company we are examining has announced that dividends will be $2.50 per share next year. We can use these numbers to compute the value of the company's equity shares as follows:

$$PV = \frac{\$2.50}{.10 - .06} = \$62.50 \text{ per share}$$

It is important to recognize that few companies ever actually have constant growth rates for dividends. Most companies may have high growth in dividends for a while. But it proves hard to sustain this, and the growth rate generally falls. Therefore, the assumption of a constant growth rate which is employed in the Gordon growth model is quite unrealistic. In fact, we are generally quite uncertain about what the future growth rate will be for most companies. And this element of uncertainty is as important as the element of time in determining value. It is to the problem of uncertainty that we turn next.

SUMMARY

In this chapter we have examined the connections between time and value. The central question which we have dealt with throughout the chapter is: How do we translate the stream of income which accrues to an asset into a value of that asset at a point in time, either today or some time in the future?

We learned at the outset that the key to determining the value of a stream of income is the rate of interest. The rate of interest measures the price we pay to forgo consumption. As long as that price is not zero we have to discount future income streams to determine value today, or present value. We also learned that the interest rate can take a number of different forms: a simple rate or a compound rate, a before-tax rate or an after-tax rate, a before-inflation rate or an after-inflation rate. Therefore, whenever we use interest rates we have to be sure that we are using the correct one—the one that fits the problem we are dealing with.

Next we discovered that all the problems involving present and future value can be divided into four basic types of problems. Real-world problems may be a simple example of one of these types or a combination of them. The solution to each problem can be stated in a relatively simple equation. Of course, these four problems are simplifications of the types of problems we meet in the real world. Therefore we examined some of the ways that our basic present and future value problems can become more complicated. First of all we may find that future income is not constant. If it is constant, then it is relatively simple to compute present or future value. But if it is not constant, then while the computations can still be made, they are more cumbersome. We also learned that we can compound interest as frequently as we choose and we learned how to alter our formulas to take this into account. We also learned how to distinguish between net present value and gross present value. Net present value provides a simple rule of thumb for determining whether an investment is worth undertaking. Finally, we learned about the internal rate of return. We found that the internal rate of return was the interest rate which resulted in a net present value of zero for a particular investment. It was emphasized that net present value and internal rate of return were simply alternative ways of thinking about the same problem— they are flip sides of the same coin. However, the internal rate of return has the potential to be quite misleading. So, whenever possible, it is best to stick with net present value.

At the end of the chapter we applied what we learned about present value and interest rates to a few examples of financial assets which we see in the marketplace. We found that we can use present value to compute the yield or price of a bond. In the process we learned what the yield and price meant. We also applied these concepts to the determination of the price of a share of stock. The important distinction here is that unlike most bonds, a share of stock has no well-defined maturity date. Therefore we employed the idea of a perpetual income stream to determine the value of the stock.

A good understanding of the subject of present value is critical for a good understanding of financial markets. Almost every decision which must be made and every aspect of the market hinges on present value. Moreover, the tools used to analyze present value are relatively concrete and easy to master. Therefore, it is worth getting a firm foundation in the subject matter of this chapter before we move on to the somewhat more difficult topic of uncertainty and value.

QUESTIONS TO IMPROVE UNDERSTANDING

1 What would be the price of an 8 percent coupon Treasury bond with semiannual coupon payments that had 14 years to maturity and a face value of $1,000 if the market interest rate is 12 percent?
2 Suppose you are considering whether to invest in some income (rental) property. You plan to hold the property for 5 years and then sell it for $140,000. You also expect to be able to collect $5,000 in rent every 6 months of that 5-year period. The first payment will be received in 6 months. The current asking price is $100,000. Suppose your alternative use of funds is to invest in Treasury bonds which yield 12 percent for a 5-year maturity. Which would you choose?
3 Reconsider question 2. Suppose you were in the 50 percent tax bracket and you could depreciate the property for tax purposes. Suppose you could deduct 10

percent of the purchase price from your taxes every year you owned the property. Now which would you choose?

4 Suppose you expect to retire in 20 years. At the time you retire you want enough money invested to be able to pay you $40,000 per year for 15 years. After 15 years you expect to be dead so you are not worried about funds after that point. Suppose that over the next 20 years you can invest funds each year at a 12 percent return. If you are going to invest a constant amount each year, how much would that be?

5 The dividend payments for IBM expressed in dollar per share for each year from 1969 to 1978 are presented in Table 2-1. Suppose your opportunity cost of funds is 12 percent. Use the Gordon growth model to compute what you think would be a reasonable estimate of the price of IBM stock as of the end of 1977.

6 Explain the difference between simple and compound interest and between simple interest and interest on a discount basis.

7 Suppose you own a Treasury bond with 5 years to maturity, a coupon rate of 8 percent, and a face value of $100,000. Suppose that when you bought the bond market interest rates were at 10 percent and they have now fallen to 6 percent. What happened to the price of your bond?

8 Suppose you were going to buy a home worth $100,000 and you intended to finance this purchase with an $80,000 mortgage. Suppose the mortgage had a maturity of 30 years and an interest of 12 percent. What would be your monthly payment? Suppose you were in the 40 percent tax bracket and could deduct interest expense. What would be the after-tax cost of your mortgage? How much would you be able to deduct during the first year of the mortgage?

9 Suppose you use a credit card with the following fees. There is a flat charge of $30 per year regardless of how much the card is used and a percentage charge of 1.5 percent per month on the balance outstanding. Suppose you had exactly $1,000 outstanding on this card for an entire year. What would be the actual annual interest rate on the $1,000?

REFERENCES

Benston, George J.: "Rate Ceiling Implications of the Cost Structure of Consumer Finance Companies," *Journal of Finance*, 32 (September 1977), pp. 1169–1194.

de Roover, Raymond: *The Rise and Decline of the Medici Bank, 1397–1494*, W. W. Norton & Company, Inc., New York, 1966.

Fama, Eugene F., and Merton H. Miller: *The Theory of Finance*, Holt, Rinehart and Winston, Inc., New York, 1972.

Hirshleifer, J.: *Investment, Interest, and Capital*, Prentice-Hall, Inc., Englewood Cliffs, N.J., 1970.

Mayer, Martin, *The Bankers*, Ballentine Books, Inc., New York, 1974.

Chapter Four

UNCERTAINTY AND VALUE

This chapter is about risk or uncertainty and the value of assets. Risk is an important element in all of our lives and in one way or another we all learn to deal with it. We each develop different attitudes toward risk. That is, some of us are more willing to accept risk than others. There are even a few people who seem to enjoy or thrive on risk. But most of us seek to avoid risk or demand to be paid in order to accept it. We demand higher pay for more risky types of employment and we demand a higher return in order to get involved in more risky types of investments. Most of us have an intuitive understanding of what it means to say that one asset or one type of employment is more risky than another. Similarly, we have an understanding of what it means to say that we demand more return to expose ourselves to more risk. But in this chapter we will get precise about what these terms mean. Specifically, we want to understand what risk means and how it can be measured. We want to know how to quantify the price that we demand to be paid to expose ourselves to risk. And we want to know how to make choices among risky assets. We will address these issues in this chapter, first of all in the restricted case where we must invest all our resources in only one investment. Then we will examine how to measure and deal with risk when we can spread our investments across a number of different assets; that is, when we can choose portfolios of assets.

SOME IMPORTANT CONCEPTS

In this chapter and the next we will be somewhat more technical, in the sense that we will make use of a lot of algebra, than we will in many other chapters in this book. Therefore, it is important to have a clear understanding of some of the words and phrases which will be used throughout these two chapters. There are five important concepts which will be used frequently in our treatment of risk and which can be described at the outset in a largely nontechnical manner. We will discuss each of them in turn.

PROBABILITY DISTRIBUTION   A *probability distribution* arrays possible outcomes of a particular event and links them with the probability that each will occur. For example, consider a horse race with five horses in the race. A probability distribution for this horse race would assign a percentage probability to the possibility that each of the five horses would win. One such probability distribution might rate the chances of each horse winning as: horse 1—10 percent; horse 2—25 percent; horse 3—5 percent; horse 4—20 percent; and horse 5—40 percent. In this book we will deal with probability distributions pertaining to economic events. Specifically, we will utilize probability distributions which define the future returns on assets. Throughout our discussion of uncertainty and the value of assets we will take these probability distributions as given. That is, in the horse race example, we will take as fact that the probability that horse number five will win is 40 percent. We simply will not question this. This is obviously unrealistic, for someone who has a better knowledge of horse racing might come along and argue that the probability horse number five will win is really only 10 percent. At this juncture we will not entertain the prospect that people might disagree about the probability distributions in the economy. However, in Chapter Six we will consider such disagreements.

EXPECTED RETURN   Because the probability distributions which we will deal with here apply to future returns on assets, we have to be careful about how we use the word return. For, if left unqualified, its meaning is ambiguous. After we observe a return we have the actual or ex post return. But before we observe the actual return we have no unique ex ante return. There is only the probability distribution on future returns. Hence, when we are speaking of return ex ante, or before an actual return is observed, we often refer to our estimate of what the future return will be. This best guess is labeled the *expected return*. In finance, the word expected is often taken for granted in referring to ex ante return. This is particularly true when speaking of "risk and return." The phrase is really risk and expected return, and it should be understood that this is what is meant when the word "expected" is omitted. Later in the chapter a more technical definition or way to measure expected return will be developed.

RISK AND UNCERTAINTY   We have used these two words quite a lot already and now we can be more explicit about what they mean. Actually the two words are often used interchangeably and they have been used that way here thus far. *Risk* and *uncertainty* simply refer to the fact that the future return on an asset is not known with certainty. Instead, the return is described by a probability distribution. In forthcoming discussions, however, we will use the word risk to refer to some quantification of the amount of uncertainty pertaining to the future return on an asset. More specifically, risk will be a measure of variability. To see what we mean by variability it is useful to reexamine Table 2-1 which shows the actual rate of return earned on IBM stock over a recent 10-year period. A person who purchased shares of IBM in 1969 could not be certain about future returns. The return might have been very high as it was in 1976, or it might have been very low, as it was in 1974. But one can look back at the historical record and see how much variation there was in the return on the stock. Later in the chapter we will examine a precise way to measure the amount of variability, and we will refer to this measure as the risk of the asset.

DIVERSIFICATION   When we consider investing in a single asset and we have no other assets to which this will be added, then the risk to us of holding this asset is the variability of the future return on this asset alone, as illustrated in the case of the IBM stock. But when we hold portfolios of assets, say some shares in General Motors and some in IBM and others, then we are literally transforming the risk that we are exposed to. The risk that any investor bears is the risk of his or her portfolio of assets. As a result, the risk of an individual asset in that portfolio is the contribution of that asset to the risk of the entire portfolio. And this is generally not the same as the risk of that asset when it is held by itself. The reason for this is because of diversification. *Diversification* occurs when assets which do not have similar probability distributions are combined in the same portfolio. Diversification is valuable because it reduces the risk to which individuals are exposed.

RISK AVERSION   Most people are averse to risk. This means that they seek and would pay to avoid it. This implies that the more risk an asset has, the less a risk-averse person would be willing to pay for it. Therefore, *risk aversion*, or people's attitude toward risk, influences the values of assets in the market. As a result, we need to be concerned not only with measuring risk and expected return but also with understanding the price that people will pay to avoid risk.

Now that we have an initial nontechnical introduction to these concepts, we can begin to examine how to measure risk and return as well as how to choose among risky investments.

MEASURING RISK AND RETURN

In order to understand how to value risky assets and how to choose among them, it is necessary to have some methodology for measuring the risk and expected return of those assets. In this section we will develop that methodology. We will start by considering an example of three investments which have uncertain future returns. Our ultimate objective is to understand how we can make well-informed choices between these investments and how we can assess their value. In this section we will examine the probability distributions on returns for each of these projects. Then we will evaluate how to measure expected return. Finally, we will develop a measurement for the risk of these assets.

The Probability Distribution on Returns

Risk and expected return are based on the probability distributions which determine the future return on each asset. Therefore we have to start with these probability distributions. We will begin by defining probability distributions for each of our three hypothetical investments that constitute our available choices. These probability distributions show five possible returns for each asset and the probability that each of these returns will occur. To explain the probability distribution we will confine our attention, momentarily, to only one of the assets, asset A. The five possible returns for this asset are shown in the column labeled "Asset A" of Table 4-1. The highest return is $8,500 and the lowest is $5,500. The probability that each outcome will occur is shown in the third column, labeled probability of occurrence of each state. In this example, the probability of both the highest and lowest return is 10 percent. The five possible returns for asset A depend on what are

TABLE 4-1

Uncertain Returns on Three Investments

STATE OF THE WORLD DESCRIPTION	NUMBER	PROBABILITY OF OCCURRENCE OF EACH STATE	RETURNS (IN $) ON EACH ASSET IN EACH STATE OF THE WORLD		
			ASSET A	ASSET B	ASSET C
Deep recession	1	0.1	5,500	3,000	13,000
Mild recession	2	0.2	6,000	5,000	11,000
Normal	3	0.4	7,000	7,000	9,000
Minor boom	4	0.2	8,000	9,000	7,000
Major boom	5	0.1	8,500	11,000	5,000

called "states of the world." These states correspond to the possible future courses of the economy, from deep recession to major boom. Actually the possible returns could have been represented more simply if only three states were considered: recession, normal, and boom. Or, the possible returns could have been represented in more detail by considering many more states. The point is you can use as many states of the world as you think are appropriate to best represent the problem under consideration.

Table 4-1 also shows the probability distributions for each of the other two assets available in our example. The alternative returns in each state of the world for assets B and C are listed in the last two columns of the table. Like asset A, the probability that each alternative return will occur is shown in the column which identifies the probability of each state of the world. The convenience of using states of the world should now be apparent. We could define a separate column of probabilities and alternative outcomes for each asset without using the states of the world. Instead, we have stated the probability of each state of the world and the outcome for each asset in each state of the world. In this way, only one column of probabilities is necessary.

It is important to understand that the probability distributions on returns for each asset are only estimated probabilities. The idea is that each investor must formulate his or her own estimates of these probabilities. There is generally substantial information available to use in formulating these estimates. But you cannot go to *The Wall Street Journal* and look up the probability distribution for future returns on IBM, although you can acquire information about IBM from *The Wall Street Journal* and utilize it to formulate a probability distribution like those in Table 4-1. But that probability distribution is still your estimate.

It will make our future work much simpler if we can develop a notation to refer to a particular asset, state of the world, probability of occurrence, and future return. Therefore we will number the states of the world 1 through 5, beginning with deep recession and ending with major boom, as shown in the second column of Table 4-1. We have already identified the assets with the letters A, B, and C. Next we will refer to the return on asset A in the first state of the world as $_1R_A$. In the example, $_1R_A = \$5,500$. We can use this notation to refer to the return on any asset in any state of the world, such as asset B in normal time—$_3R_B = \$7,000$. Finally, we need a notation for the probabilities of each of the five states of the world. We will use the symbol $P_3 = 0.4$. All the other states of the world may be referenced by adjusting the subscript; for example, $P_1 = 0.1$. Now that we have a system of notation we can utilize the probability distributions shown in Table 4-1 to measure the expected return on each investment.

Measuring Expected Return

We already know that the idea behind the expected return is that it is supposed to represent our best estimate of what the future actual return will be.

Another way to look at it is that if we had to pick a single number which would be our forecast of the future return, this would be it. One way we might try to measure the expected return is to simply take the midpoint of the possible future returns. The midpoint is half-way between the highest and lowest possible returns. But this is not a very satisfactory procedure. To see why, consider two simple gambles which are defined by probability distributions with three possible outcomes. Both of them have the same possible outcomes: $50, $100, and $150. The only difference between the two gambles lies in the probabilities assigned to each outcome. The probability distributions are illustrated in the following table:

GAMBLE NUMBER	PROBABILITY OF PAYOFF		
	$50	$100	$150
1	0.2	0.6	0.2
2	0.1	0.6	0.3

This table shows that gamble number 1, for example, has a 20 percent chance of a $50 dollar payoff, while gamble number 2 has only a 10 percent chance of a $50 dollar payoff. If we choose the midpoint as our best guess of the future outcome for both of these distributions, then they would both have the same expected return, as they both have the same midpoint. But this seems unreasonable because gamble number 2 has a lower probability of a $50 dollar return and a higher probability of a $150 return than gamble number 1. Therefore, gamble number 2 should have a higher expected return than gamble number 1. The shortcoming of the midpoint as a measure of expected return is that it ignores the probabilities that each possible outcome will occur. Therefore, we need to utilize a procedure which does not have this shortcoming.

A procedure which takes into account the entire probability distribution is to define the expected return as the weighted average of all the possible returns in the probability distribution, where the weights are the probabilities that each return will occur. Before we can define the expected return with algebra, we need some notation to represent expected return. We will use the symbol $E(R_A)$ to represent the expected return on asset A. Then we can define $E(R_A)$ as follows:

$$E(R_A) = \sum_{i=1}^{N} P_i({_i}R_A) \tag{4-1}$$

Equation (4-1) says that the expected return is equal to the sum of the products of the individual probabilities and returns for each state of the world. We can illustrate how this formula is used with the probability distribution for investment A presented in Table 4-1. The formula says that the subscript i should assume the numbers of the alternative states of the world, 1 through 5. Then the probability of each state occurring is multiplied by the return in that state. These five products are then added together as follows:

Illustration of Eq. (4-1)

$$P_1 \times {}_1R_A = 0.1 \times 5,500$$
$$P_2 \times {}_2R_A = 0.2 \times 6,000$$
$$P_3 \times {}_3R_A = 0.4 \times 7,000$$
$$P_4 \times {}_4R_A = 0.2 \times 8,000$$
$$P_5 \times {}_5R_A = \underline{0.1 \times 8,500}$$

$$\sum_{i=1}^{N} P_i \, ({}_iR_A) = 7,000$$

$$E(R_A) = 7,000$$

We can compute the expected return for each of the other projects in a similar manner. All the expected returns are presented in Table 4-2. This table illustrates that investments A and B both have the same expected return of $7,000. But investment C has an expected return of $9,000. If expected return were our only criterion for choosing or valuing investments, then we could conclude that investment C is the best one. In addition we could conclude that its value should be $9,000, for this is what it is expected to pay.

Measuring Risk

The basic idea behind measuring risk is to express in a quantitative way how much the actual return can vary. We have defined a best guess of the future return. But this best guess tells us nothing about the variability of returns or how spread out the possible returns are around the expected value. It is easiest to see what is meant by variability by examining a graphical representation of probability distributions. Before we examine plots of the distributions given in Table 4-1, it will be useful to examine some extreme cases

TABLE 4-2

Expected Return, Variance and Standard Deviation for Three Investments

INVESTMENT	EXPECTED RETURN	VARIANCE	STANDARD DEVIATION
A	$7,000	850,000	922
B	$7,000	4,800,000	2,191
C	$9,000	4,800,000	2,191

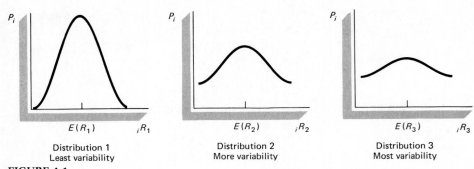

Distribution 1
Least variability

Distribution 2
More variability

Distribution 3
Most variability

FIGURE 4-1
Three probability distributions with the same expected value but different amounts of variability.

of probability distributions with different amounts of variability. An example of such extremes is presented in Figure 4-1, which illustrates three different probability distributions. The probability of each outcome is shown on the vertical axis, and the corresponding outcome is shown on the horizontal axis for each of the three distributions. All of the distributions have the same expected value, but vastly different amounts of variability. Distribution 1 has the least variability because it is the most concentrated around the expected value. In distribution 1 the probability is small that returns very far away from the expected value will actually occur. Distribution 2 has more variability. It is less peaked or concentrated around its expected value. Finally, distribution 3 has the most variability, as it is the flattest of the distributions.

Now that we have an intuitive idea of what variability means we can develop a way to measure it. The accepted measure of the variation of a probability distribution is known as the variance. First, we will examine a formal algebraic definition of the variance, and then we will examine how it is computed and interpreted by applying it to the three sample investments in Table 4-1. The standard notation for the variance is the Greek letter σ (sigma) raised to the second power, σ^2. We need to add a subscript to indicate which probability distribution we are referring to, so we will use σ_A^2 to refer to the variance of the future returns to investment A. The variance is defined as follows:

$$\sigma_A^2 = \sum_{i=1}^{N} P_i({}_iR_A - E(R_A))^2 \qquad (4\text{-}2)$$

Another similar measure which is used almost interchangeably with the variance is the standard deviation. This is simply the square root of the variance and is symbolized as σ_A.

We can utilize the probability distribution for returns on investment A to see how to compute the variance. For each of the possible returns, we subtract the expected return on the investment from that return and square the difference. Then we multiply that squared difference by the probability of that outcome. Finally, we add up all of these terms. The standard deviation is then computed by taking the square root of the variance. These computations are illustrated below for asset A, and the variances and standard deviations of all three investments are shown in Table 4-2.

Illustration of Eq. (4-2)

$$P_1 \times [_1R_A - E(R_A)]^2 = 0.1 \times (5,500 - 7,000)^2$$
$$P_2 \times [_2R_A - E(R_A)]^2 = 0.2 \times (6,000 - 7,000)^2$$
$$P_3 \times [_3R_A - E(R_A)]^2 = 0.4 \times (7,000 - 7,000)^2$$
$$P_4 \times [_4R_A - E(R_A)]^2 = 0.2 \times (8,000 - 7,000)^2$$
$$P_5 \times [_5R_A - E(R_A)]^2 = 0.1 \times (8,500 - 7,000)^2$$
$$\sigma_A^2 = \sum_{i=1}^{N} P_i [_iR_A - E[R_A]]^2 = 850,000$$
$$\sigma_A = \sqrt{850,000} = 922$$

To see how the variance and standard deviation actually measure the variation of a probability distribution it is useful to compare the variances and standard deviations of the three projects in our example with the visual impression of their variation shown in Figure 4-2. This figure shows the same type of graphical representation of probability distributions presented in Figure 4-1. We know from Table 4-2 that B and C have the same variance and standard deviation and that investment A has a smaller variance. This tells us that B and C have the same amount of risk and that they both have more risk than does investment A. Figure 4-2 indicates that investments B and C have the same amount of variation or dispersion. That is, they are

FIGURE 4-2
Probability distributions for the three investments in Table 4-1.

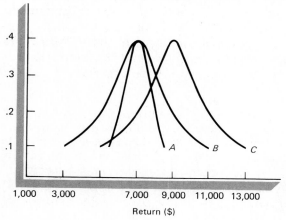

spread out to the same extent, though they have different expected returns. Judging by the standard deviations, B and C are a little more than twice as risky as investment A. This is also consistent with the figure in that the probability distributions for B and C appear to be about twice as spread out as does the distribution for A. It is misleading to judge the relative amount of risk directly from the variance because, as we can tell from Eq. (4-2), the variance includes the square of every deviation of each possible occurrence about the expected value. As a result the variance will tend to exaggerate relative riskiness. This means that if B has twice as much risk as A according to the standard deviation, it will have four times as much according to the variance.

CONCEPTUALIZING THE RISK–RETURN TRADEOFF

What Do We Do When We Have Measured Risk and Return?

To define and measure risk is not to show what to do with it or how to handle it. The basic premise upon which our analysis of investment decisions is based is that expected return is viewed as good—the more of it the better; and risk is viewed as bad—the less of it the better. The basic problem is to determine the amount of expected return a person or a market will demand in order to accept a certain amount of risk. That is, the problem is to determine the price for bearing risk. This means that we must assess the individual's and the market's tradeoffs between risk and return.

There is nothing that anyone can tell any investor about how much risk to trade for any amount of expected return. The choice between risk and return is not in any significant way different from the choice between Chevrolets and mink coats, or the choice between skiing and scuba diving, or the choice between any combination of commodities. Within some limits, one can "scientifically" measure risk and return. But once defined and measured, no one can say what is a correct choice between them. Individuals must simply make up their own minds.

In a fascinating book dealing with uncertainty and economics, Karl Borch tells a story which makes this point vividly clear. His tale helps make it possible to gain insight and understanding of the analysis we will get into shortly.

> Let us consider a big ship—an ocean liner—insured for $10 million against an annual premium of $300,000. If things go well, this insurance contract will give the insurance company a clear profit of $300,000 each year, and that means something, even to a big company. On the other hand, if the ship gets lost at sea, the company will have to pay $10 million, and that may create serious difficulties which may take the company years to overcome.

> Normally, an insurance company will not hold a contract of this kind on its own account. Usually a substantial part the contract will be "reinsured", i.e., passed

on to another insurance company. If our company "retains" only 10% i.e., reinsures 90%, the risk situation will be changed to a loss of $1 million or a profit of $30,000 (provided that reinsurance is obtained on "original terms"). The problem is then to decide how much should be reinsured.

The President of the Board of our insurance company may well ask their actuary or a statistical consultant how they should reinsure the contract. The actuary in all honesty should reply that the problem is reduced to its simplest possible form and that the Board must decide for itself when it has made up its mind how it feels about running risks.

Usually, boards don't accept such answers from highly paid actuaries. They expect the actuary to give his answer only after elaborate computations. If he is a good actuary, he should process all relevant statistics of shipwrecks and consult with engineers about the technical properties of the ship.

However, what can be the outcome of such computations? The result can be little more than a statement to the effect that the best estimate of the probability that the ship will be lost is 0.011. To this one can add some qualification. . . . But no amount of computation can give more information.

We should, however, ask ourselves if such information is useful, that is, if it really will help if these simple results are imbedded in a 50-page technical report. In one respect the situation is quite clear. What the Board really wants to know is whether the ship will sink or not. Nobody but an astrologer can tell them that.

It is told that a well-known professor of insurance once replied in this way when he was consulted by an insurance company. The company considered this for some weeks, and then invited him to join the Board. The really amusing part of the story is that the company thought that this was just what the professor wanted in the first place, and that he gave an "evasive" answer in order to get a seat on the Board. They were convinced that there was a unique solution to their problem—presumably known to a professor.

We can learn a lot about business decisions from this story even if it is not true. The story illustrates the shrewd thinking and suspicion of ulterior motives which must be very useful, if not essential, to success in business. The story, however, also gives an example of the rather naive wishful thinking which we often find in business circles and in business literature.

A businessman may often have to make difficult decisions in complicated situations. In such cases he can call upon technicians or "experts" who may be able to clarify the situation, but they cannot, in general, tell the businessman that a particular decision is the only right one. The ultimate decision as to what risks should be taken must remain the responsibility of the businessman himself. Businessmen often seem to find it difficult to accept this fact of life. A psychologist may interpret this as a search for a father figure in the person of the expert.[1]

---

[1] Excerpts from Karl Henrik Borch, The Economics of Uncertainty, (copyright © 1968 Princeton University Press), pp. 17–18. Reprinted by permission of Princeton University Press.

The point of Karl Borch's story is that there is a natural limit to the extent to which one can be scientific about investment decisions. An analyst can go to great extents to accurately measure the risk and return in alternative investments. But once these are quantified, the investor must simply decide how much a given amount of risk and return is worth. This by no means suggests that there is no reason to be systematic and rigorous in our analysis of how investment decisions are made and market value is determined. But it does mean that this analysis is more of an inquiry into how the market works than it is a practical guide to the choice of investments.

Now we want to consider how we go about making a choice between the three risky assets, A, B, and C. We know that the greater the expected return and the lower the standard deviation, the more valuable the asset. But we have no objective manner in which to say what is a sufficient expected return to compensate for a specific amount of risk. This is fundamentally up to the individual.

Regardless of whether individuals consciously state tradeoffs between risk and return, we can represent their choices between assets in terms of our measures of risk and return. To do so we will utilize a diagram with expected return on the vertical axis and standard deviation on the horizontal axis. Our purpose at the outset is merely to provide a graphical representation of the assets which we have examined in Table 4-1. The purpose of this particular graph is to facilitate comparison of the assets. Each of the three assets is plotted in Figure 4-3. Each asset corresponds to a unique point in the diagram. That point represents the expected return and standard deviation of the asset. For example, asset A plots at the point with coordinates of 7,000 and 922, corresponding to its expected return and standard deviation. We can utilize this diagram to examine the choice between the three risky investments.

FIGURE 4-3
Expected returns and standard deviations for the three investments in Table 4-1.

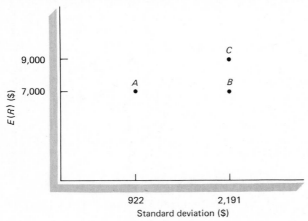

The Role of Personal Preference in Investment Decisions

To see how we go about dissecting the choice between these assets we will start by considering only the choice between assets A and B. Is one of these two assets or investments unambiguously superior to the other? That is, would you expect anyone who is risk averse to agree on which investment is superior? If all risk-averse individuals can agree, then we can conclude that personal preference is not relevant to the choice. The answer to the question is: Yes, A is unambiguously superior to B. A is superior because it has the same expected return as does B, but it has less risk. Therefore, anyone who prefers less risk to more would choose investment A over B.

Now consider the choice between assets A and C. We observe from Figure 4-3 that A and C have different amounts of both expected return and risk. Investment C has more of both than does A. This choice is not as clear-cut as the last one. The choice depends upon whether the additional return expected from investment C is sufficient compensation for the risk involved. This is strictly a matter of personal preference.

When examining investments in a diagram such as this, there is a simple way to determine whether the choice depends upon personal preference. What is necessary is to divide the diagram into quadrants centered on one of the available investments. This is illustrated in Figure 4-4, where the diagram is divided into four quadrants centered on asset A. Investments which fall in quadrant II, to the northwest of A, will always be unambiguously superior to A because they have less risk and more return. Investments which fall into quadrant IV will be unambiguously inferior to A because they have more risk and less expected return. The choice between A and any

FIGURE 4-4

This figure divides Figure 4-3 up into four quadrants centered on investment A. Investments which plot in quadrants II and IV will be unambiguously superior or inferior to A, respectively. Investments which plot in quadrants I and III will depend on the individual's attitude toward risk.

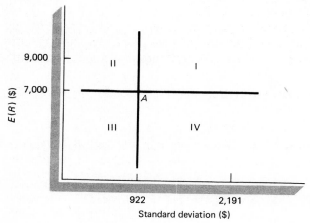

investment which falls in quadrants I and III will be a matter of personal preference because they will always have more or less, respectively, of both risk and expected return.

Now suppose that we have to make a choice between two investments like A and C, where personal preference matters. How do we do it? Is there some analytical procedure for determining which is best? The answer is no. You simply have to decide and choose!

Once we recognize that, at this juncture, the scientific method has come to the end of its usefulness as a guide for actually *making* a choice, then we can proceed with scientific procedure as a way to *represent* the way people choose. We can utilize the same type of diagram as that presented in Figure 4-3 to represent an individual's choice or tradeoff between risk and return. To do this we will introduce a curve called an indifference curve. An *indifference curve* shows the alternative investments among which an individual is indifferent. To explain the idea behind an indifference curve, we will depart momentarily from our example of investments A, B, and C, and consider five other investments. The first four of these each has more of both expected return and risk than the one before it. These investments are illustrated in Figure 4-5. An example of an indifference curve is also shown in Figure 4-5. This indifference curve slopes upward to the right and passes through the points labeled 1 through 4, which represent the first four investments. The fact that the indifference curve passes through them means that they are all equally appealing to the individual whose indifference curve this is. This means that each investment has just enough expected return to compensate for the additional risk, relative to the other investments. It is because this compensation is *just* sufficient that the indifference curve passes through these four points. This indifference curve therefore represents this particular individual's tradeoff between risk and return, or the premium or compensation demanded to bear risk. Suppose there is yet one more investment available to this individual, investment 5, which plots

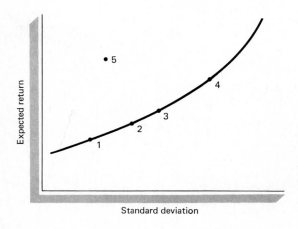

FIGURE 4-5
The upward-sloping line in this figure illustrates an indifference curve. The curve shows that an investor is indifferent between investments 1, 2, 3, 4 and finds investment 5 to be superior to each of the others.

in the diagram to the northwest of the indifference curve. This person will then prefer investment 5 to any of the investments on this indifference curve. But we can go further, for there will also be an indifference curve passing through point 5 and it will never intersect the one passing through points 1 to 4. Any investment on this second indifference curve will be preferred to any investment on the initial indifference curve. We can repeat this process indefinitely and fill the diagram with indifference curves, none of which will intersect.

A diagram with more than one indifference curve is shown in Figure 4-6. This diagram has the original three investments, A, B, and C, shown on it. A person who has the indifference curves shown in this diagram would prefer investment A to investment C because A falls on a higher indifference curve, that is, one further to the northwest. To this individual the additional expected return in investment C is not worth the additional risk. Another individual might well prefer C to A. The indifference curves of such a person are shown in Figure 4-7. This person would be less averse to risk because the additional risk would be more than compensated for by the extra expected return. This person would have flatter indifference curves than the person in Figure 4-6. The steepness of the indifference curve therefore reflects the degree of risk aversion. A person with very flat indifference curves would be less averse to risk than a person with very steep indifference curves. Another way to express this is that the indifference curve shows the tradeoff between risk and return of a particular individual. All individuals are different and each will have a different tradeoff.

Finally, we need to ask how to translate personal preference or attitude toward risk into a value that an individual will place on an asset. The value

FIGURE 4-6

This figure illustrates the choice of a relatively risk-averse individual. His or her indifference curves are sufficiently steep that for this individual investment A is a better choice than investments B or C.

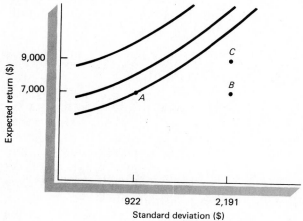

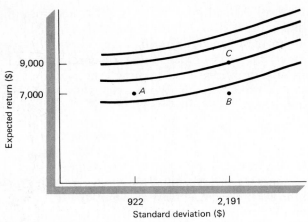

FIGURE 4-7
This figure illustrates the choice of a modestly risk-averse person. His or her indifference
curves are sufficiently flat that for this individual investment C is superior to investments B
and A. To see the effect of differences in risk aversion it is helpful to compare this figure to
Figure 4-6.

of an asset is determined by (1) the expected return on the asset, (2) the risk
of the asset as measured by the variance or standard deviation of its future
returns, and (3) the premium demanded to bear risk. Again, it is important to
emphasize that there is no hard-and-fast or scientific way to quantify how
these three factors are combined to determine value. There is no way to
quantify the premium one *should* demand to bear risk. For example, in the
case of investment A the expected return is $7,000 and the standard devia-
tion is $922. Each individual will value this asset differently, depending
upon his or her attitude toward risk. Each person must ask what amount of
money he or she would accept with certainty rather than have title to the
risky investment A. One individual might say, for example, $5,500. Another
might offer $6,000. This is the value of that asset to that particular indi-
vidual.

RISK AND RETURN IN PORTFOLIOS OF ASSETS

Until now we have presumed that the investments available in the market
were mutually exclusive, such that if you chose A, you couldn't also choose
B. But this is not always the case in the real world faced by investors.
Investors can usually choose to purchase shares in different firms, spreading
their investment across a number of assets. In this way investors construct
portfolios of assets. In this section we will examine whether there are
benefits for an investor if he or she chooses a portfolio of assets rather than
just a single asset. As we shall see, the advantage of a portfolio is that the

total amount of risk that each investor bears can be reduced through diversification. Our purpose is to understand what diversification is, how it works, and what benefits it can provide investors.

The concept of diversification is illustrated in Figure 4-8. This figure plots the returns accruing to each of the three assets, A, B, and C, in each state of the world. Note that Figure 4-8 shows that the returns on assets A and B change in the same direction from one state of the world to the next. By contrast, the return to asset C changes in the opposite direction in that the return to asset C tends to be high when the returns to A and B are low. The idea behind diversification is that if any two assets which do not change in exactly the same way are combined in the same portfolio, then their returns would tend to offset each other so that the risk of the portfolio would be less than the risk of any asset held alone. The benefit of diversification is, therefore, that it reduces the total amount of risk to which an investor is exposed. To see more specifically how this works we need to develop a way to measure the risk and expected return of a portfolio of assets.

In order to deal with portfolios of assets we need to make one important change in the example that we are carrying through this discussion. The change is that we need to deal with rates of return rather than total returns measured in dollars. The reason for this is that when we construct a portfolio of assets for an investor, that investor may purchase only a small portion of each asset or some share of each asset. Therefore we need to be able to work with the return per share or per dollar invested in the asset. To do this we have to introduce the price paid for each asset. Therefore, we will assume

FIGURE 4-8

Alternative returns for three investments in each state of the world.

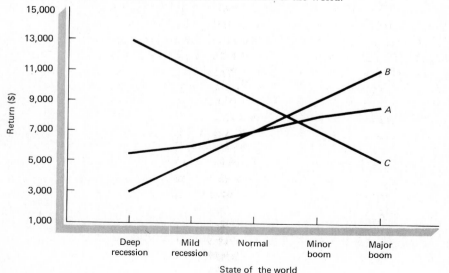

that each of the three assets initially presented in Table 4-1 can be purchased for $50,000. We can then compute the rate of return for each asset in each state of the world by dividing each payoff in Table 4-1 by $50,000. The result is presented in Table 4-3. This table contains the payoff for each asset in each state of the world in a percentage or rate-of-return form. To accommodate rates of return we need to introduce a little more notation. We will utilize the symbol $_1r_A$ to represent the rate of return on asset A in state of the world 1. Then we can simply replace the dollar return with the rate of return in all of our computations. Note that the expected rate of return for each asset is given in panel B of Table 4-3, as are the variances and standard deviations. Also note that we use the symbols $\sigma^2_{r_A}$ and σ_{r_A} for the variance and standard deviation of the rates of return.

Measuring The Relationship Between Assets

Figure 4-8 illustrates the way each of the three assets in our example is related to the others. That is, by comparing the lines in the figure we can tell whether the return on one asset will be high in the same state of the world as another asset, or whether one will have a high return and the other a low return in the same state of the world. The figure therefore provides a visual impression of how variations in two assets are related. But we will need a more precise measure of this. We will develop two of them. They are called the covariance and the correlation coefficient. Actually what we want to use

TABLE 4-3

PANEL A: UNCERTAIN RATES OF RETURN ON THREE INVESTMENTS					
STATE OF THE WORLD DESCRIPTION	NUMBER	PROBABILITY OF OCCURRENCE	RATE OF RETURN ON ASSETS IN EACH STATE OF THE WORLD		
			ASSET A	ASSET B	ASSET C
Deep recession	1	.1	.11	.06	.26*
Mild recession	2	.2	.12	.10	.22
Normal	3	.4	.14	.14	.18
Minor boom	4	.2	.16	.18	.14
Major boom	5	.1	.17	.22	.10

PANEL B: EXPECTED RATE OF RETURN, VARIANCE, AND STANDARD DEVIATION FOR THREE INVESTMENTS			
	ASSET A	ASSET B	ASSET C
$E(r)$	.14	.14	.18
σ^2_r	.00034	.00192	.00192
σ_r	.01844	.04382	.04382

*Rate of return on asset C calculated as follows: 13,000/50,000 = .26.

is the correlation coefficient. But in order to understand the correlation coefficient we must first develop the covariance.

The covariance is very similar to the variance. The *variance* of an asset is computed by subtracting the expected value from each of the possible outcomes for a particular probability distribution and then squaring that difference. The *covariance* between two assets is computed in a similar way, except the deviations of the possible outcomes from their expected values for two different probability distributions are multiplied together. The symbol for the covariance between the rates of return on two assets, A and B, is written $\sigma^2_{r_{A \cdot B}}$. The formula for this covariance is the following:

$$\sigma^2_{r_{A \cdot B}} = \sum_{i=1}^{N} P_i[_ir_A - E(r_A)][_ir_B - E(r_B)] \tag{4-3}$$

The computations involved in the covariance are illustrated below.

<u>Illustration of Eq. (4-3)</u>

$$P_1[_1r_A - E(r_A)] [_1r_B - E(r_B)] = .1 \times (.11 - .14)(.06 - .14)$$
$$P_2[_2r_A - E(r_A)] [_2r_B - E(r_B)] = .2 \times (.12 - .14)(.10 - .14)$$
$$P_3[_3r_A - E(r_A)] [_3r_B - E(r_B)] = .4 \times (.14 - .14)(.14 - .14)$$
$$P_4[_4r_A - E(r_A)] [_4r_B - E(r_B)] = .2 \times (.16 - .14)(.18 - .14)$$
$$P_5[_5r_A - E(r_A)] [_5r_B - E(r_B)] = .1 \times (.17 - .14)(.22 - .14)$$

$$\sigma^2_{r_{A \cdot B}} = \sum_{i=1}^{N} P_i[_ir_A - E(r_A)] [_ir_B - E(r_B)] = .0008$$

The covariances for the alternative combinations of investments A, B, and C are shown in Table 4-4. Recall that we are now working with rates of return rather than dollar returns; thus the numbers involved will be smaller. Suppose we try to interpret these numbers. We can see that the covariance between A and B is positive while the other two are negative. This tells us that the return on B tends to be high when the return on C is low, and the return on B is high when the return on A is high. But we would also like to be able to infer something about the strength of the relationship between the

TABLE 4-4

Covariance and Correlation Coefficients for Rates of Return of Investments A, B, and C

INVESTMENTS	COVARIANCE	CORRELATION COEFFICIENT
A · B	.0008	.99
A · C	−.0008	−.99
B · C	−.0019	−1.00

probability distributions from these numbers. That is, we would like to know whether A and B have a very close relationship so that as A goes up B goes up by a similar amount. Unfortunately we cannot judge this from the covariance. The size of the number in the covariance is not meaningful.

To remedy this problem it is possible to use what is called the correlation coefficient. The difference between these two measures of the relationship between probability distributions is that the *correlation coefficient* is computed by dividing the covariance by the product of the standard deviations of the two distributions in question. We will symbolize the correlation coefficient with $\rho_{A \cdot B}$. The formula for the correlation coefficient is as follows:

$$\rho_{A \cdot B} = \frac{\sigma^2_{r_{A \cdot B}}}{\sigma_{r_A} \sigma_{r_B}} \tag{4-4}$$

For example, the correlation coefficient between A and B can be computed as follows:

$$\rho_{A \cdot B} = \frac{.0008}{.01844 \times .04382} = .99$$

The advantage of the correlation coefficient is that it is a standardized unit of measurement, which the covariance is not. This means that the correlation coefficient is always a percentage. It never exceeds +1 and is never less than −1. A large positive fraction indicates a strong positive relationship between the two probability distributions, while a small fraction, either positive or negative, indicates a weak relationship. Finally, a large, in absolute value, negative fraction indicates a strong negative relationship. The correlation coefficients for each of the combinations of investments are shown along with the covariance in Table 4-4. We can tell from these correlation coefficients that all three of the assets have strong relationships between them. Between B and C the relationship is a perfect negative one. This means that every movement away from the expected value for B is perfectly matched by a movement in the opposite direction for C. The other relationships are not quite as close, but are still very strong.

Measuring Portfolio Risk and Return

Now we can turn our attention to the portfolio of an investor. In order to keep the example as simple as possible we will limit ourselves to portfolios which contain only two assets. Everything we do with two assets we can do with three or more. But the algebra becomes more cumbersome as we add additional assets to the portfolio.

For a portfolio with two assets, say A and B, we will assume that the investor commits x percent of his wealth to asset A and y or $(1 - x)$ percent of his wealth to asset B. Then the rate of return that he actually receives on his portfolio will be

$$r_p = xr_A + yr_B \tag{4-5}$$

where r_A is the actual rate of return which is earned by asset A and r_B is the actual rate of return which is earned by asset B. The rate of return on the portfolio is the weighted average of the rates of return on assets A and B, where the weights are the proportion of the investor's wealth which is invested in these two assets.

There are two properties of expectations of the return that make it possible to determine the equation for the expected return of the portfolio. The first property is that the expectation of a sum of two random variables is equal to the sum of the expectations of those variables. A *random variable* is one which is determined by a probability distribution; r_A is a random variable and x is not. Therefore, the expected rate of return on the portfolio, which is defined as

$$E(r_p) = E[xr_A + yr_B] \tag{4-6}$$

can be written, using this rule, as

$$E(r_p) = E(xr_A) + E(yr_B) \tag{4-7}$$

The second property is that the expectation of the product of a constant and a random variable is equal to the product of the constant and the expected value of the random variable, or

$$E(xr_A) = xE(r_A) \tag{4-8}$$

This means that the expected rate of return on the portfolio can be expressed as the weighted sum of the expected rate of return on the two assets which comprise the portfolio, where the weights are the proportion of wealth committed to each asset:

$$E(r_p) = xE(r_A) + yE(r_B) \tag{4-9}$$

For example, this implies that a portfolio which was made up of 50 percent shares in asset A and 50 percent in asset B would have an expected rate of return of 14 percent: $E(r_p) = .5 \times .14 + .5 \times .14$.

Next we need to define the risk of the investor's portfolio. To do so we need to develop an equation for the variance of the portfolio. The variance of the portfolio is extremely important because this is where diversification has its effect. Diversification reduces the variance of the investor's portfolio. To see how this happens we need to develop an expression for the variance of the portfolio which highlights the effect of diversification. To do this we will start with a definition for the variance of the portfolio which is just like the definition of the variance of the returns on any single asset. It is written as follows:

$$\sigma^2_{r_p} = \sum_{i=1}^{N} P_i[r_p - E(r_p)]^2 \qquad (4\text{-}10)$$

Next, in order to get to the form of the variance which allows us to capture the effect of diversification we have to go through considerable algebraic manipulation. Because these manipulations are not essential to understanding the ultimate result, they are relegated to a footnote.[2] The expression which results from these manipulations is the following:

$$\sigma^2_{r_p} = x^2\sigma^2_{r_A} + y^2\sigma^2_{r_B} + 2xy\rho_{A\cdot B}\sigma_{r_A}\sigma_{r_B} \qquad (4\text{-}11)$$

[2]Equation (4-11) is derived as follows. Equation (4-10) states the variance as:

$$\sigma^2_{r_p} = \sum_{i=1}^{N} P_i[r_p - E(r_p)]^2$$
$$= E[(xr_A + yr_B) - E(xr_A + yr_B)]^2$$

Using the properties discussed above, this can be rewritten as:

$$\sigma^2_{r_p} = E[(xr_A - xE(r_A)) + (yr_B - yE(r_B))]^2$$

By expanding the terms in brackets, we have:

$$\sigma^2_{r_p} = E[x^2(r_A - E(r_A))^2 + y^2(r_B - E(r_B))^2] + [2\,xy(r_A - E(r_A))\,(r_B - E(r_B))]$$

But the first and second terms are equal to $x^2\sigma^2_{r_A}$ and $y^2\sigma^2_{r_B}$ respectively, that is,

$$x^2\sigma^2_{r_A} = E[x^2(r_A - E(r_A))]^2$$

and

$$y^2\sigma^2_{r_B} = E[y^2(r_B - E(r_B))]^2$$

Moreover, the third term is:

$$2xy\sigma^2_{r_{A\cdot B}} = E[2xy(r_A - E(r_A))\,(r_B - E(r_B))]$$

By substitution it follows that:

$$\sigma^2_{r_p} = x^2\sigma^2_{r_A} + y^2\sigma^2_{r_B} + 2xy\sigma^2_{r_{A\cdot B}}$$

Recalling the definition of the correlation coefficient:

$$\rho_{A\cdot B} = \frac{\sigma^2_{r_{A\cdot B}}}{\sigma_{r_A}\sigma_{r_B}}$$

it follows that

$$\sigma^2_{r_p} = x^2\sigma^2_{r_A} + y^2\sigma^2_{r_B} + 2xy\rho_{A\cdot B}\,\sigma_{r_A}\sigma_{r_B}$$

We need to inspect Eq. (4-11) carefully. It says that the variance of the portfolio can be broken down into three terms. The first two terms are simply the individual variances of the two assets which go into the portfolio, each multiplied by the square of the proportion of wealth invested in that asset. Were it not for the last term, diversification would therefore have no impact on the variance of the portfolio. The important part of the last term is the correlation coefficient between the two assets. We know that the correlation coefficient varies between $+1$ and -1. Therefore, the smaller the value of the correlation coefficient, the smaller will be the variance of the portfolio. We can imagine a situation where we have three different assets, all with the same variances but with different correlation coefficients. Then, regardless of how we created portfolios of those assets, the first two terms in the variance would be the same. But the third term would be lower for the assets that have the lower correlation coefficients. This is where diversification comes in. Assets which have low correlation coefficients provide a greater diversification benefit and that benefit is a reduction in the variance of the portfolio of assets.

To see how this works in the case of our sample of three assets, we need to inspect Table 4-5 and Figure 4-9. The table shows the values of expected return and standard deviations for alternative portfolios of assets. Panel A of the table shows various portfolios made from investments A and C, while panel B shows portfolios made from investments B and C. The portfolios are constructed by varying the percent of wealth invested in each asset. In both panels of the table we can see from the final column that by changing the proportion of wealth in each asset we alter the risk of the portfolio. In the

TABLE 4-5

Mean and Standard Deviation of Portfolio Rates of Return

PANEL A: INVESTMENTS A AND C			
PERCENT IN A	PERCENT IN C	$E(r_p)$	σ_{r_p}
100	0	.14	.01844
75	25	.15	.00336
50	50	.16	.01285
25	75	.17	.02831
0	100	.18	.04382
PANEL B: INVESTMENTS B AND C			
PERCENT IN B	PERCENT IN C	$E(r_p)$	σ_{r_p}
100	0	.14	.04382
75	25	.15	.02191
50	50	.16	.00000
25	75	.17	.02191
0	100	.18	.04382

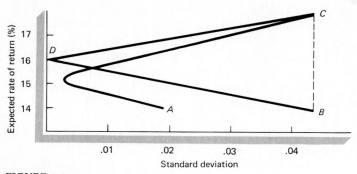

FIGURE 4-9

This figure shows the combinations of expected rate of return and risk which can be obtained by constructing portfolios of investments A, B, and C.

second panel we can actually reduce the risk to zero if resources are split 50-50 in the two assets.

Figure 4-9 illustrates, in a diagram similar to the one first used in Figure 4-3, the combinations of risk and expected return which are defined in Table 4-5. The alternative combinations of risk and expected return which result from portfolios of assets B and C are represented by the solid lines between points C, B, and D. The line segment between points C and D shows the risk and expected return of portfolios which have between 50 and 100 percent in C and zero and 50 percent in B. The lower line segment shows the other alternatives. With 50 percent in each, there is no risk at all. This occurs only when the correlation coefficient between two assets is −1. If it is even slightly larger than that, there will not be any combination of the two assets which eliminates risk entirely.

This is illustrated by the curve which goes from point A to point C. This curve shows the alternative combinations of risk and expected return which result from portfolios made up of assets A and C. We know from Table 4-4 that the correlation coefficient between A and C is −.99. As a result, there is no combination of A and C which yields zero risk.

Finally, the dashed vertical line shows the possible portfolios which would result from combinations of B and C if these assets had a correlation coefficient of +1 rather than −1. In this case, there would be no benefit from diversification with these assets. This is illustrated in the figure by the fact that as you move up or down the dashed line, regardless of how much is invested in B or C, there is no reduction in risk. There is simply a change in expected return.

Choices among Portfolios of Assets

Thus far we have defined the possible options from which we might choose portfolios. We did essentially the same thing earlier in the chapter when we had mutually exclusive choices of A, B, and C. Then we simply had to choose which one of the three assets we wanted. Now we have to choose which portfolio of assets we want. This means we have to first choose which assets to put in our portfolio and then what proportion, x and y, to invest in each asset. As in the case of mutually exclusive assets considered earlier, it may be possible to eliminate some considerations from the outset without being concerned with personal preference. An inspection of Figure 4-9 leads to the conclusion that as long as you are averse to risk, you can always do better by investing in combinations of B and C than you can by investing in A and C. This is because the line segment DC is always to the northwest of the curve between points A and C.

FIGURE 4-10
This figure illustrates the choice of portfolios for a highly risk-averse person and a modestly risk-averse person. The upper panel shows the less risk-averse individual and the lower panel illustrates the choice of the highly risk-averse individual. Panel A shows that a modestly risk-averse person finds it optimal to bear some risk rather than eliminate all risk by choosing a portfolio of equal parts in assets B and C.

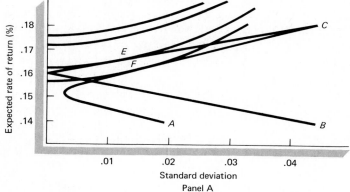

Panel A

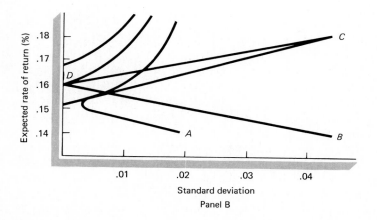

Panel B

However, the individual's attitude toward risk is the crucial determinant of the proportions to invest in assets B and C. Again, just as in the earlier case of mutually exclusive investments, there is no correct choice. You must merely decide how much risk you are willing to bear and select proportions x and y.

We can illustrate the choices of a highly risk averse person and a less risk averse person, however, just as we did earlier in the chapter. To do so we have to utilize indifference curves as we did earlier. Figure 4-10 illustrates the choices of two individuals. The individual represented in panel A is only slightly risk averse. Panel B illustrates the choice of a person who is more risk averse. The more risk averse person in panel B has steeper indifference curves than the person in panel A. These diagrams are simply the same as Figure 4-9, with indifference curves overlaid on the figure. The more risk averse person chooses to split his or her investment equally between assets B and C and bear no risk at all. He or she knows that the return on this portfolio will be .16, regardless. The person in panel A finds that the additional return which can be gained from some additional risk is worth it. But she or he demands increasing amounts of expected return to take on additional risk, so that at point E, she or he finds that enough return has been added. This figure illustrates that no single portfolio is correct for everyone. The appropriate choice depends upon an individual's personal preference for risk as opposed to expected return.

SUMMARY

In this chapter we learned how to analyze individuals' decisions when they face uncertainty. The particular kind of uncertainty which has been our concern here is uncertainty about the future returns on investments. This subject is important not only because we want to make better decisions when we are exposed to uncertainty but also because we want to know how uncertainty and peoples' reactions to it influence the value of assets.

In order to understand how to evaluate investments with uncertain returns we began by proposing a measure of uncertainty and we noted that we would refer to this measure as the risk of an investment. We also distinguished early in the chapter between the return we expected to earn on an asset and the risk or variability around that expected return. To quantify these concepts we introduced probability distributions on future returns for three example investments. Then we defined the expected return, variance, and standard deviation of the probability distributions. We centered on the variance or standard deviation as our measure of risk.

A point which was emphasized at some length is that there is a natural limit to the extent to which we can make choice under uncertainty a scientific procedure. We can measure the expected return and agree that it measures the desirable feature of an asset. Similarly, we can measure the standard deviation and agree that it measures risk, the undesirable feature of an asset. But we can define no objective way to choose between risk and expected return. The right amount of risk to tradeoff for expected return is strictly a matter of personal preference.

To this point in the chapter we were assuming that the assets in our example were mutually exclusive. This means that we could not buy shares of assets and combine them into portfolios. However, we learned that once we relaxed this restriction, a new opportunity was available. Now, through diversification, we could actually change the risk to which we were exposed. Before we could explore diversification itself we had to examine how to quantify the relationships between returns on assets. We measured this with a correlation coefficient. Then in order to see how diversification works we constructed portfolios of assets from the three assets in our example. Next we examined the variance of the rate of return on these portfolios. It is the variance or standard deviation of the portfolios which measures the risk to which an investor is actually exposed. We learned that the variance of a portfolio is dependent on the correlation coefficients between the assets in that portfolio. As a result, assets which are negatively correlated will reduce risk when they are combined in the same portfolio.

Even after we construct alternative portfolios, we still cannot define the scientifically correct portfolio to choose. Just as in the case when investments are mutually exclusive, this is a matter of personal preference. We can represent these preferences with indifference curves and portray an individual's choice of a portfolio with these curves. But such curves cannot tell us the correct investment decision.

Finally, from this discussion we can conclude that the prices of risky assets are based on the expected return to the asset, the risk of the asset, and the individual's attitudes toward risk, or the compensation one demands to bear risk.

QUESTIONS TO IMPROVE UNDERSTANDING

1   Explain what risk is. Why do we use variance to measure risk? Suppose someone told you that they felt risk was best measured by the probability of the lowest returns. That is, suppose there were two assets, one with a 5 percent chance of a rate of return less than zero and the other with a 10 percent chance of a rate of return less than zero. This person then said that the project with the greater percentage chance of a return less than zero was the more risky. What do you think of this as a measure of risk?

2   What does it mean to say that a person is averse to risk?

3   Do you think a risk-averse person is likely to buy insurance? Does a person have to have no aversion to risk to go to Las Vegas and gamble? How would you explain a person who both buys insurance and gambles in Las Vegas?

4   Suppose you have to choose between two mutually exclusive investments. Call them investments A and B. You have been told that there is a certain amount of

information about such choices which you should try to collect and analyze in a "scientific" manner. Then you reach a point where you simply have to make up your mind. Describe what you can do scientifically and then describe how you can present the personal choice you must make.

5 Consider the following two investments:

STATE OF THE WORLD	PROBABILITY OF OCCURRENCE	RATE OF RETURN ON ASSETS	
		A	B
1	.1	.00	−.12
2	.2	.05	.05
3	.4	.08	.09
4	.2	.10	.12
5	.1	.15	.24

Compute the expected return, variance, and standard deviation for each of the two investments. Compute the correlation coefficient and covariance for the two investments.

6 Draw a diagram with expected rate of return on one axis and standard deviation on the other. Plot the combinations of risk and return achieved by combining investments A and B in question 5 in different proportions.

7 The value of an asset is determined by (a) the expected return on the asset, (b) the risk of the asset, and (c) the premium demanded to bear risk. Explain what each of these means and give an example.

8 Suppose you have three assets to choose from. To keep the problem simple, suppose you can put all your wealth into any one asset or split your wealth equally between any two assets. Suppose that there are four possible rates of return for each asset corresponding to four possible "states of the world" and that each state of the world is equally probable (probability of 25 percent). The table showing possible returns is as follows:

STATE OF THE WORLD	RATE OF RETURN ON INVESTMENT		
	A	B	C
1	5	10	90
2	25	30	70
3	85	70	30
4	105	90	10

What portfolio would you prefer?

9 In question 8 show how the risk aversion of two distinctly different individuals can be illustrated with indifference curves and how the amount of risk aversion influences their choice.

REFERENCES

Borch, Karl H.: *The Economics of Uncertainty*, Princeton University Press, Princeton, N.J., 1968.

Copeland, Thomas E., and J. Fred Weston: *Financial Theory and Corporate Policy*, Addison-Wesley Publishing Company, Inc., Reading, Mass., 1979.

Fama, Eugene F., and Merton H. Miller: *The Theory of Finance*, Holt, Rinehart and Winston, Inc., New York, 1972.

Mossin, Jan: *The Theory of Financial Markets*, Prentice-Hall, Inc., Englewood Cliffs, N.J., 1973.

Sharpe, William F.: *Portfolio Theory and Capital Markets*, McGraw-Hill Book Company, Inc., New York, 1970.

Chapter Five

CAPITAL MARKET THEORY

This chapter extends the understanding we acquired in the last chapter of how risky assets are priced in financial markets. In this chapter we will examine the preeminent theory on this subject, known as the capital asset pricing model (CAPM). The purpose of the CAPM is to explain how risky assets are priced when individuals in the market choose diversified portfolios of assets. The idea behind the CAPM is that, when individuals hold diversified portfolios of assets, the relevant measure of the risk of any *individual* asset is no longer that asset's variance or standard deviation. This is not because diversification alters the total risk of individual assets. It does not. But diversification does alter the risk of portfolios of assets which investors hold. As a result, the total risk of an individual asset, as measured by its standard deviation, is not something to which investors are actually exposed. Therefore, it is no longer that risk which is relevant in determining the price of each individual asset. The purpose of capital market theory is to develop a suitable measure of the risk of individual asset when they are held in diversified portfolios and use that measure of risk to explain how those assets are priced in the market. Our purpose in this chapter is to understand how capital market theory does this.

SYSTEMATIC AND UNSYSTEMATIC RISK

We know from the last chapter that the total risk of any individual asset or portfolio of assets is measured by the variance or standard deviation of the asset's or portfolio's rate of return. Now we want to decompose the total risk of an individual asset into two components. One component is called *systematic risk*, and the other is called *unsystematic risk*. Systematic risk is the part of an asset's total risk which cannot be eliminated by forming a diversified portfolio with all assets in the market. Unsystematic risk is the residual which can be eliminated through diversification. It is important to see that diversification does not change the total risk of an individual asset, even though it does change the total risk of a portfolio of assets. The total risk of an individual asset is still its variance or standard deviation, and this is unaffected regardless of what portfolio that asset may be a part of. Therefore, as we decompose the total risk of an asset into the systematic and unsystematic parts, we must remember that regardless of what we do with this asset, the sum of the two parts is always the same.

Total risk = systematic risk + unsystematic risk

In this section of this chapter we will develop a measure of an individual asset's systematic risk. This measure is called the asset's beta (β). In order to develop beta we need to utilize what is called the market portfolio. Once we understand what the market portfolio is, then we can relate the rate of return on an individual asset to that market portfolio and derive the measure of systematic risk, beta.

Individual Assets and the Market Portfolio

In the definition of systematic risk just presented we said that the systematic risk is that portion of total risk which cannot be eliminated by forming a diversified portfolio with *all* other assets in the market. The idea of a portfolio of all the assets in the market is what is meant by a market portfolio. The market portfolio is the market as a whole. A portfolio which is made up of virtually every asset in the market offers the maximum amount of benefit from diversification. Therefore, the risk of the market portfolio is systematic risk and the systematic risk of an individual asset is that part of its total risk which is tied to the market portfolio. This phrasing may seem a little bit ambiguous, for it is not clear exactly what it means to say that the risk is tied to the market portfolio. We need to spell out the exact relationship between the return on the market portfolio and the return on a specific asset.

If we are going to take the definition of the market portfolio literally, then the market portfolio which we use to define systematic risk must actually be composed of every asset available in the market. If there were 1 million assets available in the market, then the market portfolio would be composed of shares of each of these assets. Moreover, the proportion of each of these assets in the market portfolio would be equal to that asset's proportion of total value in the market. This means that if the total value of all shares of asset number 1 available in the market is equal to 1 percent of the total value of all shares of all assets in the market, then this asset should represent 1 percent of the market portfolio. Again the idea here is that the market portfolio actually is the market.

In practice, it is impractical to construct a portfolio of *all* the assets in the market. Fortunately, this is not necessary in order to receive most of the benefits of diversification. The reason for this is that as we increase the number of assets in a portfolio, the amount of unsystematic risk in the portfolio declines fairly rapidly. Therefore, we can choose a portfolio of, say, 30 or 40 assets and that portfolio will be much like the true market portfolio. Like the true market portfolio, the risk of this portfolio will be almost entirely systematic risk, so that this portfolio gives almost as much benefit from diversification as the true market portfolio itself. This is illustrated in Figure 5-1. The figure shows what happens to systematic risk as the number of assets in a portfolio is increased. The line showing the total risk of the portfolio asymptotically or gradually approaches the line representing systematic risk. It has been shown from experiments involving portfolios with different numbers of securities that the risk of a portfolio actually declines in this manner.[1] This ensures that one does not have to include all the assets in the market in order to have an approximation of the market portfolio with most of its diversification benefit.

There is one additional requirement, however, for this to work out. That requirement is that the securities in the more modest-sized portfolio must be

---

[1] The details of these experiments can be found in W. H. Wagner and S. C. Lau, "The Effect of Diversification on Risk," *Financial Analysts Journal*, vol. 26 (November–December 1971), pp. 7–13.

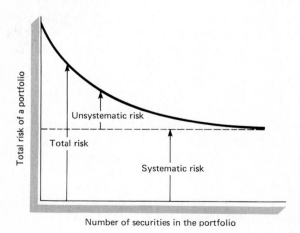

FIGURE 5-1
Systematic and unsystematic risk in a portfolio. This figure illustrates how unsystematic risk declines as randomly chosen securities are added to a portfolio.

chosen randomly. It is certainly possible to construct a portfolio of, say, 30 securities which has a lot of unsystematic risk. For example, we could choose a portfolio of all energy stocks. But if the assets are chosen randomly, then this concentration will be avoided. As a result of this approximate relationship between modest-size portfolios and the true market portfolio, well-diversified portfolios which are not really quite the total market have been used to represent the market portfolio. Two common examples which fill this role are the Standard & Poors 500 and the New York Stock Exchange Index. These are indices of returns on large well-diversified portfolios of common stock.

Thus far we have learned that an individual asset always has both a systematic and an unsystematic component to its total risk. Now we can begin to measure these components precisely by relating the return on an individual asset to the return on the market portfolio. To do so we want to specify how the rate of return on a particular asset, call it asset A, is related to the rate of return on the market. We will represent the rate of return on the market with r_M and, as in the last chapter, the rate of return on an individual asset, A, as r_A. It is important to see what we are asking for in this relationship. At this point we are not asking for a theory of how an individual asset should be priced, given the return on the market. We will come to that later in the chapter. We simply want to quantify the observable relationship between the two rates of return, r_A and r_M.

We will quantify this relationship with the following linear equation:

$$r_A = a_A + \beta_A r_M + \epsilon_A \qquad (5\text{-}1)$$

Some of the terms in the equation should be familiar by now, while a few of them need explaining. The rates of return on asset A and the market portfolio are r_A and r_M. The term β_A represents the beta of asset A; that is, β_A is a measure of the systematic risk of asset A. The term a_A is a constant which is known with certainty. This means that a_A is not defined by a probability distribution. The term ϵ_A is an uncertain or random term referred to as a residual. The exact magnitude of ϵ_A is unknown, as it is determined by a probability distribution.

To see what Eq. (5-1) means it is best to plug in some numbers and interpret its meaning in an example. Suppose that a_A and β_A have values of .02 and 2, respectively. These are the two variables we know with certainty ahead of time. Now the equation can be read as follows. The return on asset A will be equal to two times the rate of return on the market, plus .02, plus an additional random factor, ϵ_A. For example, if the rate of return on the market were zero and the random factor were zero, then the rate of return on asset A would be

$$.02 = .02 + 2 \times 0 + 0$$

If the rate of return on the market were .05 and the random factor ϵ_A were $-.03$, then the rate of return on asset A would be

$$.09 = .02 + 2 \times .05 - .03$$

Equation (5-1) is simply a way of representing how the rate of return on a particular security is generated. It is a statistical approach in that it relates the return on the particular asset in question to the return on the market where the intercept a_A and the slope coefficient β_A are the parameters in the relationship. It is not an approach that illuminates why the return on an asset is what it is. The return is actually determined by all sorts of factors pertaining to the firm involved and the products it produces. Equation (5-1) merely seeks to explain individual rates of return as having a component related to the market as a whole and a random residual component. As a result it is referred to as a single-factor model, the single factor being r_M.

Measuring the Systematic Risk of an Asset

As it stands now, it may be difficult to see how to make use of Eq. (5-1). But Eq. (5-1) is useful because it provides a basis for measuring the systematic risk of an asset, that is β. Because it is this part of total risk which an investor actually bears when he or she holds a particular asset in a portfolio, it is valuable to be able to measure systematic risk. To measure the systematic risk of an individual asset we need to use Eq. (5-1) to evaluate the variance of the rate of return on the asset. We originally defined the variance of the return on an asset in Eq. (4-2) in the last chapter. Now, in Eq. (5-1) we have redefined the rate of return on asset A as a function of the two other random variables, r_M and ϵ_A. Therefore, the variance of r_A can be written as a function of the variances of these two random variables. The resulting equation for the variance of r_A is the following:

$$\sigma^2_{r_A} = \beta^2_A \, \sigma^2_{r_M} + \sigma^2_{\epsilon_A} \tag{5-2}$$

where $\sigma^2_{r_M}$ is equal to the variance of r_M and $\sigma^2_{\epsilon_A}$ is equal to the variance of ϵ_A.

To see how Eq. (5-2) is derived we simply proceed to compute the variance of each of the three terms on the right-hand side of Eq. (5-1). The first term a_A, is a constant; thus its variance is zero. The second term is the constant β_A, multiplied by the random variable r_M. The variance of this product is β^2_A times the variance of r_M. Next, it is important to note that ϵ_A and r_M are constructed so that they are uncorrelated with each other. This means they have a correlation coefficient of zero, because the market portfolio has only systematic risk and therefore cannot be related to this residual term. As a result, the variance of the sum of r_M and ϵ_A is equal to the sum of their variances. That is, there is no covariance term which must be included. Note that there generally is a covariance term in the variance of a sum of two random variables. We have already encountered an example of this in Eq. (4-11), which shows the variance of a portfolio of two assets. But when the correlation coefficient between the two variables is zero, the covariance term drops out. And this is the case here. Therefore, the last term in Eq. (5-2) is simply the variance of ϵ_A.

Now we can use Eq. (5-2) to define the systematic and unsystematic components of the risk of asset A. The total risk of the asset is measured by the variance. The systematic component is that part of the total risk which is related to the market portfolio. Therefore, the first of the two terms in Eq. (5-2) represents the systematic risk of asset A. The equation shows that the systematic component of the variance of any asset is the product of the variance of the rate of return on the market portfolio and the square of that asset's beta. The variance of the residual ϵ_A is the unsystematic component of variance of the individual asset.

$$\sigma^2_{R_A} = \beta^2_A \, \sigma^2_{r_M} + \sigma^2_{\epsilon_A}$$

$$\text{TOTAL VARIANCE} = \frac{\text{SYSTEMATIC}}{\text{COMPONENT}} + \frac{\text{UNSYSTEMATIC}}{\text{COMPONENT}}$$

This analysis implies that beta is the appropriate measure of the systematic risk of an individual asset. If we express systematic risk in terms of standard deviation rather than variance, then the systematic risk of asset A is equal to β_A times the standard deviation of the rate of return on the market portfolio: $\beta_A \, \sigma_{r_M}$. Therefore, whatever the standard deviation of the rate of return on the market portfolio, if the beta of asset A is, say, 2, then the systematic risk of asset A is twice the risk of the market portfolio. Therefore, we can use beta as an unambiguous measure of the systematic risk of an individual asset.

Next, it is important to see how to compute beta for a given security. The procedure used is the procedure for computing the estimate of a coefficient in a linear regression model. Those familiar with linear regression should recognize that Eq. (5-1) is an example of a linear regression where r_A is being regressed on r_M. The formula for the computation of β_A is much easier to state than it is to derive. We will eschew the derivation and merely state the formula:

$$\beta_A = \frac{\sigma^2_{r_{A \cdot M}}}{\sigma^2_{r_M}} \tag{5-3}$$

where $\sigma^2_{r_{A \cdot M}}$ represents the covariance between the rates of return on asset A and the market portfolio.

As an initial illustration of the procedure involved in computing beta we can turn to the example used throughout the last chapter. To compute an estimate of beta we have to have data or observations on r_A and r_M. Table 4-3 in the last chapter presents some hypothetical data on the rates of return on three assets corresponding to five alternative states of the world. If we also had corresponding rates of return for the market portfolio in each state of the world, then we could use Eq. (5-3) to compute the beta for any of the three assets in Table 4-3. Table 5-1 presents data on the rate of return on the market portfolio in each of the five states of the world. It also repeats the probability of each state of the world and the rate of return on asset A initially presented in the earlier table.

Using the information presented in Table 5-1 and recalling the definition of covariance from Eq. (4-3) we can compute the value of β_A as follows:

$$\beta_A = \frac{\sum_{i=1}^{5} P_i(_ir_A - E(r_A))(_ir_M - E(r_M))}{\sum_{i=1}^{5} P_i(_ir_M - E(r_M))^2}$$

The numerator is equal to

$$(.1 \times .03 \times .03) + (.2 \times .02 \times .01) + 0 + (.2 \times .02 \times .01)$$
$$+ (.1 \times .03 \times .03)$$
$$= .00026$$

The denominator is equal to

$$.1 \times (.03)^2 + .2 \times (.01)^2 + 0 + .2 \times (.01)^2 + .1 \times (.03)^2 = .00022$$

TABLE 5-1

Uncertain Rates of Return on Investment A and the Market Portfolio

DESCRIPTION OF STATE OF THE WORLD	PROBABILITY OF OCCURRENCE	RATES OF RETURN IN EACH STATE OF THE WORLD	
		ASSET A	MARKET PORTFOLIO
Deep recession	.1	.11	.03
Mild recession	.2	.12	.05
Normal	.4	.14	.06
Minor boom	.2	.16	.07
Major boom	.1	.17	.09
$E(r_A) = .14$			
$E(r_M) = .06$			

This implies

$$\beta_A = \frac{.00026}{.00022} = 1.18$$

This example links the concept of systematic risk to our discussion in the last chapter of investment decisions and the value of risky assets. The example shows how to quantify the risk of each of the assets available to us when they are held as one of the assets in a large portfolio. It is important, however, to see how the concept of beta can be used to quantify the risk of an asset that is actually traded in organized markets. To do so we will examine the beta for IBM. Chapter Two contains a table, Table 2-1, which shows the annual rate of return on IBM stock from 1969 to 1978. We can use these data to compute the beta for IBM. Table 5-2 reprints the annual rate of return for IBM initially presented in Table 2-1. It also shows the annual rate of return for the Standard & Poor's Composite Index, which we will use as a proxy for the market portfolio.

The only difference between this computation and the one performed above for asset A from the example in the last chapter is that we must substitute past performance for our estimates of outcomes in alternative states of the world. Implicit in this substitution is the idea that past performance is an appropriate basis for estimating the future performance of the asset in question. If the systematic risk has changed, then this is not a useful

TABLE 5-2

Rates of Return on IBM and on the Standard & Poor's Composite Index

	RATE OF RETURN ON IBM	RATE OF RETURN ON COMMON STOCKS*
	PERCENT RETURN	PERCENT RETURN
1969	1.9	−8.5
1970	−6.8	4.0
1971	8.9	14.3
1972	18.5	19.0
1973	0.4	−14.7
1974	−30.8	−26.5
1975	−1.7	37.2
1976	37.2	23.8
1977	8.7	−7.2
1978	7.2	6.6
Average over the period	4.35	Average over the period 4.8

* Source: Ibbotson, Roger, and Rex A. Singuefield: *Stocks, Bonds, Bills and Inflation: Historical Return (1926–1978)*, Financial Analysts Research Foundation, 1979.

procedure. In effect, we are treating the past returns as sample values from the same probability distribution which will determine future returns. If this assumption is reasonable, then we can derive a measure of beta which is a valid measure of the future risk of the security.

One procedural change which must be introduced into the computations results from the fact that we have no estimates of individual probabilities as we did for the states of the world in the example in the last chapter. Therefore, when we compute the variance of the rate of return on IBM and the variance of the rate of return on the market, as well as the covariance between the two, we weight the past events equally rather than attempt to assign specific probabilities. This means that we compute the variance of the rate of return on IBM according to the following equation:

$$\sigma^2_{r_{IBM}} = \sum_{t=1}^{N} ({}_t r_{IBM} - E(r_{IBM}))^2/N$$

The subscript t now refers to the past annual observations on the rate of return rather than the alternative states of the world and N refers to the number of past observations, 10 in this case, rather than the number of states of the world. Because all past observations are weighted equally, the sum of the squared deviations around the expected rate of return is divided by N. This is equivalent to multiplying each individual deviation by $1/N$.

The computations involved in determining the variance of the rate of return on the market portfolio and the covariance between the two are not shown, though the procedure is identical. Note that the expected rate of return on IBM is 4.35 percent. Then $\sigma^2_{r_{IBM}}$ is computed as follows:

$$
\begin{aligned}
\sigma^2_{r_{IBM}} = [({}_{1969}r_{IBM} - E(r_{IBM}))^2 \quad &\text{or} \quad [(1.9 - 4.35)^2 \\
({}_{1970}r_{IBM} - E(r_{IBM}))^2 \quad &\text{or} \quad (-6.8 - 4.35)^2 \\
({}_{1971}r_{IBM} - E(r_{IBM}))^2 \quad &\text{or} \quad (8.9 - 4.35)^2 \\
({}_{1972}r_{IBM} - E(r_{IBM}))^2 \quad &\text{or} \quad (18.5 - 4.35)^2 \\
({}_{1973}r_{IBM} - E(r_{IBM}))^2 \quad &\text{or} \quad (0.4 - 4.35)^2 \\
({}_{1974}r_{IBM} - E(r_{IBM}))^2 \quad &\text{or} \quad (-30.8 - 4.35)^2 \\
({}_{1975}r_{IBM} - E(r_{IBM}))^2 \quad &\text{or} \quad (-1.7 - 4.35)^2 \\
({}_{1976}r_{IBM} - E(r_{IBM}))^2 \quad &\text{or} \quad (37.2 - 4.35)^2 \\
({}_{1977}r_{IBM} - E(r_{IBM}))^2 \quad &\text{or} \quad (8.7 - 4.35)^2 \\
({}_{1978}r_{IBM} - E(r_{IBM}))^2]/N \quad &\text{or} \quad (7.2 - 4.35)^2]/10 \\
\sigma^2_{r_{IBM}} = 2.74\% \\
\sigma_{r_{IBM}} = 16.57\%
\end{aligned}
$$

Similar computations will disclose that the value of σ_{r_M} is 18.4 percent and that the value of the covariance between the two rates of return, $\sigma^2_{r_{IBM} \cdot r_M}$, is 2.29 percent. Substituting these into the expression for the equation for the value of beta, we find that beta is equal to

$$\beta_{IBM} = \frac{2.29}{16.57 \times 18.4} = .75$$

THE CAPITAL ASSET PRICING MODEL (CAPM)

Now we will use our understanding of systematic and unsystematic risk to examine the principal existing theory used by scholars as well as by many market analysts to explain how the prices of individual risky assets are determined in the market. This theory is known as the capital asset pricing model or CAPM. The essential contribution of the theory is that it extends the concepts we developed in the last chapter about the value of risky assets to take account of the difference between systematic and unsystematic risk. The theory leads to a specific equation which explains how the market prices individual securities. In order to understand what the CAPM has to say and how we can use it, we need to start by carefully examining the key assumptions which go into the theory.

Foundation of the CAPM

There are four fundamental assumptions which form the basis of the CAPM. Once you read the assumptions you will see that they are clearly unrealistic. This should not be too troublesome, for any theory incorporates simplifications of reality which make it unrealistic. The relevant test of a theory is whether we acquire any improved understanding of how the market operates by making these admittedly unrealistic assumptions. You will have to judge that when we are finished. The assumptions are:

1 All investors are averse to risk and choose portfolios which give them the optimal combinations of expected return and risk, as measured by standard deviation.
2 Investors all agree about the probability distributions of returns on assets.
3 There exists one asset which is free of risk with a rate of return, r_F. All investors may borrow or lend unlimited amounts at this risk-free rate.
4 Assets offer a return in a single period only.

The first assumption says that people choose portfolios of assets the way we described them as doing in the last chapter. If they are risk averse, then each individual's attitude toward risk, or tradeoff between risk and return, can be represented with indifference curves in a diagram showing expected return and standard deviation of alternative portfolios of assets. These indifference curves were first illustrated in Figures 4-5 and 4-6.

We can go further than we did in the last chapter in describing the set of possible investments from which investors can choose. In Figure 4-9 in the last chapter we examined the alternative portfolios which could be constructed from the three assets in the example. We found that if two assets had a correlation coefficient of -1, then the set of possible portfolios which could be constructed looked like a V laid on its side with the bottom of the V lying on the horizontal axis. If the assets were not perfectly correlated, then the set of portfolios looked like a curve which did not reach the horizontal axis. In the real world of possible portfolios there are few assets which have correlation coefficients of -1. As a result, the possible portfolios that individuals can construct from all the assets available in the market have combinations of expected return and standard deviation which can be represented by a curve as shown in Figure 5-2. Actually the curve GH only shows the best combinations of expected return and standard deviation. This means that there are an infinite number of possible portfolios, such as the one represented by point L, which are inside the line GH. These portfolios are always inferior to some portfolio which is on the line because that portfolio on the line will have both less risk and more expected return. The line therefore represents what is called the efficient frontier. The efficient frontier includes all portfolios which are not clearly inferior to some other possible portfolio.

Assumption (1) simply says that people choose their portfolios from this efficient set and that their tradeoff between risk and return can be represented with indifference curves. We can illustrate the choice of a hypothetical individual from the efficient set with Figure 5-3. This figure shows a sample of indifference curves and the efficient set drawn in Figure 5-2. The optimal portfolio for this hypothetical individual is the one labeled P^*. This point is the point of tangency between line GH and an indifference curve of the individual. This is optimal because it is impossible to reach a higher indifference curve.

The second assumption says that all market participants agree about the estimates of future return and standard deviation for all assets in the market. This means that all individuals see the same efficient set of possible portfolios. As a result, the only thing which separates individuals is their attitude toward risk. In terms of Figure 5-3, the only thing that separates individuals is that they have different indifference curves.

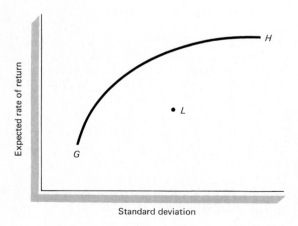

FIGURE 5-2
Efficient frontier of a portfolio. The curve GH illustrates the efficient frontier of a set of available portfolios. Portfolios to the right of the line, such as L, are available, but they are inferior to those on the frontier.

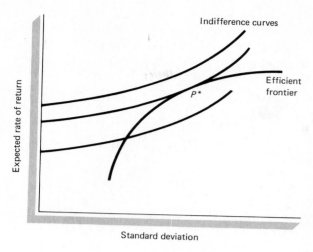

Indifference curves

Efficient frontier

P *

Expected rate of return

Standard deviation

FIGURE 5-3
Optimal portfolio on the efficient frontier. *P** illustrates the optimal portfolio for an individual with the indifference curves shown. The optimal portfolio is the point of tangency between the efficient frontier and an indifference curve.

The third assumption introduces an asset which is free of risk. In addition, it stipulates that individuals can borrow and lend at the risk-free interest rate on that asset. The real-world counterpart of the risk-free asset is a Treasury bill, which is thought to be free of default risk. The prices of Treasury bills can increase or decrease over time. But this sort of risk of price changes is not really a part of this analysis, because assumption (4) rules out multiple future periods. What the existence of a risk-free asset does is alter the set of portfolios from which individuals can choose. Figure 5-4 shows how the set of possible portfolios is altered. The key to this change is that the risk-free asset plots on the vertical axis with return at r_F because it has no risk. In addition it can be combined with any portfolio of risky assets in any proportion. The most efficient combinations are the ones which involve portfolio M and the risk-free asset. These portfolios fall on the line which intersects r_F and is tangent to the set of risky portfolios at point M. Any portfolio on this line will be superior to any portfolio beneath the line, for the same reason portfolios on the efficient frontier are superior to those inside it. An investor can move from point M in either direction by borrowing or lending at the risk-free rate r_F. Borrowing means a movement up the line away from r_F and lending or investing in the risk-free asset involves a movement down the line toward point r_F.

Now we can represent the choice of any individual for this modified set of possible portfolios, just as we did in Figure 5-3 where there was no risk-free asset. The optimal portfolio for the individual with the indifference curves shown in Figure 5-4 is the one at point N, for at this point this individual has reached the highest indifference curve possible. This portfolio represents a combination of the risk-free asset and the portfolio of risky assets at point M. The implication is that when investors agree on the

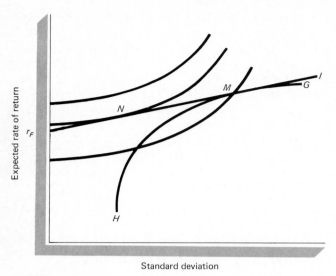

FIGURE 5-4
Portfolio choice with a risk-free asset. This figure shows how the available combinations of risk and expected return are altered when a risk-free asset is available. Everyone will now choose an optimal portfolio along the line from r_F to I. The individual in this example chooses portfolio N.

probability distributions on assets in the market, and when there is a risk-free asset which can be borrowed or lent, then no investor will ever choose a portfolio of risky assets other than the one at point M. This is the market portfolio. However, different investors will combine that portfolio in different proportions with the risk-free asset, depending upon their attitude toward risk. It is their risk-return preferences, represented by the shape of their indifference curves, which will determine how much of the market portfolio of risky assets and how much of the risk-free asset will be purchased.

The Pricing Equation

The idea behind the CAPM is that if all investors make choices in the manner just described, it leads to a mathematical statement of the way the price is determined for each asset in the market. The mathematical expression is referred to as the pricing equation. The pricing equation is usually stated in terms of expected rate of return rather than price itself. But if the expected dollar returns are known, then for the expected rate of return to increase, the price must go down and vice versa; therefore the pricing equation is really an equation for the expected rate of return. Before we state the pricing equation itself, we need to discuss its basic ingredients. The first one we have already explored. It is the beta of an asset. The second one is called the market price of risk.

When all investors behave in the way we described above, then the premium they demand, as a whole, for bearing the risk of the market portfolio is reflected in the expected rate of return of that portfolio. That is, the expected rate of return on the market portfolio $E(r_M)$ will exceed the risk-free rate of return r_F by an amount which just compensates investors for holding the market portfolio. This means that, given the expected absolute dollar returns for each asset in the market, the prices of those assets will adjust until investors are compensated for bearing the risk of the market portfolio. This difference between the expected rate of return on the market portfolio and the risk-free interest rate is called the market price of risk:

$$\text{Market price of risk} = E(r_M) - r_F$$

In the last chapter it was emphasized at some length that each individual must make up his or her own mind about the amounts of risk he or she is willing to bear. In effect, each individual has his or her own price of risk. What the capital asset pricing model does is aggregate these prices into a market price of risk. This happens because each individual holds the market portfolio of assets.

When all investors hold the market portfolio, then the price of every asset in the market is determined by three factors: the market price of risk, the systematic risk of the asset, and the risk-free rate of interest. The pricing equation which defines the expected rate of return for an asset can be written, for asset A, as

$$E(r_A) = r_F + [E(r_M) - r_F] \beta_A \tag{5-4}$$

The CAPM equation says that the expected rate of return on each asset in the market is equal to the risk-free interest rate plus the product of the market price of risk and the systematic risk of the asset. For example, if $r_F = .05$, $E(r_M) = .07$, and $\beta_A = 2$, then $E(r_A) = .09$. The risk-free interest rate represents the rate of return the asset would command in the market if it had no risk. The second term in the equation represents the compensation the market demands for risk. This compensation is equal to the measure of the systematic risk of the asset times the compensation demanded by the market to bear the same amount of systematic risk as the market portfolio. That is, if its beta were equal to one, then the price demanded to bear this risk would be the same as for the market portfolio.

This relationship is illustrated by the upward sloping line in Figure 5-5. The vertical axis in this figure measures the expected rate of return, as in Figure 5-4, but the horizontal axis measures the beta of an asset. The slope of the line is equal to the market price of risk, $E(r_M) - r_F$, and the intercept is

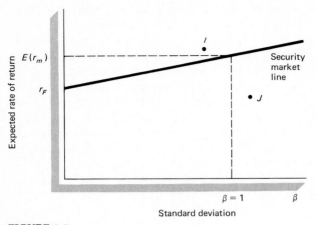

FIGURE 5-5
The security market line. This figure illustrates Eq. (5-4). Any security which has an expected rate of return above the line, such as I, has a return above that predicted by the
CAPM. If it plots below the line, as does J, then the expected return is below that predicted
by the CAPM.

equal to the risk-free interest rate. This line is called the *security market line*
because it indicates the expected rate of return demanded by the market as a
function of an asset's beta. The CAPM argues that the market should price
assets so that they fall on the security market line. If they fall on this line,
then their prices are determined according to Eq. (5-4). If an asset plots above
the line, as illustrated by point I in Figure 5-5, this means that the market is
underpricing the asset, relative to the prediction of the CAPM. This is because the expected return in the market is above that predicted by Eq. (5-4).
On the other hand, if the asset plots below the line, as illustrated by point J in
Figure 5-5, then the asset is overpriced relative to the prediction of the
CAPM.

The Usefulness of the CAPM

The greatest merit of the CAPM is its simplicity. This may seem like an
unbelievable statement if this is your first exposure to the CAPM. But it is
important to recognize that almost nothing is simple at first. Relative to the
alternative theories which seek to explain how risky assets are priced in a
market, the CAPM is really rather simple. The simplicity lies in the fact that
Eq. (5-4) has such a straightforward interpretation and is readily usable. If
this equation has not yet struck you as simple and usable, then it will be
worthwhile to interpret the equation a little more carefully.

The CAPM pricing equation decomposes the price of any risky asset into
only three factors: a risk-free factor, a price of risk, and a measure of risk.
These are the same factors which we were concerned about in the last chap-

ter when we began our discussion of the risk of an asset. In particular, when we examined assets held in isolation—that is, not in portfolios—we discovered that every individual would value assets based on these considerations. But at that juncture, the appropriate compensation for risk was a matter of personal preference. There was no right or wrong way to price risk. When we examined how assets could be combined into portfolios, we learned how to alter our measure of the risk of the portfolio, but individual assets were left hanging. We needed a way to measure the risk of an individual asset, and then we still had to price that risk. The beta of an asset resolves the first difficulty in that it measures the risk of an asset. And we can use the concept of beta as a measure of risk without ever introducing the CAPM, as we did earlier in this chapter. What the CAPM does is make use of the concept of beta in order to determine the price of an asset. What it offers is a standardized measure of the price of compensation for bearing risk. It depersonalizes the issue of how to state a proper compensation for risk. It does this by saying that the market portfolio provides the market's price of risk. The market's price of risk is the premium or difference between the expected return on the market portfolio of assets and the rate of return on the risk-free asset. Since the measure of the risk of any asset, beta, is a measure of the risk of an asset relative to the market, the compensation demanded for the risk of an individual asset should be the product of the market price of risk and the beta of an asset. The pricing equation of the CAPM quantifies this:

$$E(r_A) = r_F + \underbrace{[E(r_M - r_F)]}_{\substack{\text{MARKET PRICE} \\ \text{OF RISK}}} \cdot \underbrace{\beta_A}_{\substack{\text{RISK OF ASSET} \\ \text{A RELATIVE TO} \\ \text{THE MARKET}}}$$

A related virture of the CAPM is the ease with which this equation can be applied to the normative problem of selecting investments. To see how to do so, suppose you are the manager of a company choosing between alternative investment projects. Suppose you and your staff have prepared detailed information of the kind discussed in the last chapter for the example investments A, B, and C. From this information you have derived estimates of the variance, standard deviation, and beta of the investment projects under consideration. Finally, suppose that the ownership of your company is widely diversified, that is, you have many owners who hold widely diversified portfolios. There is no single owner who holds your company almost exclusively. What we have learned in this chapter is that the investors in this company should be concerned with systematic risk, rather than the total risk of this particular company. Therefore, if you are going to make investment decisions which are in their best interests, it is important to choose investments based on systematic risk.

The CAPM provides you with a mechanism by which you can assess the value of these competing investments based on systematic rather than total risk. To do this you need to estimate the beta for each investment, you need to estimate the rate of return on the market portfolio, and you need a measure of the risk-free interest rate. We have discussed examples of each of these throughout this chapter. The risk-free rate is usually approximated with the rate of interest on Treasury securities. And the market portfolio is usually approximated with one of a number of stock-market indices, as illustrated in Table 5-1. Using these measures, Eq. (5-4) can tell you the expected rate of return which you should demand from an investment. If the expected return which you estimate is higher than the one which you should demand, then, according to the CAPM, the investment is worth undertaking.

Shortcomings of the CAPM

While the CAPM is the preeminent analytical model of the pricing of risky assets in organized financial markets, it has its drawbacks. These drawbacks are sufficiently serious that an intense search for a superior theory of asset pricing is under way. And while there are some contenders for the throne, no coronation seems imminent.[2] The issues involved in the rivalry between alternative models are exceedingly complicated and it is impossible to cover them in any depth here. It is possible, however, to give some indication of what the shortcomings of the CAPM are and why the search for an alternative theory is proceeding. To do this we need to reexamine the assumptions of the theory. All of the assumptions are unrealistic. But some are more troublesome than others. We will start with one that proves to generate few serious problems and then proceed to consider a couple of the more troublesome ones.

One assumption is that there is a risk-free asset which every market participant can incorporate into his or her portfolio. But in reality, there is no such risk-free asset. The usual real-world counterpart for the risk-free asset is a Treasury bill. But with inflation the real returns on Treasury bills, that is, the returns after inflation, are not certain. As it turns out, it is not really necessary to have a risk-free asset to establish the CAPM. Instead, something called a zero-beta portfolio will work just as well.[3] To construct a zero-beta portfolio one has to be able to construct a portfolio of assets which is uncorrelated—that is, it has a correlation coefficient of zero—with the market portfolio. While we will not show how to construct it here, in principle this is not too difficult to do. And as long as this can be done, beta and the market price of risk retain their usefulness and can be interpreted as discussed above.

---

[2] The principal alternative is known as the Arbitrage Pricing Theory (APT). One of the first developments of this theory was in Steven Ross, "The Arbitrage Theory of Capital Asset Pricing," *Journal of Economic Theory,* vol. 13 (December 1976), pp. 341–360.

[3] See Fischer Black, "Capital Market Equilibrium with Restricted Borrowing," *Journal of Business* (July 1972), pp. 444–455, for the original development of the zero-beta portfolio and its application to the CAPM.

A more difficult problem centers on the assumption that all market participants agree on the estimates of future returns on assets available in the market. The key problem is that it is this assumption which leads everyone to hold a common market portfolio. One can still come up with an equation something like Eq. (5-4), but averages of every individual's estimates of expected returns and correlation coefficients now appear in the equation.[4] As a consequence, the resulting explanation of the prices of risky assets is not as simple and useful as the CAPM. The key to the usefulness of the CAPM is the concept of a market portfolio which lies on the frontier of all possible portfolios, as illustrated in Figure 5-4. If this portfolio does not exist in theory, or if there is no practical real-world measure of this portfolio, then the value of the CAPM is seriously compromised.

Another assumption of the theory is that investors deal in a world with only a single future period, which means there are no returns that continue on into the future. This assumption is obviously unrealistic because a central problem of financial economics is understanding how to value risky assets with returns occurring in many future periods. There is a version of the CAPM which takes care of this problem,[5] but this version of the theory has its own restrictive assumptions. In particular, it assumes that the investment opportunities themselves do not change in the future. That is, it assumes that there is no uncertainty about what future investments will be available. And this seems no more acceptable than the original assumptions of the CAPM itself.

The key difficulty which these last two assumptions only hint at pertains to problems with the CAPM which limit its testability. As we discussed in Chapter One the true test of any theory lies in its predictive power, that is, how well it can explain the real world. In the case of the CAPM, the question is whether it can explain the prices of assets better than any competing theory. We will examine some of the empirical evidence on the prices of assets using the CAPM in Chapter Eight. Here we only want to briefly consider whether the theory is really even testable. It may sound fantastic to say that the theory might not be testable, for an untestable theory is no theory at all. Some prominent scholars have argued, however, that for all practical purposes, the CAPM is not testable.[6] If this criticism is vindicated and no alternative is available, it would leave a gaping hole in financial economics, to say the least. This criticism has been a strong part of the impetus to develop a viable alternative.

Simply stated, the criticism is as follows. The crux of the problem is that we don't know what the market portfolio actually is. It is always possible to

---

[4] See John Lintner, "The Aggregation of Investor's Diverse Judgments and Preferences in Purely Competitive Security Markets," *Journal of Financial and Quantitative Analysis* (December 1969), pp. 347–400.
[5] See Robert Merton, "An Intertemporal Capital Asset Pricing Model," *Econometrica* (September 1973), pp. 867–888.
[6] See Richard Roll, "A Critique of the Asset Pricing Theory's Tests," *Journal of Financial Economics*, vol. 5 (March 1977), pp. 129–176, for the original indictment of the CAPM. Also see Richard Roll, "Performance Evaluation and Benchmark Errors," *Journal of Portfolio Management* (Summer 1980), pp. 5–12, for a less mathematical and formal discussion of the same topic.

pick some proxy for the true market portfolio with betas computed from that proxy which will satisfy Eq. (5-4). What is necessary for this to work out is that the proxy for the market portfolio must end up on the frontier of possible portfolios as illustrated in Figure 5-4, for ex post returns. That is, if we construct a frontier from actual observed returns and our proxy for the market portfolio ends up on that frontier, then Eq. (5-4) will be satisfied. If our proxy doesn't turn out to be on the frontier, then the equation will not be satisfied. In either case, it is a matter of luck. The only way we can escape this uncertainty is to know the true market portfolio, which we do not know. Moreover, if, as discussed above, people have different estimates of future returns, there is really no common market portfolio. This criticism of testability is the most pessimistic and critical appraisal of the CAPM, and it is a powerful one. The best defense of the CAPM is that while other theories seem to avoid some of the logical pitfalls of the CAPM, so far they do not have the simplicity of the CAPM and they do not appear to provide superior predictions. But, with the intense research going on in this area, this assessment may change radically in the near future.

SUMMARY

In this chapter we concluded the analysis of the pricing of risky assets which we began in the last chapter. In Chapter 4 we found that we could reduce risk through diversification, but we did not develop a measure of the risk of an individual asset when that asset is held in a portfolio and we did not develop an explicit statement of the way the market prices assets when they are held in portfolios. In this chapter we did both of these things.

We began by decomposing the risk of an asset and of a portfolio into two components, systematic and unsystematic risk. The systematic risk is that part of total risk which cannot be eliminated through diversification. Unsystematic risk can be so eliminated. In order to measure systematic risk, we relied on what is called the market portfolio. The market portfolio is a portfolio of all assets available in the market. While it is difficult to ever measure the true market portfolio, we can use indices of returns on large numbers of securities to approximate the true market portfolio. Once we have a measure of the rate of return on the market portfolio we can measure systematic risk. Systematic risk is measured by what we call beta (β). The beta of an asset measures the effect of a change in the rate of return of the market portfolio on the rate of return of an individual asset. We learned both what beta means and how we can compute it for securities which we observe in the world.

We were able to develop the concept of systematic risk and measure it with beta without ever introducing an explicit theory of how assets are priced in the market when they are held in diversified portfolios. Therefore, neither the concept nor measure of systematic risk depends upon a particular theory. However, we need an explicit theory to explain the link between our measure of systematic risk and the prices of assets in the market. The preeminent theory of this relationship is called the Capital Asset Pricing Model (CAPM).

The first thing we did in our development of the CAPM was to explicitly state and discuss the assumptions of this theory. Once we understood the assumptions, then we moved on to develop the pricing equation which follows from the theory. The pricing equation states in a mathematical manner the relationship between the price of a risky asset, its systematic risk, and the return on the market portfolio. It says that the expected return on the asset equals the return on the risk-free asset in the market plus the product of the asset's beta and what is called the market price of risk. The market price of risk is the premium the market demands to hold the market portfolio, and is equal to the difference between the expected rate of return on the market portfolio and the risk-free interest rate.

The advantage of the CAPM is the simple composition and form of this pricing equation. It says that the price of an asset is determined by only three things and the relationship among them is simple to write. However, there are potentially serious flaws with this theory of the pricing of risky assets. We briefly reviewed some of the more important flaws and appraised their significance. The most serious appears to lie in the logical difficulties involved in constructing a satisfactory method for testing the theory. This is particularly troublesome in that a theory which is inherently untestable is really no theory at all. But until a viable alternative appears, the CAPM remains the preeminent theory in this field. Moreover, the real benefit of the theory lies in the increased understanding of the market derived from understanding how the theory is developed. Even if this theory is supplanted by another, the insight it provides into the pricing of the systematic component of risk is still an important insight to acquire.

QUESTIONS TO IMPROVE UNDERSTANDING

1 The total risk of any asset can be decomposed into two parts. Explain what these two parts are. Can diversification reduce either of these parts of the risk of an individual asset? The same decomposition can be applied to a portfolio of assets. Can diversification reduce either of these parts of the risk of a portfolio? If so, then describe how this takes place.

2 How can we relate the rate of return on an individual asset to the rate of return on some index of the market? The slope coefficient in this relationship is referred to as beta. How does beta measure the systematic risk of the asset?

3 Suppose you observe the following rates of return on an asset traded in the market and an index of the performance of the entire market. Compute the beta for this asset.

	RATE OF RETURN (%)	
	INDIVIDUAL ASSET	MARKET ASSET
1974	15	07
1975	30	09
1976	05	03
1977	−10	−07
1978	08	15
1979	−22	−05
1980	10	10

4   List and describe each of the assumptions which go into the CAPM.
5   What is the market price of risk and how is it measured? How is it that the CAPM can depersonalize the tradeoff between risk and return with a single market price of risk?
6   How is beta used in the CAPM? Explain its role in the "pricing equation."
7   What is the security market line? Why is it said that "assets should price on the line"?
8   The CAPM has both serious strengths and weaknesses. What is its principal strength supposed to be? Do you agree? Why or why not?
9   Summarize the criticisms of the CAPM. What do you think of these criticisms?
10   Suppose you observed an asset that had a negative beta. What would this mean? How could you represent this with the security market line? Can you think of a real-world example of an asset that might have a negative beta?
11   Suppose you tried to find out whether real-world securities plotted on the security market line. Suppose in your investigation you discovered that the securities of small companies tended to plot above the line while those of large companies tended to plot below the line. Can you think of a rationale for this discovery?
12   Recompute the beta for IBM using the data in Table 5-2 but with only the data from 1969 to 1975. Is this beta significantly different from the one which takes advantage of the data from 1976 to 1978? What would you conclude if you found that betas tended to change significantly with time?

REFERENCES

Black, Fischer: "Capital Market Equilibrium with Restricted Borrowing," *Journal of Business* (July 1972), pp. 444–455.
Copeland, Thomas E., and J. Fred Weston: *Financial Theory and Corporate Policy*, Addison-Wesley Publishing Company, Inc., Reading, Mass., 1979.
Lintner, John: "The Aggregation of Investors' Diverse Judgments and Preferences in Purely Competitive Security Markets," *Journal of Financial and Quantitative Analysis* (December 1969), pp. 347–400.
Merton, Robert: "An Intertemporal Capital Asset Pricing Model," *Econometrica* (September 1973), pp. 867–888.
Roll, Richard: "Ambiguity When Performance is Measured by the Security Market Line," *Journal of Finance*, 33 (September 1978), pp. 1051–1069.

————: "A Critique of the Asset Pricing Theory's Tests," *Journal of Financial Economics,* 5 (March 1977), pp. 129–176.

————: "Performance, Evaluation and Benchmark Errors," *Journal of Portfolio Management* (Summer 1980), pp. 5–12.

Ross, Steven: "The Arbitrage Theory of Capital Asset Pricing," *Journal of Economic Theory,* 13 (December 1976), pp. 341–360.

Sharpe, William F.: *Portfolio Theory and Capital Markets,* McGraw-Hill Book Company, Inc., New York, 1970.

Wagner, W. H., and S. C. Lau: "The Effect of Diversification on Risk," *Financial Analysts Journal,* 26 (November–December 1971), pp. 7–13.

Chapter Six

VALUE AND THE COST
OF INFORMATION

This chapter focuses on the role of information in determining the market value of assets. In the previous two chapters the value of an asset was shown to be determined by the expected return and risk of that asset. Yet an explanation of where the estimates of expected return and risk come from was conspicuously absent. This chapter fills in that gap by exploring the concept of information about future returns on an asset and the cost of acquiring that information. After an introduction which explains the basic nature of information and its cost, the chapter explains how the *market* value of an asset is determined if individual investors have different estimates of the asset's value. This is followed by a discussion of the information-production industry. Then there is an analysis of why specialists emerge to produce information and the effect of economies in the production of information. Finally, the concept of an efficient use of information in a financial market is explained and contrasted with a situation where access to information is asymmetric. The concepts about information and financial markets developed in this chapter serve as a foundation for many of the topics developed later in the book, particularly the theory and operation of financial intermediaries and the regulation of financial markets.

THE NATURE OF INFORMATION COSTS

The previous chapters have been concerned with the way time and uncertainty influence the market value of financial assets. That is, the exposition was directed specifically at assets which generate an uncertain return over a number of periods in the future. The analysis in those chapters illustrated how each market participant can assign a value to an asset based on the expected returns of the asset, the risk of the asset, the attitude toward risk of the individual, and the risk-free rate of interest in the economy. The analysis of each of these items was carried out in an objective manner where, aside from the individual's attitude toward risk, there was no room for disagreement among individuals. There was, in fact, an explicit assumption in Chapter Five that all market participants are in complete agreement about the expected return and the risk of each asset. If these can be determined in an objective manner without room for disagreement, then any differences across individuals in the value placed on an asset must be a reflection of their different attitudes toward risk. Moreover, the only problem facing the market in aggregating individual's assessments of value into a unique market value would then be to somehow sort out these differences in attitude toward risk.

Yet it is widely believed that an important motivating factor behind many trades in any market for assets is not simply a difference in attitude toward risk, but disagreement between the buyer and the seller over the expected return or risk of an asset. This view suggests that a transaction takes place when the buyer and seller can agree on a price which is somewhere between the values that they each place on the asset. It might be possible to deal with this omission by simply supposing that different market participants assign different values to assets without tracing this to differences in probability distributions about future returns. But there is an important aspect of the operation of markets which becomes apparent when serious thought is given to the reason for diversity of opinion among investors. This aspect of the market is that it is costly to acquire information about the future returns on assets. If it were costless to acquire such information, then all investors would be willing to investigate the future returns on assets until they came to complete agreement on the probability distributions of those returns. There would simply be no cost to resolving differences among investors about the future returns on assets before a transaction took place in the market. However, since it is costly to produce estimates of future returns and, therefore, to resolve differences about those returns, transactions will be made among investors who have different estimates of an investment's expected return and risk.

A graphic but somewhat "tongue-in-cheek" example of the cost involved in resolving such differences was evidenced by the dispute between two Britons over the value of some real estate. In May 1979 John Naylor had an eight bedroom home for sale in Battle, England. His asking price was

$191,000. Kevin Reardon made him an offer of $153,000. They agreed to resolve the difference by fighting. Naylor was a former Army boxing champion. However, Reardon knocked him down 16 times in the first two rounds. Naylor offered to compromise at a price of $163,000. They agreed, apparently concluding that the marginal cost was equal to the marginal gain of further efforts to resolve their differences.

It is worth devoting some attention to exactly what is meant by the phrase, "information costs." In Chapters Four and Five the information that was important about an asset was information about the probability distribution on returns. This means information about the expected value and variance of an asset's return as well as its covariance with other assets in the market. In order to understand information costs, it is necessary to ask how information about future returns might be acquired.

There are basically two approaches to this problem. The first can be labeled the statistical approach. The basic idea is to use past returns on the asset to estimate the expected value and risk of future returns on the asset. This is the procedure we used in Chapter Five to estimate the systematic risk and expected return for IBM. The assumption which is implicit in this methodology is that the underlying probability distribution on returns does not change with time. If the probability distribution from which future returns are drawn is believed to be different from the probability distribution which generated the historical returns, then the historical data will be of very limited use. One view of information costs, then, is that they represent the costs of producing these statistical estimates. But if this is the way market participants estimate returns, there seems little room for disagreement. Given that the correct statistical procedures are well defined and the actual historical returns on an asset are not subjective estimates, all market participants should be able to agree on the estimated returns drawn from historical data.

The apparent shortcoming of this procedure is that probability distributions don't remain unchanged over time. For example, the market environment in which a firm operates changes as does its management and its cost of operation, and so forth. As a result, the second approach, and the one used by most market participants, in conjunction with the first approach, is to try to assess all the information available about an asset and make a subjective estimate of the expected return and risk of an investment. For example, this might involve, in the case of a firm's stock, assessing the market in which the firm operates and evaluating the strength of competitors or the skills of management. The cost of collecting and evaluating this information is what is referred to as information costs.

HETEROGENEOUS EXPECTATIONS AND MARKET VALUE

Before information costs themselves are analyzed, it is useful to examine the implications of the fact that individuals may have different assessments of the future returns on an asset, or what is called heterogeneous expectations. The question at issue is: How does the market aggregate individuals' assessments of the value of an asset, including their assessments of the risk and expected return and the compensation they demand for bearing risk, into a market price for the asset? In Chapter Five we explored how this aggregation takes place when all market participants have the same estimates of expected return and risk. In that chapter we developed an explicit equation for the prices of assets under this assumption. We will not go so far as to develop an alternative equation here. But we will seek to understand how value is determined when expectations differ.

To analyze the determination of market value, three experiments will be described. Each experiment corresponds to a hypothetical market for risky assets. The differences between the experiments are designed to illustrate the important determinants of market value when investors disagree about the value of an asset. These experiments are distinguished by two principal features. The first is the extent to which important characteristics of the market are assumed to be determined outside the experiment. Specifically, in the first two experiments it is assumed that the supply of risky assets is determined in this manner. A real-world example might be the sale of oil leases. If we take the supply of oil resources and, therefore of possible oil leases as determined by nature, then we can ask how the value of these oil leases is determined in a competitive market. In particular, if we know that individuals who might bid on these risky assets disagree about their value, how will their individual estimates be translated into a market value? The second principal feature is the degree to which the assets are divisible, or the relative number of investors and assets in the market. The results will generally be different if, for example, there is only one indivisible asset and many investors, than if there are many assets and many investors. Each of these three experiments has the following features in common:

1   There are 20 participants in the market who will bid on the asset or assets available. Each of these 20 participants may disagree on what he or she believes is the value of the asset or assets.
2   The payoff for each asset depends on a probabilistic event which has two possible outcomes, referred to as event A and event B. To ensure that there is room for disagreement among the participants, the outcome is assumed to be a horse race between two horses, A and B. Event A occurs if A wins and event B occurs if B wins.

Experiment 1

The unique characteristic of the first experiment is that some outsider is willing to sell to the market a single asset with the following payoffs: $200 in event A, and $100 in event B. The question is: How is the value of this risky asset determined? Each of the 20 individuals in the market must decide how much he or she would be willing to pay for this risky prospect. This depends, as discussed in Chapter Four, on the likelihood of events A and B and on the compensation each individual demands for bearing risk. Each of these 20 market participants will be willing to bid against the others until the price exceeds the value he or she places on the risky prospect. The price will, therefore, be bid up until it just exceeds the willingness to pay of all but one of the 20 market participants. The asset will, therefore, be purchased by the individual who places the highest value on it. If the variation in risk aversion among individuals is relatively slight, so that differences in value are determined by differences in the assessed likelihood of events A and B, then this means that the asset will go to the individual who is most optimistic about the occurrence of event A. This means that the market value is *not determined by the average* of the market participants' assessments of its worth. This is a logical outcome for the situation described in this market. There is only one asset available in this experiment, and it should therefore go to the individual who values its use or its possession the most highly. It is also important to note that there is assumed to be an outsider, with respect to this market, who is willing to sell the asset regardless of the price that is offered by the 20 individuals. In effect, experiment 1 ignores the incentive for anyone to supply the asset to the market, or it assumes that supply is exogenously determined.

Experiment 2

The difference between experiments 1 and 2 is that in experiment 2 the outsider offers *ten identical assets* for sale with the following payoffs: $20 in event A, and $10 in event B. The difference between this experiment and the previous one is the number and scale of the individual assets. If any one market participant purchased all ten of the assets in experiment 2, he or she would hold the same asset as the one available in experiment 1. This means that in experiment 2, shares of the gamble offered in experiment 1 may now be purchased by more than one market participant.

The question at issue here is whether the availability of shares in the asset which can be purchased by more than one person has any effect on the way the price of the asset is determined. Specifically, will the shares all be purchased by the most optimistic market participant? But, before this question is addressed, consider a slightly modified version of this experiment. Suppose that each participant in the market is restricted to the purchase of only one share. This means there are ten identical assets available, but only one per person. In this case, market value would be determined by the tenth most optimistic investor, because that person sets the value of the marginal, that is, the tenth asset. There will be nine other investors who will also be willing to pay at least the same price and, therefore, all the assets will be sold.[1]

---

[1] Edward Miller presents a detailed and interesting analysis of this case in "Risk, Uncertainty and Divergence of Opinion" *Journal of Finance*, vol. 32 (September 1977), pp. 1151–1168.

If this restriction of one share per person is dropped so that all investors can bid for the number of shares they want, then the market price will depend upon whether the value placed on assets by investors is influenced by the number of shares they hold. Suppose the price each investor is willing to pay is independent of the number of assets purchased. Then the outcome of experiment 2 is identical to the outcome of experiment 1. The most optimistic investor just outbids the second most optimistic investor for all ten shares.

However, there is a good reason why investors are likely to reduce the price they are willing to pay as the number of identical assets they purchase increases. The reason is based on the desire for diversification discussed in Chapter Four. As any investor enlarges his or her holding of a single asset, the contribution of this asset to the risk of the investor's portfolio increases. The investor's portfolio becomes less and less diversified so that the riskiness of the asset to this investor grows. Therefore, the value of the asset to the investor will not be independent of the amount of the asset purchased. This will be a minor consideration for assets which are a small portion of the wealth of the investor, but it will become more important as the asset comprises a larger portion of the individual's wealth.

This portfolio, or diversification effect, means that as the most optimistic investor increases his or her stake in the risky asset available in experiment 2, the price the investor will be willing to pay for the assets will drop. If it falls enough, then the next most optimistic investor will be willing to buy some of the assets. The market price of the asset will then fall until enough investors have been attracted to purchase all ten assets available in the market. For example, suppose there is a price at which the most optimistic investor is willing to buy six assets, the next most optimistic is willing to buy four, and none of the other investors is willing to take a position. These two investors will then set the market price of the asset.

Experiment 3

The distinguishing characteristic of the third experiment is that there is no longer a fixed supply of assets which is determined outside the experiment, regardless of the market price for the assets. In effect, there is no longer an outsider who supplies the same number of assets regardless of price. Instead participants in the market will be able to either buy or sell the assets described in experiment 2 (i.e., assets with possible payoffs of $20 and $10). This is often referred to as taking either a long or short position. If a person buys the asset, or holds positive amounts of it, he or she is said to be long in the asset. On the other hand, if he or she sells the asset, or holds negative amounts of it, he or she is said to be short in the asset. In this experiment the market participants must decide on their own how many of the assets will be traded and at what price. Therefore, supply is no longer exogenous.

In this experiment each participant no longer estimates only the number of assets he or she might purchase at each price; now an estimate must also be made of the number which would be sold at each price. For each investor, if the market price is below the estimated value of the assets, then assets will be demanded; if the price is above the estimated value, then assets will be supplied to the market. The requirement for equilibrium in this market is that there emerge a price where the quantity of assets demanded is equal to the quantity supplied. This condition can be represented by the standard type of supply and demand diagram illustrated in Figure 6-1. The demand curve intersects the vertical axis at a price just above that which the most optimistic investor would be willing to pay for one asset. The demand curve slopes down, reflecting the fact that as the price falls less optimistic people find that it becomes profitable to buy the asset. The slope of the curve is determined by the distribution of different opinions and the increased risk that these individuals bear as they add more assets to their portfolios. For example, the demand curve will be very steep to begin with if there are just a few optimistic people who buy at very high prices, and then will flatten out as the price falls far enough to bring in the people in the middle. Similarly, the supply curve intersects the vertical axis just below the price the most pessimistic investor would be willing to accept to supply one asset. The equilibrium is represented by the intersection of the two curves.

It should be recognized that no one in the market need be by nature either exclusively a supplier or a demander of assets. Everyone responds to the incentives for a profitable return. Therefore, at prices which are high enough, everyone is willing to supply assets, and at prices which are low enough, everyone is willing to demand them.

FIGURE 6-1
Demand and supply for risky assets in experiment 3. This figure illustrates that the price of risky assets is determined by the intersection of supply-and-demand curves when supply as well as demand is determined in the market. In this experiment the price represents the average value placed on the asset by all those in the market.

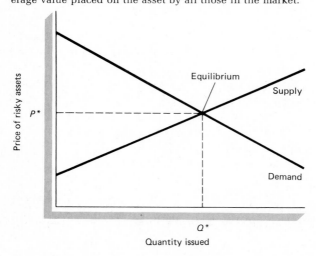

The market price which is determined in this experiment differs from those in the first two experiments in an important respect. The equilibrium price is one where the incentive to issue assets is perfectly balanced by the incentive to purchase them. This was not the case in the previous two experiments. With an arbitrary number of assets supplied, the price may be such that some investors would be willing to issue more assets at that price. On the other hand, the demand may be large enough that it exceeds what the market would be willing to supply at that price. In experiment 3, because the market must be induced to supply the assets, the price will settle at the consensus valuation of the assets of the investors in the market. Only at this price will the incentives to be either long or short in the asset become balanced.

The third experiment illustrates the important effect on market prices of the incentives to supply risky assets as well as to demand them. The important difference between the third experiment and the previous two is that value is determined by the average judgments of those in the market in the third experiment, whereas the degree of optimism is an important determinant of market value in the first two. It is often thought that experiments like the first two illustrate the effect on a market of restricting participants in a market from selling an asset short; that is, in effect, from increasing the supply of the asset. When such short-selling is restricted, the less optimistic have no way to reflect their disagreement with the market price. Experiment 3 illustrates that when short-selling is unrestricted, value reflects the consensus judgment of market participants.

These experiments show how the market combines or aggregates different individual estimates of an asset's value into a *market* value. When supply is determined outside the market, as it is, for example, in the available supply of oil, or when there are restrictions on short-selling, then the degree of optimism of participants in the market can influence the market value of assets. However, if the number of assets supplied is determined without restriction in the market, just as the quantity demanded is determined, then market value represents an average of participants' expectations. In this way the market acts as an aggregator of the diverse opinions of the investors who participate in the market. The fact that the market price reflects the average of these diverse judgments is a reassuring feature of the market. It means that, without outside restrictions on investors' actions, the price of an asset is not biased toward the judgments of either the more or less optimistic market participants.

THE INFORMATION-PRODUCTION INDUSTRY

An important feature of real-world markets which is left out of the experiments discussed above is the process through which market participants acquire information about the future returns on assets. These experiments introduce differences in estimates of value across market participants. But the experiments themselves give us no idea of where the information came from which led to these diverse judgments. Now we want to specifically examine the production of information.

An industry has developed to produce the information which investors use in assessing the value of alternative assets. Like many products in a developed economy, it would be possible for investors to produce almost all their own information and not purchase information from firms which specialize in the business of information production. Just as it is technically feasible for individuals in the United States and other developed countries to produce much of their own food, it is technically feasible for individuals to produce their own information about investment opportunities. But, as in the production of food, specialization is efficient. The economies and efficiencies in large-scale information production have led to the emergence of an industry which produces information and sells it to the consumer.

Types of Information Producers

The information-production industry in the United States is a diverse and complicated industry. At least four distinct types of information producers can be identified. They differ not so much by the nature of the production process they use as in the way they market the product which is produced. Each type of producer is discussed below.

INFORMATION PRODUCTION FOR DIRECT SALE   The most obvious type of information producer is the company which seeks information relevant to economic conditions and, therefore, investment decisions, and publishes that information for direct distribution to investors. Probably the best-known organization of this kind in the United States is Dow Jones, Inc., publisher of *The Wall Street Journal* and other business-oriented publications. Other examples of the same type of publication are *Value Line*, Standard & Poor's *Stock Reports*, and *Fortune*. Of course, much of the material found in more general publications, such as *The New York Times*, is directly relevant to investment decision making. In addition, there are newsletters, consulting services, and a large number of graduate schools of business administration which are primarily in the business of directly distributing information as well as the technical capability to assess information about investment decisions.

SALE OF A JUDGMENT ABOUT AN ASSET'S VALUE   Some information producers do not directly distribute their information, but use it to produce an estimate of the value of an asset. Then they sell that assessment of value. The most obvious example of this is the rating services provided by Moodys and Standard & Poor's. These organizations continually collect information about the riskiness of the debt obligations of corporate and municipal borrowers and distribute the conclusions they draw from this information in the form of ratings to investors. The borrowers who are being evaluated find it profitable to pay for the service. Other examples of this type of information production are real estate appraisers and film, music, and drama critics.

INFORMATION PRODUCTION BUNDLED WITH THE SALE OF AN ASSET   A number of firms produce information as a major part of their business, but only rarely sell it directly to any of their customers. An interesting example is the medical profession. Medical doctors are in the business of diagnosing illness and providing treatment. But they generally tie in the diagnosis with the treatment and do not sell the "products" separately. Only with an increased demand for second and third opinions is the diagnosis becoming known as a distinct product. The analogy with the securities brokerage industry is quite close. Securities brokers are in the business of producing information about securities to facilitate the sale of shares. However, information has not normally been sold as a distinct product. Instead, it is tied in with the service of executing a trade such that the broker's fee pays for both the transaction and the cost of information. However, as with medical services, this tie-in arrangement has been changing somewhat in recent years.

INFORMATION PRODUCTION AND INTERMEDIATION   The final type of information producer is the financial intermediary, such as the commercial bank, savings and loan association, savings bank, insurance company, or mutual fund. These institutions are in the business of investing funds for their customers. They produce information about the investments they may make and return a share of the profits from the investments they undertake to those whose funds they manage. The profits they receive on their investments may be viewed as a return on their production of information. We will explore this role for financial intermediaries in some detail in Chapter Eleven.

Problems with the Quality of Information Produced

Each of these four types of organizations is involved in collecting, processing, and, in some cases, evaluating information. They can be viewed as supplementing and/or supplanting the activity of information collection and evaluation by each investor. There is a problem which faces the information industry which is common to a number of other industries, but which may be somewhat more acute in the information industry. The problem is that there are great differences in the quality of information, and the purchaser of information is usually not in a position to effectively evaluate quality. The very nature of information as a product presumes that the purchaser of the product cannot assess quality at the time of purchase. Only with time, as the information is used and evaluated, can its quality be ascertained. Thus, there is a strong incentive for information producers to try to misrepresent the quality of information to their customers. Information producers can easily claim that they have very valuable information and try to extract a high price for it. The problem for the market is to devise a way to separate good information from bad, or price information so that price reflects quality.

The principal way that the market evaluates the quality of information is to evaluate the incentive of each producer to lie to the market. Given that it is difficult if not impossible to evaluate information directly at the time of its sale, the quality of the product is established by the market's perception of the honesty and competence of its seller. One way that the market can perceive that there is no incentive to cheat is if the information producer uses his or her own information. That is, if the information producer has a big enough stake in the outcome of the information that any incentive to cheat is offset, then the market will accept the information at its face value. A similar mechanism depends upon the economic value of a firm's reputation. If a firm has a reputation for honesty, then this will influence the value of information it sells. The market can be reasonably sure that a firm will not misrepresent information if the gain from doing so is less than the value of a lost reputation. This will often depend upon the value of future repeat sales to the firm. This suggests that the quality of information sold by a small "fly by night" operation or one with little reputation will probably be low. But it does not necessarily mean that large reputable firms that have established a track record of honesty will never lie. Some lying will take place if it is difficult to detect. Moreover, there may occasionally be a big lie as suggested by the maxim: "Be honest in all things small."[2]

ECONOMIES IN INFORMATION PRODUCTION AND THE ROLE OF SPECIALISTS[3]

It is useful to examine a little more closely the reasons why there are specialists in the production of information. The basic argument which needs to be understood is that specialization is efficient. As a result, those who specialize can produce information at a lower cost than those who do not. One example of the process of collecting or producing information is search activity. It is possible to think of search for a job or search for a house or search for an investment as the collection of information. In this context efficiency means that those who concentrate their efforts solely on search for a new job will incur lower costs of search than those who do not specialize.

Optimal Search

In order to explain the usefulness of specialists in producing information, we will concentrate on a particular example of search activity. The example concerns the sale of a house and the search involved is the search for a buyer. The problem in this example of search is presented in Figure 6-2. In Figure

---

[2] I believe that this maxim should be attributed to an anonymous but distinguished economist.
[3] The analysis presented here follows Armen Alchian's treatment of the subject very closely: "Information Costs, Pricing, and Resource Unemployment," *Western Economic Journal* (June 1969).

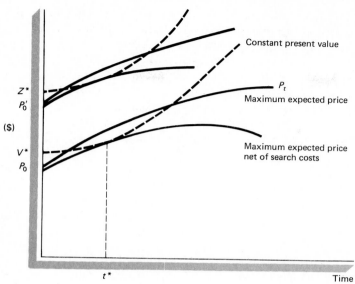

FIGURE 6-2
The value of assets and the cost of search. This figure shows two sets of curves. The lower set of curves shows the maximum expected price, maximum expected price net of search costs, and future values with the same present value for the owners of an asset who does not specialize in search. The higher set of three curves shows the same thing for a specialist who does not own the asset. The difference between Z^* and V^* represents the margin earned by the specialist.

6-2 time, measured say in days, is represented on the horizontal axis and dollars are represented on the vertical axis. Curve $P_0 P_t$ represents the maximum price which the seller expects he will be able to attract, with a constant rate of search. That is, the point P_t on the curve measures the highest offer the seller would expect to receive if he searched at a constant rate for t days. To understand the meaning of this curve suppose that a house is for sale and the seller searches for buyers at a constant rate, say 10 hours per week. With 1 week of search the maximum offer one might expect would be, say, $75,000. However, with additional days of search the chance increases that a higher offer will be received. The longer the seller searches for buyers the higher the offer he can expect to receive. However, it seems reasonable to expect that the maximum expected offer would go up by smaller amounts with greater search. Therefore, the curve $P_0 P_t$ is drawn so that it increases at a decreasing rate. This, of course, assumes that buyers don't conclude that the house must be a "lemon" if it is on the market for a long time and hence reduce their offers.

Because search is a costly activity, it is necessary to incorporate the cost of search into the analysis. The cost of search represents the opportunity cost of the time spent and resources used in the search activity. For example, suppose a person values his or her time at $15 per hour and expends an additional $10 per hour on expenses. The marginal cost per hour of search is then $25. If the search is conducted at a constant rate, or intensity, then this cost will be constant across time. Therefore, this constant cost of search per unit of time can be subtracted from the maximum expected price corresponding to the amount of time spent in search. The difference between the two can be plotted as a curve which is below $P_0 P_t$ and represents the maximum expected price, net of search costs. The two curves diverge by an increasing amount because the marginal increase in the maximum expected price declines with increased search, but there is a constant marginal cost of search.

The first question that the seller must ask is how long to search or what offer to accept at each point in time. The answer depends upon the time rate of discount or interest rate which he or she believes represents the opportunity cost. An additional curve can be drawn in the diagram which represents, for a given interest rate, the quantities of dollars in any time period t which have the same present value in time period 0. This curve, represented by the dashed line through V^* in Figure 6-2, will increase at an increasing rate as long as there is a positive interest rate, due to compounding. To see this consider an example of the future value of $10 invested at 10 percent. After 2 years the $10 is worth $12.10. After 5 years it is worth $16.11. And after 10 years it is worth $25.94. It is evident the value of the $10 is increasing at an increasing rate with time. Returning to Figure 6-2, for a given interest rate there will be an infinite number of present value lines which are parallel to one another and which intersect each point along the vertical axis. Each corresponds to a different present value and is referred to as a constant (iso) present value line.

The objective for the seller is to obtain the highest attainable present value for his or her house. Therefore, the optimal waiting time or the optimal offer to accept at each point in time is the point which attains the line of highest constant present value, given the net gain available from search. The expected waiting time will be t^* periods. At this point the curve representing maximum expected price, net of search, is tangent to the curve representing constant present value. If the seller searched longer than this he or she would be losing money because it would be more profitable to have accepted an earlier offer and invested the funds at the interest rate which represents the opportunity cost. If the seller accepted an offer earlier than optimal, he or she would be losing because he or she would expect to have gained more than the opportunity cost by waiting longer. This analysis also indicates that the value of the house which is for sale is equal to V^*, which is equal to the present value of the optimal offer.

The Role of the Specialist

The next question which must be answered is: Suppose an investor who specialized in real estate offered the seller more than V^*, today, for the house. Should the seller accept? Yes, he or she should, because V^* is the value of the house to him or her today based on the cost of search. One might ask, however, how an investor could profitably offer more than V^*. After all, presumably the investor is not buying the house to live in and, therefore, only values it based on its resale value. In order to profitably offer more than V^*, the investor must be able to do a better job of attracting offers than can the seller. This means he or she must be more efficient at processing information or searching. In fact, the investor is more efficient at this kind of information processing because he or she specializes in this particular activity. As a result, it is possible to represent the curve which the specialist sees representing the maximum expected price, net of search costs, as above that of the seller. It is shown in Figure 6-2 as the curve intersecting P'_0 and the specialist's maximum expected price, net of search costs, is shown immediately below it. The highest line of constant present value which the specialist can attain is the dashed line intersecting Z^*. Therefore, the specialist values the house at Z^* and can expect to earn a profit by buying it from the seller at V^*.

This analysis not only shows how specialized investors can profitably operate in a market but it illustrates an additional element in the determination of the prices of assets. Because there are costs of search and collection of information, assets may remain on the market for some time rather than sell immediately. Given the cost and intensity of search, there will be an optimal waiting time or an optimal offer to accept. Moreover, it is not optimal to wait until the expected increase in the maximum price offer is equal to the marginal cost of searching for a new offer. Instead, the optimal waiting time is determined when the marginal gain from additional search, net of the cost of search, is equal to the interest rate. These factors will be additional determinants of the observed prices of assets.

The fact that specialization in gathering information is efficient gives rise to all of the information producers discussed in the previous section. The basic reason these specialists exist is that they can compete with one another and earn a competitive return on producing information due to the economies which they enjoy over individual information production. Information producers can therefore be viewed as contributing to the efficiency with which the market is able to utilize information in determining the market value of assets. But this raises the question of what constitutes an efficient use of information. To answer this question it is necessary to deal with what has come to be called the efficient markets hypothesis.

MARKET PRICES AND "EFFICIENT" USE OF INFORMATION

An exceptionally important issue about the performance of financial markets is whether they make efficient use of information about the future returns on assets. The hypothesis that markets use information efficiently has come to be known as the efficient markets hypothesis. In its simplest form the hypothesis is almost intuitively obvious. It merely states that markets do not waste information. Put another way, there will never be an *obvious* good buy which the market *consistently* ignores. Because there is considerable misunderstanding about the efficient markets hypothesis, it is useful to focus attention on what the hypothesis really means. No evidence will be discussed here concerning the degree to which markets actually are efficient. That sort of evidence will be sprinkled through the remainder of the book.

The question of the efficiency of financial markets is a very popular topic among practical people as well as academicians interested in financial markets. Even a crude exposition of the hypothesis explains why. It is often said that the efficient markets hypothesis in essence says that you can't beat the market or that investment advisors can't tell you anything useful. It is evident why practitioners would not believe in such a hypothesis. It is less evident why many academicians continue to insist that markets are efficient.

Consider a little more carefully one of the arguments propounded by those who advocate the efficiency of markets. The argument is that security prices perform a "random walk." Alternatively stated, this says that if you were going to estimate the price next period of a share of stock of XYZ company, your best estimate would be today's price, and that the past behavior of the price of this stock would be of absolutely no help in predicting its future course. This past behavior will already have been incorporated in the stock's current price. This form of the efficient markets hypothesis can be stated a little more formally by saying that the expected value of next period's price, given the entire past history of the price of the stock, is equal to the current price. Therefore, there is no gain from studying past behavior. To understand what this version of the efficient markets hypothesis is saying, it is useful to examine Figure 6-3. This figure plots the performance of the price of our hypothetical XYZ company over a sample period. The random walk hypothesis says that the changes in this price through time are

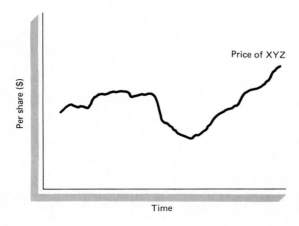

Price of XYZ

Per share ($)

Time

FIGURE 6-3
The price of XYZ Company. This figure shows the behavior through time of the price of a hypothetical company named XYZ. If the market is efficient, then there should be no discernible pattern in the change in this price.

totally random. As a result, suppose you try to forecast what the price will be at time t_2 when the current price at time period t_1 is P_1. The random walk hypothesis says that the best guess of the price at t_2 is the current price, P_1 in this example. There is nothing to be gained from studying the past behavior of the price, that is, the line in the figure to the left of t_1. The past behavior of the price will give you no clue as to its future behavior. Notice the fact that the price at time t_2 eventually turns out to equal P_2 and this is much higher than the forecast of P_1. The efficient markets hypothesis does not say that your forecast of P_1 will prove accurate with hindsight. What it does say is that at time t_1, with what you know then about the past behavior of the price of the security, you cannot come up with a better forecast than to say that the future price will equal the current price. The very fact that there is uncertainty means that this forecast will not be perfectly accurate. It should, however, be the best available forecast.

It is important to notice that information about the past behavior of the price of XYZ company is easily available to anyone as long as XYZ is a publicly traded company. Moreover, the statistical techniques needed to find any information in the past prices of XYZ are readily available to anyone who chooses to study the subject. Therefore, it is not very costly to incorporate information about the past behavior of prices into the current price. But it is not as easy to conclude that the market has incorporated other information, such as information about a secret investment project which XYZ is planning to undertake and which is known only to the board of directors of the company. The market might well not fully incorporate this kind of information into the price of XYZ company because it is very costly to obtain.

One of the reasons the efficient markets hypothesis is often misunderstood is that it is usually stated and applied with either the implicit or explicit assumption that information is not costly to acquire. The hypothesis usually makes use of the phrase, "the set of information available to the market at time t." The hypothesis then contends that the market efficiently uses all of the specified set of information. The basic strategy involved in testing such a hypothesis is to determine whether one could have expected to have made a profit on such information based on the market prices prevailing shortly after the information became available. It is logical, then, to relate the degree of market efficiency to the set of information which the market is able to use efficiently and to the time required to incorporate the information.

The degree of market efficiency is divided into three forms of the hypothesis according to the set of information which is used. These are:

1 *Weak-form Efficiency:* In this form of the efficient markets hypothesis the information set that the market is able to efficiently use is comprised of all of the past history of the *price* of a security. This is the same as the example of XYZ company discussed above.
2 *Semi-Strong-form Efficiency:* In this form of the efficient markets hypoth-

esis the information set comprises all publicly available information about a security (i.e., it is not solely restricted to price). This might include the history of dividend payout rates or bond ratings or a recent article about a company in *The Wall Street Journal.*
3 *Strong-form Efficiency:* In this form the hypothesis includes what is called insider information. This includes information which is at least initially known only to the managers of the company.

The weak-form efficient markets hypothesis is the one which has received the most attention both in the popular financial press and in academic journals. It is important to emphasize what this hypothesis does not say. It does not say that the best forecast of the next period's price of a security is this period's price. The problem with this statement is that it is unconditional; it makes no reference to a set of information. The weak-form efficient markets hypothesis says that, *based solely on the past behavior of the price of the security*, the current price is the best forecast of the future price. Additional information might well improve the forecast, but such information is not included in the set of information which is relevant to the weak-form efficient markets hypothesis.

The categories of weak, semi-strong, and strong-form market efficiency are useful for simplifying the problems created by the fact that information is costly to acquire and evaluate. The weak and semi-strong-form categories refer to information where the costs of acquisition are relatively low. This kind of information should readily be incorporated into market prices. A much stronger argument is that even information which is costly to acquire and may be known only to insiders will work its way into the market and be incorporated into prices very quickly. The implicit argument here is that the incentives to profitably use this information are so strong that it will be disclosed rapidly to the market and incorporated into prices. This argument relies on the incentives for corporate insiders to disclose information rather than the incentives for outsiders to discover or collect information. It seems likely that both kinds of forces are constantly at work to contribute to the efficiency of markets.

The real message which the efficient markets hypothesis seeks to communicate pertains to the state of competition in both the markets for information and the financial markets. That message is that one cannot *expect* to earn *monopolistic* or *excess* returns from collecting information and trading on it. The hypothesis contends that financial markets and the market for information are competitive. This does not mean that, ex post, some participants in the market will not make exceptionally large returns. This will be the case just as there will be some who will earn very low returns. What the hypothesis does mean is that one cannot expect to earn such returns, ex ante. Without barriers to competition, such excess returns will be eliminated in an efficient capital market.

THE PROBLEM OF ASYMMETRIC INFORMATION

The idea that markets are efficient means that prices of assets communicate all relevant information about the future returns on assets in the market. In the strong form this means that no one has any special information which is not accessible to everyone else. Another way of saying this is that there are no asymmetries in access to the information or that the information possessed by market participants is symmetric.

There is an alternative view, however, which maintains that there are important asymmetries in information in the marketplace. This asymmetric information argument is not really inconsistent with the available evidence on weak and semi-strong-form market efficiency. This evidence says that, on *average*, the prices of securities in the capital markets reflect publicly available information. The asymmetric information argument is really concerned with the following problem. Suppose there are two firms which have shares traded in the capital markets and the market accurately prices those shares *on average* using all information available to it. Yet the managers of one firm know that their firm is really above the average, while the managers of the other firm know theirs is really below the average. They know this because they have inside information which the market does not. The market is still right, on average, and can therefore be efficient in the weak and semi-strong form. But it is not efficient in the strong form because manager-insiders have special information. The problem that such asymmetric information raises is that managers who believe their firm is under- or overvalued will have incentives to take advantage of this situation or to try to correct it. This can lead to various observed kinds of behavior which are difficult to explain if markets are thought to be efficient in the strong form. We will encounter some of these later in this book. Moreover, in the extreme case, these asymmetries can lead to the breakdown of the market altogether.

It is interesting to consider a particular market as an example of the problems which can be created by asymmetric information. The market which will be examined is the market for used cars. The purpose of the discussion is to explain why the used car market is often thought of as a market for "lemons".[4] Suppose there are only two kinds of cars produced. One kind will be called plums because they perform beautifully, the other kind will be called lemons because they perform terribly. It will also be supposed that when the cars are new it is impossible to tell a plum from a lemon and that one can only learn the distinction by driving the car for a while. Therefore, everybody who owns a car for a while knows whether it is a plum or a lemon, but potential buyers don't know the true quality of any individual car. Also, suppose that lemons are thought to be worth $2,000,

---

[4] This analysis of the market for lemons is based on George A. Akerlof, "The Market for 'Lemons': Quality, Uncertainty and the Market Mechanism," *Quarterly Journal of Economics*, vol. 89 (August 1970), pp. 488–500.

while plums are worth $4,000, and the buyers know the number but not the identity of the lemons and plums in existence. Finally, suppose that any car owner will sell his or her car if there is a profit to be made and will hold on to it if the sale involves a loss. That is, there are no motives other than profit for selling or keeping used cars.

What will the market for used cars look like? Specifically, what will be the quality of cars which are sold in the used car market and what will be the going price for cars? If information were perfect, that is, if everyone knew whether each car was a lemon or a plum, then plums would sell for $4,000 and lemons for $2,000. But buyers don't know the quality of any car which someone has for sale. It is profitable for owners of lemons to claim they are plums and try to sell them for $4,000. But no buyer will be willing to pay $4,000 because of the probability of being sold a lemon. If half the cars in the market were lemons and half were plums, then buyers might try offering $3,000 for cars, expecting that there was a fifty-fifty chance of getting a lemon or a plum. But at $3,000, owners of plums would not sell and buyers would, therefore, realize that they would be sure to get a lemon. In fact, at any price above $2,000 buyers would be certain to lose because no plums would be offered for sale. As a result, the market for used cars will be a market for lemons and the prices of used cars will approach $2,000. This is a result of the asymmetry in information between buyers and sellers of used cars.

The problem of asymmetric information is at least potentially present in a number of markets. Essentially what is happening in this situation is that poor-quality assets are driving out high-quality assets until the market consists only of products of low quality. However, if there are relatively low-cost mechanisms for correcting the information asymmetry, the efficiency of the market can be improved. In the used car market this may take the form of inspections or tests by unbiased mechanics or good recordkeeping for maintenance and repairs.

The strong-form efficient market and the market with serious asymmetries in information may be viewed as extreme-polar characterizations of the way real markets operate. In general, there are strong incentives which tend to promote efficiency in any market. In later chapters attention will be given to the pressures and incentives that determine which characterization of a particular market is more accurate.

SUMMARY

This chapter has been about information and financial markets. The central idea dealt with in this chapter is that information about the future returns on assets is costly to acquire. We explored five separate aspects of the idea that information is costly.

HETEROGENEOUS EXPECTATIONS AND MARKET VALUE   In Chapters Four and Five we learned how the market prices assets if there is agreement among investors about the expected return and risk of the assets in the market. In this chapter we learned how differences of opinion influence the prices of assets. We learned that if the supply of an asset is limited or if the asset is unique, then the price of the asset will be determined by the most optimistic investor or investors in the market. An example of this type of risky asset would be an oil lease on a particular piece of property, because the supply of this asset is limited by nature. However, if the supply of the asset is determined in the market rather than being fixed by some outside force, then the price will reflect the average of the diverse opinions in the market. This outcome is a reassuring feature of the operation of a competitive market. It tells us that the marketplace does not have a bias in the way it combines different opinions into the market price of an asset.

THE INFORMATION-PRODUCTION INDUSTRY   Next we learned that there is a large diversified industry in the United States which produces information about assets. Moreover, we learned that this information is distributed in a number of different ways. Some information is produced for direct sale, as in the case of many business publications; sometimes it is tied in with an estimate of the impact of that information on particular firms, as in the case of rating agencies for bonds; sometimes it is tied in with the sale of an asset, as in the brokerage industry; and sometimes it is tied in with the management of funds. But regardless of the method of distributing information, it is important that the purchaser of information perceive it to be reliable. The market judges reliability by evaluating the incentive of each information producer to misrepresent the quality of its product.

ECONOMIES IN INFORMATION PRODUCTION   Next we looked more closely at why the market uses specialists in the production of information. We did this through an analysis of the cost and gain from search activity. Our example of search was the search for a buyer for a house. We learned how to analyze the optimal amount of search when search is costly. We also learned how a specialist in locating buyers for houses can generate a higher value for the house than can a nonspecialist who searches for buyers. Our analysis of search activity, as an example of information production, showed us how the specialist can operate profitably due to lower costs of search. But it also showed, incidentally, why it is often optimal to wait to sell an asset. This is the first time we have encountered this aspect of time and the value of assets thus far in this book.

EFFICIENT FINANCIAL MARKETS   Next we explored the meaning of the efficient markets hypothesis. The essence of the hypothesis is that the market makes efficient use of information. In its simplest form this means that one cannot expect to make a profit by trying to predict future stock prices by studying their past behavior. This is called the weak form of the hypothesis. The semi-strong form of the hypothesis contends that *all* publicly available information is efficiently incorporated into current prices. The strong form says that even insider information is incorporated into market prices. When we take the cost of information into account in this hypothesis, it says that we cannot expect to earn any excess return on collecting and using information to forecast future prices.

ASYMMETRIC INFORMATION Finally, we explored the implications of asymmetric information between buyers and sellers of any product or asset. We found that if the seller of an asset has superior information relative to a buyer, then the market could collapse. The reason is that the price will always be equal to the average value of all assets available for sale. As a result, the sellers of the more valuable asset will withdraw from the market in order to avoid losses. This will continue until only the lowest quality assets remain. The case of asymmetric information can be viewed as the opposite extreme of the case of a market which is efficient in the strong form.

QUESTIONS TO IMPROVE UNDERSTANDING

1 What does the phrase information costs mean? What costs are actually involved in collecting information? Can you give an example of a market besides financial markets where there is costly information?

2 What does heterogeneous expectations mean? In some markets prices are determined by the most optimistic of the market participants, and in others the price reflects the average of the diverse views in the market. What distinguishes between these two cases?

3 Some people sometimes argue that there aren't any downward-sloping demand curves in financial markets. Why do you think they argue this? What is one reason why there may well be downward-sloping demand curves? Can you explain what determines the demand curve?

4 At least four distinct types of information producers can be identified. Can you identify them?

5 Why is reputation important in the information-production industry? What has reputation got to do with the problem of so-called asymmetric information?

6 Why isn't information production a "cottage industry"? Can you explain how specialists in information can function profitably?

7 Distinguish between the weak, semi-strong, and strong forms of the efficient markets hypothesis.

8 What do you think of the following statement? If markets were really efficient, there would be no room for securities analysts.

9 Suppose you observe the price of a share of stock over a year-long period and you plot that price as in Figure 6-3. How could you use this to forecast the future price of this stock? Could you use it to forecast the price of a different share of stock? Could you use it to forecast the price of Toyota Coronas?

10 What does it mean for a market to fail or break down? Explain how this can happen if there is asymmetric information.

REFERENCES

Akerlof, George A.: "The Market for 'Lemons': Quality, Uncertainty and the Market Mechanism," *Quarterly Journal of Economics* (August 1970), pp. 488–500.

Alchian, Armen: "Information Costs, Pricing, and Resource Unemployment," *Western Economic Journal* (June 1969), pp. 109–127.

Darby, Michael R., and Edi Karni: "Free Competition and the Optimal Amount of Fraud," *Journal of Law and Economics* (April 1973), pp. 67–88.

Fama, Eugene: "Efficient Capital Markets: A Review of Theory and Empirical Work," *Journal of Finance* (May 1970), pp. 383–416.

———— and Arthur Laffer: "Information and Capital Markets," *Journal of Business* (July 1971), pp. 289–298.

Gonedes, Nicholas J.: "The Capital Market, The Market for Information, and External Accounting," *Journal of Finance* (May 1976), pp. 611–628.

Grossman, Sanford, and Joseph Stiglitz: "Information and Competitive Price Systems," *American Economic Review* (May 1976), pp. 246–252.

————, Richard E. Kihlstrom, and Leonard J. Mirman: "A Bayesian Approach to the Production of Information and Learning By Doing," *Review of Economic Studies,* (October 1977), pp. 533–547.

Klein, Benjamin: "The Competitive Supply of Money," *Journal of Money, Credit and Banking* (November 1974), pp. 423–451.

————, Robert Crawford, and Armen Alchian: "Vertical Integration, Appropriate Rents, and the Competitive Contracting Process," *Journal of Law and Economics* (October 1978), pp. 297–326.

Lintner, John: "The Aggregation of Investors' Diverse Judgments and Preferences in Purely Competitive Security Markets," *Journal of Financial and Quantitative Analysis*, vol. 4 (December 1969), pp. 347–400.

Miller, Edward M.: "Risk, Uncertainty and Divergence of Opinion," *Journal of Finance*, vol. 32 (September 1977), pp. 1151–1168.

Rabinovith, Ramon, and Joel Owen: "Nonhomogeneous Expectations and Information in the Capital Asset Market," *Journal of Finance* (May 1978), pp. 575–587.

Ross, Stephen A.: "The Determination of Financial Structure: The Incentive Signalling Approach," *Bell Journal of Economics* (Spring 1977), pp. 23–40.

THE DETERMINANTS OF
MARKET INTEREST RATES

Part Two leaves behind the question of how individual assets are valued and explores how aggregate market interest rates are determined. Throughout Part Two and the rest of this book, observed market interest rates will be referred to as nominal as opposed to real interest rates. The real interest rate is the rate of interest which is common to or underlies all observed nominal interest rates. It is the interest rate on single-period financial transactions when there is no risk, no taxation, and no inflation. In Part Two we will see that nominal interest rates can best be understood as the sum of the real rate plus premiums for each of the important factors omitted from the real rate. There are three chapters in this part of the book. The first one, Chapter Seven, explains what the real rate of interest is and how it is determined. The real interest rate is important but elusive because only rarely do we ever directly see the real interest rate. Yet the real interest rate is the underpinning of all the nominal rates in the economy, and as a result, it is important to understand the forces which determine this rate. Chapter Eight concentrates on four of the five important forces which account for the differences between nominal rates and the real rate: inflation, taxes, risk, and relative security supplies. The fifth factor, the maturity of a security and its impact on nominal interest rates is the subject of Chapter Nine. The effect of maturity on yield is referred to as the term structure of interest rates. Taken together, Parts One and Two provide a comprehensive picture of how individual prices and interest rates as well as aggregate market interest rates are determined in the U.S. economy.

Chapter Seven

THE DETERMINANTS OF
THE REAL INTEREST RATE

It is common in economic circles to hear or read a discussion of "*the* interest rate." To the uninitiated observer it would seem that everyone must understand which of the many interest rates in the world was being discussed because no one ever seems to find it necessary to identify the interest rate in question. But consider all the interest rates to which the discussion might refer. There are at least four distinct interest rates which have been discussed in earlier chapters of this book. First there is the discount rate which is used to evaluate the present value of cash flows for any investment project. Conversely, there is the internal rate of return for that investment project; that is, the discount rate which yields a net present value of zero for the project. There are also the risk-free as well as the risk adjusted interest rates which are used for determining the value of investments. These theoretical concepts of the interest rate are not always easy to relate to the interest rates which are actually observed in the marketplace.

In this chapter and the next two we will examine the factors which account for the interest rates or yields on the specific assets that are observed in the marketplace. Fortunately, the factors which interest rates have in common are generally at least as important as the factors which are particular to each financial market. Therefore, it is possible to begin the examination of interest rates which are observed in the marketplace with an abstract concept of *the* interest rate which captures the factors which are common to all interest rates, but does not correspond to any particular market rate. This chapter will be concerned with the determinants of *the* interest rate.[1] In the following two chapters attention will be directed toward the determinants of the differences between interest rates which are observed in the market.

Actually this chapter focuses on what is called the *real* interest rate. The adjective real refers to the fact that the interest rate is expressed net of inflation. At the outset it is simplest to think of the real rate as the rate which would exist if there were no inflation and financial market participants anticipated that there would be no inflation in the future. The real interest rate which is discussed here is also one which applies to a single period of time as opposed to more than one period. In addition, the real rate is free of risk and taxes. Therefore, the *real interest rate* pertains to a single-period, risk-free financial obligation where there is no inflation (or deflation).

FISHERIAN THEORY OF THE REAL RATE OF INTEREST

Our current understanding of the determinants of the real rate of interest dates back to the work of a famous economist by the name of Irving Fisher who in 1930 published a book titled *The Theory of Interest*. His principal contribution, if it is possible to succinctly summarize it, was to explicitly examine the tradeoff between goods produced, purchased, and consumed in distinct time periods. Fisher's view of the interest rate has had tremendous staying power. It has been refined, expanded, and reinterpreted. But it remains, as its name suggests, Fisherian interest rate theory.

Fisherian interest rate theory is just basic microeconomics or price theory. The basic ingredients of the analysis include the individual's preferences between goods consumed today and goods consumed tomorrow as well as the production technology which permits investment in capital goods which are used to produce consumer goods for tomorrow. The basic microeconomic problem at stake is to determine the individual's optimal amount of investment in future goods as well as that person's amount of borrowing or lending with other participants in the market. An equilibrium rate of interest is then determined where desired borrowing is equal to desired lending for all participants in the market. The purpose of the analysis is to discover and appreciate the factors that determine the real interest rate in any economy and the nature of the forces which tend to drive the market toward equilibrium.

---

[1] This chapter relies heavily on the exceptional work by Joseph W. Conard, *Introduction to the Theory of Interest*, University of California Press, Berkeley, 1959.

Time Preference

The first ingredient in the determination of the real interest rate is each individual's attitude toward consumption today as opposed to consumption tomorrow. The choice between consumption today and consumption tomorrow can be thought of as the choice between two distinct commodities. For example, there is a tradeoff between days spent skiing at Snowbird, Utah, this year and days spent there next year, just as there is a tradeoff between days spent skiing in Utah this year and days spent skiing in Wisconsin this year. Each is a distinct commodity in that the typical skier is not indifferent about the way they are substituted.

The individual's attitude toward tradeoffs between commodities, whether they are distinguished by time or other characteristics, are normally represented with indifference curves. These show the combinations of the commodities to which the individual would be indifferent. For example, a person might say that it didn't matter whether he or she had 5 days at Snowbird this year or 7 days at Snowbird next year; either option would be equally satisfying. However, if the person had to give up one of the days this year, the only way the loss would be acceptable would be if he or she could have 2 days next year. This tradeoff is illustrated with the curve labeled P_1 in Figure 7-1. This particular type of indifference curve, which is referred to as a time-preference curve, is drawn to reflect the assumption that as the individual is deprived of current consumption an ever larger amount of future consumption is required to make him or her indifferent to the exchange. The curve is therefore drawn convex to the origin.

FIGURE 7-1

Map of time-preference curves for an individual. Each curve shows the combinations of skiing this year and next to which an individual is indifferent.

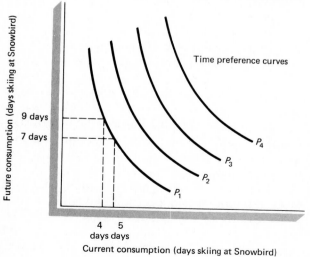

Current consumption (days skiing at Snowbird)

It is important to see that there will be an infinite number of curves for each individual. The reason for this is that each such curve represents the combinations of present and future consumption which leave the individual equally satisfied. But it is always possible to come up with combinations which create either more or less satisfaction. For example, 10 days at Snowbird this year and 10 next year is obviously better than 5 this year and 7 next year. There will be a time-preference curve which goes through the point in Figure 7-1 representing 10 days this year and 10 next which never intersects the curve drawn in the diagram which goes through the point representing 5 days this year and 7 days next. This argument can be repeated indefinitely to construct as many time-preference curves as seem pleasing.

Assuming that all individuals prefer more of almost any commodity to less (even skiing), the objective for any individual would be to attain the highest time-preference curve possible. This means that any skier would seek the most skiing possible, maintaining the tradeoff between present and future skiing. But the question arises as to what determines what is possible. What are the constraints on the individual which inhibit him or her from skiing the entire season?

Investment Opportunities

There are two types of constraints which limit any individual's opportunities to consume goods today and tomorrow. Both relate to the opportunities for the individual to transform current into future wealth and vice versa. The first is the opportunity for the individual to forgo current consumption and invest in productive activities which increase wealth. The other is the opportunity to borrow wealth from or lend wealth to other individuals. It is useful to first consider the individual's choice between current and future consumption if there are no opportunities for borrowing and lending and *only* opportunities for investment.

Thus far a few terms have been used a little loosely in order to introduce the constraints on each individual's choice. But more precise definitions of the terms saving, investment, borrowing, and lending are now in order. In common usage, saving refers to both saving as it will be defined here and lending. *Saving* is really forgone consumption. It is that portion of current income which is not consumed. Saving makes no reference to the use to which this forgone consumption is put. Income which is saved can either be invested or lent. *Investment* is the creation of new wealth or capital goods. The classical example of investment is the planting of a forest. Current income is forgone in order to plant the seeds and maintain the forest. As the trees grow the capital stock of lumber, beauty, and recreational use increases. If the forest is cut, disinvestment takes place and the capital stock is reduced by the consumption of the forest. By contrast, when the income which is saved is *lent*, a claim against future income is created, but no change in the capital stock takes place. Instead funds are exchanged today for a promise of repayment of funds tomorrow. Conversely, *borrowing* is simply the opposite side of this transaction. The individual who has acquired the funds today has issued a promise to pay tomorrow what was borrowed. With an understanding of how these words are used we can return to the problem of how to represent an individual's choice between present and future consumption.

With the aid of Figure 7-2 it is possible to examine the individual's choice between present and future consumption, where there are no opportunities to borrow or lend but where there are opportunities to invest. The horizontal axis in this figure measures the individual's current income and consumption and the vertical axis measures his or her income and consumption tomorrow. We will assume that the individual in our example starts with $30 of current income represented by the intersection of the *II'* curve with the horizontal axis. The constraint which this individual faces is defined by the set of investments which is available. The curved line labeled *II'* represents the possible combinations of current and future income the individual can reach by investing his or her initial income in real goods or services. For example, by moving to point *A* on the line *II'*, the individual gives up $2 of current income to invest in the future. This investment generates a future income of $18, and this is the coordinate of point *A* on the vertical axis.

The rate of return or yield which the individual receives on the investment can easily be calculated from curve *II'*. In the investment which moved the individual from the initial point on the horizontal axis to point *A*, the return was $18 − $2 = $16. This is a rate of return of $16/$2, or 800 percent.

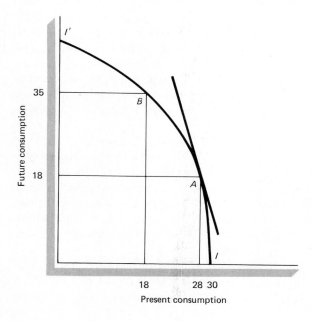

FIGURE 7-2
The investment-opportunity curve. The curve labeled *II'* represents the investment opportunities which are available to an individual or an economy. The slope of the tangent line at each point on the curve, such as the one at point *A*, represents the marginal rate of return on investment.

This is an exceptionally attractive return, but we can tell from the shape of curve II' that as the individual continues to invest more of current income, the rate of return will decline. For example, if the individual increased the investment from point A to point B, this would yield an additional $17 increase in future income. But this would require an additional investment of $10 of current income. This would yield a rate of return of ($17 − $10)/$10 or 70 percent, which is a much smaller rate of return than the initial 800 percent. If we consider an infinitely small investment, the rate of return is measured by the slope of a line drawn tangent to the curve II' at that point of investment. This is illustrated by the tangent line at point A. We can see from the shape of the II' curve that as we move farther up the curve, lines drawn tangent to the curve will have flatter and flatter slopes. This means that the more the individual invests, the lower will be the rate of return. Another way of saying this is that the individual receives diminishing marginal returns on investment.

The problem facing the individual represented in Figure 7-2 is to choose the optimal amount of investment or saving (note that saving must equal investment for each individual when there is no borrowing or lending) given the investment opportunities available. From Figure 7-2 we can conclude that it will be optimal for the individual to position himself or herself on the II' curve rather than inside it. The individual could always choose an investment opportunity which is represented by a point closer to the origin than the II' curve, but the returns from such an investment would be less than a comparable investment which is on the II' curve. And since the II' curve represents the best the individual can obtain, it is impossible to be outside it. However, it is not possible to tell from Figure 7-2 what point on the curve is best. To do this we have to incorporate time-preference curves, like those in Figure 7-1, into Figure 7-2. This is done in Figure 7-3. The optimal amount of investment in Figure 7-3 will be the point on the highest possible time-preference curve. This is represented by point A in Figure 7-3, where the II' curve is tangent to the time-preference curve P_1. This represents an optimal amount of investment and saving for the individual because it is impossible to reach a higher time preference curve, such as P_2, given the investment opportunities available.

The equilibrium which is illustrated in Figure 7-3 brings together two concepts of the real rate of interest. The first is represented by the slope of the investment opportunity curve II'. This slope represents the rate at which it is *possible* to transform current consumption opportunities into future consumption. The second is represented by the slope of the time-preference curve. This slope represents the rate of tradeoff between present and future consumption which makes the individual satisfied with the exchange. It is called the marginal rate of time preference.

The important characteristic of equilibrium in the market which is revealed by Figure 7-3 is that these two concepts of the interest rate must be the same. If this were not the case, the individual would search for a new

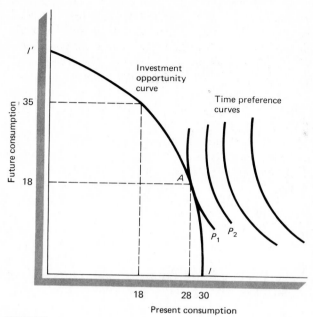

FIGURE 7-3

Optimal investment with no opportunities for borrowing and lending. This figure shows that an individual can reach the highest time-preference curve by investing until the investment-opportunity curve is tangent to a time-preference curve.

level of investment where the tradeoff between present and future consumption was more satisfactory. Therefore, the initial insight into the real interest rate is that it is the rate where each individual equates his or her marginal rate of return on investment with his or her marginal rate of time preference. In this sense, the real rate of interest represents an equilibrium.

Equilibrium with Borrowing and Lending

Now that we have seen how to describe an individual's optimal choice of consumption today and tomorrow when there are no opportunities to borrow and lend, we can expand the analysis to include borrowing and lending. To do this we have to add yet a little more to Figure 7-3. This is done in Figure 7-4. What we have to add is a straight line representing the opportunity to borrow and lend. The slope of this straight line represents the interest rate at which the individual in the figure can borrow or lend. The fact that the line is straight means that the interest rate does not change with increases or decreases in the amount of borrowing or lending. We could draw any number of these straight lines in Figure 7-4, showing opportunities to borrow and lend, just as we can fill the figure with the time-preference curves of an individual. But we will draw in only two of these lines, $B_1 L_1$ and

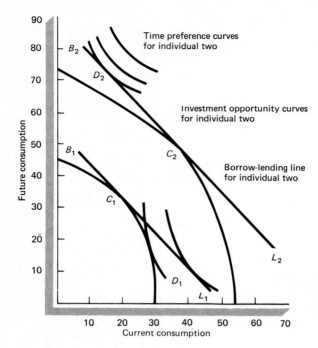

FIGURE 7-4
Equilibrium for two individuals who can borrow and lend. Individual 1 borrows and individual 2 lends.

B_2L_2. Both of these have the same slope of -1.1. This means they are consistent with an interest rate of 10 percent. Line B_1L_1 shows the borrowing and lending opportunities available to the individual whose choice we examined in Figure 7-3. Line B_2L_2 shows the borrowing and lending opportunities for another individual who is introduced in Figure 7-4. The choices of two individuals are shown in this figure so that we can see how to represent the choices of someone who chooses to borrow and someone who chooses to lend. Table 7-1 provides a legend for Figure 7-4. Panel A shows the coordinates of each of the points in Figure 7-4.

To begin with, we will concentrate on individual 1 whom we examined in the previous three figures. His or her borrowing and lending curve is B_1L_1. When borrowing and lending opportunities were not available, as depicted in Figure 7-3, it was optimal for individual 1 to invest until the investment-opportunity curve was tangent with a time-preference curve at point A. But with opportunities to borrow and lend this is no longer optimal. It will now be optimal to invest until the investment-opportunity curve is tangent to the line representing borrowing and lending opportunities, as indicated by point C_1 on line B_1L_1. Then individual 1 can borrow until he or she reaches point D_1, which is the point of tangency with his or her time-preference curve. To see that this is optimal, notice that the individual can move to any position on line B_1L_1 by either borrowing or lending. A movement up and to

TABLE 7-1
Legend for Figures 7-4 and 7-5***

Panel A	
$C_1 = 18,35$	$C_2 = 38,48$
$D_1 = 41,10$	$D_2 = 15,73$
Panel B	
$C_1' = 26,24$	$C_2' = 44,39$
$D_1' = 33,12$	$D_2' = 18,89$

* Panel A shows the coordinates of points shown in Figures 7-4 and 7-5. Panel B shows the coordinates of new points added in Figure 7-5. Current income is listed first and future income second. For example, C_1 is 18 current income and 35 future income.

the left sacrifices current income for future income and is therefore a decision to lend, while a movement down and to the right sacrifices future income for current income and is therefore a decision to borrow. By either borrowing or lending and moving along this line, the individual is able to move to a position which is tangent to a higher time-preference curve (at point D_1) than the time-preference curve which is tangent to the investment-opportunity curve at point A. In this sense, the existence of opportunities to borrow and lend makes this individual better off.

Figure 7-4 also illustrates the investment and borrowing and lending decisions of a second individual. This second individual is assumed to start with a larger initial amount of current income, $54. But this merely serves to separate the investment and borrowing and lending constraints of the two individuals in the figure so that they do not overlap. It is not an important distinction between the two. The real distinction is that the second individual chooses to lend rather than borrow. This results because his or her time-preference curve is tangent to the borrowing line *above* its tangency with the investment-opportunity curve at C_2. This individual finds it optimal to invest up to C_2 and then lend at the prevailing interest rate of 10 percent. As a result, he or she will shift toward future rather than current consumption, whereas individual 1 uses borrowing to support current rather than future consumption.

Both of these individuals have an individual equilibrium in the following sense. They have chosen a level of investment and borrowing or lending which allows them to achieve their highest time-preference curve possible. In this equilibrium, they equate the marginal rate of time preference, the marginal return on investment, and the interest rate on borrowing and lending. This follows because the straight line representing borrowing and lending opportunities is tangent to both the II' curve and the time preference curve. As a result, all three have the same slope. This means that the real interest rate is equal to all three of these alternative concepts of the rate of interest.

Market Equilibrium

We just characterized the equilibrium for a single individual. But this equilibrium will also apply to the market as a whole if total borrowing is equal to total lending in the market. In fact, for equilibrium in the whole market, the interest rate on borrowing and lending must adjust until desired lending is equal to desired borrowing. To see how this works we can use our two individuals in Figure 7-4 to represent a market of borrowers and lenders. For equilibrium to result, the desired borrowing of individual 1 must equal the desired lending of individual 2. We can see that at the 10 percent interest rate used in Figure 7-4 this condition is met. When individual 1 borrows he or she moves from point C_1 with \$18 of current income to point D_1 with \$41 of current income. This means total borrowing of \$23. Individual 2 moves from point C_2 with \$38 of current income to point D_2 with \$15 of current income. This means lending of \$23. As a result, with the interest rate at 10 percent, desired lending is equal to desired borrowing.

Thus far, the discussion of borrowing and lending opportunities for individuals in the market started with a real interest rate which was an equilibrium rate. That is, at the interest rate of 10 percent, represented by the BL lines, the amount that individual 1 wanted to borrow was the same amount that individual 2 wanted to lend. But the question arises as to how the market brings about this equilibrium. Is the market capable of adjusting toward an equilibrium if it begins in disequilibrium?

To consider this question suppose that the interest rate is initially at a higher rate represented by the $B'L'$ lines in Figure 7-5. These lines represent a higher rate because they have a steeper slope. The introduction of the new borrowing and lending lines is the only difference between Figures 7-4 and 7-5. Panel B of Table 7-1 shows the coordinates of the points added in Figure 7-5. At this higher interest rate both individuals will choose to invest a lower amount such that the marginal rate of return on investment is higher than before. Individual 1 will choose to invest to point C'_1 rather than point C_1, and individual 2 will invest to point C'_2 rather than point C_2. In addition, individual 1 will only choose to borrow \$7 at this higher interest rate as represented by the tangency between $B'_1L'_1$ and the time preference curve at point D'_1. But there will be a disequilibrium between desired borrowing and desired lending because individual 2 will choose to lend \$26 as represented by the tangency at point D'_2. To see this from the legend in Table 7-1, note that point C'_1 includes consumption of \$26, while D'_1 includes current consumption of \$33. Yet point C'_2 includes current consumption of \$44 while point D'_2 includes current consumption of \$18. In order to induce individual 1 to seek to borrow more and induce individual 2 to seek to lend less the

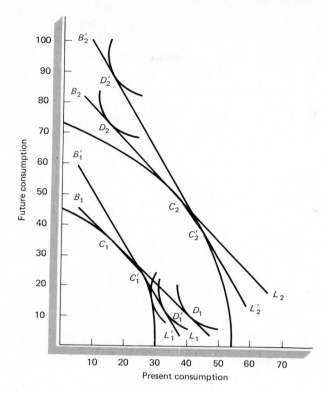

FIGURE 7-5
Illustrations of how the market reaches an equilibrium real interest rate.

interest rate will have to fall. It will fall until the real interest rate reaches 10 percent, as represented by lines BL rather than $B'L'$. At this rate desired lending is equal to desired borrowing and the market is in equilibrium. The market has an incentive to make this adjustment because, at the high disequilibrium real interest rate there is an excess supply of lending. To attract additional borrowing it is necessary to reduce the real interest rate until the incentive to borrow and to lend are equal.

In equilibrium the real interest rate captures three important factors. It is, first and foremost, the rate at which borrowing and lending are in equilibrium. But, it is also equal to the marginal rate of return on productive investment for all participants in the market. Finally, it is equal to the marginal rate of time preference for market participants; the rate at which they desire to substitute between present and future consumption. The real interest rate, therefore, reflects an equilibrium between all of these important forces in the economy which determine the economic tradeoffs across time. The real interest rate is the fundamental component of all the interest rates which are observed in the marketplace.

Finally, with the introduction of borrowing and lending opportunities we have introduced a change in the way each individual conducts investment decisions. Without opportunities to borrow and lend, the criterion for optimal investment was to invest until the marginal rate of return on investment was equal to an individual's personal rate of trading future for present consumption. Now this is no longer true. With a market for borrowing and lending, investment is undertaken until the rate of return is equal to the market interest rate. And because the market interest rate is equal for all, the rate of return on investment is equalized across the economy. In addition, the investment decision is separated from the choice of how much to consume today versus tomorrow for each individual. In this way the investment decision is depersonalized.

THE REAL RATE FROM ANOTHER PERSPECTIVE

The Fisherian theory of the real interest rate gives us a clear foundation for understanding the determinants of interest rates in the real world. It tells us that the real rate must equilibrate desired borrowing and lending and it must equal the rate of return on productive investments and the marginal rate of time preference for everyone. It is difficult to understand the world around us without understanding these concepts. On the other hand, the imagined market of the Fisherian theory is not much like the markets we actually see in the real world. One of the most glaring discrepancies between the Fisherian model and real world markets is the fact that everyone in the world does not come together to borrow and lend all at once. Instead, people are borrowing and lending in distinct financial markets all the time. This means that during any one period of time there is a large stock of outstanding financial contracts as a result of past borrowing and lending and there is new borrowing and lending which takes place during the current period. Moreover, there are often distinct markets for existing financial contracts and new financial contracts. These are called secondary and primary markets, respectively. In this section of the chapter we will use our understanding of Fisherian theory to describe how the real interest rate is actually determined in primary and secondary financial markets.

Equilibrium in a Single Market for Borrowing and Lending

Before we explicitly deal with both primary and secondary markets it is useful to translate the Fisherian theory into a simple model of demand and supply for borrowing and lending. To do this we will assume that, as in the Fisherian model, everyone comes together to borrow and lend at once. As a result there is a single market for all borrowing and lending which clears at one time. In such a market there is no outstanding stock of past borrowing and lending. At the same time that people borrow and lend they also decide how intensely to use the existing stock of real productive capital goods.

We can use a diagram to illustrate how this simple market for borrowing and lending works. Figure 7-6 shows a downward-sloping demand curve and an upward-sloping supply curve. The vertical axis in the figure measures the interest rate, while the horizontal axis measures the total volume of borrowing and lending. The downward-sloping curve shows the desired amount of borrowing by everyone in the economy at different levels of the real interest rate. We can think of this curve as the demand for funds. We know from our earlier analysis of Fisherian theory that this curve will have a negative slope because in our analysis of market equilibrium in Figure 7-5 we discovered that as the interest rate rises desired borrowing falls. The upward-sloping curve in Figure 7-6 shows the desired amount of lending in the market as a function of the interest rate. We can think of this as a supply curve for funds. We also know from our examination of Fisherian theory that this will have a positive slope.

We can use Figure 7-6 to describe the equilibrium real interest rate. The real rate is the interest rate at which desired borrowing is equal to desired lending. This is illustrated in Figure 7-6 at the point of intersection between the two curves. Of course, we also know from Fisherian theory that the equilibrium rate must also be the rate of return on productive investment opportunities or on the economy's total stock of capital. This is not explicitly shown in this figure. As a result, this figure is only a partial description of the general equilibrium in the market. Nevertheless, it is useful to translate the Fisherian concept of equilibrium into the more familiar framework of a supply and demand diagram. From this diagram we can see that anything which causes the demand for funds to shift up to the right will put upward

FIGURE 7-6
The equilibrium real interest rate and the supply and demand for funds.

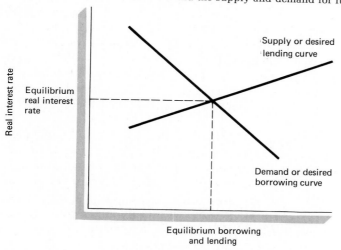

Real interest rate

Supply or desired
lending curve

Equilibrium
real interest
rate

Demand or desired
borrowing curve

Equilibrium borrowing
and lending

Total borrowing and lending

pressure on the real interest rate. Conversely, any factor which causes the supply curve for funds to shift back to the left will put downward pressure on the real rate.

We already know that an important ingredient which is left out of this simple framework is the fact that all borrowing and lending in the economy does not take place at one instant. Therefore, we need to enrich the analysis by introducing primary and secondary markets.

Equilibrium in Primary and Secondary Markets

When we introduce primary and secondary markets into our theory of the real rate of interest we do not have to make any fundamental changes in the meaning or interpretation of the real rate. But we do have to recognize that the real interest rate must now be the equilibrium rate in both primary and secondary markets. To see what this means we need to analyze the equilibrium in both types of markets, just as we analyzed the equilibrium in Figure 7-6 where everyone borrowed and lent at the same time. First we will look at the secondary market and then we will examine the primary market.

The secondary market comprises the market for outstanding financial assets. For example, the New York Stock Exchange is a secondary market for securities issued by major United States companies. The shares traded on the Exchange are shares which have previously been issued and are traded from one owner to another. In this sense they are used rather than new assets. Hence, when these assets are traded they do not represent any new borrowing and lending. Rather, there is just a redistribution of existing borrowing and lending. We can describe the equilibrium in this secondary market for assets with curves representing the total of all outstanding desired borrowing and desired lending, just as we did when we imagined a single instantaneous market. These curves now represent the total desired borrowing and lending at a point in time. In effect, they are the cumulative desired new borrowing and lending of all past periods in which financial contracts were written. This is represented in Figure 7-7. This figure shows the total desired borrowing and lending at a point in time labeled t. The real interest rate is the interest rate at which desired borrowing equals desired lending in this secondary market.

The real interest rate also has to be the equilibrium rate in the primary market. The primary market is the market for *new* borrowing and lending. It is the market where new securities are issued to obtain new funds. In many financial markets in the United States the primary and secondary markets, or the mechanisms through which new as opposed to old securities are traded, are quite distinct. However, the securities offered for sale on the primary and secondary markets are identical. And a company which sells new securities to the market to raise new funds cannot expect its new securities to command a yield which is different from the yield on outstanding identical securities. This means that the prices and yields set in secondary and pri-

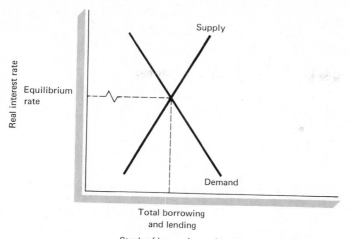

FIGURE 7-7

Equilibrium in the secondary market. This figure shows that the real interest rate must be the equilibrium rate in the secondary market where the existing stock of assets is traded.

mary markets are tied together. In terms of our analysis of the real rate of interest, this means that the real rate of interest has to be the same equilibrium rate in both the primary and secondary markets.

The relationship between the primary and secondary markets is illustrated in Figure 7-8. Panel A of this figure shows the demand and supply curves for funds at two distinct points in time, $t-1$ and t. Panel B shows the demand and supply for funds in the primary market. The demand and supply in the secondary market is the total of demand and supply at a point in time, while in the primary market it is the change in that demand and supply or desired new borrowing and lending between the two points of time that we see. This is what is illustrated in Figure 7-8. The demand and supply in the primary market can be derived from the changes in the secondary market at two different points in time. Panel A of the figure shows that both total demand and supply in the secondary market have shifted to the right between period $t-1$ and period t. The demand curve shifts from D to D' and the supply curve from S to S'. Panel B shows the new demand and supply for funds which develops between periods $t-1$ and period t.

In order to derive the demand-and-supply curves in the primary market, shown in panel B, from the changes in the demand-and-supply curves in the secondary market, we need to draw a vertical line in panel A representing the stock of assets in the market at time $t-1$. This vertical line passes through the intersection of the D and S curves. The demand curve in the primary market is determined by the horizontal distance between this vertical line and the curve D' representing demand in the secondary market at time t. Specifically, the origin in panel B corresponds to the vertical line in panel A, and the distances between the origin and point C on curve d and the vertical

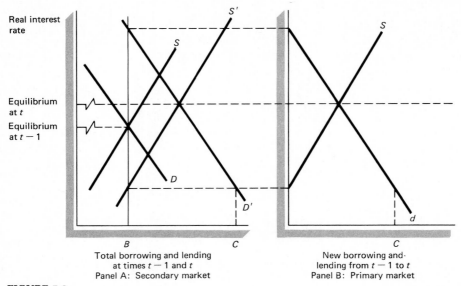

FIGURE 7-8

This figure shows how the demand and supply in the primary market is derived from the changes in demand and supply in the secondary market. The demand in panel B is equal to the quantity demanded on D'_1 less $\bar{B}$ and the supply is equal to S' less $\bar{B}$. $\bar{B}$ represents the total amount of borrowing and lending at time $t - 1$.

line and point $\bar{C}$ on curve D' (or $\bar{C}-\bar{B}$) are the same. The demand curve in the primary market, d, therefore measures the new demand flowing into the market at each level of the real interest rate. The same procedure is used to construct the supply curve s in the primary market.

The important feature of equilibrium illustrated by Figure 7-8 is that the real interest rate is the rate which equilibrates the primary market between $t-1$ and t and the secondary market at time t. You should notice that the shifts in supply-and-demand curves have been drawn so that the real interest rate changes between period $t-1$ and t. But regardless of the magnitude of the shifts in the curves and therefore of the changes in the rate, the equilibrium real rate must be the same in both markets. Therefore, when examining flows of funds in the primary market it is important to recognize that these are changes in the total stock of borrowing and lending. And the real interest rate determined in the primary market must be the same as the real interest rate determined in the secondary market.[2]

---

[2] It is important to recognize what Figure 7-8 and the accompanying discussion does not explain. It does not explain the path of the real interest rate through time nor the path of the flow of funds through time. It is as if we were using a still camera to record a continuous record of those movements. For example, we cannot tell whether the equilibrium interest rate shown in Figure 7-8 follows a straight line between the equilibrium levels at t-1 and t or follows a highly volatile path. What we do know is that new securities cannot sell at prices which differ widely from a much larger stock of identical outstanding securities as they flow into the market. But it is difficult, without considerably more analytical detail, to translate this statement into a precise statement about the *path* of the interest rate through time.

Finally, it is important to emphasize once again that, as we learned from Fisherian theory, the equilibrium real interest rate is not only the rate which equilibrates borrowing and lending; it is also the rate of return on productive investment or the rate of return on the economy's capital stock. As a result, when we examine the interest rate in the primary financial markets, in equilibrium that rate must be the same as the interest rate in the secondary market for financial assets *and* the same as the return on the economy's capital stock. This is important because it is the principal link between the financial markets in the economy and the market for real goods and services. We will explore the relationships between these two sides of the economy in some detail in Part Five of this book.

ANALYZING THE FLOW OF FUNDS

We have just learned that the real rate of interest is the equilibrium rate in both the primary and secondary markets for financial assets. We discovered that in the secondary market we were concerned with the outstanding stock of all borrowing and lending, while in the primary market we were concerned with the flow of new borrowing and lending. We will refer to this flow in the primary market as the flow of funds. Though we know the real rate is a function of what happens in both primary and secondary markets, it is often useful and interesting to focus attention on only the flow of funds in the markets. By examining the flow of funds within the economy we can tell where there are major changes in patterns of borrowing and lending. As a result we can acquire an indication of where there may be pressure on particular market interest rates. In order to make this kind of analysis possible the Federal Reserve System measures the flow of funds or new borrowing and lending between various sectors in the United States economy. These data are called the Flow of Funds Accounts.

We will analyze the flow of funds or the loanable funds market in the remainder of this chapter. To simplify our analysis we will begin by dividing the economy into four sectors. Within the Federal Reserve's Flow of Funds Accounts there are actually a much larger number of sectors. But the four sectors we will start with are the major categories of borrowers and lenders in the economy. The four sectors are labeled households, nonfinancial businesses, financial institutions, and government (including federal, state, and local).

Financial Statements for Economic Sectors

Each entity in each sector has a balance sheet and an income statement. The financial statements for all of the entities in each sector can be aggregated to form an income statement and balance sheet for the entire sector. An example of the fundamental items on such a balance sheet for the household sector is presented in Table 7-2. In this hypothetical example for the quarter

TABLE 7-2

Income Statement for Household Sector for the Quarter Ending December 31, 1978	
Current Income	$100
Current Expenditures	$ 70
Saving	$ 30

Balance Sheet for Household Sector December 31, 1978	
Assets	
Financial Assets	
Money	$ 20
Other Financial Claims	$200
Real Assets	$100
Total Assets:	$320
Liabilities	$140
Net Worth	$180
Total Liabilities and Net Worth	$320

period ending December 31, 1978, the household sector has a total current income of $100 and current expenditures or consumption of $70, which implies the total saving by this sector is $30. The hypothetical balance sheet indicates that on December 31, 1978, households had total assets of $320. The assets are broken down into two broad categories, financial and real assets. Financial assets refer to claims against future income, while real assets refer to productive capital goods. Financial assets are further divided into two categories: money and other financial claims. Liabilities or borrowing totals $140 and net worth equals $180.

A few comments are in order at this juncture as to why money is singled out as a specific type of financial claim to include on this very basic balance sheet. Money plays a key role in the U.S. economy if for no other reason than because the total quantity of it is (or could be) controlled by the government. Controversies about the institutions which distribute it—commercial banks, and the government agency which regulates it, the Federal Reserve, occupy a central position in the latter half of this book. But at this point and for the purposes of the present discussion there is nothing particularly unique about money. Money is just another form of lending or another form of holding wealth. It is introduced as a distinct type of asset so that later treatments of its significance can be more easily integrated with the present analysis of interest rates and the flow of funds.[3]

---

[3] Those readers already familiar with loanable funds analysis will note that I have avoided using the word "hoarding" to refer to the accumulation of money balances. This is because I believe the word is confusing and misleading, even for the fairly careful reader. Money balances, which are claims on financial intermediaries, are merely one form of lending. They are, however, subject to unique pressures from the government. In my judgment, the gain from dealing with hoarding at this point does not seem to be worth the cost. However, some of the problems relating to hoarding are treated in later chapters.

Sources and Uses of Funds Statements for Economic Sectors

An important distinction between the material contained in the income statement for a sector and the information contained in the balance sheet is that the income statement covers a period of time, while the balance sheet represents the sector's financial position at a point in time. The income statement reports *flows*, while the balance sheet reports *stocks*. In order to analyze the flow of funds we must convert stocks into flows. To do so it is necessary to construct a sources and uses of funds statement for each sector of the economy corresponding to a period of time. The sources and uses of funds statement for a sector of an economy is just an aggregate of sources and uses of funds statements for individuals or firms. It merely shows the changes in each item which appear on the balance sheets between two points in time, and classifies each change as to whether it is a source or use of funds. An example of a simple hypothetical sources and uses statement for the household sector is presented in Table 7-3 for the quarter ending December 31, 1978. In this statement changes in all the assets are treated as uses of funds while liabilities and net worth are treated as sources. The balance sheet identity requires that the sum of all uses equals the sum of all sources for each sector.

Each individual sector's sources and uses statement may be put together to form a flow of funds statement for the economy as a whole. An example of a hypothetical flow of funds statement for the four sectors defined above is presented in Table 7-4. This flow of funds statement illustrates that, within each sector, sources must balance uses. It follows that sources must balance uses for all the sectors combined.

The basic contribution of the flow of funds statement is that it allows us to analyze the pattern of borrowing, lending, saving, and investing for each sector and to make comparisons between sectors. In effect, it makes it possible to trace the flow of funds through the economy. In the example presented in Table 7-4 households save (90) more than they invest (64) and the excess

TABLE 7-3

Sources and Uses of Funds Statement for Household Sector for the Quarter Ending December 31, 1978

Uses		
	Money	−1
	Other Financial Claims (lending)	38
	Real Assets (investment)	64
	Total Assets	101
Sources		
	Liabilities (borrowing)	11
	Net Worth (saving)	90
	Total Liabilities and Net Worth	101

TABLE 7-4

Hypothetical Flow of Funds for Four Sectors, Quarter Ending December 31, 1978

	HOUSEHOLD SECTOR		BUSINESS SECTOR		FINANCIAL INSTI- TUTIONS		GOVERN- MENT SECTOR		ALL SECTORS	
	U	S	U	S	U	S	U	S	U	S
△Net worth (saving)		90		62		2		−5		149
△Real assets (investment)	64		85		0		0		149	
△Money	−1		3			4	2		4	4
△Financial assets (lending)	38		14		53		10		115	
△Financial liabilities (borrowing)		11		40		47		17		115
	101	101	102	102	53	53	12	12	268	268

saving is lent to other sectors. Households also acquire some financial liabilities, but lending still exceeds borrowing for this sector. Business firms, on the other hand, invest (85) more than they save (62). They acquire the necessary funds by issuing more liabilities than they acquire in financial assets. The financial institution sector saves very little and makes a negligible real investment. It largely exchanges financial assets for financial liabilities, that is, it is an intermediary. This sector is also the supplier of money (it includes the Federal Reserve System) and is, therefore, the source of money in the system. In this example governments are dissavers in that they run a deficit (−5). The deficit is financed by issuing more financial claims than are purchased.

The flow of funds table also illustrates one other important aspect of the economy. Actual investment must equal actual saving for the economy as a whole. This is definitely not true for any particular sector, as the household and business sectors make evident. However, total sources and uses must be equal for each sector and, therefore, for the entire economy. In addition, all financial claims are offsetting for the economy as a whole. Every dollar lent is offset by a dollar borrowed, so that total borrowing, which is equal to the change in liabilities, must equal total lending, which is equal to the total change in money plus other financial claims. As a result, the residuals, investment, and saving must be equal. This can be expressed in a simple algebraic form. For the whole economy:

$$\text{Investment} + \text{lending} = \text{saving} + \text{borrowing}$$

But because

$$Borrowing = lending$$

it follows that

$$Saving = investment$$

This relationship between saving and investment and borrowing and lending is not something totally new. We can draw the same conclusion from the Fisherian theory of the real interest rate. In the Fisherian theory the real rate is the interest rate which results in an equilibrium between desired borrowing and lending. At the same time, because investment plus lending must equal saving plus borrowing for the entire economy, the Fisherian theory implies that aggregate saving must equal aggregate investment. As a result, we have another way to think about the equilibrium real interest rate. The equilibrium real interest rate is the rate at which desired saving is equal to desired investment. We will utilize this approach again in Part Five of this book.

Finally, we can use flow of funds data to analyze either net or gross flows of funds between sectors. For example, the household sector illustrated in Table 7-4 is really a net lender of $26, that is, an increase in financial assets other than money of $38 plus increased money balances of −$1, less borrowing of $11. This net lending (or borrowing) is equal to the excess of savings over investment for any sector, by definition. Therefore, the analysis of *net* loanable funds is equivalent to the analysis of saving and investment. But the loanable funds actually traded in the market are gross not net loanable funds. In fact, if analysis of net loanable funds is carried out, it virtually eliminates the financial institution sector as an important part of the market because their net position is very small but their gross position is very large. In addition, the analysis of net loanable funds pretends that individuals and companies do not have motives for simultaneously borrowing and lending or, even if they do, that this is unimportant. But corporations as well as individuals do find it optimal to both borrow and lend at the same time. We all hold financial assets for their return and in case we need quick access to funds. At the same time, we generally have financial liabilities outstanding. This provides for a redistribution of risk throughout the market. As we will see in later chapters, financial intermediaries specialize in this kind of activity.

Flow of Funds for the United States in 1977

Flow of funds data are estimated on a quarterly basis for the United States economy by the staff of the Board of Governors of the Federal Reserve. A flow of funds table, similar to the simplified one presented in Table 7-4, but which shows the actual flows for the year 1977, is presented in Table 7-5. The major difference between this table of actual flows and the hypothetical example presented in Table 7-4 is the amount of detail. Table 7-5 contains both a finer division of sectors of the economy and a much more detailed breakdown of the categories of funds flows. However, the general patterns evident in the simpler table can be detected in the actual data of Table 7-5.

The first two columns of Table 7-5 pertain to the household sector. The first lines show that gross household saving in 1977 was approximately $300 billion. This saving is divided between capital consumption or depreciation allowances of $162.2 billion and net saving of $136.8 billion. The fourth line shows gross investment which does not directly correspond to any of the labels used in the earlier tables. Gross investment includes what was labeled investment in the preceding tables plus net lending. Investment as defined above is equivalent to line 5, private capital expenditures, and net lending is equal to the difference between total lending, line 12, and total borrowing, line 13. The table indicates that approximately 69 percent of investment or private capital expenditures by households was for consumer durables and that most of the remainder was for residential construction. Line 11 shows that the household sector was a net lender of funds in the amount of $68.6 billion. By comparison, the private domestic nonfinancial business sector was a net borrower of a slightly smaller amount, $61.3 billion. Approximately 51 percent of household lending was in the form of time and savings accounts with the larger portion at non-bank savings institutions. Pension funds also receive a large share. On the other hand, households withdrew funds in the amount of $5.1 billion from direct investment in corporate equities. Only about 17 percent of household lending went directly into various credit market instruments. The largest portion of this was in direct investment in residential mortgages, while obligations of state and local governments, municipal bonds, were second.

Compared to the household sector, the net saving of domestic nonfinancial businesses was relatively modest, $20.8 billion. In addition, the largest portion of business investment was in plant and equipment, $178.3 billion. The business sector loaned only about 46 percent of what it borrowed and thereby absorbed most of the surplus lending of the household sector. Most of this corporate borrowing took the form of corporate bonds, bank debt, and mortgages. A very small amount of equity, $2.7 billion, was issued.

Turning to the United States government sector, line 11 shows that the federal government ran a deficit of $54.8 billion. To finance this deficit the government sold $57.6 billion in new U.S. Treasury securities (line 28). This means that the federal government had a negative net saving of $54.8 billion. A substantial portion of this deficit was financed by foreign sources. The rest of the world sector purchased $31.5 billion in U.S. Treasury securities. In addition, the monetary authority, or the Federal Reserve, purchased another

$5.8 billion. This implies that only approximately 32 percent of the total issue of new Treasury securities had to be absorbed by domestic sectors other than the Federal Reserve.

The flow of funds tables are useful for analyzing the general pattern of investment, saving, and financing for individual sectors in the economy. But they are also useful for tracing the flows among sectors. These flows determine and are determined by the interest rates which are observed in various markets, all of which are based on the real rate examined in this chapter. An understanding of the flow of funds provides a foundation for the analysis of the yields that will be developed in the following chapters.

SUMMARY

In this chapter we analyzed the most important underlying determinant of the multitude of interest rates we observe in the world. This factor, which all market interest rates have in common, is called the real rate of interest. The real interest rate refers to the rate of interest on a single-period risk-free loan when there is no inflation or deflation and no taxes. This chapter has been devoted to explaining what determines the real interest rate.

The basic theory of the real rate of interest is referred to as Fisherian interest rate theory, after Irving Fisher, the economist who developed the analysis of the real interest rate. It shows that in equilibrium the real interest rate must equal each of three distinct concepts. The concepts are the marginal rate of return on real investment projects or the rate of return on real capital, the marginal rate at which individuals choose to exchange present for future consumption or the marginal rate of time preference, and the interest rate on borrowing and lending.

We divided the development of Fisherian theory into two parts. First, we examined what the equilibrium would be if there were no opportunities for borrowing and lending so that each person could choose only how much to invest in real productive investments. We found that each person would set the marginal rate of return on investment equal to their marginal rate of time preference. But there was nothing that would make these the same across individuals. Then we introduced the prospect that individuals could borrow and lend as well as undertake real investments. We discovered that with this additional opportunity, market participants could generally move to a position which made them better off. Those who preferred current to future consumption could borrow and vice versa. With borrowing and lending opportunities a new equilibrium real interest rate emerged. The new requirement for equilibrium in the market was that the rate of interest on borrowing and lending equal the marginal rate of return on investment and the marginal rate of time preference for all individuals. Moreover, by studying an example we found that if the market started with an interest rate that

TABLE 7.5

	HH U	HH S	BUS U	BUS S	S&L U	S&L S	TOTAL U	TOTAL S	ROW U	ROW S	USGOV U	USGOV S	
1 GROSS SAVING		298.9		177.4		16.4	492.8			20.9		-54.8	1
2 CAPITAL CONSUMPTION		162.2		156.6			318.8						2
3 NET SAVING (1-2)		136.8		20.8		16.4	174.0			20.9		-54.8	3
4 GROSS INVESTMENT (5+11)	329.1		150.8		8.5		488.3		21.9		-57.3		4
5 PVT. CAPITAL EXPENDITURES	260.4		212.0				472.5				-2.5		5
6 CONSUMER DURABLES	178.4						178.4						6
7 RESIDENTIAL CONSTRUCTION	76.3		15.7				92.0						7
8 PLANT AND EQUIPMENT	5.8		178.3				184.1						8
9 INVENTORY CHANGE			15.6				15.6						9
10 MINERAL RIGHTS			2.5				2.5				-2.5		10
11 NET FINANCIAL INVESTMENT (12-13)	68.6			-61.3	8.5		15.9		21.9			-54.8	11
12 FINANCIAL USES	213.5		52.9		35.4		301.8		48.4		10.1		12
13 FINANCIAL SOURCES		144.9		114.2		26.9		285.9		26.4		64.9	13
14 GOLD & OFF. FGN. EXCHANGE									-.2		.3		14
15 TREASURY CURRENCY										*		.3	15
16 DEMAND DEPOSITS & CURRENCY	20.3		1.3		.9		22.5		1.9		-.5		16
17 PRIVATE DOMESTIC	20.3		1.3		.9		22.5		1.9				17
18 FOREIGN													18
19 U.S. GOVERNMENT											-.5		19
20 TIME AND SAVINGS ACCOUNTS	108.3		4.8		7.0		120.1		.7		.1		20
21 AT COMMERCIAL BANKS	39.2		4.8		7.0		51.0		.7		.1		21
22 AT SAVINGS INSTITUTIONS	69.1						69.1						22
23 LIFE INSURANCE RESERVES	8.1						8.1						23
24 PENSION FUND RESERVES	55.5						55.5						24
25 INTERBANK CLAIMS											.2	6.4	25
26 CORPORATE EQUITIES	-5.1			2.7			-5.1	2.7	2.7	.4			26
27 CREDIT MKT. INSTRUMENTS	35.8		-1.5	103.3	26.4	25.9	60.6	268.7	39.5	11.9	11.8	56.8	27
28 U.S. TREASURY SECURITIES	1.5		-6.0		21.1		16.7		31.5			57.6	28
29 FEDERAL AGENCY SECURITIES	3.9		-.4	3.5	4.4		8.0				5.3	-.8	29
30 STATE & LOCAL GOVT. SECUR.	8.8		*		.2	25.7	9.1	29.2					30
31 CORPORATE & FOREIGN BONDS	1.1			21.0			1.1	21.0	3.7	5.0	-.2	-.1	31
32 MORTGAGES	11.9	94.1	3.7	36.9		.6	12.5	131.0					32
33 CONSUMER CREDIT		35.0						35.0					33
34 BANK LOANS N.E.C.		8.2	1.1	22.5			9.5	30.6	4.4	1.6			34
35 PVT. S.-T. PAPER	8.4	2.3		16.5				19.0		2.4			35
36 OTHER LOANS		3.1						2.9		3.0			36
37 SECURITY CREDIT	1.0					.2	1.0	3.1		-			37
38 TRADE CREDIT	1.3		30.9	24.8		1.0	30.9	27.1	1.7	.4	-.8	2.1	38
39 TAXES PAYABLE				-1.3			1.1	-1.3				1.6	39
40 EQUITY IN NONCORP. BUS.	-17.0		17.3	-17.0			-17.0						40
41 MISCELLANEOUS	6.6	.9		1.8		1.1	23.9	2.7	2.1	13.7	.7	-.9	41
42 SECTOR DISCREPANCIES (1-4)	-30.1		26.7			7.9	4.5			-1.1	2.5		42

Sectors: PRIVATE — HOUSEHOLDS (U, S), BUSINESS (U, S); NONFINANCIAL — STATE AND LOCAL GOVERNMENTS (U, S); TOTAL (U, S); REST OF THE WORLD (U, S); U.S. GOVERNMENT (U, S)

TABLE 7.5 (Continued)

#	Account	TOTAL U	TOTAL S	SPONS. AG. & MTG. POOLS U	S	MONETARY AUTHORITY U	S	COMMERCIAL BANKING U	S	PVT. NONBANK FINANCE U	S	ALL SECTORS U	S	DISCR. U	NATL. SVG. & INV.
1	GROSS SAVING	12.6										471.5			450.6
2	CAPITAL CONSUMPTION	5.3			.7							324.1			324.1
3	NET SAVING (1-2)	7.2										147.3			126.5
4	GROSS INVESTMENT (5+11)	20.9	6.2	.4			.2	9.2	3.2	11.1	1.8	473.9			
5	PVT. CAPITAL EXPENDITURES							4.4	2.6			476.2		-2.5	454.2
6	CONSUMER DURABLES								.6			178.4		-4.7	476.2
7	RESIDENTIAL CONSTRUCTION	-.1						4.4			-.1	91.9			178.4
8	PLANT AND EQUIPMENT	6.3							4.4	1.9		190.4			91.9
9	INVENTORY CHANGE											15.6			190.4
10	MINERAL RIGHTS														15.6
11	NET FINANCIAL INVESTMENT (12-13)	14.7	.4				.2	4.8	4.8	9.3		-2.3		2.3	-21.9
12	FINANCIAL USES	327.2										687.5			
13	FINANCIAL SOURCES	312.5	27.9	27.6		8.6	8.3	105.0	100.2	176.4	185.7	689.7		2.3	26.4
14	GOLD & OFF. FGN. EXCHANGE	*										.6		-.3	48.4
15	TREASURY CURRENCY	.6				.6	*					.3			
16	DEMAND DEPOSITS & CURRENCY	1.6	28.6	.1			4.9	.5	23.7	25.5	1.0	28.6		3.1	
17	PRIVATE DOMESTIC	1.6	25.8	.1			8.3	.5	17.5	24.1	1.0	25.8		1.6	
18	FOREIGN		1.9				*		1.9	1.9		1.9			
19	U.S. GOVERNMENT		1.0				-.3		4.3	-.5	1.0	1.0		1.5	
20	TIME AND SAVINGS ACCOUNTS	3.5	124.5					54.6	54.6	69.9	3.5	124.5			
21	AT COMMERCIAL BANKS	2.7	54.6					54.6	54.6	54.6	2.7	54.6			
22	AT SAVINGS INSTITUTIONS	.8	69.9						.8	69.9	.8	69.9			
23	LIFE INSURANCE RESERVES		7.9							7.9		8.1			
24	PENSION FUND RESERVES		49.1							49.1		55.5			
25	INTERBANK CLAIMS	5.4	5.4			1.4	3.5	4.0	1.9	5.5	5.4	5.4			
26	CORPORATE EQUITIES	6.2	.6						.6	*	.8	3.8			
27	CREDIT MKT. INSTRUMENTS	283.7	58.2	26.9	26.3	7.1		85.8	163.8	26.5		395.6			
28	U.S. TREASURY SECURITIES	9.5		-3.4		5.8		-.9	8.0	8.0		57.6			
29	FEDERAL AGENCY SECURITIES	13.3		-.4	27.4	1.4		-.8	11.6	11.6		26.7			
30	STATE & LOCAL GOVT. SECUR.	20.0						9.2	10.9	10.9		29.2			
31	CORPORATE & FOREIGN BONDS	31.3						-.1	31.4	29.2		36.1			
32	MORTGAGES	121.7		24.0				27.4	70.3	36.1	9.6	134.0			
33	CONSUMER CREDIT	31.4						17.0	14.3		3.1	35.0			
34	BANK LOANS N.E.C.	32.2	*					32.2				32.2			
35	PVT. S.-T. PAPER	*								9.5	5.3	19.8			
36	OTHER LOANS	5.9	14.4	.4					4.9	12.0	4.3	25.1			
37	SECURITY CREDIT	18.4	3.1	6.4	-1.2			.6		2.8	1.3	4.4			
38	TRADE CREDIT	3.4	1.3									29.6		-3.4	
39	TAXES PAYABLE	1.1	.7						1.1	1.1	.7	-.6		-.1	
40	EQUITY IN NONCORP. BUS			.9	1.3					33.0	-.5	-17.0		3.0	
41	MISCELLANEOUS	21.8	36.1			-.6	-.6	14.1	14.0	48.5	20.9	51.5			
42	SECTOR DISCREPANCIES (1-4)	-8.4	.4	.4				-6.0	-2.7	-2.7		-2.5		-2.5	-3.7

was too high or low for equilibrium, market forces would drive the rate toward equilibrium. This concept of equilibrium underlies all the different interest rates we observe in the marketplace.

Next we examined the real rate from an alternative perspective. We briefly examined the aggregate supply and demand for funds in the market in the context of the traditional supply–demand diagram. We used the Fisherian theory to develop supply-and-demand curves which determined the real interest rate. Moreover, we found that in the real world there are two basic types of markets which simultaneously determine the real interest rate. These are referred to as primary and secondary markets. The secondary market represents the market for the outstanding stock of borrowing and lending at a point in time. The primary market is the market for new borrowing and lending flowing into the market during any period of time. Because new assets must trade at the same rate of return as old assets, the real interest rate must be an equilibrium in both markets. Therefore, though in practice we often concentrate on the flow of funds in the economy or the primary market, we must remember that this is a part of a larger secondary market.

Finally, with this understanding of the link between primary and secondary markets we examined the flow of funds in the United States economy. We constructed hypothetical financial statements for sectors of the economy and from these developed a statement of the sources and uses of funds in the economy as a whole. Within this framework, we explored the differences between borrowing, lending, saving, and investment in the aggregate economy, and we examined the basic equilibrium condition that for the economy as a whole, saving must equal investing. After using this hypothetical construction to understand what the flow of funds measures, we examined the actual flow of funds in the United States economy during 1977.

QUESTIONS TO IMPROVE UNDERSTANDING

1 What is the real rate of interest?
2 In equilibrium the real interest rate is equal to three distinct concepts. Explain what these are.
3 What is a time-preference curve? What does it show? How does it differ from the indifference curve used when we dealt with risk and expected return in Chapters Four and Five?
4 Investments are often said to have diminishing marginal returns. How can we represent diminishing marginal returns in a diagram which also includes time-preference curves? Construct an example to illustrate diminishing marginal returns.
5 Suppose you had two individuals with distinct investment-opportunity curves and distinct time-preference curves and with no opportunities to borrow and lend. Could there be a distinct equilibrium real interest rate for each of them?

Why would this be an equilibrium for each individual but not a market equilibrium?

6 Using the example presented in Figure 7-5 and Table 7-1, explain what would happen to desired borrowing and lending if the interest rate were 5 percent. Why is 5 percent a disequilibrium in this example?

7 What is a primary as opposed to a secondary market? Why does the primary market refer to the flow of funds while the secondary market refers to the stock of funds? What does this mean? What is wrong with concentrating on only one of these two markets in order to analyze the determinants of the real interest rate?

8 Explain the differences between lending, investing, and saving for an individual and for an economy.

9 In this chapter it was explained that in equilibrium saving must equal investment. Why is this true for the economy as a whole but not for an individual sector of the economy? Can you identify these categories in the U.S. flow of funds for 1977 shown in Table 7-5?

10 What is the difference between net and gross flows of funds. Why does the financial institution sector of the economy have very large gross flows of funds but very small net flows of funds?

REFERENCES

Conard, Joseph W.: *Introduction to the Theory of Interest*, University of California Press, Berkeley, 1959.

Fisher, Irving: *The Theory of Interest*, The Macmillan Company, New York, 1930.

Hirshleifer, Jack: *Investment, Interest and Capital*, Prentice-Hall, Inc., Englewood Cliffs, N.J., 1970.

Van Horne, James C.: *Financial Market Rates and Flows*, Prentice-Hall, Inc., Englewood Cliffs, N.J., 1978.

Chapter Eight

FACTORS AFFECTING
NOMINAL INTEREST RATES

In the last chapter we learned about the real interest rate. Unfortunately, it is very rare that we actually observe the real interest rate. The real rate is a bit like the nucleus of an atom. It is very difficult to actually see it, but it is the foundation of everything we do observe. Now that we understand what goes into this foundation we need to fill in the gaps between the foundation and the interest rates we actually observe in the world. We will refer to these observed rates as nominal rates, to distinguish them from the underlying real interest rate. In this chapter and the next we will examine five factors which account for the difference between the real rate and observed nominal rates. They are:

Inflation
Risk
Taxes
Relative security supplies
Maturity

We will deal with the first four of these factors in this chapter. The final one, maturity, is sufficiently detailed and important that it requires an independent treatment. Therefore, the next chapter is devoted to it.

MEASURING AND COMPARING NOMINAL YIELDS

In this chapter we will seek to explain the basic determinants of observed nominal interest rates. To see more specifically what is meant by explaining observed rates, it is helpful to examine a diagram which plots the levels of various yields over a specific historical period. Figures 8-1 and 8-2 show the level of a collection of yields from 1970 to 1978. Figure 8-1 plots yields on debt securities, including bonds issued by private corporations, the U.S. government, and state and local governments (municipal bonds). Figure 8-2 plots yields on a selection of equity securities for the same period. The figure shows that municipal bonds generally had the lowest yield of all the debt securities indicated. The next highest yields were on 20-year Treasury bonds and 90-day Treasury bills, at different times during the period. Finally, the

FIGURE 8-1

Yields on selected debt securities from 1970–1978 (yield shown is yield to maturity).

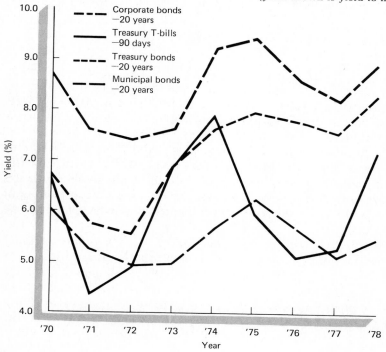

FIGURE 8-2

Rates of return on three equity securities.

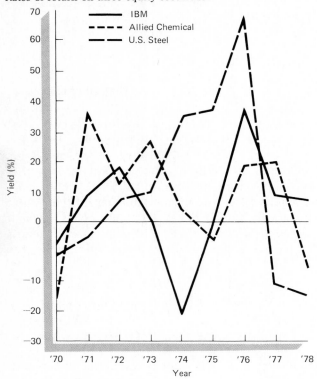

yields on corporate bonds were consistently higher than the yields on Treasury bonds. By contrast, the selection of equities shown had widely different
and sometimes volatile yields.

The yields shown in the two figures reflect two different concepts or
ways of measuring yield. It is important that we carefully distinguish between the two from the outset. The yields on the debt securities in Figure 8-1
are called yields to maturity, while those on the equity securities shown in
Figure 8-2 are known as holding-period yields. We will examine the
holding-period yield first.

The *holding-period yield* is the yield that a security holder actually
receives if he or she holds the security for a particular length of time, say 1
year. We must therefore define the holding-period yield according to the
time interval involved. The yield is then defined as the internal rate of
return, given the price that was paid for the security, the price at which it
was sold, and the stream of dividends or interest payments received during
the holding period. For example, if a particular security was purchased in

time period 1 at price P_1, sold in time period 5 at price P_5, and dividends of D_t were earned in each of the five periods, then the yield would be the interest rate r, which satisfied the following present value equation:

$$P_1 = \sum_{t=1}^{5} \frac{D_t}{(1 + r)} + \frac{P_5}{(1 + r)^5}$$

The important thing to observe about this relationship is that all of the prices and dividend payments are past observations and therefore known with certainty when the holding-period return is calculated. The holding-period return is therefore a measure of past experience, not an estimate of the yield that will be earned in the future. This type of yield is what is illustrated in Figure 8-2.

The alternative is to measure the yield that would be earned over some future period. This is close to impossible with some securities, such as equities, because the stream of dividends or interest payments and the future price are totally uncertain. However, it is not nearly as difficult in the case of a bond, because a bond has a clearly specified price at maturity and, if it is a coupon bond, a well-defined stream of coupon payments until maturity. It is therefore possible to calculate the yield that an investor would earn if the bond were purchased at the current price and held to maturity. This is known as the *yield to maturity*, and it is identical to the yield computed in the example of pricing a bond presented in Chapter Three. Almost invariably a bond's yield is calculated as a yield to maturity. This type of yield is illustrated in Figure 8-1.

Using either of these measures of yield to make comparisons between securities has its difficulties. The principal problem with holding-period yields is taken up in the discussion of risk premiums in equity securities later in the chapter. One of the principal difficulties involved in using the yield to maturity to compare bonds is that investors may have intended holding periods which are much shorter than the maturities of the bonds under comparison. For such investors, the yield to maturity is simply irrelevant. These investors are more interested in the price of the bond at the point in time when they expect to sell it. Studies of yield spreads between bonds based on yield to maturity may then be quite misleading. Whether this problem is of tremendous practical importance is difficult to determine. It may not be for comparisons between types of bonds where the holding periods are roughly the same, though shorter than the time to maturity. But if the holding periods are significantly different for the types of bonds in question, then comparisons of yield to maturity will be less meaningful.

Despite the limitations of yield to maturity, it is still used frequently in studies of the pricing of bonds. Later in this chapter a selection of these studies is examined and the results which are summarized are based largely on yield to maturity. By and large, the problems with yield to maturity are not thought to be tremendously serious for most empirical applications. But caution must be taken when examining empirical evidence using this measure of yield.

INFLATION AND NOMINAL INTEREST RATES

The real interest rate, as indicated in the last chapter, is defined net of inflation. It is similar to real income or real gross national product in that the effect of inflation has been extracted. This does not mean that inflation has no impact on interest rates so that it is safe to ignore it. Inflation, or more precisely, the *anticipated* rate of inflation is an important determinant of the interest rates which are observed in the world. When the interest rate is referred to inclusive of the effect of inflation, it is called the nominal interest rate.

The Real and Nominal Rates Defined

The *real interest rate* is the equilibrium rate at which claims to future income are traded for current income. The real rate of interest is expressed without reference to prices. If the quantity of goods and services available for consumption in time periods 1 and 2 are represented by Q_1 and Q_2, respectively, then the real rate of interest is

$$\text{Real interest rate} = \frac{Q_2 - Q_1}{Q_1} \tag{8-1}$$

This means that the real interest rate is the real rate of growth in available goods and services.

The *nominal interest rate*, on the other hand, takes into account the change in the price of goods and services. That is, the nominal interest rate values the quantity of goods and services in each time period at their going price. If the aggregate price level of all goods and services is represented by P_1 and P_2 in periods 1 and 2, respectively, then the nominal interest rate can be expressed as

$$\text{Nominal interest rate} = \frac{P_2 Q_2 - P_1 Q_1}{P_1 Q_1} \tag{8-2}$$

In addition, the rate of inflation between periods 1 and 2 can be defined as

$$\text{Inflation rate} = \frac{P_2 - P_1}{P_1} \tag{8-3}$$

There is a relationship between the real and nominal rates which follows directly from these definitions. The nominal interest rate can be expressed as the sum of the real interest rate, the rate of inflation, and the product of the real interest rate and the rate of inflation:

$$\frac{P_2Q_2 - P_1Q_1}{P_1Q_1} = \frac{Q_2 - Q_1}{Q_1} + \frac{P_2 - P_1}{P_1} + \left[\frac{(Q_2 - Q_1)}{Q_1} \times \frac{(P_2 - P_1)}{P_1}\right] \quad (8\text{-}4)$$

Nominal rate = real rate + inflation rate + (real rate × inflation rate)

To see this it is easiest to expand the right-hand side of Eq. (8-4) and cancel terms until this expression for the nominal interest rate reduces to the one on the left-hand side of the equation.[1]

There is a convenient simplification for this equation which results in a simple and usable relationship between the nominal rate and the rate of inflation. The simplification relies on the fact that the last term is the product of two small fractions. As a result, it is likely to be so small that it can be harmlessly dropped. For example, suppose that the real rate is 3 percent and the inflation rate is 10 percent, then the product of the two will be .003. Generally, this is simply too small to make much of a difference. Therefore, the simple expression for the nominal interest rate is that the nominal rate is equal to the sum of the real interest rate and the rate of inflation:

$$i_N = i_R + \Delta P \quad (8\text{-}5)$$

where i_N is the nominal rate, i_R is the real rate and, P is the inflation rate. For example, if the inflation rate is 10 percent and the real rate is 3 percent, then the nominal rate is 13 percent.

It is important to recognize that thus far no economic hypothesis has been offered about the relationship between real and nominal interest rates. The expression which has just been developed follows directly from the definitions of the real interest rate, the nominal interest rate, and the infla-

---

[1] We can rewrite Eq. (8-4), after expanding the final term, as follows:

$$\frac{P_2Q_2 - P_1Q_1}{P_1Q_1} = \frac{Q_2 - Q_1}{Q_1} + \frac{P_2 - P_1}{P_1} + \frac{P_2Q_2 - P_2Q_1 - P_1Q_2 + P_1Q_1}{P_1Q_1}$$

Next, we will multiply numerator and denominator of the first term by P_1 and the second term by Q_1. We then have:

$$= \frac{P_1Q_2 - P_1Q_1}{P_1Q_1} + \frac{P_2Q_1 - P_1Q_1}{P_1Q_1} + \frac{P_2Q_2 - P_2Q_1 - P_1Q_2 + P_1Q_1}{P_1Q_1}$$

Now we can cancel all the products of price and quantity which do not have the same time subscripts. What is left is the following:

$$= \frac{-P_1Q_1}{P_1Q_1} - \frac{P_1Q_1}{P_1Q_1} + \frac{P_2Q_2}{P_1Q_1} + \frac{P_1Q_1}{P_1Q_1}$$

Finally, the first and last terms cancel and the expression for the nominal rate remains.

tion rate. It therefore says nothing about how financial markets respond to inflation. In order to develop an hypothesis about financial markets and inflation, it is necessary to recognize that at any point in time the inflation rate is uncertain. The economic issue, then, is how anticipations of inflation affect the market.

Ex Ante and Ex Post Inflation and Real Interest Rates

It is exceptionally important to distinguish between anticipated and unanticipated inflation, or, alternatively stated, between the ex ante expected rate of inflation and the ex post observed rate of inflation. Irving Fisher offered an hypothesis some years ago about the relationship between nominal interest rates and the market's ex ante expected inflation rate. That hypothesis is exceptionally relevant today. At first glance the hypothesis looks the same as Eq. (8-5) above. But it is not. Equation (8-5) followed directly from the definitions specified above when uncertainty about the inflation rate was ignored. Fisher's hypothesis can be stated as follows:

$$i_N = i_R + \Delta P^e \qquad (8\text{-}6)$$

Nominal interest rate = The ex ante real interest rate +
the market's ex ante expected rate of inflation

The hypothesis asserts that the equilibrium nominal interest rate is such that lenders receive a compensation equal to the real interest rate plus an amount which perfectly offsets the *expected* rate of inflation. If the nominal interest rate provided less compensation than this, then lenders would be expected to lose in real terms on financial transactions. Because, in equilibrium, lenders should not expect to lose on financial contracts, the nominal interest rate will have to rise to just cover the market's expectation of inflation plus the real interest rate.

Because the inflation rate is uncertain, the ex post or realized real return may be either more or less than the real interest rate demanded ex ante. To see what this means it is helpful to examine a modified version of Eq. (8-6). Equation (8-7) says that the ex post real interest rate which a lender actually receives, symbolized by i'_R, is equal to the nominal rate which was initially set for the financial transaction i_N, less the actual inflation rate which occurred during the period in question, symbolized by $\Delta P'$:

$$i'_R = i_N - \Delta P' \qquad (8\text{-}7)$$

In any given time period the ex post real interest rate may be calculated from the actual nominal interest rate and the actual rate of inflation. But this ex post real interest rate is not the ex ante real interest rate in Fisher's theory. The ex post real interest rate will reflect the market's errors in guessing the inflation rate. For example, the ex post real interest rate earned by holding 90-day Treasury bills for 1977 are shown in Table 8-1. These were computed according to Eq. (8-7). For example, in January i_N = 4.6 percent, P′ = 10.2 percent, so that i'_R = 4.6 percent − 10.2 percent = −5.6 percent. These returns reflect the actual returns, after inflation, from holding Treasury bills during this period. But they do not necessarily give any indication of the value of the ex ante real interest rate demanded by lenders. We simply do not see the ex ante real rate, in spite of its importance in lenders' decisions.

The Behavior of the Ex Ante Real Rate and the Efficient Markets Hypothesis: Some Unresolved Questions

There are at least two interesting and important questions which should be asked about the observed behavior of the nominal interest rate. The first question is: How much of the changes in the nominal interest rate are due to changes in the real rate of interest as opposed to changes in the expected rate of inflation? The second question is: Does the market efficiently use all available information in assessing the future inflation rate? The answers to these questions are not obvious. There is considerable disagreement not only about the correct answers but also on how to go about determining the correct answers. Still, these questions are important and worth considering, at least briefly, even if no definite answers can be provided.

Irving Fisher is widely perceived to have argued that the real rate of interest is essentially constant. (Unfortunately, he is not around now to

TABLE 8-1

Ex Post Real Returns on Three-Month Treasury Bills for 1977

THREE-MONTH TREASURY BILL RATE ISSUED IN MONTH:		SUBSEQUENTLY OBSERVED INFLATION RATE* (%)	EX POST REAL INTEREST RATE (%)
MONTH	RATE (%)		
January	4.6	10.2	−5.6
February	4.7	8.1	−3.4
March	4.6	8.3	−3.7
April	4.5	6.9	−2.4
May	4.9	6.1	−1.2
June	5.0	4.9	0.1
July	5.1	4.2	0.9
August	5.5	4.7	0.8
September	5.8	3.5	2.3
October	6.2	4.0	2.2
November	6.1	6.6	−0.5
December	6.1	8.2	−2.1

* This is computed from the 3-month change in the consumer price index, that is, for January this is the annualized change from January to April.

explain what he really meant.) According to Fisher, fluctuations in the nominal rate of interest basically represent changes in the expected rate of inflation. It should be understood that the real rate of interest is probably never exactly constant. The argument is that fluctuations in the real interest rate are relatively small. Therefore, when there are periods of fairly sizable changes in nominal interest rates, these changes should be attributed to changes in the expected rate of inflation. The alternative view is that there can be, and often are, rather large changes in the real interest rate. Therefore, changes in nominal rates cannot be attributed entirely to changes in inflation expectations.

The significance of the constant real rate hypothesis should not be underestimated. This view suggests that it is largely fruitless to worry about such things as analysis of the loanable funds market and the flow of funds. Changes in desired borrowing and lending basically all come out in the wash and equilibrate at the same real interest rate. The argument that is really behind this is that the real interest rate also represents the marginal rate of return on the economy's capital stock. That capital stock is very large and changes only very slowly. Hence, changes in the real interest rate cannot be very large, at least in the short run.

The alternative view is that, for substantial periods of time, shifts in the supply or demand curves for loanable funds, which influence the real interest rate in financial markets, can take place. Only in a very long-run equilibrium do these changes have to induce similar changes in the real rate of return on the economy's capital stock. This argument implies that the real interest rate in the loanable-funds market can move above or below the real return on capital for periods that may be as long as a year or two. For the purpose of understanding monthly, quarterly, or annual changes in interest rates on financial contracts, it is important to examine changes in the real rate of interest.

The second question, regarding market efficiency, is not quite so controversial. In this instance, the efficient markets hypothesis asserts that all available information is efficiently used by the market in assessing future inflation rates. This seems easy enough to accept, but it is very difficult to verify. The reason is that it is impossible to ever directly observe the market's expected rate of inflation. This is true for the same reason that it is impossible to ever directly observe the market's ex ante real interest rate. It is possible to observe the ex post real interest and inflation rates, but these are not the direct subject of the efficient markets hypothesis.

It is possible to draw some conclusions about market efficiency from the ex post real interest rate, however. One implication of the efficient markets hypothesis is that the market should not make *systematic* errors in guessing the inflation rate. This means, for example, that if there is some pattern in the way the actual inflation rate moves through time, then the market should figure out the pattern and it should not show up in the behavior of the market's ex post real return. This means that if you looked at a graph of the ex post real interest rate, it should wander around without any definable pattern.

This hypothesis has been tested statistically by Eugene Fama in a controversial but interesting study.[2] Fama shows that there is an identifiable pattern in the behavior of the inflation rate. He also shows, however, that when the real return on Treasury bills is computed, as in Table 8-1, the pattern does not show up in these returns. He concludes that the market efficiently uses the information contained in the consumer price index in assessing the future changes in that index. Other researchers have criticized some of Fama's methodology and have challenged his conclusions. This is a challenging and difficult topic, and more definitive conclusions about the market's efficiency in this instance may be hard to come by.

PREMIUMS FOR RISK AND DEFAULT

Chapters Four and Five developed the basic theory of the value of risky assets. In this section we will draw upon and extend that theory in order to explain the observed differences in yields on different securities. The theory in those chapters argued that securities should differ in price or yield according to the perceived riskiness of the income streams accruing to those securities. A higher yield will be demanded on assets that are thought to be more risky. In this section we shall explore how well the theory does in explaining actual observed yields. First we will turn our attention to the market for debt securities and then to that for equity securities.

Risk Premiums in the Market for Debt Securities

The task of examining the premiums demanded to bear risk in the market for debt is in one respect simpler, while in another more complicated, than in the market for equity. It is simpler because we observe nominal ex ante promised yields and we can directly compare those to risk-free and other presumably less risky interest rates. It is more complicated because we must take into account the prospect of default which is not an issue with equity securities. First, consider the simplifying fact that we can directly observe the promised yield on debt securities and make direct comparisons between them. For example, Figure 8-1 shows the values over time of promised yields on a selection of debt securities. The difference in each period between the level of yields on corporate bonds and comparable-maturity Treasury bonds is, in part, determined by the risk of default of corporate bonds, since Treasury securities are assumed to be free of default risk. It is this premium that we will now concentrate on.

[2] See Eugene F. Fama, "Short-Term Interest Rates as Predictors of Inflation," *American Economic Review* (June 1975), pp. 269–282.

The unique factor in debt securities is the possibility of default. To understand the role of default it is necessary to examine the probability distribution on uncertain returns to the asset on which the debt is a claim. Suppose, for example, that we are examining the risk premium on a bond issued by the American Express Company. The bond is really a claim on the income stream which will accrue to American Express. The uncertainty surrounding the payments on the bond is determined by the uncertainty of the future earnings of American Express. As long as the earnings are sufficient to pay the promised return due the bondholders, then the bondholders will have no problem. But if the earnings are less than the promised amount, then the bondholders will be paid only as much as the firm has earned. We can therefore deduce the probability distribution for returns to the bondholders from the probability distribution on earnings for the company. Examples of this are shown in panels A and B of Figure 8-3.

Panel A shows a hypothetical probability distribution for returns measured in dollars on a particular asset. Three distinct amounts of dollar returns are marked on the horizontal axis, labeled x_1, x_2, and x_3. If we presume a specific face value of the debt claim on this income stream, say $100,000, then x_1 represents the amount of earnings that the firm would have to generate in order to pay the debtholders the risk-free rate of interest on their debt. If the risk-free rate were 10 percent, then x_1 would equal $110,000. But the bondholders do face risk. The probability distribution shows that their returns could be much lower than this $110,000. As a result, they will demand a contract interest rate which gives them an expected return which is higher than the risk-free rate of interest. Based on their estimate of the risk involved, they will demand an expected dollar return of say x_2. If the risk were such that the expected rate of return they demand were say 13 percent, then x_2 would be $113,000. The difference between x_2 and x_1 represents the same sort of premium for risk as was developed in Chapter Four. That is, it is the compensation demanded to bear the risk of the bond.

But with the probability distribution given, the factor that actually determines the debtholders' expected return is the contract or promised interest rate. Investors will demand a contract interest rate which gives them an expected dollar return of x_2. In order to have an expected return of x_2, they must set the contract interest rate higher than x_2 because, if they set the contract return at x_2 and there were any probability of default, that is, a payment less than x_2, then the expected return could not be as large as x_2. There will always be a contract return, symbolized by x_3, which will lead to an expected return of x_2. For the probability distribution in panel A, the probability that return on the bond will equal x_3 is represented by the area under the curve to the right of the vertical line originating at x_3. The probability distribution to the left of this line shows the probabilities of return less than x_3. Finally, the distance between x_2 and x_3 represents the default margin.

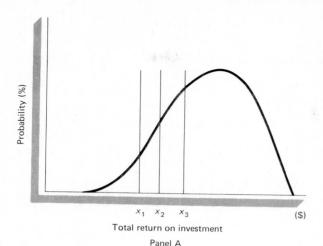

Total return on investment

Panel A

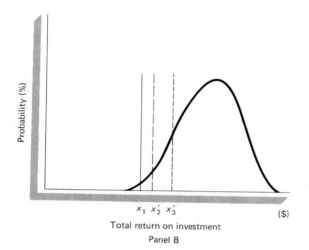

Total return on investment

Panel B

FIGURE 8-3
Uncertain returns on bonds and the assets on which they are claims. Panels A and B show probability distributions on two different assets. The debt claim in panel A is more risky than the one in B. X_1 shows the risk-free return on debt claims on these assets. X_2 and X_2' show the expected return demanded. X_3 and X_3' show the promised interest-rates demanded.

As a result, the observed yield spread or risk premium, represented by the difference between x_3 and x_1, can be divided into two parts. First, there is the compensation for bearing risk which is equal to $x_2 - x_1$. Second there is the default margin which is equal to $x_3 - x_2$:

Risk premium of a bond = compensation for bearing risk + default margin

The same thing is shown in panel B of Figure 8-3, but in that case the probability distribution on returns is more concentrated around its expected value. As a result, the observed risk premium, measured as $x_3' - x_1$, is smaller than in the example shown in panel A.

It is one thing to understand what is captured, in the observed risk premium on a bond. It is quite another to be able to assess the uncertain returns and determine the appropriate size of the risk premium for a particular bond. Because of the difficulties involved and the economies generated by specializing in this sort of activity, two firms provide ratings of most bonds sold in the market. The ratings are prepared and published by Moody's and Standard & Poors. The expense of preparing the rating is paid by the companies being rated rather than by the users of the service. The ratings provide a qualitative judgment of the risk of each bond. The various rating categories employed by the agencies are shown in Table 8-2. The highest rating is a triple A. The two rating agencies usually agree on ratings and the market generally is thought to have high regard for the rating agencies' judgments.

Over the years academicians have conducted empirical studies to see whether they can pin down the basic determinants of the risk premiums on different types of bonds. Some of the earlier studies tried to explain the differences in risk premiums across a number of different individual bonds at given points in time. More recent studies have attempted to identify the reasons why the risk premiums on bonds with different ratings vary through time. The most well-known study of the differences in risk premiums across

TABLE 8-2

Bond Ratings Produced by Moody's and Standard & Poor's

MOODY'S	EXPLANATION
Aaa	Best quality
Aa	High quality
A	Higher medium grade
Baa	Medium grade
Ba	Possess speculative elements
B	Generally lack characteristics of desirable investment
Caa	Poor standing; may be in default
Ca	Speculative in a high degree; often in default
C	Lowest grade

STANDARD & POOR'S	EXPLANATION
AAA	Highest grade
AA	High grade
A	Upper medium grade
BBB	Medium grade
BB	Lower medium grade
B	Speculative
CCC-CC	Outright speculation
C	Reserved for income bonds
D	In default

firms was conducted by Lawrence Fischer in the 1950s.[3] In his classic study Fischer attempted to explain the differences in risk premiums as a function of three factors: the historical variability of the company's earnings, the company's ratio of debt to equity securities, and the length of time since any suspension of payments to creditors. Using these variables and a measure of the marketability of the firm's bonds, Fischer was able to explain approximately three-quarters of the variation in observed risk premiums for samples drawn in five different years. Fischer's was the first major study of the principal determinants of risk premiums. Moreover, it remains the definitive evidence on the subject.

More recent studies have concentrated on trying to account for the changes in risk premiums through time. Either of two basic factors can lead to such changes: either the perceived probability of default can change or the degree of risk aversion of the market can change. Increases in either of these items will lead to increases in observed risk premiums. In recent years a number of researchers have attempted to measure these changes. One method has used a survey-based measure of consumer sentiment called "MOOD" to quantify investors' risk aversion. Not surprisingly, these studies have found that as consumers become more optimistic, risk premiums tend to decline. In addition, measures of the level of economic activity also tend to have a positive impact on observed risk premiums, suggesting that the perceived probability of default varies with the level of economic activity.[4]

Risk Premiums in the Market for Equity Securities[5]

As explained in Chapter Five, the preeminent theory of the determinants of risk premiums on equity securities is the capital asset pricing model (CAPM). The basic question at issue in an examination of risk premiums for equity securities is whether the CAPM provides an adequate explanation of the differences in observed premiums. That is, can the risk premiums on equity securities observed in the market be adequately explained as a function solely of the systematic risk of the securities? If they can, then it is possible to accept the CAPM as a reasonably good description of reality. If they cannot, then some additional factors other than systematic risk must be included in the analysis.

To be specific about what we mean by the risk premium on equity securities and by systematic risk, we return to the CAPM as stated in Chapter Five. The CAPM asserts that all assets will be priced so that their expected return is equal to the risk-free interest rate plus the product of the beta of the

---

[3] See Lawrence Fischer, "Determinants of Risk Premiums on Corporate Bonds," *Journal of Political Economy*, vol. 67 (June 1959), pp. 217–237.

[4] See Dwight M. Jaffee, "Cyclical Variations in the Risk Structure of Interest Rates," *Journal of Monetary Economics*, vol. 1 (1975), pp. 309–325; also Timothy Q. Cook and Patrick H. Hendershott, "The Impact of Taxes, Risk and Relative Security Supplies on Interest Rate Differentials," *Journal of Finance*, vol. XXXIII (September 1978), pp. 1173–1186.

[5] This section draws on the capital asset pricing model developed in Chapter Five. It can be omitted without loss of continuity.

security and the excess of the rate of return on the market portfolio over the risk-free interest rate or, for asset A, according to Eq. (5-4)

$$E(r_A) = r_F + [E(r_M) - r_F]\beta_A$$

This can be transformed into an equation for testing the determinants of risk premiums simply by moving the risk-free rate to the left-hand side of the equation, and by introducing an additional intercept term (α), which becomes the subject of the test:

$$E(r_A) - r_F = \alpha + [E(r_M) - r_F]\beta_A \tag{8-8}$$

The CAPM asserts that the risk premium of a particular security is equal to the market price of risk $[E(r_M) - r_F]$ times the measure of the security's risk (β_A). But Eq. (8-8) incorporates an additional term, α. The α acts as a proxy for other factors which might be important for risk premiums but which are excluded from the CAPM and which cannot be specifically measured by other available data. The object of the test is to determine whether α is equal to zero. If tests indicate that it is equal to zero, then these factors are judged to be insignificant. Another thing which can be measured is the security's unsystematic risk. The security's variance can be used to measure this.

But there is one other serious problem which must be dealt with before such tests can be performed. The problem is that Eq. (8-8) includes the *expected* rate of return on security A and on r_M, and these are never observed in the market. The actual ex post return is observed each period, but the ex ante expected return is not. Those who have conducted statistical tests of the CAPM have dealt with this by assuming that, over the long run, all assets constitute what is called a "fair game." In a fair game the expected rate of return is equal to the average actual return over the long run. In any single period, the actual return may be above or below the expected return. But over time, in a fair game, high returns will balance low returns and on an average, the asset will actually return its expected value. The idea of a fair game is essentially the idea of an efficient market, as discussed in Chapter Six. If the market were not a fair game, then you could expect to earn excess returns and the market would not be efficient. Therefore, tests of the determinants of risk premiums based on the CAPM also implicitly assume that markets are efficient. As a result, it is possible to rewrite the empirically useful form of Eq. (8-8) without the expectation for the return on asset A, as long as it is recognized that this holds only for average returns over long periods:

$$r_A - r_F = \alpha + (r_M - r_F)\beta_A \tag{8-9}$$

where r_A and r_M are the actual ex post rates of return on assets A and M.

Tests of this type of equation for observed risk premiums on equities have been conducted by a number of researchers. The results of these tests have led to a general consensus on at least two basic conclusions. First, measures of unsystematic risk do not significantly contribute to the explanation of observed risk premiums. By and large, whenever the variance of the security's return is added to Eq. (8-9) it does not add significantly to the statistical explanation of the risk premium. On the other hand, these tests uniformly conclude that α is not equal to zero.

An example of this kind of empirical test is presented in Figure 8-4.[6] This figure shows the average monthly returns on 10 portfolios of securities (vertical axis) graphed against the systematic risk of the portfolios (horizontal axis) for the 35-year period from 1931 to 1965. The slope of the line in the figure is an estimate of the market price of risk ($r_M - r_F$), just as ($r_M - r_F$) measures the slope in Eq. (8-9). The intercept term in the figure is an estimate of α and it is greater than zero.

These kinds of results compel us to reject the capital asset pricing model as a completely satisfactory description of the way equity securities are priced.[7] Evidently something has been left out. While there is considerable conjecture about what the missing factor or factors may be, at this time there is little consensus or reliable evidence.

[6] See Fischer Black, Michael C. Jensen, and Myron Scholes, "The Capital Asset Pricing Model: Some Empirical Tests," in Michael C. Jensen (ed.), *Studies in the Theory of Capital Markets*, Praeger Publishers, New York, 1972, p. 104. Copyright Holt Rinehart & Winston. Figure reprinted by permission.
[7] For other empirical studies of the capital asset pricing model, see Eugene Fama and James Macbeth, "Risk, Return and Equilibrium: Empirical Tests," *Journal of Political Economy* (May–June 1973), pp. 607–636; also Marshall Blume and Irwin Friend, "A New Look at the Capital Asset Pricing Model," *Journal of Finance*, vol. 28 (March 1973), pp. 19–33.

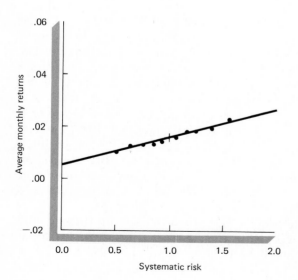

FIGURE 8-4
Average monthly returns versus systematic risk for the 35-year period 1931–1965 for ten portfolios and the market portfolio.

TAXES AND THE YIELDS ON SECURITIES

The third factor which has an influence on observed interest rates is taxes. The effects of taxes on the prices and yields of securities and on the investment decisions that are made in the market are as varied and complicated as are the tax laws themselves. Basically, investors treat taxes like other costs; they try to minimize them. As a result, when judging investments, investors are interested in *after-tax returns*. And this means that the price and yield of an asset are determined by its after-tax returns rather than by the returns it pays before taxes are accounted for. Moreover, because investors are taxed at different rates, an asset with a particular before-tax return will often yield a different amount after taxes to two investors; therefore, it is important to take into account not only the fact that different securities are treated differently in the tax law but also the fact that individuals are taxed at different rates.

In this section we will examine two effects of the tax laws on the yields on different securities. These are not the only effects of taxes in financial markets, but they are instances where the effects of taxes can be directly observed in the yields on debt securities. The first tax effect we will examine is the exemption of interest income on municipal securities from federal income taxes. Second, we will examine the effect of differential taxation of interest income and capital gains on the yields on debt securities. Taxes will also be taken up in Parts Three and Four of this book, when we discuss financial institutions.

The Tax Exemption of Municipal-Bond Income

Bonds issued by state and local governments are referred to as municipal bonds. In an effort to reduce the cost of borrowing for state and local governments across the country, the U.S. government has made the interest income on municipal bonds exempt from federal income taxes. In addition, each state has declared that the interest income on its own bonds will be exempt from its state income taxes. Finally, some states and localities have given tax-exempt status to bonds issued by other states on a reciprocal basis.

The tax-exempt feature of the interest income on municipal bonds has made them attractive to individuals and institutions which have high tax rates. Individuals who face a progressive income tax schedule (see Table 2-2 and accompanying discussion of progressive income taxes) find that the higher the tax bracket, the more advantageous is the tax-exempt feature of municipals. Corporations have a constant marginal tax rate of 48 percent (as long as their taxable income is over $25,000) and therefore do not find that the attractiveness of municipal securities varies directly with their income level in the same way as do individuals. In addition, some institutions with sizable amounts of funds to invest, such as pension funds and tax-exempt foundations, do not pay taxes and therefore find the tax-exempt feature of municipals totally unattractive.

The attractiveness of municipal bonds hinges on the difference in yields between the municipal security and an otherwise comparable security which is fully taxable. For example, suppose that a municipal bond and corporate bond are identical in every respect except the tax-exempt status of the municipal bond. Also suppose that the yield on the corporate bond is 10 percent and the yield on the municipal is 6 percent. At what tax rates will it be profitable for an investor to hold the municipal rather than the corporate bond? The answer can be computed from the following formula:

$$1 - \frac{.06}{.10} = .40 \tag{8-10}$$

To see why this is true we must return to the statement that investors are interested in *after-tax returns*. The problem facing the investor is to determine the yield he or she will receive after taxes on a taxable bond paying 10 percent. The corporate and municipal bonds will yield identical after-tax returns if

$$r_c (1 - \ell) = r_m \tag{8-11}$$

where ℓ is his or her tax rate, r_m is equal to the yield on the municipal bond, and r_c is equal to the yield on the otherwise equivalent taxable corporate bond. This means that for a given yield on both the municipal and corporate bonds, we can solve for the minimum marginal tax rate where the municipal bond produces the higher after-tax yield:

$$\ell = 1 - \frac{r_m}{r_c} \tag{8-12}$$

This is exactly the same equation as the example in Eq. (8-10). It implies that anyone with a tax rate over 40 percent, in the example, will find the municipal bond to be a better investment than the corporate bond.

From the observed yields on municipals and roughly comparable securities that are taxable, it is possible to compute the implied marginal tax rate, as in this example. Figure 8-5 shows the recent yields on high-quality municipal bonds with a maturity of 20 years. It also shows the yields on long-term corporate bonds over the same historical period. Using the corporate bonds as the "comparable security," it is possible to compute the marginal tax rate at which the municipal security becomes preferable, over the same historical period. The marginal tax rates are shown in panel B of the figure. There is considerable fluctuation in the computed marginal tax rate over the historical period. On the other hand, the figure shows that the marginal tax rate does not wander aimlessly. It tends to fluctuate around an average of roughly 35 percent. This means that yields on municipals have tended to be roughly 65 percent of yield on other comparable bonds.

It is not obvious why this yield spread has been around 65 percent rather

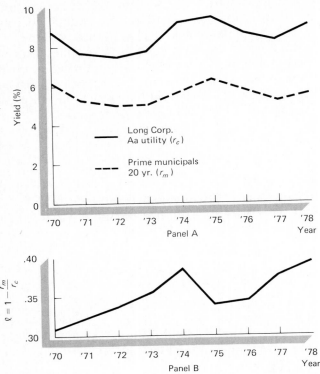

FIGURE 8-5
Yields on municipal (r_m) and corporate bonds (r_c) and the yield spread: $\ell = 1 - r_m/r_c$. Panel A shows the levels of yields and Panel B shows ℓ.

than some higher or lower amounts, such as 75 percent or 55 percent. The size of the spread depends largely on who is attracted to hold municipals and who is not. Most municipal bonds are held by commercial banks, fire and casualty insurance companies, and high tax-bracket individuals. Because commercial banks have the largest position in the municipal-bond market, it has been argued that their decisions to buy or sell municipals are an important, if not the most important, determinant of the marginal tax rate.[8] It is argued that as banks, which have a 48 percent marginal tax rate, move into or out of the market, they increase or decrease the total demand for municipals. The slack must be taken up by individuals who face a progressive tax schedule. Therefore, when they must pick up additional slack, the marginal tax rate must fall to induce more individual investors to buy municipals.

The movement of banks into and out of the market is sometimes said to provide a "segmented market" explanation of observed yield spreads. The

[8] See Tim S. Campbell, "On the Extent of Segmentation in the Municipal Securities Market," *Journal of Money, Credit and Banking*, vol. XII (February 1980), pp. 71–82.

empirical significance of this effect is in some dispute, however. One study tried to directly estimate the magnitude of this effect and found that it was insignificant.[9] That is, changes in banks' holdings of municipal securities were not found to have a significant long-run effect on differences between low-risk municipal and Treasury yields. But, as yet, not enough insight or empirical evidence has been developed to completely resolve the question.

There are also other difficulties in linking a particular yield spread to the investment decisions of specific purchasers of municipals.[10] One reason for this is that it is difficult to identify securities which are comparable to municipals in all other respects except tax treatment. For example, the risk of default and the options open to security holders in the event of default are somewhat ambiguous with regard to municipal securities. The effective default of New York City in the late 1970s and the limited options open to investors due to the political nature of the problem highlighted the potential difficulties involved in municipal debt. Premiums for risk may therefore vary widely for even the most highly rated municipal securities, especially when the maturities are long. Another problem is that there are a number of peculiar pressures on commercial banks which may alter the apparent tax advantage of municipals for banks. For example, depending upon the type of pressure applied by the Federal Reserve System when it tightens monetary policy, banks may find it necessary to liquidate municipal bonds to satisfy the commitments they have made to extend commercial loans. This prospect of untimely liquidation will alter the perceived return to banks from holding municipal bonds. These factors and others make it exceptionally difficult to measure true after-tax yield spreads between municipal and other securities as perceived by commercial banks.

Taxation of Interest and Capital Gains: The Advantage of Discount Bonds

The tax laws treat income derived from interest and income derived from capital gains differently. Capital gains income is taxed at a lower rate than interest income. Generally the capital gains rate is one-half of an individual's regular rate, but for high-income individuals the difference is smaller. Moreover, since 1976 an asset must be held for more than a year to qualify for the capital gains rate.[11]

The implication of the differential taxation of interest and capital gains is that the price and yield of a bond can be influenced by shifting the income in a bond from coupon interest to capital gains. To see precisely what this means it is necessary to reconsider the price of a coupon bond, as developed in Chapter Three, and introduce taxes into the present value equation which

[9] See James C. Van Horne, *Financial Market Rates and Flows*, Prentice-Hall, Englewood Cliffs, N.J., Chap. 8, 1978.

[10] See Cook and Hendershott, op, cit., pp. 1173–1186.

[11] See *1978 Security Transactions*, Commerce Clearing House, Clark, N.J., 1978, for a relatively recent review of the pertinent tax law.

determines its value. The value of an N period coupon bond with a value at maturity of $1,000 can be defined as

$$PV = \sum_{t=1}^{N} \frac{A}{(1 + r)^t} + \frac{1,000}{(1 + r)^N} \qquad (8\text{-}13)$$

where r is the discount rate and A is the periodic coupon interest payment. Equation (8-13) implies that, given a discount rate or value for r, the price of the bond can be determined. Or, given a price for the bond, the equation implies a yield for the bond.

Once we try to take taxes into account, this equation still represents the relationship between the observed price and the observed before-tax yield, but it no longer tells us how the price is really determined. This is because investors are concerned with after-tax yields and returns. Therefore, the value of the bond will be determined by investors discounting their after-tax returns at the after-tax discount rate they demand. We can imagine the market working in the following manner. Investors consider the returns on alternative investments on an after-tax basis. They bid for securities which look attractive after taxes. The prices of securities come to reflect investors' after-tax yields.

In order to specify how the price is determined, we have to state the relationship between price and the *after-tax* income stream accruing to the asset. To do this we will need some additional notation. We will represent the tax rate on regular income with the symbol ℓ, as we did above, the tax rate on capital gains with the symbol g, and the after-tax interest rate demanded by investors as r_a. Now we need to state an equation for the present value of after-tax returns discounted at the after-tax rate r_a. This equation can be written as follows:

$$PV = \sum_{t=1}^{N} \frac{(1 - \ell)A}{(1 + r_a)^t} + \frac{1,000}{(1 + r_a)^N} - \frac{(1,000 - PV)g}{(1 + r_a)^N} \qquad (8\text{-}14)$$

The first term is the present value of the coupon payments after taxes. The second term is the present value of the maturity value. The third term is the present value of the future capital gains tax. This equation determines the price that an investor will place on an asset based on its after-tax returns.

In order to illustrate how this equation is used to determine the price, we need to move the PV in the last term on the right-hand side of the equation to the left-hand side so that we can solve for PV. When we do this we have the following somewhat more complicated expression:

$$PV = \left[\sum_{t=1}^{N} \frac{(1 - \ell)A}{(1 + r_a)^t} + \frac{1,000\ (1 - g)}{(1 + r_a)^N} \right] \left[\frac{(1 + r_a)^N}{1 + (1 + r_a)^N} \right] \qquad (8\text{-}15)$$

However, while it is more complicated, we can plug a number into everything on the right-hand side. To illustrate, suppose that the tax rate on regular income is 50 percent, the tax rate on capital gains is 25 percent, and the after-tax discount rate is 5 percent. Also suppose this bond pays annual coupon payments of $50 and there are 10 years to maturity. Then we can solve for the price as follows:

$$PV = \left[\sum_{t=1}^{10} \frac{25}{(1.05)^t} + \frac{1,000\,(1 - .25)}{(1.05)^{10}} \right] \left[\frac{1.05^{10}}{1.05^{10} - g} \right]$$

$$= [193 + 460][1.18]$$

$$= 771$$

Equation (8-14) shows how the price of a coupon bond is determined with taxation of interest income and capital gains at different rates. In spite of the importance of after-tax yields to each investor, however, we observe only the before-tax yield of the bond quoted in the market. The before-tax yield is the one which is determined by Eq. (8-13). And we can compute it by solving Eq. (8-13) for the internal rate of return when the price is $771. The before-tax yield is still used by the market as just another way of stating the price of the security. But it no longer represents a yield which is demanded by security holders. The yield actually demanded is the after-tax yield r_a.

The effect of the differential tax rate on capital gains and interest income is to create a preference for bonds which have low coupon rates.[12] These are called discount bonds because they sell at low or discount prices. The idea behind a discount bond is to shift income from coupon payments to capital gains in order to take advantage of the lower tax rates on capital gains. To see how this works we want to examine two bonds that have the same yield before taxes, but have different proportions of capital gains as opposed to coupon interest income. The first bond has coupon payments which are virtually equal to the market interest rate. The second bond has much lower coupon payments. If these two bonds were traded in a world where there were no taxes, then the first bond would have no capital gain, because its current value would be exactly equal to its value at maturity. In order to maintain the same yield, the price of the second bond would have to fall until the capital gain was large enough to promise the same yield to investors as the first bond. Now suppose that interest income and capital gains are taxed, but with the capital gains rate lower than the rate on interest income. The decrease in coupon payments on the second bond would then create a tax savings. We can see how this happens from Eq. (8-14). As we decrease the coupon payments, the value of the bond declines and the capital gain in the third term increases to compensate. However, due to the tax savings, the value of the bond does not have to fall as much as it otherwise would to maintain the same after-tax yield. Because the price of the bond does not go down as far as it otherwise would, the before-tax yield, which is computed from Eq. (8-13), should be lower for a discount bond than for a bond with a coupon rate close to the before-tax market interest rate.

[12] For a more detailed discussion, see Van Horne, op. cit., pp. 196–202.

This is, in fact, what is observed in the market. For example, on November 23, 1979, the prices and yields on two Treasury bonds were as follows. One was a discount bond which matured in February 1990, and had a coupon rate of 3.5 percent. The other offered little discount with a coupon rate of 8.25 percent and a maturity date of May 1990. Because these bonds are nearly identical except for the distinct coupon rates, they would have roughly the same market yield, were it not for the tax treatment of capital gains. The discount bond was priced at $75.20 with a before-tax yield of 6.69 percent. The bond with little discount was priced at $86.2 with a before-tax yield of 10.39 percent. The tax treatment of capital gains therefore drove down the before-tax yield on the discount bond because the price did not have to fall as much as it would were it not for the tax savings on capital gains.

THE IMPACT OF RELATIVE SECURITY SUPPLIES ON NOMINAL YIELDS

The impact of relative supplies of securities on nominal yields hinges on the extent of segmentation in securities markets as opposed to the strength of substitution between different securities. The segmentation and substitution theories are polar extreme characterizations of the way financial markets operate. Basically, the *segmentation theory* argues that different securities or groups of securities have distinct markets with impenetrable barriers between them while the *substitution view* says that such barriers are nonexistent or minimal and that all investors substitute back and forth between securities as they detect opportunities for excess returns. The implication of the segmentation view is that observed yield spreads are largely determined by changes in demand or supply for a given segment of the market. On the other hand, the substitution theory implies that factors which affect the real return to investors, such as risk and taxes, account for the observed differences in yields. The initial task is to fully understand the differences between these two views.

Segmentation Theory

The fundamental tenet of the segmentation theory is that specific securities have some characteristics which cause particular clienteles of investors to be interested in those securities and other investors to avoid holding them. The characteristics which lead to the formation of clienteles, or to segmentation of the market, are usually thought to be something external to the innate risk and return characteristics of the security. They may be related to the tax treatment of some securities or to some government restriction on the investments of financial institutions or to some characteristics of the investors themselves which might make them choose securities on some basis other than the risk and return of the security. This segmentation of the market into groups of investors who are willing to hold only particular types of securities is illustrated in Figure 8-6. The diagram shows the total population of investors divided into two groups according to some criterion which is unrelated to the actual returns on the securities. Each group holds only one type of security. As a result, there are effectively two markets with no links between them.

The empirical implication of the segmentation theory is that investors will be insensitive to changes in risk and return across the barrier which divides the markets. Therefore, factors which influence the distribution on returns for securities in different segments of the market will not explain the spreads between the yields on these securities. What will explain these yield spreads is the relative strength of supply and demand in the various segments of the market. The segmentation theory implies that the observable links between securities markets or between different assets is weak. It implies that where segmentation exists, observed yields essentially follow their own independent paths and are not closely related.

Substitution Theory

The substitution theory argues that relative supplies and demands are not important determinants of security prices. Rather, all securities are priced to reflect the market's assessment of their risk and return. In this view, observed yield spreads are determined by all the factors which affect the return distributions on each security and any costs of substituting back and forth between securities. For example, if the income from different securities is treated differently for tax purposes, then this will affect the after-tax returns to investors, which will, in turn, influence the observed yields on these securities. The difference in yield will reflect the *cost* to investors of the differential tax treatment of the income of the securities. The substitution

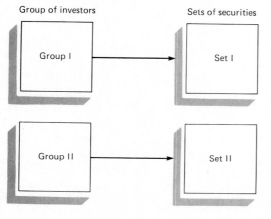

FIGURE 8-6
Segmented market. The figure shows that in a segmented market investors are divided into groups that hold distinct sets of securities.

theory leaves no room for seemingly arbitrary or unexplained divisions of securities or investors into groups or clienteles which determine the yields on securities. It therefore argues that relative supply and demand will be unimportant in explaining differences in yields. The essence of this theory is that yield spreads must be due to perceived real differences in future returns.

Evidence on Segmentation and Substitution

There are two types of evidence on the extent of segmentation in financial markets. One is an indirect type of evidence, while the other is direct. Indirect evidence is drawn from attempts to account for observed differences in yields on different securities based on the factors which directly affect the future returns to those securities. This indirect evidence does not try to directly test the impact of relative security supplies. Instead it attempts to explain yield spreads with the facts which the substitution theory asserts are relevant. If this explanation proves adequate, then the segmentation theory is judged unimportant. Unfortunately, there is no unambiguous criterion as to what is an adequate explanation. It is impossible to fully account for observed yield differences in empirical studies. Therefore, what seems adequate to one person who reviews the evidence may seem inadequate to another. For example, Marshall E. Blume and Irwin Friend conclude after an extensive analysis of risk premiums on equity securities (using the capital asset pricing model) that the ability to explain observed differences in yields is sufficiently poor that "the evidence points to segmentation of markets as between stocks and bonds."[13] In general, a failure to adequately explain observed yield spreads with the identifiable factors affecting returns has led to the conclusion that there must be some segmentation.

Fortunately there is also some specific evidence on the impact of the relative supply and demand for securities. One of the most recent and most comprehensive studies of yield spreads on bonds which attempted to directly test the importance of relative supplies of securities was conducted by Timothy Cook and Patrick Hendershott.[14] They examined the yield spreads between long-term corporate and Treasury bonds. They made extensive adjustments for tax and technical factors influencing the yield data, and then attempted to isolate the influences of risk and relative security supplies on the observed yield spreads. However, their measures of relative supplies of corporate and Treasury bonds have no perceptible effect once risk and taxes are accounted for.

But, as Cook and Hendershott point out, the segmentation view requires that there does not exist a large group of investors who are indifferent at the margin between the two securities in question. Even if this is not the case for high-grade corporate and Treasury bonds, it may be true for other securities. The discussion earlier in this chapter suggests that one more likely candi-

[13] See Blume and Friend, op. cit., p. 32.
[14] See Cook and Hendershott, op. cit., pp. 1173–1186.

date might be the market for municipal securities. In that case, some have argued that the tax treatment of municipal bonds has created a segmented market which is dominated by commercial banks. In this case, the evidence is not as clear-cut. In a recent study of regional markets for municipal bonds, Hendershott and Kidwell found evidence of segmentation in the yield spreads between yields in the regional market and yields on nationally distributed bonds which could not be attributed to risk and other factors affecting returns.[15] But in another study of 20 years worth of aggregate national yield data for municipal bonds and Treasury bonds as well as between municipal bonds of different risk and maturity, no evidence was found of segmentation resulting from changes in banks' holdings of those securities.[16]

Finally, John S. Bildersee examined yield spreads between Treasury securities and other securities backed by the U.S. government but issued by other agencies within the federal government and called agency securities. Bildersee's study attempted to determine the extent of segmentation between the markets for these types of securities and identify the factors which accounted for changes in yield spreads over time. This particular issue has attracted some attention from market observers because the underlying securities are so similar, yet there are persistent yield spreads between the securities. Bildersee concluded that "the yield spreads separating these markets are most consistently related to economic liquidity measures . . . and to market measures such as relative transaction rates and market size." Bildersee also draws an important conclusion about the general problem of segmentation and substitution in financial markets. He points out that "it appears that the major questions that must be answered about the bond markets are not whether they are continuous and integrated or segmented. Instead, the questions must revolve around the issues of how continuous and integrated these markets are, how this continuity can be defined and how it changes through varied economic conditions."[17]

Markets become more segmented when there are barriers or costs to substituting between alternative types of investments. This includes the cost of evaluating the yield spread to determine whether it is justified by anticipated real returns and the transactions cost of selling one security and buying another. It seems exceptionally reasonable that such costs exist in substituting between various regional markets. It also seems reasonable that these costs may be large in the short run. This means that a short-run change in yield spreads may be slow to induce investors to alter their portfolios and make the adjustments necessary to force the yield spread back to what they believe is an equilibrium. This may be particularly true when a large change

[15] See Patrick H. Hendershott and David S. Kidwell, "The Impact of Relative Security Supplies; A Test with Data from a Regional Tax-Exempt Bond Market," *Journal of Money, Credit and Banking*, vol. 10 (August 1978), pp. 337–347.

[16] See Campbell, op. cit., pp. 71–82.

[17] See John S. Bildersee, "U.S. Government and Agency Securities: An Analysis of Yield Spreads and Performance," *Journal of Business*, vol. 51 (July 1978), p. 520. Copyright © 1978 by the University of Chicago.

in investments may be necessary, which occasionally occurs in the municipal-bonds market.

But these costs should dissipate over time. In effect, as the disequilibrium yield-spread persists, more investors are able to make the substitutions which will return the yield spread to equilibrium. Segmentation therefore results when the costs of substituting between assets are large. As these costs diminish across time, or regional boundaries become less significant, segmentation diminishes.

SUMMARY

In this chapter we have moved from the theoretical concept of the real interest rate, which was the subject of the last chapter, to deal with the principal features of observed market interest rates, referred to as nominal rates. We analyzed four of five factors which account for the differences between nominal rates and the real interest rate. These are inflation, risk, taxes, and relative security supplies.

Probably the most important difference between nominal rates and the real rate for the decades of the 1970s and 1980s has been and will be the premium the market demands for inflation. We learned that excluding risk, taxes, and relative security supplies, the nominal rate is equal to the sum of the real rate and the market's expectation of inflation. Therefore, in a time of high inflation there will be a large difference between observed nominal rates and the underlying real rate. We also evaluated some of the available evidence on the degree to which the market efficiently incorporates publicly available information regarding future inflation rates into nominal interest rates. We found that the available evidence suggests that the market is efficient in this weak-form sense.

Next we examined premiums for risk in both equity and debt securities. We found that with debt securities there is both a premium for bearing risk, in the sense that we understand from Chapter Four, and a premium for default. Both of these premiums represent differences between the contract or promised interest rate on a debt security and the expected rate of return on the investment that debt security is financing. Both of these factors in combination account for the difference between observed promised rates on debt securities and the risk-free real interest rate. Regarding equity securities the central question is whether we can adequately account for observed nominal rates of return on equity securities using the capital asset pricing model developed in Chapter Five. We found that there appears to be some factor left out of the CAPM which is an important determinant of actual observed rates of return. At this time, it is not known what that factor may be.

Next we explored the effects of taxes on nominal yields. In this discussion we limited our attention to two important examples of the effects of taxes on yields, the exemption from federal income taxes of interest income on municipal bonds and the taxation of capital gains at a lower rate than regular interest income. We found that the tax treatment of municipal bonds tends to decrease municipal bond yields relative to yields on comparable securities with taxable income until the after-tax yields are the same. Furthermore, this tax treatment tends to concentrate investments in municipals in the hands of those who have the least preferential tax treatment, particularly high tax-rate individuals, commercial banks, and property and casualty insurance companies. Regarding the tax treatment of capital gains, we found that when capital gains are taxed at lower rates than regular income, it is possible to raise the after-tax yield of a bond by reducing the coupon payments so that more of the income takes the form of capital gains. Such bonds are known as discount bonds because they have low prices and low coupon payments. We learned how to examine the after-tax yield of a discount bond and why it is after- rather than before-tax yield which determines market prices.

Finally, we examined the impact of relative security supplies, or the segmentation argument. The segmentation argument asserts that there are clienteles of investors in the market who prefer specific types of securities at the exclusion of others. The source of the formation of such clienteles is often thought to be due to something external to the factors which determine a particular security's future returns. The alternative theory, which was characterized as perfect substitution, asserts that no such external forces exist and each security's price and yield are determined by the return it is expected to offer and the risk surrounding that return. We found that evidence on segmentation often comes from two sources. Often times, when it is difficult to empirically explain observed prices or yields with available measures of the future returns, this disparity is attributed to the presence of segmentation. The other evidence is based on the contribution to yields of changes in the volume of supply or demand for securities. Most such direct evidence points to segmentation only in the short run or in markets which have great regional dispersion.

This chapter emphasizes that observed nominal yields are a result of a number of factors. In the chapter we attempted to summarize both what these factors are and the empirical evidence on their importance. With an understanding of these factors, it is much easier to make some sense out of the multitude of interest rates observed in the market.

QUESTIONS TO IMPROVE UNDERSTANDING

1 Explain the difference between "holding period yield" and "yield to maturity"?
2 What is the difference between the ex ante and the ex post real interest rate? Why can we observe one and not the other? Why do many economists argue that the real interest rate is essentially constant? Do you think that the real interest rate is just as likely to be constant in the very short run (a week, a month, a quarter) as in the long run? Why?

3 What does it mean to say that the market efficiently uses available information about the future inflation rate in setting nominal interest rate? Why is it difficult to directly test whether this is true?

4 In this chapter we have differentiated between two components of the premium for risk in a bond. What are these two components and what do they mean? Suppose market participants became more averse to risk. Which of these two components of the premium would this affect?

5 Suppose you noticed that the yields on Treasury bonds with 20 years to maturity and municipal bonds of the highest quality and also with 20 years to maturity had yields of 12 percent and 9 percent respectively. What would be the marginal tax rate at which you would find it profitable to hold municipal rather than Treasury bonds?

6 What does it mean to say that a financial market is segmented? Many people who have studied segmentation of financial markets have concluded that segmentation is a transitory or short-run phenomenon. In the very long run there really is little or no segmentation. Does this make sense? Why?

7 The capital asset pricing model says that only systematic risk of an asset should affect its price. How have tests of the CAPM attempted to test this proposition? What have they found? They have also led to some important conclusions about the magnitude of the factor in the model referred to as α (alpha). What have they concluded about α and what do you think it means?

8 Can you summarize the factors that lead to observable changes in nominal interest rates over time? What do you think has probably been the most important factor causing changes in nominal rates in the 1970s and early 1980s?

REFERENCES

Bildersee, John S.: "U.S. Government and Agency Securities: An Analysis of Yield Spreads and Performance," *Journal of Business,* 51 (July 1978), pp. 499–520.

Black, Fischer, Michael C. Jensen, and Myron Scholes: "The Capital Asset Pricing Model: Some Empirical Tests," in Michael C. Jensen (ed.), *Studies in the Theory of Capital Markets,* Praeger Publishers, Inc., New York, 1972.

Blume, Marshall, and Irwin Friend: "A New Look at the Capital Asset Pricing Model," *Journal of Finance,* 28 (March 1973), pp. 19–33.

Campbell, Tim S.: "On the Extent of Segmentation in the Municipal Securities Market," *Journal of Money, Credit and Banking,* XII (February 1980), pp. 71–82.

Cook, Timothy Q.: "Some Factors Affecting Long-Term Yield Spreads in Recent Years," *Monthly Review of the Federal Reserve Bank of Richmond,* 59 (September 1973), pp. 2–14.

——, and Patrick H. Hendershott: "The Impact of Taxes, Risk and Relative Security Supplies on Interest Rate Differentials," *Journal of Finance,* XXXIII (September 1978), pp. 1173–1186.

Fama, Eugene, and James Macbeth: "Risk, Return and Equilibrium: Empirical Tests," *Journal of Political Economy* (May–June 1973), pp. 607–636.

Fischer, Lawrence: "Determinants of Risk Premiums on Corporate Bonds," *Journal of Political Economy,* 67 (June 1959), pp. 217–237.

Jaffee, Dwight M.: "Cyclical Variations in the Risk Structure of Interest Rates," *Journal of Monetary Economics*, 1 (1975), pp. 309–325.

Hendershott, Patrick H., and David S. Kidwell: "The Impact of Relative Security Supplies; A Test with Data from a Regional Tax-Exempt Bond Market," *Journal of Money, Credit and Banking*, 10 (August 1978), pp. 337–347.

Van Horne, James C.: *Financial Market Rates and Flows*, Prentice-Hall, Inc., Englewood Cliffs, N.J., 1978.

Chapter Nine

THE TERM STRUCTURE OF
INTEREST RATES

An important characteristic of debt securities which was not dealt with in the last chapter is the maturity of the security. The impact of maturity on yield is an important enough topic that it warrants a treatment which is separate from the other factors influencing yield. In this chapter we will examine this relationship between the yield on a debt security and its maturity, a relationship referred to as the term structure of interest rates. It is important to recognize that the term structure deals only with debt securities because only debt securities have a stated maturity. In addition, the term structure refers to the relationship between maturity and yield for securities which are alike in all other respects; for example, in their risk and tax treatment. Therefore, the term structure is normally applied to Treasury securities because of their high degree of homogeneity across maturities.

The term structure of interest rates is an important topic both because it contributes to a general understanding of financial markets and because one of the most critical financial decisions facing any corporation hinges on a proper understanding of the term structure. If the financial manager of a company is attempting to assess whether to obtain funds with short-term debt or with long-term debt, his or her choice will be determined by the yields available at the alternative maturities. If the short-term interest rate is higher than the long-term rate, as it was in 1974 for 1- and 10-year maturities, for example, then he or she might conclude that long-term borrowing will be better. But one of the theories of the term structure which we will examine in this chapter, the unbiased expectations theory, argues that the long-term rate is determined solely by the market's expectations of future short-term rates. If the unbiased expectations theory is correct, then the financial manager cannot expect to save by borrowing at the longer rate because it is lower. The point is that an understanding of the term structure is of tremendous practical importance.

YIELD CURVES AND FORWARD RATES

The bulk of this chapter is devoted to an examination of three alternative theories of the term structure of interest rates. But before we get into the theories themselves we need to develop some concepts which are important for all three of these theories. First, we need to understand what a yield curve is. Second, we need to understand both what forward interest rates are and the relationship between current rates and forward rates.

What Is the Yield Curve?

The term structure of interest rates is normally represented by what is called a yield curve. The yield curve shows the yields prevailing at a given point in time for bonds which differ only by maturity. As a result, there is a different yield curve or term structure in existence at any such point. Examples of different yield curves that have existed in recent years are shown in Figure 9-1. The figure shows that the yield curve which prevailed in December 1968 had a relatively flat slope, while the one which prevailed in September 1974 had a largely downward slope. A largely upward-sloping yield curve prevailed in June 1975, which means that short-term interest rates were generally below long-term interest rates during that month, the result being an upward-sloping yield curve.

Before we begin the more detailed analysis of the term structure, it is fruitful to briefly examine the behavior of the yield curve through time. For example, consider the changes that occurred in the yield curve during the 1974–1975 recession. September 1974 was near the peak of short-term interest rates which occurred during that recession. During that time short-term interest rates reached record high levels, though that record has since been shattered. For example, 90-day Treasury bill rates went as high as 9.33 percent. By comparison, long-term Treasury bond rates were not nearly as explosive, reaching a peak of approximately 8.5 percent. This is reflected in the shapes of yield curves observed at different points, as illustrated in Figure 9-1. At the peak of short-term interest rates in the 1974 recession, the yield

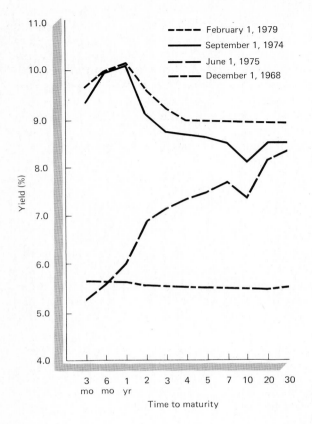

FIGURE 9-1
Yield curves for Treasury
securities.

curve was negatively sloped. Later in the recession, short-term interest rates fell relative to long-term interest rates and the yield curve became positively sloped, as illustrated for June 1975.

This pattern of relatively volatile short-term interest rates and less volatile long-term interest rates has been a common feature of business cycles in the United States. The basic reason for this is that long-term rates reflect the markets expectations of what will transpire over a long period of time, probably including a number of business cycles. Hence, these rates reflect an average of those expected future events. But the short-term cost of credit is directly reflected in short-term rates. These rates rise and fall to reflect the equilibrium demand and supply for short-term funds. Long-term rates would have patterns that are as volatile as short-term rates only if the market expected the trends in short-term rates to continue. That is, if the market expected the short-term rate to increase and stay at that higher level, then long-term rates would make a similar adjustment. The volatility of short-term relative to long-term rates reflects the market's belief that changes in short-term rates will remain a short-run phenomenon.

It is particularly interesting to examine the shape of the yield curve in late 1979, as illustrated in Figure 9-1. Short-term interest rates again reached record high levels. Again the yield curve had a negative slope in that long-term rates were substantially below short-term rates. This was a time when the rate of inflation had accelerated sharply and was running in excess of 13 percent per year. And it was widely perceived that short-term rates were rising in order to incorporate the expectations of inflation. But the fact that long-term rates were still substantially below short-term rates apparently reflected the market's belief that inflation rates would not remain in the long run at the levels experienced in 1979. The only alternative explanation of such low long-term rates would be that the market was willing to accept an expected long-run negative real return. In order to see more precisely the way the market incorporates its expectations into the term-structure it is necessary to develop an understanding of forward rates.

The Meaning and Computation of Forward Rates

The *term structure* of interest rates is the relationship between the *current* long-term interest rate and the *current* short-term interest rate. But underlying this there is really a relationship between the current long-term rate and the rates on current *and future* short-term loans. To see what this means suppose that there is a market for future short-term loans. In such a market you could arrange for a loan to begin, say, 1 year from now and receive a promise today of the interest rate you would have to pay 1 year from now. Such rates are called *forward rates*. And forward rates, or interest rates prevailing today for future loans, are an important part of the term structure relationship.

In order to understand the role of forward rates in the term structure, consider the choice between two types of debt contracts. One type of contract is a long-term bond at a single interest rate for N periods. The rate prevailing for such a contract today will be symbolized by $_tR_N$. The capital R means that it is a current rather than a forward rate. The subscript t means that it is the rate which prevails at time period t. The other contract involves N single-period loans, all contracted for at time period t. The rate of the first period will be $_tR_1$, which is the rate for single-period loans beginning today. The rate for loans in each future period which can be contracted for today, is a forward rate. The forward rates will be symbolized as $_{t+1}r_1$, where the lower case r indicates it is a forward rate; the subscript $t + 1$ indicates that the loan begins in period $t + 1$; and the subscript 1 indicates it is a one-period loan. Figure 9-2 shows the time periods to which the forward rates and current rates apply in the case where $N = 5$. This figure illustrates that there are four forward rates which apply to the four year-long intervals between the maturity of the 1-year bond and the maturity of the 5-year bond. For example, the forward rate $_{t+1}r_1$ measures the interest rate prevailing today for a 1-year loan beginning 1 year from now.

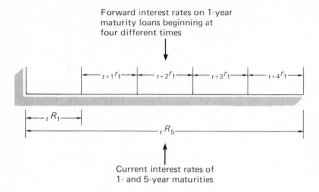

Forward interest rates on 1-year
maturity loans beginning at
four different times

Current interest rates of
1- and 5-year maturities

FIGURE 9-2
Illustration of the time periods
covered by forward interest
rates (small r's) and current
interest rates (large R's).

If we relate this notation to the yield curve, the first thing to notice is that we directly observe the Rs on the yield curve, but we do not observe the rs. We can see this from Figure 9-1. For example, we can identify the rates prevailing in June 1975 for Treasury securities of different maturities. A selection of these interpreted from the figure are listed below. (Note that the right-hand subscript measures years to maturity and t means June 1975):

$$_tR_1 = 6.04 \qquad _tR_{10} = 7.38$$
$$_tR_5 = 7.49 \qquad _tR_{20} = 8.17$$

The yield curve directly measures the rates prevailing today for current loans with different maturities, the Rs. On the other hand, the forward rates, the rs, are not directly shown in Figure 9-1.

Since we do not observe the forward rates on the yield curve, the natural question is where do they come from? The answer is that we can compute forward rates from current rates of different maturities. To see how to do this we need to think about the choice between the two debt contracts we have just described, the long-term contract at a single interest rate and the alternative contract with a number of single-period future loans. We need to define the condition under which the two contracts would have the same cost or the same future value. The two will have the same cost if the current and forward rates have the following relationship:

$$(1 + {_tR_N})^N = (1 + {_tR_1})(1 + {_{t+1}r_1})(1 + {_{t+2}r_1}) \cdots (1 + {_{t+N-1}r_1}) \quad (9\text{-}1)$$

Equation (9-1) means that the value of the interest payments will be the same for either debt contract. Another way of looking at this is to say that the long-term rate implies a sequence of forward rates and Eq. (9-1) defines the relationship between them. For example, if the interest rate on a 5-year bond is 12.8 percent and the rate on a 1-year bond is 10 percent, then the following sequence of forward rates will satisfy Eq. (9-1):

$$_{t+1}r_1 = .12, \, _{t+2}r_1 = .12, \, _{t+3}r_1 = .15, \, _{t+4}r_1 = .15$$

We can make sure of this by substituting them in Eq. (9-1). We find that both sides of the equation equal 1.82:

$$(1.128)^5 = (1.1)(1.12)(1.12)(1.15)(1.15) = 1.82$$

When we observe the current interest rates on bonds with different maturities at a given point, we can use Eq. (9-1) to solve for the forward rates which these current rates imply. Suppose, for example, that we observe the current interest rate on 9-year bonds and 10-year bonds. We can use these to compute the forward rate for a 1-year loan beginning 9 years from now. The formula for the forward rate is as follows:

$$_{t+9}r_1 = \frac{(1 + {}_tR_{10})^{10}}{(1 + {}_tR_9)^9} - 1 \tag{9-2}$$

We can satisfy ourselves that this is correct by moving the 1 to the right-hand side of Eq. (9-2) and substituting from Eq. (9-1) for the values of ${}_tR_{10}$ and ${}_tR_9$:

$$1 + {}_{t+9}r_1 = \frac{(1 + {}_tR_1)(1 + {}_{t+1}r_1)(1 + {}_{t+2}r_1) \cdots (1 + {}_{t+8}r_1)(1 + {}_{t+9}r_1)}{(1 + {}_tR_1)(1 + {}_{t+1}r_1)(1 + {}_{t+2}r_1) \cdots (1 + {}_{t+8}r_1)} \tag{9-3}$$

The equation is satisfied because the first nine terms in the numerator and denominator cancel out. To see how this can be used in an example, suppose that ${}_tR_{10} = .12$ and ${}_tR_9 = .11$. Then we can solve for ${}_{t+9}r_1$ as follows:

$$_{t+9}r_1 = \frac{(1.12)^{10}}{(1.11)^9} - 1$$

$$= \frac{3.106}{2.558} - 1$$

$$= .21$$

So the rate for a 1-year loan beginning 9 years from now is .21.

Thus far we have dealt with forward rates which applied to future loans lasting only one period. In terms of our notation, the right-hand subscript on the forward rate has always been 1. But there is no reason to deal only with single-period loans. We can contract for a future loan to last any number of periods. And we can solve for the forward rate on such a loan from the rates on current loans just as we did for single-period forward rates. From now on we will refer to the length of the future loan as K periods.

The formula for the forward rate on a K-period loan is similar to Eq. (9-2), but with a complication introduced by the difference of K periods. If we observe current rates on an N-period bond and an $N + K$-period bond, then

$$_{t+N}r_K = \sqrt[K]{\frac{(1 + {}_tR_{N+K})^{N+K}}{(1 + {}_tR_N)^N}} - 1 \tag{9-4}$$

To see why this is equal to the forward rate on a K-period loan, we can examine the expression inside the radical ($\sqrt{}$). This can be rewritten as:

$$\frac{(1 + {}_tR_{N+K})^{N+K}}{(1 + {}_tR_N)^N} = \frac{(1 + {}_tR_1)(1 + {}_{t+1}r_1)(1 + {}_{t+2}r_1) \cdots (1 + {}_{t+N+K-1}r_1)}{(1 + {}_tR_1)(1 + {}_{t+1}r_1)(1 + {}_{t+2}r_1) \cdots (1 + {}_{t+N-1}r_1)} \quad (9\text{-}5)$$

The difference between the numerator and the denominator is that the numerator includes the last K forward rates for single-period loans which are not included in the denominator. After cancelling terms in both the numerator and denominator, we are left with

$$\frac{(1 + {}_tR_{N+K})^{N+K}}{(1 + {}_tR_N)^N} = (1 + {}_{t+N}r_1)(1 + {}_{t+N+1}r_1) \cdots (1 + {}_{t+N+K-1}r_1)$$

But using the reasoning in Eq. (9-1), the product of these rates on the right-hand side of the equation will be the same as the forward rate on a K-period loan, raised to the Kth power. That is

$$(1 + {}_{t+N}r_K)^K = (1 + {}_{t+N}r_1)(1 + {}_{t+N+1}r_1) \cdots (1 + {}_{t+N+K-1}r_1) \quad (9\text{-}6)$$

This means that the expression in the radical in Eq. (9-4) is equal to

$$\frac{(1 + {}_tR_{N+K})^{N+K}}{(1 + {}_tR_N)^N} = (1 + {}_{t+N}r_K)^K \quad (9\text{-}7)$$

Equation (9-3) follows readily from Eq. (9-7) in the special case where $K = 1$. The implication of this is that whenever we observe current rates with maturities which differ by K periods, we can compute the forward rate for a K-period loan which begins at the maturity of the shorter of the two bonds.

To illustrate these computations suppose we observe a sequence of current interest rates on bonds with maturities ranging from 1 to 5 years. An example of such rates is given in the left-hand column of Table 9-1. These current rates can be used to compute the equivalent forward rate on future loans over this 5-year period. For example, the current rates on 1- and 2-year bonds imply a forward rate for a 1-year loan beginning 1 year from now of

$$_{t+1}r_1 = \frac{(1.11)^2}{(1.12)} - 1 = .10$$

Similarly the current rates on 3-year and 5-year bonds imply a forward rate for a 2-year loan beginning 3 years from now:

$$_{t+3}r_2 = \sqrt{\frac{(1.10)^5}{(1.105)^3}} - 1 = .09$$

TABLE 9-1

Example of Current and Corresponding Forward Interest Rate

CURRENT INTEREST RATES FOR SELECTED MATURITIES	A SELECTION OF FORWARD RATES WHICH CAN BE COMPUTED FROM CURRENT RATES
$_tR_1 = 12.0\%$	$_{t+1}r_1 = 10.0\%$
$_tR_2 = 11.00\%$	$_{t+2}r_1 = 09.5\%$
$_tR_3 = 10.5\%$	$_{t+3}r_1 = 09.5\%$
$_tR_4 = 10.25\%$	$_{t+4}r_1 = 09.0\%$
$_tR_5 = 10.00\%$	$_{t+1}r_4 = 09.5\%$
	$_{t+2}r_3 = 09.3\%$
	$_{t+3}r_2 = 09.3\%$

Other forward rates that can be computed from the first column of Table 9-1 are presented in column 2 of the table.

Thus far we only have the basic mechanics of the relationship between current interest rates of different maturities and the forward rates with which they are consistent. Now we need to examine the various theories about forward rates and current long-term rates.

THEORIES OF THE TERM STRUCTURE OF INTEREST RATES

There are three basic theories which are designed to explain the term structure of interest rates. Two of the theories are extreme alternatives and the third is a hybrid of the first two. The theories are labeled:

Unbiased expectations theory

Segmentation theory

Preferred habitat theory

In this section of the chapter we will examine each of these theories to see how they explain observed yield curves. We will conclude that neither the unbiased expectations theory nor the segmentation theory provides a completely adequate description of the term structure of interest rates. Hence, we are led to the hybrid preferred habitat theory.

Throughout our investigation of each of these theories we will rely upon our understanding of yield curves and forward interest rates. Thus far we have looked at forward rates as interest rates prevailing today for loans which will actually take place at some time in the future. For example, $_{t+3}r_2$ is the rate available today on a two-period loan which will begin three periods from now. However, in the real world there may not actually be contracts for such future loans. Fortunately, even if such future contracts do not actually exist, we can still make profitable use of the concept of the forward interest rate. It will become apparent how we do this as we develop each of the theories.

If there are no explicit contracts for future loans, then investors and borrowers cannot face a choice between a long-term bond today and a sequence of future single-period loans all contracted for today. The second option is no longer available. The choice now facing investors and borrowers is between a long-term bond today and a sequence of future short-term loans, each contracted for *when that loan begins*. This means that if a borrower chooses to borrow a year from today for 1 year, he must wait to pay the rate prevailing at that time rather than set that rate now.

To see more clearly what this means, consider the problem facing an investor who wants to lend money for 5 years. If there are no futures markets in loans, then the investor has the following three options. The simplest option is to buy a bond with a 5-year maturity. Then the maturity of the bond he or she holds is exactly the same as the maturity desired. However, the investor could buy a short-term (1-year) bond each year for the next 5 years. As a result, he or she will earn the short-term interest rate that prevails in each future year. The investor's third alternative is to buy with a maturity longer than 5 years, say 10 years, and sell after 5 years. It is clear that the first option, that of buying a 5-year bond, is the simplest in that the only transaction is the initial purchase. But without knowing the interest rates today and in the future, and ignoring any costs involved in making transactions, it is not apparent which alternative will turn out to be the most profitable investment.

As we discuss the various theories of the term structure of interest rates, we will be examining the question of how to choose between the kind of options just described. The first theory of how to choose between these options and the prices or yields on bonds which result from this choice is called the unbiased expectations theory. We will examine it next.

The Unbiased Expectations Theory

The best alternative open to the investor who wants to lend his or her funds for 5 years depends upon his or her expectations of the rates that will prevail in the future for short- and long-term bonds. Suppose we use the forward interest rate to represent the investor's best guess of what the future short-term interest rate will actually be. For example, $_{t+1}r_1$ would represent the one-period interest rate that is expected to prevail one period from now. We can express this algebraically as

$$_{t+i}r_1 = E\ (_{t+i}R_1) \tag{9-8}$$

where $_{t+i}R_1$ represents the interest rate on a one-period loan which will be observed in period $_{t+i}$, or i periods from now, and E represents the market's best guess or expectation.

The unbiased expectations theory says that the investor in this example will find that he or she is indifferent between the option of buying five one-period bonds or one five-period bond if the following relationship holds between the long-term rate $_tR_5$ and the forward rates:

$$(1 + {}_tR_5)^5 = (1 + {}_tR_1)(1 + {}_{t+1}r_1) \cdots (1 + {}_{t+4}r_1) \qquad (9\text{-}9)$$

This equation is merely an example of the more general equation in (9-1). But now the forward rates are equal to the expected future short-term rates. If Eqs. (9-8) and (9-9) hold, then the investor will not expect to be able to gain by choosing either of these two options. More generally, if Eqs. (9-1) and (9-8) hold for any maturity or any value of N, not just 5, then each of the three options open to the investor will be expected to yield the same payoff. This means that an investor cannot buy a bond with a maturity of 5 years and sell it or cash it in at maturity and expect to earn more than he or she could by buying five 1-year bonds at yearly intervals. This is what Eqs. (9-1) and (9-8) say.

It is important to see the incentive that the investor faces and the reaction of the market as a whole to his or her actions if Eq. (9-1) does not hold but Eq. (9-8) does, or when forward rates equal expected future rates. If, for example, a large number of investors believe the left-hand side of Eq. (9-1) exceeds the right-hand side, then these investors will shift investments from short-term bonds to long-term bonds because they can expect to earn a higher return by doing so. This substitution from short- to long-term bonds will increase the price and decrease the yield of long-term bonds. This process will continue until Eq. (9-1) is satisfied. As a result, the incentive to substitute between bonds of different maturities forces yields into an equilibrium where long-term rates reflect the market's expectations of future short-term rates and Eq. (9-1) holds. The process of substitution and the equilibrium to which it leads are represented by Eqs. (9-1) and (9-8). These equations constitute the unbiased expectations theory of the term structure.[1]

A useful way to interpret each of the three theories of the term structure of interest rates which we will deal with pertains to the implication of each theory for the shape of the yield curve. Each theory offers a different explanation for upward-, flat-, and downward-sloping yield curves. The *unbiased expectations theory* says that long-term interest rates are determined by the market's expectations of future short-term interest rates. Therefore, this theory implies that the market's expectations account for the slope of the yield curve. For example, the unbiased expectations theory suggests that the upward-sloping yield curve which existed in 1975, shown in Figure 9-1,

---

[1] Irving Fisher first articulated the substance of the unbiased expectations theory in "Appreciation and Interest," *Publications of the American Economic Association*, vol. XI (August 1896), pp. 23–29 and 91–92. It was further refined by J. R. Hicks in *Value and Capital*, Oxford University Press, London, 1946.

implies that the market expected future short-term interest rates to increase. By contrast, the downward-sloping yield curve observed in 1974 reflected expectations that short-term rates would decline.

The unbiased expectations theory can be an accurate description of the term structure only if there are no barriers or costs to substituting between bonds with different maturities. If it is costly to execute transactions, that is to buy and sell bonds, then when Eqs. (9-1) and (9-8) hold, the returns from buying one new one-period bond *each year* will have to be lower than the returns from buying a *single* long-term bond. This is because Eq. (9-1) ignores these costs of transacting. Such costs include brokers fees and the cost of time spent in arranging the transaction. In most markets these costs are reasonably small and therefore Eqs. (9-1) and (9-8) can still potentially be good approximations of the actual relationship between yields.

The unbiased expectations theory is an example of the perfect substitution view of the way financial markets work. Bonds of different maturities are viewed as perfect substitutes for one another. As a result, the difference in their prices should be totally determined by the differences in the market's expectations for the time periods they cover. Any other factors should be irrelevant because investors will substitute between bonds until an equilibrium which reflects only expectations is reached.

But there are alternative explanations of the term structure of interest rates, where bonds of different maturities are not viewed as perfect substitutes. The polar extreme alternative is the segmentation view. We will examine this theory next.

The Segmentation Theory of the Term Structure

Some people have argued that the markets for bonds of different maturity are segmented, just as the markets for securities which differ by tax treatment or risk are sometimes thought to be segmented.[2] As in these other cases, the fundamental implication of the *segmentation theory* of the term structure is that the yield at each maturity is determined by the relative strength of supply and demand for bonds at that maturity. If, for example, a large number of borrowers wants to issue bonds with maturities of 10 years, but there are few investors who want to purchase such bonds, then the promised yield will be driven up until there is an equilibrium between supply and demand at that maturity. As a result, in this theory the shape of the yield curve represents the relative strength of supply and demand for particular maturities. A downward-sloping yield curve means a shortage of demand in the shorter maturities. On the other hand, an upward-sloping yield curve means a shortage of demand for the longer maturities.

The segmentation theory of the term structure, like all examples of the

---

[2] One of the original proponents of the theory was J. M. Culbertson, "The Term Structure of Interest Rates," *Quarterly Journal of Economics*, vol. LXXI (November 1957), pp. 489–504.

segmentation theory, requires that there be few investors who are willing or able to substitute between securities of different maturity. Without such arbitragers in the market, yield spreads could deviate widely from the market's expectations of future short-term rates. But if investors are willing to substitute between maturities when they expect such substitution will be profitable, then yield spreads that are inconsistent with the market's expectations of future rates will not persist. Therefore, the segmentation theory in its strongest form hinges on the existence of barriers which prevent or discourage investors from any substitution across maturities.

One reason investors refrain from such substitution is to reduce or hedge some of the risks of their portfolios. This motive is most often attributed to financial institutions, though it may really be applied to other corporations and individuals as well. But financial institutions generally have some of the best opportunities for arbitraging differences in yields and, therefore, their motives are of particular interest. The type of risk that financial institutions are often thought to hedge is the risk of losses incurred because liabilities and assets do not have maturities that are matched. When an institution totally matches the maturities of both sides of its balance sheet, it is said to be in a hedged position.

To see more precisely what the risk is that the hedge eliminates we need to more carefully consider our example of how best to invest funds with a 5-year maturity. What we have failed to consider as yet is the risk involved in the choice. One option is to purchase a bond with a maturity shorter than 5 years, say 1 year, and purchase another one when that one matures. The risk involved here is that interest rates could fall below expectations at the end of a year and the investor would stand to lose income on the second bond. Another option is to purchase a bond with a maturity longer than 5 years and sell it prior to maturity. But the price prior to maturity will fluctuate with market interest rates. The risk is that the price could be very low at the time when the bond must be sold. The strategy which eliminates all such risk is to buy a bond with a maturity of exactly 5 years. The bond will be redeemed at maturity and the maturity value is *known with certainty*. Therefore this type of risk can be eliminated by matching the maturities of assets and liabilities.

If most market participants perfectly hedge the maturity risks of their balance sheets, then there will be relatively little substitution between maturities. The segmentation theory argues that investors will choose to hedge *regardless of how attractive* the opportunities for substitution may become. Essentially the theory says that the incentive to avoid risk by hedging will be so strong that it will dominate any incentive to seek profits by substitution. A less extreme version of the theory asserts that if the incentive to substitute is large enough to compensate the investor for the risk borne, then substitution will take place. This represents a compromise between the pure segmentation and unbiased expectations theories and is known as the preferred habitat theory of the term structure. We will examine this next.

The Preferred Habitat Theory of the Term Structure

The *preferred habitat theory* is a blend of the unbiased expectations theory and the segmentation theory in that it takes into account what each of those theories omits. The unbiased expectations theory ignores the risk that investors expose themselves to when they substitute across maturities. On the other hand, the segmentation theory ignores the expected profits of such substitution and concentrates exclusively on the incentive to avoid risk. But we know that investors will bear risk if properly compensated to do so. Therefore, there is a third theory of the term structure which incorporates the premiums that investors demand to bear risk.

The basic tenet of the preferred habitat theory is that each investor has a preferred maturity or habitat at which he or she would like to borrow or lend.[3] The maturity is determined by the nature of the business he or she is engaged in. For example, if the borrower wants to borrow money to build a factory with a long, useful life, he or she will have a natural preference for a bond with a long maturity. Similarly, if a financial institution needs to obtain funds to lend to a customer for 6 months, it will generally seek to borrow for 6 months. The preferred habitat theory asserts that if the total amount of desired borrowing is equal to the total amount of desired lending *at each maturity*, then the term structure will be determined by the unbiased expectations theory. Because there is no imbalance between supply and demand at any maturity, investors at each maturity demand an interest rate which is fair, based on the market's expectation of future interest rates. All investors avoid risk because they are all borrowing or lending at their desired maturity; hence, no premiums for risk are reflected in the term structure.

However, it is unlikely that total desired lending is very often exactly equal to desired borrowing at each maturity. The more likely possibility is that there are imbalances at most all maturities most of the time. To see what happens when such imbalances arise we can return to the example of an investor with a desire to invest for 5 years. Suppose there is an excess supply of such investable funds with this 5-year maturity. This means that with a 5-year interest rate which is consistent with the unbiased expectations theory, there is a shortage of bonds with 5-year maturities. Therefore, the investor must lower the interest rate he or she is willing to accept for 5-year bonds until the supply of such bonds increases or else try to obtain bonds with either a shorter or longer maturity. The question at issue is: What happens to the prices and yields on bonds with different maturities when this kind of imbalance develops?

The answer to this question is that interest rates will adjust until the investor in the example, and the market as a whole, are no longer willing to substitute between maturities. If investors are averse to risk, they will demand a premium to substitute between maturities. The interest rates on

[3] See Franco Modigliani and Richard Sutch, "Innovations in Interest Rate Policy," *American Economic Review*, vol. LVI (May 1966), pp. 178–197.

bonds of different maturities will adjust to a new equilibrium where investors will be compensated for bearing the risk of being out of their preferred maturity. In this example, the investor will have to pay a price for a 5-year bond which provides an inducement to some borrower to alter his or her desired maturity. Suppose, for example, that there is another participant in the market who wants to borrow $100,000, but with a maturity of 10 years. If this person borrows by issuing a 5-year bond now and another 5 years later, the risk is that in 5 years interest rates will increase more than expected and the costs will go up for the second bond. The lender will demand to be paid a premium by the investor to accept this risk of fluctuations in interest rates. This premium will take the form of a lower interest rate on the 5-year bond than on the 10-year bond.

This example provides an illustration of how markets work in the aggregate. If there is an excess supply or demand for bonds at any particular maturity, then an incentive has to be provided to induce investors to shift maturities and eliminate the excess supply or demand. The greater the excess supply or demand, the greater the premiums will have to be, because more investors will be exposed to more risk of fluctuation in interest rates or bond prices. The market will be in equilibrium when the premiums offered in the term structure are just sufficient to induce enough investors out of their preferred habitats to equilibrate desired borrowing and lending at each maturity.

This preferred habitat theory of the term structure can be represented by Eq. (9-1) and a modified version of Eq. (9-8). Equation (9-8) requires that the forward rates exactly equal the market's expectations of future short-term rates. But now we know that the forward rates can differ from expected future rates. In equilibrium, the difference will be a compensation for risk which equilibrates desired lending and borrowing at each maturity. We can represent this premium, which is referred to as a liquidity premium, with the symbol $_{t+i}L_1$. This represents the liquidity premium for a one-period loan beginning in period $t + i$. More specifically, it is the premium demanded by the market to stretch its maturity one period, from $t + i - 1$ periods to $t + i$ periods. Under the preferred habitat theory, each forward rate is equal to the sum of the market's expectation of what the future interest rate will be *and* the market's liquidity premium:

$$_{t+i}r_1 = E(_{t+i}R_1) + _{t+i}L_1 \tag{9-10}$$

The implication of the preferred habitat theory is that the yield curve does not necessarily give a clear signal of the market's expectations of future interest rates. The preferred habitat theory implies that the yield curve is determined both by the market's expectations and by the imbalances in preferred habitats. If those imbalances are large, then premiums demanded to bring about an equilibrium will also be large. If those imbalances are small, then the premiums will be small and the observed yield curve will be determined largely by expectations.

For example, suppose that there is a pattern in the liquidity premiums such that the longer the maturity, the larger the premium. The liquidity premiums would then satisfy the following inequalities:

$$0 < {}_{t+1}L_1 < {}_{t+2}L_1 < \cdots < {}_{t+N}L_1 \qquad (9\text{-}11)$$

If liquidity premiums increased with maturity in this manner, then the yield curve would tend to have a positive slope. This means that even if the market expected that short-term interest rates would remain constant, the yield curve would be upward sloping. The upward slope would be a reflection of the increasing liquidity premiums. You can see this if you substitute Eq. (9-10) into Eq. (9-1) for bonds with longer maturities. The fact that the liquidity premiums are increasing will cause rates to increase with maturity even if expected future rates are all the same.

We can illustrate this with an example. To keep the example simple we will deal with only a 5-year time period. Suppose that the market expects future short-term rates to be constant at the current rate of 6 percent. But the market also requires the following liquidity premiums:

$$\begin{array}{ll} {}_{t+1}L_1 = .01 & {}_{t+3}L_1 = .03 \\ {}_{t+2}L_1 = .02 & {}_{t+4}L_1 = .04 \end{array}$$

Using Eq. (9-10) and these premiums, we can compute the forward rates beginning 1, 2, 3, and 4 years from now as follows:

$$ {}_{t+1}r_1 = .06 + .01 = .07 $$

$$ {}_{t+2}r_1 = .06 + .02 = .08 $$

$$ {}_{t+3}r_1 = .06 + .03 = .09 $$

$$ {}_{t+4}r_1 = .06 + .04 = .10 $$

Now we can use these data to compute the current rates on bonds with maturities of 2 to 5 years:

$$\begin{aligned} {}_tR_2 &= [(1.06)\,(1.07)]^{1/2} - 1 \\ &= .065 \\ {}_tR_3 &= [(1.06)\,(1.07)\,(1.08)]^{1/3} - 1 \\ &= .07 \\ {}_tR_4 &= [(1.06)\,(1.07)\,(1.08)\,(1.09)]^{1/4} - 1 \\ &= .075 \\ {}_tR_5 &= [(1.06)\,(1.07)\,(1.08)\,(1.09)\,(1.10)]^{1/5} - 1 \\ &= .08 \end{aligned}$$

We can see from this example that the yield curve will increase if expected future rates are constant but liquidity premiums are increasing. We can also infer that if liquidity premiums are increasing and the yield curve is flat, the market must expect future short-term rates to fall.

Some people have argued that liquidity premiums do in fact satisfy the inequalities in Eq. (9-11).[4] The reason that they use to support this argument is that they believe that lenders predominantly prefer to lend short rather than long. Therefore, longer premiums have to be offered to bear the additional risk of longer maturity loans. Others argue that there are enough investors with little or no risk aversion that liquidity premiums are really equal to or close to zero. This view contends that the unbiased expectations theory of the term structure is essentially accurate and that the yield curve represents the market's expectations of future short-term rates.

Most of the available evidence supports the view that there are liquidity premiums in the term structure of interest rates. Some of the original tests for these liquidity premiums conducted during the 1960s left considerable doubt as to which theory was essentially correct.[5] But, more recently, tests of the ability of long-term interest rates to forecast future short-term interest rates have made it almost impossible to escape the conclusion that liquidity premiums do exist. However, there remains little convincing evidence on the size and pattern of liquidity premiums over time. Next, we will examine some of the evidence on the forecasting ability of long-term rates.

INTEREST-RATE FORECASTS AND THE TERM STRUCTURE

Thus far we have learned that unless the term structure of interest rates is completely explained by the segmentation theory, then the yield curve incorporates the market's expectations of future short-term interest rates. This means that long-term interest rates are determined, at least in part, by expectations. We know that the yield curve does not provide a perfect clue to the market's expectations as long as liquidity premiums are incorporated in the term structure. But, it is fruitful to ask what we can learn about expectations by studying yield curves. In this section of this chapter we will examine three aspects of this question. First, we will examine whether the market efficiently incorporates information about future interest rates into long-term interest rates. Second, we will examine various theories of the way expectations are formed. Third, we will explore how we can make practical use of yield curves as forecasts of future rates in financial decisions.

The Efficient Markets Hypothesis and the Term Structure of Interest Rates

Anytime the financial market incorporates a best guess of a future event into a price or interest rate we can ask whether, in so doing, the market efficiently

[4] This was originally argued by Hicks, op. cit., pp. 146–147. He referred to this as "normal backwardation."
[5] See James C. Van Horne, *Financial Market Rates and Flows*, Prentice-Hall, Englewood Cliffs, N.J., 1978, for a review of the historical development of empirical evidence on this subject.

uses available information. We first explored this concept of market efficiency in Chapter Six, where the basic idea behind the hypothesis was explained. Then in Chapter Eight we examined the hypothesis that nominal interest rates efficiently incorporate available information about future inflation rates. In this chapter we will briefly examine the hypothesis that long-term interest rates efficiently incorporate all available information about the values of future short-term interest rates.

In order to see exactly what the efficient markets hypothesis regarding the term structure is, let us temporarily suppose that the unbiased expectations theory of the term structure holds. This means that the forward rates which are implied by the yield curve observed at any point in time represent the market's expectation of the future short-term interest rate, or as stated in Eq. (9-8),

$$_{t+i}r_1 = E(_{t+i}R_1)$$

The efficient markets hypothesis then implies that if we try to forecast future short-term interest rates with forward rates computed from yield curves, these forward rates ought to provide the best forecasts we can find. There should exist no other mechanism, based on publicly available data, which provides a better forecast of the future short-term interest rates. For if the market is efficient, then any such forecasting mechanism should be incorporated into the forecast that is in the yield curve.

Eugene Fama has conducted a test of this hypothesis by comparing the forecasting ability of forward rates computed from the yield curve with alternative forecasts of short-term interest rates.[6] One very simple alternative is to assume that short-term interest rates are expected to remain constant for one period ahead or that the best forecast of tomorrow's short-term rate is today's short-term rate. Fama shows that the forward rates computed from yield curves provide forecasts which are *inferior* to the forecasts derived from this simple alternative forecast of the behavior of the short-term interest rate. At first glance, this might seem to be damning evidence against market efficiency. But it must be remembered that the forward rate should be equal to the market's best forecast of the corresponding future short-term interest rate only if the market views securities of different maturities as perfect substitutes; that is, if there are no liquidity premiums. And if there are liquidity premiums in the term structure, then forecasts of future short-term rates provided by the forward rates will be in error, on average, due to the existence of these liquidity premiums.

In order to develop more satisfactory tests of market efficiency Fama attempted to measure the liquidity premiums present in the term structure of interest rates, and extract those premiums from the forward rates in order to derive the market's true forecast of the future short-term interest rate. He

[6] See Eugene F. Fama, "Forward Rates as Predictors of Future Spot Rates," *Journal of Financial Economics,* vol. 3 (1976), pp. 361–377.

then compared this forecast to the simple alternative forecast of the future short-term rates based on the current short-term rate. Fama concluded from these types of comparisons that the forecasts of future short-term rates, which are embedded in the long-term rate, do as well as the simple alternative forecasting model. But the performance of the term-structure model is not noticeably superior to the performance of the alternative model with which it is compared. This is evidence, albeit weak evidence, in favor of market efficiency. The fundamental difficulty involved is in deriving accurate measures of the liquidity premiums demanded by the market. Thus far, no very satisfactory measures of these premiums have been devised. Without better measures of liquidity premiums it may well prove difficult to devise better tests of this dimension of market efficiency.

An alternative way to evaluate whether long-term interest rates efficiently incorporate information about future short-term rates pertains to the behavior through time of yield on debt securities with different maturities. We should recall from our original discussion of the efficient markets hypothesis that the weak form of the hypothesis implies that the past value of the price of a share of stock should be no clue to the future level of that price. That is, the best forecast of tomorrow's stock price is today's. The same argument applies to the yields on long-term bonds such as 20-year U.S. Treasury bonds. But it does not apply to short-term Treasury debt, such as 90-day Treasury bills.

To see why this is true we need to examine the difference between long-term bonds and short-term bonds. We will use 20-year and 90-day Treasury obligations as our example. Remember that what we observe in the market are the yields on both types of securities at discreet intervals. In terms of the notation we have used in this chapter, we observe the yield on 20-year bonds at time t, then $t + 1$, then $t + 2$, and so forth. The interval between these dates is generally a week or a month or a quarter, but it could be any interval which you wanted to choose. In an efficient market, the yield on a 20-year bond at time t, $_{t+2}R_{20}$, will incorporate all information known to the market pertaining to the interval from t to $t + 20$, that is, for the next 20 years. But the interest rate on the 20-year bond will not necessarily provide an efficient forecast of a 20-year rate observed at time period $t + 1$. This is because the periods of time which these two rates cover do not perfectly overlap. This distinction between the time periods covered by two consecutive 20-year interest rates is illustrated in Figure 9-3. The figure shows that the periods covered by each rate differ by a single period at both the beginning and the end of the 20-year period.

The relevant question is whether this difference in periods of coverage influences the ability of the current interest rate to forecast the interest rate in the next period. Suppose that we are actually dealing with interest rates on 20-year bonds which are observed 1 month apart. Then the lack of overlap amounts to 2 months out of 240 months in the total 20-year interval. In this case, the lack of overlap is a minor problem. But suppose we are talking

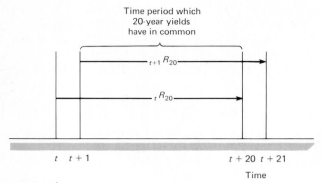

FIGURE 9-3
This figure shows the overlap in time included in the maturities of two 20-year bonds when the yields on these bonds are observed one period apart.

about 90-day Treasury bills. Now, out of the 3-month maturity on two bills observed a month apart, there are only 2 months in common or 60 out of 90 days. As a result, one would not expect the current 90-day bill rate to predict the future 90-day bill rate simply because, to a large degree, each is covering a different time period.

The actual empirical evidence on the predictive ability for 20-year bonds and 90-day bills confirms these arguments. If we try to predict future rates on 20-year bonds, we find that we cannot significantly improve the predictive ability of the current rate by adding past rates to the prediction as the efficient markets hypothesis implies. But the current rate on 90-day Treasury bills is not as good a predictor of the future 90-day Treasury bill rate. Here, past rates do add to the power of the current rate as a predictor as the argument above suggests.[7] The available evidence therefore suggests, that like stock prices, long-term interest rates efficiently incorporate publicly available information. This is further evidence that financial markets efficiently use all *publicly* available information.

Theories of the Formation of Expectations

Except in the case of the pure segmentation theory, an important determinant of the term structure of interest rates is the market's expectations of future short-term interest rates. This has caused a number of scholars to try to explain how the market forms its expectations of future rates. Various theories have been proposed about the way the market uses past information to form its expectations and these theories have been tested to see which is the best explanation of the available data on the term structure. This issue of

---

[7] For evidence which is consistent with this position, see Fama, op. cit., and Tim S. Campbell, "On the Extent of Segmentation in the Municipal Securities Market," *Journal of Money, Credit and Banking*, vol. 12 (February 1980), pp. 71–83.

how expectations are formed is an extremely important question in almost all branches of economics. Expectations of the future influence almost all economic decisions, and it is therefore exceptionally important to have some systematic understanding of how these expectations are formed.

There are two principal hypotheses about the formation of expectations which are referred to as "extrapolative" and "regressive" expectations. These two hypotheses are not mutually exclusive. In fact, many people argue that a combination of the two is the best available explanation of how interest-rate expectations are formed. Extrapolative expectations simply mean that in the short run (i.e., for interest rates which will be realized just a few months in the future) the market extrapolates its current experience; that is, it expects currently observed patterns to continue. But in the long run (i.e., for rates well beyond a few months in the future) the market expects the rate to regress toward a "normal" rate of interest based on historical experience. This normal interest rate is usually described as a weighted average of past observed interest rates where the weights decline with time. This implies that more recent experience has a larger impact on the market's concept of the normal rate than does less recent experience. When the regressive and extrapolative hypotheses are combined, expectations are thought to be extrapolative in the short run and regressive in the long run.

In a sequence of studies published in the late 1960s and early 1970s Franco Modigliani, Richard Sutch, and Robert Shiller argued that a term structure relationship could be constructed based on both the theories of regressive and extrapolative expectations.[8] This relationship can be expressed in the following algebraic form:

$$_tR_L = \sum_{i=0}^{m} w_i \,_{t-i}R_s \qquad (9\text{-}12)$$

where the subscripts L and s represent long and short maturities. Equation (9-12) says that the current long-term rate (e.g., the 20-year Treasury bond rate) can be expressed as a weighted average of past short-term interest rates (e.g., the 90-day Treasury bill rate). In their formulation, the combination of regressive and extrapolative expectations resulted in a particular form of Eq. (9-12) where the weights w_i follow a pattern which looks like an inverted U, as illustrated in Figure 9-4. The inverted U shape for the weights indicates that very recent short-term interest rates have little effect. This is because, for short maturities, the regressive and extrapolative expectations tend to cancel each other out. But as the time lag involved increases, extrapolative expectations become unimportant and the weights reflect only regressive expectations. Regressive expectations place less emphasis on events further removed in the past; hence the weights gradually decline as illustrated in the figure.

---

[8] See Modigliani and Sutch, op. cit., and Franco Modigliani and Robert T. Shiller, "Inflation, Rational Expectations and the Term Structure of Interest Rates," *Journal of Political Economy* (Feburary 1973), pp. 12–43.

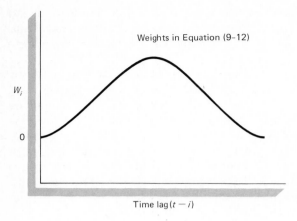

Weights in Equation (9-12)

W_i

0

Time lag $(t - i)$

FIGURE 9-4
Weights in Eq. (9-12) which are
consistent with regressive and
extrapolative expectations. The
weights are small for short lags,
then rise and fall again as the time
lag increases.

Modigliani, Sutch, and Shiller have amassed a substantial amount of
statistical evidence which purports to show that the actual relationship between the current long-term interest rates and past short-term interest rates
is the one predicted by Eq. (9-12), where the weights have the inverted U
shape. They argue that this is evidence which shows that the market's expectations are a combination of regressive and extrapolative elements. Recently,
however, there has been substantial criticism of the empirical evidence presented by Modigliani et al.[9] The essence of the criticism is that it is difficult if
not impossible to produce statistically reliable estimates of the weights in
Eq. (9-12), hence difficult to confirm or reject the hypothesized inverted U
shape. A development of the statistical problems involved here is beyond the
scope of this treatment. But the important point about this controversy is that
if the criticism is correct, it will be difficult to ever develop reliable evidence
as to whether the market combines regressive and extrapolative expectations. This means that despite the plausibility of the argument, for practical
purposes this may well be an untestable hypothesis.

It should be recalled, however, that whatever mechanism best characterizes how the market forms expectations, if the market is efficient, those
expectations are incorporated in the current interest rate or price of the asset.
Again, the implication is that long-term interest rates incorporate the market's best forecast of future rates, regardless of how these expectations are
formed.

The Usefulness of the Yield Curve

It is exceptionally important to understand, as a participant in financial
markets, what the yield curve is telling you. The yield curve is often a rather
maligned device because individuals ask too much of it. People often think

[9] See Llad Phillips and John Pippenger, "The Term Structure of Interest Rates in the MIT-PENN-SSRC Model:
Reality or Illusion?" *Journal of Money, Credit and Banking*, vol. 11 (May 1979), pp. 151–164.

that the yield curve is supposed to give them a forecast of future short-term interest rates. That is, they think of the yield curve as a forecasting device that can be used by individuals, business firms, or financial institutions to construct estimates of future rates. But we have learned that the yield curve only has this practical use if it is determined by the unbiased expectations theory. Only then will the forward rates implied by the yield curve represent the market's forecast of future short-term interest rates. But if, as the available evidence suggests, there are liquidity premiums in the term structure, then without good measures of these premiums, the market's forecast will be difficult to extract.

The nagging question which this leaves is: Of what use is the theory of the term structure? The answer is that term structure theory explains how prices and yields on assets which differ by maturity are determined in a competitive market. And it can be used as a practical tool in the following manner. An investor with his or her own forecast of future rates in hand can compute forward rates from the observed yield curve and compare these forward rates to his or her independent estimate of future rates. If the difference is large enough to compensate the investor for the perceived risk involved in betting on future rates, then an investment outside of a preferred habitat will look profitable. This is the substitution process at work, which leads to liquidity premiums that are an equilibrium compensation for the risk of betting on future interest rates. The yield curve therefore provides a standard of comparison by which an individual can tell whether an investment across maturities is profitable. In this sense, the yield curve is useful. And it is because it is useful in this way, that the term structure can be explained with the theories developed in this chapter.

INNOVATIONS IN DEBT CONTRACTING FOR DIFFERENT MATURITIES

A number of innovations have developed in American financial markets which tend to increase the possible options for debt contracting across different maturities. Two of these innovations will be discussed in this final section of the chapter. The first is the development of a futures market in Treasury bills. The second is the advent of floating-rate loans. Both of these represent relatively new types of financial contracts which increase the options available to participants in the financial markets.

The Treasury Bill Futures Market

Futures markets are not a recent innovation in the U.S. economy. Futures markets in various commodities have existed for some years. The basic purpose of the futures market is to provide a mechanism for reducing the risk to which producers of commodities, particularly agricultural commodities, are exposed. The wheat farmer, for example, may contract for the sale of his or her wheat prior to harvest and thereby eliminate uncertainty about the price of the product. The farmer pays a price for this, of course, in that a speculator must be paid to bear the risk of that price fluctuation.

One relatively new element in the futures markets in the United States is the development of a market for futures contracts in Treasury bills. Since January 1976 a futures market in 3-month Treasury bills has operated on the International Monetary Market of the Chicago Mercantile Exchange.[10] The futures market in Treasury bills performs essentially the same functions as a futures market in a commodity. Individuals with funds which will be available at a future time, say 6 months distant, can contract now to purchase a Treasury bill in 6 months at a prespecified price. On the other side of the transaction, the seller of the futures contract guarantees to deliver a Treasury bill at the prespecified price, 6 months hence. The seller of the contract bears the risk of fluctuations in the price of Treasury bills because he or she must acquire a Treasury bill, regardless of the price, to satisfy the contract.

The interesting feature of the Treasury bill futures market is that investing in the market, that is, selling contracts, is essentially the same as betting on future interest rates by buying Treasury bills with different maturities. To see that this is the case suppose we entered the futures market and promised to sell a 3-month Treasury bill, with a maturity value of $10,000, 6 months from now at a price of $9,500. The $9,500 is referred to as the price of the contract. But notice that it is not a price which we pay today, as is the price of a Treasury bill. Instead, it is the price at which we promise to deliver a Treasury bill in the future. We will break even on this bet if the actual price of Treasury bills 6 months from now is exactly equal to the price we promise, or $9,500. If the price is higher, we will lose and if it is lower, we will make a profit on the bet. We can restate the nature of our gamble in terms of yield rather than price, as follows. At the price of $9,500, a 3-month Treasury bill would have to yield 21 percent. The yield is computed as the interest rate r, which solves the following present value equation:

$$\$9,500 = \frac{\$10,000}{(1 + r/4)}$$

Therefore, we are betting that interest rates on 3-month bills will be greater than 21 percent 6 months from now when we promise to supply a bill at a price of $9,500. In effect, this interest rate is the forward rate that we defined at the beginning of this chapter. We can observe this rate directly in the futures market, but we can only infer it from the yield curve.

The same bet can be made by buying a 9-month Treasury bill and selling it in 6 months. The investor would expect these investments to pay the same return if the forward rate for a 3-month Treasury bill 6 months in the future,

[10] For a more detailed description of the market, see Albert E. Burger, Richard W. Lang, and Robert H. Rasche, "The Treasury Bill Futures Market and Market Expectations of Interest Rates," *Review*, Federal Reserve Bank of St. Louis, vol. 59 (June 1977), pp. 2–9.

computed as in Eq. (9-4), were exactly 21 percent. Therefore, the Treasury bill futures market provides a vehicle for investing on the basis of future interest rate expectations, just as does substituting between different maturities.

Another way to see this relationship is the following. Suppose we consider two Treasury bills, one maturing in 6 months and one in 9 months, as well as a futures contract with a 6-month maturity. Suppose the price of the 6-month bill is P_6 and that of the 9-month bill is P_9. We are interested in determining what the price of the futures contract will be if there are no profitable opportunities to substitute between the bills themselves and the futures contract. We will represent this equilibrium price by the symbol P^*. In our example, this means that $P^* = \$9,500$. Suppose that an investor buys the 9-month bill for the price of P_9 and then sells a futures contract to obtain a certain price for the bill in 6 months of P^*. He or she now holds what is the equivalent of a 6-month bill. The only difference is that the certain payment to be received in 6 months is now P^* instead of the $10,000 face value of the bill. If the annualized yield demanded by the market is, say, 16 percent, the value today of the 6-month Treasury bill is determined according to the present value equation as follows:

$$P_6 = \$10,000 \Big/ \left(1 + \frac{.16}{2}\right) \qquad (9\text{-}13)$$

But the value of the 9-month bill sold in the futures market must be such that it gives the same 6-month yield as the 6-month bill:

$$P_9 = P^*/(1 + .16/2) \qquad (9\text{-}14)$$

If the price in the futures market of the 3-month bill to be delivered 6 months hence is set, as in our example, at $9,500, then we can use this equation to determine the price of the 9-month bond today. It is

$$\$8,796 = \$9,500 \Big/ \left(1 + \frac{.16}{2}\right)$$

We can restate this in a way that emphasizes the relationship between the futures market and the market for Treasury bills of different maturities by combining Eqs. (9-13) and (9-14). Taken together, these two equations imply that

$$\frac{\$10,000}{P_6} = \frac{P^*}{P_9} \qquad (9\text{-}15)$$

This means that the price of the 6-month bill must be in the same proportion to its maturity value as the price of the 9-month bill is to the price of the futures contract. If this were not true, then there would be sure profits to be made by either buying or selling futures contracts and 9-month Treasury bills, depending upon the direction of the imbalance. The profit opportunities ensure that, in equilibrium, the market will price futures contracts according to Eq. (9-15).

This relationship will be only approximately true if there are costs involved in buying and selling Treasury bills and futures contracts. In a recent empirical study of whether the actual prices of futures contracts in Treasury bills conform to this relationship, Rendlemen and Carabini[11] concluded that there were some persistent but small opportunities for profitable trading between Treasury bills and futures. But they found that the opportunities were sufficiently small that if you included all of what they counted as the "indirect costs" for most market participants of conducting such trading, that the opportunities would not be profitable. In other words, Eq. (9-15) is a very close approximation of the actual relationship between Treasury bill prices and the prices of Treasury bill futures.

Floating-Rate Loans

Another relatively recent development in financial markets is the advent of the *floating-rate loan*. This is a multiperiod loan contract where the interest rate is adjusted each period with the changes in short-term interest rates. This type of debt agreement has a long-term maturity just like a standard long-term bond, but unlike a standard long-term bond, the interest rate is not fixed for the entire maturity. This kind of debt agreement has become common practice for loans granted to commercial and industrial customers by commercial banks. For example, during 1977 for loans with original maturities of 1 year or less, approximately 60 percent of the commercial and industrial loans by larger banks in the United States (representing about half of the total loan volume in that year) were made with floating interest rates. The normal mechanism used by these banks to adjust the rates on their floating-rate loans is to tie the interest rate to the prime rate. A particular loan customer will therefore have a loan which is priced at, say, 1 percent above the prime rate. Therefore, when the prime rate changes, so will the interest rate on that particular loan.

Banks have been particularly interested in this type of debt contract because most of the funds they obtain have very short maturities. Therefore, if they extend long-term loans at fixed interest rates, they bear considerable risk of fluctuations in interest rates. As changes in short-term interest rates have become more extreme in recent years, banks have become less willing to bear this type of risk without substantial additional compensation. As a result, the predominant form of the loans extended by the larger banks throughout the country has become the floating-rate loan.

This type of debt contract has also become more common in other markets. The variable-rate mortgage (VRM) is another example of this type of

[11] See Richard J. Rendlemen and Christopher E. Carabini, "The Efficiency of the Treasury Bill Futures Market," *Journal of Finance*, vol. 34 (September 1979), pp. 895–914.

debt agreement. Here the mortgage rate that the borrower pays fluctuates with an index of the cost of funds to savings and loans. This type of contract is particularly attractive to savings and loans for the same reason it is attractive to commercial banks—savings and loans obtain most of their funds at very short maturities from savers. When they make mortgage loans with fixed rates, they are exposed to substantial interest-rate risk. One way to reduce this risk has been to adjust the terms of the mortgage with fluctuations in their costs of funds. Thus far, however, the VRM has met with only limited success. This topic will be discussed further in Parts Three and Four of this book.

SUMMARY

In this chapter we learned how debt securities, which differ only by their term to maturity, are priced. This relationship between debt securities of different maturity is referred to as the term structure of interest rates. We discovered that the pricing of debt securities of different maturities entails another application of the theory of pricing of risky assets which we explored in Chapter Four. In essence, the prices and yields of long-term securities are determined by the market's expectation of future short-term rates, the risk involved in betting on future short-term rates, and the amount of risk aversion of market participants.

We found in this chapter that before we could understand the theories which have been offered to explain the term structure, we first had to learn how to quantify the relationship between long- and short-term interest rates. To do this we relied on the use of forward interest rates. And we quantified the relationship between any long-term rate and the sequence of forward rates corresponding to the same time period. This relationship serves as the foundation for our entire development of the term structure.

Next we considered three theories of term structure. Each theory presents a distinct explanation of the relationship between long- and short-term interest rates. The first theory, known as the unbiased expectations theory, says that the forward rates in the term structure relationship represent the market's expectation of future short-term rates. This theory hinges on the hypothesis that investors will substitute between maturities until the expected return from all maturities are the same. In effect, it assumes that investors are not averse to the risk that they bear in performing such substitution. The second theory is the extreme alternative to the first. This theory, known as the segmentation theory, says that investors find substitution between maturities to be so risky and they are so averse to this risk that they avoid any substitution out of their preferred maturity. In the segmentation theory forward rates are unimportant because the yield at each maturity is determined by supply and demand at that maturity. The third theory, known as preferred habitat, is a blend of the first two. It argues that individuals will substitute out of their preferred maturities, but only if they are paid a sufficiently large premium to compensate them for the risk they bear. This theory concludes that forward rates equal the sum of the market's expectation of future short-term rates plus the appropriate premiums for bearing risk.

All these theories are concerned with the ability of the market to forecast future short-term interest rates. It is natural then to ask how successfully the market does this and to inquire into how the market forms expectations. We reviewed the available evidence on the efficiency of the market's forecasts of future short-term rates contained in long-term rates. We concluded that the evidence is rather weak on this subject. The evidence does suggest that the market is efficient in the weak sense, but the difficulties involved in measuring liquidity premiums make it difficult to evaluate the forecasting ability of the market. Statistical difficulties also appear to be substantial in drawing definite conclusions on the way the market formulates expectations. One popular theory is that the market extrapolates short-term behavior and regresses to a notion of a normal interest rate in the long term. Unfortunately, there are significant obstacles involved in evaluating this theory with statistical evidence. Yet these negative conclusions pertaining to forecasting ability do not necessarily render the term structure a useless concept. The practical value of the yield curve is that it gives each of us a bench mark against which to compare our forecasts and our price for bearing risk.

Finally, we examined some recent innovations in debt contracting. One of these innovations is the recent development of a futures market in some debt instruments. The futures market provides a market where future borrowing and lending is directly priced. That is, the futures market directly sets the forward rate which we used in examining the term structure. With the development of futures markets it is now possible to bet on future rates either through buying debt securities of different maturities, as was discussed in the development of the term structure, or directly in the futures market. Therefore the prices and yields in the two markets should be linked together. In this last section of the chapter we discovered how these two markets are linked.

The other innovation is a way of avoiding the risk of long-term debt securities at fixed interest rates. This is known as the floating-rate loan. In a floating-rate loan the loan itself may have a long maturity, but the interest rate on the loan changes with short-term interest rates. With the increased volatility of interest rates in recent years, floating-rate loans have become considerably more common.

QUESTIONS TO IMPROVE UNDERSTANDING

1   What is the yield curve? What does it mean to say that the yield curve is upward or downward sloping? How does the yield curve usually change over the business cycle? What happened to the yield curve during the 1980 recession? (You won't find the answer to this last question in this book.)

2   Suppose you observed the following current rates from the yield curve: $_tR_{20} = .15$, $_tR_{15} = .14$, $_tR_{10} = .10$, and $_tR_5 = .05$. Compute all the forward rates you can from these current rates.

3   Explain what a forward rate is. Explain why you can use the procedure you did in question 2 to compute forward rates.

4   The unbiased expectations theory of the term structure is often referred to as the perfect substitution theory. Explain the connection between the ideas of perfect substitution and unbiased expectations. How does perfect substitution lead to unbiased expectations?

5   Explain the segmentation theory. Why is this referred to as a case of extreme risk aversion?

6   Compare the interpretations that would be placed on the slope of the yield curve if either the unbiased expectations theory or the segmentation theory were correct. How would these interpretations change if the preferred habitat theory were correct? Why do increasing liquidity premiums lead to a bias toward a positive slope in the yield curve? Explain what this means.

7   In what way is the preferred habitat theory a hybrid of the unbiased expectations and segmentation theories? What does the liquidity premium measure and how does it affect forward rates?

8   The efficient markets hypothesis says that long-term interest rates should make efficient use of public information about future short-term interest rates. What does this mean? Why is it difficult to devise a very satisfactory direct test of this hypothesis?

9   What are extrapolative and regressive expectations? Suppose the market forms its expectations in a combination of an extrapolative and regressive manner. What would this say about the relationship between long-term and short-term interest rates?

10   What is a Treasury bill futures market? How would you make use of the Treasury bill futures market if you know you will have funds to invest in 3 months and you want to reduce the risk about the return you will receive on those funds?

11   Suppose you observe the prices of 6-month and 9-month Treasury bills with maturity values of $10,000. These prices are $9,500 and $9,700, respectively. What can you conclude should be the price of a Treasury bill futures contract with 6 months to maturity? Why?

12   What is a floating-rate loan? Why have they become more popular in recent years?

REFERENCES

Burger, Albert E., Richard W. Lang, and Robert H. Rasche: "The Treasury Bill Futures Market and Market Expectations of Interest Rates," *Review*, Federal Reserve Bank of St. Louis, 59 (June 1977), pp. 2–9.

Campbell, Tim S.: "On the Extent of Segmentation in the Municipal Securities Market," *Journal of Money, Credit and Banking*, 12 (February 1980), pp. 71–83.

Culbertson, J. M.: "The Term Structure of Interest Rates," *Quarterly Journal of Economics*, LXXI (November 1957), pp. 489–504.

Elliott, J. W., and M. E. Echols: "Rational Expectations in a Disequilibrium Model of the Term Structure," *American Economic Review*, LXVI (March 1976), pp. 28–44.

Fama, Eugene R.: "Forward Rates as Predictors of Future Spot Rates," *Journal of Financial Economics*, 3 (1976), pp. 361–377.

———: "Inflation, Uncertainty, and Expected Returns on Treasury Bills," *Journal of Political Economy*, 84 (June 1976), pp. 427–448.

Fisher, Irving: "Appreciation and Interest," *Publications of the American Economic Association*, XI (August 1896), pp. 23–29 and 91–92.

Hicks, J. R.: *Value and Capital*, Oxford University Press, London, 1946.

Meiselman, David: *The Term Structure of Interest Rates*, Prentice-Hall, Inc., Englewood Cliffs, N.J., 1962.

Modigliani, Franco, and Richard Sutch: "Innovations in Interest Rate Policy," *American Economic Review*, LVI (May 1966), pp. 178–197.

———: "Debt Management and the Term Structure of Interest Rates: An Empirical Analysis of Recent Experience," *Journal of Political Economy*, 75, Supplement (August 1967), pp. 569–589.

———, and Robert J. Shiller: "Inflation, Rational Expectations and the Term Structure of Interest Rates," *Journal of Political Economy* (February 1973), pp. 12–43.

Nelson, Charles R.: *The Term Structure of Interest Rates*, Basic Books, Inc., New York, 1972.

Pesando, James E.: "On the Random Walk Characteristics of Short- and Long-term Interest Rates In an Efficient Market," *Journal of Money, Credit and Banking*, XI (November 1979), pp. 457–466.

Phillips, Llad, and John Pippenger: "The Term Structure of Interest Rates in the MIT-PENN-SSRC Model: Reality or Illusion?" *Journal of Money, Credit and Banking*, 11 (May 1979), pp. 151–164.

Rendlemen, Richard J., and Christopher E. Carabini, "The Efficiency of the Treasury Bill Futures Market," *Journal of Finance*, 34 (September 1979), pp. 895–914.

Roll, Richard, *The Behavior of Interest Rates: An Application of the Efficient Market Model to U.S. Treasury Bills*, Basic Books, Inc., New York, 1970.

Van Horne, James C.: *Financial Market Rates and Flows*, Prentice-Hall, Inc., Englewood Cliffs, N.J., 1978.

FINANCIAL MARKETS AND INSTITUTIONS IN THE UNITED STATES

Part Three moves away from the questions of how assets are valued and market interest rates are determined and explores how the markets themselves operate. This part of the book has two basic purposes. The first is to create a taxonomy or organizational structure for financial markets so that it is possible to make sense out of the multitude of different markets which can be observed in the U.S. economy. The second is to survey the various markets which serve the consumer, business, and government sectors of the economy. Part Three is comprised of five chapters. The first of these, Chapter Ten, deals with two of the three basic types of markets which can be found in the United States—auction markets and over-the-counter markets. This chapter explains the general characteristics of these two types of markets and discusses some examples. Chapter Eleven deals with financial intermediation or intermediated markets. Financial intermediaries have come to play an extremely important role in the financial markets of the United States, and this chapter lays out the nature of the services which they provide. This chapter also examines the features of the dominant type of financial intermediary, the commercial bank, and explores a few special issues pertaining to financial intermediaries. The final three chapters draw upon the structure and organization which is established in Chapters Ten and Eleven in order to analyze the contemporary markets serving consumers, businesses, and government. Chapter Twelve focuses on the principal forms of borrowing and lending available to consumers. Chapter Thirteen explores the various forms of corporate financing. And Chapter Fourteen examines the extent and type of borrowing undertaken by federal as well as state and local governments. Each of the chapters in Part Three presents a real-world view of how U.S. financial markets are organized and how they operate.

Chapter Ten

THE ORGANIZATION AND STRUCTURE
OF FINANCIAL MARKETS

To the uninitiated, even to some of the initiated, financial markets look like a maze. There are so many different types of assets, institutions through which these assets are bought and sold, and participants in the markets, that just categorizing these diverse elements is a large task. Therefore, the purpose of this chapter is to explain how financial markets are organized. This chapter focuses on what are called auction and over-the-counter markets. These labels are intended to characterize the way the markets operate. An auction market involves some kind of centralized facility where buyers and sellers, or their commissioned agents, come together to execute trades. Over-the-counter markets differ from auction markets in that there is no centralized mechanism or facility for trading. An over-the-counter market is composed of dealers who stand ready to buy and sell assets with anyone who chooses to trade.

Auction and over-the-counter markets are, by their nature, public markets. Anyone who finds it economical to do so can buy or sell. There is another type of market which we think of as a private market where securities are issued only to a financial intermediary and the intermediary issues its own liabilities in order to supply the funds for these private borrowers. In an intermediated market financial intermediaries perform the function of a dealer, but they also change the nature of the asset being traded. This means that financial intermediaries acquire one type of asset, create a claim on themselves which is a new asset, and sell that asset. Financial intermediaries are by no means restricted to dealing only in such private distributions. They also purchase from public auction or over-the-counter markets.

In this chapter we will examine the basic characteristics of auction and over-the-counter markets as well as the operations of dealers. We will also examine primary and secondary markets and how they are related to the market's mode of operation. Then we will examine some examples of these types of markets in the U.S. economy.

The subject matter in this chapter should be viewed as an introduction and precursor to the material in the remaining chapters in this part of the book and for the material on regulation of financial markets in Part Four. In the next chapter we will contrast intermediated markets, that is, markets where financial intermediaries play a large role, with over-the-counter and auction markets. And in the final three chapters of Part Three we will encounter all these types of market organization as we explore the markets for business, consumer, and government financing.

MARKET ORGANIZATION AND THE FUNCTION OF BROKERS AND DEALERS

Introduction

It is useful to recognize that there are a number of ways to decompose financial markets, and that each such taxonomy sheds a little more light on the operation of markets. It is also important to recognize that no taxonomy is perfect. There will always be exceptions or special cases which do not quite fit the taxonomy. But it is much easier to understand financial markets if they are organized into some kind of structure, even an imperfect one. The one we will settle on in this chapter is not perfect. We will find exceptions which do not quite seem to fit. But in spite of the imperfections, we gain much more than we will lose by utilizing this taxonomy.

Probably the most obvious way to classify financial markets corresponds to the types of securities traded in those markets. Equities, mortgages, bonds, short-term debt instruments, deposits, and the like, are often treated as having distinct markets, and we have done so throughout this book. Another possibility is to classify markets according to who wants to borrow and who wants to lend. This is an extremely useful way to look at financial markets and we will use precisely this organization in the last three chapters of Part Three. But both of these taxonomies for financial markets fail to emphasize the mode of operation of the market and this is what we will explore here.

We can start examining the market itself, rather than the securities traded or the people trading them, by identifying the basic functions which a market serves. A market provides essentially three functions. First, it provides the facility or the mechanism through which funds flow from those who want to lend to those who want to borrow. This means that the market provides the means by which assets can be exchanged and the recordkeeping function that goes with this flow of funds. Second, the market provides the vehicle by which prices are set both for new assets that accompany newly lent funds, and for the existing stock of assets. In this sense, the market serves the function of valuing assets. Finally, the market acts as a collector of information. The market is the facility used to process and aggregate information about the values of assets and the flows of funds from lenders to borrowers. To a large extent, it is the costs of collecting and aggregating information which determine the type of market organization which will emerge. Now that we have identified the functions of a market, we can look more carefully at the characteristics of auction and over-the-counter markets.

The Characteristics of Auction Markets

The essence of an auction market is that there exists some kind of centralized and open competitive bidding process where all trades in an asset take place. This kind of exchange process cannot operate successfully in every financial market. There are four basic requirements necessary for such an auction market to be viable. They are

A central trading facility

Homogeneous assets

A minimum volume of buy and sell offers

A profitable market-maker

We will examine each of these in turn.

At one time it might have been relatively simple to picture exactly what a central trading facility would look like. It would be one large room where buyers and sellers of assets or their representatives could meet to make their bids and exchange assets. But in some cases technology has rendered this conception obsolete. A centralized trading facility need no longer always be a central physical location where people who want to trade, or their representatives, congregate as, say, the New York Stock Exchange. Instead it can be a computerized trading facility where all trades are processed, but none of the traders has to be physically present. The essence of the requirement that there exist a central trading facility is that all trades must be executed through a mechanism which preserves ready access. This means that the central trading facility makes known all trades and prices to all market participants on an ongoing basis and there are no trades which are priced and executed away from the central facility. The central facility relieves the market participants of the burden of searching for individual prices. All the market's information about prices and exchanges is centralized in one location.

The second requirement for an auction market to operate successfully is that assets must be reasonably homogeneous. The centralized trading facility in an auction market collects information about bids and prices of assets. If each asset is a distinct asset and cannot be succinctly described, a central market cannot successfully collect this kind of information. But, if assets are homogeneous, then the cost of collecting information can be spread over a number of homogeneous assets so that a central distribution of this information becomes economical. For example, consider the market for mortgages on residential real estate. Mortgages on residential property have traditionally not been distributed through an auction market. One of the principal reasons is that each asset is so distinct. A centralized auction market could not economically process all the information which would be necessary to describe each mortgage which was offered for sale. The same could be said for equity shares in corporations were it not for the provision of limited liability. Limited liability means that the value of a share of equity stock is independent of who holds it. If liability were not limited in this way, then the value of the security would change if a rich person sold it to a poor person simply because the personal assets which would stand behind the security would be reduced. Limited liability has meant that all equity claims on a particular company are homogeneous assets.

A closely related requirement to that of homogeneity is that the market not be too "thin" in an asset. This means that there must be some minimum volume of transactions in the asset and there must be a desire to exchange the asset. If there are too few shares of a homogeneous asset or most of the shares are held by individuals who choose not to trade in the asset, then the centralized facility does not work effectively. The costs of collecting and maintaining access to an asset in a centralized facility are largely fixed costs, in that they do not rise and fall with the volume of trading. Therefore, it is difficult to maintain a centralized market in an asset that is traded only infrequently.

Finally, there must be some market-maker, someone or something which serves the function of an auctioneer. To function in the long run this market-maker must be profitable. At one time the market-maker was literally an auctioneer who called out prices bid and asked. But now, to a large extent, the auctioneer's function can be mechanized. The function may be limited to that of bringing together all the buyers and sellers without the market-maker ever holding stocks of the assets which are traded. On the other hand, the market-maker may also function as a dealer, purchasing securities for resale. The distinction between an auction market and an over-the-counter market is not as pure as it might be, if what we call dealers can operate in auction markets. The fact that a market-maker may purchase securities for resale and therefore become a dealer does not in itself alter the auction nature of a market. What distinguishes an auction market from others is the presence of a centralized facility through which exchanges are made and the lack of private exchanges between individual parties or trades off the centralized exchange. When trading off the central exchange becomes significant, we have an over-the-counter market. We might say that the presence of dealers in an auction market only diminishes the "purity" of the market form.

Auction markets can be further divided into two types of auctions, referred to as call and continuous markets. A call market operates with simultaneous offers to buy and sell all placed at one time. All the bids and offers are then collected and exchanges take place at once. The market then ceases to function until there is sufficient demand for another round of exchanges, at which time the market operates again with simultaneous offers to buy and sell and exchanges. The alternative type of auction market is a continuous market. In such a market offers to buy or sell can be placed at any time while the market is in operation and exchanges take place on a continuous basis. The advantage of the continuous market is that it increases the flexibility of the market participants so that they are not constrained to wait until the times when the market operates, as is the case in a call market. However, in a continuous market the offers to buy or sell may be quite spread out in time. As a result, there will be opportunities for imbalances between offers to buy and sell, or what are called trading imbalances, to develop. The market price can rise or fall as excesses of buy or sell offers develop. These imbalances create the opportunity for dealers to enter the market.

The Characteristics of Over-the-Counter Markets and the Roles of Brokers and Dealers

There are two important features of an over-the-counter market. First there is no central exchange facility as there is in the case of an auction market. Second, the market operates through middlemen (or women) who stand ready to buy or sell a given security upon request. These middlemen are referred to as dealers. Dealers are distinguished from brokers on the one hand and financial intermediaries on the other. Brokers do not buy and sell assets on their own. Rather they act as salespersons and receive commissions. Dealers are distinguished from financial intermediaries in that the former are principally engaged in selling the same securities they buy, whereas financial intermediaries create and sell new claims on themselves in order to fund their holdings of the securities they purchase. Dealers' holdings of securities are small relative to their turnover of those securities.

In this sense they operate like the typical retailer. They buy assets not to hold them for long periods, but to sell them quickly so that the stock of assets that they hold at any one time is an inventory maintained for resale.

In many respects, an auction market and an over-the-counter market can be quite similar. An over-the-counter market functions better the more homogeneous the assets and the larger the volume of trades, as does an auction market. In addition, dealers may perform a useful function in either market. In a continuous auction market dealers will be able to operate profitably if there are periodic imbalances between orders to buy and sell and if market participants are willing to pay to reduce the impact on prices of those imbalances. The reason that an auction market arises in one instance and an over-the-counter market in another hinges on the benefits perceived by the participants in the market of a centralized exchange facility. Such a facility serves essentially as a collector of information and a means of economizing on the costs of searching for alternative prices from dealers. Therefore, if communication among dealers and participants in a market is good enough and competition is intense, a centralized facility may be an unnecessary luxury.

The important feature of an over-the-counter market involves the nature of the service provided by dealers, though this service may be rendered in auction markets as well. The service provided by dealers has been referred to as "immediacy."[1] The dealer allows the buyer or seller of an asset to make the exchange when he or she desires, rather than waiting to locate a party who wants to be on the other side of the transaction. It is important to emphasize the distinction between the service provided by a dealer and a broker. A broker acts as an agent in executing a transaction and collects a commission. The broker goes hunting for the party on the other side of the transaction. His incentive to hunt efficiently is improved if his fee is tied to the outcome, so it is usually stated as a percentage of the sale price. On the other hand, the dealer holds an inventory of the assets in which he or she deals and, therefore, stands ready to execute the transaction when the buyer or seller desires.

Whether in an auction market or an over-the-counter market, dealers must be able to operate profitably in providing the service of immediacy. The costs that the dealer faces can be broken down into three components:[2]

Holding costs

Order costs

Information costs

---

[1] The concept of immediacy was articulated by Harold Demsetz, "The Cost of Transacting," *Quarterly Journal of Economics*, vol. 82 (February 1968), pp. 33–53.

[2] This breakdown is found in Hans R. Stoll, "The Supply of Dealer Services in Securities Markets," *Journal of Finance*, vol. 33 (September 1978), pp. 1133–1151.

Holding costs represent the costs that any investor would bear for holding a portfolio of assets which is not an optimal combination of risk and return. In order to make a market in a particular asset, a dealer must hold an inventory that is larger than he or she would hold if the dealer were investing in the asset on his or her own. Dealers demand a compensation for holding an excess amount of such assets. In contract, *order costs* are costs of transacting. These involve all the costs of handling securities and the fixed costs of office and staff, recordkeeping, and so forth, involved in executing transactions. Finally, *information costs* arise because some investors will trade with a dealer based on special information which is not available to the dealer. The dealer knows that some portion of his or her transactions are with parties who have superior information and the dealer expects to lose on such transactions. These expected losses represent his or her information costs.

The dealer earns returns from the *spread* between offers to buy and sell. This simply means that the dealer attempts to buy low and sell high, on average. The difference between the price paid for assets and the price received is the spread. In markets where dealers are involved, the spread is a function of the dealer's costs and the degree of competition in the market. Later in the chapter we will examine some evidence on spreads and returns to dealers in selected U.S. financial markets.

Primary and Secondary Markets

Primary markets are the markets where new securities are bought and sold. This does not mean that there can exist no other securities like the new ones being sold. It simply means that the particular securities which are being distributed have not been owned before. For example, a primary market exists in the stock of a particular company when it issues new shares, despite the fact that it may already have shares outstanding. We think of the primary market as the market for the *new* shares as opposed to the often virtually identical *old* shares. A *secondary market* is a market where the old (used) securities are traded. This means that in a secondary market securities are not being sold principally by the party upon which they are a claim and therefore involve no new lending or borrowing. For example, all IBM shares sold in the secondary market would not be offered for sale by IBM. They would be sold by the parties who own them.

Primary markets are essentially a distribution device and act as the conduit through which new capital or funds can be acquired. The method of operation for these markets is whatever method is best suited to the purpose of collecting information and facilitating this initial distribution. The secondary market provides the similar function of being a vehicle for exchange. The difference is that the exchange opportunities offered by a secondary market provide liquidity for those who hold the security as well as a mechanism for valuing the outstanding stock of assets. In other words, the outstanding stock of assets has some market value and the market value is determined through the secondary market. The asset need not actually change hands in order for the asset to be valued, as long as there is a secondary market in which similar assets are traded. Therefore, the market serves even those who do not directly use it during a particular period of time.

There is no necessary reason why primary or secondary markets would operate as auction or over-the-counter markets. Either form of operation is potentially feasible and, in the next section, we will identify examples of each possibility. With either primary or secondary markets, the essence of the auction form of operation is the centralized exchange facility. And such a facility can exist as an efficient means of collecting and processing information in either type of market. This facility is efficient only when there are a large number of assets distributed in the market on a regular basis. Therefore, an auction market will not work in a primary market where particular types of assets are distributed infrequently or where the market needs to process a large amount of special information with the distribution of an asset. But a primary market can be an auction market if new homogeneous securities are issued regularly. A secondary market can operate as an auction market if there is a volume of securities which are actively exchanged, that is, if the turnover of securities is sufficiently frequent. But it need not act as an auction market unless the centralized trading facility provides some efficiencies over a dealer system. All of these possible forms of organization are found in American financial markets.

Primary and secondary markets in the same security are not always different markets with distinct methods of operation, although they usually are. One case in which the two markets are virtually the same is the market for equity obligations of a few very large corporations. In this case, some corporations are large enough that they can offer their new securities directly to the secondary market, as would someone who had used securities of such a corporation to sell. In either case, a broker might be involved, but there would be no need for the particular type of dealer usually involved in the primary equity market, the investment banker. Such cases are not that frequent, however. In most instances the primary market operates in a somewhat different manner from the secondary market. The differences usually depend upon the number of securities to be sold relative to the volume and distribution of outstanding securities and the amount of information possessed by the market about the securities for sale.

AUCTION AND OVER-THE-COUNTER MARKETS
IN THE UNITED STATES

In this section we will examine examples of the kinds of markets we have been discussing. The purpose is to learn how auction and over-the-counter markets actually work. The examples we will take up are not exhaustive.

That is, we are not going to deal with all the auction markets we can discover in the country or even all the important ones. Instead, we will deal with three examples which illustrate the alternatives. First, we will examine one of the purest auction markets in the country, pure in the sense that dealers have no part to play. This is the *primary* market in Treasury bills. Second, we will examine one of the larger markets where dealers play an important role, the secondary market for corporate equities. Within this we will look at the New York Stock Exchange, an auction market, and the market for over-the-counter stocks. Finally, we will examine an over-the-counter market, the money market. Each of these markets will come up again in later chapters. But at this juncture our purpose is to see how different market structures operate, rather than to explore all relevant facets of the example markets.

The Primary Treasury Bill Market—Pure Auction

The primary Treasury bill market is one of the few pure call auction markets for financial assets in operation. Auctions of Treasury bills are conducted by the U.S. Treasury at regular weekly intervals. The Treasury decides ahead of time what volume of bills it intends to issue and then auctions those bills to the highest bidders. At one time the Treasury operated in the reverse manner by setting a price and then seeking buyers, but this was abandoned some years ago in favor of the auction procedure.

Two types of offers to purchase bills are entertained by the Treasury. They are referred to as competitive and noncompetitive tenders. Competitive tenders constitute an offer to buy a specific volume of Treasury bills at a specific price. Buyers who make such offers are generally dealers in the secondary market in government securities or other large institutions which buy in volume and can afford to invest the time and effort to study the market and forecast what the best offer price will be. If they guess high, they will be assured of being able to secure their bid. If they bid low, then there may be sufficient offers at higher prices to exhaust the Treasury issue. Noncompetitive tenders contain no specific offer of a price. Instead, they constitute an offer to buy a specific volume of securities at the average price prevailing in that auction, whatever it may be. The Treasury places maximum limits on the size of noncompetitive tenders for bills. This stood at $500,000 in the late 1970s. By comparison, the average size of competitive tenders often exceeds $20 million.

The procedure used in the Treasury bill auction to determine whose orders will be accepted is as follows. The Treasury accepts all noncompetitive tenders first and then turns to the competitive tenders. It proceeds through the competitive tenders from highest to lowest bid until all the bills available have been sold or until the issue is fully subscribed. It then computes the average price of all competitive tenders and applies that price to the noncompetitive tenders.

While neither the Treasury nor the Federal Reserve has collected historical data on the composition of noncompetitive tenders, the Federal Reserve Bank of New York did conduct a special study of those making noncompetitive tenders in the New York Federal Reserve district for the auction of bills which occurred on July 20, 1978. This information is useful because noncompetitive tenders for bills increased in the 1970s as market interest rates increased and the general public became increasingly interested in short-term Treasury obligations. The magnitude of this increase is shown in Figure 10-1, which records the total volume of noncompetitive tenders for bills during the 1970s. In this 1978 auction more than 85 percent of the total number of noncompetitive tenders came from individuals as opposed to financial institutions or corporations and this represented 70 percent of the total dollar volume of such tenders. Of these tenders from individuals more than 40 percent of the volume came in amounts in excess of $100,000, though many of these large offers came from estates or trust accounts managed by commercial banks.[3]

The purity of the primary auction market for Treasury bills leaves no room for dealers. Dealers are certainly one of the more important customers in this primary market. They purchase new Treasury bills to support their inventories for resale in the secondary market, which is an over-the-counter rather than an auction market. But the auction procedure utilized in the primary market leaves no room for dealers in the primary distribution. Unlike the secondary market in equities which we will discuss next, the trading process is not continuous, so no imbalances develop between buyers and sellers which can be resolved by dealers. In the primary Treasury bill market imbalances are resolved by the low bidders going without. They can then wait for the next primary auction or they can turn to a dealer in the secondary Treasury bill market.

Secondary Markets in Equities—Auction and Over-the-Counter Markets

The secondary market for equity securities provides an excellent example of the differences between auction and over-the-counter markets. The reason is that auction and over-the-counter markets operate side by side for different equity securities. Moreover, the costs of collecting and processing information about equities and conducting exchanges in equities are changing sufficiently rapidly that the market is evolving quickly. It has been possible, as a result, to witness significant changes in these markets in relatively short intervals of time.

Most corporate equities are traded in one or more of the major stock exchanges in the United States. Of all the exchanges, the greatest publicity is given to the New York Stock Exchange because it dwarfs the other exchanges in volume of trades executed in any year and in the value of the

[3] See Charles M. Sivesind, "Noncompetitive Tenders in Treasury Auctions: How Much Do They Affect Savings Flows?" *Quarterly Review*, Federal Bank of New York, vol. 3 (Autumn 1978), pp. 34–38.

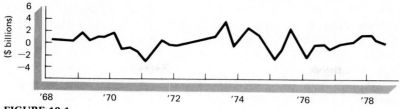

FIGURE 10-1

Volume of noncompetitive tenders for Treasury bills. Source: Charles M. Sivesind, "Non-competitive Tenders in Treasury Auctions: How Much do They Affect Savings Flows?" *Quarterly Review*, Federal Reserve Bank of New York, Autumn 1978, p. 38.

securities listed on the exchange. But there are a number of other stock exchanges which operate in the United States. The second largest is the American Stock Exchange (AMEX). While it is not tremendously far behind the NYSE in the total number of securities listed, the total value of these securities is a fairly small portion of the total value of securities listed on the NYSE. The other exchanges are far behind the NYSE both in number of securities and in total value. The same ranking prevails based on data on the volume of trading. Trading volume for the NYSE and AMEX is illustrated in Figure 10-2, for most of the decade of the 1970s. This figure indicates that daily trading volume for the NYSE averaged around 30 million shares in the late 1970s, while volume on the AMEX was approximately 5 million shares.

The NYSE is essentially a continuous auction market, but it incorporates a few features of a call-auction market, and dealers play a significant role in the market. The market is not continuous in the sense that it does not operate

FIGURE 10-2

Number of shares traded per day on the New York and American stock exchanges. Source: *Federal Reserve Monthly Chart Book*, August 1979.

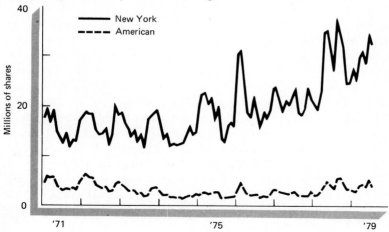

24 hours per day, 365 days per year. Rather the market conforms to normal business hours. When the market opens, all business which has accumulated during its close is handled as if it were a call market. From there on, throughout the trading day, the market operates in a continuous manner. The market-maker in the NYSE is referred to as a specialist. Specialists are so named because they operate as dealers in particular stocks rather than in all the stocks listed on the exchange. The rules of the exchange are designed to limit the specialist's role as a dealer in order to minimize the costs of executing trades on the exchange. Specialists are required to give priority to the execution of orders between public investors rather than trades with themselves. This means that when a specialist receives an order to buy or sell a stock he or she must first seek to match it with an opposite order from a nonspecialist. The specialist is permitted to execute his or her own order first only if its bid price is higher, or its offering price is lower than the prices of any public order on the exchange. As trading imbalances develop, the dealer is permitted to trade on his or her own account.

There has also long been a market in equities which does not operate through one of the organized stock exchanges. Banks traditionally acted as dealers in these securities (though they no longer do this) and the securities were literally sold over-the-counter. Hence, this market became known as the "over-the-counter" market. In 1971 the National Association of Securities Dealers, the trade association of securities brokers, implemented an automated quotation system (NASDAQ) for these over-the-counter securities. NASDAQ is a computerized nationwide communications system which provides price quotes for major dealers in over-the-counter securities. As of 1977 the total number of securities which were listed on the NASDAQ system was 2,575 issues, compared to about 1,500 on the NYSE. A total of 1.9 billion shares were traded during that year. The NASDAQ system is not exactly identical to the over-the-counter market. Many over-the-counter stocks, usually those which are infrequently traded, are not listed on NASDAQ and a few NYSE stocks are listed on NASDAQ. But as a rough approximation it is useful to think of NASDAQ as the system through which over-the-counter stocks are traded.

Individual dealers in the NASDAQ market hold inventories in the securities listed on NASDAQ and trade in those securities as they receive offers to buy or sell. Brokers or others who have access to the NASDAQ system have computer terminals which provide information on prices bid and asked by these dealers. The terminals report the median bid and median asked price of all dealers in the system who trade in a particular stock. In addition, users can obtain the bid and asked price of each dealer in the system. The essential difference between NASDAQ and an exchange like the NYSE is that the NASDAQ system does not carry out or record transactions. It merely lists information on dealers' quotations. Exchanges must be completed by telephoning the dealer and carrying out the transaction. This is one important feature which distinguishes the over-the-counter from the auction market.

The fundamental differences between the securities listed on the NYSE and the NASDAQ system or other exchanges pertain to the volume of securities outstanding and the frequency of trades in those securities. The NYSE lists only securities which have a large enough volume and are traded frequently enough to warrant the cost of a centralized exchange facility. The NASDAQ system will list bids on stocks which meet much less stringent requirements, because the service they provide is less expensive. To be listed on the NASDAQ system securities must have at least two dealers willing to make a market in that security. Listing also involves a fee for the corporation whose stock is listed. In the mid-1970s there were a little over 500 dealers who listed stocks on the NASDAQ.

Some interesting evidence on the pricing of dealer services on the NASDAQ market has been collected since the market began. This market is of particular interest because the market allows multiple dealers in each stock or direct competition among dealers, whereas the NYSE has not allowed this. The NYSE has long permitted only one dealer in each stock. As a result, it is difficult to collect any direct evidence on whether competition could reduce the price of dealer services, or the spread between bid and asked prices, on the NYSE. But the NASDAQ market provides a better opportunity to examine this question as well as to study the other determinants of dealer prices.

Probably the most comprehensive study of this question was conducted by Hans Stoll.[4] He analyzed the data on the spreads in the NASDAQ market and their determinants for a 6-day period in July 1973. Some background data on the characteristics of the market for selected dates preceding his sample period are shown in Table 10-1. The table indicates that the middle of 1973 was not a particularly good time for the securities industry. Between April 1972 and July 1973, trading volume and average prices fell substantially. In response, percentage spreads between bid and asked prices increased dramatically, from 5.1 percent to 10.0 percent for the typical industrial stock and from 2.7 percent to 4.2 percent for the typical financial stock. However, the median number of dealers in each stock did not change much at all, remaining four or five throughout the period. This means that the average dealer experienced less trading activity.

During his 6-day sample period Stoll attempted to explain the variation in observed bid-ask spreads across securities as a function of the following factors: the riskiness of the stock, measured by the variance of its price; the amount of trading which is based on superior information or the information cost of the dealer, measured by trading volume relative to the number of shares outstanding on the grounds that this should rise when some people

[4] See Hans R. Stoll, "The Pricing of Dealer Services: An Empirical Study of NASDAQ Stocks," *Journal of Finance*, vol. 33 (September 1978), pp. 1152–1172.

TABLE 10-1

Background Information on the Operation of the NASDAQ Market on Selected Dates During 1972 and 1973

| | | | DATE | | | | |
| | | 1972 | | | 1973 | | |
VARIABLE	4/3	6/27	9/28	12/26	3/27	6/27	7/11
1 NASDAQ composite price index	128	130	129	131	117	100	103
2 NASDAQ share volume for week containing date (millions)	53	38	40	32	33	23	27
3 Median % spread							
Financial stocks	2.7	2.8	2.9	3.0	3.6	4.2	4.2
Industrial stocks	5.1	5.6	6.3	6.7	8.0	10.5	10.5
4 Median $ volume ($100)							
Financial stocks	101	79	74	80	75	54	101
Industrial stocks	75	48	32	39	21	15	22
5 Median price							
Financial stocks	26	25	26	26	23	19	19.4
Industrial stocks	11	10	8.9	8.5	7.3	5.9	5.9
6 Median number of dealers listed							
Financial stocks	5	5	5	5	5	5	5
Industrial stocks	5	5	5	5	4	4	4

Note: Median calculated across all non-third-market common stocks.

Source: Hans R. Stoll, "The Pricing of Dealer Services: An Empirical Study of NASDAQ Stocks," *Journal of Finance*, vol. 33 (September 1978), p. 1156.

start to trade on special information; the level of order costs; the willingness of dealers to bear risk, measured by a proxy for dealer wealth; and the lack of competition among dealers, measured by the number of dealers in each stock and the concentration of their trading in that stock. As any of these factors increases, so should observed spreads between bid and asked prices.

Using these measures of dealer cost and competition, Stoll was able to account for 80 percent of the variation in observed bid-ask spreads. Furthermore, he showed that each of the factors itemized above has a significant impact on actual spreads in the NASDAQ market. Of particular interest is his conclusion that increased competition does cause a significant decline in the spreads.

As time has passed, the differences between the NYSE and the other segments of the secondary market in equities have blurred or diminished. With the advent of NASDAQ the over-the-counter market has become increasingly like the NYSE itself. Congress has recently mandated changes in this market structure which promise a further blending of these markets. We will examine this congressional mandate when we study regulation of auction and over-the-counter markets in Chapter Sixteen.

The Money Market—An Over-The-Counter Market

Another example of an over-the-counter market is the so-called money market. In one sense this is a misnomer because money per se is not traded in this market. Money is composed essentially of cash or currency and demand deposits or checking account balances. And these items are not traded in the money market. But the closest substitutes to money which the financial markets have to offer are traded in the money market. As a result, it is useful to think of the money market as determining the yields on these close substitutes for money and thus indirectly on money itself.

The money market refers to the market for a wide variety of short-term debt instruments, where short-term generally means securities having maturities of 1 year or less. The money market is a combination of primary and secondary markets. The important feature here is that the asset must be relatively liquid. This means that it can be turned over quickly at low cost. Also this normally means that it is necessary for the asset to be able to be resold. With assets with very short maturities, however, the resale provision may not be all-important as long as there is little probability of default. As a result, the money market is composed of assets which are perceived to be liquid, either because they have short maturities with low default risk, or because there is an active secondary market in the asset. To qualify under either of these accounts, an asset must be reasonably homogeneous or standardized and have a sufficient trading volume to make it profitable for dealers to hold it in their inventories. To understand the money market one has to understand the nature of the securities traded in it. We will briefly examine some of these securities next.

TREASURY BILLS   The most important type of security in the money market in terms of volume of securities outstanding is the bills issued by the U.S. Treasury. These bills are part of the secondary rather than the primary market in Treasury bills and are available in denominations as low as $10,000, though most Treasury bill trading is in larger denominations. The maturities available range from 30 days to 1 year, and the interest rates in the secondary market are closely related to the rates on new issues of Treasury bills.

COMMERCIAL PAPER   This is the name given to the unsecured short-term financial obligations sold to the market by corporations or financial institutions. Trading in commercial paper is principally a primary rather than a secondary market. Commercial paper is generally issued with denominations of at least $100,000 and may have a maturity of up to 270 days. Publicly issued securities with longer maturities must be registered with the Securities and Exchange Commission, and that is a costly process which would raise the cost of these short-term debt instruments (see Chapter Thirteen). The market for commercial paper is generally limited to the more creditworthy corporations and financial institutions. As a result, commercial paper is thought to be a relatively low-risk investment.

However, defaults have not been unknown on commercial paper. In 1970 the Penn Central Railroad defaulted on $82 million worth of commercial paper. The market did not suffer any serious long-term difficulties due to this default of a major borrower, though it did encourage lenders to carefully analyze the risks involved. One mechanism used to limit the amount of risk is for borrowers to have their commercial paper backed by commitments from commercial banks to extend loans, if necessary, at the time the commercial paper matures. Commercial paper which is backed in this way is called "prime commercial paper."

CERTIFICATES OF DEPOSIT   These securities, known as CDs, are a marketable type of time deposit originally issued by commercial banks. CDs are issued with a specific maturity and have a minimum denomination of $100,000. The market for CDs began to develop in the early 1960s as a secondary market where existing CDs could be resold. Prior to this time, investors were reluctant to commit large amounts of funds to bank time-deposits because of the penalty which had to be paid if the funds were withdrawn prior to maturity. But with the advent of a secondary market, this problem was essentially eliminated. Still, CDs, like other bank deposits, were subject to restrictions of maximum interest rates which could be paid (see Chapters Twelve, Seventeen, and Eighteen). They were therefore unattractive in periods when interest rates on other money market securities were above these limits. But between 1970 and 1973, the Federal Reserve phased out these restrictions on the interest rates which could be paid on deposits over $100,000 or on CDs. With this change, CDs became an important part of the money market, both when interest rates were high and when they were low.

BANKER'S ACCEPTANCE   Historically, bankers' acceptances were one of the first short-term highly marketable assets. They have been used for trade for virtually hundreds of years. A banker's acceptance is created to finance goods which have not yet been transported from the seller to the buyer. The buyer of the goods promises to pay a prespecified amount within a limited period of time, say 90 days. The promise is given credibility if the bank "accepts" it because the bank then commits itself to make the payment should the seller of the product default. The *banker's acceptance* is therefore a commitment from a merchant and from a bank to pay a specified amount at a particular time. This makes these securities of rather low risk. Bankers' acceptances have functioned as a highly liquid short-term asset for many years.

FEDERAL FUNDS AND REPURCHASE AGREEMENTS   Federal funds and repurchase agreements constitute probably the most liquid and the shortest maturity assets available in the money market. The federal funds market started as a market where commercial banks which were members of the Federal Reserve System could borrow and lend excess reserves among one another. Excess reserves are funds which banks hold on deposit with the Federal

Reserve to satisfy the requirements for reserves imposed by the System. If one bank finds it has an excess in deposits at the Federal Reserve, it can loan these funds to another bank and the exchange is made by the Federal Reserve through what is called its wire transfer service. This is an electronic mechanism through which funds can be transferred instantly from one bank to another. There is no delay for a check to clear as in the case of other types of transactions. As a result, it became possible to have virtually overnight maturities on federal funds. The market for federal funds has gradually grown to be much broader than merely the borrowing and lending of excess reserves between banks which are members of the Federal Reserve System. The federal funds market now involves borrowing and lending between a variety of financial institutions. The fundamental characteristic of the market is that it involves "immediately available funds," or funds cleared through the Federal Reserve's wire transfer service.

A closely related market is the market for repurchase agreements (RPs). A repurchase agreement involves the sale of a security, usually a Treasury bill, with the simultaneous agreement by the seller to repurchase the security at a prespecified later date. A repurchase agreement is therefore similar to a collateralized loan. The seller of the Treasury bills is borrowing funds for a prespecified period. Repurchase agreements are generally of very short maturities, sometimes 1 day, but most often 3 to 14 days. Because of this they are very similar to federal funds. One distinction is that they involve a larger market. In addition, RPs are used as a substitute for federal funds because of the flexibility of negotiating maturities. Financial and nonfinancial corporations as well as governments borrow and lend through repurchase agreements.

The money market is an over-the-counter market, as is the NASDAQ market in corporate equities. But the technology utilized by the dealers in this market is substantially different. The money market operates over the telephone and most all transactions are carried out by large institutions or corporations such that the transaction size is relatively large. Because the central purpose of the market is to provide highly liquid short-term borrowing and investment opportunities to corporations and financial institutions, the market is particularly concerned with the ability to execute fast and efficient transactions.

An order is placed in this market through a phone call to a dealer who quotes a bid or asked price. An order can be placed immediately with a dealer or a customer may shop around for quotations from other dealers. Once an order is placed the dealer arranges for transfer of title to the securities and an exchange of funds through the customer's bank. Some of the dealers in this market are commercial banks and others are brokerage firms. In either case, they stand ready to quote a price and execute the transaction over the phone.

In terms of the volume of securities outstanding, the largest component of the money market is made up of Treasury bills. Moreover, because RPs are often collateralized by Treasury bills and federal funds are closely related to

Treasury bills, government securities are the dominant portion of the market. This is illustrated in Figure 10-3, which shows the volume of the principal money market securities outstanding during the 1970s. The figure shows that Treasury bills have been consistently the largest volume security throughout the decade. Because of the prominence of government securities in the money market, the over-the-counter market in these money market assets is closely tied in to the whole secondary market in government securities, not just the secondary market in Treasury bills. We will examine closely the entire dealer market in government securities in Chapter Fourteen.

The money market differs from other markets in that it is really a conglomeration of markets for distinct securities which have some common characteristics. The common features are their short maturity, low default risk, and high degree of liquidity. The securities are sufficiently similar that it is feasible in most cases for a dealer in one to be a dealer in all of them. Yet they are not sufficiently homogeneous to make an auction market an efficient method for trading them. As a result, they have come to be traded in what operates like a single over-the-counter market.

FIGURE 10-3

Outstanding volume of principal types of money market securities. Source: *Federal Reserve Bulletin*, various issues.

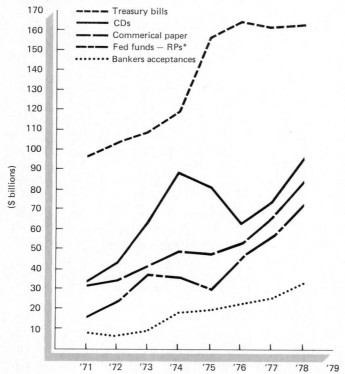

SUMMARY

In this chapter we have examined two of the three principal forms of market organization which we observe in financial markets in the United States. The two types of markets we have discussed are auction and over-the-counter markets. The important distinction between them is that in an auction market all trades or exchanges take place through some kind of centralized facility. At one time this meant that all buyers and sellers, or their brokers, had to meet in one location to trade in a competitive bidding process. But with modern computer technology a centralized exchange facility no longer requires that brokers meet in a single physical location. An auction market now requires only that there be a single facility through which all trading takes place or all transactions are recorded.

The alternative to the auction market is called an over-the-counter market. The name derives from the portion of the equity market where shares in smaller companies were traded "over-the-counter" at commercial banks. Now the name is used to describe the method of operation of any market which has no centralized trading or exchange facility, but instead has all trades handled by dealers. We noted that dealers can also operate in an auction market. A dealer is a person who maintains an inventory of a particular security and buys and sells for that inventory with anyone who enters the market. In this way the dealer provides immediacy to the market by offsetting imbalances between supply and demand. This service can be valuable in both an auction and over-the-counter market. The important distinction is that in an auction market all trading with dealers takes place through a centralized facility, while trading is decentralized in an over-the-counter market.

We enumerated four requirements for a market to become centralized like an auction market. First, the market must have an economical centralized facility for conducting exchanges. Second, the assets which are traded must be homogeneous so that a centralized trading facility is feasible. Third, there must be enough volume of trading in the assets to make it efficient to operate the centralized facility. Finally, there must be some kind of market-marker, a dealer, for example, who can operate profitably in the market. All of these requirements derive from the function of a market as a collector and processor of information. If the assets traded in a market are homogeneous with a large trading volume, then the process of collecting information and bringing it together can be centralized in an efficient manner.

In this chapter we also considered the distinction between primary and secondary markets. We learned that primary markets are markets for new securities and secondary markets are the markets for used securities. There is no necessary connection between the primary-secondary classification and the auction versus over-the-counter classification for markets. Both primary and secondary markets can operate as either auction or over-the-counter markets. And in the chapter we considered examples of each combination.

We examined four examples of different markets. First, we examined the primary market in Treasury bills and found that this was a pure auction market. It operates as a call auction market with no dealers. Next, we examined the secondary market for equity securities. We found that there are two distinct markets operating within this general label. First, there are the organized exchanges like the New York Stock Exchange, which function as auction markets. The other equity market, the NASDAQ market, uses an automated quotation system to distribute information on dealers' prices for different securities. But the system does not handle actual transactions in the securities. Hence, we still consider it an over-the-counter market. Finally, we examined the money market. This is an example of an over-the-counter market which operates without a single automated system for displaying price information from dealers. The money market includes a number of different types of securities, all of which are short-term, highly liquid debt securities.

This chapter has tried to fit the wide variety of different types of financial markets which exist in the United States into an organized structure. We see such a variety of securities because participants in financial markets have such diverse needs and because a competitive economy responds to these needs by creating distinct securities and distinct markets in which these securities can be traded. The diversity which we see is so great that some sort of classification system or taxonomy is necessary to make sense out of the marketplace. The taxonomy we have used here not only provides a useful classification system, but it also helps us understand how the markets themselves work. This understanding will prove very useful as we proceed through Parts Three and Four of this book.

QUESTIONS TO IMPROVE UNDERSTANDING

1 What are the important characteristics of an auction market? Why is the auction market held out as the economists' ideal of a market organization?
2 What is an over-the-counter market? Compare this form of organization to an auction market.
3 What is the service provided by a dealer? Explain the costs incurred by a dealer in providing this service?
4 Distinguish between a continuous and call-auction market.
5 Distinguish between a primary and secondary market. Can a primary and secondary market be either an over-the-counter or an auction market? Why or why not?
6 Explain how the primary market for Treasury bills operates. What makes this market so pure?
7 The NYSE is a continuous auction market with dealers. How do dealers function in such an auction market?
8 Compare the organizational structure of the money market with the NASDAQ market. How do they differ?

9   What are the basic determinants of the spreads earned by dealers in the NASDAQ market?
10 What is the difference between an intermediated market and an over-the-counter market?

REFERENCES

Demsetz, Harold: "The Cost of Transacting," *Quarterly Journal of Economics*, 82 (February 1968), pp. 33–53.

Epps, Thomas W.: "The Demand for Brokers' Services: The Relation Between Security Trading Volume and Transaction Cost," *Bell Journal of Economics*, 7 (Spring 1976), pp. 163–194.

*Garbade, Kenneth D.: "Electronic Quotation Systems and the Market for Government Securities," *Quarterly Review*, Federal Reserve Bank of New York, 3 (Summer 1978), pp. 13–20.

————, and William L. Silber: "Price Dispersion in the Government Securities Market," *Journal of Political Economy*, 84 (1976), pp. 721–740.

————, and ————: "Structural Organization of Secondary Markets: Clearing Frequency, Dealer Activity and Liquidity Risk," *Journal of Finance*, 34 (June 1979), pp. 577–594.

*Hervey, Jack L.: "Bankers' Acceptances," *Business Conditions*, Federal Reserve Bank of Chicago (May 1976), pp. 3–11.

*Lucas, Charles, Marcos T. Jones, and Thom B. Thurston: "Federal Funds and Repurchase Agreements," *Quarterly Review*, Federal Reserve Bank of New York (Summer 1977), pp. 33–48.

*Merton, William C.: "The Market for Large Negotiable CD's," *Quarterly Review*, Federal Reserve Bank of New York (Winter 1977–1978), pp. 22–34.

*Sobel, Robert: *The Big Board*, The Free Press, New York, 1965.

*Sivesind, Charles M.: "Noncompetitive Tenders in Treasury Auctions: How Much Do they Affect Savings Flows?" *Quarterly Review*, Federal Reserve Bank of New York, 3 (Autumn 1978), pp. 34–38.

Stoll, Hans R.: "The Supply of Dealer Services in Securities Markets," *Journal of Finance*, 33 (September 1978), pp. 1133–1151.

————: "The Pricing of Dealer Services: An Empirical Study of NASDAQ Stocks," *Journal of Finance*, 33 (September 1978), pp. 1152–1172.

Tinic, Seha M.: "The Economics of Liquidity Services," *Quarterly Journal of Economics*, 86 (February 1972), pp. 79–93.

————, and Richard West: "Competition and the Pricing of Dealer Services in the Over-the-Counter Market," *Journal of Financial and Quantitative Analysis*, 7 (June 1972), pp. 1707–1727.

*References marked with an * provide additional institutional detail and make excellent supplementary reading.

Chapter Eleven

FINANCIAL INTERMEDIATION

In this chapter we will examine the process of financial intermediation and the roles that intermediaries play in financial markets. In today's economy a very large percentage of all financial transactions involve some kind of financial intermediary. So it is very important to understand what intermediaries are all about.

Like the last chapter, this chapter is designed to explain the basic structure of financial markets. In the previous chapter we explored the characteristics of auction and over-the-counter markets. In this chapter we will examine the basic features of intermediaries which act as conduits into those markets and provide for the private distribution of financial claims outside of those public markets. With an understanding of the various forms of market organization in hand, we will be able to concentrate on the characteristics of the markets for consumer, business, and government financing in the coming chapters.

We will begin by defining the concept of financial intermediation and by evaluating various services that financial intermediaries provide for the participants in financial markets. Next, we will consider the various types of financial intermediaries which exist in the American economy. We will examine the aggregate data on the flow of funds through these various intermediaries and we will explore the basic structure of the balance sheet of the most important type of intermediary, the commercial bank. Finally, we will examine two interesting and important issues regarding the operation of intermediaries, the questions of how to determine the value of an intermediary and how intermediaries manage liquidity.

THE CONCEPT OF INTERMEDIATION

It is useful to begin by comparing a financial intermediary with a dealer. We know that a *dealer* buys and sells assets and lives off the "spread." A dealer does not acquire assets for the long term. Rather, assets are held only for the purposes of providing an inventory, though some dealers may also speculate for themselves and hold some assets for such purposes. As a result, the dealer's role as a middleman does not involve any changes in the assets which are traded or the creation of any new or distinctly different types of assets. Precisely the opposite is true with a financial intermediary. *Intermediaries* purchase most assets as long-term investments. This means that intermediaries' holdings of assets do not serve essentially as inventories. Instead of reselling the assets they purchase, they create new assets and sell them to the market. The new assets constitute a financial claim on the intermediary rather than on the party who originally issued the asset purchased by the intermediary. Therefore, unlike the dealer, the intermediary does more than provide immediacy or absorb temporary trading imbalances. The intermediary creates and distributes new financial claims upon itself. This alteration of the nature of the financial claim that is distributed to the market is the concept behind the word intermediation.

The distinction between dealer and intermediary is relatively clear-cut and easy to grasp. The distinction between an intermediated market and either an auction market or an over-the-counter market is not quite as straightforward. An intermediary may participate in either an auction or an over-the-counter market. For example, commercial banks all buy and sell Treasury bills on a regular basis. Hence, depending upon whether they use the primary or secondary market, they are participating in an auction or an over-the-counter market. But commercial banks also participate in a private loan market. That is, they stand ready to make loans to business customers out of the funds they raise by offering various types of deposit accounts. This private loan market is certainly not an auction market. Yet it does operate much like an over-the-counter market. The important difference between this market and an over-the-counter market is that the suppliers of loans are intermediaries rather than dealers. The same distinction applies to the liabilities offered by intermediaries. The market for the liabilities of an intermediary operates like an over-the-counter market, but the suppliers are intermediaries; that is, institutions which create new and distinct liabilities to fund their assets. Therefore, we will call these *intermediated markets*. The important concept here is that financial intermediaries are distinct entities because they create new financial claims. But they may participate in all the types of markets we have identified. Hence, they create a distinct or new type of market, but they also bridge the gaps between markets. Next, we need to explore why their services are in such great demand.

It is not at all obvious why the services of a financial intermediary are needed. An intermediated market is more complicated than either an auction or over-the-counter market because an intermediary creates an entirely new set of assets. It therefore seems implausible that intermediaries provide a service that is essentially the same as the one provided by a dealer—that of immediacy. The question then becomes: What sorts of benefits do intermediaries offer to the economy which lead to some markets being dominated by intermediaries and others not? There is no single answer to this question. Intermediaries come in various forms and provide a number of distinct services to the market. These services can be grouped into two broad categories. First, intermediaries act as investment managers. They accept funds from those who wish to lend funds, issue these lenders liability claims, select the appropriate investments for those funds, and monitor those investments. In order to prosper as investment managers, intermediaries must be able to do something for the investors they serve that those investors cannot do on their own. That is, there must be something inherent in the process of the intermediary managing funds for investors which generates some economies or efficiencies for the intermediary. Then, as long as there is competition among intermediaries, these efficiencies will be passed on to the suppliers of funds. The second category of services involves activities which can easily be tied in with the task of managing investments. These services are not really a necessary part of intermediation per se. That is, some other type of firm could provide these services as well. But in performing the investment management function, the intermediary finds that these other services are naturally complementary with the investment management function.

THE SERVICES PROVIDED BY FINANCIAL INTERMEDIARIES

Financial intermediaries provide six services for the financial markets. They are:

Risk reduction through diversification
Maturity intermediation
Reduction in the cost of contracting
Information production
Management of the payments system
Insurance

Almost all intermediaries provide some reduction of risk through diversification. But the other five services are more specialized. Some intermediaries provide two or more of these additional services, while others are more narrow. We will examine each of these services closely.

Risk Reduction Through Diversification

All financial market participants are interested in reducing risk through diversification. We learned in Chapters Four and Five that by choosing a portfolio of investments, rather than investing all one's resources in a single asset, the total risk that an individual is exposed to can be reduced. The concept behind constructing a diversified portfolio is illustrated in Figure 11-1, which shows a hypothetical combination of expected return and risk measured by the variance of the portfolio, σ^2. Various portfolios may be selected by allocating one's wealth in different proportions across the assets available in the market and each such selection corresponds to a point in the shaded area to the right of line DD' in the figure. The curve labeled DD' represents the so-called efficient frontier of the possible portfolios one might choose. This means that any combination of the available assets which does not plot on that curve is inferior to some portfolio that does plot on the curve, because not enough risk has been diversified away. The implication is that any risk averse person will find it optimal to choose a portfolio of assets from the set of portfolios which is on this line. The optimal portfolio for any individual to choose is the one which provides what that individual perceives to be the best combination of expected return and risk from those combinations which plot on line DD'.

While this is a very useful representation of what constitutes any optimal portfolio and of the impact of diversification, it is not necessarily a very practical guide for choosing investments. In order to use this as a practical guideline, one has to have estimates of the risk and return on each asset one

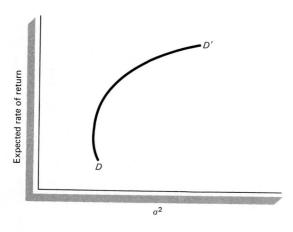

FIGURE 11-1
Efficient frontier of portfolios of risky assets.

might choose and the relationships between these assets, or between individual assets and some representative market portfolio. As a result, portfolio theory recommends that individuals who have no special knowledge should choose a portfolio which closely approximates the market as a whole. As a practical matter, if one randomly chooses 20 or more equity securities from the market and spreads one's available funds across these securities, the resulting portfolio will be a close approximation of the return on the market as a whole. As one adds more randomly chosen securities to this portfolio, the benefits from diversification increase slightly. In the limit, one could choose to invest a small amount in virtually all securities in the market and thereby have a completely diversified portfolio.

The only difficulty with following this advice directly is that it does not take into account the fact that it is costly to buy and sell securities in order to construct such a diversified portfolio. To illustrate the nature of the problem, suppose an individual had $10,000 to invest and wanted a highly diversified portfolio. In order to accomplish this, suppose that the person went to a broker with an order to purchase equal shares in each of the largest 100 corporations in the United States. Suppose the broker said that the brokerage fee would be $5 per share. The investor would then be able to purchase $95 worth of each of these 100 companies, and the total cost for conducting the transaction would be $500. If he or she wanted to liquidate half of these holdings 6 months later, yet still wanted to maintain the same degree of diversification, additional large transactions costs would be incurred.

Financial intermediaries can economize on such transactions costs by providing diversified portfolios for their customers. The financial intermediary pools the funds of a number of investors and acquires a large diversified portfolio. Then it sells claims on the entire portfolio of assets to individual investors. In this way, the individual who has $10,000 to invest and desires a diversified portfolio can purchase a portion of the larger portfolio of the intermediary. The intermediary does not have to buy small portions of each asset when individuals add or withdraw their claims on the intermediary. Instead, the intermediary holds an inventory of assets which can be liquidated at low cost and uses these to provide funds to individuals when they withdraw. Similarly, it adds to this pool of low-transactions-cost assets when new funds are provided to it. As long as there is some balance between the inflow and outflow of funds, the intermediary can reduce the costs of transacting for all market participants who seek diversified portfolios.

Maturity Intermediation

Many financial intermediaries currently provide the service of intermediating across maturities or borrowing short and lending long. This means that they accept funds from investors who desire to lend their funds with a short maturity, and lend those funds out to borrowers who desire a long maturity. Borrowers and lenders who have different preferred maturities are thus not compelled to agree on a common maturity. But as we know from the theory of the term structure of interest rates (see Chapter Nine), this cannot be accomplished without cost. By intermediating across maturities, financial intermediaries bear the risk of fluctuations in short-term rates. Lenders who supply funds to the intermediaries and receive short maturities are provided with liquidity that they would otherwise have to forgo or else purchase directly from borrowers without an intermediary in the transaction. When lenders deal with an intermediary, they still have to pay a price for this liquidity. Moreover, the risk involved is not a risk that can be reduced by diversification. Diversification is beneficial when assets can be combined that have probability distributions on their returns which are less than perfectly correlated. The risk borne by an intermediary which borrows short and lends long is the risk that nominal short-term interest rates will rise, and it will have to match these rates in order to retain its funds. But if these rates rise above the rate of return on outstanding long-term loans, then the intermediary loses money. The risk of an increase in short-term rates is not a risk which can be diversified.

The risk can be transferred or sold off to another party and in this way reduced. Futures markets (see Chapter Nine for a discussion of Treasury bill futures) can be utilized to hedge the risk of these changes. But whether sold or held, a price will be charged as a compensation for bearing this risk. In spite of the fact that the intermediary cannot reduce the underlying risk involved in bridging the gap between preferred habitats, it can often perform this function more efficiently than might other forms of market organizations. To do so the intermediary must be able to generate some kind of economies by specializing in lending long and borrowing short for large numbers of borrowers and lenders. These economies come from two sources. First, individuals who supply funds in small amounts cannot easily estimate the risks involved in arranging long-term contracts. By specializing in this function, intermediaries are better able to assess these prospects. Second, they are able to package short-term liabilities and long-term loans in economical units. This means that a borrower who is not large enough to effectively sell debt claims in a dealer market, but who is large enough to require funds from a sizable number of lenders, will find it efficient to utilize the services of the intermediary.

Reduction in the Cost of Contracting

One way to view the service provided by financial intermediaries in almost all the financial arrangements in which they engage is as a reduction in the cost of contracting. There are two distinct types of costs included under the label of contracting costs. The first is simply the cost of writing and understanding the contract in the first place. The second is the cost of monitoring the activities of the parties to the contract to ensure that the contract terms are observed and enforcing these terms if they are not.

Financial intermediaries are able to reduce the costs of writing contracts in cases where lenders or borrowers find highly standardized contracts to be unsuitable. The intermediary is able to write a contract which is tailored to the needs of individual borrowers at a lower cost than it would be possible to do in an auction or over-the-counter market. In these markets contracts are usually highly standardized, without special provisions tailored to individual borrowers. To some extent, such special provisions make it difficult for the market as a whole to evaluate the financial instrument. Moreover, when specialized contracts are written with an intermediary, the borrower is also able to renegotiate the terms of the contract with relative ease, whereas this would be costly and difficult if financial claims were widely distributed to the public.

The financial intermediary can reduce the costs of monitoring and enforcement by centralizing these functions in one agent rather than distributing them across all holders of bonds. This centralization is efficient because each bondholder, acting on his or her own, has a limited incentive to expend effort in monitoring and enforcement activities. The same advantage in centralization leads to the use of trustees in public distributions of bonds who are given certain monitoring and enforcement tasks. Moreover, because the intermediary's own return is tied to the success of monitoring and enforcement activities, there is an incentive to perform those duties in a reliable manner. A trustee could also be compensated in a way that provides such an incentive, but the fact that the intermediary's return comes from the asset and that it is not sold off as a dealer would sell it, accomplishes this as well.

Finally, the intermediary can provide a service for lenders if they are relatively unsophisticated, compared to borrowers. The intermediary is interjected between a sophisticated party, usually the borrower, and an unsophisticated party, usually the lender. The intermediary is therefore in a position to write, monitor, and enforce contracts with greater skill than the individual lender. In effect, lenders find it profitable to pool their resources and hire a financial intermediary in the same way they would hire a lawyer.

Information Production

An important service provided by financial intermediaries is the production of information about the value of assets. Intermediaries are certainly not the only type of information producer in the financial markets. The news media, brokerage houses, bond rating agencies, and other entities all produce information. But intermediaries do too. Intermediaries expend considerable resources collecting, processing, analyzing, and interpreting facts and opinions about the future profits of the firms they finance. Investors could do this on their own and to a certain extent they do. But it is also efficient to hire specialists in the production of information just as it is efficient to hire specialists to monitor the terms of contracts. The unique aspect of the financial intermediary as an information producer is that the intermediary generally does not redistribute information to the market as a whole. In other words, the intermediary does not collect information for direct resale to the market as does *The Wall Street Journal*. Instead, the intermediary collects information and uses it to guide the investment decisions it makes for those who supply it with funds. Therefore it can be thought of as tying the production of information in with the management of investments.

One of the major concerns about financial intermediaries as information producers is whether they perform this function in a reliable manner. The investor does not ever directly see the information and therefore needs some assurance that the intermediary is not in effect being bribed to invest in firms at prices that are too high. In this case, a bribe is some kind of extra payment that is paid to owners or managers of an intermediary to induce them to loan funds to a firm that might not qualify, or to provide funds on terms which are not in the interest of the intermediary's suppliers of funds. The principal insurance that the investor has that the intermediary will perform reliably is the stake that the owners and/or managers of the intermediary have in the investments that they choose for the intermediary's customers. The larger the amount of capital that the intermediary's owners contribute to the intermediary, the more the owners have to lose if they place their investments where they know they will not pay off. The market is therefore able to judge by the size of the intermediary's capital stock, the extent of its reliability in gathering information and using it to guide investment decisions.

Intermediaries also provide another service to the market which goes hand in hand with their production of information. They are often recipients of information from corporate borrowers who seek to protect the confidentiality of their information. It is useful to think of confidential or inside information as being of two types—technological information and strategic information. *Technological information* might include the knowledge of how to construct a Polaroid camera or a videocassette recorder. With a technological advance the product itself can be revealed to the market without revealing the method of production, and the market may be able to assess its value fairly. Moreover, the value of technological information is frequently protected by patent rights so that disclosure is possible. However, much inside information is of a strategic rather than a technological nature. *Strategic information* refers to marketing and advertising strategies, collusive price agreements of an overt or a covert nature, organizational techniques, and research and development procedures. The important characteristic of the latter information is that if the strategy is completely disclosed its value is diminished.

Firms which seek to protect such confidential information will find it advantageous to finance their activities from internal funds if and when they can. When they can't they will find it advantageous to go to sources of financing where the information they have can be revealed in order to secure financing but where confidentiality will be protected. Financial intermediaries provide this option. They therefore sell financing as well as the protection of confidential information.

Management of the Payments System

The services discussed thus far are provided by almost all intermediaries engaged in the management of investments. Now we will examine two important but more specialized services. The first, *management of the payments mechanism*, has long been provided by commercial banks. This means that banks provide the bookkeeping function of keeping track of receipts and disbursements for their customers as well as handling the exchange of funds. There is no necessary reason why the management of payments has to be handled by a financial intermediary which also manages funds. For example, some European countries have payments systems referred to as giro which are not linked to commercial banks. Although these systems are not all alike, such systems allow individuals to authorize payments to a number of parties through the giro. Usually the giro system allows a user to specify a list of payments to be made and a bank account number from which the funds can be drawn. The bank is then notified of the total funds used. Automated giro systems are sometimes more closely related to the postal system in such countries than to commercial banks. The postal system handles the exchange of funds and provides the customer with a record of these exchanges and the commercial bank merely maintains the balances of funds for the customer.

In the United States management of the payments mechanism became tied in with the banking industry early in the history of the country. In the first half of the nineteenth century the banking industry issued what were called bank notes. These were like a bank's own currency. These notes did not always trade at the same value. That is, the notes issued by a very strong and reputable bank would exchange at a higher value than would notes issued by a weak and risky bank. Each bank was willing to accept the notes of other banks at what they thought was a fair rate of exchange and this constituted the payments mechanism. In the latter part of the century notes were replaced by demand deposits or checking accounts. This meant that banks now began to keep records of transactions from demand deposit accounts and that they had to establish procedures for clearing checks back and forth. Banks set up clearing houses to handle these exchanges and large urban banks began to provide many of the collection and recordkeeping services for smaller banks. These larger banks became known as correspondent banks. In the twentieth century, after the Federal Reserve System was created, it began to provide many of these check-clearing services for the banking industry.

More recently, innovations have dramatically changed the economics of the payments system. These changes are continuing at a rapid pace. First of all, credit cards are actively competing with checks as an efficient means of making payments. The credit card includes the advantage of providing the customer with a direct link to a source of credit. But it also alters the method of recording and accounting for transactions. It increases reliance on automated recordkeeping and seeks to economize on the amount of paper which must change hands. Probably the most significant potential change in the payments mechanism is the prospect of an electronic funds-transfer system. Such a system would go further toward minimizing the amount of paper which changes hands in the payments system while relying on electronic recordkeeping to the maximum extent possible. There are large potential economies in such a system. But it is difficult to estimate how rapidly we will progress toward a completely electronic system of funds transfer.

Insurance

Another service provided by some financial intermediaries is insurance. Insurance is a service which, like management of the payments mechanism, is easily tied in with the function of managing investments. In the process of insuring various contingencies, insurance companies receive premiums which they invest, just as commercial banks invest the funds they receive in the course of managing payments for their depositors. While it might be possible to utilize a separate investment manager for the funds collected by an insurance company, this is a less efficient means of providing the service of insurance than is combining the two services.

The basic idea behind insurance is essentially similar to the idea of diversifying risk in the stock market. Individuals and corporations are subject to risks that they would like to be able to avoid or shift to other parties. The risk may be the economic hardship imposed on a family in the event of a death or the loss incurred if there is damage to property. Those who are exposed to these risks are generally willing to pay a fee to have someone else bear at least part of that risk. This shifting of risk becomes economical when the risk is diversifiable. To see what this means consider the case of a company exposed to the risk of a fire. A company that is interested in insuring against a fire faces a small probability that a fire will occur and there will be a large loss, and a large probability that no fire will occur and there will be no loss at all. A company which insures other companies against fire knows that some fires will always occur, but it knows that the probability that a large number of fires will occur at once is exceptionally small. As long as the insurance company has a large number of customers which are spread out geographically, it diversifies the risk of fire facing each customer. Therefore, the insurance company is able to offer customers a price for insurance which the customer views as better than the prospect of no cost as long as no fire occurs, but large losses if it does.

From the standpoint of the economy, this kind of risk shifting is beneficial because it induces people to undertake productive activities which they otherwise would perceive as too risky. The owners of a company might well be averse to constructing an expensive manufacturing plant if they alone had to bear the risk of its burning down. Therefore, risk shifting in general, and insurance in particular, serve a socially useful function.

FINANCIAL INTERMEDIARIES IN THE UNITED STATES ECONOMY

Now that we know why financial intermediaries exist, or at least the services which they provide in financial markets, it is important to acquire an understanding of the different types of intermediaries which operate in the United States capital markets. There is a wide variety of types of intermediaries providing distinct services. In part this variety is a response to the market's demand for different financial services. But in part it is also due to government regulation. Government regulation has led to a more fragmented set of institutions than would be likely were it not for that regulation. We will not discuss the regulatory system per se in this chapter, but as we examine the basic structure of financial intermediaries, the fact that regulation has a strong influence on this portion of the financial markets should be kept in mind. In this section we will first survey the different financial institutions which can be found in the U.S. economy. Then we will examine the flow of funds through these intermediaries. Finally, we will take a closer look at the largest and most diverse type of financial intermediary, the commercial bank.

Types of Financial Intermediaries

COMMERCIAL BANKS   Commercial banks are probably the oldest, largest, and most diversified of financial intermediaries. They have been the dominant source of business credit for centuries. In the United States commercial banking was a large and important enterprise before the New York Stock Exchange had even been founded. Today commercial banks are still fundamentally business lenders. Moreover, they have traditionally provided mainly short-term debt financing to business borrowers. This traditional role has been assumed in order to limit the risk of intermediating across time. This risk is potentially significant for commercial banks because most of their funds are obtained in the form of highly liquid deposits. Banks offer demand deposits; savings deposits, which are interest-bearing accounts with no stated maturity; and time deposits, which are interest-bearing accounts with a prespecified maturity. There are two features which have distinguished commercial banks from other financial intermediaries. First, they alone have been able to offer demand deposits. As a result, they alone have been involved in managing the payments mechanism. Second, they are the most diversified of financial intermediaries. They make loans to businesses, consumers, farmers, and governments. Some loans are uncollateralized while others have collateral in the form of machinery, securities, automobiles, real estate, and so forth. No other financial intermediary offers quite the variety of financing opportunities that the commercial bank offers.

SAVINGS AND LOANS   Savings and loans are depository institutions which specialize in making mortgage loans. This means that they obtain funds through deposit accounts, both savings and time deposits, and they extend loans to finance residential property. They do hold a small number of highly liquid securities, but these are held to maintain liquidity and not as profitable investments. In offering this specialized service to the market, savings and loans have invested principally in fixed-rate long-term mortgages. Yet their deposits have very short maturities. As a result, they provide the market with the service of intermediating across time. We will look closely at these institutions in the next chapter.

MUTUAL SAVINGS BANKS (MSBs)   These institutions are a sort of cross between commercial banks and savings and loans, with some additional unique features. MSBs originated during the late nineteenth century in the New England states as an alternative to the commercial bank where working men and women could save funds and seek loans when needed. At that time commercial banks did not commonly extend loans to consumers to the extent they do today. Hence MSBs filled a distinct gap in the market. As a result of this purpose they were organized as cooperative or mutual organizations. This means that the depositors are the owners of the organization. In MSBs depositors do not hold fixed interest claims with all residual income accruing to separate equity owners. Instead, the earnings of the MSB are paid to depositors. MSBs are similar to savings and loans in that a large portion of the loans are committed to home mortgages. MSBs also provide other types of consumer loans to their members, and they invest a sizable portion of their funds in corporate bonds. Almost all MSBs in existence today are located in the New England states and in New York. They have not spread to the rest of the country, probably because of the growth in savings and loans and credit unions which serve an essentially similar purpose.

CREDIT UNIONS   Credit unions are very much like mutual savings banks. They are organized as a mutual or cooperative organization and their purpose is to provide an alternative to commercial banks where consumers can save and obtain loans when needed. Credit unions do not invest heavily in first mortgages, largely because they are restricted from so doing. But they do finance most other types of consumer purchases. Credit unions got their start in the early part of the twentieth century and existed in 38 states by 1934. But their largest growth occurred after World War II. Since that war, they have had the highest rate of growth of any financial intermediary in the country. The real distinction between a credit union and a mutual savings bank is that there is supposed to be some common bond among the members of a credit union, usually, but not necessarily, their place of employment.

FINANCE COMPANIES   These are a type of intermediary which makes both business and consumer loans. Many of them are owned by commercial banks or by nonfinancial corporations which produce or distribute consumer products. Many specialize in making consumer loans, often to more risky customers than banks deal with on average. These institutions have evolved largely to circumvent many of the existing regulations on depository financial institutions. For example, many larger banks operate finance companies which have offices outside of the territory in which these banks are permitted to operate, in order to evade restrictions on branch banking and to be prepared in the event that commercial banks are ever allowed to have branches nationwide.

INVESTMENT COMPANIES   Investment companies, or mutual funds, act as managers of investment portfolios for their customers. They provide all the services which go hand in hand with managing investments, such as reduction of risk through diversification, information production, and reduction in the cost of contracting. There are a variety of different types of investment companies, or mutual funds. We will discuss the differences between two major types of funds, closed- and open-end funds, toward the end of the chapter. An increasingly important type of investment company is the pension fund. Pension funds are essentially investment companies which accept funds from individuals during their working lifetime, invest those funds, and pay them back to the individuals upon retirement. Like other intermediaries, they channel funds from lenders to borrowers. Their unique feature is that the contingency which triggers repayment of the funds which are lent is the retirement of the lender. There are a number of different types of pension funds and a number of different types of pension contracts or sets of terms for determining the amount of funds lent and the conditions of repayment.

INSURANCE COMPANIES   It is not always obvious that insurance companies perform a financial intermediary function similar to that of commercial banks or the nonbank intermediaries described above. But they do. There are basically two types of insurance companies, life insurance and property and casualty insurance companies. These institutions differ according to the type of risk they insure and the type of investments they tend to make, but not by the basic function they provide in the economy. Insurance companies accept funds in the form of premiums from those they insure and stand ready to pay off on the risks they insure. However, they also invest the funds they receive, thus acting as a lender. As a consequence, they act much like a commercial bank or other intermediary that channels funds from lenders to borrowers.

The Flow of Funds Through Financial Intermediaries

It is exceptionally important to appreciate the significance of these various intermediaries in the financial markets. The market for corporate equity securities often attracts such attention in the popular press, as well as among scholars who study financial markets, that it is easy to underestimate the relative importance of financial intermediaries in the financial markets. Figure 11-2 shows the proportion of all funds supplied to any borrower in the United States from any private domestic source which involved a financial intermediary during the decade of the 1970s. A private domestic source means that these data exclude funds which come either from the government or from some foreign source. In every year shown in the figure the proportion of funds passing through some kind of financial intermediary comprises over two-thirds of all borrowing and lending which took place in the U.S. economy. The implication is that financial intermediaries are the rule rather than the exception in contemporary U.S. financial markets. The figure also shows that, in most years, the largest portion of these funds has passed through commercial banks. The years when the commercial banks' share of the market declined substantially were generally the years following a recession, when the demand for funds through commercial banks was at a cyclical low point. This pattern is analyzed in more detail in Chapter Thirteen.

FIGURE 11-2

Proportion of private domestic flow of funds involving financial intermediaries. Source: Flow of Funds Accounts.

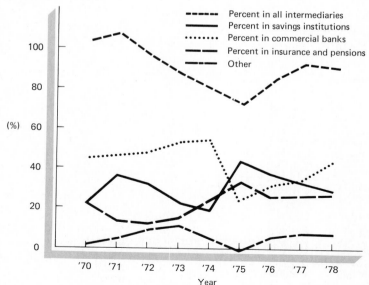

It is important to recognize that the large role for financial intermediaries does not mean that auction and over-the-counter markets are unimportant. Because the flow of funds passes through a financial intermediary does not mean that those funds ultimately are not used to purchase a security in an auction or dealer market. Financial intermediaries act as agents for the customers to whom they issue liabilities and they may use those customers' funds either to purchase publicly traded securities or to provide private financing in the form of loans. It is only the private financing that is completed without any purchase or sale of securities in a dealer or auction market. Therefore, financial intermediaries acquire funds from lenders and distribute those funds in the form of both public and private securities.

A Closer Look at Commercial Banks

It is useful to examine commercial banks a little more closely, both because they are the largest financial intermediary in the market and because they are the most diversified intermediary. In the coming chapters we will examine all of the financial intermediaries in more detail, but an initial scrutiny of commercial banks provides an important sense of perspective.

The asset side of the balance sheet of commercial banks is composed largely of loans with a little less than a third of total assets typically invested in marketable securities. Figure 11-3 shows the composition of the asset side of all commercial banks taken together during 1977 and 1978. The figure illustrates that commercial banks extend a wide variety of different types of loans. The largest component of the loan portfolio is made up of commercial

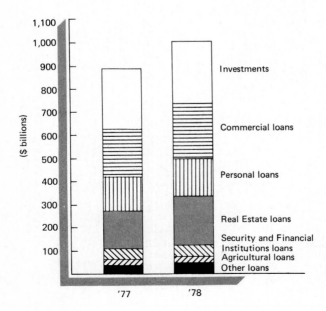

FIGURE 11-3
Loans and investments of commercial banks. Source: *Federal Reserve Bulletins*, various issues.

or business loans, followed by mortgage loans. Bank investments (that is, their holdings of publicly traded securities) are almost exclusively in two types of securities, Treasury bonds and bills and municipal bonds. Banks hold Treasury securities because of their high liquidity. They hold municipal bonds because of their tax advantages. Municipal bonds are free of corporate income taxes and this feature is attractive to commercial banks which, unlike such investors as pension funds, are subject to income taxes. In fact, commercial banks and insurance companies are the largest holders of municipal bonds in the economy. Figure 11-4 shows the relative volume of Treasury and municipal investments of commercial banks. The figure indicates that bank holdings of municipal bonds have been increasing relative to holdings of Treasury securities. This reflects decreased reliance on Treasury securities as a source of liquidity and increased emphasis on the contribution to after-tax earnings of municipal bonds.

On the liability side of the balance sheet, commercial banks derive almost all their funds from various types of deposit accounts. Of the three

FIGURE 11-4

Total volume of U.S. Treasury securities and municipal securities held by commercial banks.
Source: *Federal Reserve Chart Book*, 1979.

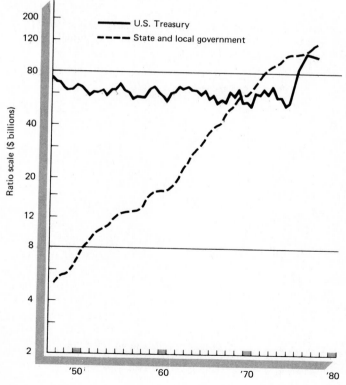

types of accounts—demand deposits, savings deposits, and time deposits—demand deposits have been declining in relative importance in recent years. This reflects the decreased attractiveness of demand deposits in times of high inflation. On the other hand, banks' holdings of time deposits have not suffered as much because interest rates on these accounts have been able to rise with general market rates, though sometimes with some lag. The various types of deposits offered by banks as well as by other intermediaries are highly dependent upon the decisions of regulators because the interest rates banks can offer on these accounts are controlled by the government. As a result, these trends are heavily influenced by regulatory decisions. Banks have also come to rely more heavily on various nondeposit sources of funds. In recent years these have become a larger portion of total bank liabilities. Finally, bank equity capital provides depositors with a cushion against declines in bank earnings. The size of this cushion is controlled by regulators and it has declined somewhat, as a proportion of total liabilities and capital, in recent years. Figures 11-5 and 11-6 illustrate some of these trends in deposits and capital relative to total bank liabilities. They show the decline in demand deposits and rise in time deposits as sources of funds and they illustrate the relative decline of capital accounts.

FIGURE 11-5

Trends in commercial bank demand and time deposits. The figure shows the total stock of demand and time deposits as a proportion of total bank liabilities and capital for all commercial banks. Source: *Federal Reserve Chart Book*, 1979.

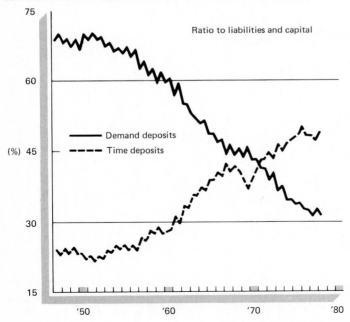

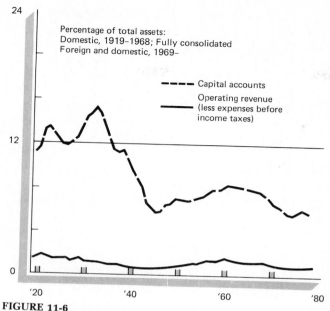

FIGURE 11-6

The trend in bank capital. The figure shows the total volume of bank capital as a percent of total assets for banks which are members of the Federal Reserve System. Source: *Federal Reserve Chart Book*, 1979.

SPECIAL ISSUES IN INTERMEDIATED MARKETS

There are a large number of important issues regarding the operation of intermediaries in the financial system. A good number of them deal with how intermediaries are regulated. But two interesting issues which we can take up before we confront the regulatory system deal with the market's valuation of financial intermediaries and liquidity management by intermediaries.

Valuing Financial Intermediaries

There are a number of special problems encountered in trying to value a financial intermediary. An intermediary functions as a portfolio manager and derives its revenues from the assets which it holds in its portfolio. As a result, the value of the intermediary is dependent upon the value of those assets. Yet as we learned above, these assets often have some special characteristics. In many cases, the assets have no secondary market so that they cannot be resold; thus there is no market which sets the value of these outstanding assets. This is true of most loans held by commercial banks and many types of loans held by other institutions. In addition, intermediaries, particularly commercial banks, may have acquired special information about the assets or loans they hold which the outsider valuing the bank may not have. Most financial intermediaries are also highly regulated and this regulation has a material impact on the value of the intermediary. Finally, like nonfinancial firms in the economy, most intermediaries have other assets which are a necessary part of the firm's ongoing business. Many of these institutions, particularly commercial banks and savings and loans, have extensive plant and equipment which they use to serve their customers. As in valuing any other firm, these assets must be taken into account.

One type of financial intermediary where all of these problems are kept to a minimum is the investment company. These institutions are one of the simplest types of financial intermediaries because the service they provide is essentially one of diversification. Investment companies offer diversified portfolios of securities in which investors can buy shares. These funds are managed by individuals who seek to provide combinations of risk and return which will be attractive to different groups of investors. For example, some funds, loosely known as "go-go" funds, emphasize more risky securities, while others do not. Some funds are bond funds in that the investments are only in bonds; some are municipal-bond funds, which are attractive to high-tax-bracket investors; and some are money market funds, investing only in money market securities.

Two broad types of investment funds are of particular interest for the purposes of valuing intermediaries. One is referred to as an open-end fund and the other as a closed-end fund. Both types of funds invest in marketable securities. In an *open-end fund* the owners of the fund hold direct claims on the securities managed by the fund. This means that if an investor wants to cash in his or her share of an open-end fund he or she receives a pro rata share of the value of the fund's portfolio at the time of cashing in. In a *closed-end fund* the investor owns a share of the fund as a separate entity and the fund owns the securities it manages. Closed-end funds therefore have a market value of their own as distinct from the value of the securities which they manage. When a person buys into the fund or sells his or her shares in the fund, then those shares are exchanged at the price of the fund's shares, regardless of the prices of the securities owned by the fund. The closed-end fund is similar to most other types of intermediaries in that it owns assets and individuals hold claims on the intermediary rather than directly on the assets. The differences are first, that the closed-end fund does not issue deposit claims as do many other intermediaries. Deposit claims are debt claims which are insured by the government. Therefore the closed-end fund is not subject to the same kind of regulation as are depository intermediaries. Second, the closed-end fund also holds assets with active secondary markets so that unlike other intermediaries, the market value of the assets can be readily determined. The closed-end fund therefore provides an interesting opportunity to examine the market's valuation of financial intermediaries, because it is possible to directly compare the value of the assets held by a closed-end fund with the market value of the fund itself.

It is interesting to observe that the value of a closed-end fund is not always the same as the value of the assets owned by that fund. Differences between the market value of the securities owned by the fund and the market value of the fund itself are referred to as *premiums* or *discounts*. The fund is said to be selling at a premium if the value of the fund exceeds the value of the securities in the fund. In this case, investors who wish to purchase shares in the fund must pay more than they would pay if they purchased those shares for themselves in the market. The fund is said to be selling at a discount if the value of the fund is less than the value of the securities in the fund. This means that investors can pay less than the value of the securities owned by the fund if they purchase shares in the fund.

At first glance one might suspect that, aside from potential difficulties surrounding the accounting procedures in these funds, there ought not be either premiums or discounts. That is, the value of a fund should be the same as the value of the assets which it owns. But this is simply not the case. Closed-end funds sell at widely different premiums or discounts. There is both substantial variation across funds at one time and in the premium or discount for individual funds at a different time. This variability is illustrated in Table 11-1. The table shows the discounts (positive sign) and premiums (negative sign) for a selection of funds which existed from 1960 to 1975. The table indicates tremendous variability in the size of the premium or discount. The interesting question is why this occurs.

There are at least four plausible explanations for these premiums and discounts. One possibility is that there are sufficient tax considerations that there will be wide and variable differences between the value of the fund and the value of its assets. This argument relies on the idea that there are different capital gains in different funds, because the gains are based on the prices at which the securities were previously acquired. These capital gains will be taxed when the fund shares are sold and the income realized. The magnitude of these unrealized capital gains might account for premiums and discounts. A second possibility is that the difference between the two values is a result of economies in accomplishing diversification of the fund relative to the cost incurred by individuals. This argues that the value of the shares owned by the fund does not include the cost of acquiring them. The third possibility is that the value of the fund includes the capitalized value of the skill of its managers. This will be a positive amount, and thus generate a premium, if the managers are believed to be able to outperform the market. It will be a negative amount, and lead to a discount, if the market believes they will fail to outperform the market, but will generate expenses in so doing. Finally, there is the possibility that the market is simply inefficient in appraising the value of funds and does not act on clear opportunities to trade profitably.

While no one has yet determined exactly what the answer is, some

TABLE 11-1

Year-End Discounts* for a Sample of Large Closed-end Funds in the Years from 1960 to 1975 (%)

ID NO.	60	61	62	63	64	65	66	67	68	69	70	71	72	73	74	75
3	14	3	4	9	10	12	6	6	-10	-6	6	15	14	14	25	23
1	30	39	35	34	10	-5	-12	-77	-54	15	-37	-10	6	-26	9	-48
8	12	2	7	8	6	11	19	21	12	14	18	20	17	19	16	22
11	19	10	-1	3	6	7	11	-1	-14	-8	8	12	4	17	13	26
14	-1	-5	-4	-1	6	11	9	-16	-23	-16	-14	8	13	20	22	20
15	2	-23	-28	-13	-3	-2	-18	-19	-32	-51	-16	3	19	34	29	30
18	12	-6	3	6	0	8	12	11	-8	-12	-5	13	7	4	-4	4
16	-2	3	-2	2	10	2	-14	-33	-26	15	12	15	27	39	43	37
19	0	0	5	6	3	-6	0	3	-7	-4	3	14	4	8	10	-2
21	4	5	3	12	21	24	20	19	7	14	15	26	28	23	25	28
22	22	16	19	24	26	33	29	17	7	11	3	7	3	21	26	25
23	23	13	15	21	24	23	25	16	4	2	5	14	19	13	14	22
13†	E	E	34	15	32	27	32	9	-5	-6	-11	-7	8	31	43	16
Average	11	5	7	10	12	11	9	-3	-11	-2	-1	10	13	17	21	16

* Discount = (NAV − MV)/NAV, where NAV is the net asset value of the fund, and MV is the market value of the fund's outstanding stock.

† E = fund not traded.

Source: Rex Thompson, ''Information Content of Discounts and Premiums on Closed-End Fund Shares,'' *Journal of Financial Economics*, vol. 6 (1978), p. 158. Reprinted with permission.

interesting evidence on the question has been collected. Essentially this evidence indicates that closed-end funds which sell at discounts tend to generate higher returns than the market average, after adjustments for risk.[1] That is, one can devise simple rules for trading in the market, utilizing funds which sell at discounts and significantly outperform the market as a whole. This is consistent with either the tax argument, the diversification argument, or the inefficiency argument, though it seems unlikely that taxes and diversification can account for it. This conclusion suggests that either there is some kind of market inefficiency which leads to premiums and discounts or that there is some significant factor determining the prices of risky assets which financial economists have not yet been able to include in their tests. The problem of understanding how intermediaries are valued remains an intriguing and important puzzle.

Financial Intermediaries and Liquidity Management

One of the most important tasks facing most financial intermediaries is liquidity management. Most intermediaries not only manage portfolios for their customers but they offer those customers access to that portfolio with little cost of transacting. This is particularly important for intermediaries which intermediate across time, such as savings and loans and commercial banks, and less so for those which do not, such as insurance companies. In fact, as discussed early in the chapter one of the principal reasons intermediaries are able to prosper is because they can offer economies in the costs of transacting to their customers. But the intermediary is then left with the task of providing this liquidity and it is useful to consider the basic approaches to dealing with this problem.

Intermediaries derive their profits from investing in assets which are often times not highly marketable. This is particularly true of commercial banks, as they cannot sell their loans in secondary markets. These institutions face a continual inflow and outflow of funds or cash. They must be prepared for the contingency that there will be a larger outflow than inflow. The situation is illustrated in Figure 11-7, which shows a hypothetical pattern of net cash flows for an intermediary over a given time period. The figure shows that during some periods there is a net inflow of funds but during others there are large cash drains on the intermediary. The intermediary has essentially three methods available to deal with this problem. They are:

Liquidate assets

Borrow funds in the money markets

Hedge cash-flow risks in the futures markets

---

[1] See Rex Thompson, "The Information Content of Discounts and Premiums on Closed-End Fund Shares," *Journal of Financial Economics*, vol. 6 (1978), pp. 151–186.

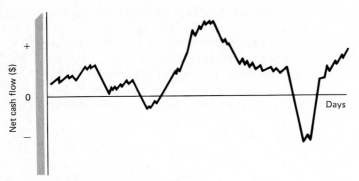

FIGURE 11-7
Illustration of net cash flow for a financial intermediary. When the line is above the horizontal axis, this represents positive cash flow, and when it falls below the axis, this represents negative cash flow.

We will discuss each of these alternatives in turn.

The first choice the intermediary has is to liquidate existing assets. With many types of loans, this may be either virtually impossible or exceedingly costly. Some loans simply have no secondary markets. Others have secondary markets, but the loss involved in liquidating those assets may be very large. The cost can be reduced if active secondary markets can be developed and in some cases this has happened in recent years. For example, there has developed a large secondary market in the mortgage industry which has improved the liquidity position of savings and loans. But to a substantial degree the principal loans of most financial intermediaries remain largely illiquid. As a result, most financial intermediaries invest in a second type of asset which is highly liquid. Treasury securities are generally used for this purpose because of the active secondary market in these securities.

The decision on how extensive should be the holdings of liquid assets, such as Treasury securities, depends upon the costs of holding these securities compared to the alternative means of meeting cash outflows. There are two components to this cost. The first is the opportunity cost of revenue lost by not holding more lucrative but less marketable loans or investments. This is really the spread between the rate of return on the liquid asset and the rate of return on the more profitable loan or investment. The second is the brokerage or transaction cost of selling the liquid asset to satisfy cash outflows. This includes not only the actual cost of selling the asset but the capital losses incurred if the price of the asset has fallen when it is sold. As either of these costs increases, this alternative will become more expensive.

The maintenance of reserves of liquid assets has been the traditional tool used by financial intermediaries to deal with the liquidity problem. This method has generally been referred to as asset management because the decision is one of how to split assets between the less and more liquid forms. But during the 1970s intermediaries came to rely less intensively on asset management and more on the other two alternatives. This is reflected in the decline in commercial bank holdings of Treasury securities, relative to the less marketable municipal securities, shown in Figure 11-4. The reason for this shift is due to the development of the money markets and more recently the futures markets which give intermediaries efficient alternatives to asset management.

The option to turn to the money market to satisfy cash outflows is simply the option to borrow short-term funds when they are needed to satisfy cash drains. During the late 1960s and all of the 1970s, the money markets developed into efficient sources of very short-term borrowing and lending. Financial intermediaries are able to borrow large amounts of funds with maturities as short as 1 day through federal funds and repurchase agreements. This constitutes an over-the-counter market in what is referred to as "immediately available funds." The risk that an intermediary bears in relying on the money market as opposed to its own holdings of liquid assets is that the cost of obtaining funds in the money market may be high at times when cash flows are least favorable. The advantage of this liability as opposed to asset management is that there is no ongoing opportunity cost of investing in low return assets. The choice between the two alternatives depends upon one's assessment of the relative costs.

The third possibility available to deal with liquidity allows the intermediary to hedge some of the risk involved in the other alternatives by using the futures markets. Futures markets in financial obligations are a relatively recent but important innovation in the U.S. capital markets. The essence of how they operate was described in Chapter Nine. Here we want to see how they can be used to hedge or reduce the risk of increases in the future cost of obtaining funds. Suppose a financial intermediary is concerned that there will be a net cash outflow of say $5 million in 4 weeks. If the manager of the intermediary waits to see whether it develops and finds that it does, he or she will have to borrow the $5 million in the money market and pay the going interest rate 4 weeks from now, whatever that may be. Suppose the manager observes that the current interest rate is 9.65 percent and he or she is concerned that this rate will increase. The manager can go to the futures market in Treasury bills and sell a $5 million futures contract in Treasury bills to be delivered 4 weeks later. This means that he or she contracts today to deliver a Treasury bill at a prespecified price or yield 4 weeks later. Now suppose that interest rates do increase above the current level of 9.65 percent, so that it becomes more expensive to borrow funds when they are needed. At the same time, this rise in interest rates will mean a fall in the price of Treasury bills. Therefore, when the Treasury bill futures contract matures it will be possible to buy a Treasury bill and sell it at the contract price for a profit. The profit on the Treasury bill futures contract will offset the increase in the cost of borrowing in the money market. If, on the other hand, interest rates go down (and prices of bills go up), then there will be a loss on the futures contract, but it will be offset by the reduced cost of borrowing in the money market. In this way, the financial intermediary is able to hedge its risk of future changes in interest rates.

Even before futures markets developed it was still possible to construct such a hedge. The manager in the example could hedge by borrowing (the same as selling short) a 3-month Treasury bill and simultaneously selling it. Then after 4 weeks he or she would buy a Treasury bill with the same maturity date. If interest rates corresponding to that maturity rose so that the price of bills fell, then the manager would profit from the transaction and thereby offset the increase in the cost of borrowing. If rates fell he or she would lose on the short-sale transaction, but the cost of borrowing would fall to offset it. The difficulty is that this short-sale procedure for hedging is often more cumbersome and costly than using an organized futures market. Hence the attraction of the futures market is that it makes hedging behavior easier.

Futures markets developed in the United States at a rapid pace during the 1970s. As of 1980 there were markets in Treasury bills, Treasury bonds, and securities issued by the General National Mortgage Association or GNMA securities (see Chapters Twelve and Fourteen for discussions of these securities). Thus far most of the trading in these markets is more for the purpose of speculating on the future course of interest rates. During 1979 financial intermediaries and other businesses not specializing in the futures industry accounted for less than 30 percent of the futures trading volume in each of these three securities. This low participation is probably due, in part, either to regulatory restrictions or to ambiguity regarding regulators' attitudes toward participation in the market.[2] Nevertheless, this market holds out the opportunity of an important new avenue for the hedging of risks for financial intermediaries.

SUMMARY

In this chapter we examined the third type of market organization besides auction and over-the-counter markets, the intermediated market. An intermediated market is one where financial intermediaries play a dominant role. A financial intermediary differs from a dealer in that an intermediary purchases assets and holds them as an investment rather than purchasing for resale and holding only an inventory. The intermediary acquires funds for these investments by selling claims on itself to the public. Therefore, unlike a dealer, the intermediary creates a new security and sells it to the market rather than reselling the securities it purchases.

We examined six services which financial intermediaries provide to financial markets. The first few services are provided by almost all intermediaries. But the latter services are more specialized.

[2] See Marcelle Arak and Christopher J. McCurdy, "Interest Rates Futures," Federal Reserve Bank of New York, *Quarterly Review*, 4 (Winter 1979–1980), pp. 33–46.

RISK REDUCTION THROUGH DIVERSIFICATION Financial intermediaries construct diversified portfolios of securities and then sell claims on themselves to the market. In this way, they provide diversification to the investor. This is profitable because intermediaries find it less costly to construct a large diversified portfolio and sell small portions of it than would individual investors if they had to construct their own small diversified portfolios.

MATURITY INTERMEDIATION Many intermediaries sell claims with very short maturities. This is referred to as intermediating across time or maturity intermediation. The intermediaries will demand a price for this which compensates them for the risk which they bear in bridging the gap between desired maturities.

REDUCTION IN THE COST OF CONTRACTING There are two principal costs involved in utilizing financial contracts. The first is the cost of constructing the contract, including the expertise required to know how best to structure the contract. The second is the cost of monitoring the behavior of the party to the contract to be sure the terms are observed. Investors who supply funds to financial intermediaries would find these costs to be quite large if they had to write, monitor, and enforce contracts with borrowers themselves. But financial intermediaries can lower these costs by specializing in financial contracting.

INFORMATION PRODUCTION Financial intermediaries produce information about the borrowers who are supplied with funds. But they differ from other types of information producers in that they do not directly distribute this information to the market. Hence, much of the information they receive is confidential.

MANAGEMENT OF THE PAYMENTS SYSTEM A service historically provided by commercial banks is to keep records and provide for exchange of funds through demand deposits. Other types of intermediaries are increasingly competing with commercial banks in providing this service in the United States. This service is tied in with other services involved in managing investments for individuals and companies.

INSURANCE Many types of financial intermediaries provide insurance against particular contingencies. The principal types of such intermediaries are life insurance and fire and casualty insurance companies. These companies act as financial intermediaries in that they invest the funds received as premium income and repay these funds in the event of some event, such as fire, accident, or death. Though the management problems of insurance intermediaries are quite different from those of deposit intermediaries, they serve as a market for borrowing and lending just as do other financial intermediaries.

Next we surveyed the types of financial institutions which operate in the U.S. economy. The largest and most diversified financial intermediaries are commercial banks. Commercial banks are also the oldest type of financial intermediary which attracts funds in the form of deposit accounts. Other, more specialized intermediaries which rely on deposits include savings and loans, mutual savings banks, and credit unions. Savings and loans invest almost exclusively in mortgages due to regulatory restrictions. Mutual savings banks exist almost exclusively in New England. They evolved to provide consumers alternative sources of borrowing and lending. Credit unions are similar to savings and loans in their purpose and origin. However, today their lending is almost exclusively non-mortgage lending to consumers, while mutual savings banks also invest heavily in corporate bonds and mortgages. We also found that there are investment companies which essentially sell risk reduction and information as they manage investments. Finally, there are finance companies. These exist largely to circumvent regulations on the other types of financial intermediaries.

Finally, we examined two of the more interesting and important issues regarding financial intermediaries, aside from aspects of how they are regulated. First, we examined the problem of how to value a financial intermediary. In particular, we examined the magnitude of discounts and premiums on closed-end funds. These are one of the simplest types of intermediaries we encounter in the market and therefore should present one of the simpler problems of valuation. We found that closed-end funds often sell at significant premiums and discounts, but we found it difficult to fully account for these pricing patterns. This remains an interesting and important problem. Second, we examined some of the alternative ways intermediaries manage their liquidity. We found that there are essentially three options available: liquidate assets, borrow funds in the money market, and hedge cash flows in the futures market. While the first option was widely used at one time, we found that the second two have since become much more important. With the improvement of futures markets and the increased volatility of interest rates in recent years, hedging may become even more popular in the years ahead.

QUESTIONS TO IMPROVE UNDERSTANDING

1   Investors on their own, without the aid of an intermediary, can diversify portfolios and purchase securities with different maturities. Under what circumstances would they seek to use intermediaries to do this for them?

2   What does it mean to say that intermediaries can reduce the cost of contracting? What is included in the cost of contracting? What is the difference between an intermediary and the trustee of a bond?

3   What is the incentive for a financial intermediary to produce reliable information? How does the market on its own deal with the problem of unreliable production of information by financial intermediaries?

4   What is the "payments system"? How do commercial banks in the United States manage the payment system? Can you imagine an alternative, equally efficient system.

5   Insurance leads to a redistribution of risk. How can such a redistribution be socially beneficial?

6   What distinguishes commercial banks from other types of financial intermediaries? Are these differences intrinsic in commercial banking or could other financial intermediaries become essentially identical to commercial banks?

7   Explain the differences between savings and loans, mutual savings banks, and credit unions.

8   What are the fundamental difficulties involved in valuing a financial intermediary? What are closed-end funds? Why do they provide an interesting opportunity to explore how financial intermediaries are valued by the market?

9   Explain how intermediaries can use either asset or liability management to handle their liquidity problem.

10 How can intermediaries use futures markets to "hedge"?

REFERENCES

Arak, Marcelle, and Christopher J. McCurdy: "Interest Rate Futures," *Quarterly Review*, Federal Reserve Bank of New York, 4 (Winter 1979–1980), pp. 33–46.

Arrow, Kenneth J.: "Insurance, Risk and Resource Allocation," in Kenneth J. Arrow (ed.) *Essays in the Theory of Risk-Bearing*, Markham Publishing Company, New York (1971), pp. 134–143.

Baltensperger, Ernst: "Alternative Approaches to the Theory of the Banking Firm," *Journal of Monetary Economics*, 6 (January 1980), pp. 1–38.

Benston, George, and Clifford Smith: "A Transactions Cost Approach to the Theory of Financial Intermediation," *Journal of Finance*, 31 (May 1976), pp. 215–231.

Campbell, Tim S.: "Optimal Investment Financing Decisions and the Value of Confidentiality," *Journal of Financial and Quantitative Analysis*, 14 (December 1979), pp. 913–924.

———, and William A. Kracaw: "Information Asymmetries, Signalling and the Theory of Financial Intermediation," *Journal of Finance*, 35 (September 1980), pp. 863–882.

Leland, Hayne E., and David H. Pyle: "Informational Asymmetries, Financial Structure and Financial Intermediation," *Journal of Finance*, 32 (May 1977), pp. 371–387.

Malkiel, Burton G.: "The Valuation of Closed-End Investment-Company Shares," *Journal of Finance*, 32 (June 1977), pp. 847–859.

*Mayer, Martin: *The Bankers*, Weybright and Talley, Inc., New York, 1974.

*McKinney, George W., Jr.: "Liability Management: Its Cost and Its Uses," *The Bankers Magazine*, 161 (January–February 1978), pp. 50–58.

Miller, Merton, and Daniel Orr: "A Model of the Demand for Money by Firms," *Quarterly Journal of Economics*, 80 (August 1966), pp. 413–435.

Pyle, David H.: "Descriptive Theories of Financial Institutions Under Uncertainty,"

---

* References marked with an * provide additional institutional detail and make excellent supplementary readings.

Journal of Financial and Quantitative Analysis, 7 (December 1972), pp. 2009–2029.

————: "On the Theory of Financial Intermediation," *Journal of Finance*, 26 (June 1971), pp. 737–747.

*Schweser, Carl, Joseph Cole, and Lou D'Antonio: "Hedging Opportunities in Bank Risk Management Programs," *Journal of Commercial Bank Lending* (January 1980), pp. 29–41.

Thompson, Rex: "The Information Content of Discounts and Premiums on Closed-End Fund Shares," *Journal of Financial Economics*, 6 (1978), pp. 151–186.

Chapter Twelve

THE MARKET FOR CONSUMER BORROWING AND LENDING

In the late 1970s the market for consumer financing became the largest in the United States. In 1979 consumers borrowed approximately $160 billion to finance purchases ranging from houses and automobiles to gold and vacations. Not only has the volume of consumer debt become larger than other types of borrowing in the economy, but, at least in the latter part of the 1970s, the rate of growth in consumer debt was larger than in the corporate or government sectors. These trends are illustrated in Figure 12-1. It shows the total volume of funds borrowed by major sectors within the U.S. economy, as shown in the flow of funds accounts for the decade of the 1970s. Sheer size alone makes this market important. But it is also interesting because it is closer to each of us as consumers than the other markets in the economy. In addition, parts of this market have been in turmoil in recent years. And in this chapter we will find out why.

In this chapter we will explore the financial markets in which consumers borrow and lend. We will examine the various forms in which consumers borrow and the institutions which serve this market. Then we will turn our attention to the various ways in which consumers lend. We will examine the types of securities which consumers purchase, the trends in this side of the market, and the prospects for change in the future.

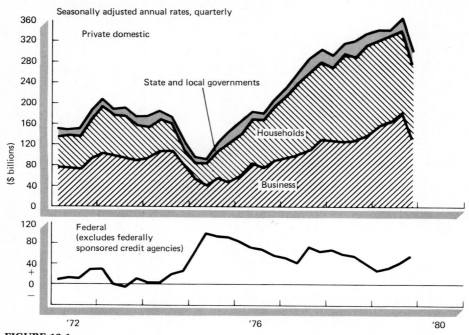

FIGURE 12-1

Net funds raised by major sectors of the economy. Source: *Federal Reserve Chart Book*, 1979.

OVERVIEW OF CONSUMER FINANCING

To start our investigation of the consumer-related financial markets we will focus on the basic patterns in consumer borrowing, on the types of assets consumers have acquired and on the institutions they have used over the last decade. With an understanding of the important components of the market in hand, it is possible to analyze the major components of this market in somewhat more detail.

The largest single component of consumer financial markets is the mortgage industry. For most individuals the purchase of a home is the largest transaction they will make, and the mortgage which finances that home is the largest financial obligation they will ever incur. Figure 12-2 shows the dollar magnitudes involved. It shows the amount of funds raised through home mortgages during most of the 1970s, compared to other forms of household borrowing. But the volume of home mortgage financing is also quite large compared to most other types of securities issued by either governments or businesses. In the last few years of the 1970s, funds raised by consumers through home mortgage loans exceeded 25 percent of all funds raised in the financial markets by any source. The second largest portion of total financial markets was composed of Treasury securities, which represented approximately one-half of the total funds raised through home mortgages. Second to mortgage debt, the other important component of consumer debt is labeled consumer installment credit. The total volume of installment credit incurred during the 1970s is shown in Figure 12-2. This debt includes a variety of different types of debt contracts, generally with financial institutions, which are used to finance purchases of commodities and services for personal consumption. Later we will examine the types of consumer installment debt, what they are used for, and the institutions which supply them.

On the other side of the aggregate household balance sheet there have been some significant changes in the types of financial assets consumers have chosen to hold. The basic trends in the holdings of financial assets by consumers are shown in Figure 12-3. This figure shows the total stock of household assets broken down into three components. The first component, deposits and credit market instruments, represents the total sum of all deposits held with financial intermediaries plus all debt instruments purchased without an intermediary, largely Treasury bills. Corporate equities represent personal holdings of all equity shares issued by corporations. Finally, life insurance and pension fund reserves represent the claims of individuals against life insurance and pension funds. All of these holdings are represented as a percentage of personal disposable income, that is, income after taxes. The most dramatic thing shown in this figure is the large decline in personal holdings of corporate equities. Private individual's holdings of

FIGURE 12-2

Principal forms of household borrowing. Source: *Federal Reserve Chart Book, 1979.*

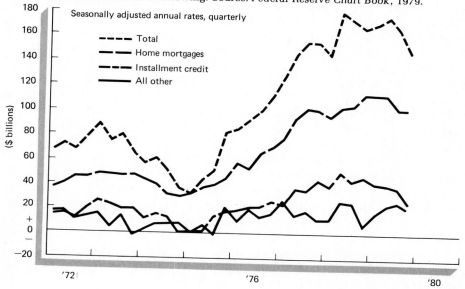

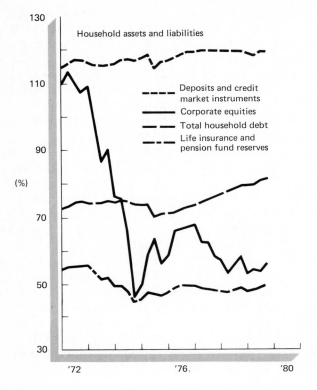

FIGURE 12-3
Principal financial assets held by households expressed as a percent of disposable personal income. Source: *Federal Reserve Chart Book,* 1979.

equities have declined dramatically as a proportion of total disposable income, while claims on financial intermediaries and credit market instruments have held their own or increased. This has meant that a larger proportion of household financial claims are now on financial intermediaries, rather than direct claims on securities issued by the ultimate borrower of funds. With the decline in consumers holding of equities, deposits and credit market instruments now represent the overwhelming share of personal financial assets, with deposits representing the larger portion. Moreover, within the category of deposits, there have also been tremendous changes, and that is likely to continue in the future.

All segments of the market for consumer borrowing and lending are dominated by financial intermediaries. Virtually the only significant portions of these markets which involve direct participation in auction or over-the-counter markets by individuals are the purchase of corporate equity and market credit instruments. But as indicated above, direct household participation in the equity market has been declining rapidly. Moreover, holdings of credit instruments are relatively small compared to total deposits.

The principal intermediaries which serve consumers are commercial banks and savings and loans. But there is increasing competition from other intermediaries, including credit unions, mutual savings banks, and other thrift institutions. Moreover, many nontraditional suppliers of credit have been penetrating this market. Many retail companies such as Sears derive sizable portions of their revenues from their credit services. In effect, they tie the financing and sale of consumer products together. In the following sections, as we analyze the types of borrowing and lending in the market we will also examine the nature of the institutions which operate in the market.

THE RESIDENTIAL MORTGAGE MARKET

In this section of the chapter we will examine the residential mortgage market. We will start by examining how the demand for mortgage credit has changed in recent years. Then we will turn our attention to the various institutions which supply mortgage funds to the market. Finally, we will explore how the mortgage industry is changing and how mortgage contracts themselves are undergoing a major overhaul in the 1980s.

The Changing Demand for Mortgage Credit

It is easy to get the impression that people take out home mortgage loans almost exclusively for the purpose of acquiring homes. This is simply not the case. In fact, it is necessary to look back approximately 10 years to find a time when this was the case. Figure 12-4 shows the volume of increases in mortgage debt on 1 to 4 family units and new construction of such units,

FIGURE 12-4

New construction and new mortgage debt for 1 to 4 family and multifamily units. Source: *Federal Reserve Chart Book*, 1979.

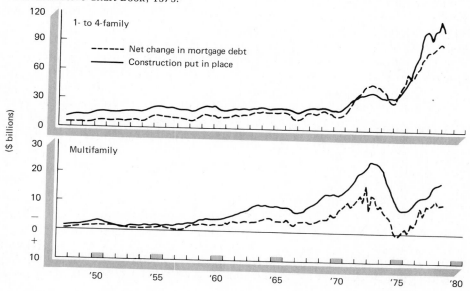

from 1948 to 1979. The figure shows quite a striking change. In the early part of the postwar era mortgage debt was consistently less than the volume of new construction. During this period mortgage debt was used to finance the acquisition of new housing. But by the early 1970s the volume of new mortgage financing outstripped the increase in new residential property. Mortgage debt began to be used for all sorts of purposes from financing education to funding vacations. It has become a source of consumer financing for a number of purposes.

This change did not occur simply because the United States emerged from a time of tremendous unsatisfied demand for housing, as was the case in the early 1950s. It occurred because there was a tremendous increase in the value of real property, coupled with a decline in the *real* cost of existing mortgages. In other words, over the last 10 years, residential property owners found that the market value of their property increased while their mortgage payments remained fixed. The fixed terms of the mortgage at interest rates which proved, with hindsight, to be quite low, meant that the real cost of the mortgage was declining. As a result, homeowners chose to borrow against the increased value of their property and use the funds to finance other expenditures. For most individuals in the 1970s, their homes turned out to be the best investment they ever made. Figure 12-4 shows the extent to which they have borrowed against that value.

Intermediaries in the Mortgage Financing Industry

What has been good for the borrower has not necessarily been good for either the ultimate supplier of funds or for the private institution which acts as the intermediary between borrower and lender. With the advent of high inflation rates in the 1970s, which to a large degree were unanticipated, there have been wealth transfers from lenders to borrowers. Those who acquired mortgage debt at fixed rates early in the inflationary process have benefited, while those who funded those mortgages have been hurt. To understand the nature of the difficulties which have developed we have to look closely at the industry which funds mortgages in the United States.

Not only is the mortgage market large, it is also one of the more complicated financial markets in the United States, at least in terms of the number of institutions which make up the mortgage industry. The single most important type of institution which provides home mortgage funds is the savings and loan. In addition, commercial banks, mutual savings banks, insurance companies, mortgage bankers, and a number of governmental and quasi-governmental institutions supply mortgage funds both for single-family dwellings and for multifamily units and commercial property. Some of these institutions specialize in particular parts of the mortgage market. For example, life insurance companies invest heavily in commercial mortgages, but have a relatively small investment in mortgages for single-family residential property. On the other hand, savings and loans are almost exactly the opposite—most of their funding goes to single-family dwellings and very little to commercial real estate. Commercial banks' mortgage loans are probably the most diversified, with a sizable investment in each category. While the share in residential mortgages occupied by multifamily units has been growing in recent years, the bulk of financing still is committed to what is termed 1 to 4 family units, that is, single-family homes or multiple units which contain no more than four separate residences. We will concentrate on this portion of the market and refer to it as home mortgage financing.

The total amount of home mortgage debt held by each type of institution during the decade of the 1970s is shown in Table 12-1. The table shows that throughout the decade the largest portion of home mortgages was held by savings and loans. Commercial banks' holdings of home mortgages have been on the increase, while those of mutual savings banks have grown at a slower rate than the market as a whole. Of the private intermediaries commercial banks are the most diversified in their total loan portfolio. For example, in 1979, real estate loans represented just 30 percent of the loans of all commercial banks. Savings and loans, on the other hand, are constrained by federal regulation to invest almost exclusively in residential mortgages. In addition to these private intermediaries, by the end of the decade participation in the industry by a group of quasi-governmental agencies through direct purchase of mortgages and through mortgage pools (explained below) had become quite sizable, representing 18 percent of all home mortgage debt in 1979.

There are three major quasi-federal agencies which act as financial intermediaries in the mortgage market. There are also two agencies, the Federal Housing Administration and the Veterans Administration, which offer government subsidies on mortgages to qualified borrowers. All of these entities are distinct from the government agencies which regulate the savings and loan industry. The three financial intermediaries are named the Federal National Mortgage Association (FNMA or "Fannie Mae"), the Federal Home Loan Mortgage Corporation (FHLMC or "Freddie Mac") and the General

TABLE 12-1

Sources of Total Supply of Home Mortgage Debt (Billions of Dollars)

YEAR	TOTAL 1-4 FAMILY	COMMERCIAL BANKS	MSBs	S&Ls	FEDERAL*	POOLS	OTHER
1979	872	146	65	394	53	102	112
1978	761	27	62	356	44	76	97
1977	657	105	58	311	36	61	87
1976	556	86	53	261	36	42	78
1975	491	77	50	224	38	28	74
1974	449	75	49	201	33	19	72
1973	416	68	49	187	25	14	72
1972	372	57	46	166	24	11	67
1971	307	48	39	142	26	—	52

* Excludes Federal Home Loan Bank Board advances.

Source: *Federal Reserve Bulletin*, various issues.

National Mortgage Association (GNMA or "Ginnie Mae"). These agencies are referred to as quasi-governmental because they were initially started as federal agencies, but have been transformed into privately owned companies with a mandate from the federal government. They each have some form of public supervision and are constrained to pursue public policy objectives. Moreover, they issue their own securities, known as *agency securities*. Agency securities are securities issued by agencies of the federal government other than the U.S. Treasury.

The oldest of the three quasi-federal agencies is Fannie Mae. It was originally created in the late 1930s in order to assist the home mortgage industry by purchasing mortgages which were insured by the Federal Housing Administration. Freddie Mac was established in 1970 in order to fulfill essentially the same purpose but with conventional mortgages, that is, mortgages that are not backed by FHA. Both of these agencies initially operated by selling agency securities in the market and using the funds to directly purchase mortgages from savings institutions. The majority of support provided by Fannie Mae still comes in this way. But more recently, Freddie Mac and Ginnie Mae, which was created in 1968 to supplement the activities of Fannie Mae, have created what are called *mortgage pools*. A mortgage pool is essentially a portfolio of mortgages which serves as collateral for securities issued to the market. The securities issued by the pool represent a share of all the mortgages in the pool. The pool provides a reduction of risk through diversification, which ownership of a single mortgage does not. Ginnie Mae was the largest issuer of mortgage pools and Freddie Mac was second, with about $76 and $12 billion, respectively. These agencies insure the payment of principal and interest on the pools and then sell participations in the pools to the public.

The principal contribution of these quasi-federal agencies to the mortgage industry has been the creation of a secondary market. Whether these quasi-federal agencies directly buy mortgages or sponsor mortgage pools, they are creating a secondary market where mortgages are traded as a security. That is, these agencies have made it possible for the primary lenders to resell mortgages which they originate. As this market has developed, private as well as quasi-governmental lenders have been able to participate as buyers in the secondary market. The largest part of their contribution is contained in the "Other" category in Table 12-1. The difficulty which long had inhibited the development of a secondary market is that mortgages are not homogeneous assets. Individual homes are quite distinct and do not represent a standardized commodity. However, with the advent of mortgage pools and government backing, the secondary market in mortgages now flourishes. As a consequence, savings and loans, commercial banks, and mutual savings banks are now viewed as the principal originators of mortgages, but not necessarily as the ultimate owners of the mortgages they originate. This means that they perform the functions of meeting with the borrower, granting the loan, and servicing the loan over its life. But they may well sell off that loan to another party and not actually hold it themselves.

The Conventional Mortgage and the Savings and Loan: A Closer Look

The dominant lenders in the home mortgage market are savings and loans and the dominant form of mortgage, at least at the end of the 1970s, was the conventional (i.e., nongovernment-insured) long-term fixed-rate mortgage. A conventional fixed-rate mortgage has an interest rate and a monthly payment which are fixed over the life of the mortgage. While this conventional mortgage was still the principal type of mortgage loan as of the end of 1979, there were some interesting and significant changes in the average terms of such loans during the 1970s. This decade was characterized by a significant increase in the rate of inflation, both in the economy in general and in home prices in particular. Along with that increase in the inflation rate went an increase in most interest rates, including the mortgage rate. Therefore, consumers seeking to use mortgage financing faced both higher prices for homes and higher financing costs. Both the average interest rate on conventional mortgages for new homes which prevailed during most of the 1970s and the average price of a new home are shown in Figure 12-5. Figure 12-6 shows the impact of these changes on various terms of mortgage loans. Panel A in this figure shows that the average loan amount on a conventional mortgage ap-

FIGURE 12-5

Prices on new homes and interest rates on new mortgages. The purchase price represents the average price on newly constructed single-family homes. The interest rate is the effective rate on conventional mortgages under the assumption that the mortgage is prepaid in 10 years. Source: *Federal Reserve Bulletin*, various issues.

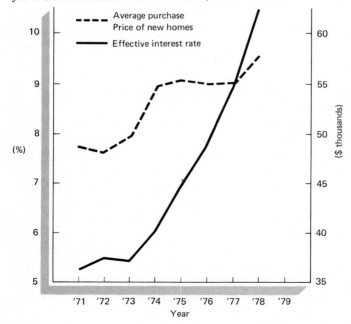

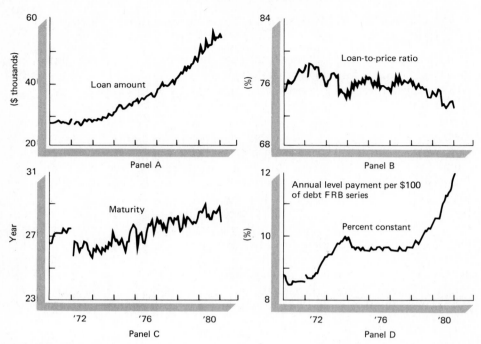

FIGURE 12-6
Terms on conventional mortgage loans on new homes. Source: *Federal Reserve Chart Book*, 1979.

proximately doubled from 1972 to 1979, from just under $30,000 to almost $60,000. In order to accommodate this increase in the average size of the loan, the maturity of the loan gradually increased, as shown in panel C, and the ratio of the amount of the loan to the price of the property was reduced, as shown in panel B. Finally, the average payment on the mortgage increased, as shown in panel D, and that increase was particularly dramatic in the latter part of the decade.

The high interest and inflation rates which characterized the 1970s have created serious problems for the savings and loan industry. Yet the underlying difficulty facing the industry is not inflation itself. Instead, the difficulty results from two important features of the balance sheets of savings and loans. The first is the fact that savings and loans invest almost exclusively in residential mortgages. This is not a matter of their own choice, but a product of government regulation which restricts them to this type of investment. The second feature is the fact that their mortgage loans have been made largely at fixed rates and have very long maturities, while their liabilities have very short maturities. As a result, they perform the function of intermediating across time. Taken together these two features have left the typical savings and loan exposed to a tremendous amount of risk; risk that short-term interest rates will increase but that the returns on their loans will not. And this is precisely what happened during the decade of the 1970s.

The data presented in Table 12-2 provide a little more insight into the nature of the problem. The table shows the outstanding volume of savings deposits at the end of each year for all savings and loans in the United States during the 1970s and comparable data on the total inflow of new savings during each year. The ratio of the inflow of savings to the end-of-year total shows the proportion of total deposits which were new during each year or which turned over during the year. This ratio is labeled the savings turnover rate. The data indicate that in excess of 50 percent of total savings turned over in any given year, and in the more recent years the percentage has grown. This implies that if savings and loans have to compete with interest payments in order to attract savings, the total cost of their savings deposits will change very rapidly. That is, with the short maturity or high turnover of savings, their cost of funds will closely follow the changes in short-term interest rates, if they have to compete for funds with interest payments.

On the other hand, quite the opposite situation applies to the turnover of their loan portfolios. The turnover of their loan portfolios, which is computed in the same way, is generally between 20 and 30 percent. As a result, when interest rates rise, loans which were taken out at what prove to be low interest rates remain in the portfolio of the savings and loan much longer than do savings which were initially deposited at the same time. This problem is referred to as the dilemma of lending long and borrowing short. To some extent, commercial banks also engage in this kind of intermediation, but they have a substantially more diversified portfolio of loans than do savings and loans. As a result, their situation is generally less precarious when interest rates increase than is that of the savings and loan industry. The twin facts that the maturities of their mortgage loans are long and the maturities of their liabilities are short, and that they are concentrated almost

TABLE 12-2

Turnover of Savings Accounts and Mortgage Loans

YEAR	GROSS SAVINGS RECEIVED DURING YEAR	END-OF-YEAR SAVINGS BALANCE	SAVINGS TURNOVER RATE	MORTGAGE LOANS CLOSED	END-OF-YEAR TOTAL LOANS	LOAN TURNOVER RATE
1979	360.6	470.2	.77	100.5	475.8	.21
1978	270.9	431.0	.63	110.3	432.9	.25
1977	218.2	386.8	.56	107.4	381.2	.28
1976	184.2	333.9	.55	78.8	323.0	.24
1975	154.6	286.0	.54	55.0	278.6	.20
1974	125.9	243.0	.52	39.0	294.3	.13
1973	113.2	227.0	.50	49.5	231.7	.21
1972	95.9	206.8	.46	51.4	206.2	.25
1971	78.2	174.2	.45	39.4	174.3	.23

Source: *Federal Home Loan Bank Board Journal*, various issues.

exclusively in mortgage loans, has created a serious problem for the savings and loan industry. Moreover, the problem became acute in the late 1970s and early 1980s as inflation accelerated.

The principal method which has been used to deal with these problems is to limit interest-rate competition for savings through regulation and to increase federal support for the industry. We will evaluate this regulatory system in Chapter Eighteen. The solution that is likely to be increasingly applied during the 1980s is the use of alternative mortgage contracts that limit the amount of the risk of the interest-rate changes that is transferred from the borrower to the intermediary. We will examine some of these alternative mortgage instruments next.

Alternative Mortgage Contracts

The essential idea behind the alternatives to the conventional mortgage is to limit the extent to which the financial intermediary is intermediating across maturities, or the extent to which it is borrowing short and lending long. Most of the alternative mortgages tend to call for interest rates on the mortgage to adjust with short-term market rates. One obstacle which has stood in the way of widespread use of alternative mortgages is consumer understanding and acceptance. These mortgages are generally more complicated than the conventional mortgage and they have often met with considerable consumer resistance. The other obstacle has been reluctance on the part of regulators to permit the use of such mortgages. A few of the alternatives have been used in some parts of the country. But at the beginning of the 1980s they were not yet widespread. The principal alternatives are described below.

FIXED-RATE MORTGAGE WITH A DUE-ON-SALE CLAUSE   The *due-on-sale clause* stipulates that a mortgage lender can declare the mortgage due when the property is sold. Such mortgages are said to be nonassumable. This clause means that when the mortgage is initially written the lender does not anticipate that the mortgage will have to be held until its original or stated maturity. Because most property turns over or is sold prior to this, the lender can anticipate a substantially shorter maturity than would otherwise be the case. This tends to limit the guarantee of a fixed interest rate provided by a fixed-payment mortgage that has no due-on-sale clause. In times of high mortgage interest rates, such as prevailed during much of 1980, a mortgage that is assumable is considerably more valuable than one which is not. However, that value is gained at the lender's expense.

THE GRADUATED-PAYMENT MORTGAGE   A graduated-payment mortgage has a fixed interest rate and maturity just like a conventional mortgage. The distinction is that the schedule of monthly payments is not constant. The early payments are usually designed to be less than the later payments. This is a popular option when most people expect that their nominal income will rise. With this mortgage the scheduled monthly payments increase so that higher payments will be incurred when it is anticipated that the available income will be larger. In effect, this makes a mortgage with a particular fixed interest rate more affordable, especially for relatively young individuals. But it does not change the interest rate on the mortgage.

THE ROLLOVER MORTGAGE   This kind of mortgage has a long-term maturity, but the interest rate on the mortgage is fixed for a much shorter period of time, say 5 years. At the end of every 5-year period the borrower has the choice of either paying off the mortgage or continuing the mortgage at the new prevailing interest rate. This is referred to as rolling over the loan. If interest rates have fallen, this will be to the advantage of the borrower. But if they have increased, it will be to the advantage of the lender. The advantage of this mortgage is that the payment schedule is based on a long-term maturity, but the lender's commitment to insure the borrower against increases in interest rates is limited.

THE VARIABLE-RATE MORTGAGE   The variable-rate mortgage is a long-term mortgage like the rollover mortgage, but the interest rate is tied to a short-term market interest rate or index of market rates and therefore fluctuates over the life of the mortgage. It is conceivable that the rate on the mortgage could be adjusted as frequently as payments are made, generally every month. And in fact, in April 1981, the Federal Home Loan Bank Board authorized federally chartered savings and loans to offer mortgages with adjustments as often as every 30 days. When the interest rate changes the borrower has essentially two options. One is to alter the maturity, so that if the rate increases the maturity is stretched out. However, this method can absorb only rather modest increases in rates. The alternative is that the monthly payment must increase. With a variable-rate mortgage the financial intermediary is no longer insuring borrowers against fluctuations in interest rates; the lender is no longer intermediating across maturities.

SHARED-APPRECIATION MORTGAGE   Under this arrangement the lender has title to some portion, say one-third, of the total capital gain (or loss) on the property whenever it is sold. In exchange, the lender provides the borrower with a lower interest rate than would be offered on a conventional fixed-rate mortgage.

NONMORTGAGE CONSUMER DEBT

In this brief section we will take a look at the other types of debt used by consumers. First, we will examine the two classes of nonmortgage consumer debt. Second, we will examine the intermediaries which provide funds for nonmortgage consumer debt.

Types of Nonmortgage Consumer Debt

Consumers utilize debt, other than mortgage debt, to pay for a wide variety of goods and services. This nonmortgage debt is divided into two broad categories that are based on the nature of the agreement to repay the loan. The most important type is what is called *installment credit*. Installment credit involves a contract to pay off the principal of the loan in periodic payments, usually on a monthly basis. Such payments are referred to as *installment payments*. All consumer credit which is scheduled to be repaid in a lump sum, or a single-payment loan, is broken into a second category. The predominant form of nonmortgage borrowing by consumers is installment credit. Table 12-3 shows the total volume of this kind of borrowing from 1971 to 1979. By the end of 1979 a total of somewhat more than $300 billion in installment debt was outstanding.

In the latter part of the 1970s consumers were willing to take on installment debt at an unprecedented rate; the rate of growth in installment debt was close to 20 percent per year for the 4 years between 1975 and 1979. To a large degree this was a result of the accelerating rate of inflation during those years. Consumers concluded that it was cheaper to buy goods on credit, before prices increased, and pay later with deflated dollars. This proves to be a good strategy as long as the rate of inflation continues to exceed the market's expectations. However, it also leaves the consumer sector as a whole exceedingly vulnerable should there be a decline in income available to meet the obligations on outstanding debt. Hence the risk to which the consumer sector and the economy are exposed increases, with large increases in installment debt motivated by a beat-inflation strategy.

Sources and Uses of Installment Debt

Historically, consumers have used installment debt to finance purchases of durable goods. Such goods include any commodities which are not fully

TABLE 12-3

Consumer Installment Credit by Type of Lender (Millions of Dollars)

YEAR	TOTAL	COMMERCIAL BANK	FINANCE COMPANY	CREDIT UNION	RETAILER	OTHER
1979	311.1	149.6	68.3	48.2	27.9	17.1
1978	275.6	136.2	54.3	45.9	24.9	14.2
1977	230.8	112.4	44.9	37.6	23.5	12.5
1976	194.0	93.7	38.9	31.2	19.3	10.9
1975	162.2	78.7	36.7	25.4	18.0	3.5
1974	155.4	75.8	36.2	22.1	17.9	3.3
1973	146.4	71.9	35.4	19.6	16.4	3.1
1972	126.8	60.9	31.4	16.9	14.8	2.8
1971	111.2	51.6	28.4	14.8	13.9	2.5

Source: *Federal Reserve Bulletin*, various issues.

used up during the quarter or the year in which they are purchased. Durable goods include such things as refrigerators, television sets, furniture, and automobiles. The largest single use of installment credit is to finance automobile purchases. Slightly more than one-third of all outstanding installment debt finances automobiles. Beyond this, there is no other large single use. Moreover, with the growth of bank credit cards in recent years, it is more difficult to account for the uses to which installment credit is put.

A number of different types of financial institutions act as intermediaries supplying installment credit. The largest suppliers are commercial banks. As indicated in Table 12-3, they provided slightly less than one-half of all the installment credit outstanding at the end of 1979. Consumer finance companies, many of them owned and operated by commercial banks, provided the next largest share of the market. Credit unions and retailers are third and fourth, respectively. Retailers provide a relatively large share of the nonautomobile market but provide very little financing for cars. On the other hand, credit unions are not particularly specialized in what they finance, as is the case for commercial banks.

The market for installment credit does not have quite the complexities and problems that face the market for mortgage debt. To a large degree, this is because there is not as much intermediation across time in this market. The maturities of most installment loans are usually very short compared to mortgage loans, and this is the key to the problem in the mortgage market.

CONSUMER ACQUISITION OF FINANCIAL ASSETS

In this section we will examine the other side of the consumer's balance sheet—the financial assets acquired by consumers. This section is divided into two parts. First, we will examine deposit accounts at financial intermediaries and consumer acquisition of credit market instruments. Second, we will examine consumer investment in pension funds, life insurance companies, and the equity markets.

Deposits and Credit Market Instruments

According to the data shown in Figure 12-3, consumers hold most of their financial assets in the form of time and saving deposits and credit market instruments. Yet this is still a fairly broad category of assets and the aggregate data on this category camouflage a number of important changes. A more detailed picture of this particular segment of the financial markets is presented in Figure 12-7. This figure separates deposits and credit market instruments and divides deposits into three components: deposits at nonbank depository institutions, time and savings deposits at commercial banks, and demand deposits, all expressed as a proportion of disposable income. The figure indicates that relative to disposable income, the biggest growth has been in deposits at nonbank institutions, while time and savings

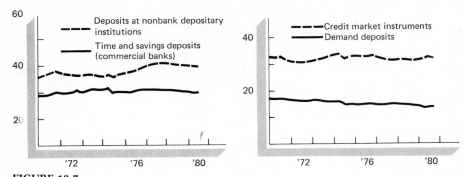

FIGURE 12-7

Deposits and credit market instruments held by households expressed as a percent of disposable income. Source: *Federal Reserve Chart Book*, 1979.

deposits at commercial banks have been roughly constant and demand deposits have declined. The basic story that Figure 12-7 has to tell is that there has been a gradual shift away from demand deposits into time and savings deposits, particularly at nonbank depository institutions. Commercial banks' share of the total deposit market has therefore declined. The losses that commercial banks have suffered have not been in their own time and savings deposits, but rather in their demand deposits.

To understand the reasons for these changes it is necessary to acquire a more detailed understanding of exactly what time and savings deposits are. Savings accounts generally refer to those deposits which earn interest, but which have no specific maturity. More specifically, these accounts are called passbook savings accounts. On the other hand, time deposits are accounts with specific maturities ranging from 30 days to 8 years or longer. For many years the maximum interest rates payable on all of these accounts have been set by federal regulation. Such interest rate ceilings are generally referred to as regulation Q ceilings, which is the regulation on interest-rate ceilings imposed on commercial banks by the Federal Reserve Board. In recent years the interest rates paid by these institutions have almost always been the legal maximum. For example, Table 12-4 illustrates the interest-rate ceilings applicable as of February 29, 1980. The table shows that time deposit accounts with longer maturities have higher legal interest rates. This structure of yields is based on the fact that the yield curve observed in the market is generally upward sloping.

During the 1970s consumers increased their holdings of time deposit accounts, mainly because the alternatives were not particularly attractive. Early in the decade there were relatively few opportunities for savers with small amounts of funds, particularly less than $10,000, other than these types of accounts. Hence small savers were attracted to time deposit accounts. Moreover, as interest-rate ceilings gradually increased, consumers shifted their funds out of demand deposits into time deposits. In effect, as

TABLE 12-4
Maximum Interest Rates on Deposit Accounts

Type and maturity of deposit	Commercial banks				Savings and loan associations and mutual savings banks			
	In effect Feb. 29, 1980		Previous maximum		In effect Feb. 29, 1980		Previous maximum	
	Percent	Effective date	Percent	Effective date	Percent	Effective date	Percent	Effective date
1 Savings	5¼	7/1/79	5	7/1/73	5½	7/1/79	5¼	(1)
2 Negotiable order of withdrawal accounts[2]	5	1/1/74	(3)	....	5	1/1/74	(3)	....
Time accounts[4]								
Fixed ceiling rates by maturity								
3 30–89 days	5¼	9/1/79	5	7/1/73	(3)	....	(3)	....
4 90 days to 1 year	5½	7/1/73	5	(5)	5¾[6]	(1)	5¼	1/21/70
5 1 to 2 years[6]	6	7/1/73	5½	1/21/70	6½	(1)	5¾	1/21/70
6 2 to 2½ years[6]			5¾	1/21/70			6	1/21/70
7 2½ to 4 years[6]	6½	7/1/73	5¾	1/21/70	6¾	(1)	6	1/21/70
8 4 to 6 years[7]	7¼	11/1/73	(8)	....	7½	11/1/73	(8)	....
9 6 to 8 years[7]	7½	12/23/74	7¼	11/1/73	7¾	12/23/74	7½	11/1/73
10 8 years or more[7]	7¾	6/1/78	(3)	....	8	6/1/78	(3)	....
11 Issued to governmental units (all maturities)	8	6/1/78	7¾	12/23/74	8	6/1/78	7¾	12/23/74
12 Individual retirement accounts and Keogh (H.R. 10) plans (3 years or more)[9]	8	6/1/78	7¾	7/6/77	8	6/1/78	7¾	7/6/77
Special variable ceiling rates by maturity								
13 6 months money market time deposits[10]	(11)	(11)	(11)	(11)	(11)	(11)	(11)	(11)
14 2½ years or more	(12)	(12)	(13)	(13)	(12)	(12)	(13)	(13)

1. July 1, 1973, for mutual savings bank; July 6, 1973 for savings and loan associations.

2. For authorized states only. Federally insured commercial banks, savings and loan associations, cooperative banks, and mutual savings banks in Massachusetts and New Hampshire were first permitted to offer negotiable order of withdrawal (NOW) accounts on Jan. 1, 1974. Authorization to issue NOW accounts was extended to similar institutions throughout New England on Feb. 27, 1976, and in New York State on Nov. 10, 1978.

3. No separate account category.

4. For exceptions with respect to certain foreign time deposits see the FEDERAL RESERVE BULLETIN for October 1962 (p. 1279), August 1965 (p. 1084), and February 1968 (p. 167).

5. Multiple maturity: July 20, 1966; single maturity: September 26, 1966.

6. No minimum denomination. Until July 1, 1979, a minimum of $1,000 was required for savings and loan associations, except in areas where mutual savings banks permitted lower minimum denominations. This restriction was removed for deposits maturing in less than 1 year, effective Nov. 1, 1973.

7. No minimum denomination. Until July 1, 1979, minimum denomination was $1,000 except for deposits representing funds contributed to an Individual Retirement Account (IRA) or a Keogh (H.R. 10) Plan established pursuant to the Internal Revenue Code. The $1,000 minimum requirementwas removed for such accounts in December 1975 and November 1976, respectively.

8. Between July 1, 1973, and Oct. 31, 1973, there was no ceiling for certificates maturing in 4 years or more with minimum denominations of $1,000; however, the amount of such certificates that an institution could issue was limited to 5 percent of its total time and savings deposits. Sales in excess of that amount, as well as certificates of less than $1,000, were limited to the 6½ percent ceiling on time deposits maturing in 2½ years or more.

Effective Nov. 1, 1973, ceilings were reimposed on certificates maturing in 4 years or more with minimum denomination of $1,000. There is no limitation on the amount of these certificates that banks can issue.

9. Accounts maturing in less than 3 years subject to fixed rate ceilings.

10. Must have a maturity of exactly 26 weeks and a minimum denomination of $10,000, and must be nonnegotiable.

11. Commercial banks, savings and loan associations, and mutual savings banks were authorized to offer money market time deposits effective June 1, 1978. The ceiling rate for commercial banks is the discount rate on most recently issued 6–month U.S. Treasury bills. Until Mar. 15, 1979, the ceiling rate for savings and loan associations and mutual savings banks was ¼ percentage point higher than the rate for commercial banks. Beginning Mar. 15, 1979, the ¼ percentage point interest differential is removed when the 6–month Treasury bill rate is 9 percent or more. The full differential is in effect when the 6–month bill rate is 8¾ percent or less. Thrift institutions may pay a maximum 9 percent when the 6–month bill rate is between 8¾ and 9 percent. Also effective March 15, 1979 interest compounding was prohibited on 6-month money market time deposits at all offering institutions. For both commercial banks and thrift institutions, the maximum allowable rates in January and February were as follows: Jan. 3, 11.880; Jan. 10, 11.858; Jan. 17, 11.783; Jan. 24, 11.886; Jan. 31, 11.846; Feb. 7, 11.985; Feb. 14, 12.256; Feb. 21, 13.013; Feb. 28, 13.629.

12. Effective Jan. 1, 1980, commercial banks, savings and loan associations, and mutual savings banks are authorized to offer variable ceiling accounts with no required minimum denomination and with maturities of 2½ years or more. The maximum rate for commercial banks is ¾ percentage points below the yield on 2½ year U.S. Treasury securities; the ceiling rate for thrift institutions is ¼ percentage point higher than that for commercial banks. In February, the ceiling at commercial banks was 10.40 percent, and the ceiling at thrift institutions was 10.65 percent. Effective March 1, a temporary ceiling of 11¾ percent was placed on these accounts at commercial banks; the temporary ceiling is 12 percent at savings and loan associations and mutual savings banks.

13. Between July 1, 1979, and Dec. 31, 1979, commercial banks, savings and loan associations, and mutual savings banks were authorized to offer variable ceiling accounts with no required minimum denomination and with maturities of 4 years or more. The maximum rate for commercial banks was 1¼ percentage points below the yield on 4–year U.S. Treasury securities; the ceiling rate for thrift institutions was ¼ percentage point higher than that for commercial banks.

NOTE: Maximum rates that can be paid by federally insured commercial banks, mutual savings banks, and savings and loan associations are established by the Board of Governors of the Federal Reserve System, the Board of Directors of the Federal Deposit Insurance Corporation, and the Federal Home Loan Bank Board under the provisions of 12 CFR 217, 329, and 526, respectively. The maximum rates on time deposits in denominations of $100,000 or more with maturities of 30–89 days were suspended in June 1970; such deposits maturing in 90 days or more were suspended in May 1973. For information regarding previous interest rate ceilings on all types of accounts, see earlier issues of the interest rate ceilings on all types of accounts, see earlier issues of the FEDERAL RESERVE BULLETIN, the Federal Home Loan Bank Board *Journal* and the *Annual Report* of the Federal Deposit Insurance Corporation.

Source: *Federal Reserve Bulletin*, March, 1980.

interest rates went up, the cost of holding demand deposits increased as well, because demand deposit accounts earned no interest, again due to government restriction. For consumers with funds to lend in excess of $10,000 there were other alternatives. The principal one was to purchase Treasury bills, which have a minimum denomination of $10,000. Such investments are as free of default risk as government-insured deposits at commercial banks or savings and loans, yet the interest rate is not restricted by government regulation. And to a large extent, consumers did purchase Treasury bills when the interest rate on Treasury bills rose above the government-mandated ceilings on deposit accounts. During the 1960s and 1970s this happened periodically as interest rates peaked. Figure 12-8 shows the behavior of the interest rate on 90-day Treasury bills and the ceiling rate on time deposit accounts. During those periods when the Treasury bill rate

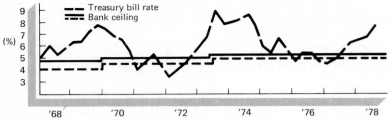

FIGURE 12-8

Treasury bill rates relative to ceilings on deposit interest rates. The higher ceiling in the figure represents the ceiling on passbook accounts at thrift institutions and the lower ceiling pertains to passbook accounts at commercial banks. Source: *Federal Reserve Bulletin*, various issues.

was above the ceiling rate, many individuals with funds greater than $10,000 shifted out of savings institutions and into Treasury bills. This process is referred to as *disintermediation*.

The Advent of Money Market Certificates

The problem of disintermediation was serious enough during the 1960s and early 1970s, but by the late 1970s it had become acute. Due to high and volatile inflation rates, market interest rates had also become high and volatile, and the prospect of massive disintermediation became a serious possibility. In addition, a number of new types of alternatives began to be made available to consumers with less than $10,000 to invest. Principal among these was the money market mutual fund. An account with a money market mutual fund is much like a passbook savings account, except that the funds are invested principally in Treasury bills or certificates of deposit and commercial paper issued by banks at competitive rates. And the proceeds, less a small fee, are returned to the depositor. Money market mutual funds offer market rates that are not restricted by ceilings to savers with only a few thousand dollars to invest. With the high interest rates which prevailed during the late 1970s this was a very attractive option and money market mutual funds prospered.

In response to these developments the federal regulatory agencies created a new type of time deposit which commercial banks and savings and loans were permitted to offer, called a money market certificate. The money market certificate is a time deposit with a denomination of $10,000 and a 6-month maturity. It earns an interest rate equal to the Treasury bill rate prevailing at the time it is issued. In effect, it is very close, though not exactly identical, to a 6-month Treasury bill. The purpose of creating such a time deposit is to give commercial banks and savings and loans the ability to compete for consumer deposits in times when market interest rates exceed the ceilings on other deposit accounts. However, it also has the effect of greatly increasing the cost of funds for all depository institutions.

The money market certificate has become tremendously popular, as evidenced by the data in Table 12-5. This table documents the impact of the money market certificate on the composition of deposits for savings and loans. The table shows the net change in money market certificates as opposed to savings accounts and other time deposit accounts subject to interest-rate ceilings, during the 2-year period starting in October 1977, shortly before the money market certificate was first authorized. During this period there was a net decrease in savings accounts of $8,381 million and a net decrease in time deposit accounts subject to interest-rate ceilings of $14,820 million. Yet money market certificates grew by $101,911 million. This indicates that consumers were withdrawing their funds from accounts with ceilings and switching to accounts which did not have these ceilings, to a massive degree. With this change in the composition of deposits has come tremendous political pressure for a complete elimination of interest-rate ceilings on deposit institutions. In 1980 pressure for change led to the enactment of major new legislation, the Depository Institution Deregulation Act of 1980. Among the many provisions of the act is a gradual elimination of these ceilings.

It now seems evident that the market for time and savings deposits which existed in the 1960s and 1970s, one dominated by the impact of deposit rate ceilings in a time of increasing inflation, will not survive the 1980s. Many students of the behavior of these markets have long argued for the abolition of interest-rate ceilings, and with the enactment of the Depository Institution Deregulation Act of 1980, it now appears that the demise of the system of deposit-rate ceilings is at hand. How the market for consumer savings will work in the absence of these ceilings is not yet obvious and there remains the possibility that the steps toward reform included in this legislation could be rescinded. But if the actions called for in the 1980 act are carried out, then the system of interest-rate ceilings will be elimi-

TABLE 12-5

Changes in Savings and Time Deposits and Money Market Certificates

	NET CHANGE IN DEPOSITS AMOUNTS OUTSTANDING (MILLIONS OF DOLLARS)				
	OCT. 1977– MAR. 1978	APRIL 1978– SEPT. 1978	OCT. 1978– MAR. 1979	APRIL 1979– SEPT. 1979	TOTAL DEPOSIT AS OF SEPT. 30, 1979
Savings accounts	3,795	−4,191	−11,861	3,876	126,324
Money market certificates	0	19,337	53,877	28,697	101,911
Other time deposits subject to ceilings	15,364	3,814	−17,121	−16,877	195,785

Source: *Federal Home Loan Bank Board Journal*, January 1980, p. 24.

nated by the mid-1980s. The details of these reforms, a more complete explanation of the regulatory system they modify, and speculation on what the future may hold are presented in Chapters Seventeen and Eighteen.

Pension Funds, Life Insurance, and Household Participation in the Equity Market

The principal avenues through which households can acquire financial assets, other than through claims on depository institutions and direct purchase of market debt instruments, are through insurance companies, pension funds, and direct purchase of equity securities. In the broadest sense, insurance companies and pension funds are simply another type of financial intermediary which invests funds for consumers. The special characteristic of these institutions, as compared to depository intermediaries, is that some event triggers the repayment of the funds to the household. With pension funds the event is retirement and with insurance companies it is death or the occurrence of some kind of accident. But the principle behind the operation of these institutions is that the funds which are paid in premiums or pension contributions are invested. Hence, these institutions function as financial intermediaries channeling funds from consumers to lenders.

The aggregate pattern of household use of pension funds, insurance companies, and direct investment in equities was documented in Figure 12-3. This figure shows household equity holdings and the sum of household claims against life insurance companies and pension funds as a percentage of disposable income. The figure indicates that direct equity investments have fallen precipitously, while claims against pension funds and insurance companies have approximately held their own. Actually this figure camouflages almost as much as it reveals. A little more detail on this situation is presented in Figure 12-9, which shows the dollar increase in household claims on pension funds and on life insurance companies from 1970 to 1979. This figure indicates that household claims on pension funds have grown by much larger amounts than have the claims on life insurance companies. If one looks back to the early years of the postwar period, this was not the case. During that time pension fund claims were a very small portion of household assets and the value of life insurance policies represented a much larger portion. In effect, many people chose to use life insurance as a vehicle for savings as well as for insuring their lives. This was reflected in the strong preference for what are called *whole life insurance policies* as opposed to *term policies*. Whole life policies offer savings benefits where the insured party can draw on the policy prior to his or her demise. The policies are a combination of a savings plan and a life insurance policy. Term insurance excludes the savings provisions. In recent years more households have turned away from whole life policies as pension fund claims have increased.

This shift has created an interesting change in the financial markets, principally as a result of the fact that pension funds invest largely in corpo-

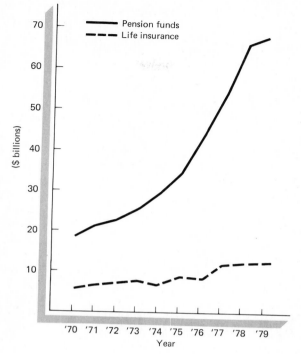

FIGURE 12-9
Net increase in claims of
households on pension funds
and life insurance companies.
Source: Flow of Funds
Accounts.

rate equity securities, while life insurance companies invest largely in bonds
and mortgages. The result has been that individuals have withdrawn from
direct participation in the equity markets, reduced their investment in life
insurance policies, and switched to an indirect participation in the equity
market through pension funds. This has meant that the largest single source
of funds for investment in equities has come from private and governmental
pension funds. Figure 12-10 shows the extent of this investment in the
1970s. The figure shows the dollar volume of new equity issues distributed
to the public from all corporate sources, the liquidations of equities by
households, and acquisitions by private and state and local government
pension funds. For example, in 1975 there were $10.7 billion in new issues
and household liquidations of $3.5 billion. Of the total of $14.2 billion, $8.2
billion or 58 percent were acquired by pension funds. These new equity
holdings of pension funds account for most of their total new investments.
Finally, the data indicate that pension funds are now playing an increasingly
important role in the financial markets as a whole and in the consumer
sector. During the 1970s these institutions had imposed upon them extensive new federal regulation. We will examine this regulatory system in
Chapter Eighteen.

   The other side of the pension fund story has been the decline in direct
participation by individuals in the equity markets. This seems to be only a
part of the trend which has developed over the entire postwar period of

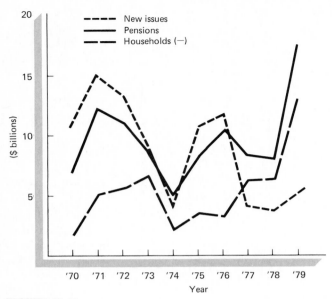

FIGURE 12-10
Acquisition and sale of equity securities by pension funds and households. The figure shows new equity issues, acquisitions by pension funds, and sales by households. Source: Flow of Funds accounts.

increasing reliance on financial intermediaries by consumers. Considerable attention has been devoted to trying to explain the withdrawal of individuals from direct participation in the equity markets. Some have argued that this is due to the poor performance of equities in general or to the poor performance of individuals managing equity portfolios. Others argue that most individuals simply find it cheaper to hire financial intermediaries to manage their investments than to manage them themselves. Some rather interesting evidence has been collected on the returns experienced by those who have chosen to persist in managing their own equity investments. A study has been conducted which analyzes the returns of individual investors who maintained accounts with a major national brokerage house from 1964 to 1970.[1] The study found that on average the returns of these individuals were slightly higher than returns on the market as a whole and on various kinds of mutual funds, even after brokerage fees on these accounts were deducted. Assuming this evidence is representative, it suggests that those people who persist in managing their own equity investments do not suffer measurably from doing so. However, the answers to questionnaires sent to these individuals revealed that the average individual spent between 5 and 10 hours

[1] See Gary G. Schlarbaum, Wilbur G. Lewellen, and Ronald C. Lease, "The Common-Stock-Portfolio Performance Record of Individual Investors: 1964–70," *Journal of Finance* (May 1978), pp. 429–441.

per month collecting information and selecting securities. It would seem that those who enjoy this process and find it rewarding, and possibly those who think they know something the market does not, may be those who continue to directly participate in the equity markets. In any event, this seems to have been a declining portion of the population in recent years.

SUMMARY

In this chapter we examined the market for consumer borrowing and lending. We explored the important trends on both the asset and liability side of consumer balance sheets and we examined the major financial markets serving consumers. A large part of the chapter was devoted to an examination of the mortgage market. This market deserves so much attention both because it is the largest financial market serving consumers and because the market underwent such significant change in the late 1970s and early 1980s. In addition to exploring the mortgage market we briefly examined the characteristics of nonmortgage consumer debt and we analyzed the market for consumer lending and saving in some detail.

We began our discussion of the mortgage market by noting the changing relationship between the volume of new residential construction and the volume of new residential mortgage financing. During the early years of the post-war era new construction consistently exceeded the volume of new mortgage financing. But beginning in the early 1970s, as inflation drove up the value of residential real estate, mortgage financing was used to support a wide variety of purchases and the volume of new mortgage financing consistently exceeded the volume of new residential construction.

The most important financial intermediary providing mortgage financing is the savings and loan. But in addition to savings and loans, commercial banks, other thrift institutions, and a variety of quasi-governmental agencies also supply funds to the mortgage market. The central difficulty facing the mortgage market pertains to the constraints which have been placed on savings and loans by the federal government. Historically, savings and loans have been constrained to invest almost exclusively in conventional long-term fixed-rate mortgages. Yet savings and loans support most of their mortgages with short-term funds obtained through deposits. This has meant that if interest rates increase, as they did quite dramatically during the late 1970s, savings and loans become exceedingly vulnerable.

The changes which are being instituted to deal with these difficulties were only partially explained in this chapter. The story is completed in Chapter Eighteen which deals with the regulation of financial intermediaries. But the long-run solution, assuming inflation continues, will almost certainly involve much less reliance on the conventional fixed-rate mortgage. Alternative mortgage contracts which shift more of the risk of interest-rate fluctuations to consumers were discussed in this chapter. These alternative mortgage contracts will be much more common in the 1980s than they ever have been before.

The changes in the composition of the asset side of consumer balance sheets during the 1970s has been quite interesting and dramatic. A large portion of consumers' assets continue to be held in deposit accounts with financial intermediaries. However, during the 1970s there was a shift away from demand deposits at commercial banks toward time deposits at banks and other thrift institutions such as savings and loans, credit unions, and mutual savings banks. In addition, the types of time deposit accounts have also changed considerably. In 1977 the federal regulators allowed depository financial intermediaries to begin to offer money market certificates. These are deposit accounts with interest rates which are tied to the Treasury bill rate prevailing at the time the account is issued. These accounts have been tremendously popular with consumers and have become a major portion of all deposit accounts at financial intermediaries. With the advent of money market certificates it became possible for all financial intermediaries to compete for consumers' funds when interest rates were high. Prior to the introduction of these new instruments, when interest rates rose above ceilings on deposit accounts enforced by the government, funds flowed out of the intermediaries. But with the introduction of money market certificates, the problem of borrowing short and lending long which faced savings and loans became more acute and the need for alternative mortgage instruments increased.

Interesting changes have also occurred during recent years regarding the role of nondeposit assets in consumers' portfolios. Probably the most important changes have involved consumer investment in pension funds, life insurance companies, and the equity markets. Consumers have been net sellers of equities in recent years and consumers' investments in life insurance companies have declined. The shift out of insurance investments has occurred in large part because consumers have switched from whole life to term insurance policies, which involve no savings program tied in with life insurance. At the same time these declines have occurred, pension funds have been a growth industry. This has meant that consumers' claims on pension funds have increased dramatically. Pension funds, in turn, invest heavily in the equity markets. As a result, consumers have switched from a direct participation in the equity markets to an indirect investment in the equity markets, managed by pension funds.

The changes that have occurred in financial markets in the last decade should not be viewed in isolation. Significant changes will also undoubtedly take place during the 1980s as well. The important force behind most of these changes has been inflation and it seems likely that inflation will continue to be a problem during the 1980s. The nature of the additional changes which will occur in the 1980s is hard to forecast. But it seems evident that more of the risks of fluctuating interest rates will be shifted to consumers and the deposit market will be essentially free of interest-rate ceilings by the end of the decade.

QUESTIONS TO IMPROVE UNDERSTANDING

1 Explain the role of the so-called quasi-governmental agencies in the home mortgage industry. Is it accurate to say that the total volume of funds provided by these agencies through either direct purchases of mortgages or mortgage pools (see Table 12-1) represent government subsidy of the mortgage industry? Explain why or why not.

2 What makes the typical savings and loan such a unique type of financial intermediary? Explain what it means to borrow short and lend long. What happened to savings and loans in the 1970s as a result of the fact that they borrowed short and loaned long?

3 What kinds of alternatives have been considered for the conventional long-term fixed-rate mortgage? Compare how these alternatives would work.

4 What does it mean to say that a mortgage loan does not necessarily constitute a loan to finance the acquisition of residential property? What has been the long-term trend in the use of mortgage financing? Can you explain why this trend has occurred?

5 What has happened to consumers' use of installment debt during the 1970s? Why? How might you evaluate what constitutes too much consumer debt for the economy as a whole?

6 Discuss the principal changes in recent years in the types of claims that individuals hold on financial intermediaries. What do you think might be the major factors which could cause these trends to continue or to change in another direction?

7 What is disintermediation and why has it taken place?

8 What are money market certificates and why have they become such popular vehicles for consumer investment?

9 How have individuals shifted from direct participation in the equity market to indirect participation through intermediaries. Why do you think individuals have chosen to pull out of the equity markets to such an extent?

REFERENCES*

Crane, Dwight B., and Michael J. Riley: "Strategies for a Now-Account Environment," *Bankers Magazine* (January–February 1979), pp. 35–41.

Melton, William C.: "Graduated Payment Mortgages," *Quarterly Review*, Federal Reserve Bank of New York (Spring 1980), pp. 21–28.

————, and Diane L. Heidt: "Variable Rate Mortgages," *Quarterly Review*, Federal Reserve Bank of New York (Summer 1979), pp. 23–31.

Mishkin, F. S.: "What Depressed the Consumer? The Household Balance Sheet and the 1973–75 Recession," *Broolsings Papers on Economic Activity*, 1, 1977, pp. 123–174.

* All the references listed above provide additional institutional detail and make excellent supplementary readings.

Palash, Carl J.: "Household Debt Burden: How Heavy Is It?" *Quarterly Review*, Federal Reserve Bank of New York (Summer 1979), pp. 9–12; also see references at end of Chapter Eighteen.

Schlarbaum, Gary G., Wilbur G. Lewellen, and Ronald C. Lease: "The Common-Stock-Portfolio Performance Record of Individual Investors: 1964–1970," *Journal of Finance* (May 1978), pp. 429–441.

Sivesind, Charles M.: "Mortgage-backed Securities: The Revolution in Real Estate Finance," *Quarterly Review*, Federal Reserve Bank of New York (Autumn 1979), pp. 1–10.

Chapter Thirteen

THE MARKET
FOR CORPORATE FINANCING

In this chapter we will examine the various ways in which corporations finance their activities. This is an immense topic and we can acquire only a very broad perspective in a single chapter. Therefore, this chapter seeks only to explain how corporations have in fact financed themselves in recent years and to document some of the major changes which have taken place in corporate financial markets. We will try to avoid consideration of what determines optimal financing decisions for individual corporations as much as possible. The theory and empirical evidence regarding what constitutes optimal financing strategies has traditionally been the domain of corporate finance and corporate finance per se is not the subject of this book. In a sense, our focus here is more on the history, most of it relatively recent, of what has happened in corporate financial markets in the aggregate, rather than on the theory of how financing decisions should be made.

In spite of the fact that we will stay away from assessing the pros and cons of various financing decisions as viewed by individual firms, the fundamental financing decisions which all corporations must make provide the shopping list of topics which are addressed in this chapter. Corporations can utilize internally generated funds or they can raise funds externally; if external, they can issue either debt or equity, or even some hybrid of the two; if debt, they can commit to a short or a long maturity. Regardless of the type of external financing, however, they must decide whether to distribute the securities publicly or to seek a private placement. In this chapter we will examine to what extent each of these options has been utilized in recent years.

The chapter is organized into four major sections. The first section lays out the basic financing options available to corporations and presents aggregate data on the recent use of each option. It also defines the principal uses to which this financing has been put. The next two sections examine specific financing options. Section two deals with retained earnings and equity financing. Section three focuses on the various forms of debt. The final section examines the changing use of each of these methods of financing over the business cycle. Specifically, this latter section concentrates on the brief historical period surrounding the 1974 recession and explains how that recession affected corporate financing.

OVERVIEW OF THE SOURCES AND USES OF CORPORATE FINANCING

The Financing Options

The financing options facing any corporation can be viewed as a sequence of four decisions. They are, in order, (1) the dividend decision, (2) the leverage decision, (3) the maturity decision, and (4) the placement decision. This sequence of decisions and the financing options associated with each decision are illustrated in Figure 13-1. All of these decisions take the firm's investment needs as given. That is, it is presumed at the outset that the managers of the firm have decided what investments will be undertaken and that they know what funds will be needed to support these investments. The four decisions listed above influence the way these funds will be raised. In a sense, the assumption that investment needs are known is exceedingly unrealistic. Managers sometimes think they know what investment needs will be and then circumstances change and new financing must be obtained. But we will postpone consideration of such difficulties until the end of the chapter when we examine how changes in the economy during 1974 influenced corporate financing.

With knowledge of investment needs in hand, the first financial decision the managers of the firm must make is the dividend decision. This decision allocates after-tax profits between dividends and retained earnings. Retained earnings comprise one of the two sources of internal funds, the other being depreciation allowances. It is generally thought that most firms prefer to finance with internal funds; hence, retained earnings are often considered one of the first sources of financing. However, retained earnings

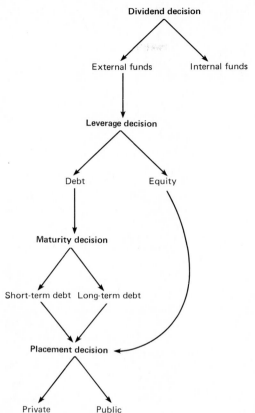

FIGURE 13-1
Financing decisions facing corporations.

come at the expense of dividends and, in spite of the fact that earnings which are paid in dividends are taxed, both when they are earned by the corporation and again when they are distributed to owners as income, at least some people seem to prefer dividends.

When internal funds are insufficient to finance the firm's investments, as is generally the case for most corporations, the management must turn to some form of external financing. The first decision affecting external financing is the leverage decision, the decision on whether debt or equity financing will be used and the relative amounts of each. Equity is a residual claim on the earnings of the firm. That is, equity holders receive compensation after all other claims against the firm are paid. The principal alternative form of external financing is debt. And debt can be issued in a tremendous variety of forms. If debt is chosen, the next decision is the maturity decision. Debt can be issued with almost any maturity desired, ranging from virtually overnight to 30 years. The line which generally divides what is classified as short-term from long-term debt is 1 year.

The final decision, the placement decision, affects both debt and equity. The placement decision pertains to whether external financing should be obtained through some kind of intermediary or dealer, or whether securities should be sold directly to the market. The nature of a placement through an intermediary varies from one type of security to another. With short-term debt the choice is basically between bank loans and commercial paper. With longer maturity debt, the choice is between a private placement with, say, an insurance company and the option of selling bonds directly to the market. With equity, the choice is whether to sell securities directly to the market, principally through what is called a rights offering to existing shareholders, or whether to sell the securities to an investment banker who in turn sells them to the market.

The Volume of Alternative Sources of Financing

There is no particular pattern followed by all corporations in drawing upon alternative sources of financing. Some corporations rely almost exclusively on internal funds and equity financing. Others are highly levered, some with long maturity debt and some with short. But, while it is difficult to profile the sources of financing for the typical corporation, we can examine the extent to which each type of financing is used in the aggregate; that is, for all nonfinancial corporations taken together. To begin with, the volume of external and internal funds used by all nonfinancial corporations in the United States during the 1970s is shown in Figure 13-2. Internal funds are broken down into two components, *capital consumption allowance* and *retained earnings*. The figure shows that the largest consistent source of funds was the capital consumption allowance. This allowance refers to the earnings of corporations which are allocated to depreciation and, hence, are a source of funds for maintaining plant and equipment owned and operated by corporations. It is important to note that the capital consumption or depreciation allowance provides no funds for expansion or for new investments. It merely provides for the replacement of existing capital. Moreover, to a large extent, the magnitude of the allowance is determined by the tax laws so that it is not a matter of choice; hence, it is not included in Figure 13-1 as a financing option. Compared to either external financing or the capital consumption allowance, aggregate retained earnings were rather small during the 1970s. Moreover, total internal financing grew fairly consistently over the decade, while external financing did not. It is also apparent from Figure 13-2 that total external financing can be rather volatile. We will examine why this occurs later in the chapter.

Aggregate data on the major components of external financing are shown in Figure 13-3. The figure shows that equity financing was a rather small portion of the total, ranging from roughly 5 to 25 percent. The figure also shows the volume of short-term debt issued to banks and finance companies versus commercial paper sold directly to the market. Bonds and

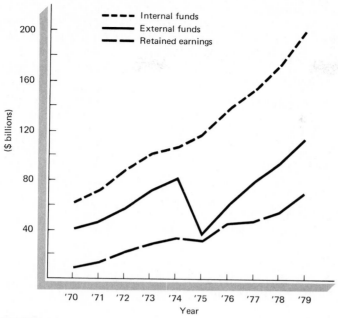

FIGURE 13-2

Major sources of funding for nonfinancial U.S. corporations. The figure shows total internal funds, total external funds, and retained earnings. The difference between total internal funds and retained earnings represents capital consumption allowances. Source: Flow of Funds Accounts.

mortgages have consistently been a sizable portion of the total, while the volume of bank loans has been extremely volatile. Bank loans increased considerably in the early part of the decade and were liquidated in 1975 and 1976. It is apparent from the figure that commercial paper represents a relatively small portion of the aggregate market for short-term debt. The proportion of private and publicly placed bonds is documented in Figure 13-4. This figure shows that, generally, more than half of the corporate bonds are publicly distributed.

On the whole, during the 1970s, corporations used more internal than external funds; they used more debt than equity; more long-term debt than short-term debt; and most debt was privately rather than publicly distributed. Next, we need to examine the uses to which these funds were put.

The Uses of Corporate Financing

The funds which corporations raise, both internally and externally, have four principal uses. The largest uses of funds are to finance the acquisition of plant and equipment and new construction, all of which are referred to as

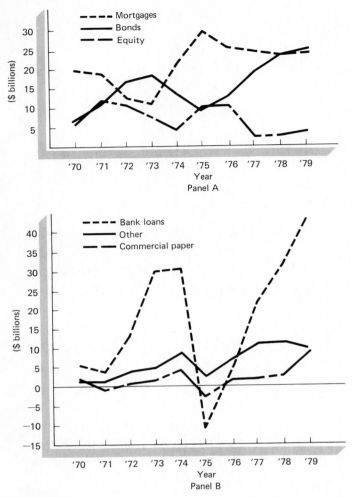

FIGURE 13-3
Major sources of external financing for nonfinancial corporations. Panel A shows
long-term and Panel B short-term financing. Source: Flow of Funds Accounts.

fixed investment. The other uses are to finance the acquisition of inventories,
to support trade credit supplied by one nonfinancial corporation to another,
and to permit the acquisition of liquid financial assets. Figure 13-5 shows the
relative importance of each of these uses. It is apparent from the figure that
fixed business investment is the largest component of the total. Most firms
try to plan their fixed investment expenditures far ahead and thereby avoid
significant peaks and valleys in investment expenditures. Inventories, on the
other hand, act essentially as a shock absorber in order to smooth production

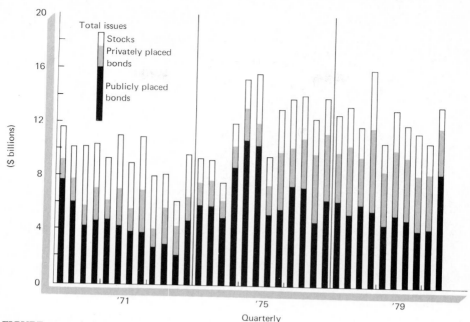

FIGURE 13-4

Volume of corporate securities issued, 1971–1979. The figure shows the proportion of stocks, privately placed bonds, and publicly placed bonds. Source: *Federal Reserve Chart Book*, 1979.

activity. As a result, inventory investment can change dramatically in a short period as sales activity changes. Liquid assets serve a similar function, providing a financial shock absorber and, therefore, are also quite volatile.

INTERNAL FUNDS AND EQUITY FINANCING

The sources of financing available to corporations if they avoid leveraging themselves are internal funds and equity financing. As Figures 13-2 and 13-3 evidence, if we compare the total volume of internal funds with the total volume of new equity financing over the last decade, internal funds represent a much larger share of the total. Yet the bulk of these internal funds is not available to support real expansion of corporate assets. Without debt, it is really retained earnings and new equity which are available to support the real growth of corporations. In this section we will look more closely at retained earnings and the equity portion of external financing in order to determine the major forces influencing these financing sources during the 1970s.

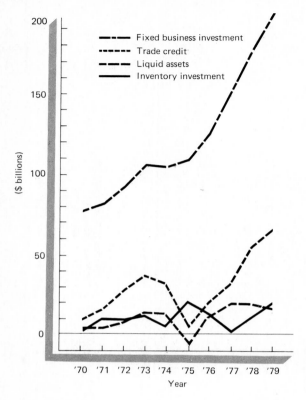

FIGURE 13-5
Principal uses of funds raised by
nonfinancial U.S. corporations.
Source: Flow of Funds Accounts.

Corporate Reliance on Internal Funds

Corporate managers often express a great preference to be able to finance
new expenditures with internal funds. This is often a sign that past investments have been successful enough to generate substantial profits which are
then available to be reinvested in the firm. It also reflects a preference held by
some managers to avoid financial commitments to others. The ultimate
source of all internal funds is corporate profits. There are only two items
which are subtracted from corporate profits in order to arrive at total internal
funds. These are taxes and dividends. The basic accounting procedure for
computing retained earnings and gross internal funds is shown in panel A of
Table 13-1 using data for years at each end of the last decade (1971 and 1979)
for all corporations in the United States. Aside from taxes and dividends, the
other important item in this panel is depreciation.

THE ROLE OF DEPRECIATION   In order to understand the effect of depreciation
on the internal funds of American corporations, it is necessary to grasp the
distinction between real or economic depreciation and accounting depreciation. Real depreciation is the real decline in value of capital goods over a

TABLE 13-1

Panel A: Accounting for Internal Funds for American Businesses (Billions of Dollars)

	1971	1979
Profits before taxes and depreciation	143.6	368.2
less depreciation expense	60.3	131.1
Profits before taxes	83.3	237.1
less taxes	37.3	92.9
Profits after taxes	45.9	144.5
less dividends	25.4	52.7
Retained earnings	20.5	91.8
plus depreciation expense	60.3	131.1
Internal funds	80.8	222.9

Panel B: Adjusted Profits, Retained Earnings, and Internal Funds (Billions of Dollars)

	1971	1979
Profits before taxes and depreciation	143.6	368.2
less depreciation expense	60.3	131.1
inventory valuation adjustment	4.7	41.8
capital consumption adjustment	1.8	16.7
Adjusted profits before taxes	76.8	178.6
less taxes	37.3	92.9
Adjusted profits after taxes	39.5	85.7
less dividends	25.4	52.7
Adjusted retained earnings	14.1	33.0
plus depreciation expense	60.1	131.1
capital consumption adjustment	1.8	16.7
Adjusted internal funds	76.0	180.8

Panel C: Impact of Revised Tax Treatment on Internal Funds (Billions of Dollars)

		1971		1979
Adjusted profits before taxes		76.8		178.6
less adjusted taxes				
actual taxes	37.3		92.9	
less adjustments*	3.0		26.9	
adjusted taxes		34.3		66.0
Tax corrected after tax profits		42.5		112.6
less dividends		25.4		52.7
Tax corrected adjusted retained earnings		17.1		59.9
plus depreciation expense		60.1		131.1
capital consumption adjustment		1.8		16.7
Tax corrected internal funds		79.0		207.7

* 48 percent of the sum of the inventory adjustment and the capital consumption adjustment.

Source: *Federal Reserve Bulletins, GNP Accounts.*

period of time. Accounting depreciation is the amount of depreciation actually recorded in the accounts of a firm and it is usually dictated by what the tax laws will permit. With a firm's profits (before taxes and depreciation) determined, the effect of an increase in accounting depreciation is to reduce that firm's tax liability, thereby increasing the gross internal funds available to the firm. While this increase in accounting depreciation also reduces retained earnings, the net effect on total internal funds is still positive because the decrease in retained earnings is exactly offset by the increase in depreciation, leaving the tax savings as the net change.

One of the most important developments affecting retained earnings and gross internal funds during the 1970s pertains to this difference between real depreciation and that which is claimed for tax purposes. The problem is that depreciation allowed for tax purposes (the numbers listed in panel A of Table 13-1) has increasingly understated the real depreciation which was experienced during the decade of the 1970s. The underlying culprit which has generated this problem is inflation. Inflation creates two problems which distort stated corporate profits after depreciation expense and hence tend to increase the tax liabilities of U.S. corporations. Inflation has also created some significant problems for the market value of corporate equities which are discussed in detail in Chapter Twenty-two. One of these pertains directly to the depreciation of capital equipment and the other to the portion of profits which are due to the misstatement of the value of inventories. The first problem occurs because inflation increases the replacement cost of existing capital assets, which means that the real depreciation rate must be increased to reflect this increased replacement cost. Yet allowable accounting depreciation has not been adjusted to take this effect of inflation into account. Throughout the 1970s allowable depreciation expense was based on the historical rather than the replacement cost of assets. This tends to understate depreciation and overstate profits. A similar problem pertains to inventories. As the replacement cost of inventories increases with inflation, profits tend to be inflated because costs are measured on an historical basis.

INFLATION ADJUSTMENTS   Both of these problems were relatively insignificant at the beginning of the last decade, but have increased in significance as inflation has increased. The effects of these problems on corporate profits and retained earnings for 1971 and 1979, as well as a procedure for adjusting profits and retained earnings, are shown in panel B of Table 13-1. The entry labeled "inventory valuation adjustment" adjusts profits for the effect of inflation on inventories and thereby corrects for what have come to be called inventory profits. The capital consumption adjustment corrects accounting depreciation so that it reflects replacement rather than historical cost. This panel shows that, while these adjustments were inconsequential in 1971, in 1979 the adjustments totaled $58.5 billion and reduced retained earnings by 64 percent. The effect of these adjustments on profits and re-

tained earnings is illustrated further in Figure 13-6, which shows reported
profits and retained earnings as well as adjusted profits and adjusted retained earnings as a percent of gross national product, for the years 1971 to
1979. It is evident from the figure that profits, both adjusted and unadjusted,
have declined significantly from the levels achieved during much of the
1960s. (Again, see Chapter Twenty-two for an investigation of the impact of
this development on the value of corporate equities.) This has tended to
reduce the ability of American corporations to finance investments with
internal funds.

TAXES AND INTERNAL FUNDS   There is yet one more aspect of the way these
two adjustments influence retained earnings and internal funds. The problem is that corporate profits taxes are based on unadjusted rather than adjusted profits. As a result, profits taxes are higher than they would be if the
effects of inflation were properly accounted for. Panel C of Table 13-1 shows
the size of the discrepancy, again for the years 1971 and 1979. The computations in this table assume that the tax benefit which would be generated if
profits were taxed at adjusted levels is equal to 46 percent (which is the
nominal corporate tax rate) of the sum of the two adjustments. The table

FIGURE 13-6

The effect of adjustments for inflation on retained earnings and profits of U.S.
corporations. The figure shows before-tax profits (π) and retained earnings (RE) as a
proportion of gross national product. It also shows adjusted before-tax profits and
retained earnings. Source: *Federal Reserve Bulletin*, various issues.

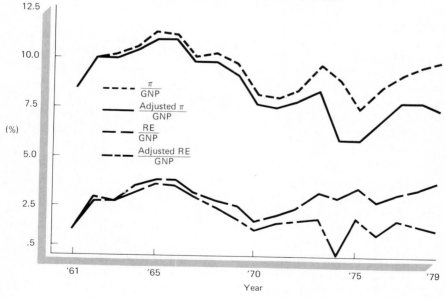

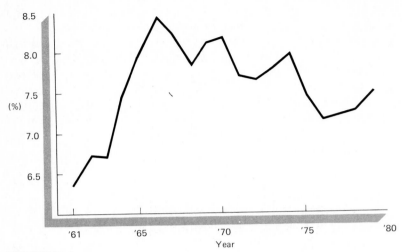

FIGURE 13-7
Investment in plant and equipment by nonfinancial U.S. corporations as a percentage of gross national product. Source: *Federal Reserve Bulletin*, various issues.

shows that in 1979 corporate taxes would have been reduced by $26.9 billion or 29 percent and retained earnings would have been increased by the same dollar amount and percent had taxes been based on adjusted profits.

The implication of these trends toward declining profits and retained earnings is that corporations are compelled to either reduce investment expenditures or rely more heavily on external funds. Corporations seem to have chosen a little of each. In the latter half of the 1970s capital expenditures on plant and equipment by American corporations were somewhat sluggish, particularly relative to the high levels of investment experienced in the mid-1960s. This is illustrated in Figure 13-7, which shows plant and equipment investment as a percent of GNP. Many observers of American capital markets fear that the level of investment in the U.S. economy is too low to sustain the kind of economic growth the economy has maintained during most of the post-World War II era. Whether this pattern in investment spending is the beginning of a long-run trend or a response to more short-run difficulties is a controversial question on which there is little consensus at this time.[1]

New Equity Financing

If a corporation has insufficient internal funds to finance its investments, then it must turn to external funds and decide whether to issue debt or

[1] See Burton G. Malkiel, "The Capital Formation Problem in the United States," *Journal of Finance*, 34 (May 1979), pp. 291–306.

equity. As a practical matter, over the last 25 years sizable new issues of equity were offered to the market when the stock market was doing well and prices were perceived to be high. When prices were low and the market was in a slump, the volume of equity issues was relatively small. Figure 13-8 illustrates this pattern of new equity issues. The lower panel of the figure shows the volume of new stock issues from 1956 to 1979, while the top panel shows the Standard & Poor's 500 stock index for the same period. Through most of the late 1950s and 1960s the supply of internal funds was more plentiful than it has been in recent years and the volume of new equity issues was correspondingly low. In the 1970s, as retained earnings became scarce, equity issues increased, but only when the stock market was moving out of a slump. This happened during 1971 and 1972, after the stock market trough of 1970, and again in 1976 and 1977, after the stock market trough in the recession of 1974. When prices are depressed, as they were in 1970 and 1974, corporate managers are reluctant to issue new equities because new buyers are allowed to acquire shares in the firm at what managers believe to be bargain-basement prices.

Most of these new equity issues have gone to financial intermediaries, particularly pension funds and insurance companies, with pension funds absorbing the majority. In addition, a growing portion of these new equity

FIGURE 13-8

New equity issues and market performance. The top part of the figure shows the Standard & Poor's 500 Index of prices of equity securities. The bottom part shows the annual new equity issues. Source: *Federal Reserve Bulletin*, various issues.

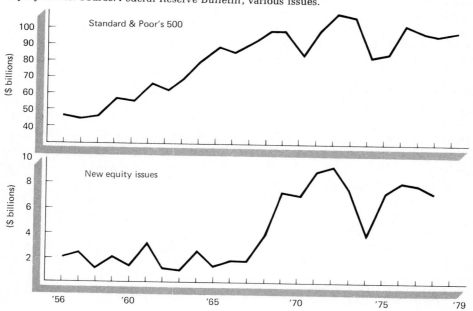

issues have been sold to foreign purchasers. As documented in the preceding chapter, individuals have not been directly acquiring equity securities during recent years. In spite of this, individuals' direct holdings of equities are still very large, larger than the equity holdings of any other single segment of the economy.

THE PLACEMENT OF EQUITY   The placement decision for equity securities centers on whether to utilize the services of an investment banker or whether to sell the securities directly to the market. In recent years most issues of new equity securities have been handled by an investment banking firm. But there have always been some issues which have been distributed without an investment banker through what is called a rights offering or privileged subscription. In addition to privileged subscriptions, in the latter part of the decade a few large firms have chosen to bypass investment bankers and issue securities directly to anyone in the market. We will consider the rights offering first.

A *rights offering* or, equivalently, a *privileged subscription*, is an offering of new equity to existing shareholders at a reduced price. The basic idea behind a privileged subscription is that existing shareholders are given the opportunity to maintain their proportional ownership in the firm at a time when the firm is raising new equity capital. This is accomplished by offering each shareholder the right to purchase a proportionate amount of the new securities to be issued, at a slightly reduced price. The greater the price reduction, the greater the chance that all the new equity shares will be sold to existing owners. But at the same time, the greater the price reduction, the smaller the amount of funds that will be raised by issuing a given number of new shares. The name rights offering is applied to this kind of new issue because, in many instances, the charter of a corporation specifies that existing shareholders will be given the right to preserve their proportionate ownership of the firm when new equity securities are issued. The actual value of such a right, however, depends upon the amount of price reduction offered to existing owners.[2]

Another possibility which avoids reliance on an investment banker is to sell securities directly to the market, without a rights offering and without the services of a specialist like the investment banker. This direct market offering has been attempted infrequently, but in recent years a few large companies have chosen this option and have been quite successful. In particular, some of the larger oil companies have chosen to bypass their investment bankers and occasionally sell securities directly to investors.[3]

The most frequent method chosen for issuing new equity is to utilize an investment banker. An *investment banker* performs essentially the same services as any other type of dealer. The investment banker acquires the

[2] A clear discussion of the value of a right and the amount of the discount can be found in Richard Brealey and Stewart Myers, *Principles of Corporate Finance*, McGraw-Hill, New York, 1981.
[3] See W. Robertson, "Future Shock at Morgan Stanley," *Fortune* (February 27, 1979), pp. 174–186.

securities which a company wants to issue and then redistributes them to the market. Unlike a commercial bank or a savings and loan, the investment banking firm does not change the security itself. That is, the investment banking firm does not buy equity securities and issue deposit claims, as a commercial bank accepts loans and issues deposits. Instead the investment banker redistributes the same securities. He or she does not act merely as the seller of these securities by only arranging the sale, but instead takes a position in the asset. The investment banker is said to be an "underwriter" because he or she bears the risk of changes in the price of the equity issue during the period in which it is distributed. Investment bankers are willing to bear this kind of risk because they specialize in locating customers for new security issues and in understanding the factors which can determine the success of a new offering. The typical corporation which utilizes an investment banker issues equity securities only infrequently and therefore finds itself at a disadvantage in handling this kind of proceeding on its own. On the other hand, investment banking firms are generally not willing to bear the risk of distributing any particular new equity issue on their own. Instead, they generally form syndicates in order to spread or diversify the risk involved. The investment banking firm which originates the issue or forms the syndicate usually manages the distribution and takes the largest portion of it.

The company which is issuing new securities to the market has two basic options when deciding what arrangement to make with investment bankers. One option is to offer the securities for competitive bids by investment bankers. Technically speaking, it is this procedure which gives rise to syndicates. The company invites bids from investment bankers and the investment banking firms divide into competing syndicates to bid on the issue. The name syndicate may be somewhat unfortunate in that it gives the impression that investment bankers form a relatively permanent association held together by the threat of various and sundry penalties. This is generally not the case. Any particular investment banking firm may be involved in a number of different syndicates on a typical day. The syndicate is merely a device for diversifying portfolios.

The second option open to the issuing company is referred to as a *negotiated offering*. Under this arrangement the company selling the securities locates a particular investment banking firm which it wants to handle its issue. This procedure has the disadvantage that there is no competitive bidding procedure. On the other hand, the investment banking firm is then in a position to give advice to the company on the optimal way to structure its security offering. These arrangements between firms and investment bankers are often long-term relationships where the continuing advice of the investment banker is valued.

While the vast majority of new equity securities are sold through investment banking firms without a rights offering, there is some evidence which indicates that this is a considerably more costly alternative. Clifford

Smith studied the costs of issuing equity through an investment banker versus the cost of using a rights offering for a sample of 578 issues of securities filed with the Securities and Exchange Commission between 1971 and 1975. He concluded that the average cost of securities issued through an underwriter was 6.17 percent of the proceeds of the issue, while the cost for rights offerings with no underwriter averaged 2.45 percent.[4] It is not entirely clear why underwriting is so popular if it is, in fact, so costly. Some speculate that investment bankers act as a disciplining force on managers so that managers are compelled to utilize them in spite of the additional cost. Others argue that firms try to increase their value by utilizing investment bankers with prestigious reputations. At this juncture the actual answer is unclear.

CORPORATE DEBT FINANCING

If a corporation chooses to use external financing and chooses to obtain at least some of that in the form of debt, then it must decide on the maturity and the placement of that debt. But as we will discover shortly, these are really only the first of a number of options available once the decision to utilize debt has been made. The market for corporate debt can be divided into three broad categories based on maturity and placement: the market for long-term debt, commercial bank financing, and nonbank short-term financing. Actually the division of debt between long-term and bank debt is somewhat arbitrary because banks now provide debt to corporations in a wide variety of maturities. But traditionally, commercial banks almost exclusively offered short-term loans to business customers. They are still principally oriented toward short-term loans, but their corporate loan portfolio is now more varied than it once was.

Long-term Debt Financing

Long-term debt financing by corporations takes basically two forms, bonds and mortgages. The volume of both of these securities issued in the last decade was shown in Figure 13-3. Taken together, in most years bonds and mortgages represent the largest form of external financing. Roughly half of the bonds sold are publicly rather than privately distributed. The proportion of public and private bonds issued during the 1970s was shown in Figure 13-4.

The principal purchasers of corporate bonds during the 1970s have been life insurance companies and pension funds. In earlier years individuals also purchased sizable portions of the bonds issued. But as in the equity market, individual participation in the bond market has declined in recent years.

[4] See Clifford W. Smith, "Alternative Methods for Raising Capital: Rights versus Underwritten Offerings," *Journal of Financial Economics*, 5 (December 1977), pp. 273–307.

Figure 13-9 shows the relative shares of newly issued corporate bonds acquired by major suppliers of funds during the 1970s.

The largest single purchaser of corporate bonds is the life insurance industry. Utilizing the funds they acquire from life insurance contracts, life insurance companies purchase corporate bonds as well as mortgages. Figure 13-10 illustrates the proportion of their total assets which have been invested in corporate bonds and mortgages during the 1970s. Life insurance company investments in corporate bonds are more volatile than their investments in mortgages or in policy loans because they are somewhat of a residual. Policy loans are loans to holders of life insurance policies and generally carry rather low interest rates. As a result, when market interest rates rise, policy loans increase and funds available for bond investments decline. In addition, mortgage loans are generally made on the basis of commitments a number of months ahead of time. Hence, once a commitment is made the funds must be provided, again sometimes at the expense of funds for bonds.

Of the other institutions which purchase corporate bonds, pension funds have increased their investments while mutual savings banks have maintained a more stable share. Pension funds have grown tremendously during the 1970s as more individuals have come to utilize such institutions to manage their retirement investments, rather than do so themselves or

FIGURE 13-9

Major purchasers of corporate bonds. This figure shows that life insurance companies are the largest single purchaser of corporate bonds. Source: Flow of Funds Accounts.

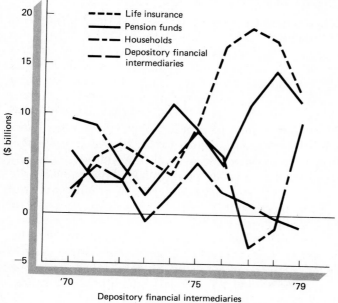

Depository financial intermediaries

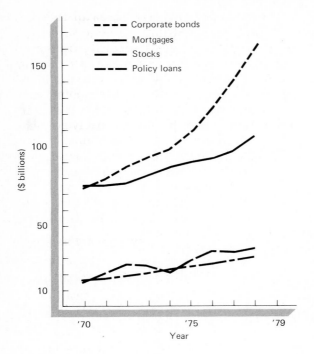

FIGURE 13-10
Principal types of life insurance company investments. The figure indicates the total volume of life insurance company investments in corporate bonds, mortgages, equity securities, and policy loans. Source: *Federal Reserve Bulletin*, various issues.

provide nothing at all for retirement. Pension funds have been one of the most important new intermediaries to develop in recent years and they participate heavily in both the equity and bond markets.

The principal factor which distinguishes corporate bonds is their placement, private or public. Publicly issued bonds tend to be larger and more standardized than do privately issued bonds and are often issued by well-known companies. The advantage of issuing privately generally hinges on the flexibility it provides. Privately placed bonds often have complicated features which would be difficult to incorporate in public bonds. These features often require that the borrower return to the intermediary which holds the bond to renegotiate various terms. Such flexibility is virtually impossible with public debt. Almost all privately placed bonds are distributed to insurance companies and most of these to a fairly small number of large companies. By contrast, most publicly distributed bonds are sold to pension funds. Insurance companies have long specialized in analyzing the investments of the corporations in which they invest and in this respect serve a purpose similar to that of commercial banks. The principal distinction is that insurance companies generally lend for relatively long maturities, largely because their liabilities have long maturities. By contrast, commercial banks provide shorter maturity loans which are more closely matched to the maturity of their liabilities.

The costs of private versus public placement of bonds with roughly comparable characteristics do not diverge by tremendous amounts. In a recent study of the private-placement market for bonds it was reported that between 1961 and 1977 the yield on privately distributed bonds exceeded that on publicly distributed bonds by an average of 50 basis points (one-half of one percentage point), and varied between a spread of 5 basis points and 94 basis points.[5] This study points out that higher flotation costs in public offerings and increased flexibility of private offerings can probably account for the average yield difference. Furthermore, the study accounts for the variation in this spread as a result of slow adjustment of private interest rates to changes in conditions in public markets.

Business Financing from Commercial Banks

Commercial banks have long been the principal source of funds available to most businesses for short-term debt. The proportion of new commercial bank loans relative to total, newly acquired, external financing is shown in Figure 13-3. In peak years, such as 1973 and 1974, commercial bank financing was larger than any other single form of external financing. In other years, such as 1975, following the 1974 recession, there was a net liquidation of commercial bank loans. This volatility of bank loans results from the principal use to which bank loans are put. The most important single purpose for which commercial banks extend loans to businesses is to finance inventories. As inventories increase in the early stages of a recession, such as 1974, bank loans rise to finance those inventories. As those inventories decline, bank loans generally do so as well.

Commercial and industrial loans from banks take a number of different forms. Such loans vary in maturity and size and according to whether the loan is made under some form of prearranged commitment, as well as whether the interest rate on the loan floats with the prime interest rate. The major characteristics of commercial and industrial loans are documented in Table 13-2 for loans made in early November 1979. These data on commercial and industrial loans are drawn from a survey of commercial banks conducted by the Federal Reserve on a quarterly basis to document the terms of bank lending. The table indicates that most loans reported in the survey were short-term rather than long-term loans. In addition a little over half of these loans were made under a commitment and had interest rates which floated with the prime rate. Furthermore, the average maturity of most short-term loans was only 3 months. Finally, the largest number of these loans was very small, but most of the dollar volume was extended in loans with amounts over $1 million.

LOAN COMMITMENTS   There are two major types of commitments which may be agreed upon by borrowers and commercial banks. The purpose of the

[5] See Burton Zwick, "Yields on Privately Placed Corporate Bonds," *Journal of Finance*, 35 (March 1980), pp. 23–30.

TABLE 13-2

Item	All sizes	Size of loan (in thousands of dollars)					
		1–24	25–49	50–99	100–499	50–999	1,000 and over
SHORT-TERM COMMERCIAL AND INDUSTRIAL LOANS							
1 Amount of loans (thousands of dollars)	8,107,372	696,629	369,217	431,935	1,724,393	685,208	4,199,992
2 Number of loans	128,317	97,398	11,174	6,984	10,369	1,062	1,330
3 Weighted average maturity (months)	3.0	3.6	3.3	3.3	3.5	3.9	2.5
4 Weighted average interest rate (percent per annum)	15.81	14.77	14.92	15.93	15.40	16.01	16.19
5 Interquartile range[1]	15.25–16.82	12.68–16.99	13.21–16.83	14.58–17.48	13.65–16.91	15.25–16.86	15.31–16.70
Percentage of amount of loans							
6 With floating rate	52.6	17.1	21.7	44.7	36.4	66.6	66.3
7 Made under commitment	49.4	19.6	26.1	38.4	43.6	61.1	58.0
LONG-TERM COMMERCIAL AND INDUSTRIAL LOANS							
8 Amount of loans (thousands of dollars)	1,646,325		325,742			204,389	137,391	978,803
9 Number of loans	28,827		27,356			1,020	206	244
10 Weighted average maturity (months)	48.5		35.1			39.0	35.7	56.7
11 Weighted average interest rate (percent per annum)	15.55		14.76			15.66	15.43	15.81
12 Interquartile range[1]	15.25–16.50		13.00–16.14			15.00–17.23	15.25–17.00	15.25–16.25
Percentage of amount of loans							
13 With floating rate	71.7		27.8			66.4	74.1	87.0
14 Made under commitment	63.3		33.1			60.3	62.0	74.1

commitment is to provide some insurance to the borrower that funds will be available if and when they are needed. One type of commitment is referred to as a *line of credit*. This is an informal agreement between borrower and lender to provide funds up to a prespecified amount over a prespecified time interval. Most lines of credit stipulate that the interest rate the borrower will receive floats with the prime rate and hence are referred to as *floating-rate agreements*. Lines of credit which commit a bank to a specific rate in the future, or *fixed-rate agreements*, are now fairly uncommon. Lines of credit are informal agreements in the sense that they are not legally binding upon the bank. Banks scrupulously try to honor most such agreements because their reputation for reliability is at stake, but this type of agreement is not enforceable in court and banks can legally refuse to honor it. Banks generally require that borrowers with a line of credit maintain balances with the bank as a means of compensating the bank for a line of credit. These balances serve in lieu of a fee paid for the line of credit.

The alternative type of commitment is a *revolving credit agreement*. Unlike the line of credit, the revolving credit agreement is a legally binding commitment to provide funds on prespecified terms. As a result, revolving credit agreements often include more detailed specifications which the borrower must meet than are included in a line of credit. In addition, banks generally require that fees be paid to secure a revolving credit agreement.

FLOATING-RATE LOANS   A number of years ago it was not too uncommon to see fixed-rate commitments extended to business borrowers by commercial banks, but as interest rates became more volatile during the 1970s, this became an increasingly risky provision. It is now relatively standard practice to tie the interest rate on commitments to the prime interest rate. As a result, with floating-rate commitments, corporate borrowers are essentially purchasing insurance against the prospect that the markup over prime they might have to pay will go up, or against the prospect that they may be virtually unable to obtain banks funds, regardless of the rate they are willing to pay. If a firm is virtually unable to obtain additional financing regardless of the rate it is willing to agree to, then financing is said to be *rationed*.

With the advent of increased use of floating-rate bank loans, the prime interest rate has received increased attention. For borrowers with floating-rate loans, it is the prime interest rate which is the principal determinant of the actual interest rate they pay. Until relatively recently the prime interest rate charged by most banks was changed rather infrequently; that is, it was not tied directly to the level of any single rate or group of money market interest rates. But this also has changed in recent years. Figure 13-11 shows the prime rate and the rate on prime commercial paper (see Chapter Ten for a discussion of commercial paper) from the early 1960s to the end of 1979. In the early years of this period changes in the commercial paper rate were accompanied by little if any change in the prime interest rate. The prime rate was set by individual banks and they chose to adjust this rate only with major movements in market interest rates. But as interest rates became more volatile in the late 1960s and 1970s and more loans became tied to the prime rate, most banks began to adjust the prime rate with changes in the commercial paper rate. Some banks even announced that their rates were determined according to a weighted average of market rates. By the end of the 1970s the prime rate was changing dramatically in very short periods, as did money market rates in general.

FIGURE 13-11

Prime interest rate and rate on prime commercial paper. Source: *Federal Reserve Chart Book*, 1979.

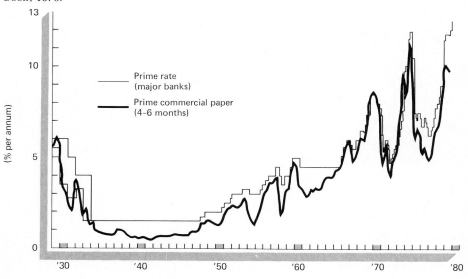

There is another important ingredient in the forces which led to more flexible prime rates and to increased use of floating-rate loans. This is the increased reliance of commercial banks on sources of funds with highly volatile interest rates. The traditional sources of funds for commercial banks have been demand, savings, and time deposits. But, as explained in the previous chapter, during the 1960s and 1970s consumers shifted out of demand deposits and, at cyclical peaks in interest rates, also tended to shift out of time deposits. At the same time this shift in the sources of funds was taking place commercial banks found themselves bound to honor previously made commitments to extend loans. The result was that they were compelled to seek new sources of funds, other than deposits subject to interest-rate ceilings. One source was the market for federal funds and RPs (defined in Chapter Ten); another was funds obtained from foreign sources; another was large certificates of deposit which were exempt from interest-rate ceilings; a final source was bank commercial paper issued directly to the market. Figure 13-12 shows the ratio of all of these sources of funds, except commercial paper, relative to total commercial bank liabilities and capital for the period from 1972 to 1979. This figure shows the increase, sometimes not so gradual, in the importance of funds which are not subject to federal interest-rate ceilings. The largest growth in funds not subject to interest-rate ceilings occurred during periods of peak interest rates, such as 1974–1975, when

FIGURE 13-12
Significance of nondeposit sources of funds for commercial banks. The figure shows the ratio of total nondeposit sources of funds relative to total bank liabilities for all domestically chartered commercial banks. Source: *Federal Reserve Bulletin*, various issues.

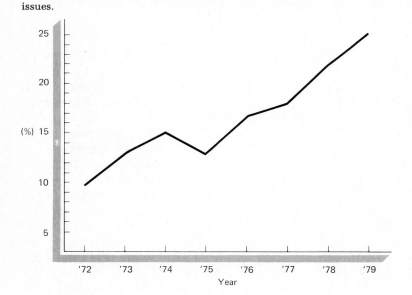

banks found it necessary to honor loan commitments but traditional sources of funds were in short supply. In the decade of the 1980s the changes in the nature of banks' sources of funds may be even more significant if interest-rate ceilings are in fact relaxed as called for in legislation of 1980. Whatever the speed of these changes, the banking markets of the 1980s are likely to be distinctly different from those of the 1960s and 1970s.

Alternative Sources of Short-term Debt

Corporations have increasingly found new sources of short-term debt which have provided additional competition for commercial banks. Probably the three most important sources of such financing are commercial paper, finance company loans, and leasing. Figure 13-3 shows the relative importance of commercial paper and finance company lending (included in the other category) in total external financing. It is difficult to measure total leasing volume, as it is a kind of "off-balance-sheet" financing. That is, it does not show up as a debt claim on the balance sheet of most corporations. This has long been one of the principal attractions of leasing, aside from some tax advantages.

Probably the most interesting and most important developments concerning nonbank sources of short-term financing pertain to the development of the commercial paper market. In the late 1960s and early 1970s commercial paper grew to become a significant part of the total supply of corporate financing. To a very large extent the growth of the commercial paper market was a response to attempts by the federal government to regulate credit markets. The real impetus for growth of the commercial paper market resulted from attempts to avoid the impact of restrictions imposed by the Federal Reserve. The first real surge of growth in the commercial paper market occurred after the interest-rate peak and credit crunch of 1966. During 1966 money market interest rates rose above interest-rate ceilings on deposit accounts and both banks and corporate borrowers found it necessary to scramble for funds. One option chosen by many larger companies was to issue their own short-term debt to the public, just as they issued corporate bonds. The largest most creditworthy borrowers who were continually in need of such short-term funds found it efficient to issue commercial paper directly to the market, while smaller companies (though still large corporations) chose to utilize an investment banker for such distributions. Once the 1966 credit crunch got this practice started, it continued to grow.

It is conceivable that the volume of commercial paper issued might have become much larger than it did in the late 1970s had it not been for two events in the beginning of the decade. The first was the default on outstanding commercial paper by a large borrower, the Penn Central Railroad. This brought the market to a temporary halt, for all but the most highly creditworthy borrowers. It is difficult to assess the long-term effects of this development because in the few years after this the second event occurred—the

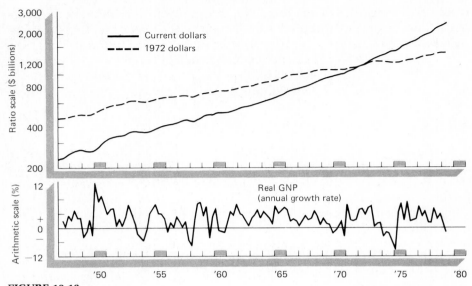

FIGURE 13-13
Gross national product. The upper panel shows the nominal and real (1972 dollars) GNP and the bottom panel shows the rate of growth in real GNP. Source: *Federal Reserve Chart Book*, 1979.

Federal Reserve announced regulatory changes which improved the competitive position of commercial banks vis-a-vis the commercial paper market. By 1973 the Federal Reserve relaxed the restrictions on interest rates applying to deposits of $100,000 and more, or certificates of deposit. This greatly improved the ability of commercial banks to compete for money market funds and reduced the advantage to corporate borrowers of turning to commercial paper. The development of the commercial paper market encouraged banks to price their loans to corporate borrowers in a manner that was not only competitive with other commercial banks but also with the terms in the commercial paper market. As a result, the rates on commercial paper, on large certificates of deposit, and on the prime interest rate now move closely together.

A roughly comparable situation developed regarding financing from nonbank finance companies during the latter part of the 1970s. Finance companies, often subsidiaries of large industrial companies (as, say, the General Motors Acceptance Corporation is a subsidiary of General Motors), found it possible to issue their own commercial paper to the market and then use the proceeds to loan to other corporate borrowers. Like trade credit, this is essentially a mechanism whereby the large nonfinancial corporations provide credit to other, usually smaller companies. However, in this case the loans were not a result of a sale of a product. In effect, the finance company was an intermediary much like the commercial bank. The principal difference was that finance companies were unregulated and, specifically, did not have to maintain reserves behind the funds they obtained from the market. As a result, they had a competitive advantage over many commercial banks. During the late 1970s finance companies became an increasingly important part of the market for loans to large nonfinancial corporations. The regulatory changes embodied in the Depository Institutions Deregulation Act of 1980 will have some impact on this part of the market, though at this juncture the exact nature of that impact is uncertain.

CORPORATE FINANCING THROUGH THE BUSINESS CYCLE: A LOOK AT THE 1974 RECESSION

The Pattern of Business Financing Over the Business Cycle

During most of the postwar era the U.S. economy has experienced cycles of recession and expansion in business activity. Figure 13-13 illustrates these cycles. The upper panel shows the level of both nominal and real gross national product and the bottom panel shows the rate of growth of real gross national profit (nominal gross national product adjusted for inflation) attained by the U.S. economy each year from 1947 to 1979. A recession is defined as a period of at least two consecutive quarters of negative growth in real gross national product. Figure 13-13 shows that the economy vacillated between recession and boom with some regularity during the 1950s and early 1960s and then experienced a period of nearly continual expansion until the early 1970s. The 1974 recession, which brought this period to an end, was the most severe experienced by the United States since World War II.

During most of these business cycles there has been a rather well-defined pattern of changes in business financing. At the onset of a recession most firms, particularly producers of durable goods, find that sales decline and inventories increase. At the outset it is usually not obvious that a recession is at hand and firms often refrain from cutting production immediately in the hopes that sales will quickly rebound. So they turn to increased short-term financing, often by drawing down loan commitments from banks, to finance additional inventories. And they draw down stocks of short-term financial assets. With declining sales, profits and internal funds deteriorate and the need for short-term financing is increased. This increased demand for credit tends to drive up short-term interest rates, and to a lesser extent long-term rates, and declining profits tend to cause stock prices to decline. High interest rates and a poor equity market discourage issuance of new long-term debt or equity securities, so that the reliance of firms on short-term sources of funds, particularly from commercial banks, is acute. It is, to a large degree, because of this prospect that firms find loan commitments and their relationships with their bankers to be so important. As credit demands decrease and sales rebound in the latter stages of a recession, interest rates tend to decline and most companies return to the equity markets and long-term debt markets in order to lengthen the maturity of their debt and decrease their leverage. Therefore, as the economy comes out of the recession, long-term debt and equity financing generally expand. In addition, firms generally rebuild their stock of short-term liquid financial assets which were utilized during the recession.

The 1974 Recession

The 1974 recession was unique in a number of respects. It was the largest or deepest of all the recessions since World War II. This means that there was a larger decline in real gross national product than in previous recessions. In addition, though this is difficult to measure with any precision, it was probably more of a surprise than any other downturn. It brought to an end virtually an entire decade of expansion—one without parallel since the 1920s. The recession was a classic inventory recession, which means that manufacturers accumulated stocks of inventories as sales declined and then production levels had to be reduced until those inventories were eliminated. The magnitude of the inventory expansion in late 1974 through 1975 is documented in Figure 13-14, which shows the ratio of inventories to total sales for durable goods manufacturers and all businesses, from 1971 to 1979. The peak in the diagram corresponds to the 1974 recession. By and large, the recession was brought about by a decline in consumer purchases, which in turn was caused at least in part by the oil embargo instigated by OPEC during the Arab-Israeli war.

The decade of expansion which preceded this recession was a time when the gap between corporate expenditures and internal funds widened. As a result, business had to depend more heavily on external sources of funds, particularly debt. The unprecedented expansion apparently caused many to be less concerned about the potential risk associated with high degrees of leverage and low degrees of liquidity than might otherwise have been the case. This meant that when the relatively severe recession of 1974 arrived, many corporations had to hustle in order to meet their financing needs. As Figures 13-3 and 13-6 show, 1974 was a year of very low profits and retained earnings and of extensive acquisition of loans from commercial banks. During this period corporations also drew upon liquid assets to an unprecedented degree. All of this led to a retrenchment in capital expenditures until the end of the recession. The situation is summarized in the diagram presented in Figure 13-15. This figure shows the volume of capital expenditures and of gross internal funds from 1967 until 1976. The difference between these two lines represents what has often been called the "financing gap," the amount of capital expenditures which must be funded with external funds. The figure indicates that the gap widened in the late

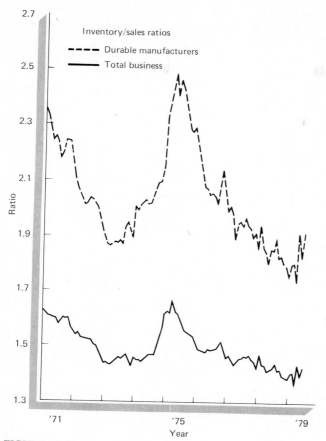

FIGURE 13-14

Inventory/sales ratio for U.S. corporations. This figure shows the ratio of total inventories to sales for manufacturers of durable goods and for all businesses. For the period shown, the peak in both ratios occurred during the 1974–1975 recession. Source: *Federal Reserve Chart Book*, 1979.

1960s, narrowed somewhat in the first few years of the 1970s, and then grew to an unprecedented magnitude in 1974 as capital expenditures increased dramatically and internal funds nosedived. This led to the cutback in capital expenditures shown in the figure, which rebounded again in late 1975 as the economy recovered from the recession.

The reaction to the 1974 recession by U.S. corporations was as significant as the recession itself. In 1975 and 1976 corporations replaced much of their short-term bank debt with equity and corporate bonds, thus decreasing their vulnerability to future squeezes in credit markets. Moreover they added significantly to their stocks of short-term financial assets in order to

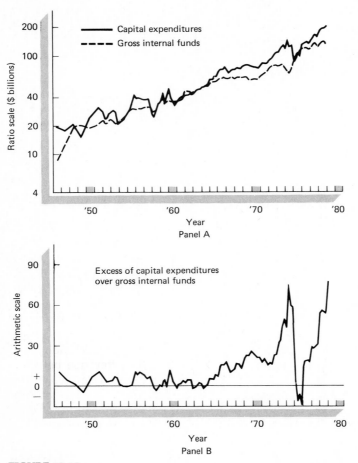

FIGURE 13-15
The gap between internal funds and capital expenditures of nonfinancial U.S. corporations. Panel A shows the levels of capital expenditures and internal funds. Panel B shows the difference or gap between these two. Source: *Federal Reserve Chart Book*, 1979.

have additional reserves in the event of another squeeze. However, there was little that corporations could do to alter the forces which were leading to deterioration in internal funds. Inflation continued to lead to large inventory profits and to large discrepancies between allowable depreciation and the replacement cost of assets. As explained earlier, this led to decreases in internal funds for purposes other than replacement of existing equipment and to increased taxes on corporate profits.

Some observers have concluded that the 1974 recession taught corporate managers a lesson, and that for at least a while financial risk induced by highly levered positions will not rise to the level it was prior to the 1974 recession. This remains to be seen.

SUMMARY

In this chapter we have examined the types of financing used by U.S. corporations during the 1970s. All corporations have four basic decisions to make regarding the types of financing they will utilize. These choices are: the amount of earnings to retain in the firm; the amount of debt as opposed to equity to utilize; the maturity of the debt which is issued; and, finally, the placement of new securities—either public or private. In this chapter we did not delve into the theory of how each of these choices should be made. Instead, we examined how these decisions have been made by U.S. corporations in the 1970s. We also looked at some of the important features of each of the segments of the financial markets serving U.S. corporations.

We began by analyzing the supply of internal funds. Internal funds represent the largest source of funds for corporate investment. Internal funds can be divided into two parts, depreciation allowances and retained earnings. Depreciation allowances represent the accounting profits set aside to replace the capital stock which is used up in the production of current goods. Retained earnings are the earnings of the firm which are retained for new investment after depreciation allowances, taxes, and dividends have been subtracted from corporate profits. The important difference between depreciation allowances and retained earnings is that depreciation allowances are tax deductible while retained earnings are not. In recent years there has been a considerable discrepancy between true or economic depreciation and the depreciation which has been allowed for tax purposes. This has been a result of the fact that inflation has raised the replacement cost of assets, yet allowable depreciation for tax purposes has not been based on replacement cost. A similar problem has developed in accounting for inventories. As a result of these difficulties corporate taxes have been higher and internal funds lower than they otherwise would have been.

One important alternative to internal funds is new equity financing. As a practical matter most corporations offer new equity securities to the market when the market is in a boom period and refrain from issuing new securities when the market is doing poorly. In recent years most of these equity issues have been purchased by financial institutions, particularly pension funds. In the equity market the placement decision involves the choice of selling securities directly to the market or utilizing an investment banker. Most issues involve investment bankers, although the cost of using an investment banker is rather high.

During the 1970s the largest portion of external financing was in the form of debt rather than equity securities. Once a corporation has chosen to use external financing it must decide on the maturity of the new debt. Debt issues with a maturity of longer than 1 year are considered long-term. Long-term debt can assume two forms, either bonds or mortgages. Most corporate bonds and mortgages issued during the 1970s were purchased by life insurance companies and pension funds, with life insurance company acquisitions representing the largest share of the market. Corporate bonds may be publicly or privately placed. One of the principal advantages of private bond financing is the flexibility it provides or the ease with which the terms of the agreement may be renegotiated.

The principal source of short-term debt for U.S. corporations has long been commercial banks. The most striking feature of bank financing provided to corporations, relative to other types of corporate financing, is its volatility. Corporations utilize bank loans as a kind of shock absorber in that they rely on bank loans when internal funds are scarce and longer term financing is unattractive. This was particularly evident in the 1974–1975 recession when the volume of bank loans increased and then fell off dramatically as the economy went into recovery. Because of the desire to rely on bank loans when other financing is unavailable or unattractive, formal agreements between banks and their corporate customers have become popular. These agreements, known as lines of credit and revolving credit agreements, provide guarantees of the availability and terms of bank loans.

During the 1970s there was tremendous growth in alternative types of short-term debt financing. One such alternative is commercial paper. Commercial paper is a short-term debt obligation issued directly to the market or sold through a dealer. Another alternative is offered by private finance companies such as the General Motors Acceptance Corporation. These nonbank finance companies can issue their own commercial paper to the market and then provide financing to corporations just as do commercial banks.

The market for corporate financing has a tremendous variety of securities and contracts as well as market participants. It illustrates the ability of a competitive marketplace to innovate and generate financing arrangements which satisfy the demands of the market. Compared to the markets for consumer financing, which we examined in the last chapter, corporate financial markets face problems which may be less severe. Markets for corporate financing have not been influenced by regulations, particularly in the form of ceilings on interest rates, to the extent found in the mortgage market. The market for corporate financing in the United States shows how smoothly a competitive capital market can operate in a complicated and diverse economy.

QUESTIONS TO IMPROVE UNDERSTANDING

1 The typical corporation must make four fundamental decisions regarding financing. They involve decisions on dividends, leverage, maturity, and placement. Explain the choices involved in each of these decisions.

2 Explain the major trends in the last decade in the major components of corporate financing, that is, internal versus external, debt versus equity, private versus public placement. Why is private debt so volatile relative to some other categories?

3 Explain the distinction between real and accounting depreciaticn. Ten years ago there was little practical difference between these two, but this is no longer true. Why?

4 Explain what "adjusted" retained earnings are and how you would compute them. What are "adjusted" internal funds and "adjusted" taxes? How big were these adjustments in the late 1970s?

5 The annual volume of new equity issues is not a smooth and constant amount. Instead it is fairly volatile. Can you give a plausible explanation for this volatility?

6 What is the difference between a commercial banker and an investment banker? What does it mean to say that an investment banker functions as an underwriter? What is the purpose of forming a syndicate of investment bankers?

7 Commercial banks offer a large portion of their corporate loans through either lines of credit or revolving credit agreements. Explain what these are and how they work.

8 What is the difference between a fixed-rate and floating-rate loan? Why have floating-rate loans become more common in recent years?

9 If a corporation is seeking to issue short-term debt, what are the principal alternatives to utilizing a commercial bank?

10 Explain the basic pattern in the use of different types of corporate financing over the business cycle. Why have recessions like the 1974 recession been referred to as inventory recessions?

REFERENCES

Baron, David P., and Bengt Holmstrom: "The Investment Banking Contract and New Issues: Asymmetric Information and the Incentive Problem," unpublished, Northwestern University.

Campbell, Tim S.: "A Model of the Market for Lines of Credit," *Journal of Finance*, 32 (March 1978), pp. 231–244.

Cox, John C., Jonathan E. Ingersoll, Jr., and Stephen Ross: "An Analysis of Variable Rate Loan Contracts," *Journal of Finance*, 35 (May 1980), pp. 389–404.

*Harris, Maury: "Finance Companies as Business Lenders," *Quarterly Review*, Federal Reserve Bank of New York, 4 (Summer 1979), pp. 35–39.

*Hurley, Evelyn M.: "The Commercial Paper Market," *Federal Reserve Bulletin*, 63 (June 1977), pp. 525–536.

Kidwell, David S., and Charles A. Trzcinka: "The Risk Structure of Interest Rates and the Penn-Central Crisis," *Journal of Finance*, 34 (June 1979), pp. 751–760.

Lewellen, Wilbur G., M. S. Long, and J. McConnell: "Asset Leasing in Competitive Capital Markets," *Journal of Finance*, 31 (June 1976), pp. 787–798.

Malkiel, Burton G.: "The Capital Formation Problem in the United States," *Journal of Finance*, 34 (May 1979), pp. 291–306.

* References marked with an * provide additional institutional detail and make excellent supplementary readings.

Shapiro, Eli, and C. R. Wolf: *The Role of Private Placement in Corporate Finance*, Division of Research, Graduate School of Business Administration, Harvard University, Boston, 1972.

Smith, Clifford W.: "Alternative Methods for Raising Capital: Rights versus Underwritten Offerings," *Journal of Financial Economics*, 5 (December 1977), pp. 273-307.

———, and Jerold B. Warner: "On Financial Contracting: An Analysis of Bond Covenants," *Journal of Financial Economics*, 7 (1979), pp. 117-161.

Zwick, Burton: "Yields on Privately Placed Corporate Bonds," *Journal of Finance*, 35 (March 1980), pp. 23-30.

*———: "The Market for Corporate Bonds," *Quarterly Review*, Federal Reserve Bank of New York (Autumn 1977), pp. 27-36.

*"Recent Changes in the Liquidity of Major Sectors of the U.S. Economy," *Federal Reserve Bulletin*, 62 (June 1976), pp. 463-469.

*"Recent Developments in Corporate Finance," *Federal Reserve Bulletin*, 61 (August 1975), pp. 463-472.

Chapter Fourteen

THE MARKET FOR
GOVERNMENT FINANCING

Government financing has been one of the key growth industries of the twentieth century. Early in the century the volume of government financing was so small as to be an inconsequential part of the total economy. But by the time the post-World War II era began in the United States this was simply no longer the case. During the late 1960s and throughout the 1970s the market for government financing developed tremendously. In the 1970s it also became a focal point for political attention as inflation increased and the debate about how to curtail inflation intensified. Yet to most people government financing remains a mystery and, with the increases in taxes in recent years, a painful mystery. In this chapter we will try to unravel some of the intricacies of government financing. We will try to understand the demand for government financing by the federal and state and local governments, the types of securities these levels of government distribute, and how the markets for these securities operate. Today, possibly more than ever, it is important to understand how our various levels of government are financing their activities.

FEDERAL GOVERNMENT FINANCING

There are two distinct types of markets through which the federal government and its agencies obtain financing. The largest market is the market for
Treasury securities. Treasury securities are issued largely to fund the deficit
of the U.S. government. The other market is known as the agency security
market, and it is composed of securities sold by a collection of federal and
federally sponsored agencies. In this section we will examine the types of
securities issued in each market and the uses of funds obtained from these
securities. In the next section, then, we will examine how the markets for
these securities operate.

The Purpose and Volume of Treasury Financing

The U.S. Treasury borrows from the public in order to finance its deficit.
Therefore, in order to understand the reasons for the growth in Treasury
financing we must explore the trends in the budget of the U.S. government.
In 1979 federal expenditures exceeded $450 billion. This was approximately
ten times greater than federal expenditures at the end of World War II. This
growth is illustrated in Figure 14-1 which shows the volume of government
expenditures and receipts from 1940 through the end of the 1970s. The
difference between receipts and outlays or expenditures represents the
surplus or deficit of the federal budget. The figure illustrates that, with

FIGURE 14-1
Receipts and expenditures of the federal government. Source: *Federal Reserve Chart
Book*, 1979.

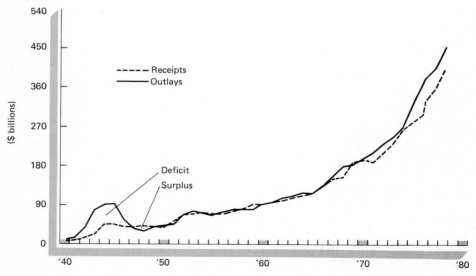

TABLE 14-1

Deficit of the United States Treasury (1970–1979)

FISCAL YEAR	ANNUAL DEFICIT ($ BILLION)
1979	40.162
1978	59.166
1977	53.647
1976	66.446
1975	45.108
1974	4.689
1973	14.849
1972	23.772
1971	23.033
1970	2.845

Source: *Federal Reserve Bulletin*, various issues.

the exception of the period of World War II (1941–1945), receipts and outlays were roughly in balance until the mid-1960s. Since 1965, expenditures have almost always exceeded receipts. Table 14-1 documents the magnitude of the deficit incurred each year since 1970. An additional perspective on the size of the federal budget is acquired by examining the budget as a proportion of gross national product. This percentage is shown in Figure 14-2. The figure shows that since the mid-1960s, federal expenditures have consistently represented in excess of 20 percent of gross national product.

Figure 14-3 gives some indication of where these federal expenditures are going. It breaks total federal outlays into five components: defense

FIGURE 14-2

Federal expenditures as a percent of gross national product. Source: *Federal Reserve Bulletin*, various issues.

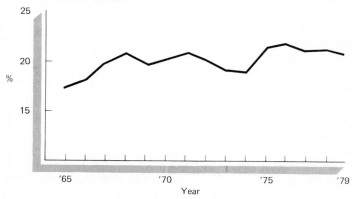

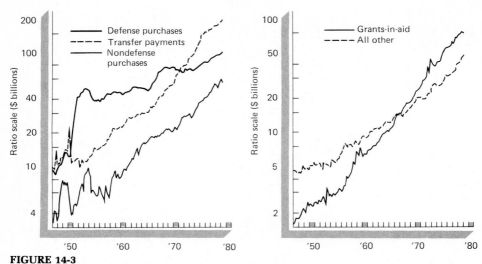

FIGURE 14-3
Major categories of United States government expenditures. Source: *Federal Reserve Chart Book*, 1979.

purchases; transfer payments, which represent payments to individuals through welfare and other programs; nondefense purchases; grants-in-aid, which are grants to state and local governments; and all others. This figure illustrates a tremendous increase in defense purchases in the early 1950s at the time of the Korean war, and another increase in the mid-1960s at the time of the Vietnam war. Until 1970 defense purchases represented the largest single item in the budget. But in that year, transfer payments exceeded defense purchases and they remain the largest part of the federal budget. Transfer payments and grants-in-aid have had the highest rate of growth of any components of federal spending. Many of the programs included in these categories are now tied to the level of inflation as measured in the Consumer Price Index (CPI). Hence, as the CPI increases, legally required expenditures for these programs must increase as well.

Because the federal government's tremendous growth in outlays has not been matched by an equal growth in its revenues, it has had to obtain funds from the credit markets in increasing amounts. The magnitude of the funds obtained from the capital markets by the Treasury and the proportion of all funds raised in the capital markets by any nonfinancial source are shown in Figure 14-4. The figure illustrates that in the early 1970s Treasury borrowing represented roughly 10 percent of total borrowing. But in some years since that time the percentage has gone as high as 40 percent. The volatility of this percentage is a result of the impact of recessions in economic activity on private and government borrowing. During a recession federal tax revenues decline and government expenditures increase, largely because of increases in transfer payments triggered by the recession. When a recession ends private borrowing declines as corporations attempt to restructure their balance sheets, but the federal deficit, and therefore federal financing, are at their peak. This was the situation in 1975 when funds raised by sources other than the federal government fell to $125 billion, yet federal financing rose to $86 billion.

The magnitude of the increase in the federal government's demand for financing has caused serious concern in recent years for a number of reasons. One of the most important reasons relates to the role of these deficits in causing the high rate of inflation in the United States in recent years. We will examine this in Chapter Twenty-two. Another pertains to what has come to be called the *crowding out* effect. This refers to the fact that as the government demand for funds increases, it tends to crowd out private demand for funds. The way this works is that as government demand for funds increases, market interest rates tend to rise. With higher costs of funds it becomes more expensive to finance private investment projects. Hence some private investments which would be profitable at lower interest rates become unprofitable. As a result government borrowing comes to replace private borrowing and to reduce the magnitude of private investment. It is difficult to ever produce a precise estimate of how much private spending may be crowded out, because it is difficult to know how much would have been spent had interest rates been lower. However, if government deficits and borrowing continue to increase, this is certain to become a more serious problem.

FIGURE 14-4
New funds raised by the U.S. Treasury expressed in dollars and as a proportion of total funds raised by all nonfinancial sectors of the economy. Source: Flow of Funds Accounts.

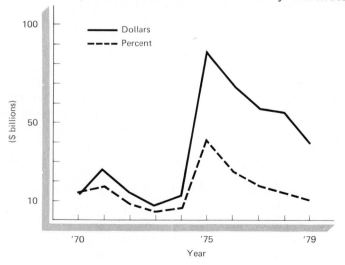

Type and Ownership of Treasury Debt

The debt of the U.S. Treasury incorporates a number of different types of securities. The broadest classification is between marketable and nonmarketable securities. As shown in panel A of Table 14-2, as of the end of 1979 marketable debt accounted for approximately 63 percent of outstanding Treasury obligations. Marketable debt is divided into three types of debt obligations: bills, notes, and bonds. The difference between them is essentially their original maturity. Bills are issued with a maturity of 1 year or less, notes with 1 to 7 years, and bonds with 7 years or more. Panel A of Table 14-2 shows that notes represented the largest component of marketable debt, followed by bills, and then bonds. The table also shows a number of different types of nonmarketable debt, the most voluminous being the government account series and savings bonds and notes. The government account series represents securities sold almost exclusively to government agencies and trust funds. Savings bonds and notes represent nonmarketable government debt sold in small denominations, largely to individuals. This type of Treasury obligation has not grown rapidly in recent years because of the low yields and lack of marketability of these assets compared to savings opportunities available to small savers at financial intermediaries.

Panel B of Table 14-2 shows the ownership distribution of marketable Treasury debt as of the end of 1979. The table shows that roughly 25 percent of the total marketable debt outstanding is held either by the Federal Reserve System or by other federal agencies. Roughly 21 percent of the debt is held by various types of corporations, including financial intermediaries and nonfinancial corporations. Of all of these institutions, commercial banks have the largest holdings of these securities. The rest of the securities are listed in a residual category, including individual and foreign holdings. This category accounts for roughly 55 percent of all Treasury security holdings.

Agency Securities

Agency securities refer to the securities issued by a number of institutions which are either part of the federal government or are privately owned quasi-governmental institutions. Each of these institutions was created under federal law to serve an explicit purpose and authorized to issue their own securities. Some of these agencies have remained part of the federal government, while others have become private institutions, generally with some government control or regulation. As a result, some of the securities issued by these agencies are virtually government debt, while others have less explicit government backing. The agency security market is now a large market for debt securities with active secondary trading. Figure 14-5 shows the total volume of outstanding agency securities over the last decade. As of the end of 1979 the volume of agency securities outstanding represented about 20 percent of the volume of outstanding Treasury securities.

TABLE 14-2

Panel A: Composition of Treasury Debt Outstanding (December 1979)

TYPE OF SECURITY	DOLLAR VOLUME OUTSTANDING ($ BILLIONS)	PERCENT OF TOTAL
Marketable	530.7	63
Bills	172.6	20
Notes	283.4	34
Bonds	74.7	9
Nonmarketable	313.2	37
Foreign issues	28.8	3
Savings bonds and notes	79.9	9
Government account series	177.5	21
Other	26.8	3
Total (interest bearing)	844.0	100

Panel B: Ownership of Marketable Treasury Debt (December 1979)

OWNER	DOLLAR VOLUME HELD ($ BILLIONS)TOTAL	PERCENT OF
U.S. government agencies	11.1	2
Federal Reserve	117.5	22
Commercial banks	69.1	13
Insurance companies	11.5	2
Savings and loans and MSBs	5.4	1
Nonfinancial companies	8.4	2
State and local governments	15.7	3
Other	291.1	55
Total	529.8	100

Agency securities serve a somewhat different purpose than do Treasury securities. Treasury obligations are issued essentially to fund the deficit of the U.S. government. Therefore, the larger the gap between federal expenditures and revenues, the larger the volume of Treasury securities which must be issued. But the volume of agency financing does not represent any accumulated deficit. Instead, most of the institutions which offer agency securities act essentially like private financial intermediaries. They issue securities of their own to the public and utilize the proceeds of those securities to purchase various other types of assets. The largest portion of the agency securities market provides financing for residential construction; that is, most agency securities are issued by institutions which purchase mortgages in the secondary mortgage market. Figure 14-5 shows the volume of this portion of the agency security market. It is evident from the figure that agency securities devoted to mortgage financing have become an increasingly important part of the total market during the 1970s.

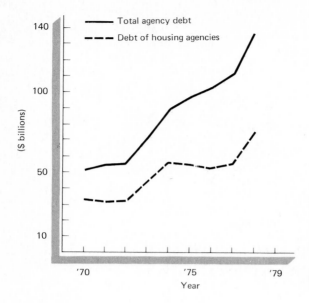

FIGURE 14-5
Agency securities outstanding.
The figure shows both the total
volume of agency securities
issued during the 1970s and the
volume of securities issued by
the agencies involved in housing
finance. Source: *Federal Reserve
Bulletin*, various issues.

There is such a variety of institutions issuing securities in the agency market that it is difficult to give a complete characterization of each of them. Table 14-3 presents a list of the names of the principal agencies along with the acronyms by which they are known. It also indicates which are government institutions as opposed to government-sponsored institutions. The bulk of the agency securities outstanding are issued by the federally sponsored agencies rather than the federal agencies. This is because most of the mortgage-related agencies are federally sponsored. The other important purpose served by the federally sponsored agencies is funding for agriculture. The institutions directed toward this purpose include the Banks for Cooperatives, the Federal Farm Credit Banks, and the Federal Land Banks.

The federal government does not directly guarantee the securities of the federally sponsored agencies. However, it is generally thought that the government would not allow wide-scale defaults on the securities of these agencies. Despite their independent status, many of these institutions have strong government control. For example, the three directors of the FHLB are appointed by the President with the consent of Congress; and FNMA is regulated by the Department of Housing and Urban Development, and five of its fifteen directors are appointed by the President. The FHLB is as much a regulator of the savings and loan industry as a supplier of funds to that industry, and has a status roughly comparable to that of the Federal Reserve Board.

Since 1974 the federal agencies, as opposed to the federally sponsored agencies, have issued no new securities of their own. Instead, they have borrowed through the U.S. Treasury; specifically, through a division of the

TABLE 14-3

The Borrowers in the Agency Security Market and their Acronyms

FEDERALLY SPONSORED AGENCIES	
Banks for Cooperatives	BCs or COOPs
Federal Farm Credit Banks	FFCBs
Federal Home Loan Banks	FHLBs
Federal Home Loan Mortgage Corporation	FHLMC or Freddie Mac
Federal Intermediate Credit Banks	FICBs
Federal Land Banks	FLBs
Federal National Mortgage Association	FNMA or Fannie Mae
FEDERAL AGENCIES	
Export-Import Bank	EXIM
Farmers Home Administration	FmHA
General Services Administration	GsA
Government National Mortgage Association	GNMA or Ginnie Mae
Postal Service	PS
Tennessee Valley Authority	TVA
OTHER	
Washington Metropolitan Area Transit Authority	WMATA

Treasury known as the Federal Financing Bank (FFB). The FFB was created by an act of Congress in 1974 in order to consolidate borrowing activities in the agency market. The FFB is responsible for funding all the activities of the federal agencies which were then issuing their own securities. Rather than issue its own securities, the FFB borrows from the Treasury and then funds the activities of the federal agencies which are dependent upon it. As a result, the outstanding debt of these agencies, contained in the total shown in Figure 14-5, includes only those securities which had already been issued when the FFB began operation. As these securities mature, no new ones are issued. This change means that eventually the agency security market will be comprised only of securities issued by federally sponsored agencies.

There is one other type of security which should be discussed at this point because it is very similar to the securities in the agency market and because the outstanding volume of this type of security is becoming quite large. This type of security is called a GNMA pass-through. A GNMA pass-through represents a claim on a pool of mortgages. The name comes from the fact that the cash flow from the mortgages is passed through to the owners of the security. This type of security is also referred to as a mortgage-backed bond, though GNMA pass-throughs are only one example of a mortgage-backed bond. The GNMA pass-through is not actually issued by GNMA. It is, therefore, not directly a claim on the agency itself. Instead, GNMA guarantees the timely payment of principal and interest from the mortgage pool to the owners of the security. The security is generally issued by a private mortgage company and is not considered an agency security. In addition, the mortgages included in pools for GNMA pass-throughs are mortgages which are insured by the Federal Housing Administration or the Veterans Administration. As a result of these features, the owner of a GNMA pass-through is provided with a regular cash flow and very low default risk on securities backed by mortgages. The advent of the GNMA pass-through has brought about a significant change in the mortgage market. These securities have become extremely attractive to institutional investors which previously found it difficult to invest in mortgages. As a result, the outstanding volume of these securities has grown tremendously and an active secondary market has developed. These securities were first issued in 1970 and the total amount outstanding as of 1979 was in excess of $75 billion. When this volume is added to the total volume of agency securities outstanding, the size of the market for government-sponsored securities becomes significantly larger than it is when agency securities alone are taken into account.

THE MARKETS FOR TREASURY AND AGENCY SECURITIES

In this section we will examine the operation of markets for Treasury and agency securities. To a large degree these two markets function as one integrated market. This is because the securities traded in them are very close substitutes and many of the same dealers operate in both markets. Therefore, we will concentrate on describing the Treasury market and then point out the important differences between the agency and Treasury markets. Before we turn to the actual operation of the market itself we will examine how Treasury securities are priced.

Pricing of Bills

We know from our discussion of market interest rates in Part Two of this book that the nominal yield on any security, including a Treasury security, is determined by a number of factors. These include the real interest rate in the economy on a single-period loan, the market's expectation of inflation, a premium for default risk, a premium reflecting tax treatment, a premium reflecting the impact of relative security supplies, and a liquidity premium depending upon the maturity of the security. These are the forces which determine the compensation demanded by the market for holding a particular type of security and these forces are reflected in the observed yield on the security. At this juncture we want to take these forces, and the yield they determine, as given and examine the mechanics of how the market sets the price of bills, notes, and bonds. This is essentially an exercise in present value computations. Once we understand this price-setting process, then we can turn our attention to an examination of the operation of the market for Treasury debt.

First, we will examine the pricing of Treasury bills. Aside from their maturity, Treasury bills are distinguished from Treasury notes and bonds by the fact that there are no coupon interest payments on Treasury bills. The yield on holding a Treasury bill is determined solely by the price appreciation of the bill, and this is taxed as current income rather than as capital gains. This is not the case with notes and bonds, which include semiannual coupon payments. The difference in maturity also means that any gains on Treasury bills are, for tax purposes, treated as regular income rather than as capital gains, while long-term gains on notes and bonds can be treated as capital gains if they meet the holding-period requirements of the tax code.

The short maturities on Treasury bills and the lack of coupons mean that it is simpler to price bills than it is notes and bonds. The marketplace competitively determines the price of a bill so that it will provide the yield which the market demands. The yield is computed in one of two ways, either on a discount basis or on what is called a coupon issue yield equivalent. The yield on discount is virtually the same as the interest rate on a discount loan (see Chapter Three). To see how this yield is computed we will refer to a bill as having a par or maturity value of 100 and a discount yield of r_d. Then r_d is equal to

$$r_d = \frac{100 - P}{100} \cdot \frac{360}{\text{number of days to maturity}} \qquad (14\text{-}1)$$

where P is the price of the bond. Here the anount of price appreciation is divided by the maturity or par value of the bill rather than by its price, which is consistent with the procedure in any discount loan. In addition, the interest rate is adjusted by its maturity, measured in days, relative to a 360-day year.

There are two differences between the coupon equivalent yield and the discount yield. The first is that the price of the bond rather than the par value is used as the basis for determining return, and a 365-day year rather than a 360-day year is used for adjusting the time interval. The formula for the coupon equivalent yield r_c is therefore

$$r_c = \frac{100 - P}{P} \cdot \frac{365}{\text{number of days to maturity}} \qquad (14\text{-}2)$$

Quotations of the yields on Treasury bills in the secondary market are printed each day in *The Wall Street Journal*. An example of these quotations is presented in Table 14-4. The table shows the yields on bills of different maturities which were traded on November 23, 1979. For each bill, the maturity date, the yield that was bid, the yield asked, and the actual yield on the bill are indicated in the table. Using Eq. (14-1) it is possible to calculate

TABLE 14-4

Treasury Issues

* * *

Bonds, Notes & Bills

Friday, November 23, 1979
Over-the-Counter quotations; sources on request.
Decimals in bid-and-asked and bid changes represent 32nds; 101.1 means 101 1/32. a-Plus 1/64. b-Yield to call date. d-Minus 1/64. n-Treasury notes.

Rate	Mat.	Date	Bid	Asked	Bid Chg.	Yld.
7⅛s,	1979	Nov n	99.28	100	+ .1	0.00
7⅛s,	1979	Dec n	99.15	99.19	+ .1	11.24
7½s,	1979	Dec n	99.16	99.20	+ .1	11.25
7½s,	1980	Jan n	99.2	99.6	+ .1	11.90
4s,	1980	Feb	98.2	98.10	+ .2	11.83
6½s,	1980	Feb n	98.21	98.25	+ .4	12.03
7⅝s,	1980	Feb n	98.23	98.27	+ .5	12.02
7½s,	1980	Mar n	98.9	98.13	+ .6	12.22
7¾s,	1980	Apr n	98	98.4	+ .6	12.31
6⅞s,	1980	May n	97.18	97.22	+ .6	12.08
8s,	1980	May n	97.29	98.1	+ .4	12.11
7⅝s,	1980	Jun n	97.15	97.23	+ .10	11.71
8¼s,	1980	Jun n	97.26	97.30	+ .11	11.95
8½s,	1980	Jul n	97.18	97.22	+ .10	12.14
6¾s,	1980	Aug n	96.16	96.20	+ .15	11.77
9s,	1980	Aug n	98	98.8	+ .4	11.60
8⅜s,	1980	Aug n	97.4	97.8	+ .9	12.26
6⅞s,	1980	Sep n	95.24	96	+ .10	11.99
8⅝s,	1980	Sep n	97.7	97.11	+ .10	12.04
8⅞s,	1980	Oct n	97.8	97.16	+ .10	11.80
3½s,	1980	Nov	93.18	93.26	+ .10	10.38
7⅛s,	1980	Nov n	95.17	95.25	+ .13	11.87
9¼s,	1980	Nov n	97	97.8	.....	12.22
5⅞s,	1980	Dec n	94.6	94.14	+ .16	11.43
9⅞s,	1980	Dec n	98.11	98.19	+ .15	11.28
9¾s,	1981	Jan n	97.30	98.6	+ .18	11.44
7s,	1981	Feb n	95.6	95.14	+ .14	11.10
7⅜s,	1981	Feb n	95.10	95.12	+ .16	11.54
9¾s,	1981	Feb n	97.28	98.11	+ .18	11.39
6⅞s,	1981	Mar n	94.4	94.12	+ .18	11.51
9⅝s,	1981	Mar n	97.2	97.10	+ .6	11.85
9¾s,	1981	Apr n	97.14	97.22	+ .16	11.55
7⅜s,	1981	May n	94.12	94.20	+ .16	11.46
7½s,	1981	May n	94.12	94.20	+ .14	11.59
9¾s,	1981	May n	97.12	97.20	+ .18	11.51
6¾s,	1981	Jun n	93.12	93.20	+ .24	11.22
9⅛s,	1981	Jun n	96.7	96.15	+ .18	11.61
9⅜s,	1981	Jul n	96.10	96.18	+ .16	11.69
7s,	1981	Aug	93.6	94.6	+ .28	10.79
7⅝s,	1981	Aug n	93.14	93.22	+ .9	11.78
8⅜s,	1981	Aug n	94.28	95.4	+ .15	11.58
9⅝s,	1981	Aug n	96.22	96.30	+ .24	11.60
6¾s,	1981	Sep n	92.2	92.10	+ .18	11.49
10⅛s,	1981	Sep n	97.12	97.20	+ .22	11.59
12⅝s,	1981	Oct n	101.15	101.19	+ .23	11.68
7s,	1981	Nov n	92.2	92.10	+ .20	11.47
7¾s,	1981	Nov n	93.22	93.30	+ .24	11.27
7¼s,	1981	Dec n	92.7	92.15	+ .19	11.39
6⅛s,	1982	Feb n	90.2	90.10	+ .16	11.17
6⅜s,	1982	Feb	90.9	90.25	+ .19	11.18
7⅞s,	1982	Mar n	93.7	93.15	+ .23	11.12
7s,	1982	May n	91.5	91.13	+ .23	11.07
8s,	1982	May n	93.7	93.15	+ .21	11.10
9¼s,	1982	May n	96.12	96.20	+ .25	10.85
8¼s,	1982	Jun n	93.22	93.30	+ .24	11.00
8⅛s,	1982	Aug n	92.26	93.2	+ .14	11.15
9s,	1982	Aug n	94.28	95.4	+ .14	11.13
8⅜s,	1982	Sep n	93.21	93.29	+ .29	10.92
7⅛s,	1982	Nov n	90.12	90.20	+ .28	10.91
7⅞s,	1982	Nov n	92.7	92.15	+ .29	10.91
9⅜s,	1982	Dec n	95.29	96.5	+1.1	10.87
8s,	1983	Feb n	92.2	92.10	+ 1	10.89
9¼s,	1983	Mar n	95.4	95.12	+ .30	10.94
7⅞s,	1983	May n	91.13	91.21	+1.3	10.82
11⅝s,	1983	May n	101.31	102.7	+1.3	10.84
3¼s,	1978-83	Jun	81.12	82.12	+ .30	9.18
8⅞s,	1983	Jun n	93.28	94.4	+ .28	10.89
9¾s,	1983	Sep n	96.13	96.21	+ .29	10.84
7s,	1983	Nov n	87.22	87.30	+ .8	10.82
7¼s,	1984	Feb n	88.14	88.22	+ 1	10.65
9¼s,	1984	May n	94.20	94.24	+ 1	10.76
6⅜s,	1984	Aug	84.29	85.29	+ .5	10.21
7¼s,	1984	Aug n	87.22	87.30	+ 1	10.56
8s,	1985	Feb n	89.18	89.26	+ .30	10.59
3¼s,	1985	May	74.26	75.26	+ .16	8.94
4¼s,	1975-85	May	76.26	77.26	+ .18	9.55
8¼s,	1985	Aug n	89.20	89.28	+1.4	10.41
7⅞s,	1986	May n	86.20	86.28	+ .24	10.51
8s,	1986	Aug n	87.14	87.22	+1.4	10.61
6⅛s,	1986	Nov	82	83	+ 1	9.52
9s,	1987	Feb n	91.13	91.21	+1.1	10.69
7⅝s,	1987	Nov n	84.22	84.30	+1.4	10.46
8¼s,	1988	May n	87.2	87.10	+1.2	10.55
8¾s,	1988	Nov n	89.28	90.4	+1.12	10.47
9¼s,	1989	May n	92.22	92.30	+1.6	10.44
10¾s,	1989	Nov n	101.14	101.18	+1.10	10.49
3½s,	1990	Feb	75.20	76.20	+ 1	6.69
8¼s,	1990	May	86.2	86.18	+ .18	10.39
4¼s,	1987-92	Aug	76.10	77.10	+ .31	6.97
7¼s,	1992	Aug	78.11	78.27	+1.3	10.27
4s,	1988-93	Feb	75.8	76.8	+ .28	6.74
6¾s,	1993	Feb	75.12	76.12	+1.2	10.01
7⅞s,	1993	Feb	82.3	82.19	+1.9	10.32
7½s,	1988-93	Aug	79	80	+1.2	10.25
8⅝s,	1993	Aug	87.1	87.17	+1.13	10.35
8⅝s,	1993	Nov	87.8	87.24	+1.14	10.30
9s,	1994	Feb	89.29	90.13	+1.12	10.30
4⅛s,	1989-94	May	75.14	76.14	+2.6	6.69
8¾s,	1994	Aug	88.6	89.6	+1.20	10.18
10⅛s,	1994	Nov	98.6	98.22	+1.15	10.30
3s,	1995	Feb	75.10	76.10	+ .30	5.28
7s,	1993-98	May	75.2	76.2	+1.12	9.84
3½s,	1998	Nov	75.18	76.18	+2.3	5.51
8½s,	1994-99	May	85.20	86.4	+1.18	10.15
7⅞s,	1995-00	Feb	79.30	80.6	+1.16	10.21
8⅜s,	1995-00	Aug	83.30	84.6	+1.12	10.23
8s,	1996-01	Aug	81.7	81.23	+1.17	10.09
8¼s,	2000-05	May	82.20	82.28	+1.14	10.14
7⅝s,	2002-07	Feb	77.9	77.17	+1.7	10.05
7⅞s,	2002-07	Nov	84.2	84.18	+ .27	9.45
8⅜s,	2003-08	Aug	83.19	83.27	+1.5	10.11
8¾s,	2003-08	Nov	87	87.8	+1.18	10.12
9⅛s,	2004-09	May	90.16	90.24	+1.13	10.11
10⅜s,	2004-09	Nov	101.18	101.26	+1.14	10.17

U.S. Treas. Bills

Mat. date	Bid	Asked	Yield	Mat. date	Bid	Asked	Yield
	Discount				Discount		
-1979-				-1980-			
11-29	11.59	10.77	10.93	3-13	11.56	11.36	11.95
12- 6	11.13	10.45	10.62	3-20	11.57	11.37	11.99
12-11	11.10	10.46	10.65	3-27	11.64	11.36	12.01
12-13	10.98	10.48	10.68	4- 1	11.65	11.47	12.15
12-20	10.89	10.35	10.56	4- 3	11.63	11.45	12.14
12-27	10.89	10.35	10.58	4-10	11.64	11.48	12.20
-1980-				4-17	11.68	11.50	12.25
1- 3	11.16	10.76	11.03	4-24	11.72	11.54	12.32
1- 8	11.24	10.82	11.11	4-29	11.72	11.56	12.36
1-10	11.27	10.89	11.19	5- 1	11.68	11.52	12.33
1-17	11.28	10.94	11.27	5- 8	11.68	11.50	12.33
1-24	11.33	11.03	11.39	5-15	11.65	11.47	12.33
1-31	11.35	11.05	11.43	5-22	11.44	11.34	12.21
2- 5	11.60	11.36	11.78	5-27	11.63	11.41	12.31
2- 7	11.56	11.36	11.79	6-24	11.53	11.35	12.26
2-14	11.57	11.37	11.82	7-22	11.52	11.34	12.29
2-21	11.34	11.24	11.71	8-19	11.44	11.26	12.25
2-28	11.51	11.29	11.79	9-16	11.32	11.16	12.20
3- 4	11.62	11.40	11.96	10-14	11.13	11.01	12.10
3- 6	11.61	11.41	11.98	11- 6	10.91	10.83	11.95

the actual price of the bill corresponding to the market yield it commanded. For example, the bill marked with an * in the table matures on January 3, 1980 and therefore has 40 days to maturity (11-23-79 to 1-3-80). It has a market yield of .1103. We can use this yield on a discount basis to compute the price of the bill as follows:

$$\frac{100 - P}{100} \cdot \frac{360}{40} = .1103$$

This implies that the price of the January 3 bill is:

$$P = 100 - (40/360)\,(.1103)\,(100) = 98.77$$

Pricing of Bonds and Notes

The important distinction between pricing of bonds and notes and pricing of Treasury bills is that bonds and notes have coupon payments as well as possibilities for capital gains and losses. Moreover, bonds and notes have longer maturities than do bills. Therefore, in order to properly price the bond we must properly specify the present value equation which includes coupon payments and price appreciation. The coupon interest rate is stated in terms of a percentage of the face value of the bond. Coupon payments are made every 6 months. For example, if the bond has a par value of $10,000 and a coupon rate of 6 percent, then coupon payments of $300 are made every 6 months. If the coupon payment is represented by A, the maturity value by M, and the number of years to maturity by N, then the present value equation for the bond can be specified as follows:

$$PV = \sum_{t=1}^{2N} \frac{A}{(1+r/2)^t} + \frac{M}{(1+r/2)^{2N}} \tag{14-3}$$

Here PV is equal to the current price of the bond and r is the annual yield on the bond under the assumption that the bond is held to maturity. Notice that the bond will be priced at $10,000 if the coupon rate and market yield are the same. But even if they are identical when the bond is issued, thereafter the market yield and the price of the bond will fluctuate.

The price of the bond can also be computed at any time prior to maturity (but after it has been issued) by taking proper account of the time remaining to maturity. For example, if there are exactly 3 years to maturity, then the price of the bond would be

$$PV = \sum_{t=1}^{6} \frac{A}{(1+r/2)^t} + \frac{M}{(1+r/2)^6} \tag{14-4}$$

When the price is determined at times other than exact 6-month intervals from maturity, then proper accounting must be made of accrued interest and the equation must be slightly modified.

Daily quotations on the prices and yields on Treasury notes and bonds are published each day in *The Wall Street Journal*, just as they are for Treasury bills. A selection of these quotations drawn from *The Wall Street Journal* of November 26, 1979, covering the business day of November 23, 1979, are presented in Table 14-4. These data are released daily by the Federal Reserve Bank of New York and are compiled from dealers' quotations collected that day.

It is useful to examine one of the securities in some detail. For example, there is a 9 3/8 note which matures in July 1981. The 9 3/8 refers to the coupon interest rate on the bond which, by convention, is measured in eighths. The column labeled "Bid" shows the price that dealers were paying for this particular note on November 23, 1979. The number to the right of the decimal point in the price is a fractional amount expressed in 32s rather than 100s. In this case, the price is 96 10/32. Though this seems unusual it is a long-standing practice in the Treasury security market. The price is also expressed as a percentage, that is, 96 10/32 percent, of the maturity value of the bond rather than in absolute dollar terms. The "Asked" price is the price at which dealers would be willing to sell the bond or note. The difference is referred to as the spread and it constitutes the earnings of the dealer for making a market in the security. In this case, the dealer's spread is 8/32 of the par value of the security. The column labeled "Bid Chg." indicates the change in the bid price from the previous day. The "Yield" represents the yield to maturity if the bond is purchased at the asking price and held to maturity. The yield is computed according to Eq. (14-3), where the price is $965,625 for a note with maturity value of $1 million (96 18/32 × 1,000,000).

The Market for Treasury Securities

The market for Treasury securities consists of distinct primary and secondary markets. The primary market is a pure auction market where the Treasury auctions off bills, notes, and bonds to the highest bidders. The operation of the primary market for bills was described in Chapter Ten and the primary market for coupon issues (notes and bonds) operates in a similar manner. We will therefore concentrate here on the secondary market. The secondary market is an over-the-counter market. It is one of the most efficient and active over-the-counter markets in the world because such a large volume of homogeneous securities with minimal default risk are available to be traded.

DEALERS IN THE MARKET   To be a dealer in the Treasury securities market takes on special meaning. The official dealers in Treasury securities are those firms which the Federal Reserve Bank of New York (FRBNY) classifies as dealers. The FRBNY has a central position in this market because it conducts all trades in Treasury securities for the Federal Reserve System. And the principal mechanism through which the Federal Reserve conducts monetary policy (as we will learn in Chapter Nineteen) is through the purchase and sale of Treasury securities. As a result, the FRBNY has, in effect, become the regulator of the dealers in this market. The FRBNY receives daily statistical reports from all dealers which it recognizes and trades with. In addition it maintains daily phone contact with these dealers and visits the firms periodically. The number of dealer firms was roughly 20 during the 1960s, with a few dropping off and a few being added. By the end of 1977 there were 36 dealers reporting to the FRBNY, of which 12 were commercial banks and 24 were nonbank dealers. A firm is invited to join the official list when the FRBNY concludes that it has sufficient volume of business across the maturity spectrum of available securities, and that it is adequately capitalized and managed. The fact that there are a specific number of official dealers does not mean that these are the only firms which actually function as dealers.

The total trading volume in the secondary market expanded dramatically during the 1970s. The average daily volume of trades by all official dealers increased from less than $1.5 billion per day in 1960 to over $16 billion in 1979. Throughout this period most trading was in securities with less than 1 year to maturity, though trading in the longer maturities also increased in importance during this period. Part of the reason for this increase in trading volume was simply the increase in the volume of total Treasury debt. But it was also apparently due to an increased tendency on the part of many investors to trade in Treasury securities for a profit, rather than to use them simply as a secure liquid asset. With the decline in prices on the stock market over this period and with the increase in Treasury yields, the secondary market in Treasury securities became more attractive and volume increased.

Trading in the market is generally broken down into the interdealer market and the customer market. The *customer market* includes trading with all other nondealer participants. The *interdealer market* includes trades directly between dealers and trades between dealers arranged through a broker. Trading through a broker is attractive because it offers anonymity to the dealers. Direct dealer trades declined in significance throughout the 1970s, but trading with brokers increased. The sum of the two represented approximately 40 percent of all trades in the late 1970s.

Dealers in this market earn their profits principally off the spread between bid and asked prices on the securities they trade and from the gains or losses they experience on positions they take in particular securities. In addition, dealers attempt to earn a higher rate of interest on their inventory of securities than they must pay for funds to support that inventory. When this yield spread is favorable to the dealer, it is referred to as a "positive carry." Their ability to generate a positive carry hinges on the shape of the yield curve. This is because their investments tend to be spread across the maturity spectrum, while their funding is obtained with a very short maturity. The profit earned from trading depends upon the magnitude of the spread in the market and how successfully dealers have managed their positions; that is, whether they experience large capital gains or losses on their inventories.

Dealers have been able to reduce their holdings of inventories in recent years at the same time that transactions volume increased. In large part this probably reflects a reaction to the increases in the level and volatility of interest rates during the 1970s. These increases caused dealers to seek to manage their inventories more carefully, which led to lower ratios of inventory to trading volume. The total inventory position and the ratio of inventory to trading volume for dealers recognized by the FRBNY are shown in Figure 14-6. The figure illustrates that the ratio fell from 1.46 in 1972 to .26 in 1979. The total volume of dealer financing has not shown a similar downward trend. Instead, dealers have consistently maintained highly levered positions. The largest single source for dealer financing has usually been commercial banks. Dealer financing is obtained either through re-

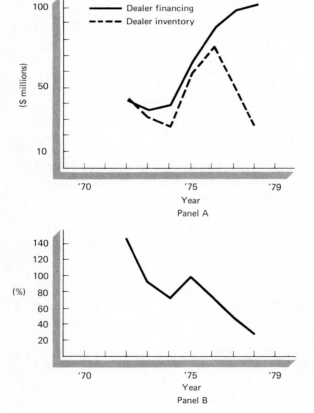

FIGURE 14-6
Key statistics on government securities dealers. Panel A shows total dealer inventories and financing. Panel B shows the ratio of inventory to trading volume. Source: *Federal Reserve Bulletin*, various issues.

purchase agreements (RPs) or through direct loans with Treasury securities as collateral.

STRUCTURE OF THE MARKET   The secondary market in Treasury securities is referred to as an over-the-counter market in that there is no centralized exchange facility to which all market participants have access. But this market underwent tremendous changes in the 1970s and it is now much closer to an auction market than it once was. In fact, the interdealer portion of the market now functions essentially as an auction market due to the implementation of an automated exchange process. Moreover, electronic quotation systems have also led to significant changes in the remainder of the market.

In the early 1960s and 1970s the market operated over the telephone. The traders working for each dealer firm would quote prices and make exchanges with other dealers, with brokers, or with other customers. Customers would have to search for the best price to buy or sell by calling separate firms and asking for quotes. There was no centralized facility for exchange or for displaying quotations of bid or ask prices. Beginning in the mid-1970s this system began to change. At that time dealer firms began to implement automated quotation systems. These systems were not introduced by regulators but were a result of private entrepreneurial activity. The automated quotation system involved two separate systems, one used in the interdealer market and one available to dealers and nondealer customers of brokers. The system, used exclusively in the interdealer market, facilitates automated quotation of bid and ask prices as well as automated execution of trades. It eliminates the need for dealers to search for the best prices among themselves. Like the similar system envisioned for the NYSE, it provides automatic exchanges at the best available prices. With the use of this facility the interdealer market has become essentially an auction market.

The billboard system used outside the interdealer market provides only display of bid and ask prices. There is no ability to actually conduct an exchange through the system. A dealer displays his or her price on the quotation system and a customer interested in an exchange at that price must call the dealer to conduct the exchange. These billboard systems are available for a rental fee for anyone interested in the market. A billboard system like this is essentially an advertising device. It reduces the cost of searching for alternative prices which are borne by the customers in an over-the-counter market. This type of billboard system proves to be most economical for securities that are very actively traded. For securities with a smaller volume, it may be too costly to list them on the automated system.

The Market for Agency Securities

There is no centralized auction market for agency securities. The wide variety of distinct agency securities, particularly if one includes GNMA pass-throughs, leads to a variety of different marketing arrangements. All of these securities are traded in an over-the-counter market, generally for both primary and secondary issues. In the primary market, there is what is called a fiscal agent which handles the distribution of new securities to dealers and institutions. In the market for mortgage-backed securities, private agents known as mortgage bankers act as dealers in new and old securities. Most of the federally sponsored agencies distribute new issues of securities on a quarterly basis. The maturity of most agency debt is in the intermediate range of 1 to 10 years. There is a much smaller volume of very short maturity securities than is the case in the Treasury market. The secondary market in agency securities is essentially similar to the secondary market in Treasury obligations. Treasury security dealers usually also act as dealers in agency obligations and report trading volume in these securities to the Federal Reserve Bank of New York. The reported volume of trading in agency securities was roughly one-fifth of the volume in Treasury debt at the end of 1979.

The yields on agency securities are quite close to the yields on Treasury securities of comparable maturity. Throughout most of the 1970s the yields on agency securities exceeded the yields on Treasury securities, for maturities of 5 to 7 years where there is a large volume of both types, by between 15 and 65 basis points (100 basis points equals 1 percentage point). This yield spread may be accounted for in part by perceived differences in risk, costs of arbitraging differences in yields, and relative imbalances in supply and demand. Generally, the yield spreads between Treasury and agency securities have tended to narrow as the market for agency securities has developed over the decade and a broader participation in the market has occurred.

STATE AND LOCAL GOVERNMENT FINANCING

In this final section of the chapter we will examine the market for financing of state and local governments. We will begin by examining the securities issued by these governments and the market in which they are traded. Then we will examine the forces which influence supply and demand for municipal bonds. Finally, we will evaluate the effectiveness of the tax-exemption feature of municipal bonds as a mechanism for subsidizing state and local governments.

Characteristics of Municipal Bonds

The debt obligations of state and local governments are known as municipal bonds. The name municipal is applied regardless of whether the issuer is a state, a county, a city, or some kind of special district, such as a school district, a water district, or a publicly owned airport. Municipal bonds are also often referred to as tax-exempt securities and the market in which they are sold as the tax-exempt market. They are referred to in this manner because the interest income they generate is free of federal and often state income taxes. In part, this federal tax exemption results from constitutional separation of state and federal governments, but it is also motivated by a desire to subsidize state and local governments by reducing their cost of obtaining funds.

There are two basic types of municipal bonds: revenue bonds and general obligation bonds. Municipal revenue bonds are backed by the revenues generated from specific investments, such as a toll road or a mass-transit system. The owners of these bonds have no claim on the issuing unit of government beyond the claim to the revenues of the specific project which is funded by the bond. As a result, the risk of the bond is dependent on the risk of the investment it finances, as the risk of a corporate bond is largely the risk of the investments undertaken by the company issuing the bond. A general-obligation bond, however, has the backing of the unit of government issuing the bond. That is, the taxing authority of the government stands behind the bond. These are often called "full faith and credit" obligations. In the late 1950s and much of the 1960s revenue bonds represented a very small portion of total municipal issues. But during the 1970s the volume of revenue bonds issued to the market grew tremendously. In 1979 revenue bonds represented just under 75 percent of all new issues of municipal debt.

There is no single well-organized market for all municipal debt. Instead, there are essentially two distinct markets differentiated by the size and quality of the municipal issue. The primary market for the issues of larger well-known state and local governments operates in a manner similar to that of the primary market for corporate bonds. New issues are distributed to the market through investment bankers. The investment bankers form syndicates to bid on the issues and then distribute the bonds to their ultimate purchasers. There is also a secondary market in these issues which operates as an over-the-counter market. The secondary market is able to function because of the volume and homogeneity of outstanding securities. However, the largest number of bond issues which are sold each year are issued by small not-so-well-known local governments. These bonds are generally sold in the region in which the local government is located and are handled as a private placement without a syndicate. Due to the lack of volume, there is no secondary market in these securities.

As in any primary market, the cost to the issuer of a new bond depends on prevailing interest rates and on the extent of competition in the primary market for the security. Moreover, both the number of competing bidders on a new bond issue and the intensity with which they search for information about the new issue tend to reduce the cost of the issue. This role of competition in the bidding process is of particular interest in the municipal-bond market because the government prohibits commercial banks from acting as underwriters of revenue bonds. Statistical evidence collected over a number of years shows that the cost to municipalities of issuing revenue bonds would be reduced if this restriction were eliminated.[1] Moreover, with the increase in the volume of new revenue versus general-obligation bonds, this issue becomes increasingly important. But, thus far, commercial banks are still precluded from assuming the role of underwriters.

The Supply and Demand for Municipal Bonds

Most state and local government borrowing is directly linked to the financing of specific capital investments. This link between financing and a specific capital investment is now particularly evident with the growth of revenue bonds as opposed to general-obligation bonds in which the purpose of the financing is not as clearly defined. In the late 1970s most of the proceeds from new issues of municipal bonds were devoted to social welfare projects, government-financed utilities, and education.

The actual decision made by a state and local government as to whether to issue a municipal bond depends upon the balance between revenues and expenditures experienced by that unit of government as well as the stock of its liquid financial assets. If tax and other revenues are sufficient to fund expenditures and to maintain desired levels of liquid assets, then bonds will not be issued. However, lower levels of revenues will dictate a larger reliance on municipal debt. Historically, until the early 1970s state and local governments as a whole ran a deficit. However, in 1972 and 1973 a surplus was recorded in the aggregate budget of all state and local governments for the first time in 20 years. Deficits were recorded again in the recession years of 1974 and 1975, but with the end of the recession surpluses again appeared. This change altered the need for state and local governments to rely on municipal bonds to fund their deficits. The factor which accounts for this change is the increase in grants-in-aid extended by the federal government to state and local governments. The volume of this aid increased from roughly $24 billion in 1970 to approximately $80 billion in 1979. This increase proved sufficient to erase the aggregate deficit for state and local governments as a whole. Figure 14-7 shows the magnitude of the surplus and deficit for the decade of the 1970s.

There was another interesting change in the financial situation of state and local governments during the 1970s: They added significantly to their holdings of financial assets throughout this period, including Treasury and agency securities as well as time deposits with financial institutions. In 1965 state and local governments held about $50 billion in financial assets, and they added roughly another $20 billion by 1970. But, as Figure 14-7 illus-

[1] See Reuben Kessel, "A Study of the Effects of Competition in the Tax-Exempt Bond Market," *Journal of Political Economy*, 79 (July–August 1971), pp. 706–738, and Michael H. Hopewell and George G. Kaufman, "Commercial Bank Bidding on Municipal Revenue Bonds: New Evidence," *Journal of Finance*, 32 (December 1977), pp. 1647–1656.

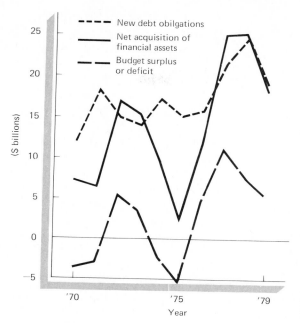

FIGURE 14-7
Financial trends for state and local governments. The figure shows the total volume of new financing and the net acquisition of financial assets by state and local governments. It also shows the total surplus or deficit (−) of all state and local governments in the aggregate. Source: Flow of Funds Accounts.

trates, from 1972 to 1979, with the exception of the recession years of 1974 and 1975, they acquired financial assets in a volume which roughly matched the annual increase in total financial liabilities. This represented a significant increase in their total stock of liquid assets.

It is not fully understood why this has occurred, but at least part of the explanation lies in the incentive created by the tax-exempt status of municipal debt. Because of the tax treatment, municipal bonds command a lower yield in the market than do comparable Treasury or corporate bonds. For example, during the first quarter of 1979 long-term Treasury bonds earned an average of 9.03 percent interest, while comparable municipal bonds earned 6.37 percent. This creates an incentive for a municipal government to issue its own securities at the municipal-bond rate and buy Treasury securities at a higher rate. This happened to an increasing extent during the 1970s. In effect, to the extent that this occurs, it creates an additional subsidy for state and local governments and leads to an increase in the volume of municipal debt.

The principal purchasers of municipal bonds are commercial banks, property and casualty insurance companies, and individuals in relatively high tax brackets. The reason for the concentration of ownership of municipal debt among these investors is that they have relatively high tax rates so that the tax-exemption feature of interest income on municipals is attractive to them. Important segments of the investing public have low or zero tax rates and are therefore simply not interested in municipal bonds. This applies to pension funds, most nonbank thrift institutions, such as mutual savings banks, credit unions, and life insurance companies.

The volume of acquisitions of municipal bonds by each of the major types of investors can be fairly volatile from one year to the next. Figure 14-8 shows the total acquisition of municipal bonds by all investors and by commercial banks, households, and property and casualty insurance companies from 1970 to 1979. The figure illustrates that commercial banks' commitment to municipals tends to vary periodically and the gap tends to be filled by households. In addition it shows that property and casualty companies have had a reasonably steady increase in their purchases of municipal bonds over the decade.

There are a number of reasons for this variation in the volume of purchases of municipal bonds by commercial banks. Foremost among these is the tax-shelter incentive. Like all investors, commercial banks commit themselves to municipal bonds principally because of the tax benefits. As a result, their demand for municipals is largely a function of the amount of taxable income they need to shelter. As this income rises, they increase their demand for municipal bonds. In one study of the demand for municipal bonds by financial institutions, roughly 60 percent of the variation in purchases of municipals was accounted for by fluctuations in taxable income.[2] But banks

[2] See Patric H. Hendershott and Timothy W. Koch, "The Demand for Tax-Exempt Securities by Financial Institutions," *Journal of Finance*, 35 (June 1980), pp. 717–728.

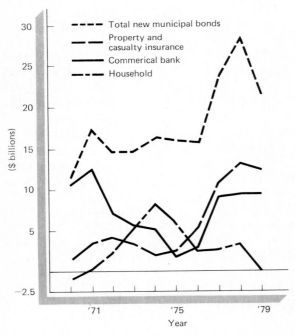

FIGURE 14-8
Major purchasers of new municipal bonds. The figure shows that banks were the largest purchaser of new municipal bonds in the first half of the 1970s but were supplanted by property and casualty insurance companies late in the 1970s. The figure also shows that bank acquisitions have tended to rise and fall in an opposite pattern relative to household acquisitions. Source: Flow of Funds Accounts.

do not utilize municipal bonds alone to shelter income from taxes. To an increasing extent during the 1970s they also utilized leases in order to take advantage of the investment tax credit[3] and deductions for depreciation. In addition, foreign operations provide deductions for taxes paid to foreign governments. These factors are generally thought to account for the fact that in 1975 and 1976 commercial banks' acquisitions of municipals bonds were rather low. The conventional wisdom at that time had it that commercial banks invested in municipal bonds almost exclusively as a residual after loan demand was satisfied. The inference was drawn that when loan demand was soft, banks should purchase municipals. This inference ran counter to the 1975–1976 experience in that commercial banks' loan demand was down *and* so were their purchases of municipal bonds. The actual reason for the 1975–1976 episode appears to be a diminished incentive to utilize municipal bonds as a tax shelter.

The Effectiveness of Tax Exemption as a Subsidy for State and Local Governments

The federal government uses its tax policy not only to raise revenue but also to provide subsidies and to generate incentives for productive activities. There are numerous such subsidies and incentives built into the tax system. For example, the government utilizes the investment tax credit, which provides tax credit for capital investment expenditures, to attempt to encourage capital spending in the economy. As we will discover in the next part of the book, the government also uses tax policy to attempt to influence the investments of various financial institutions. The tax-exempt status of municipal bonds is another tool utilized by the federal government to subsidize a particular sector of the economy and thereby encourage capital expenditures by that sector. However, there is considerable sentiment that the method utilized to accomplish this subsidy (i.e., granting tax-exempt status to municipal bonds) is an inefficient device for accomplishing this purpose.

To understand the criticism of the tax exemption on municipal bonds we need to examine the incentives to purchase tax-exempt securities by those who face a constant as opposed to a progressive income tax. Personal income taxes in the United States are based on a progressive tax schedule. This means that the tax rate increases as taxable income increases or that the marginal tax rate exceeds the average tax rate. However, after some minimum level of income, corporate income taxes are not based on a progressive tax schedule. Instead, it is taxed at a constant 46 percent rate. As a result, individuals and financial corporations subject to the full corporate

---

[3] The investment tax credit is a credit on federal income taxes for new investments. The amount of the credit is a percentage of the cost of the investment. But some investors do not have sufficient taxable income to utilize all of the investment tax credit. They can pass on the tax credit, however, if they lease the equipment to which the investment tax credit applies from another party which has sufficient taxable income. Banks have found this arrangement to be attractive.

income tax may have quite different incentives to purchase municipal bonds.

To see how the demand for municipal bonds will differ between individuals and corporations, we need to examine the spread between yields on municipals and other comparable bonds. (See Chapter Eight for a separate treatment of yield spreads between municipal and other bonds.) We will start by examining the incentive to purchase municipal bonds as opposed to comparable corporate bonds by anyone, either an individual or a corporation, subject to an arbitrary tax rate l. A party subject to a tax rate l will have no preference between corporate and municipal bonds that are comparable except for their tax treatment if the *after-tax* yield on the corporate bond is equal to the yield on the municipal bond. If we designate the before-tax yield on the corporate bond as r_c and the yield, both before and after taxes, on the municipal bond as r_m, then the investor will be indifferent if

$$r_m = (1 - l)\, r_c \qquad (14\text{-}5)$$

If the after-tax yield on the corporate bond exceeds the yield on the municipal bond, then this investor will prefer the corporate bond and vice versa. For example, an investor in the 50 percent tax bracket will be indifferent to municipal and comparable corporate bonds which have yields of 5 percent and 10 percent, respectively.

We can rewrite this condition so that it is stated in terms of the ratio of the yields. Then Eq. (14-5) can be expressed

$$\frac{r_m}{r_c} = 1 - l \qquad (14\text{-}6)$$

This means, for example, that the investor in the 50 percent tax bracket won't have a preference between the two bonds as long as the municipal yield is 50 percent of the corporate bond yield.

Now we can examine the distinction between the demand for municipal bonds by financial corporations subject to the full corporate tax rate and individual investors facing a progressive tax schedule. As long as financial institutions expect that their investments will be subject to full corporate taxes, then they will prefer municipal bonds over comparable corporate bonds if the yield on municipals is at least 5 percent of the corporate yield. This assumes that no other tax shelters are available for this income so that the full 46 percent tax rate will be paid if the municipal bond is not utilized. The fact that there is a constant tax rate means that as long as the ratio of the municipal- to the corporate-bond yield is *exactly* equal to one minus that constant tax rate, then municipal bonds are as good as corporate bonds in terms of their after-tax yields. Moreover, there are no corporate investors with higher tax rates to be induced into the municipal market by offering higher yields. Therefore, if yields rise above the ratio of 54 percent, this would tend to increase the gain to corporate investors above what is sufficient to induce them to enter the market. Moreover, this gain comes at the expense of issuers of municipal bonds. For as the yield they have to pay increases relative to prevailing corporate yields, the subsidy they derive from tax exemption declines. As long as the ratio of the yields remains at 54 percent, then municipal governments pay no more than is necessary to attract investors subject to the corporate income tax and they maintain the maximum amount of their subsidy.

The situation is different, however, with a progressive as opposed to a constant tax schedule. To see why consider the incentive to shelter income with municipal bonds for individuals in the 60 as opposed to the 40 percent tax bracket. The individual in the 60 percent bracket will find it profitable to purchase municipal bonds as long as their yield exceeds 40 percent of the yield on a taxable bond. On the other hand, 40 percent tax bracket individuals require that the municipal yield rise to 60 percent of the corporate bond yield to induce them to purchase municipals.

Another way to see this is to compute the relative gain that an individual in a particular tax bracket would reap by investing in municipal rather than corporate bonds, depending upon the ratio of the yields. For example, if a person who is in the 60 percent tax bracket invested in corporate bonds, he or she would reap an after-tax return equal to 40 percent of the corporate-bond interest rate r_c. If the ratio of the yields is also 60 percent, $r_m/r_c = .60$, then the return from municipals is equal to 60 percent of the corporate bond rate. As a result, a person in the 60 percent bracket gains 20 percent of the corporate bond rate by investing in municipals. If the corporate bond rate is 10 percent, then this gain represents 200 basis points (or 2 percent interest). We can repeat these calculations for individuals in different tax brackets and for different yield spreads to see what the amounts of the gains and losses will be. The results of these computations are presented in Table 14-5. Table 14-5 shows that as the ratio of the yields rises, individuals in lower tax brackets are induced to purchase municipal bonds and the demand for municipal bonds rises.

We can represent this relationship with a demand curve for municipals by individuals as a function of their marginal tax rates. Such a demand curve is illustrated in Figure 14-9. It shows that individual demand rises as the ratio of yields rises, or as the marginal tax rate at which municipals become profitable *l* falls. Now suppose that the ratio between the two yields is 60 percent, so that the critical tax rate at which it is profitable to invest in municipal bonds is 40 percent. All investors with marginal tax rates above 40 percent would be willing to buy municipals at yield spreads less than 60 percent. For example, the 60 percent bracket individual would be willing to purchase municipals if the municipal yield declined to 40 percent of the corporate yield. As shown in Table 14-5, at any yield spread greater than 40 percent this individual would reap some gain.

As a result, at any particular tax rate *l* in Figure 14-9, the individual with exactly that tax rate breaks even on corporate or municipal bonds and the higher tax bracket individuals receive a surplus. The surplus is the amount

TABLE 14-5

Gain (or Loss) from Investing in Municipal Bonds

r_m/r_c	TAX BRACKET		
	40%	46%	60%
20%	$-.4\ r_c$	$-.34\ r_c$	$-.2\ r_c$
40%	$-.2\ r_c$	$-.14\ r_c$	0
54%	$-.06\ r_c$	0	$.14\ r_c$
60%	0	$.06\ r_c$	$.2\ r_c$
80%	$.2\ r_c$	$.26\ r_c$	$.4\ r_c$

Gains on municipal bond investments relative to corporate bonds — gains are expressed as a multiple of the corporate bond rate. Each gain is computed as:

$$\left[\frac{r_m}{r_c} - (1 - l)\right] r_c$$

of interest income they would be willing to give up and still hold municipal bonds. In effect, this is a transfer of the federal subsidy from the state and local governments to the individuals in very high tax brackets. The total amount of this surplus, in the case where the ratio of the yields is 60 percent or l equals 40 percent, is represented in Figure 14-9. The surplus is the shaded area under the demand curve above the horizontal line at the 40 percent marginal tax rate.

It is because of this *bondholders' surplus* that tax exemption is criticized as an inefficient subsidy. Rather than returning all the subsidy to state and local governments, this system diverts part of it to high-tax-bracket individuals. This is viewed as an undesirable result by those who seek to maintain a progressive tax system. Moreover, recently the ratio of yields on municipals to other securities has been increasing significantly. (See Figure 8-5 in Chapter Eight.) This increase has caused concern that the magnitude of the bondholders' surplus has increased and that the efficiency of the tax-exemption system as a subsidy has declined. This increase in relative yields has generated renewed interest in alternatives to the tax-exempt status for municipal bonds.

The principal idea behind the alternative proposals is to replace the tax exemption with a direct subsidy to state and local governments, thereby eliminating the bondholder's surplus. One such proposal was offered by the administration of President Carter in 1978. This proposal, referred to as the Taxable Bond Option (TBO), would have allowed state and local governments to issue either tax-exempt bonds or taxable bonds, with a direct subsidy from the federal government. The Carter proposal included an initial 35 percent subsidy, with the stipulation that it would rise to 40 percent within 1

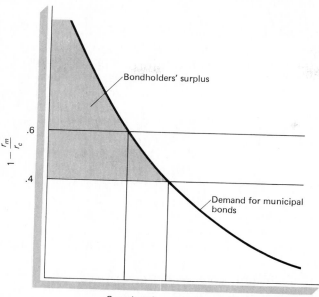

FIGURE 14-9

Bondholders' surplus. The downward-sloping line in this figure represents the demand for municipal bonds by individuals who face a progressive income tax. The marginal tax rate l implied by the ratio of municipal and corporate bond yields is on the vertical axis and the demand for municipal bonds is on the horizontal axis. The area under the demand curve above the horizontal line at .4 represents the bondholders' surplus if the marginal tax rate is .4 or the ratio of the yields is .6.

year. Neither this proposal nor others like it met with success during the 1970s.

SUMMARY

This chapter has dealt with the financial markets which serve the federal, state, and local governments. The markets through which the federal government obtains financing are known as the Treasury security market and the agency security market. State and local governments obtain financing through the municipal-bond market. All of these markets have experienced significant growth in the last decade as well as throughout this century, as government-funded activities have become a larger portion of the entire economy. In this chapter we have examined the basic trends in the financing demands of each level of government as well as the securities and markets through which they obtain their financing.

To finance its debt the Treasury issues three types of marketable securities (known as bills, notes, and bonds) in addition to some nonmarketable obligations. The volume of U.S. Treasury financing is largely dictated by the magnitude of the deficit of the federal government. And the federal government consistently ran a deficit during the 1970s. As a result, the volume of Treasury financing consistently increased throughout the decade. The demand for financing by the Treasury has been highest in recession years when the deficit has peaked. During 1 year in the 1970s, new Treasury financing represented as much as 40 percent of total new funds raised in the capital markets. There has been considerable concern that this large demand for Treasury financing tends to raise interest rates and crowd out private financing of profitable investments.

Another type of federal financing is known as agency debt. Agency securities are issued by a number of governmental or quasi-governmental institutions. As of the end of 1979, the volume of agency securities outstanding represented about 20 percent of the volume of outstanding Treasury securities. Most of the agency securities are issued by institutions created to support either agriculture or the housing industry. These agencies do not issue securities for the same reason that the Treasury does. That is, they do not obtain financing to fund a deficit. Instead, they act like a financial intermediary in that they issue their own securities and then purchase assets, largely claims on residential or agricultural property.

The market for Treasury bills, notes, and bonds provides one of the clearest examples of how present value procedures are used to price securities. Of these three securities Treasury bills are the easiest to price because they offer no coupon interest. Therefore, the yield on a Treasury bill is determined solely by the amount of price appreciation which occurs when the bill matures. The price of a bill is determined by the number of days to maturity and the yield demanded in the market corresponding to that maturity. The important distinction between pricing of bonds and notes and pricing of Treasury bills is that bonds and notes have coupon payments as well as possibilities for capital gains and losses. Therefore, the value of a bond or note is the present value of the future coupon payments plus the payment at maturity.

The market where Treasury securities are traded consists of distinct primary and secondary markets. The primary market is a pure auction market (the primary market for Treasury bills was described in Chapter Ten). The secondary market is an over-the-counter market with a large number of active dealers. To be an official dealer in Treasury securities requires recognition by the Federal Reserve Bank of New York. Though the secondary market still operates essentially as an over-the-counter market, this market underwent tremendous changes in the 1970s in that the trading procedure is now highly automated. Rather than relying on the telephone for price quotes as well as to conduct exchanges, the market now has an automated quotation system. For trades among dealers the system can actually be used to conduct exchanges, but for trades between dealers and other customers it acts as a "billboard" displaying price quotations. In contrast to the Treasury security market, the agency market is strictly an over-the-counter market where private dealers make the market.

Financing for state and local governments is provided through the municipal-bond market. The important characteristic of municipal bonds is that the interest income they generate is free from federal and most state income taxes. This means that the yields on municipal bonds are lower than the yields on comparable corporate or Treasury bonds which do not have the tax-exemption feature. It also means that municipal bonds are attractive principally to those with high tax rates, including some individuals, commercial banks, and insurance companies. There are two principal types of municipal bonds which are known as general-obligation bonds and revenue bonds. General-obligation bonds are backed by the general taxing authority of the issuing government, while revenue bonds are claims on the revenues of a particular project, such as a toll road. Historically, state and local governments issued municipal bonds to finance major long-term investments and to fund any deficits. Until the early 1970s state and local governments ran a fairly consistent deficit in the aggregate. However, with the advent of increased federal grants during the 1970s these deficits have been less frequent. In spite of this, municipal-bond issues did not decline and it appears that state and local governments have been issuing municipal bonds, in part, to fund their holdings of Treasury securities with higher yields. The tax-exemption of interest income on municipal bonds has attracted considerable criticism because it is viewed as an inefficient means of subsidizing state and local governments. Instead of state and local governments reaping all the benefit of the tax exemption, individuals with high tax rates receive part of the subsidy. Proposals to change this system abound, but by the early 1980s none has met with success.

QUESTIONS TO IMPROVE UNDERSTANDING

1   Why has there been such tremendous growth in the outstanding volume of Treasury debt? What have been the major uses of these funds in recent years? What is the relative volume of the various types of Treasury debt outstanding?
2   What are agency securities? Which agencies borrow through the FFB? What is the dominant purpose for which agency securities are sold?
3   What are GNMA pass-through securities? Explain how the market for these securities operates and why they have been so successful.
4   How would you compute the price of a Treasury bond which had a 6 percent coupon rate, 8 years to maturity, and a market yield of 9.5 percent? What is the yield on a coupon basis for a Treasury bill with a maturity value of $10,000 that is selling for $9,885 with 84 days until maturity? What is the yield on a discount basis?
5   Explain how the introduction of automated quotation systems has altered the over-the-counter market in Treasury securities. What is the difference between the systems used in the interdealer market and the rest of the secondary market?

6 What is the role of the Federal Reserve Bank of New York in the over-the-counter market in Treasury securities? What constitutes an official dealer? What has happened to dealer volume and inventories in recent years? Why?

7 How does the primary market in municipal bonds operate? What is the distinction between revenue and general-obligation bonds? How might competition in the primary market for revenue bonds be increased?

8 Why did state and local governments show a surplus in most of the 1970s? Has this surplus meant that they have had no need for municipal debt? What has been the trend in their acquisition of liquid assets? Why has this trend developed?

9 Why is there such a narrow market for municipal securities? What tends to cause commercial banks' holdings of municipals to fluctuate as they do?

10 Explain what bondholder's surplus represents. Why is a progressive as opposed to a constant tax rate necessary for there to be a bondholder surplus? Why is the bondholder surplus used to argue that the tax exemption of municipal bonds is an inefficient way to subsidize state and local governments?

REFERENCES

*Banks, Lois: "The Market for Agency Securities," Quarterly Review, Federal Reserve Bank of New York, 3 (Spring 1978), pp. 7–19.

Benson, Earl D.: "The Search for Information by Underwriters and Its Impact on Municipal Interest Cost," Journal of Finance, 34 (September 1979), pp. 863–870.

Fortune, Peter: "Tax-Exemption of State and Local Interest Payments: An Economic Analysis of the Issues and an Alternative," New England Economic Review, Federal Reserve Bank of Boston (May/June 1973), pp. 3–20.

*Garbade, Kenneth D.: "Electronic Quotation Systems and the Market for Government Securities," Quarterly Review, Federal Reserve Bank of New York, 3 (Summer 1978), pp. 13–20.

———, and William L. Silber: "Price Dispersion in the Government Securities Market," Journal of Political Economy, 84 (1976), pp. 721–740.

Hendershott, Patrick H., and Timothy W. Koch: "The Demand for Tax-Exempt Securities by Financial Institutions," Journal of Finance, 35 (June 1980), pp. 717–728.

Hopewell, Michael H., and George G. Kaufman: "Commercial Bank Bidding on Municipal Revenue Bonds: New Evidence," Journal of Finance, 32 (December 1977), pp. 1647–1656.

Kessel, Reuben: "A Study of the Effects of Competition in the Tax-Exempt Bond Market," Journal of Political Economy, 79 (July–August 1971), pp. 706–738.

*McCurdy, Christopher J.: "The Dealer Market for U.S. Government Securities," Quarterly Review, Federal Reserve Bank of New York, 2 (Winter 1977–1979), pp. 35–47.

*Resler, David H., and Richard W. Lang: "Federal Agency Debt: Another Side of Federal Borrowing," Review, Federal Reserve Bank of St. Louis, 61 (November 1979), pp. 10–19.

*Rosenbloom, Richard H.: "A Review of the Municipal Bond Market," Economic Review, Federal Reserve Bank of Richmond (March–April 1976), pp. 10–19.

Sorenson, Eric H.: "Negotiated Municipal Bond Issues: Implications for Efficiency," Journal of Money, Credit and Banking, 3 (August 1979), pp. 366–370.

* References marked with an * provide additional institutional detail and make excellent supplementary readings.

REGULATING FINANCIAL
MARKETS AND INSTITUTIONS

Part Four deals with government regulation of financial markets. There is a large and diverse government regulatory system for financial markets. Some important parts of this system came into existence as early as the mid-nineteenth century, but the major portions were enacted into law as a response to the Great Depression of the 1930s. The regulatory system put in place in the 1930s has remained largely intact until the present time. However, with the advent of high inflation rates in the 1970s, major weaknesses in this system have become apparent. Portions of this system are now undergoing a major overhaul. The chapters in Part Four seek to explain why regulation has been imposed in financial markets, to lay out the basic features of the regulatory structure which has existed since the 1930s, and to put the ongoing changes in this system in historical perspective. The first chapter of Part Four, Chapter Fifteen, presents a theory or a rationale for the regulation of financial markets which forms the basis of the analysis in the remaining four chapters in Part Four. Chapter Sixteen deals with the regulation of auction and over-the-counter markets, or securities markets. The next two chapters examine the regulatory system for financial intermediaries.

Chapter Seventeen focuses on commercial banks. Chapter Eighteen examines how other financial intermediaries, such as savings and loans, credit unions, pension funds, and insurance companies, are regulated. Finally, the last chapter in Part Four serves as a transition into the subject matter of Part Five. It deals with how the Federal Reserve regulates the total supply of money in the economy.

Chapter Fifteen

THE RATIONALE FOR
REGULATING FINANCIAL MARKETS

In this chapter and the next four we will deal with government regulation of financial markets. In general, financial markets are among the most heavily regulated of all the markets in the United States. Yet, both the extent and type of regulation varies tremendously across these markets. For example, the largest and most important type of financial intermediary, the commercial bank, is highly regulated with virtually every decision of the commercial banker subject to scrutiny by one or more government agencies. On the other hand, insurance companies are relatively free of regulation. In the case of commercial banks and most other deposit intermediaries, regulation takes the form of government insurance for depositors against the prospect of losses and government supervision of loans and investments. In auction and over-the-counter markets, such as the market for corporate equities, regulation is directed principally at ensuring the disclosure of relevant information to the public and at maintaining a competitive market.

The regulatory system which governs financial markets is also complicated and often confusing. It is difficult to imagine that, if we could start over with a new regulatory system, we would create something exactly like what we have today. The system we have now evolved only gradually in response to situations which were perceived to be crises at the time. Regulations which effectively dealt with these crises were preserved and the government institutions which were in charge of implementing those regulations grew. Oftentimes, however, institutions and regulations which failed were also preserved so that many features of the system we observe in operation today are rather difficult to justify.

Regulation is a timely topic for the 1980s. From the onset of the Great Depression of the 1930s until the late 1970s, the trend was toward increasing regulation in almost every industry in the country. But in the late 1970s the desirability of increased regulation came to be seriously questioned, not just by those who had obvious interests in reversing the trend, but by an increasingly broad cross-section of Americans and their political representatives. This new sentiment has already had its impact on the regulation of financial markets and it is likely that, throughout the 1980s, the regulatory system will continue to change in significant ways.

In order to understand why this is happening and what it portends, it is necessary to have a clear understanding of what constituted the regulatory system in existence at the beginning of 1980 as well as how and why it came to be. In the next few chapters we will try to develop this understanding. In this chapter we will concentrate on developing an understanding of the underlying rationale for the regulation of financial markets. Then in the remaining chapters of this part of the book, we will examine specific aspects of the regulation of auction, over-the-counter, and intermediated markets.

AN INITIAL PERSPECTIVE ON REGULATION

Before we get involved in the motives for and structure of regulation of financial markets, it is useful to acquire a broad perspective on the reasons for regulating any kind of market, not merely the market for financial assets. The purpose of exploring the more general problem of regulation in any market is not to meander away from the principal issue at hand. Instead, it is to provide a meaningful context in which to place the special problems which have led to regulation of financial markets.

Regulation and the Competitive Marketplace

The ideal kind of market is one which is perfectly competitive. The opposite extreme from this ideal is a market which is monopolistic. It is exceptionally important to have a clear understanding of what constitutes a competitive as opposed to a monopolistic market in order to understand why and how markets are regulated.

An industry is competitive if there are many firms in that industry all selling their products at the lowest price they can, such that they still find it profitable to remain in the industry. In this situation the firms are said to be earning no excess or monopoly profits. A more technical characterization of a competitive price is that it is equal to marginal cost. This means that the price charged by each firm is equal to the cost of producing the last unit of the firm's product. Where all firms price at marginal cost and where any firm that chooses can enter the industry and compete for customers, monopoly profits will not exist and the industry will be perfectly competitive.

When an industry is controlled by a monopoly, the price charged by the monopoly will be greater than the price that would exist if that industry were perfectly competitive. In addition, the monopoly will reduce the quantity of goods produced in the industry relative to what would exist if the industry were perfectly competitive. By so doing the monopolist earns more profits than firms would earn if the industry were competitive. By keeping other firms out the monopolist is able to raise price, lower quantity, and increase profits beyond the level that would be just sufficient to keep the monopolist in the industry. In order for a monopoly to be successful some mechanism must be devised to keep out the competition, that is, the monopolist must maintain a barrier to entry.

The rationale for regulation in a competitive economy is to, in some instances, encourage and in others supplant the competitive marketplace. When used to encourage competition, it tries to prohibit practices by firms which interfere with the operation of a competitive market. When regulation is applied for this purpose, the presumption is that the market can operate competitively if the proper regulations are enforced. But regulation is also used to supplant the operation of a competitive market when a competitive marketplace is not feasible. In this instance the competitive market is said to have failed. Most regulation which we observe in the United States can be traced to some kind of perceived or real market failure.

Market failure occurs when, for some reason, the private marketplace ceases to function at all or is *unable* to operate in a *competitive* manner, taking into account all the costs or benefits from production of a good. Market failure does not include the possibility that some firm or group of firms is able to establish a monopoly, unless there is something inherent in the market which ensures that competition cannot survive. There are three important ways in which market failure can occur and we will discuss each of them in turn. They are labeled:

Natural monopoly

Externalities

Asymmetric information

Natural Monopoly

Most regulation in the United States has been developed to deal with industries subject to a particular kind of market failure called natural monopoly.

Natural monopoly refers to a situation where an industry is inherently a monopoly. The principal natural monopolies are public utilities. For example, consider the prospect of competing electric companies providing service to the same community. Each company would have to build generators and construct electrical lines throughout the community. This is simply not feasible. It is much cheaper and more efficient to have a single set of electrical lines and generating facilities. The economist refers to an industry with a natural monopoly as a decreasing-cost industry or one subject to continuing *economies of scale*. This means that the cost of production, per unit of output, decreases as the volume of output increases. When an industry has economies of scale it is difficult to rely on competition to police prices. The electrical utility is by nature a monopoly and this monopoly, if left to its own devices, would establish monopolistic prices. The solution to this problem has been to regulate the industry. Generally, public utility commissions are formed which have the responsibility for determining "fair" prices and rates of return for the industry. How this might be accomplished in an objective manner is still something of a mystery, for the definition of "fair" is always debatable. Yet, this form of regulation has been applied to most electric power, gas, and communication utilities.

Externalities

A second type of market failure results from what are referred to as externalities. *Externalities* are costs which are not properly accounted for in the prices which are established in a competitive market. When externalities are present there is said to be a divergence between social costs or benefits—that is, the total costs or benefits derived from the production of a product—and the private returns or costs derived by the purchaser or producer of the product.

Externalities can cut both ways. Social costs or benefits may be greater or less than private costs or benefits. The principal example of a situation where social benefits exceed the private return from producing a product is referred to as the case of public goods. A public good is a product which people want to use or consume, but it is difficult or impossible to compel them to pay the price of their consumption. The problem involved in public goods is best illustrated with an example. Suppose national defense were produced in a competitive market instead of produced by the government and paid for through taxes. While most individuals would prefer to consume some amount of national defense and would be willing to pay for it as they pay for other products, they know that if everyone else pays for national defense they can consume that defense without paying their share. In effect, they can free-ride on the system, but when everyone recognizes the possibility of being a free-rider, it is difficult for private producers of national defense to induce anyone to pay for their consumption. As a result, the production of national defense is less than most everyone would like. The root problem with a public good is that it is impossible to exclude from the consumption of such a good someone who has not paid for the right to use it. Hence, access to the good is public. Another way to view the problem is that the private return to the producer of defense is below the social return because of the free-rider problem. The externality involved in public goods leads to underproduction of those goods, and the role of regulation is to increase production to a level perceived to be socially optimal.

When an externality cuts the other way, the problem is that the private return from producing a product exceeds the social return from that product. This results when there is some social cost borne by the society as a whole resulting from the production of a particular product, but the market does not compel the producer of the product to bear that cost. The principal contemporary example of this divergence between social and private cost is provided by pollution. A wide variety of industrial products contribute to the pollution of the environment. But, in general, the market does not include the cost of that pollution in the private cost of producing those products. The problem is to devise a way to make the producers, and therefore ultimately the consumers, of the products which pollute bear the cost of that pollution.

There are two ways regulation can be used to accomplish this purpose. The first is to hold the producers liable for social costs or impel them to directly reduce the amount of pollution and hence the social cost of that pollution. The second is through taxes which transform the social costs into private costs. In this instance, unlike the case of the public good, the market produces too much rather than too little of a product because of the divergence between social and private cost. In both instances, government regulation is prompted in order to alter the level of production and the distribution of returns or costs.

Asymmetric Information

The final type of market failure in competitive markets which has led to government regulation is a topic which was introduced earlier in this book, asymmetric information (see Chapter Six). The earlier discussion of asymmetric information was couched in the example of the so-called "lemons" problem. The essence of the lemons problem is the following. Suppose there is a product for sale which is subject to a large variation in quality. Also, suppose that the quality of each such product is known to the seller but not to the buyer. For example, the products might be automobiles, refrigerators, or medical services. If sellers only sell products when the price yields them a profit and buyers only buy when they believe they are getting a fair price, then this market may be subject to a particular type of failure. Buyers know that every seller is likely to claim he has the highest quality product in the market. They know that most of these sellers are lying, but they do not know who is lying and who is telling the truth. The price they will be willing to pay will reflect the quality of the average product available in the market.

It is in this sense that the price is fair. The sellers who actually have high-quality products will be unwilling to sell at this price, as they must expect to take a loss by so doing. Hence, only the liars will be willing to trade at this average price. Recognizing that the sellers with high-quality products will drop out, the buyers will revise their idea of a fair price downward until all the higher quality products have been driven out of the market. In this kind of extreme situation, where nothing intervenes to alleviate the asymmetry of information, the market fails to deliver anything but low-quality products. In such instances, regulation may be useful to correct the information asymmetry and provide ways for buyers to discriminate among high-quality and low-quality products.

The Motives for Regulating Financial Markets

Much of the existing regulatory structure which applies to markets other than financial markets has evolved to deal with the problems of natural monopoly and the types of externalities described above. But this is not true in financial markets. Financial markets are heavily regulated. Yet virtually no financial industries are natural monopolies. Moreover, while there certainly are externalities in financial markets, the externalities related to pollution, safety, and health which have led to such extensive regulation in other industries are not present.

In this chapter we will identify four distinct rationales for regulation of financial markets. Three of these rationales pertain to difficulties arising from imperfections in the distribution of information, the most serious of which is market failure due to asymmetric information. The other rationale is one of those which has led to regulation in other markets—the desire to limit monopoly power and promote competition. The labels we will give to these rationales are:

1 Promote competition and prevent monopolistic practices
2 Prevent or limit expropriation
3 Control the actions of agents
4 Prevent market failure

These four basic rationales for regulation, the problems which they create, and the types of regulation they have spawned are briefly summarized in Table 15-1. This table provides a useful frame of reference for the discussion of regulation in the rest of this chapter and in the rest of the chapters in this part of the book.

The remainder of this chapter is devoted to discussions of each of these four reasons for regulation. The next section is concerned with item number

TABLE 15-1

Summary of the Rationale for Regulation of Financial Markets

MOTIVE FOR REGULATION	NATURE OF PROBLEM	REGULATION TO DEAL WITH THE PROBLEM
1 Limit monopoly power and promote competition	1 Cartel behavior promotes monopolistic practices	1 Promulgate and enforce rules designed to prevent monopolistic practices
2 Limit opportunities for expropriation when there is a difference in information between contract parties	2 Unsophisticated parties—generally consumers—may be unable to adequately protect themselves against expropriations	2 Limit allowable contracts and require disclosure of information (truth-in-lending)
3 Limit opportunities for agents to act against the interests of their employers	3 Agents who have special information may be able to use that information for their own advantage at the expense of their employers	3 Mandate disclosure of information and limit opportunities for insiders to trade on information
4 Avoid market failure due to asymmetric information	4 With unregulated financial intermediaries, depositors periodically withdraw from the market if they fear for the safety of their funds	4 Provide insurance on deposits *and* control the risk of financial intermediaries

1. The following section concentrates on items 2 through 4—those which arise from problems with the distribution of information.

REGULATION AND MONOPOLY POWER IN FINANCIAL MARKETS

We will begin this section by examining how monopoly power can develop in financial markets and then we will explore the ways that regulation can be used to limit monopoly power.

Sources of Monopoly Power in Financial Markets

A significant amount of the regulation applied to financial markets is designed to promote competition or restrict practices which are perceived to be monopolistic. There are examples of this kind of regulation in auction and over-the-counter markets as well as in intermediated markets. The prospect that a monopoly might exist in financial markets in the United States has long been viewed as exceptionally pernicious, maybe more so than in most nonfinancial markets. The reason is probably that an important part of the structure of any democratic society is the concept that no citizens should be arbitrarily restricted from access to capital. A monopoly in the market for capital holds out the prospect that capital may be distributed in an arbitrary manner and, even if access is not restricted, prices will be set at monopolistic levels. As a result, it has been a strong part of the democratic tradition for the government to take actions which assure access to financial resources and to explicitly forbid practices which are clearly monopolistic.

In financial markets one of the principal devices which can be used to promote monopoly power is the trade association. A *trade association* is a club or organization formed by the firms in an industry to promote the good of the industry and to deal with common problems. A trade association can serve many useful purposes—setting rules of behavior, promoting the industry, representing the industry in government proceedings, and performing research and educational tasks for firms in the industry. But a trade association can also be the front for a cartel. That is, it can serve as the means by which the industry establishes a monopoly and compels the firms in the industry to behave in a monopolistic manner. To serve this purpose it needs to set rules of behavior which are to the joint benefit of all the firms in the industry acting in concert as a monopoly. The rules are needed because it is always to the benefit of any one firm in a cartel to cheat on the agreed behavior of the cartel. For example, the rules of the cartel may stipulate a minimum price for a product. If all firms in the cartel but one observe this minimum price and this one firm cheats by lowering its price in secret, it will attract business from the other firms and earn higher profits than it would if it observed the minimum price. However, if all firms in the cartel behave in this way the cartel is doomed. Therefore, in order to be successful, a cartel needs to have enforceable rules of behavior.

Auction markets provide exceptionally good opportunities for the operation of cartels if these markets operate with brokers and dealers. In the purest of auction markets, without any brokers or dealers, the opportunities for cartel behavior are limited. Such a market is probably the closest in the real world to the economists' conception of perfect competition. But in auction markets where all sales are made by brokers or where dealers function to absorb temporary trading imbalances, there is a potential for a cartel to flourish. Essentially what is involved is forming a trade association in which one must be a member to act as a broker or dealer. If such a trade association is used to promote a cartel, then its principal objective will be to establish restrictions on permissible behavior which tend to generate monopoly profits for all the brokers or dealers in the association. Enforcement of such rules comes through the ability to revoke membership in the association to violators of rules. The rules may directly govern pricing of the services that member brokers and dealers are allowed to provide or the amount of information which they can divulge to customers. All of these things will tend to establish monopoly power.

Another possibility for cartel behavior occurs in the distribution process of new securities, that is, in primary markets which do not function as auction markets. In the primary markets securities are often distributed through investment bankers who come together to form syndicates in order to purchase and distribute securities. The purpose of the syndicate is to distribute the risk of a particular security issue across separate investment bankers. The diversification motive is a very legitimate purpose of syndicates. However, there is at least the potential that the syndicate form of organization can be used to monopolize the primary markets. The success of such a cartel depends upon the competitive forces at work in the industry, particularly the willingness of the issuers of securities to circumvent the cartel. In this case, as in the case of a trade association of brokers or dealers in an auction market, the cartel must have some mechanism for stipulating and enforcing rules.

In order for a cartel to be successful in the long run, it usually requires some kind of legal sanction. The legal sanction must not apply merely to the existence of the association which serves as the front for the cartel, but also to the rules and enforcement procedures used by the cartel. This is principally where regulation comes to bear in promoting competition in financial markets. Few financial markets are so dominated by a single firm that the firm can create a monopoly on its own without the support of a cartel. As a result, monopoly power in financial markets largely depends on cartel behavior. And regulation can be used to limit the ability of cartels to operate successfully. These regulations are directed at legitimate trade associations to be sure that they do not directly fix prices, that they do not restrict the services which members can offer, and to be sure that they do not restrict access to information which would lead to more competitive pricing.

Regulation to Promote Competition

It is useful to divide the regulatory actions taken to promote competition in financial markets into those which deal with auction and over-the-counter markets and those which deal with intermediated markets. While the issues are not totally separate, there are considerable distinctions.

Regulation in over-the-counter and auction markets is directed toward preventing cartel behavior. Responsibility for regulating these markets lies principally with the Securities and Exchange Commission (SEC). A good portion of this regulation is directed at the New York Stock Exchange. In part this is because it is the oldest and largest auction market in the country and in part because it has been perceived as one of the ripest possibilities for cartel behavior. The SEC now explicitly prohibits minimum prices for brokers' services and closely supervises dealer activities on the exchange. In addition it has major responsibility for determining what type of market organization will actually be used in the secondary market for corporate equities and bonds. These issues will be examined closely in the next chapter.

The task of promoting competition is less complicated in auction and over-the-counter markets than in the markets where intermediaries play a large role. This is because the problems pertaining to the distribution of information, which have led to the regulation of intermediaries, are not so severe in these markets. In auction markets, such as the New York Stock Exchange, the central problem is to be sure that the brokers and dealers who comprise that market offer competitive prices for their services. This is not significantly different from the issues regarding competitive versus monopolistic pricing which arise in other (nonfinancial) industries.

In the intermediated markets, such as commercial banking, the fundamental difficulty is that many actions which tend to increase competition and lower prices also tend to interfere with the regulatory system which is designed to prevent market failure. A competitive market is one in which the weak and inefficient firms fail to survive. But in banking, such failure has often come all at once for a large number of institutions in response to a financial panic. Such failures threaten the stability of the whole industry and the economy. The regulatory system which has evolved to deal with the problem of market failure tends to ensure the survival of at least some banks which would not be profitable in a more competitive environment. Unfortunately, there seems to be no practical way to eliminate this conflict. As a result, the regulators of financial intermediaries often argue about how much competition to allow and they often disagree with the Justice Department on these questions. These disputes are further complicated by the fact that it is possible to attempt to justify, as a necessary part of the regulatory system designed to prevent market failure, restrictions which do not really serve this purpose at all, but which tend to reduce competition and increase the profits of existing financial institutions.

The important issues regarding competition in the intermediated markets relate primarily to the types of activities in which various intermediaries will be allowed to engage and to the amount of competition permitted in any region. Each type of intermediary is restricted as to the types of activities in which it may engage. Many of these restrictions are designed to prevent conflicts of interest or to limit risk and thereby protect depositors. But they also all tend to limit competition. The central issue is how much fragmentation of markets should be enforced by regulation versus how much competition should be encouraged. There appears to be no simple answer. With regard to regional competition, the underlying issue is essentially the same. As we will discover in Chapter Seventeen, regulations on bank branching and bank holding companies tend to restrict the amount of competition in any given geographic area. Many of these regulations are determined at the state rather than the federal level. Again, they tend to restrict competition apparently in order to reduce risk, though the motives here may be more to protect established regional monopoly positions than to protect the interests of depositors.

REGULATION AND THE PROBLEM OF EXPROPRIATION

Now we will consider the rationales for regulation of financial markets which result from imperfections in the distribution of information—items 2 through 4 on our list. As we have learned throughout the book, an essential function of financial markets is to aggregate information about the future returns on assets and set the prices of those assets. It is natural, then, that we should be concerned about how effectively an unregulated competitive marketplace can perform this job. We learned in Part One of the book that if all participants in a market have equal information, then the market can process information and set prices in a manner with which we can find little fault. But if participants in a financial market have significantly different information, then the market can have difficulties and those difficulties *may* justify some regulation by the government or another third party. The most serious difficulty is that the market may fail as described in the "lemons" paradigm. But even short of market failure, an imperfect distribution of information may lead to difficulties which give rise to regulation. And, in fact, this is what has occurred in the U.S. economy in the twentieth century.

In the remaining sections of this chapter we will analyze three types of difficulties which can arise in a financial market when there is an unequal distribution of information. The most severe problem, market failure, has already been discussed. Our purpose here is to understand more thoroughly why and how regulation has been used to avoid market failure. The other two problems pertain to what we will call expropriations which can be carried out in financial markets and to the closely related problem of agency. In analyzing these topics we will try to understand how an unregulated competitive market deals with them, and then how regulation may be used as well. Our purpose in this discussion is not to justify the extent of regulation we observe in the financial markets of the 1980s; instead, it is to try to understand why and how our present regulatory system evolved.

Expropriation in Private Contracts

Virtually all financial assets involve some kind of legal contract. Legal contracts serve to both promote and protect the interests of all the parties involved. But whenever such contracts are agreed to, there are opportunities available for one party to take actions which tend to hurt or to expropriate the other party or parties. In fact, it is often because of these possibilities that such contracts are necessary. For example, consider the relationship between the owners of equity securities and the owners of debt securities in a particular firm. One way that equityholders might try to expropriate debtholders is to rob the firm of its assets by paying themselves excess dividends. This action increases the likelihood that the firm will be unable to meet its contractual obligation to debtholders and thereby expropriates their value. Another possible form of expropriation involves the relationship between security holders and the managers of a firm. Managers may try to expropriate wealth from the firm's security holders through various forms of embezzlement. Such embezzlement may be through the more explicitly illegal form of actually stealing funds from the firm, or it may involve excess consumption of perquisites such as hunting lodges, yachts, and other valued services provided by the company to management.

Market Mechanisms to Deal with Expropriation

The unregulated market has essentially three methods for dealing with these expropriation activities. But each of these methods has costs and hence may well not be used to completely eliminate such expropriation. The first method is called *ex ante pricing* of expropriation. This means that those who expect to be expropriated charge a price when the contract is agreed upon which compensates them, ex ante, for the expropriation which they expect will take place in the future. For example, in the case of the stockholders who are expected to pay themselves excess dividends, the bondholders who anticipate that this will occur will be unwilling to pay a price for the debt of this firm which is as high as they would pay for an otherwise identical firm where the expropriation was not expected. That reduction in the price the debtholders will pay represents the charge demanded, ex ante, for the future expropriation. Once they have paid the price for this expropriation, the equityholders will be compelled to actually go through with the expropriation, so that this method of dealing with the problem does not curtail the expropriation itself. This method may work rather well when there is little ambiguity about the incentive of equityholders to actually expropriate—that is, when debtholders are able to perfectly anticipate the future expropriation—but if equityholders can estimate such expropriation opportunities better than debtholders, then ex ante pricing will only work imperfectly.

The second method the market uses to deal with expropriations is to include provisions in legal contracts which limit the ability of one party to expropriate the other. In the case of relations between equityholders and debtholders, such *covenants* would include restrictions on equityholders which limit the amount of dividends they can choose to pay themselves. Such restrictions are, in fact, often included in debt contracts. Unlike the method of ex ante pricing, these covenants are designed to actually prevent the expropriation from occurring rather than to seek compensation for it. The problem with covenants is that, as a rule, they involve costs which must be borne by the parties to the contract. The most obvious cost is that it is necessary to monitor the party whose action is restricted to make sure that the covenant is observed. In many instances these covenants may be quite complicated and therefore such monitoring can be quite expensive. A second cost is that the covenant may limit the flexibility of the restricted party in a way that is detrimental to that party's interests above and beyond the limits it places on his or her ability to expropriate. For example, covenants which restrict the amount of additional debt a firm may acquire may restrict a firm's ability to engage in a new and profitable investment which becomes available when the stock market is at a low point and additional equity financing is exceedingly expensive. If the firm has to finance in a poor equity market, it might find the investment to be unprofitable and, with a restriction requiring it to use at least some new equity, its flexibility is reduced. It is because of this kind of difficulty that debt agreements between corporations and private lenders such as banks and insurance companies are often renegotiated if the covenants begin to harm the borrower. But again, this renegotiation process is costly, so that the method of restricting expropriations with covenants cannot perfectly restrict all conceivable expropriations.

The final method utilized by the market for dealing with expropriations is referred to as *ex post settling up*. This might be thought of as the legal solution. It is really the opposite of ex ante pricing. It simply means that if an expropriation takes place, then the courts will be used to extract damages from the party who does the expropriating. If ex post settling up can work perfectly, then the incentive to expropriate is eliminated; but if there are costs or difficulties involved in such settling up, then at least some expropriation will take place, regardless. Returning to the example of the relationship between debtholders and equityholders in a firm, consider the problem of deciding when an expropriation has taken place due to a payment of excess dividends. The problem is that it is difficult to establish, in any objective manner, what is excessive and what is not. If the value of the securities owned by the debtholders goes down, they may claim it was because excess dividends were paid. But the equityholders may claim that it was because of some totally unrelated event. It is difficult, if not impossible, to establish who is correct in such cases. In addition to these kinds of difficulties, it is costly to use the courts. Legal expenses mean that there will always be room for some expropriation where the gains from litigation are not worth the cost.

Regulating the Terms of Contracts

The market's methods for dealing with expropriations are costly and complicated, even when parties to contracts are sophisticated and have a thorough understanding of how the market operates. But if some potential parties to financial contracts are what we might term unsophisticated or naive, then the opportunities for expropriation are enhanced. In contracts between representatives of corporations, the general presumption is made that parties are sophisticated or at least should be. But in contracts with consumers this is not the case. Consumers engage in financial contracts on a relatively infrequent basis and therefore do not often have the opportunity to learn the ways they may be expropriated and the methods they may use to protect themselves.

This possibility has provided a motivation for regulation which directly protects or helps the consumer to be self-protecting. The motivation for this kind of protection arises from what is called the *doctrine of conscionability*.[1] This legal doctrine holds that some contracts or actions by parties to contracts may be unjust, immoral, or unconscionable. From an economic viewpoint, this means that a relatively sophisticated party is attempting to take advantage of an unsophisticated party. The doctrine of conscionability leads to two general types of regulations. One type involves restrictions on the allowable contracts which are legally binding. This means that some contract provisions may be completely prohibited because they are viewed as unconscionable. The second type of regulation is to impose requirements of disclosure on the relatively sophisticated party which tend to educate or increase the sophistication of the unsophisticated party. Both of these are supplements to the methods utilized by the private market to deal with expropriation opportunities in contracts.

A number of regulations imposed by the government are designed to prevent unconscionable contracts. Some of these regulations directly restrict the types of contracts in which market participants may engage. In other cases, the regulations are designed to improve the access to information of all parties to contracts. There are a number of examples of each kind of regulation.

One example of a direct restriction on permissible contracts is provided by the limitations on the types of mortgage contracts which can be offered by savings and loans in the United States. These contracts are restricted by both state law and by federal regulators. Until very recently, mortgage contracts other than the standard mortgage, with an interest rate which is fixed for the life of the mortgage, were prohibited by regulation. While many regulators saw additional justifications for these restrictions apparently the principal motive was to protect consumers from mortgage contracts which they might not understand. This kind of protection has often been criticized as more paternalism than real protection, but it is difficult to identify an objective criterion for what amount of regulation may be appropriate in this domain. Another example of this kind of restriction is provided by usury ceilings. As discussed in Chapter Two, usury ceilings appear to be an outgrowth of the religiously motivated restrictions on interest rates prevalent in Europe in the Middle Ages. The idea is that there are interest rates that are so high that people should be prevented from agreeing to them even if they understand the contract and choose to agree to its terms.

[1] See Richard A. Epstein, "Unconscionability: A Critical Appraisal," *Journal of Law and Economics*, 18 (October 1975), pp. 302–320.

In recent years there has been a trend toward regulations which improve access to information rather than toward those which leave the uninformed in their unfortunate state, and restrict the kinds of contracts to which they are allowed to agree. Principal among these regulations is truth-in-lending. Significant truth-in-lending legislation was first adopted by the U.S. Congress in the early 1970s. Essentially, it requires that any firm which lends to consumers must comply with federal regulations regarding disclosure of the terms of the loan. In particular, the legislation requires that lenders present the true cost of the loan in a simple and understandable manner. This kind of legislation tends to limit the room for unconscionable contracts while still keeping paternalism to a minimum. The drawback, however, is that such disclosure is costly. Many economists argue that, in most instances, the market will generate the optimal amount of disclosure if left to its own devices. But where relatively uninformed consumers are involved, this argument may well be weak. Yet the opposite extreme, one of extensive disclosure requirements, is also socially suboptimal, for truth-in-lending legislation raises the cost of providing credit, and all borrowers bear that additional cost.

REGULATION AND THE CONCEPT OF AGENCY

A special but important case of the problem of expropriation discussed above is labeled the *problem of agency*. The idea of an agent applies to a wide variety of contractual relationships in our economy. Managers of firms are agents who make the decisions of the firm which are delegated to them by the stockholders. This applies to financial firms as well as nonfinancial firms. In an ideal world, agents would act in the best interest of those who hire them, without having to be induced to do so. But the world is often not ideal and the interests of agents often diverge from those of their employers. As a result, it is necessary for those who hire agents to devise mechanisms to induce them to behave as they should. Actually, it is hopeless to try to induce an agent to act against his or her own interest in the long run. The trick is to make the agent's interests coincide with the interests of his or her employer to as great an extent as possible. The difficulties involved in accomplishing this trick are what constitute the agency problem.

Sources of the Agency Problem

There are three sources of differences between the interests of agents and their employers. First, employers and agents have different attitudes toward the effort expended by managers. Employers view more effort on the part of their agents as unambiguously better in that it leads to higher returns or lower costs for the investment that the agent controls. The agent, on the other hand, sees the positive effect of effort that his or her employer sees, but also sees more effort as less leisure. The agent, therefore, wants to balance effort and leisure, while the employer derives no benefit from the agent's leisure.

The second source of difference, and probably the most important one for our purposes, pertains to information which the agent possesses about the investments he or she controls for his or her employers. Agents generally have better information about the value of the investments they manage than do owners, because they specialize in the acquisition of that information. Only if there were no barriers to disseminating that information to the market would this provide them with no particular advantage. But it is often necessary for managers to limit access to a considerable amount of information, generally to keep it away from the firm's competitors. But, once much information remains private, managers must then choose the investments of the firm without the owners being able to review or observe those choices. The problem facing the employers is to provide an incentive for managers not to withhold information, unless it is in the interest of the employers to do so, and then to use that information to the advantage of the employers. It is not obvious that the market has any effective way for resolving this problem.

The final source of difference between agents and their employers is essentially a problem of embezzlement. If agents observe the actual returns on an investment which they manage and are responsible for reporting that return to their employers, then they are provided with an opportunity to embezzle. They can report lower earnings than actually accrued and keep the difference for themselves. One impediment which deters such behavior, or presumably does, is the threat of criminal prosecution for theft. The other method utilized to prevent this problem is for the employers of agents to hire accountants to audit the agent's reported earnings and ensure that embezzlement does not occur. There is, of course, the question of the reliability of such auditors. They may also find embezzlement to be profitable. If the gain is large enough, there will always be an incentive to cheat so that no such inspection system can be perfect. But, in general, the smaller the gap in information between agents and employers, the smaller the incentive for embezzlement.

Regulating Agents

Regulation which deals with the problem of agency is principally designed to decrease the disparity in information between agents and those people they represent. This type of regulation is referred to as *disclosure regulation*. Like truth-in-lending, it requires managers of firms to disclose information to the capital markets about the value of their firms' investments.

Existing disclosure regulations come under the domain of the Securities and Exchange Commission (SEC). They can be divided into two basic kinds. One kind of regulation requires disclosure to the market of information about a firm and its investments through periodic filing of financial statements as well as in the form of a prospectus when securities are issued to the market. These rules apply to all companies with 500 stockholders or $1 million in assets. Hence, they apply to all but the smallest corporations in the United States. These disclosure restrictions are designed to provide a common basis of information for all current and potential owners of the firm's securities. The second kind of disclosure regulation is referred to as rule 10b-5 of the Securities and Exchange Commission. Rule 10b-5 requires that all managers of corporations or other insiders—that is, people with access to the managers' information—must disclose all trading in the stock of the firm they manage. This rule is designed to prevent managers, and those in whom they confide, from using their special or inside information to buy or sell the shares of their firm when they know something which the market does not. While it might be possible to restrict such trading altogether, the government has opted largely for disclosure rather than total restriction of trading.

In the years since 1934, when the Securities and Exchange Commission was created and this type of regulation was first implemented, there has been considerable debate as to whether disclosure regulation of this kind is actually needed. As in the case of truth-in-lending legislation, many argue that the market will disclose, on its own, an appropriate amount of information. Because generation and disclosure of information are costly, increased disclosure is not necessarily better. In the next chapter we will examine this debate about the need for the SEC's disclosure rules.

REGULATION TO LIMIT MARKET FAILURE

The prospect of a significant collapse of financial markets has been the prime mover behind regulation of financial markets in the United States for over 150 years. During most of this period, such concerns centered around the banking industry because banks were involved in almost all financial transactions in one way or another. The country simply did not have the highly diverse types of markets and financial institutions which exist today. The problem which plagued commercial banks throughout the nineteenth century and into the early decades of the twentieth century was the periodic occurrence of financial panics. That is, financial markets periodically experienced varying degrees of market failure.

As indicated early in the chapter, the market failure which occurred was not due to natural monopoly or externalities such as pollution. Instead, it was principally a result of the difference in information between those who owned and managed financial intermediaries and those who had deposits in those intermediaries. Though the panics and failures were due to problems arising from differences in information, markets did not fail exactly as the "lemons" parable suggests. That is, firms with valuable assets did not withdraw from the financial markets. Instead, depositors in possession of little information about the value of an intermediary's assets and fearing that their deposits would be lost, withdrew their funds from financial intermediaries and hoarded them. Once the withdrawal of deposits began, the stability of the financial intermediaries was threatened and the incentive to withdraw funds increased. This kind of panic could, and in the early 1930s did, lead to the breakdown of the entire system, or to market failure. In Chapter Seventeen we will look more closely at how and why these panics occurred.

The principal form of regulation which has evolved to deal with this problem involved a fundamental change in the nature of the financial contract to which individuals agree when they deal with a financial intermediary. The most important single feature of this regulatory system is insurance of deposits. Deposits with commercial banks and with savings and loans are now insured by the federal government up to a maximum of $100,000. This means that individual depositors at commercial banks need no longer fear that their funds will be misused when they are dealing with a financial institution which has vastly superior knowledge about financial markets and financial contracts. There is no longer a need to withdraw funds from a bank because of a distrust of the banker's incentive to act in the depositor's interest. The regulation imposed in the form of insurance means that the government guarantees the banker's performance so that the underlying problem which leads to market failure is, at least in part, eliminated.

If deposit insurance alone were the only form of regulation used to eliminate the prospect of failure in financial markets where intermediaries play a large role, then it would not be successful. The reason is that the insured depositor no longer has any incentive to collect information and evaluate the performance of the banker. In effect, the banker is no longer an agent of the depositor, but is now an agent of the government which provides the insurance. The government must now perform all the functions that any sophisticated private party would perform who has contracted with the financial intermediary. The government has to devise schemes to protect against expropriation and monitor the activities of the banker to see that his or her interests coincide with those of the government as much as possible. As we will discover in Chapter Seventeen most of the regulations imposed upon financial intermediaries are designed to accomplish these purposes.

In those financial markets which are not dominated by financial intermediaries, regulation designed to prevent market failure is much less extensive. This is true for two reasons. First, these markets tend to be ones where the social cost of market failure is less than it is in the markets dominated by intermediaries. Specifically, market failure involving the commercial banking system has historically threatened almost all markets in the country. This results from the fact that banks provide the mechanisms of payment, through demand deposits and cash, which are used throughout the economy. When the banking system is threatened, the viability of the entire system for exchanging all goods and services is also threatened. Second, financial intermediaries exist and prosper in financial markets where there is a useful role to be served by some kind of specialist. These services which intermediaries provide were discussed in Chapter Eleven. Most of these services involve some sort of collection and processing of information for the parties who want to borrow and lend. This means that, by its very nature, the intermediary comes to possess information which is not possessed by all the parties with which it deals. It is in precisely this kind of situation that there is the greatest potential for market failure. In those markets where differences in information are relatively slight, there is neither the need for a financial intermediary nor as significant a prospect that there will be substantial market failure. Therefore, by and large, market failure is a problem which pertains to financial intermediaries, and the regulations which seek to prevent it are regulations which are imposed upon financial intermediaries.

SUMMARY

In this chapter we have examined the rationale behind the regulation of financial markets. We began by surveying the reasons for regulation of any type of market, not just financial markets. We found that one reason for regulation is to limit monopolistic practices in a market and another is to supplant a competitive market when it would be subject to market failure if unregulated. There are three basic types of market failure. The first is natural monopoly. This occurs when there are economies of scale in an industry so that the natural form of organization for the market is a monopoly. The second is when a market has significant externalities which create a divergence between private and social cost in the industry. The third results when asymmetric information causes market participants to withdraw from the market. Much of the regulation which developed in the 1960s and 1970s was directed toward the problem of natural monopoly and externalities, such as pollution, health, and safety. But these problems are relatively insignificant in financial markets.

Financial markets are regulated for two principal reasons. First, much regulation is designed to limit monopolistic practices and promote competition. Second, regulation is directed at problems which result from asymmetries in information, the most serious of which is the prospect of virtual collapse or failure of financial markets. In this chapter we have examined each type of regulation, beginning with regulation to limit monopolistic practices.

Monopoly power in financial markets arises largely out of the potential for cartels to develop which control access to a market. In financial markets one of the principal entities which can function as a cartel is a trade association. To function as a cartel a trade association must be able to enforce rules which prevent individual members from cheating on the cartel. To be successful in the long run such rules generally require legal sanctions. Trade associations are common in financial markets, both in intermediated markets and in auction and over-the-counter markets. One which has been the subject of considerable attention is the New York Stock Exchange. This is because it is one of the oldest and largest auction markets in the country and because it has had practices which have been viewed as supportive of a cartel. One of these practices is the maintenance of minimum prices for brokerage services, but this practice is now restricted by the Securities and Exchange Commission. The SEC has the principal responsibility of regulating to prevent monopoly in auction and over-the-counter markets.

Problems in the distribution of information and the regulation to which they give rise can be broken down into three important categories. First, there is the general problem of expropriation between parties to a financial contract. The market has its own ways of dealing with expropriation, including ex ante pricing, restriction through protective covenants, and ex post settling up, but each of these approaches may be costly and imperfect. In cases where some parties to a transaction are unsophisticated or have inferior information, the market's methods for dealing with expropriation have been viewed as inadequate. This is often the case in financial contracts with consumers. Hence, the government has come to regulate the allowable terms of contracts and to require the disclosure of information to minimize the chances for expropriation.

The next problem which has led to substantial regulation is referred to as the problem of agency. An agent is someone who is employed to perform some action in the best interest of his or her employer. Managers of non-financial firms and of financial intermediaries are agents of the owners of those companies. The agency problem is the problem of inducing the agent to act in the owner's best interests or minimizing the differences between the interests of the agents and owners. These differences include different attitudes toward the effort of agents and differences in information possessed by agents and owners. The goal of regulation has been to reduce the differences in information and limit the conflicts which those differences may create. The principal approach to this issue has been to impose disclosure rules on agents and to define the legal responsibilities of agents to those whose interests they represent.

The last, and historically most serious problem arising from asymmetries in information has been the prospect that financial markets may virtually collapse. In the United States this largely took the form of banking panics where depositors at banks periodically withdrew their funds en masse. The principal form of regulation which has evolved to deal with this problem involves a fundamental change in the nature of the financial contract to which individuals agree when they deal with a financial intermediary. This change took place in 1933 when deposits at commercial banks became insured. The regulation later became extended to other financial intermediaries. This means that the depositor now has a contract with the government rather than merely with a private financial institution. With the change in the contract came a system of government supervision and control of risk, a system that is now the central feature of our regulatory system in intermediated financial markets. We will look closely at this system in Chapter Seventeen.

QUESTIONS TO IMPROVE UNDERSTANDING

1 Distinguish between perfect competition and monopoly. What is the purpose of a cartel? How does "anti-trust" deal with monopolies and cartels? Compare this with the way regulation is intended to influence cartels.

2 Explain what an externality is. How can an externality "cut both ways." How are externalities related to the concept of social cost?

3 In the simplest version of the so-called "lemons" problem, sellers of all high-quality assets immediately withdraw from the market and only the lowest quality assets are left. But this may well not happen directly and immediately in real-world markets. Explain why.

4 In any financial contract there may be methods for each party to try to do in or expropriate the other party. The unregulated marketplace has ways for dealing with this problem. What are they? Why are they not likely to stop such expropriation altogether?

5 How have financial markets been regulated to prevent market failure? Why is the regulation designed to prevent market failure oriented more toward inter-mediated financial markets than toward auction or over-the-counter markets?

6 Regulation can reduce the instances of so-called unconscionable contracts in two ways. Explain and evaluate them.

7 What is an "agent"? How does the marketplace, if left to its own devices, try to control the actions of agents? How is regulation used to influence agents?

8 Why are those who are strong advocates of the efficient markets hypothesis, particularly the strong form of the hypothesis, opposed to many regulations which are imposed upon financial markets?

REFERENCES

Akerlof, G.: "The Market for 'Lemons': Qualitative Uncertainty and the Market Mechanism," *Quarterly Journal of Economics*, 89 (August 1970), pp. 488–500.

Campbell, Tim S., and William A. Kracaw: "Information Production, Market Signalling, and the Theory of Financial Intermediation," *Journal of Finance*, 35 (September 1980), pp. 863–882.

Coase, Ronald H.: "The Problem of Social Cost," *Journal of Law and Economics*, 3 (October 1960), pp. 1–44.

Epstein, Richard A.: "Unconscionability: A Critical Appraisal," *Journal of Law and Economics*, 18 (October 1975), pp. 302–320.

Fama, Eugene F.: "The Effects of a Firm's Investment and Financing Decisions on the Welfare of its Security Holders," *American Economic Review*, 68 (June 1978), pp. 272–284.

————: "Agency Problems and the Theory of the Firm," *Journal of Political Economy*, 88 (April 1980), pp. 288–307.

————: "Banking in the Theory of Finance," *Journal of Monetary Economics*, 6 (June 1980), pp. 39–59.

Leland, Hayne: "Quacks, Lemons, and Licensing: A Theory of Minimum Quality Standards," *Journal of Political Economy*, 87 (December 1979), pp. 1328–1346.

Ross, Stephen: "The Economic Theory of Agency: The Principal's Problem," *The American Economic Review*, 63 (May 1973), pp. 134–139.

————: "Disclosure Regulation in Financial Markets: Implications of Modern Finance Theory," in F. P. Edwards (ed.), *Key Issues in Financial Regulations*, Columbia University Center for Law and Economic Studies, Columbia University, New York, 1978.

Smith, Clifford W., and Jerold B. Warner: "On Financial Contracting: An Analysis of Bond Covenants," *Journal of Financial Economics*, 7 (1979), pp. 117–161.

Chapter Sixteen

REGULATION OF
THE SECURITIES MARKETS

In this chapter we will examine the regulatory system which applies to auction and over-the-counter markets. A little less technical name for these markets is securities markets. The issues which we will address in this chapter are the ones which were raised in the last chapter. Specifically, we will examine how securities markets have been regulated to promote competition and limit monopolistic practices and to improve the distribution of information. While, as consumers, we do not all come in personal contact with securities markets, they are still extremely important to our economy. It is vital for all of us that they work efficiently and competitively and that the public perceive that these markets are fair. The regulatory system is intended to accomplish all of these goals. But it has met considerable criticism in recent years. In this chapter we will examine how the system works and we will evaluate some of the criticism.

In our investigation of the regulation of securities markets we will focus principally on the primary and secondary markets for corporate equities and bonds. This is because these markets have attracted the most attention from regulators and the more controversial issues pertain to these markets. We will not consider intermediated markets here, for these markets are the concern of the next three chapters. We will also leave the market for government securities largely untouched. The government has not found it necessary to impose extensive regulations on this market as an outside third party, probably because it is so intimately involved in these markets as a demander of funds. In effect, the government regulates as it participates in the market for government securities. But in many other auction and over-the-counter markets in the United States the government plays an active role as a regulator. In this chapter we will look closely at what that role is and how well that job is done.

OVERVIEW OF THE REGULATORY SYSTEM FOR SECURITIES MARKETS

In this section we will outline the structure of the regulatory system which governs securities markets in the United States. In addition, we will explore how this system came to be. The securities laws which govern auction and over-the-counter markets in the United States were written largely in 1933 and 1934. They have been amended since then, but have remained essentially intact. Probably the most important amendments are contained in the Securities Acts Amendments of 1975. And we will examine these laws, the events that led to them, and the regulatory institution they created.

But before we get involved in the historical development of the existing regulatory system for securities markets, we need to recall the basic rationale for regulation that was introduced in the last chapter. We learned in that chapter that there are four central problems which have led to regulation. These were summarized in Table 15-1. These four reasons for regulation are:

1 Promote competition and prevent monopolistic practices
2 Prevent or limit expropriations
3 Control the actions of agents
4 Prevent market failure

As we learned in Chapter Fifteen the last three of these purposes for regulation arise from problems in the distribution of information, while the first one arises from various factors which present opportunities for monopolies to form in auction and over-the-counter markets. We will use these four purposes as a checklist in this chapter. As we analyze the specific types of regulations which are imposed on securities markets, we will refer back to these basic problems so that the central reason for each particular regulation is clear. And when it is not clear that there is any good reason or when the reason is hotly disputed, we will try to take note of that as well. If you have read Chapter Fifteen carefully and understand the arguments behind each of these points, then the connection behind the rationale and each piece of regulation should be relatively easy to grasp. We will find that the big problems in securities markets, as opposed to intermediated markets, are items 1 and 3 on our checklist. In these markets the problem of market failure and the need to protect consumers from expropriations are much less important than they are in intermediated markets.

The Events Leading Up to the Securities Acts of 1933 and 1934

From the end of World War I until late 1929 the United States experienced tremendous prosperity. This was an unprecedented time in U.S. history. It was the period when laissez faire capitalism was at its pinnacle. Businesses and individuals were not only prosperous, they were also optimistic. That optimism was reflected in the performance of securities on the organized securities markets. The decade of the 1920s was an almost constant bull market. While the market experienced some short periods of retrenchment during the decade, it always rebounded very strongly. For example, the New York Stock Exchange experienced a decline during the first 3 months of 1928, but then, between April 1928 and September 1929, the Dow Jones index increased by nearly 50 percent.[1] But October 24, 1929, known as Black Thursday, was the beginning of the end. On that day the market began its now-famous collapse.

The collapse of the securities market and the Great Depression which followed were a puzzle at the time. No one knew precisely why these events occurred. Time has increased our understanding, but has by no means perfected it, for the underlying causes of the Great Depression and the appropriate measures to ensure that there will be no recurrence are still issues on which reasonable people differ. However, it became evident at the time and it is still evident today that a part of the cause of the collapse was the opportunity for abuse of the securities markets by those who had inside information or by those who sought to take advantage of less sophisticated parties. Whether the abuses which came to light after the crash were in fact one of its major causes can still be debated. But the crash did focus attention on these abuses and this ultimately led to an assortment of regulations governing almost every phase of the operation of securities markets.

It is fruitful to examine a few examples of the types of practices which took place on the exchanges during the 1920s. One of the most often cited abuses was a particular scheme to manipulate prices. This scheme is referred to as a pool. A pool is essentially a device to push up the price of a stock by disseminating false information about that stock. The pool gets its name because, in order to be successful, such ventures usually require the efforts of more than one party. Hence, individuals come together to pool their resources in such an effort. When a pool is formed the members try to acquire as many of the shares of some particular security as they can. The idea is to try to pay as low a price as possible for these shares, so it is desirable to keep

[1] See Robert Sobel, *The Big Board: A History of the New York Stock Market*, The Free Press, New York, 1965, p. 262.

the intentions and identity of the pool secret. Such purchases are usually facilitated by the dissemination of negative information about this security, whether that information is accurate or not. Once a large enough position in the stock has been acquired, then the whole process is reversed. Now the attempt is made to try to drive up the price of the stock. So favorable information and hot tips are distributed about the security. In addition, the members of the pool can sell back and forth to each other at high prices to make it look as though the market value of the stock is actually increasing. When the price has been driven up, then the members of the pool sell their holdings.

Anyone might try to operate such a pool. But the ability of the average investor to accomplish this sort of manipulation is quite limited. This may not be the case, however, if brokers or dealers get together to form a pool. They can be in a position to distribute information to the market which will have an appreciable effect on the prices of securities and they may also have the resources to support a successful pool. But because brokers are agents of the public, they also have a clear conflict of interest. When they engage in such activities, they are not acting in a way that tends to promote the efficient operation of the market and they are not acting in the interests of the customers who employ them. This is an example of problem 3 on our checklist.

A second abuse pertained to the distribution of information regarding new issues of securities. Insiders stood to make extraordinary profits and investors extraordinary losses if securities could be sold to the public based on false or inadequately disclosed information. The essence of the problem in this regard was that there was no standard for what constituted false information, no requirement for disclosure of all pertinent information, and essentially no legal recourse on the part of the investor for misinformation or inadequate information. Investigations conducted by the Federal Trade Commission of security distributions from utility corporations disclosed a number of instances of questionable practices of this kind.

A final example of the kinds of abuse which occurred at this time pertains to the provision of loans by banks and brokers to investors to fund the purchase of securities. Such loans are called *margin loans* or loans to purchase securities on margin. When the stock market crash occurred during 1929 a large volume of securities had been purchased on margin. This meant that when the prices of securities dropped, investors would face margin calls, and if they had no additional cash, would be compelled to sell their securities. To see what this means, suppose securities have been purchased at a price of $1,000. Suppose further that they are financed with $200 from the investor and $800 borrowed from a broker. If the market price falls below $800, the broker will demand the difference through what is called a *margin call*. If the owner cannot pay the difference, then the broker will sell the security. If many investors purchase securities on very high margins, then relatively small declines in market prices can lead to widespread margin calls. If those investors cannot produce the cash to cover the margin calls, then the brokers are forced to sell and this depresses market prices even further.

During the late 1920s a large number of investors financed their securities holdings with large amounts of borrowed funds. There were no explicit restrictions at the time on the portion of stock purchases which could be funded on margin accounts or through loans from a broker. In many cases, the actual proportion was quite large. The role of margin accounts in the crash is illuminated by the precipitous decline in the total volume of such margin loans beginning in October 1929. Loans from brokers to customers had risen to over $8.5 billion in 1929 and this actually represented only a part of all the leveraged funds used to purchase securities. Within 10 days after Black Thursday $3 billion of these loans had been wiped out through margin calls or other means. Then the Depression set in and by August 1932 total loans from brokers had dropped to $242 million.[2]

Shortly after Franklin Roosevelt became President, a subcommittee of the Senate Committee on Banking and Currency hired a man named Ferdinand Pecora as the committee's chief counsel and directed him to investigate abuses in the securities markets. The Pecora Committee, as it came to be called, was able to document 107 cases of pools on the New York Stock Exchange during 1929 alone, as well as a number of other abuses. The revelations of the Pecora Committee rival the revelations of the modern-day Watergate investigation in terms of the public attention and demand for reform to which they led. (And they did not even have television coverage.) It was in this time of economic instability, political change, and public desire for reform that the securities laws were drafted.

The Securities Acts of 1933 and 1934

The demand for reform of the securities markets precipitated by the crash of 1929 and the subsequent Depression led to the enactment of two extremely important pieces of legislation, the Securities Act of 1933 and the Securities Exchange Act of 1934. (It also led to the Banking Act of 1933, which we will discuss later.) The first act was followed shortly thereafter by the second act because of apparent omissions and inadequacies in the initial legislation. The contents of these acts define the regulations governing securities markets which still apply today. The Securities Exchange Commission (SEC) was also created in this legislation and given the power to administer most of the provisions of both acts. We will not be particularly concerned with identifying which law is responsible for what reform; instead, we will discuss the two acts together. In addition, where appropriate, we will examine some more recent changes or interpretations of the laws by the courts.

[2] See Irwin Friend and E. S. Herman, "The S.E.C. Through a Glass Darkly," *Journal of Business*, University of Chicago, 27 (October 1964), p. 389.

DISCLOSURE IN PRIMARY DISTRIBUTION   The principal purpose of the 1933 act was to require disclosure of information in primary distributions of securities. The principal vehicle used to accomplish this purpose is to require the issuers of new securities to file a registration statement with the SEC and issue a prospectus to the public. What goes into the prospectus is stipulated by the SEC. Essentially, it serves to acquaint the potential investor with all relevant information pertaining to the new issue. The law requires that the issuer must wait 20 days after the prospectus is filed before securities may be sold. During this waiting period the investment banker for the new issue may engage in predistribution solicitations, but actual sales may not take place. If the SEC has not notified the issuer of flaws in the registration statement within the 20-day period, then the issue may be sold. During this interval before SEC approval, it must be designated in red ink on the front of the prospectus that the SEC has yet to approve it. Such a prospectus is known as a *red herring*.

There are a number of exemptions from this registration procedure. A firm which issues less than $1.5 million per year in new securities is exempt. If the security is privately rather than publicly distributed, then it need not be registered. If the security is issued in exchange for outstanding stock in a merger, it is exempt. Finally, if the security is a debt instrument with a maturity shorter than 270 days, it is exempt. These exemptions are designed to minimize the burden of preparing registrations and yet still protect investors who might be unsophisticated.

DISCLOSURE FOR PUBLICLY TRADED FIRMS   The securities laws also require disclosure on a regular basis for firms which have publicly traded securities outstanding. Three types of financial statements must be filed with the SEC. The first is referred to as form 10k. This constitutes detailed balance sheets, income statements, and supporting documents which must be filed on an annual basis. Second, form 9k, which includes less detailed statements, must be filed semiannually. Third, a short report, form 8k, must be filed at the end of any month in which what the SEC calls "significant" events have occurred. These include such things as major changes in legal liability, changes in control of the corporation, or major changes in the value of assets. In 1964 these disclosure requirements were applied to all corporations with at least 500 stockholders or $1 million in assets. This includes most publicly held corporations in the United States.

SEC CONTROL OF SECONDARY MARKETS   The securities laws give the SEC the authority to regulate all organized exchanges for trading of securities, such as the NYSE. The SEC has the authority to set rules governing conduct of brokers and dealers on the exchange and to disapprove the rules of any association of brokers or dealers. It can take legal action against members of the exchange and it has the authority to close down any exchange if it chooses. This authority has led to a large number of specific rules governing conduct on the major exchanges.

MARGIN REQUIREMENTS   The securities laws gave the Federal Reserve the authority to regulate margin loans extended by brokers, dealers, and commercial banks. The Federal Reserve rather than the SEC was given this authority because it was believed that this was more closely tied to its general responsibility for regulating the supply of money and credit than to the responsibilities of the SEC. The Federal Reserve sets margin requirements through its regulations T and U. These requirements are altered by the Federal Reserve from time to time, but generally remain between 50 and 80 percent. This means, for example, that if the margin requirement is 75 percent, then the maximum amount of funds that can be borrowed to support securities purchases is 25 percent of the value of the securities.

INSIDER ACTIVITIES   The securities laws take the position that those endowed with inside information about the value of publicly traded securities should not personally profit from that information at the expense of the general public and the existing owners of the corporation. The procedure used to limit such opportunities is to require disclosure not of the inside information itself but of the investments of those who have access to such information. The SEC also prohibits short selling by insiders and it has the authority to sue corporate officials who it believes have used inside information to acquire personal profits at the expense of the company's owners and the investing public. The SEC has utilized this authority and, through the courts, it has clarified what practices are permitted and what are not. The principal such clarification was provided in the early 1960s in the Texas Gulf Sulphur Case. This involved a case where Texas Gulf located an exceptionally valuable mineral deposit. Information about the deposit was not distributed to the general public, largely to prevent competitors from acquiring property which was adjacent to the site. However, during the period that the information about the discovery remained confidential, a number of employees of Texas Gulf purchased stock at what turned out to be bargain prices. The courts held that such trading was fraudulent and that it inflicted damages on those who sold to the employees with inside information.

CORPORATE GOVERNANCE   A closely related realm of responsibility pertains to the SEC's authority to determine the system of corporate governance. By this it is meant the methods by which boards of directors supervise the activities of the corporation for shareholders and the accountability of those directors. The SEC has established rules to govern the solicitations of votes of shareholders, or proxies, to be exercised during shareholders' meetings. The purpose of these rules has been to make the process of governance of corporations as democratic as possible. In addition, the SEC encourages the use of outside members for boards of directors. This is a portion of the SEC's responsibility which is evolving rapidly at this time.

ANTIFRAUD REGULATION   The securities laws stipulate that certain practices, which were believed to be common during the 1920s, are illegal. These include such things as dissemination of fraudulent information, as well as various schemes to manipulate prices, such as pools. Furthermore, the courts have interpreted these antifraud provisions such that it is not always necessary to prove fraudulent intent under the law. Instead, the courts have held that when securities are distributed, all persons responsible for that information, including accountants and underwriters, must exercise "due diligence" in determining that the information is factual. If they do not, they are liable.

REGULATION OF INVESTMENT COMPANIES   The SEC has been given the authority to exercise almost complete control over investment companies and investment advisors. Investment companies are firms which are organized to manage investments for individuals. In this instance, a system of disclosure was not deemed adequate to protect against conflict of interest or fraud. The SEC has long supervised every aspect of this business. This power was not granted in the original securities acts but was conferred in two laws passed in 1940, the Investment Company Act and the Investment Advisor Act.

SEPARATION OF COMMERCIAL AND INVESTMENT BANKING   A final aspect of the regulatory system for securities markets, which was not a part of the securities acts of 1933 and 1934, is the requirement that commercial banks and investment banks must be separate. This requirement was a part of the Banking Act of 1933. Prior to this time, commercial banks and investment banks were often divisions of the same firms. This created a potential conflict in that the investment banker could sell securities to his or her own bank—in effect, to depositors. Because the investment banker acted as both an agent for the firm distributing securities and for the depositors who supplied funds, there was a clear potential for conflict of interest. To remedy this, the Banking Act of 1933 required all commercial banks to divest themselves of their investment banking operations.

Reform of the Securities Markets in the 1970s

The securities laws, particularly the rules governing organized exchanges, stayed largely intact from the 1930s until the 1970s. But by the early 1970s some major changes had taken place in the secondary market for corporate securities which led to major changes in the regulation of this market. The most important development was the withdrawal of individual investors from direct participation in the equity market and the growth of institutional participation in the market (see Chapter Twelve for some details). Through-out the 1960s more and more individuals channeled their investments to-ward institutions, particularly pension funds, and diminished their direct participation in the market. This led to a significant increase in the portion of trading volume on the exchanges which involved institutions rather than individuals. For example, by the mid-1970s the proportion of total trading volume on the New York Stock Exchange which involved institutions reached 60 percent. This meant that an increasing portion of all trades were what are called block trades. Such trades involve large blocks of stock, usu-ally in excess of 10,000 shares. Block trades represented less than 5 percent of total volume in the early 1960s, but approached 25 percent of total volume by the late 1970s.

With the rise in importance of institutional investors in the market came increased pressure for competition in the pricing of brokers' services. His-torically, the NYSE has been governed by a number of rules, sanctioned by the SEC, which tended to inhibit direct price competition by brokers. One such rule stipulated minimum commissions which could be charged by member brokers of the NYSE. In effect this allowed the NYSE to function as a cartel. This is an example of item number 1 on the checklist at the beginning of the chapter. Other rules tended to limit the entry of new brokers onto the Exchange and to inhibit the ability of member brokers to try to conduct exchanges off the NYSE. For example, NYSE Rule 394 prohibited members of the NYSE from sending orders off the Exchange to be traded elsewhere. All of these rules were subject to some criticism prior to the growth of institutional participation in the market. But institutions which traded in blocks were in a better position than individuals to search for low-cost means of conducting exchanges. As a result, the increased growth of institu-tions put increased pressure on the rules governing brokers which were enforced by the NYSE.

Institutional investors sought a number of routes around the rules of the NYSE. For instance, brokers increasingly offered a variety of services to institutions to attract their business because they couldn't compete with prices. In addition, many of the institutions set up their own brokerage facility in one of the regional exchanges. In some cases, these brokers han-dled the transactions of the institution. In other cases, they handled business for a broker who was a member of the NYSE in exchange for handling trades of their parent institution on the NYSE. Another method was to move trades to the so-called "third market." The third market was formed by a group of brokers who were not members of the NYSE in order to trade NYSE-listed securities off the exchange. They competed directly with the NYSE and without minimum commissions for conducting trades.

All of these actions to circumvent the rules of the NYSE led to fragmen-tation of the secondary market in corporate securities. Such fragmentation tended to change a highly centralized auction market into a collection of over-the-counter markets. It also tended to decrease public access to the prices at which assets were trading and generally to increase the cost of conducting transactions; that is, the cost that would have been incurred were the Exchange not subject to rules limiting competition.

These developments led to reactions on the part of the regulators and the Congress which ultimately led to major changes in the rules under which the NYSE operates. Moreover, these changes have by no means completely run their course. One of the first events which seriously threatened the NYSE rules was a challenge to the practice of minimum commissions which was brought by the Justice Department. In 1968, when the NYSE made a relatively routine request for the SEC's approval of an increase in the level of minimum commissions, the Justice Department challenged this practice as illegal under the antitrust laws. This and other events prompted the SEC to open an intensive investigation of this practice and of the broader problem of institutional investors in the secondary market for corporate securities. The SEC's study, known as the Institutional Investor Study, was one of the most important major investigations of the securities industry ever undertaken. It was submitted to Congress and published in 1971.[3] After some consideration the SEC ruled in 1975 that minimum commissions would no longer be permitted. This prohibition became effective on May 1, 1975, known as "May Day" on Wall Street.

Later in 1975 the Congress passed what is probably the most significant securities legislation since the original acts of 1933 and 1934. These regulations were intended to increase competition in the securities markets. The Securities Acts Amendments of 1975 made fixed minimum commissions illegal. It also mandated that the SEC facilitate the development of a National Market System. The National Market System is intended to be an auction market for all outstanding securities which can feasibly be included. It is to be an automated system, with public access, linking all markets throughout the country. The exact design of such a system was not specified in the 1975 legislation. Rather the legislation is a statement of intent and a mandate to the SEC to see that this intent is carried out. The SEC is currently studying and moving in the direction of such a National Market System.

The auction and dealer markets for securities in the United States have undergone tremendous changes in recent years. In part this is due to advances in technology which have made new methods for conducting exchanges possible. And in part it is because of changes in the composition of those who trade securities as well as changes in the attitudes of regulators. It is unlikely that these changes will stop or even slow down appreciably. With some sense of the evolution of the regulatory process in hand, we can examine some of the more controversial issues regarding the effectiveness of the regulatory system.

[3] See *Institutional Investor Study, Report of the Securities and Exchange Commission*, 92d Congress, 1st Session, House Document No. 92-64, 1971.

PROMOTING COMPETITION IN SECURITIES MARKETS

In this section we will examine the two principal issues of the last decade which affect the extent of competition in the secondary market for corporate securities. First, we will examine the impact of the elimination of fixed minimum commissions on the NYSE. Then we will explore the possible forms which a National Market System might take.

The Impact of Eliminating Minimum Brokerage Commissions

Those who advocated that minimum brokerage commissions should be abolished argued that the NYSE functioned as a cartel. The essential features of the cartel were that it limited entry to the Exchange, fixed prices for utilizing the Exchange, and compelled its members to trade only on the Exchange all securities listed on the Exchange. In any cartel there is an incentive for members to break price-fixing agreements or cheat on the cartel. Because of this, a cartel is generally unstable unless a strong mechanism for enforcement of its rules can be devised. In the case of the NYSE, the ultimate method of enforcement was to deny a brokerage firm membership in the NYSE if it did not observe the Exchange's rules. Because the SEC had long agreed to these rules, the Exchange had the legal authority to enforce its restrictions. Hence, it had most of the prerequisites of an effective cartel. But a cartel also requires that it be able to prevent effective competition from competitors outside the cartel. In this case, such competition came from regional exchanges and brokerage houses which were not members of the NYSE and traded in the so-called third market. The difficulty facing the third market was that there were sufficient economies inherent in operating a single, large exchange that the NYSE could operate at lower cost than potential competitors which were considerably smaller. With large size come fewer trading imbalances and greater liquidity and because many of the costs of the market are fixed costs, it is desirable to spread them over larger volume. Therefore, the opponents of fixed commissions argued that, in order to ensure a competitive securities market, it was important to eliminate the ability of the Exchange to enforce fixed commissions.

In the debate which developed about fixed commissions the NYSE maintained that they were a necessary part of a healthy stock exchange. To support their case they made essentially two arguments. The first was that without fixed commissions there would be a reduced incentive for membership in the Exchange, leading to its gradual disintegration. In effect, they argued that it was important to the economy to have a single central exchange. Moreover, an essential part of the nature of the Exchange was as a brokerage industry with a number of prosperous firms which had an incentive to behave reliably and honestly. If membership were not valued, the Exchange itself would disintegrate and so would the security and reliability of the market. The second argument was that competitive commission rates would lead to a large degree of consolidation in the brokerage industry, with a few large firms dominating the market. Here they argued that the economies in the industry were sufficiently substantial that if price competition were permitted, most brokerage firms would be driven out. Their argument was essentially that the brokerage industry was a natural monopoly and that, because of this, prices needed to be regulated, with a price floor enforced by the NYSE.

We already know that the NYSE lost the debate. But in addition, the historical record since 1975 seems to add additional evidence against the NYSE's case. First of all, it is important to see what the actual reduction in commissions amounted to after the May Day change. There is no doubt that elimination of fixed commissions has led to a significant reduction in the cost of buying and selling securities, particularly for the large institutional investors who can negotiate lower prices for higher volume. In its 1978 annual report the SEC assessed the impact on prices of the May Day change as of the end of September 1978. It reported that:

> . . . individual investors' effective commission rates when measured as a percent of principal value declined 13.9 percent. Institutional customers, due to their larger average order size and greater bargaining power, have negotiated discounts averaging 48.8 percent from the exchange prescribed minimum rates.[4]

The evidence suggests that the NYSE's role as the principal marketplace for trading equities has been maintained. The demise of fixed commissions has led to neither a decline in the amount of trading on the floor of the Exchange, nor in the proportion of all stocks traded which this represents. Furthermore, there has been no noticeable decline in the membership on the NYSE and only a slight decline in the total number of members engaged in brokerage business with the public, from 413 at the beginning of 1975 to 361 at the end of 1978.

The evidence also shows no significant consolidation of the brokerage industry, with a few large firms emerging in a dominant position. This does not mean that brokerage firms were unaffected by the change, but the effect depended largely on the extent to which they served institutional rather than individual investors. Some firms which did a large portion of their business with institutions merged with more diversified firms. In addition, a group of so-called discount brokers entered the industry. In a review of the impact of the elimination of fixed commissions on the brokerage industry published at the end of 1979, Seha Tinic and Richard West conclude:

> To be sure, national full-line firms and institutional brokerage firms have increased their aggregate shares of commission business, gross revenue, and net pretax income during 1976–1978. But even more dramatic gains have been made

[4] See *Securities and Exchange Commission Annual Report*, Washington, D.C., 1978, p. 7.

by regional firms which primarily conduct an agency business. The securities commission revenues and pretax incomes of regional firms have increased at substantially higher rates than any other class of NYSE brokerage firms.

Data recently released by the SEC also show that discount brokers are 'proving to be one of the most profitable and fastest growing segments of the brokerage industry.' At the end of 1978 there were at least 55 discounters in business, 20 of which were started after the demise of fixed rates. Overall, their profit rates for 1978 were superior to those of NYSE member firms as a whole. Clearly, then, the brokerage industry has not been one in which economies of scale have dictated that under competitive pricing, the largest four or five firms, or a particular group of firms, would grow inexorably at the expense of the rest.[5]

It now appears highly probable that competitive commission rates will be a permanent aspect of the securities industry.

The National Market System

Of even greater potential importance for the operation of securities markets is the prospect that a National Market System (NMS) for securities will emerge. The Securities Acts Amendments of 1975 mandated that the Securities and Exchange Commission should move as directly as possible to develop and implement such a system. This was motivated by a desire to ensure the most competitive type of financial markets possible, that is, point 1 on our checklist. The idea behind a National Market System is to bring into existence a central computerized system for recording and executing all transactions in publicly available securities. It is not clear at this juncture exactly what features of the present system of trading securities would be retained and what would be replaced if and when a National Market System is placed in operation. But it is certain that such a system would drastically alter the structure and probably significantly improve the performance of the industry. Essentially, what is involved in such a system is some kind of consolidation of all the regional and national stock exchanges as well as the over-the-counter market. All brokers would be given the right to access this market, which would encourage additional competition in the industry.

Some progress has already been made in implementing the system. The initial step was to make available a composite list of price quotations, drawing on the national and regional exchanges as well as the over-the-counter market. This information has been printed in the daily press since 1976. The second step was to develop a consolidated system for price quotations so that all brokers have the same list of prices and they do not have to hunt for price quotes on the floor of an exchange. Considerable progress has been made on this issue in the last few years. The final step is to develop a system

[5] See Seha M. Tinic and Richard R. West, "The Securities Industry Under Negotiated Brokerage Commissions: Changes in the Structure and Performance of New York Stock Exchange Member Firms," *Bell Journal of Economics*, 11 (Spring 1980), pp. 34–35.

that records all orders for purchases and sales of securities and to develop regulations relating to the disclosure of these orders. Little real progress had been made on this final step by the end of the 1970s.

As currently envisaged, the NMS can take one of two possible forms. One form involves separate display of prices and execution of transactions, and functions essentially as a communication link between separate exchanges. We will refer to this as the Intermarket Trading System (ITS). The other form involves a single integrated system for recording orders and executing transactions without regard for physical location. This plan leaves less room for a meaningful role for separate exchanges. A system of this kind began operation on the Cincinnati Stock Exchange as an experiment in early 1978. As a result, this system is often labeled CSE.

The NYSE and many of the other exchanges have come out in favor of an ITS. One apparent reason for their stand is that this system preserves the separate exchanges as meaningful trading centers. This system would work very much like the automated system in the secondary market in government securities discussed in Chapter Fourteen. One component of the system is an automated display capability for bid and ask prices. This mechanism would display for anyone to observe all offers to buy and sell arriving in the system. A separate automated mechanism would handle actual orders. The initial version of this system operating on the NYSE in 1978 and 1979 allowed a broker on a particular exchange to check to see if a price available on his or her exchange was the best in the system. If it was not, he or she could use the system to trade on the exchange with the best available price.

One potential pitfall with this kind of system involves what are known as limit orders. *Limit orders* are orders from a customer to a broker to buy or sell a stock at a maximum or minimum price. For example, a customer might stipulate that a broker should sell a stock when the price rises to $50 per share. The difficulty here is that the SEC has proposed that the NMS incorporate nationwide protection of limit orders. This means that, for example, if a limit order to sell at $50 is given a broker on one exchange, the order should be executed when the stock rises to $50 per share on any exchange where it is traded, not merely the one where the broker is initially located. If brokers kept those limit orders themselves and watched the display terminal to see when anyone on any exchange was quoting a $50 price, this might work effectively. But traditionally those limit orders have gone to dealers on the floor of the exchange who handle their execution and the dealers' limit orders have not generally been public knowledge. These dealers pay attention only to their exchange and, hence, cannot execute limit orders on a nationwide priority. As a result, it is necessary to change that part of the dealer system and in some manner record all limit orders to be executed based on priority of price and time of arrival on the system.

It appears that the CSE system is inherently more capable of accomplishing this objective. In the experimental CSE system there is a central computerized system which records all bid and ask prices and automatically arranges transactions based on the priorities given to the system. The priorities which govern trades are that purchases are made at the lowest price offered and sales at the highest and if prices are equal, then priority is given to time of entry. Anyone can purchase access to the system from anywhere in the country and need never actually be present at the exchange. This kind of system can potentially carry all limit orders in the automated system and execute them in any priority. In addition, it provides a ready method of verifying transactions to ensure observance of SEC rules and regulations.

One thing which is left unclear if a CSE system were implemented for all the exchanges is the role of dealers in such a market. Traditionally dealers on the NYSE have derived a significant portion of their revenue from handling limit orders. If this function were automated, it is not clear whether there would arise some other specialized function which would supplant this service. If it did not, the dealer's actual role in the market might be reduced to that of purely providing liquidity or absorbing temporary imbalances between supply and demand.

Probably even more fundamental is the future role of the separate exchanges themselves. Traditionally the central exchange offered the advantage of a single facility where brokers could meet for face-to-face auction of securities. If the face-to-face nature of the auction becomes obsolete, then so too may the concept of an exchange tied to any single location.

REGULATING THE DISTRIBUTION OF INFORMATION

The other important area of responsibility given to the SEC in the securities laws, aside from the task of regulating the exchanges and promoting competition, is to prevent the kinds of abuses which occurred prior to 1934. Most of these arise from problems pertaining to access to information. To deal with these problems the SEC has attempted to minimize the potential for conflict of interest arising from the agency problems discussed in the last chapter. Of all of these functions, probably the one that has aroused the most controversy, at least in economic circles, is the attempt to improve the distribution of information, or disclosure regulation. In this section we will examine the pros and cons of regulations designed to compel the manager-agents of corporations to disclose financial information. Then we will examine various controversial issues surrounding regulation to limit conflicts of interest between agents and owners of firms.

Is Disclosure Regulation a Good Thing?

One of the principal forms of regulation imposed upon securities markets by the SEC is the requirement that corporations disclose a wide variety of information to the public. Though these disclosure requirements date back to the Securities Exchange Act of 1934, during much of the 1960s and 1970s there was considerable sentiment for tightening of these disclosure requirements. It is easy to get the impression that without government mandated disclosure requirements there would be tremendous secrecy. But it is by no means obvious that this is true. Prior to the enactment of the 1934 act, a considerable amount of information was disseminated to the market by managers of firms with publicly traded securities. Moreover, it is almost certain that if the disclosure laws were repealed, there would still be considerable voluntary disclosure of information to the market. And it is also evident that required disclosure is costly. Real resources are expended by all the firms which must comply with the SEC regulations and by the SEC itself to enforce these disclosure requirements. The question therefore arises as to whether required disclosure actually contributes in any significant way to the successful operation of the market. There are powerful arguments and considerable statistical evidence on both sides of this question.

Over the years a number of economists have attracted attention as critics of the SEC's disclosure regulations. But in recent years one of the most cogent cases against disclosure has been made by George Benston.[6] Because he has become one of the most well-known critics of disclosure we will closely examine the criticisms he offers and a rebuttal to his charges by some other well-known observers of the system. The essence of his position is that, since 1934, required disclosure has led to no measurable increase in the efficiency of financial markets. In effect he argues that competitive markets are efficient on their own, so that required disclosure adds nothing. And because required disclosure is costly, it is best to eliminate or substantially reduce the requirements. Benston has been criticized, particularly by Irwin Friend and Randolph Westerfield,[7] both for the strength of his case concerning market efficiency and for the fact that he is unable to satisfactorily examine what they contend is probably the most important justification for the disclosure legislation. It is fruitful to examine these issues fairly closely.

Benston's criticism of disclosure requirements hinges on the idea that the information which is disclosed must be perceived as valuable by the market as a whole. This means that the disclosed information must be information which is new and valuable to the market. The operational criteria for determining whether information is new and valuable is to determine whether the disclosure leads to observable and significant changes in the prices of the securities to which that information pertains. The bulk of Benston's case is devoted to the collection and assessment of evidence as to whether such a cause and effect relationship can be established between required disclosure and the observed prices of securities.

[6] See George J. Benston, "Required Disclosure and the Stock Market: An Evaluation of the Securities Exchange Act of 1934," *American Economic Review*, 63 (March 1973), pp. 132–155.
[7] See Irwin Friend and Randolph Westerfield, "Required Disclosure and the Stock Market: Comment," *American Economic Review*, 65 (June 1975), pp. 467–477.

Benston uses three approaches to do this. The first approach is to select some time interval since the implementation of required disclosure and collect data on the prices of securities as well as the financial data which were disclosed according to SEC requirements over this time interval. In addition, he attempts to account for other factors which would affect the prices of these securities during the period, such as general market conditions and unanticipated changes in dividends. With these factors accounted for, the next step is to determine whether there is any significant statistical relationship between the disclosure and the prices of the securities in the sample. Benston conducts such a test for the year of 1964 and reviews other researchers' tests of the same proposition. He concludes that there is no economically significant impact of disclosure.

Friend and Westerfield criticize Benston both for apparent shortcomings in his procedure and for the conclusion he draws from the evidence. Criticism of methodology aside, Friend and Westerfield argue:

> He in effect considers not too relevant for stock prices knowledge about changes in financial variables, in spite of the fact that he finds an increase of 100 percent in the annual rate of net sales is associated with an increase in price of 10.4 percent in the month of the announcement, and that changes in other variables are also associated with significant though proportionally smaller changes in price.[8]

Thus, the important disagreement hinges on what constitutes an economically significant effect of disclosure. While it seems inappropriate to totally dismiss the effect cited by Friend and Westerfield, it does not seem overwhelming. If this is the case upon which required disclosure regulation rests, it seems a weak case indeed.

Next Benston argues that his first test may understate the impact of disclosure for the following reason:

> It is often claimed that the detailed reports required by the SEC are more useful to trained analysts than to the ordinary stockholder. The analyst then passes on his information to his clients, or, in any event, trades on the information, thereby bringing its effect to the market. But does it get there by means of the financial reports required by the SEC?[9]

Benston reviews the studies of a number of researchers who have investigated the ability of analysts to make use of special information. Again, he concludes that information disclosed through the SEC is of no real value to the analysts and therefore to the market.

Benston pursues an additional avenue to test the impact of required disclosure and it is based on the following potential flaw which he sees in his first two tests:

[8] Ibid., p. 468.
[9] Benston, op. cit., p. 140.

Even though the evidence reviewed does indicate that the financial reports re-quired by the SEC, when made available, have almost no information content, this does not prove that the required disclosure is not valuable to investors. One might argue that the statements provide a confirmation of data previously re-leased. Because investors know that a corporation's sales, operating expenses, extraordinary gains and losses, assets and liabilities will be reported, they may have some assurance that the preliminary reports, press releases, etc., are not prevarications. Thus when the financial statements are made public the data they contain are fully anticipated. But had it not been for the SEC's disclosure requirements, such a state of affairs might not exist. [10]

In order to account for this possibility, Benston turns to an examination of the actual impact on the prices of securities of the initial 1934 enactment of the legislation requiring disclosure. He collected data on the prices of a sample of securities for a period prior to and after the date the legislation went into effect and concludes, again, that required disclosure had no ob-servable impact on the prices of securities traded in 1934.

The most telling criticism of these conclusions which Friend and West-erfield have to offer pertains more to the issues which Benston was not able to test than to any specific problems pertaining to the tests which he did conduct. His tests did not pertain to what these authors refer to as the "fair-ness" of the market as between the public and insiders. Their concept of fairness is close, if not identical, to the concept of asymmetric information discussed throughout this chapter. They argue that prior to the enactment of required disclosure, there were numerous opportunities for relatively well-informed insiders to take advantage of less well-informed investors. This allegedly led to numerous instances of actual expropriation or fraud and to a perception by investors that insiders had special information which pro-vided them with an advantage in the market. They further argue that the instances of these kinds of abuse and presumably therefore the potential for such abuse were reduced by required disclosure.

Benston's response to this criticism highlights one of the most pressing difficulties facing those who are concerned with the efficiency and fairness of our regulatory system. His response is that their criticism is based on their *impressions* drawn from conversations with people in the industry and their reading of the historical record. He retorts:

I have reviewed most of the cited materials and have found no more than anec-dotes and assertions . . . . Apparently we both have formed very different im-pressions based upon roughly the same 'evidence.' [11]

---

[10] Ibid., p. 141.

[11] See George J. Benston, "Required Disclosure and the Stock Market: Rejoiner," *American Economic Review*, 65 (June 1975), p. 476.

The inherent difficulty is that, at this juncture, the issue which Friend and Westerfield raise is exceedingly difficult to test in the scientific manner in which Benston's tests were conducted. But decisions about the extent of regulation must be made, with or without such tests. And the consensus judgment of those with responsibility for that regulation seems to have been in support of the position taken by Friend and Westerfield.

How Much Should We Limit Potential Conflicts of Interest?

One of the important purposes of the securities laws is to limit the instances where there can arise significant conflicts of interest. Conflicts of interest are the essence of the problem of agency discussed in the last chapter (point 3 in our checklist). An agent is someone who is employed to work in the best interests of another party. A conflict of interest develops when either the interests of the agent and his or her employer diverge, or when there are simultaneous agency relationships such that the interests of the parties who are employing an agent are in conflict. The securities laws have created different regulatory solutions for different cases of conflict of interest. In some instances the method employed has been to require disclosure so that the market can be fully informed about the actions of an agent who may face conflicts. In other cases the securities laws have simply eliminated simultaneous conflicting agency relationships altogether.

THE SEPARATION OF COMMERCIAL AND INVESTMENT BANKING   From an historical standpoint, one of the greatest conflicts of interest has been between commercial and investment bankers. Commercial bankers provide loans to corporate customers and often receive special or inside information as a part of the loan relationship. The majority of the funds for most commercial banks comes from various deposit accounts. As a result, the banker acts as the agent of the depositors who supply funds for business loans. On the other hand, investment bankers are dealers in the primary market for corporate securities. As such, they act as the distributors of new corporate debt and equity securities. Their principal responsibility is to the corporations whose securities they distribute. Moreover, they generally purchase these securities from the issuing company and then bear the risk involved in distributing them to the market. Conflict arises when the same company operates both as a commercial bank and an investment bank. If an investment banker who experiences difficulty in distributing securities to the market is also a commercial banker, there is a great temptation to eliminate the difficulty in distribution by purchasing the securities for the commercial bank. In effect, the investment banker would have sold the securities to the depositors.

In order to eliminate the opportunities for such conflicts, Congress passed the Banking Act of 1933, which mandated that henceforth no company would be allowed to engage in both types of business.[12] This led to a major change in the commercial banking industry and primary securities markets as they then existed. Most companies chose to stay with their major line of business and close down or sell off their secondary line. For example, the First National Bank of Boston created a separate entity known as the First Boston Corporation, which remains active as a major investment banker. The bank founded by J. P. Morgan eventually broke into separate organizations now known as Morgan Guaranty and the investment banking firm of Morgan Stanley. Since 1934 the SEC and the bank regulators have devised an additional set of rules to enforce a separation between commercial banking and the sales distribution of marketable securities.

The Banking Act of 1933 and the separation it created between commercial and investment banking has probably become more controversial in the 1970s than in any period since its inception. Neither commercial banking nor investment banking are quite the same industries they were in the 1930s. Commercial banks now provide a wide variety of services both for corporations and consumers which did not exist in the 1930s. At one time commercial banks were unique in that they were the principal institutions which offered demand and savings deposits. These deposits were perceived by individuals and by the regulators as distinctly different from the more risky investments which individuals might make in marketable securities. Hence, it was possible to create a real separation between these distinct types of investments and the institutions that offered them. But as time has passed these distinctions have blurred. In today's financial market brokerage houses which deal in the secondary markets for securities also function as investment bankers and offer securities to consumers in the form of money market mutual funds and other accounts which are exceedingly close to demand deposits. At the same time, the large national commercial banks are continually seeking expanded authority to manage investments in securities traded on organized markets and to provide a wide variety of services to corporations which come very close to being those offered by an investment banker. Therefore, competition and innovation in the financial markets has made this separation, which was once fairly clear and real, more and more difficult to both rationalize and enforce.

As they currently exist the rules which restrict commercial bank activities in the securities markets sometimes draw some very fine distinctions. It is useful to consider at least one example. Banks are not permitted to act as brokers in any corporate securities traded in over-the-counter markets or on an organized exchange. However, under certain circumstances, they may, for customers, place orders for such securities with brokers, but they cannot act as brokers themselves. The brokerage houses contend that banks provide

---

[12] This act is also popularly referred to as the Glass-Steagall Act. However, a less important piece of legislation passed in February 1932 is actually more accurately characterized with this name. While Senator Glass and Congressman Steagall had a principal role in both pieces of legislation, we will refer to the 1933 act as the Banking Act of 1933.

investment services normally provided by brokers and that this is unfair competition. The brokerage houses argue that they should also be allowed to offer services normally reserved for commercial banks. These distinctions are difficult enough to rationalize now, but as a National Market System becomes more of a reality, this kind of distinction may be hard to maintain.

In the years ahead it is likely that commercial banks and firms that function as securities brokers and investment bankers will be granted increased powers to offer services which were previously denied them. Some of this seems inevitable in view of the market forces which are moving toward decreased fragmentation in all financial markets. But with all these changes, the original restriction contained in the Banking Act of 1933, which prohibits commercial banks from acting as underwriters who bear the risk of primary distributions, is likely to remain intact. As brokerage houses invade the deposit market with various types of funds, the more interesting question may be whether the restrictions which they will face will be closer to those under which commercial banks have traditionally operated.

REGULATING THE USE OF CONFIDENTIAL INFORMATION A second source of conflict of interest in the securities markets pertains to the use of confidential information or inside information. The facts that such inside information exists and that its confidentiality is often valuable to the corporation, create potential conflicts. The conflicts center on the use of such information for personal gain by those who possess it. The principal restriction imposed by the regulators to deal with this conflict is the SEC's disclosure rule (rule 10b-5), which requires reporting of security trades by corporate insiders. This is distinct from the corporate disclosure requirements discussed above. This rule, as interpreted by the courts (see the discussion of Texas Gulf Sulphur earlier in this chapter), in effect requires those who come into possession of such inside information to "disclose or abstain" from trading in the security.

This disclosure rule has created substantial controversy, just as has the one pertaining to corporate disclosure. Some who have examined the subject argue that there should be no disclosure of insider trading. It is insider trading, they say, which causes prices to fully reflect all information (or which brings about strong-form market efficiency). Those who defend the requirement do not necessarily dispute this argument. Rather they argue that the method by which the information gets transmitted to the market is unfair to the party on the other side of the trade. Just as in the earlier discussion of disclosure, this is usually about where the argument stops, with a comparison of the concept of fairness and the overall efficiency of the market. The conflict here is between the personal interests of the insiders and the interests of the public owners of the firm. Trading on the part of the firm's insiders tends to make the price a more accurate reflection of all information, but it also leads to a transfer of wealth from outside owners to insiders. The law's view has been that such conflicts should be held to a minimum.

Many discussions of disclosure of insider trading do not explicitly take up the prospect that it may be in the best interests of the firm's shareholders to maintain the confidentiality of information. Some information is useful only if competitors do not know about it. For example, in the case of the discovery of mining deposits it may be best to keep competitors in the dark about the facts or even existence of such a discovery. If competitors find out, they will tend to take actions which decrease the value of the find. Such confidential information is, in fact, a commonplace thing in the world. And many financial arrangements are designed to protect the confidentiality of information. Two relatively frequent recipients of such confidential information are commercial banks and investment banks. Commercial banks receive it in the course of the decision on the terms of loans to be extended to corporate borrowers. And investment banking firms receive it in the course of helping design and distribute new issues, generally private placements, or for other services, say relating to mergers.

The existence of such confidential information has created a clear potential for conflict of interest. The recipient of the information, the commercial or investment bank, can utilize it for its own trading or to distribute to other customers. In the case of a commercial bank these problems have attracted particular attention because banks operate trust departments which are required to be separate from the rest of the commercial banking operation. As a result, information acquired by a loan officer is not to be transmitted to someone in the trust department. These divisions of the bank are to be treated as if they were separate companies. They are to maintain what are referred to as "Chinese Walls" to separate these two sections of a bank. Investment bankers claim that the same Chinese Walls exist between those personnel working for different customers. In the case of commercial banks the separation is created by regulation. In the case of investment banks, the question increasingly being asked is whether an expanded role for regulation is called for.

A number of instances came to light in the late 1970s where the Chinese Wall had apparently been penetrated. Most of these cases involved the use of inside information in recommending or financing a bid to take over a company. Probably the most interesting and potentially important of these cases involved Morgan Stanley, one of the most prestigious investment banking firms in the country. It also involved Kennecott Copper, Olinkraft, and Johns-Manville. The essential ingredients of this episode, as reported in the press, are the following. In October of 1977 Morgan Stanley took part in a merger discussion between Olinkraft and Kennecott, as a representative of Kennecott. In the course of these negotiations, Olinkraft allowed Morgan Stanley access to internal projections of earnings which constituted confidential information. The merger negotiations were unsuccessful but Morgan Stanley retained the inside information on Olinkraft. In 1978 Johns-Manville asked Morgan Stanley to produce a list of acquisition prospects. Olinkraft was included on that list. The confidential information in the hands of Morgan Stanley was eventually turned over to Johns-Manville, after another firm, Texas Eastern Airlines, made a competitive offer to purchase Olinkraft. It was also revealed that during this period Morgan Stanley had maintained its own position in the stock of Olinkraft, or what is referred to as an arbitrage position. At one time Morgan Stanley held 149,200 shares of Olinkraft, worth roughly $7 million.

Morgan Stanley's actions raised at least two questions about the appropriate use of inside information. First, are there any circumstances under which inside information should be revealed and should the desire to serve another client qualify as such a reason? Second, had the separation between the portion of the firm handling mergers and that managing the firm's arbitrage position, another so-called Chinese Wall, broken down? Circumstantial evidence made many observers suspicious that it had. Normally if an investment banking firm has such a position, the client, in this case Johns-Manville, is informed at the outset and it is also disclosed as early as possible in reports filed with the SEC. In this instance, this was not done. In addition, Morgan Stanley chose to defend itself, once the circumstances became public through the luck or diligence of a *Wall Street Journal* reporter, by arguing that there can arise unusual circumstances when confidentiality can be broken. However, to the apparent chagrin of the investment banking industry, it later altered its position and contended that it never had a confidentiality agreement, written or oral, with Olinkraft; hence, it was free from the outset to do as it pleased with this information. In one news report on these events the reaction to this contention of another investment banker was quoted: "Every conversation, every piece of paper, that a corporation gives to an investment banker is understood to be confidential. We would expect that, of *all* firms, Morgan Stanley would be hollering this philosophy the loudest."[13]

It is evident from this incident alone that there are substantial opportunities for conflicts of interest in the investment banking business, even if separation from commercial banking is maintained. An important issue in the years ahead is likely to be whether Chinese Walls and the desire to protect a reputation can serve as adequate protections against such conflicts. The alternative will be increased regulation, presumably by the SEC, of the activities of investment bankers. This is likely to be an interesting and important issue in the regulation of securities markets in the 1980s.

SUMMARY

In this chapter we have examined how securities markets—that is, auction and over-the-counter markets—are regulated. We began by relating the discussion of regulation of securities markets to the various rationales for regulation presented in Chapter Fifteen. We found that most regulation of

[13] See John Thackray and Cary Reich, "The Credibility Crisis at Morgan Stanley," *Institutional Investor* (February 1979), pp. 30–38.

securities markets is designed either to promote competition and limit monopoly practices or to deal with the agency problem which grows out of imperfections in the distribution of information in the marketplace. In the rest of the chapter we tied each aspect of regulation back to these underlying problems. Table 16-1 summarizes this relationship by listing each of the major forms of regulation in securities markets which we examined in the chapter and relates them to the appropriate underlying purpose for regulation.

With this framework in hand we then looked into the origins of the securities laws which created our present regulatory system. A large part of this regulatory system emerged in response to the financial collapse of 1929 and the Great Depression which followed. This collapse was viewed by many to be at least in part a result of abuses which were possible in the unregulated markets of the 1920s. As a result, the Securities Acts of 1933 and 1934 and the Banking Act of 1933 were passed. These laws created a regulatory system which has remained largely intact to this day. Important features of these laws included new rules for disclosure of information on an ongoing basis by publicly held firms and for new securities which are distributed to the market, creation of the Securities and Exchange Commission with power to regulate the operation of secondary markets, imposition of margin requirements for stock purchases, restrictions on insider trading, regulation by the SEC of the methods of corporate governance, definition of fraudulent activities, regulation by the SEC of investment companies, and the separation of commercial and investment banking. In the years since the early 1930s there have been some relatively minor changes in the laws, but the most important changes came in the Securities Acts Amendments of 1975. The important features of these amendments were the elimination of minimum commissions on the New York Stock Exchange and the mandate for a National Market System.

TABLE 16-1

Summary of Principal Regulations in Securities Markets

REGULATION TO PROMOTE COMPETITION
1 SEC control of the rules of an exchange (e.g., NYSE) authorized in the Securities Acts of the 1930s.
2 Prohibition of minimum commissions on NYSE—1975.
3 Congressional mandate for a National Market System—1975.
REGULATION TO CONTROL AGENTS
1 Disclosure requirement for new security issues and for publicly held firms.
2 Regulation of insider trading.
3 Laws restricting fraudulent activities.
4 Regulation of investment companies.
5 Separation of commercial and investment banking.

The issue of minimum brokerage commissions on the New York Stock Exchange took on such significance because of the changes which had taken place in the Exchange during the 1960s and early 1970s. During this period trading by individual investors declined in importance relative to trading by large institutions, and large institutions were often in a better position to demand competitive pricing of brokerage services on the Exchange than were individuals with small trading volume. As a result, the long-standing rule of the Exchange which fixed minimum commissions began to cause the market for equities to fragment. This focused attention on the role of this minimum-price rule as a device for supporting a cartel. After action by the U.S. Justice Department and by the Securities and Exchange Commission, Congress declared this minimum-price rule illegal.

The other important feature of the 1975 Act may have tremendous significance for the operation of securities markets in the long run. The Act includes a mandate to the SEC to see that the markets move as fast as possible toward the implementation of a National Market System. The idea behind a National Market System is to bring into existence a central computerized system for recording and executing all transactions in publicly available securities. It is not clear at this juncture exactly what features of the present system would be retained if and when a National Market System is implemented, but some experiments which have already begun give a clue as to what the system might be like. One form for the system involves the preservation of separate exchanges as they now exist, with automated display of prices and execution of transactions essentially as a communication link between separate exchanges. The other form involves a single integrated system for recording orders and executing transactions without regard for physical location.

Many of the provisions of the securities laws have been controversial virtually since their inception. One feature which has attracted considerable recent attention is the set of disclosure requirements enforced by the SEC. The essence of the criticism of required disclosure is that it has led to no measurable increase in the efficiency of financial markets. The argument is that competitive markets are efficient on their own, so that required disclosure adds nothing. The conclusion is that because required disclosure is costly it is best to reduce or eliminate it. There are two basic responses to this argument. The first response is to quarrel with the contention that there is no measurable increase in efficiency. This portion of the debate involves the collection and evaluation of statistical evidence as to whether disclosure leads to observable and significant changes in the prices of the securities to which that information pertains. The second counterargument is that required disclosure has reduced the opportunities for well-informed insiders to take advantage of less well-informed investors. Unfortunately, the evidence on this point is largely subjective and therefore can be interpreted quite differently by those on opposite sides of the issue. In any event, the debate on required disclosure promises to continue in the future.

Another important point of contention in the securities laws regards how extensively potential conflicts of interest should be limited by regulation. An important opportunity for conflicts of interest was eliminated in the 1930s when commercial and investment banking were separated. However, during the 1970s this separation also began to receive closer scrutiny. The reason for this change in attitude is that the operational distinctions between the two types of institutions have become less well defined. In today's financial market brokerage houses which deal in the secondary markets for securities also function as investment bankers and offer securities to consumers in the form of money market mutual funds and other accounts which are quite close to demand deposits. At the same time, large commercial banks are seeking expanded authority to compete with brokerage houses in their traditional lines of business. Whether it will be possible to maintain a meaningful separation in the future is hard to predict.

A final potential conflict of interest which may become the subject of more, rather than less, regulation pertains to the use of confidential information. Many financial institutions receive confidential information on a regular basis and they contend that they limit potential conflicts by erecting Chinese Walls around those who have such information. During the 1970s, however, a number of instances where such walls had been penetrated came to light. This may be an interesting issue during the 1980s.

QUESTIONS TO IMPROVE UNDERSTANDING

1 Explain how a "pool" works and why it is considered an abuse of the securities markets? What kind of conflict of interest does a broker or banker have who participates in a pool?

2 What are margin loans? How did margin loans contribute to the stock market crash of 1929?

3 Explain the attitude of the securities laws of 1933 and 1934 toward disclosure. What do you believe might be the feasible alternatives to these disclosure rules?

4 Describe the circumstances or events which led up to the enactment of major amendments to the securities acts in 1975. What were the fundamental features of these amendments?

5 Summarize the case made by the NYSE for preserving minimum commissions. What were the major arguments against this case? Compare and evaluate the two positions.

6 What is the National Market System? Describe the two basic ways such a system might operate. What are the most difficult issues involved in choosing between these alternatives?

7 Why have some people chosen to criticize disclosure regulation? What is the essence of their argument against this type of regulation?

8 Why is the concept of a "fair" capital market one which causes so much disagreement? Can you give a precise definition of what fair means in this context? How would you go about collecting evidence to assess fairness? Suppose you couldn't collect any such evidence, yet you were responsible for choosing what

regulations should be maintained and what ones should be eliminated. Would you feel "fairness" was relevant?

9 Why have commercial and investment banking been separated? Why may this separation be more difficult to enforce in the future than it has been in the past?

10 What are "Chinese Walls"? How do they get penetrated? Should there be more regulation to enforce these barriers? What might be an appropriate approach to this issue?

REFERENCES

Benston, George J.: "Required Disclosure and the Stock Market: An Evaluation of the Securities Exchange Act of 1934," *American Economic Review*, 63 (March 1973), pp. 132–155.

Campbell, Tim S.: "Optimal Investment Financing Decisions and the Value of Confidentiality," *Journal of Financial and Quantitative Analysis*, 14 (December 1979), pp. 913–924.

Francis, Jack Clark: *Investments: Analysis and Management*, McGraw-Hill Book Company, New York, 1972.

Friend, Irwin, and E. S. Herman: "The S.E.C. Through a Glass Darkly," *Journal of Business*, University of Chicago, Chicago, 27 (October 1964), pp. 382–405.

————, and Randolph Westerfield: "Required Disclosure and the Stock Market: Comment," *American Economic Review*, 65 (June 1975), pp. 467–477.

Melton, William C.: "Corporate Equities and the National Market System," *Quarterly Review*, Federal Reserve Bank of New York, 3 (Winter 1978–1979), pp. 13–25.

Offer, A. R., and A. Melnik: "Price Deregulation in the Brokerage Industry: An Empirical Analysis," *Bell Journal of Economics*, 9 (Autumn 1978), pp. 633–641.

Sobel, Robert: *The Big Board: A History of the New York Stock Market*, The Free Press, New York, 1965.

Stigler, George: "Public Regulation of the Securities Markets," *Journal of Business*, 37 (April 1964), pp. 117–142.

Thackray, John, and Cary Reich: "The Credibility Crisis at Morgan Stanley," *Institutional Investor* (February 1979), pp. 30–38.

Tinic, Seha M., and Richard R. West: "The Securities Industry Under Negotiated Brokerage Commissions: Changes in the Structure and Performance of New York Stock Exchange Member Firms," *Bell Journal of Economics*, 11 (Spring 1980), pp. 29–41.

Securities and Exchange Commission Annual Report, Washington, D.C., 1979.

Chapter Seventeen

THE REGULATION OF
COMMERCIAL BANKS

This chapter deals with the historically dominant type of financial institution in the United States, commercial banks. More specifically, it deals with the regulation of commercial banks. The debate about the appropriate way to regulate commercial banks is probably the oldest public-policy question pertaining to financial markets in the United States. It is also still one of the most important. In a sense, after the Great Depression the principal issues of bank regulation, which had raised such tremendous political controversies for over a century, were thought to be laid to rest. This was because the system put in place in the first presidential term of Franklin Roosevelt was perceived to be so immensely successful. But in the 1970s some of the perennial issues have begun to come to the fore again. The underlying reason for this is intimately linked to the problem of inflation.

In this chapter we will try to develop some understanding of the long-standing controversies concerning bank regulation. Then we will examine some of the more contemporary problems of regulation with the advantage of some historical perspective. The historical material presented in this chapter is not intended to serve merely as a transition. In this instance the history is really as important as current events. In the next decade we may experience changes in the regulatory system which will be as dramatic as those which happened in the 1930s. Only with a sense of historical perspective can these potential changes be understood. And because the success of our system for regulating banks and other intermediaries is so tied up with the problem of inflation, in this chapter we will only begin to expose part of the plot. The final answer to this who-done-it comes in the last chapter of the book, the one devoted to the problem of inflation.

OVERVIEW OF THE BANK REGULATION SYSTEM

It is important at the outset to recall our list of reasons for regulation in financial markets which we developed in Chapter Fifteen and used again at the beginning of Chapter Sixteen. There are four underlying problems or motives for regulation which comprise our checklist. They are:

1 Promote competition and prevent monopolistic practices
2 Prevent or limit expropriation
3 Control the actions of agents
4 Prevent market failure

In Chapter Sixteen we found that the big issues in regulating auction and over-the-counter markets were 1 and 3. In this chapter we will find that the big, even overwhelming, issue in regulating financial intermediaries is number 4. Actually, it is not quite that simple. The underlying problem with financial intermediaries is the potential for expropriation by the intermediary, that is, by the agent who owns or operates the intermediary. In financial intermediaries these problems can become so severe that they threaten failure of the market. Hence the real goal which has motivated regulation of financial intermediaries is the desire to avoid or ensure against market failure. Unfortunately, as we will discover, the regulations which have evolved to deal with market failure have made it more difficult to promote competition and prevent monopolistic practices. As a result, there is a tradeoff between objective number 1 and objective number 4 on our checklist. We will explore this tradeoff in this chapter.

The problems which have led to regulation of financial intermediaries are not strictly a matter of recent history. Instead, they have been with this country virtually since its birth. During most of the history of the United States there were periodic liquidity crises or panics where citizens sought to withdraw their funds from financial institutions and hoard them. In effect, the banking industry was prone to market failure. Various methods were instituted by the government over the years in order to deal with these crises. With each additional approach to the problem, the regulatory system grew in complexity. It is imperative, in order to avoid getting lost in the maze of agencies and regulations which currently exist, that we examine the historical evolution of the existing regulatory system and only then assess its effectiveness.

To appreciate the complexity of the current system for regulating commercial banks, it is helpful to start with an outline of the major regulations which currently exist. Then we can turn to an account of the historical evolution of these regulations and the rationale behind them. The regulations are listed roughly in the sequence in which they came into existence and in an order which will facilitate a logical explanation of their purpose.

FRACTIONAL RESERVE BANKING AND NATIONAL CURRENCY   The National Banking Act of 1863 created a system of government-required reserves for nationally chartered banks, though no provision was made for expansion or contraction of those reserves. The legislation which followed shortly after led to the extinction of the multiple currencies issued by state banks which existed throughout the earlier portion of the nineteenth century.

ELASTIC CURRENCY   In 1913 the Federal Reserve System came into existence and with it a provision for government control of the volume of currency and of bank reserves. The Federal Reserve was designed to serve as a lender of last resort for commercial banks experiencing liquidity difficulties or to provide what is called an elastic currency.

RESTRICTION OF INTEREST PAYMENTS ON DEPOSITS   Beginning in the Great Depression, with the Banking Acts of 1933 and 1935, the federal government imposed limits on the interest rates that could be paid on demand, savings, and time deposit accounts in order to limit competition. Interest payments on demand deposit accounts were entirely prohibited, while the Federal Reserve has periodically adjusted interest-rate ceilings on savings and time deposits.

DEPOSIT INSURANCE   Since the Depression, deposits at commercial banks, as well as savings and loans, have been insured by the United States government. This insurance is provided for commercial banks by the Federal Deposit Insurance Corporation.

RESTRICTIONS ON PERMISSIBLE ACTIVITIES OF COMMERCIAL BANKS   Banks are restricted as to the activities they can engage in and investments they can make. These restrictions began to be imposed in the 1930s and have been modified more recently as banks formed holding companies.

CAPITAL REQUIREMENTS   The government imposes minimum capital requirements on all commercial banks.

ENTRY RESTRICTIONS   Permission must be obtained from the banking regulators in order to create a new bank or a new branch of an existing bank.

Moreover, banks are not allowed to cross state lines. Each state has the right to determine whether banks will be permitted to have branch offices.

INSPECTION AND CONTROL OF RISKINESS   The government examines commercial banks in order to assess the riskiness of their deposit liabilities and can compel bank management to alter policies which are found to be too risky.

With this outline of the existing regulatory system for commercial banks as an introduction, we can examine in more detail the underlying reason why banks have been subject to so much instability and the historical evolution of the regulatory system designed to correct it.

BANKING REGULATION THROUGH THE GREAT DEPRESSION

The Underlying Issue: Convertibility and Stability

The fundamental problem facing depository institutions, virtually throughout history, results from the peculiar nature of deposits as a financial asset. In the broadest sense, deposits are simply another type of debt claim, such as a bond or a loan. As we discussed in Chapter Fifteen, one of the problems with any debt claim, including deposits, is that there are opportunities for the issuer of the debt claim, in this case the commercial bank, to engage in activities which tend to expropriate the holder of the claim. The most obvious kind of expropriation is for a borrower to take a lender's funds, issue a promise to repay, and simply disappear, or spend the money and then claim bankruptcy. But there are a number of other more devious methods to accomplish essentially the same thing, as will soon be evident from the banking arrangements which existed in the United States in the nineteenth century. As pointed out in Chapter Fifteen, in order to prevent such problems most formal debt contracts issued by corporations include covenants which constrain the borrower or require collateral which the lender can claim if an expropriation is attempted. The covenants restrict such things as future dividends and debt issues in order to limit the borrower's ability to divert funds from the corporation to equity owners, or to increase the debt of the company and therefore the risk to which existing debtholders are exposed.

The unique characteristic of depository claims on banks is that it is exceedingly difficult to devise effective means to protect against such expropriations. To see why this is true it is necessary to examine a little more closely one of the principal ways such an expropriation may be accomplished. Suppose that a firm finances its activities 50 percent by debt and 50 percent by equity securities. At the time the debt is sold, the debtholders understand that the proportion of debt and equity will be 50-50 and they price the bonds that they purchase accordingly. This means that the riskiness they believe they are exposed to is based on the assumption that there will be a 50 percent equity cushion. Next, suppose that once this debt is sold, the equity owners of the firm decide to increase the amount of debt financing to, say, 75 percent of the financing of the firm. This decreases the equity cushion of existing debtholders and increases the risk to which they are exposed. One way to deal with this problem is for people to borrow and lend only when they trust each other enough that a lender can believe the promise of a borrower not to expropriate. Another way is for lenders to write covenants into the bond agreement which restrict the borrowers' activities so that expropriations of this kind become impossible. In this example, such a covenant would directly restrict the ability of the borrower to issue further debt without the permission of the original debtholders.

The problem with expropriations regarding depository institutions is that it is exceedingly difficult to construct covenants which adequately protect against future increases in the debt issued by the institution. The reason for this is that the business of a bank is to issue deposits. In order to be able to function effectively it must have the freedom to increase or decrease deposits as the need arises. It would be totally infeasible for the initial depositors to restrict the ability of the bank to issue additional deposits. The volume of deposits fluctuates from day to day, and virtually must do so if the bank is to be able to profitably serve its customers. Moreover, this same flexibility makes it impossible to assign collateral to specific deposits. But this creates an opportunity for the kind of expropriations described above to be carried out.

The method which first evolved for dealing with this problem was for banks to back their deposits, or the antecedents of deposits called *notes*, with gold. Under such a system banks promised to redeem their notes or deposits in gold at a prespecified price. As a result, notes or deposits were titles to gold, and gold essentially fulfilled the role of collateral. But the promise to convert notes into gold on demand was a promise which could easily be broken, so that the fundamental nature of the problem was not really changed. Banks only invested a small portion of their funds in gold. Most of their funds were committed to loans and other investments. As a result, the commitment to convert the deposits to gold could only be honored if a small portion of the total volume of deposits was presented for conversion at once. In essence, banks held gold as a reserve to satisfy the volume of conversions which were anticipated, plus some amount as a cushion. But because banks earned their profits from loans, the more gold they held in reserve, the less profitable they could expect to be.

This problem of balancing liquidity against profitability has always been the fundamental choice facing commercial banks. Throughout the history of the United States banking industry, panics developed when the public perceived either that banks were trying to expropriate them or that they had become too illiquid or were running too short on gold. If the panic became serious enough, it virtually guaranteed that the liquidity which did exist would be insufficient and the system would become unstable. We will explore some of the historical episodes of instability in the banking system as we examine how the regulatory system we now have evolved to deal with them.

Early Regulation and the Wildcat Banking Era

Shortly after the United States became an independent country, the government sought to establish a government-sponsored bank which could serve as the government's bank and could regulate the note issues of independent state-chartered banks. This bank, known as the First Bank of the United States, was chartered for a 20-year life in 1791. At that time each independent bank issued what amounted to its own currency, referred to as bank notes. These were paper notes which circulated largely in the geographic area in which each bank operated and which the banks promised to redeem in gold. The First Bank of the United States issued its own notes and offered deposits. But it also sought to regulate the issue of notes by state banks. It did this by regularly redeeming state banks' notes for gold rather than always recirculating the notes. The bank also was intended to serve the Treasury of the United States, and it did this by maintaining deposits for the Treasury and executing its payments.

The charter of the First Bank was not renewed in 1811 due to increased political opposition to the bank. A large element of the population distrusted banks and felt that the United States government should not sponsor a bank. For a while, at least, they won. Unfortunately, without the bank, the private banking system almost immediately experienced great instability as the volume of private bank notes expanded. In 1814 this led to a general suspension of convertibility of notes into gold. Moreover, the United States entered the War of 1812 with Britain almost immediately after the charter of the First Bank expired and the demise of the bank made it difficult for the Treasury to finance the war. After 5 years, in 1816, Congress reversed its earlier decision and chartered the Second Bank of the United States.

The Second Bank of the United States performed a function essentially similar to that of the First Bank. But in the end its fate was the same. President Andrew Jackson was vehemently opposed to the bank and, in 1836, he permitted its charter to expire. Andrew Jackson represented largely agrarian southern and western groups, as opposed to the more industrial eastern part of the country. By and large, this constituency felt that the Second Bank of the United States, particularly its able and powerful president, Nicholas Biddle, was not acting in their best interests. The bank consistently returned notes issued by southern and western banks for conversion to gold in an attempt to try to establish a national currency. Jackson's constituency objected strenuously to this policy and succeeded not only in reversing the policy but in eliminating the bank.

From the time of the demise of the Second National Bank until the Civil War, the banking industry was virtually unregulated at the national level.

Some states chose to impose relatively tight regulations. One state (Iowa) went so far as to outlaw banking altogether.[1] But in spite of the restrictions that were imposed in a few states, this period was one of almost totally unfettered competition. There were thousands of state banks throughout the country, each issuing its own bank notes. The notes of each bank were exchanged at whatever price the market would bear. Bank notes often traded at their par value of a dollar note for a dollar note if the exchange took place in the same immediate locale of both banks and if both banks were thought to be reputable. But notes often deteriorated in value with distance from the issuing bank because the perceived risk of being able to convert the note to gold increased. There even emerged a small industry to collect information about the value of notes and the exchange rates between the notes of different banks. This information was published in newspapers and in catalogues called bank note reporters.

Most of the time most banks maintained convertibility of their notes into gold. But a number of banks tried to develop schemes which would minimize the chance that such conversion would be attempted. For example, it is said that some banks located their offices far out in the woods "where only the wildcats lived," yet they distributed notes in more populated areas. Such banks were the source of the name for this era in banking history. The opportunity for this kind of expropriation was at its height during this time because the system was essentially one of "buyer beware." The market developed methods for trying to assess the risk of nonconvertibility, but no guarantees were available and the responsibility for assessing risk and deciding on the appropriate notes to use belonged totally to the individual.

It is important to recognize that during this time period there was virtually no national currency as we know it today. Each bank issued its own notes or currency and the only common denominator among these bank notes was their link to gold. The price of gold was fixed in dollars and, assuming that convertibility was maintained, each dollar note could be converted to a dollar in gold. But individual notes often exchanged at values well below $1. This system of "competing monies" came to an end with the onset of the Civil War and has not existed in this country since.

Reform: The National Banking Act

By 1863 the United States had experienced nearly 30 years of what some people thought was virtual chaos in the banking industry. There was, therefore, considerable sentiment that the system was ripe for reform. But had it not been for the Civil War, this sentiment might not have been sufficient to bring about any significant changes. The government found banking reform

---

[1] See Robert Craig West, *Banking Reform and the Federal Reserve 1863-1923*, Cornell University Press, Ithaca, N.Y., 1974, for a description of the attitudes of individual states toward banks during the wildcat banking era.

to be a convenient way to create a market for the government bonds needed to finance the war. As a result, the National Banking Act was first passed in 1863 and amended in the years immediately following.[2]

The most important and permanent accomplishment of the National Banking Act was the creation of a national currency and the elimination of competing notes issued by state banks trading at different values. But this was not accomplished by directly distributing a government-produced currency as we have today. Instead, the National Banking Act provided for the chartering of national banks which could issue notes backed by government bonds. These banks were not government banks like the First and Second Banks of the United States. They were simply privately owned commercial banks with a national rather than a state charter. The act as it was amended in 1866 also imposed a 10 percent tax on the notes of state banks. This virtually eliminated state bank notes. As a result, the notes of the nationally chartered banks became the national currency. Unlike the notes of state banks issued during the wildcat banking era, national bank notes always traded at par. This was because they were not really backed by the promises of the individual banks which issued them. Instead, the volume of these notes was directly linked to the bank's holdings of government securities, bearing what was called a circulation privilege. Hence the national bank notes were really an indirect form of government-issued money. With this system the government created, at one time, both a ready market for its bonds and a uniform currency.

This method alone was not sufficient for financing the war so the government also issued a currency of its own which had no backing of gold. This currency came to be known as "greenbacks." Greenbacks and national bank notes circulated simultaneously, though not necessarily at the same value. Moreover, banks still generally promised to redeem deposits in gold. But the government did not officially back its own greenback currency with gold. Hence, there was a period during and after the Civil War when the promise of the government to settle its claims in gold was abandoned. The resumption of government payments in gold came in 1879. From then until the creation of the Federal Reserve in 1913, the system remained largely the same.

In addition to establishing a national currency, the National Banking Act also created the basic structure of banking regulation that we have today. First, it required nationally chartered banks to hold reserves behind their deposits in a fixed proportion which depended on the size and location of the bank. This is why it is called a *fractional reserve* banking system. These reserves were maintained in the form of either cash or deposits with other banks. The major difficulty with this system was that these reserves were virtually unavailable when problems of liquidity arose because there was no provision for adjusting reserve requirements or for extending loans to banks.

---

[2] See Ibid. for a perspective on the forces which led to the National Banking Act of 1863.

These reserves were simply not available when they were needed. Large banks often fulfilled the role of a lender for smaller banks, but when the liquidity problems spread to the larger banks the system did not work well.

The National Banking Act also created the office of the Comptroller of the Currency, which still exists today. The comptroller was empowered to maintain minimum capital requirements for national banks and to inspect and restrict the activities and investments of such banks. This laid the foundation for the more elaborate regulatory structure we have today.

The Federal Reserve System

The banking system created by the National Banking Act operated without major changes until the panic of 1907, when the solvency of the financial system came into serious question. This crisis in financial markets led to a major reexamination of the banking system. That analysis culminated in the passage of the Federal Reserve Act of 1913.

The Federal Reserve System was created out of a dissatisfaction with the existing system for ensuring the stability of the banking system. The nineteenth century was comprised of a number of banking panics where people would run on the banks demanding redemption first of their notes in gold and, later, their deposits in either gold or currency. But if the run on virtually any bank is large enough, that bank will be unable to satisfy the demand for conversion, regardless of how sound its loans may be. Even the strongest bank does not hold nearly enough highly liquid assets to satisfy its depositors' demands to convert deposits to currency if enough of them show up at once. Therefore, even a bank which has made no attempt to expropriate its depositors, in the sense discussed early in this chapter and in Chapter Fifteen, may still be unable to fulfill its promises if a large number of depositors simultaneously demand that those promises be kept. Such liquidity problems surfaced every few years throughout the nineteenth century and were particularly severe in 1907. The system created under the National Banking Act was ill-suited to deal with these liquidity problems. As described above, it did lead to the end of an era of competing monies, but it did almost nothing to assist banks in maintaining their liquidity. The Federal Reserve System was therefore created to fill this void.

The important feature of the Federal Reserve System was that a central bank was given the power to control the supply of reserves and therefore the liquidity of commercial banks. As it has developed since 1913, the most important method for exercising this control is through the purchase and sale of United States government securities by the Federal Reserve. But the other method, which was of critical importance at that time, was the ability of the Federal Reserve to extend loans or discounts to member commercial banks. This meant that the Federal Reserve had the ability to increase or decrease the liquidity of member commercial banks by extending or contracting its loans to these banks. Banks did not and do not now rely on the

Federal Reserve as a major source of their funds. Rather, this discounting function of the Federal Reserve provided flexibility in the amount of currency outstanding or in the liquidity of the banking system, as the Federal Reserve was able to act as a "lender of last resort."

From 1913 until 1929 the economy in general and the Federal Reserve in particular were both in their prime. After World War I ended the economy experienced tremendous growth and prosperity and the banking system experienced tremendous stability. The Federal Reserve was perceived as a great improvement in bank regulation and there was little sentiment for further change. But in 1929 the stock market crashed, the Great Depression began, and the Federal Reserve's heyday came to an end.

Any reasonable assessment of the Federal Reserve's track record in preserving the liquidity of the banking system during the early years of the Depression must conclude that the System was a dismal failure. Between 1929 and 1933 approximately 9,000 banks failed, roughly half of the total number of banks in existence in the United States at the time. This was virtually unprecedented in the history of the country. While there were a number of banking panics throughout the nineteenth century, a general suspension of all banking business in the country for a period as long as a week had never taken place before this. Such a banking holiday was declared on March 6, 1933, however, and all banks, including the Federal Reserve System, closed down for a week. Milton Friedman and Anna Schwartz, in their book on U.S. monetary arrangements, *A Monetary History of the United States*, point out the irony of the whole situation:

> The central banking system, set up primarily to render impossible the restriction of payments by commercial banks, itself joined the commercial banks in a more widespread, complete, and economically disturbing restriction of payments than had ever been experienced in the history of the country. One can certainly sympathize with (President Herbert) Hoover's comment about that episode: 'I concluded (the Reserve Board) was indeed a weak reed for a nation to lean on in time of trouble.'[3]

It is difficult to provide a concise explanation for the failure of the Federal Reserve to maintain the stability of the banking system during this period. The banking system collapse developed in stages, between 1930 and 1933. At each stage confidence in the system was further shaken and the crisis became more severe. The initial bank failures in the early stages were probably due to bad loans as much as anything else. But as the crisis deepened, the demand for conversion of demand deposits into cash intensified. This occurred at a time when the bond market had collapsed, so that the current market value of a large portion of bank assets was unusually low.

---

[3] Excerpts from Milton Friedman and Anna Schwartz, *A Monetary History of the United States 1867–1960*, copyright Princeton University Press, Princeton, N.J., 1963, pp. 327–328. Reprinted by permission of Princeton University Press.

This did not necessarily mean that there would be default if those bonds were held to maturity, but it did mean that many banks would become insolvent if they had to liquidate those bonds at current low market prices in order to satisfy demands for conversion of demand deposits to currency.

The Federal Reserve could have extended loans on a massive scale to banks facing this difficulty. But it did not. Friedman and Schwartz attribute this failure to a lack of understanding of the situation, and it seems difficult to come to any other conclusion:

> The major reason the System was so belated in showing concern about bank failures and so inactive in responding to them was undoubtedly due to a limited understanding of the connection between bank failures, runs on banks, contraction of deposits, and weakness of the bond markets—connections we have tried to spell out earlier in this chapter. The technical personnel of the New York Bank understood these connections, as undoubtedly many other individuals in the System did also; but most of the governors of the Banks, members of the Board, and other administrative officials of the System did not. They tended to regard bank failures as regrettable consequences of bad management and bad banking practices, or as inevitable reactions to prior speculative excesses, or as a consequence but hardly a cause of the financial and economic collapse in process.[4]

The Banking Legislation Spawned by the Depression

When President Franklin D. Roosevelt took office in 1933 action was taken to alter the situation in the financial markets. The principal piece of legislation which was adopted at that time, and which has fundamentally altered commercial banking since, is the Banking Act of 1933. The most important element of this act was the provision of federal insurance of deposits. Under this law the federal government provided insurance of deposits, originally up to $2,500 and today up to $100,000, for commercial banks which became members of the new agency called the Federal Deposit Insurance Corporation (FDIC). The FDIC became the third federal regulatory agency, in addition to the Comptroller of the Currency and the Federal Reserve. Federally chartered banks were required to join the FDIC, but nearly 97 percent of all (which includes state as well as federal) commercial banks became insured by the FDIC. This percentage has increased to nearly 100 percent in the intervening years.

Deposit insurance has been tremendously successful. Panics and liquidity crises were a recurring problem in the United States from the administration of George Washington until the Great Depression. But they have been virtually nonexistent since that time. The problem was not resolved by imposing a national currency and creating reserve requirements, nor by giving a central bank the authority to expand and contract that currency. But

[4] Ibid., p. 358.

deposit insurance did the job. The impact on the stability of the banking industry is documented in Figure 17-1. It shows the number of bank failures between 1921 and 1978. The table clearly shows the dramatic effect that the creation of the FDIC had on bank failures.

The Banking Act of 1933 also compelled banks to divest themselves of their investment banking activities. This activity was separated from commercial banking because of the perception that there was an inherent conflict of interest between the two functions. In addition to the separation of com-

FIGURE 17-1
Number of bank failures (includes only insured banks after 1935). Source: *Annual Report of the Comptroller of the Currency*, 1979.

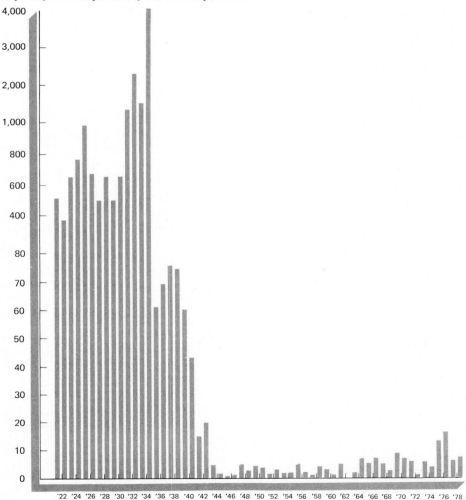

mercial and investment banking (which was discussed in the previous chapter), at least three other important changes were instituted at this time. The first was the prohibition of any interest payments on demand deposits and on time deposits above a ceiling set by the Federal Reserve. This prohibition was instituted in order to prevent what many perceived as dangerous competition among banks for depositors' funds. When allowed to compete with interest payments, it was believed that banks would be compelled to seek highly risky investments in order to earn enough return to compensate their depositors. The increased competition was therefore perceived to be the source of excessive risk taking. By restricting payment of interest on deposits it was believed that risk would be reduced.

Second, the government finally phased out entirely the national bank notes which originally came into existence with the National Banking Act of 1863. This was accomplished by retiring the remaining U.S. bonds which, when held by nationally chartered commercial banks, gave them the authority to issue notes. National bank notes had gradually come to be replaced by Federal Reserve notes anyway. These are still the form of currency used in the United States. With this change the evolution was complete from a currency produced by private institutions, as was the case during the first half of the nineteenth century, to a government monopoly currency.

A final and very important change which took place at that time regarded the role of gold in the banking system. Throughout the history of the United States the stability of the banking system hinged on the believability of the promise to redeem notes or deposits in gold. In the nineteenth century banks directly converted notes to gold upon demand. But by the late 1920s the conversion was principally from deposits to currency and the government stood ready to convert currency to gold, if the demand was made. But in 1933 President Roosevelt essentially nationalized gold. By this it is meant that it was made illegal, through the power of existing statutes, for private citizens and institutions within the United States to hold gold. All gold was turned over to the U.S. Treasury at the existing legal price at that time of $20.67 per ounce.

The Significance of the Changes in the 1930s

The implications of the nationalization of gold and the enactment of deposit insurance were substantial. Bank deposits, and earlier, bank notes, had virtually always been a type of private security. This means that they involved the obligations of private parties alone, and not the federal government. The unique characteristic of this security was its high degree of liquidity. This liquidity led to the problem of stability and potential failure (item 4 on our checklist) which plagued the banking industry for over a century. But gradually the note and then the deposit were transformed. First the transformation involved only the formation of a national currency linked directly to United States government securities, through the National Banking Act.

But currency and deposits were still linked to gold and the contract or promise between a bank and its depositors was still essentially a private contract. With the institution of deposit insurance and the nationalization of gold, the backing behind the deposits of banks became a government promise rather than essentially a promise of the individual bank. Individual banks no longer backed their deposits with gold. Rather, they were compelled to maintain convertibility of their deposits into government-issued currency, which in turn was backed by the good will of the government.[5] But because depositors were insured if private banks reneged on that promise, depositors no longer had an incentive to carefully assess the believability of promises made by individual banks. That responsibility now lay with the government. And in order to fulfill that responsibility a more elaborate system of regulation and control of risk was necessary.

DEPOSIT INSURANCE AND ACCOMPANYING REGULATION

When the FDIC was created in 1933 it not only took on the responsibility of providing insurance to commercial banks but it began to regulate banks in order to minimize the chance it would have to pay off on that insurance. Over the next few years a much more stringent system of regulation emerged and it has remained essentially intact to this day. In addition to the innovation of deposit insurance by the FDIC, the three bank regulatory agencies— the Comptroller of the Currency, the Federal Reserve, and the FDIC—share the responsibility for enforcing regulations in three basic areas: government control and examination of the quality of loans and investments, restrictions on entry and expansion of facilities and types of activities, and maintenance of minimum capital requirements.

Deposit Insurance and Control of Risk

The deposit insurance provided to commercial banks by the FDIC is not free. The FDIC charges an insurance premium which is nominally set at one-half of 1 percent of a bank's total domestic deposits. This is the nominal rate because the FDIC allows a credit on this amount so that the effective rate is generally less than half of this. These premiums are used to build a fund of investments managed by the FDIC which can be drawn upon in the event a bank fails and the FDIC has to take it over. This fund has grown fairly rapidly throughout the 1970s and stood at approximately $8.8 billion as of 1978.

There are a number of interesting and controversial questions pertaining to how the system of deposit insurance ought to operate. The system has undergone relatively little change during its existence, despite continuing

---

[5] See Benjamin Klein, "The Competitive Supply of Money," *Journal of Money, Credit and Banking*, November 1974, pages 423–453, for an analysis of banking regulation in the United States which emphasizes the significance of forced convertibility.

discussions of how the system might be altered. And without a major crisis to precipitate change, it seems likely that the system will remain essentially as it is now. Nonetheless, it is worth examining some of these issues.

PRICING OF DEPOSIT INSURANCE   The first issue is how deposit insurance should be priced. Currently the price is linked to the total volume of a bank's domestic deposits. No attempt is made to tie the premium to the riskiness of the bank. Compared to any private insurance scheme or to the pricing of securities in the financial markets, this is quite unusual. Almost all private insurers are keenly interested in ascertaining the true risk of those they insure. If everyone pays the same premiums, regardless of actual risk, then the low-risk prospects end up subsidizing the high-risk prospects. Private insurance markets seek to minimize this as much as possible, and some people argue that deposit insurance should seek to do the same thing. The regulators have not been particularly sympathetic to this argument, not because of lack of concern for equitable pricing, but essentially for two other reasons. The first is that it is exceptionally difficult to develop a meaningful criterion for distinguishing the riskiness of banks with any precision. Even if this difficulty could be overcome, their second reason may be more important. This reason is that such a pricing mechanism would focus public attention on the riskiness of banks which could decrease the stability of the system. The regulators' purpose is not only to prevent banking defaults as a result of bad loans and mismanagement but also to avoid banking panics which could precipitate widespread failures. In fact, from an historical standpoint, this is the very reason for their existence. Hence, pricing based on risk, while a more equitable pricing system, may be inconsistent with the ultimate motive of the agency.

The second issue is who should be covered. Under the present system all depositors are insured to $100,000. This means that no one with deposits less than this can avoid insurance and no one with greater deposits in a single bank can obtain more insurance. Some people argue that everyone should have 100 percent compulsory insurance and others argue that all insurance should be optional but that those who use it should be charged. The second proposal has a serious flaw. The flaw is a type of free-rider problem (see Chapter Fifteen). Each individual knows that if the deposit insurance system is working well, then the risk of failure of any individual bank is very low. As a result, the benefit to him or her of deposit insurance is low, as long as the system of deposit insurance and regulation is working well. But, on this basis no individual has a strong private incentive to purchase insurance, though everyone would like the system as a whole to work. This incentive of individuals to "free-ride" threatens the stability of the entire system. Therefore, the regulators have felt that a choice about deposit insurance is counterproductive. On the other hand, the regulators have chosen to place a ceiling on the amount of deposit insurance. The apparent justification for this is that it provides an incentive for those with large deposits to scrutinize the riskiness of the bank in which they place their funds. This presumably helps the regulators in their task of limiting risk. The counterpart is that large depositors tend to bail out if and when a bank has difficulty, and this can add to the problems of such a bank, increasing the probability that the bank will ultimately go into receivership. Such a bailout occurred when Franklin National Bank failed in 1974. This might be the ripest area for change in the deposit insurance system.

Finally, some criticism can be heard to the effect that if there ever really were another banking panic, the FDIC would have insufficient resources to rescue large numbers of banks. It is important to recognize that the FDIC maintains reserves which are intended to be sufficient for a reasonable number of bank failures. It would be a waste of resources to maintain such large reserves that the FDIC could instantly cover massive losses in a major banking panic. The ultimate source of insurance behind the FDIC is the taxing authority of the United States government. The government has made a contract with depositors to insure them against losses, up to a limit, on deposit accounts. That insurance is as good as, and only as good as, the United States government.

GOVERNMENT CONTROL OF RISK With deposit insurance must come government control of risk. The three federal regulatory agencies all conduct examinations of the loans and investments of commercial banks. The division of authority for examination of banks among these agencies is rather complicated. The Comptroller of the Currency examines all nationally chartered banks; the Federal Reserve examines all state chartered banks which are members of the Federal Reserve; and the FDIC examines all banks which are not members of the Federal Reserve System. In addition, each state has state examiners which examine the banks in that state.

All of these bank examiners are looking for problems in bank loans and investments which threaten the stability of the bank and the value of depositors' claims against the bank. Such problems may result from fraud or, more frequently, they may simply be a result of mismanagement. The FDIC, in cooperation with the other two federal regulators, maintains a list of banks which it judges may become insolvent. This list of "problem banks" is used to assess the probability that FDIC insurance will have to be used. The agencies utilize the examination procedure to try to spot difficulties early enough that corrective action can be taken to alter the problem. When the examiners discover loans or investments which violate the law or which they consider unsound they meet with bank management and the board of directors of the bank and insist upon changes. The ultimate penalty which the regulators wield is to prosecute managers or bank owners for explicit violations of the laws or to take over the bank if they judge that the bank is becoming insolvent.

If and when a bank does go into receivership, the FDIC takes over the operations of that bank so that there is virtually no interruption in service to the customers of the bank. The FDIC then finds a new owner for the bank and the bank may continue to exist or it may be merged with another bank. Any losses are absorbed by the FDIC, except for those on deposits which exceed the federal insurance limit, currently $100,000. The largest recent example of a bank failure involved the Franklin National Bank of New York. This bank was the twentieth largest in the country and it failed in 1974. The FDIC took over this bank and later sold it to a consortium of foreign banks. The depositors of Franklin experienced no losses on deposits which were insured by the FDIC.

Restrictions on Entry and Expansion

From the time the Office of the Comptroller was created, in 1863, until 1933, it was relatively easy to start a bank. Most state governments were quite willing to grant charters and the Comptroller was equally willing to grant federal charters. As a result, by the late 1920s there were nearly 20,000 banks in the United States. Many of these were small state chartered banks and these had to meet very limited regulatory standards. After the establishment of the FDIC, however, all banks which wanted deposit insurance had to meet the standards of this new agency. And nearly all banks needed deposit insurance to be perceived as credible and, therefore, to survive. But the FDIC began to demand proof that there was an actual need for the services of a bank in order for it to be insured. This concept of need has become the standard criterion for the creation of a new bank today. To show need one must demonstrate that a given market is inadequately served by existing banks and that a new bank will be able to operate profitably.

The simultaneous existence of banks with federal charters and banks with state charters persists to this day and is generally referred to as the dual banking system. This system has evolved so that each state has the authority to determine what the banking industry in that state will look like. The system is enhanced by the fact that the federal government prohibits any banks from crossing state lines and permits each state to set its own laws on branch banking within the state. As a result, each state has a separate banking industry and the rules for creation of new banks or expansion of existing banks vary widely across states. Some states, such as Illinois, are unit banking states. Banks in these states can operate in only one physical location. In other states, such as California, statewide branch banking is permitted. Some states, such as Virginia, have only limited branch banking. But in all cases, for a new bank to be started or a branch to be opened, a need must be shown for the new service or the federal regulatory agencies will not agree to the new bank or branch.

Many banks have sought to evade the restrictions on branching within a state and across state lines by forming bank holding companies. These holding companies can buy banks which operate in different states or can operate different banks in the same state somewhat like branch offices. According to the Bank Holding Company Act of 1956 and its amendments in 1966 and 1970, all bank holding companies are subject to regulation by the Federal Reserve Board. The Federal Reserve restricts the amount of direct control of an individual bank which can be exercised by the holding company. But the Federal Reserve also restricts the other activities in which these holding companies are engaged.

In recent years this has become an issue of substantial importance in the commercial banking industry because banks have formed holding companies and the holding companies have diversified into a number of alternative types of businesses. The Federal Reserve Board has been concerned about this diversification of activities because it perceives that it may increase the risk to which deposits are exposed. As a result, the Federal Reserve has exercised strict control over the lines of business in which bank holding companies are allowed to enter. These restrictions initially were included in the Bank Holding Company Act of 1956. This law gave the Federal Reserve Board the power to approve or disapprove requests to engage in traditionally nonbanking businesses, but the original law had a number of loopholes and significant amendments were added in 1970.

One of the more interesting loopholes was that the law was worded to restrict *multibank* holding companies. Holding companies with *only one* bank were left unrestricted. This encouraged a large number of banks to form single-bank holding companies and then the holding companies could engage in other businesses as they pleased. It also meant that nonbanking firms could seek to acquire banks. This loophole was closed in 1970 when the law was expanded to cover single- as well as multibank holding companies. Today, the Federal Reserve maintains a list of activities which are permissible for bank holding companies and a list of those which are specifically forbidden. Many of the permissible activities are in the general financial area, such as mortgage banking, leasing, financial advisory services, credit cards, and data processing services.

In order to limit the risk in bank investments there are also restrictions on many of the banking activities of banks. Principal among these are the requirements that banks cannot invest in equity securities or directly in real estate. In addition, bank loans to any one customer are constrained so that they cannot exceed 10 percent of the capital of the bank. Furthermore, bank investments in bonds are restricted to the higher rating categories. These rules are enforced through the process of bank examination.

Minimum Capital Requirements

The final important element of bank regulation is the minimum capital requirement. The regulators do not attempt to enforce a standard capital requirement across all banks in the United States. That is, they do not require that all banks must finance, say, 10 percent of the total assets through equity capital. Rather they try to see that capital is adequate, given the risk of a bank, or a particular class of banks. Furthermore, the agencies utilize a number of different measures of adequacy of capital. One such measure is the ratio of total capital to total assets of a bank, where total capital includes both the equity value of the bank and long-term debt (not deposits). Many people believe that long-term debt should not be counted as capital for regulatory purposes and, hence, measure capital adequacy with the ratio of equity, including common and preferred stock and retained earnings, to total assets. Both of these measures of capital adequacy have been declining in recent years in the United States. In 1978 (September) the ratio of equity to total assets for insured banks was 7 percent.[6] This is lower than it has been for some time. Figure 11-6 in Chapter Eleven shows the fluctuations in this ratio from the 1920s to the late 1970s. It is difficult to determine whether this trend will continue or whether regulators will tighten their requirements for capital in commercial banks.

The question of what constitutes an adequate or optimal supply of capital for a bank is an exceptionally difficult one. There is not even a clear understanding of what constitutes an optimal capital structure, or mix of debt and equity, for a nonfinancial firm. But for banks, where failure in large numbers imposes a substantial social cost, the problems are even more difficult. In a competitive capital market the market will price all securities to reflect the market's perception of risk and return. As a result, the market extracts a premium from firms that use more risky debt and prices the equity capital of the firm to reflect that risk. But the elements of secrecy surrounding commercial banks, insurance of deposit liabilities, and restrictions and examinations of riskiness make the assessment of such premiums a difficult task for the marketplace. As a result government regulators seek to use capital to provide an additional cushion or protection for depositors against mismanagement, conflicts of interest, and fraud committed by commercial bankers. As such, capital requirements are one more tool used by the regulators to minimize the prospect of major instability in the banking system. How much is adequate or optimal, however, is a difficult and tricky question upon which there is likely never to be complete agreement.

THE RECENT PERFORMANCE OF THE REGULATORY SYSTEM

The Track Record on Bank Failures and Stability

The principal purpose of the regulatory system which has evolved in the United States is to avoid the instability which plagued the banking industry and the economy throughout the nineteenth century and ultimately to avoid market failure. The system has been tremendously successful in accomplishing its objectives. Figure 17-1, which was discussed earlier, shows that after

---

[6] The total assets and equity of insured commercial banks as of September 30, 1978, were $1,198,495 million and $85,540 million, respectively. See the *Federal Reserve Bulletin*, March 1980, pp. A18 and A19.

the institution of deposit insurance, bank failures almost completely ceased. In the last few years there have been more problems with bank failures than has been the case since 1935. But relative to the experience prior to 1933, the numbers are still very small.

The number of bank failures alone does not tell the whole story. Since deposit insurance has been instituted, the kinds of panics which periodically gripped financial markets during the nineteenth century, and which led to the Depression of the 1930s, have virtually been eliminated. That does not mean that the economy has not experienced times of recession and boom. It does mean that financial panics where citizens feared their deposits would become worthless and, therefore, ran on the banks, seem to have been eliminated. More recently we have experienced problems in financial markets, including what we call liquidity crises. But thus far, they have not led to the kinds of panics which occurred prior to the advent of deposit insurance.

The Cost in Lost Competition

This improved track record has not been accomplished without cost. One of the costs which has been imposed by this regulatory system, is the cost of forgone competition. While we know that one of the basic reasons for regulation in financial markets is to promote competition and prevent monopolistic practices (see point 1 in the checklist at the beginning of the chapter), the regulatory system for financial intermediaries, in part, seeks to reduce competition in order to minimize the chances of bank failure and financial panic. Competition leads to lower prices and more efficient services. The essence of competition is that the inefficient simply do not survive. So a regulatory system which places top priority on survival of most participants inherently sacrifices some competition. This is an inherent conflict for which there seems to be no easy solution.

Unfortunately, it is difficult if not impossible to accurately measure the amount of competition, or efficiency resulting from competition, that is sacrificed due to the regulatory system. In a more competitive system it is likely that prices for most banking services would be lower simply because the most efficient would set the standard for the industry, but it is difficult to estimate how much reduction in prices might be accomplished. One clearly observable result of limits on competition from the existing regulatory system is the size distribution of banks in the United States. Unlike other western countries, the United States has a very large number of banks. In part, this is probably just a result of historical circumstances. But it is also due to the laws which prohibit banks from crossing state lines and the restrictions on branching. These laws have led to the continued existence of a relatively large number of very small banks.

Figures 17-2 and 17-3 illustrate this size distribution. Figure 17-2 shows the distribution of bank deposits by size of bank. This figure indicates that

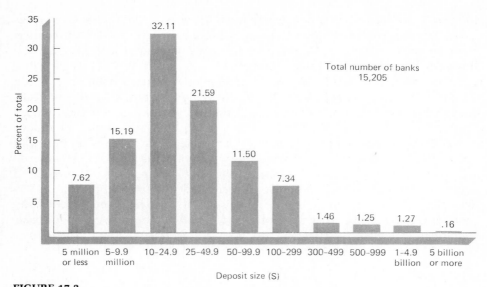

FIGURE 17-2
Size distribution of commercial banks. The figure shows the percentage of the total
number of banks in size classes measured by total deposits. Source: *Federal Reserve
Bulletin*, various issues.

the majority of banks have less than $25 million in deposits. Only a very
small portion of the total number of banks have total deposits of $1 billion.
Figure 17-3, however, shows that most of the total deposits in the country are
in the large banks. The top 0.2 percent of the banks hold 37 percent of all the
deposits. To most people who have examined this question, it seems that the
large number of small banks would not continue to exist were it not for
regulatory restrictions, particularly regarding branching.

The laws on branching and the prohibition on banks operating in more
than one state are viewed by many as exceptionally archaic restrictions. This
view contends that commercial banking is much like a "mom and pop" store
and that it is inefficient as a result. Those who advocate this view point to the
size distribution of banks shown in Figure 17-2 and argue that the large
number of small banks simply cannot be justified on economic grounds. The
branching laws are viewed as more a protection of entrenched monopoly
position than anything else. But if and when these laws change there is
likely to be a large amount of consolidation in this industry. Those who are
worried about this bring to bear considerable political pressure to preserve
the present system. Whether they will be successful throughout the 1980s
remains to be seen.

One other way to evaluate the relative efficiency of small and large
banks is to directly analyze the cost of providing banking services as a
function of the size of the bank. Most studies of this subject have concluded

that there are some economies involved in larger scale banking operations. Two such economies that result from increasing bank size are lower labor costs per unit and increased access to more sophisticated automatic processing systems. For example, George Benston[7] has estimated that with a 100 percent increase in bank output, costs would increase by 93 percent, on average. This gain tends to be reduced once a bank reaches an intermediate size so that medium-size banks are probably as efficient as very large banks. This means that the banking industry is not subject to the same kinds of problems or economies of scale as characterize the public utilities industry.

Pressures for Change in the Regulation of Commercial Banks

The process of evolution in the system of regulation for commercial banks did not stop with the major reforms accomplished in 1933. The most significant revisions in regulations since the Depression have recently been enacted and new changes are likely to be forthcoming in the near future. The underlying reason for this change is that much of the regulatory system which has existed for nearly 50 years is incompatible with an economy

[7] See George J. Benston, "Economies of Scale in Financial Institutions," *Journal of Money, Credit and Banking* (May 1972), pp. 312–341.

FIGURE 17-3

Distribution of deposits across commercial banks. The figure shows, for example, that the banks with 5 billion or more in deposits have approximately 37 percent of total deposits. *Federal Reserve Bulletin*, various issues.

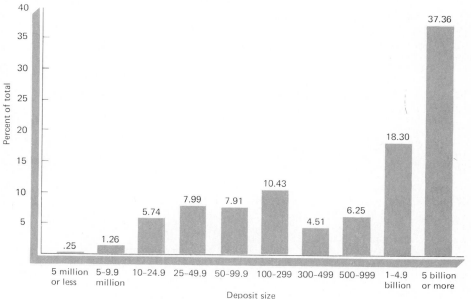

which is experiencing high and volatile inflation rates. To understand the difficulty which inflation creates we will have to examine the system of barter used in commercial banking or the system of exchanging services for balances. This system has resulted from two factors. The first is the restriction of interest payments on deposit accounts. The second is the Federal Reserve's policy of requiring reserves which do not earn interest and providing services in exchange.

Since its inception the Federal Reserve System imposed reserve requirements on commercial banks which are members of the system. The exact percentage of reserve requirements can be altered by the Federal Reserve Board and it differs, at any point, according to the size of the bank and the type of deposit. The reserve requirements which were in effect in February 1980 are shown in Table 17-1. These reserves amount to a tax on the bank because the Federal Reserve pays no interest on the reserves. The banks could invest these funds in Treasury bills or other securities and earn a rate of return, if they were not held in reserve. But in exchange for these reserves the Federal Reserve provides a package of services to commercial banks without charge. These services include a wide variety of things which the banks generally value, including check clearing and electronic transfer of funds upon which the federal funds market is based.

TABLE 17-1

Member Bank Reserve Requirements

TYPE OF DEPOSIT, AND DEPOSIT INTERVAL ($ MILLIONS)	REQUIREMENTS IN EFFECT FEBRUARY 29, 1980		PREVIOUS REQUIREMENTS	
	PERCENT	EFFECTIVE DATE	PERCENT	EFFECTIVE DATE
Net Demand				
0–2	7	12/30/76	7-½	2/13/75
2–10	9-½	12/30/76	10	2/13/75
10–100	11-¾	12/30/76	12	2/13/75
100–400	12-¾	12/30/76	13	2/13/75
Over 400	16-¼	12/30/76	16-½	2/13/75
Time and Savings				
Savings	3	3/16/67	3-½	3/2/67
Time				
0–5, by maturity				
30–179 days	3	3/16/67	3-½	3/2/67
180 days to 4 years	2-½	1/8/76	3	3/16/67
4 years or more	1	10/30/75	3	3/16/67
Over 5, by maturity				
30–179 days	6	12/12/74	5	10/1/70
180 days to 4 years	2-½	1/8/76	3	12/12/74
4 years or more	1	10/30/75	3	12/12/74

Source: *Federal Reserve Bulletin.*

The question is how valuable are these services to the banks which use them. When interest rates were relatively low, as they were by current standards in the late 1960s, these services were not very expensive. This is because the cost of holding reserves was not as large as it has been in more recent years, as interest rates have risen appreciably. The result of the rise in interest rates has been that the cost of these services has gone up, but the benefit which the commercial banks believe they derive from these services has not gone up to match. Banks which are members of the Federal Reserve have therefore chosen, in increasing numbers, to simply withdraw from the Federal Reserve System. They no longer receive the services, but they also do not have to hold reserves which earn no interest.

A similar type of problem has developed in the relations between commercial banks and their depositors. As explained earlier in this chapter, restrictions were imposed in 1935 on the ability of commercial banks to pay interest on deposit accounts. Specifically, banks were prohibited from paying any interest on demand deposits. But banks have found ways to circumvent this restriction to some extent. Instead of directly paying interest they provide services, free of charge. The most important service is to refrain from directly charging for processing transactions through a checking account. This is a system very much like the one that operates between commercial banks and the Federal Reserve. The Federal Reserve requires deposits by member commercial banks on which it pays no interest. But it does provide services in exchange.

The difficulty here, just as with the Federal Reserve, is that as interest rates have risen with inflation in recent years, depositors have been less willing to accept these services in exchange for deposits. There has been increased pressure on banks to pay direct interest on demand deposits for fear of losing these deposits. Moreover, this is not an idle fear. In recent years a number of nonbank financial institutions have offered liability accounts to consumers that are virtually identical to demand deposits, but which also pay interest. One example of this is what is called the money market mutual fund. Another is the so-called NOW accounts offered by mutual savings banks and savings and loans (see Chapter Eighteen). A money market mutual fund offers what is essentially a demand deposit and invests the funds in a selection of money market instruments. The earnings of the fund are then paid to depositors, less a relatively small management fee. Figure 17-4 shows the recent growth in these funds. They have been particularly attractive in the last few years as short-term interest rates have increased dramatically.

The Deregulation Act of 1980

These difficulties have been at least partially dealt with by the Depository Institutions Deregulation and Monetary Control Act of 1980. This legislation, which was passed by the Congress and signed by President Jimmy

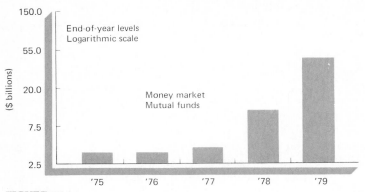

FIGURE 17-4

Growth of money market mutual funds. This figure shows the total assets of money market mutual funds from 1975 to 1979. Source: *Annual Report of the Federal Reserve Bank of New York*, 1979.

Carter in March 1980, involves four principal changes in the regulatory system which affect these problems:[8]

1 It requires *all* depository institutions, not simply commercial banks which are members of the Federal Reserve System, to maintain reserves. The law stipulates that banks which were members of the Federal Reserve in 1980 cannot escape current reserve requirements by withdrawing from the System. It also defines a gradual phase-in for reserve requirements on depository institutions which were not previously subject to reserve requirements, that is, which were not member banks in 1980.
2 It requires that the Federal Reserve directly price those services which are provided to commercial banks and make them available to all depository institutions.
3 It provides for what amounts to payment of interest on demand deposits by authorizing automatic transfer accounts, NOW accounts, and share drafts. Automatic transfer accounts provide for automatic transfer from savings to checking accounts, NOW accounts are essentially interest-bearing accounts from which checks can be written, as are share drafts at credit unions. It further specifies that all of these accounts will be subject to reserve requirements.
4 It requires the gradual elimination of interest-rate restriction on deposit accounts over a 6-year period.

These changes in the regulatory system will have significant and long-term effects. The central question is whether events will overtake these changes so that the gradual phase-in of the changes will not be fast enough.

---

[8] For a detailed statement of the provisions of this law, see *Depository Institutions Deregulation and Monetary Control Act of 1980*, Conference Report, 96th Congress, 2d Session, Report No. 96-640, March 21, 1980.

In addition, the one potentially crucial change which this law does not include is some provision for including interest payments on reserves. Reserves will soon be required of all depository institutions and none of those reserves will earn interest. The long-standing complaint of many participants in this industry is that if they are going to be regulated, they should at least all have to compete under the same regulations. With the Monetary Control Act of 1980, all depository institutions will be facing the same form of taxation through the requirement that non-interest-bearing reserves be maintained. Whether this will prove to be a viable change remains to be determined.

This problem of interest payments on reserves is a particularly difficult one because it involves a significant change in federal tax revenues. Before this story can be completed, it will be necessary to examine the links between the Federal Reserve control of the money supply and the rate of inflation in the United States. We will explore this in Chapter Twenty-two, and we will examine why reserve requirements contribute to what is called the "inflation tax."

SUMMARY

In this chapter we have examined the regulatory system for commercial banks. A large portion of this chapter has been devoted to explaining how and why this regulatory system evolved. This is important because without an understanding of the history of banking regulation *and* what it means it is difficult to make sense out of the regulatory system we have inherited. With the history as background we were then able to examine the current regulatory system and discuss some of the important issues concerning its operation. Finally, we were able to place the significant regulatory changes which will be phased in during the early 1980s into perspective.

Of the four rationales for regulation which we introduced in Chapter Fifteen, the fundamental problem facing depository institutions is the prospect that instability in the banking system may lead to market failure. This results from the peculiar nature of a deposit as a debt obligation. Like any debt security, the value of the deposit can be influenced by expropriations instigated by the issuer of the claim. The problem with expropriations regarding depository institutions is that it is exceedingly difficult to construct covenants which adequately protect against future increases in the debt issued by the institution. The reason is that in order to be able to function effectively a depository institution must have the freedom to increase or decrease deposits as the need arises. This same flexibility makes it impossible to assign collateral to specific deposits.

The method which first evolved for dealing with this problem was for banks to back their deposits with gold. But because banks earned their profits from loans, the more gold they held in reserve, the less profitable they could expect to be. During the Civil War this system of strictly private backing for deposits was augmented. The Banking Act of 1863 created nationally chartered banks with backing by government bonds which were in turn backed by gold. It also created a system of reserves for banks. But banking panics still developed and in 1913 the Federal Reserve System came into existence. The Federal Reserve was given the power to control the supply of reserves in the banking system and, therefore, the liquidity of commercial banks. But in spite of the structure created through the Federal Reserve to provide bank liquidity, the largest banking crisis in U.S. history occurred—the stock market crash of 1929—and the Federal Reserve was unable or unwilling to prevent it.

As a result of this failure of the Federal Reserve System to adequately solve the stability problem of deposit intermediaries, the system was fundamentally altered with the Banking Act of 1933. The changes entailed government insurance of the value of bank deposits and government supervision and control of the risk of depository intermediaries. With the institution of deposit insurance, the backing behind the deposits of banks became a government promise rather than essentially a promise of the individual bank. And because depositors were insured if private banks reneged on their own promise, depositors no longer had an incentive to carefully assess the believability of promises made by individual banks. That responsibility now lay with the government. The system of regulation of commercial banks has been left essentially unchanged until 1980.

On the whole, the system instituted in the 1930s has worked rather well in that banking panics have apparently become obsolete. But there remain a number of issues about the operation of this system which were examined in this chapter. Moreover, we found that as inflation accelerated during the 1970s, some of these issues became so important that they led to the most important changes in the regulatory system since the 1930s. Some of the issues include how deposit insurance should be priced; how extensively the risk of deposit institutions should be regulated; what sorts of barriers to regional and product-line diversification should be allowed; what minimum capital requirements should be required.

But probably the most important issues of the 1970s and 1980s pertain to the restrictions on competition for deposits and the barter system to which those restrictions led. The barter system involved two important elements. First, since the early 1930s the government has imposed restrictions on the interest rates that could be paid on deposit accounts, including restriction of interest on demand deposits. Second, the government required banks which were members of the Federal Reserve System to hold reserves with the System which earned no interest. In return the Federal Reserve provided services to member banks. But as inflation drove market interest rates up, these restrictions became more severe and member banks increasingly withdrew from the Federal Reserve System and sought ways to circumvent the interest-rate restrictions on deposit accounts. In the late 1970s these problems became sufficiently acute that new legislation was passed to deregulate financial intermediaries in important ways. Essentially, the law allows many types of financial institutions to offer demand deposits, allows them to pay interest on those deposits, requires them all to hold reserves behind those deposits, and gradually phases out interest-rate restrictions on deposit accounts. However, it does not provide for interest payment on reserves. It is too early to tell how this system will work.

QUESTIONS TO IMPROVE UNDERSTANDING

1 What does "convertibility" mean? Explain the nature of the convertibility problem which faced banks throughout most of the nineteenth century.

2 Explain what commercial banking was like during the era of wildcat banking. Why is this period referred to as a time of "competing monies"?

3 During the wildcat banking era bank notes traded at whatever rate of exchange the market demanded. After the Civil War bank notes of nationally chartered banks traded at par value. Why did this change occur?

4 Contrast the nature of the solution to banking panics contained in the Federal Reserve Act with the nature of the solution which came with the FDIC. How did the FDIC fundamentally change the nature of the financial contract between a bank and its depositors?

5 The banking reform legislation of the early 1930s is sometimes said to have nationalized gold. What does this mean and what is its significance?

6 Deposit insurance and regulatory control of risk are said to go hand in hand. Why is this so?

7 How might the current system for pricing and coverage of deposit insurance be changed? Evaluate the pros and cons.

8 How does the regulatory system restrict bank branching? How do the banks seek to avoid these restrictions? What are the consequences of branching restrictions for the size distribution of commercial banks?

9 What does it mean to say that there has been a "barter system" operating between banks and their customers and between banks and the Federal Reserve? Why is this barter system under such pressure? What is the role of interest payments on reserves for this barter system?

10 Summarize the provisions of the Depository Institutions Deregulation Act of 1980.

REFERENCES

Benston, George J.: "Economies of Scale in Financial Institutions," *Journal of Money, Credit and Banking*, 4 (May 1972), pp. 312–341.

Black, Fischer, Merton H. Miller, and Richard A. Posner: "An Approach to the Regulation of Bank Holding Companies," *Journal of Business*, 51 (1978), pp. 379–412.

Chase, Samuel B., and John J. Mingo: "The Regulation of Bank Holding Companies," *Journal of Finance*, 30 (May 1975), pp. 281–292.

Friedman, Milton, and Anna Schwartz: *A Monetary History of the United States 1867–1960*, Princeton University Press, Princeton, N.J., 1963.

Juncker, George R.: "A New Supervisory System for Rating Banks," *Quarterly Review*, Federal Reserve Bank of New York, 3 (Summer 1978), pp. 47–51.

Kareken, John H., and Neil Wallace: "Deposit Insurance and Bank Regulation: A Partial-Equilibrium Exposition," *Journal of Business*, 51 (1978), pp. 413–438.

Peltzman, Sam: "Capital Investment in Commercial Banking and Its Relationship to Portfolio Regulation," *Journal of Political Economy*, 78 (1970), pp. 1–26.

Pringle, John: "The Capital Decision in Commercial Banks," *Journal of Finance*, 29 (1974), pp. 779–795.

Santomero, Anthony M., and Ronald D. Watson: "Determining an Optimal Capital Standard for the Banking Industry," *Journal of Finance*, 32 (September 1977), pp. 1267–1282.

West, Robert Craig: *Banking Reform and the Federal Reserve 1863–1923*, Cornell University Press, Ithaca, N.Y., 1974.

U.S. Congress: *Depository Institutions Deregulation and Monetary Control Act of 1980*, Conference Report, 96th Congress, 2d Session, Report No. 96-640, March 21, 1980.

Chapter Eighteen

REGULATION OF NONBANK
FINANCIAL INSTITUTIONS

In the last chapter we examined the important features of the regulatory system which has evolved to ensure the stable operation of the commercial banking system. During the nineteenth and the early decades of the twentieth century commercial banks constituted almost the entire financial intermediation industry in the United States. The only other types of financial institutions which had any significant role in the market were insurance companies. Moreover, while panics and failures plagued the commercial banking industry and threatened the stability of the rest of the economy, the insurance industry continued to function without much public attention. As a result, it operates today without a complex federal regulatory system like that imposed on commercial banks. But during the twentieth century a number of new types of financial intermediaries have emerged. None of these intermediaries are quite like commercial banks and they are certainly not like insurance companies. Actually each of them performs some but not all of the functions of commercial banks as they exist today.

These institutions have become such an important part of the economy that it is very important to closely examine the regulatory systems which govern them. A distinct regulatory system has developed for each of these institutions. While these systems are generally quite similar to the system which has evolved for commercial banks, there are some interesting and important differences. In this chapter we will explore the features of these nonbank financial intermediaries and the regulatory systems which govern their operation. The basic functions of these institutions have been described in Part Three of this book. So the emphasis here will be on describing the regulation of these financial intermediaries. Because many of these institutions are so new, they present some of the most interesting and difficult regulatory issues which may be confronted in the 1980s.

OVERVIEW OF THE REGULATION OF NONBANK FINANCIAL INTERMEDIARIES

It is important to begin this chapter, just as we did the last two, by itemizing the four basic reasons for regulation in any financial market. They are:

1   Promote competition and prevent monopolistic practices
2   Prevent or limit expropriations
3   Control the actions of agents
4   Prevent market failure

As in the last chapter we will find that most regulation of nonbank depository financial intermediaries is designed to avoid market failure. This regulation is essentially the same as the insurance system designed for commercial banks. In addition, many of the nonbank depository intermediaries are regulated as much to protect them as entities distinct from commercial banks as to avoid the social cost of failure which we have come to associate with commercial bank failures. We need to look carefully at this motive because it does not fit neatly into our list of *economic* rationales for regulation. In the case of nondeposit intermediaries, such as insurance companies and pension funds, regulation is motivated more by the other three items on our list. Before we get involved in the details of the regulation of each type of intermediary, it is important to get an overview of the special problems and issues in the regulation of nonbank financial intermediaries.

The first important issue pertains to the social cost of the failure of nonbank financial intermediaries. As discussed in the last chapter, the system of regulation which has emerged for commercial banks is principally designed to prevent periodic panics in banking and the near collapse of the banking system, as occurred in the 1930s. In the period between 1860 and 1934, when the regulatory system evolved, banks, insurance companies, and brokerage houses were virtually the only games in town. In the 1930s the FDIC was created for the banks, the SEC was created for the brokerage houses and investment bankers, and the insurance companies were largely left alone. Since that time, new nonbank intermediaries have become more important and, in most cases, they have been treated much like commercial banks.

It is not obvious, however, that these institutions need government-supplied insurance and control or inspection of risk, as do the commercial banks. Recall that the original motivation for the extensive regulation of banking was that failure of the banking industry imposed a large social cost on the rest of the economy because banks are involved in virtually all trans-actions in the economy. Banks have long provided the medium of exchange used in the economy and if access to that medium of exchange is threatened, then so is the stability of the entire economy. Other nonbank financial inter-mediaries have not necessarily played such a central role in the economy. As long as they remain distinct institutions, with limited roles in accepting savings and providing credit, then the motivation for regulating them must hinge on one or both of two other arguments. One possibility is that any financial problems experienced by one of the specialized nonbank inter-mediaries may spread to the commercial banking industry. The other is that there is some socially beneficial purpose of a particular nonbank inter-mediary which warrants regulation and protection.

This second possibility constitutes the second important issue regard-ing the regulation of nonbank financial intermediaries. The issue is how extensively should the specialized set of nonbank financial intermediaries which has emerged in the United States be protected by government regula-tion. Many of the nonbank intermediaries have been shielded from compe-tition, either through special advantages created and maintained by the government or through restrictions placed upon potential competitors, par-ticularly commercial banks. When a particular type of institution is initially protected by the government it is often done with an intent to accomplish some social benefit. The difficulty, of course, is that nearly everyone can imagine a special purpose which he or she believes should be protected and promoted. This can justify extensive regulation and protection of the entire financial industry when there is really no underlying economic rationale of the kind developed in Chapter Fifteen and used in Chapters Sixteen and Seventeen to explain the regulation of securities markets and commercial banks.

An example should help clarify the nature of the difficulty. The savings and loan industry is a, if not the, prime case. Savings and loans have been nourished and protected by the government to promote and encourage the construction of housing. But as time has passed, the savings and loan and construction industries themselves have developed a vested interest in con-tinuing the protection. Hence, it eventually becomes difficult to separate the original purpose, that of providing additional housing for the citizens of the country, from the desire of the housing construction and finance industries to promote their own well-being.

The central question is: What amount of net benefit is generated for society by creating specialized and protected financial intermediaries designed to serve a particular segment of the market? One view holds that there is relatively little benefit. Those who hold this view would eliminate most of the protection currently afforded particular institutions and allow all financial intermediaries to compete on an equal basis. This view has come to be labeled the unisex financial institutions movement. The nonbank institutions which we examine in this chapter probably exist as we know them today principally because of the protection they are afforded. Without that protection, competition would probably result in considerable consolidation and possibly elimination of some of these institutions as distinct entities.

It is difficult to draw an objective conclusion as to the extent of regulation and protection which is appropriate for each type of financial intermediary because the social costs involved in a failure are often difficult to quantify and measure. Despite this difficulty, as nonbank intermediaries are examined in the rest of this chapter, the question of the appropriate extent of regulation should be kept in mind.

REGULATION OF SAVINGS AND LOANS AND THE PROBLEM OF DISINTERMEDIATION

In this section we will explore the basic features of the regulatory system which governs the savings and loan industry and we will focus attention on the central problem regarding regulation in this industry, disintermediation. *Disintermediation* refers to a trend of withdrawals from financial intermediaries which occurs when savers choose to place their funds directly into market instruments rather than to utilize the services of intermediaries. Disintermediation means a loss of funds for savings and loans and, therefore, also for the housing industry. There have been a number of relatively brief periods of disintermediation in the United States which have occurred when market interest rates have peaked. There is an interesting and intricate explanation for why this occurs, which will be presented in this section.

Outline of the Regulatory Structure for Savings and Loans

The federal regulator of savings and loans is the Federal Home Loan Bank Board (FHLBB) and the federal insurer is the Federal Savings and Loan Insurance Corporation (FSLIC). Like commercial banks, savings and loans can be chartered by the state in which they operate and hence regulated by that state, or they can be federally chartered and regulated at the federal level. Of the roughly 4,700 savings and loans in operation at the end of the 1970s, slightly less than 50 percent were federally chartered, but more than 90 percent were insured by the FSLIC and these insured institutions account for 98 percent of all deposits.

The regulatory system operated by the FHLBB, the FSLIC, and the individual states is quite similar to the system which applies to commercial banks. Like commercial banks, savings and loans are prohibited from branching across state lines and must acquire permission for branching within their state. In most states branching restrictions are more liberal for savings and loans than they are for commercial banks. In part this is because the FHLBB has taken a fairly liberal attitude toward branching and because there are probably fewer long-established vested interests in this industry which are threatened by branching than there are in commercial banking. The regulators of savings and loans have responsibility for inspecting and controlling risk, as do the bank regulators. They also enforce capital requirements and requirements on reserves. Finally, they impose minimum interest-rate ceilings on the various types of deposit accounts that savings and loans offer.

While most of the regulations which have historically been imposed upon savings and loans are nearly identical to similar regulations imposed upon commercial banks, there are also some very important differences. The differences have been motivated by the long-standing intent of the federal government to support housing finance. The important differences boil down to the following five points:

Savings and loans have been required to place all but a small portion of their assets into residential mortgages.

Savings and loans have been authorized to pay higher interest rates (historically ranging up to one-half of 1 percent) than commercial banks on various deposit accounts.

The FHLBB has provided a continuing source of funds to savings and loans in the form of advances.

Congress has granted special tax treatment to savings and loans.

The FHLBB has restricted the types of mortgage contracts which savings and loans can offer.

It is important to recognize that this is the system which existed throughout the 1960s and 1970s, but with the regulatory changes which were enacted in 1980 (and summarized in the previous chapter), this system is now undergoing some fundamental changes. In this section of the chapter we will examine the special features of the regulatory system which have existed for savings and loans, and then we will review the major features of the changes enacted in 1980.

The requirement that savings and loans invest only in residential mortgages, aside from some holdings of liquid assets such as Treasury bills, is one of the most direct steps taken by the government to support housing construction. This has meant that roughly 80 percent of all savings and loan assets are invested in mortgages. The idea has been that by establishing a lender which is restricted to invest almost exclusively in mortgages, more funds will flow into home mortgages than would otherwise be the case. But the potential problem with this kind of restriction is that a private institution which is constrained in this way is unlikely to be able to compete effectively in the long run with institutions which are not so restricted. In order to offset this disadvantage, as well as the fact that, unlike commercial banks, savings and loans have historically been unable to offer demand deposits, the FHLBB has permitted savings and loans to pay higher interest rates on deposit accounts than those paid by commercial banks. In the early 1970s this margin amounted to one-half of 1 percent on most types of deposits. In 1973 the margin was dropped to one-quarter of 1 percent. It will be eliminated by 1986.

In addition to this margin, the FHLBB has come to assume a supportive role with savings and loans which the bank regulatory agencies, particularly the Federal Reserve, do not provide for commercial banks. The FHLBB is a direct supplier of funds to savings and loans through what are called advances. These advances have come to represent a sizable portion of the total source of funds for savings and loans. The Federal Reserve provides a service which is similar in some respects through what is called the discount window. But loans extended to commercial banks through the discount window of the Federal Reserve are intended as temporary sources of funds, to be used only when a bank has a short-term liquidity problem. Continued reliance on the discount window is a sign of trouble which attracts the bank examiners. But this has not been true with savings and loans' use of advances. Advances have been a more permanent source of funds and therefore, in effect, a way of providing federal support for mortgage loans. This is in addition to the secondary market provided by quasi-governmental agencies like the Federal National Mortgage Association. The total volume of advances, as well as total savings and loan deposits are shown in Figure 18-1.

These institutions are also regulated through tax laws. Tax breaks provided to various institutions act as subsidies or methods of protecting those institutions. The tax system also creates incentives which guide many financing decisions in the economy. For example, we learned in Chapter Fourteen that municipal bonds are held in large quantities by commercial banks because the tax-exemption feature is attractive to these institutions. Commercial banks have enough flexibility in their portfolio decisions to take advantage of the tax treatment of municipal-bond income. But savings and loans do not. Because they deal almost exclusively in mortgage loans, this method of tax avoidance has not been a viable option.

Until the early 1960s savings and loans as well as other thrift institutions, excluding commercial banks, had little need for such tax-evasion schemes because other techniques were successful in avoiding almost all taxes. It was not until 1952 that savings and loans and mutual savings banks became subject to the federal corporate income tax. From 1952 until 1962 these institutions were able to avoid almost all federal income taxes through liberal use of so-called bad-debt reserves. Bad-debt reserves represent funds which are set aside to cover possible future defaults on loans. The tax advan-

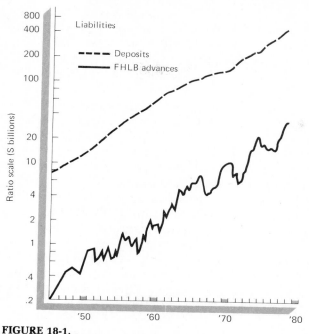

FIGURE 18-1.
Volume of deposits and advances from the Federal Home Loan Bank Board at savings
and loan associations. Source: *Federal Reserve Chart Book*, 1979.

tage they provide is that income is tax deductible when it is placed in the
bad-debt reserve rather than when a bad debt is actually realized. Therefore,
by diverting funds to bad-debt reserves these institutions were able to offset
almost all taxable income.

Initial revisions in the tax laws pertaining to the deductibility of these
expenses were made in 1962 and more extensive revisions were made in the
Revenue Act of 1969. The changes incorporated in these acts were significant and led to a sizable increase in the effective tax rates on savings and
loans. The effective tax rate for savings and loans rose from approximately
0.4 percent in 1962 to approximately 24.8 percent in 1974. The 1969 act
provided for a more uniform system of taxation for all financial institutions,
particularly with regard to bad-debt reserves. Both the 1962 and 1969 laws
defined a number of allowable procedures for computing bad-debt reserves
which might be chosen by any financial intermediary and left one additional
method open only to savings and loans and mutual savings banks. But the
law set requirements for use of this method: savings and loans must have 82
percent of their assets and mutual savings banks 72 percent in residential
mortgages, cash, government securities, and passbook loans. These restrictions were first instituted in 1962 and were liberalized in the 1969 law to the
extent that an institution which had 60 percent of its assets in these invest-

ments could deduct a smaller percent of its income using the percentage-of-income method. Below 60 percent, the method could not be used. The income method allows an institution to transfer up to 40 percent of annual income as of 1979, and a higher percent in earlier years, to bad-debt reserves. This generally allows greater deductions than do other methods allowed by the IRS.

The last unique feature of this regulatory system is that the FHLBB has historically restricted the types of mortgages which federally chartered savings and loans may offer and the state regulators have restricted the allowable contracts for state chartered savings and loans. It is somewhat difficult to pin down the exact motive for such a restriction. In part it is motivated by a desire to control the risk assumed by insured institutions and in part it is designed to prevent exploitation of unwary consumers. The specific nature of the restriction has been that savings and loans, until recently, have been allowed to invest solely in fixed-rate mortgages. Alternative mortgage instruments, which provide for more flexibility in the interest rate, are now allowed and are becoming increasingly popular with savings and loans. To fully appreciate why these alternatives have attracted such attention we need to come to understand what causes disintermediation and the cures for this problem which the regulators have tried in recent years.

Problems with the Regulatory Strategy for Savings and Loans

The essential problem faced by savings and loans in the last 20 years results from the fact that they borrow short and lend long. That is, the average maturity of their loans is considerably longer than the average maturity of their deposit liabilities. (This problem was discussed at some length in Chapter Twelve. See, for example, Table 12-2.)

When savings and loans extend mortgage loans with maturities of 30 years, at a fixed interest rate, they are making a commitment to provide insurance to the borrower against future changes in interest rates. If the lender's liabilities had the same maturity as its mortgage loans, then it would bear no risk in providing that insurance. But when its funds are obtained with an average maturity that is substantially shorter than the maturity of its loans, then it bears the risk that the cost of its funds will increase while the return on its mortgages remains unchanged. In a time when inflation is accelerating and much of that inflation is unanticipated, short-term interest rates will tend to increase and the rates of return on existing long-term mortgages will remain unchanged. If this kind of development persists long enough it can mean disaster for financial intermediaries which invest almost exclusively in fixed-interest-rate mortgage loans.

It is important to recognize that the source of the problem for savings and loans is that they have been restricted by government regulation to invest almost exclusively in long-term fixed-rate mortgage loans. Hence, they are precluded from taking the kinds of steps which an unrestricted lender might take to reduce exposure to the risk of increasing short-term interest rates. Other institutions, such as commercial banks, have chosen not to become so heavily committed to mortgages and, thereby, have limited the amount of risk they bear. But to permit savings and loans this option has been inconsistent with the objective of promoting housing construction, and this objective has guided government policy toward savings and loans.

Until very recently the solution to this problem chosen by the regulatory authorities and by Congress was to restrict the ability of the institutions which compete for consumer deposits from doing so with interest rates. That is, rather than let the cost of deposits rise with short-term market interest rates, the government chose to place ceilings on the interest rates which savings and loans and commercial banks could pay to depositors. The ceilings were actually intended to protect savings and loans, and to a lesser extent commercial banks. It was infeasible to attempt to protect savings and loans alone, because commercial banks would then have a sufficient advantage in the market for consumer deposits that savings and loans presumably would not be viable institutions. So the government chose to impose a regulation which specified interest-rate ceilings on both commercial banks and savings and loans. Regulation Q is the regulation of the Federal Reserve Board pertaining to deposit ceilings and it applies only to commercial banks. However, a similar regulation has been coordinated with regulation Q and imposed by the FHLBB on savings and loans. All of these ceilings are somewhat loosely referred to as regulation Q ceilings.

The potential problem with ceilings on deposit rates is that when market-controlled interest rates rise above those ceilings, depositors have a strong incentive to withdraw their funds and invest in credit market instruments that are not restricted. When deposit rate ceilings were first implemented this was only a potential and not an actual problem. The reason was that market interest rates were not particularly volatile and generally remained at levels that, from the vantage point of the late 1970s, seem rather low. However, this state of affairs did not last, so the potential problem with deposit ceilings became an all-too-vivid reality. By the middle 1970s interest rates on short-term U.S. Treasury bills, the principal alternative to deposit accounts with interest-rate ceilings, rose to unprecedented levels. As a result, there was a tremendous incentive for depositors who had at least $10,000, the minimum amount needed to buy a Treasury bill, to do so. This led to unprecedented declines in the flows of deposits into both savings and loans and commercial banks, or disintermediation. The spreads between Treasury bill rates and deposit ceilings are illustrated in Chapter Twelve, Figure 12-8, where the effect of ceilings on the market for deposits was first explained.

With the advent of high and volatile inflation and interest rates during the 1970s, the potential problem with deposit rate ceilings became its fatal flaw. The regulators became persuaded that something had to be done to deal with the problem of disintermediation or housing would probably suffer such severe problems that the whole purpose for creating and protecting savings and loans would be compromised. A partial solution to the problem which the government utilized during the 1970s was to encourage the development of the secondary mortgage market through the quasi-governmental agencies which purchase mortgages and issue their own securities. Of particular significance during the past decade have been the mortgage pools developed by GNMA which grew to over $75 billion by 1979. The development of a more efficient secondary market attracted investors, who were not previously involved, into the mortgage market, thereby improving the flow of funds into mortgage financing.

But by the late 1970s, after the experience of the 1974–1975 recession, the bank and savings and loan regulators concluded that some more fundamental change in the system was needed. What they did was to partially undo the system of deposit ceilings, but not eliminate it altogether. The way they did this was to create the money market certificates, which we first examined in Chapter Twelve. Essentially, money market certificates allow banks and savings and loans to compete with Treasury bills. Money market certificates are very similar to Treasury bills. In particular, the interest rates on new money market certificates are tied to the rate prevailing each week on Treasury bills. As a result, when interest rates rise, depositors who would otherwise have had an incentive to withdraw their funds and place them in Treasury bills, no longer have good reason to do so.

The problem which these certificates have created for the financial institutions is the precise problem which deposit ceilings were designed to prevent. That is, the profitability of savings and loans is seriously threatened when short-term interest rates increase and the rate of return on existing mortgages remains unchanged. Until the federal regulators created money market certificates, savings and loans had been protected from this problem, but since 1977, with the advent of money market certificates, the situation facing savings and loans has become more precarious. This became particularly evident in late 1979 and early 1980 when short-term interest rates hit their post-World War II peak. Had interest rates remained at the very high levels they reached in early 1980 and had federal support not been available to ease savings and loans through this interest-rate peak, numerous savings and loans could have been threatened with insolvency. However, the precipitous decline in short-term interest rates between April and June 1980 eased the situation, at least temporarily.

The most recent step taken by the federal regulators to deal with the problems which confronted savings and loans during the 1970s is contained in the Depository Institution Deregulation Act of 1980, summarized in the previous chapter. As pointed out in that chapter, essential features of the act include a 6-year phase-out of regulation Q interest-rate ceilings on savings and time deposit accounts and the authorization of all depository intermediaries to offer interest-bearing transaction accounts, such as NOW accounts. It has also granted savings and loans some limited ability to diversify their investments; they have been allowed to invest in some shorter term assets and some consumer loans. The regulators have also permitted greater use of alternative mortgage instruments. In particular, in April 1980, the FHLBB authorized federally chartered savings and loans to offer variable rate mortgages. Whether these changes will be sufficient for the savings and loan industry to prosper in the long run as a distinct component of the financial intermediation industry is hard to determine at this time.

It is important to understand the basic rationale behind the regulatory system which has been applied to savings and loans and which has undergone such significant change in recent years. In effect, the government supported housing by designing a system where the consumer did not directly bear the inherent risk of the changing costs of funds. Instead, through federal support and restrictions on savings and loans, the costs of bearing this risk were shifted around, and in a rather confusing way. This worked without too much difficulty as long as inflation and interest rates were low, but by the mid-1970s it became apparent that fundamental changes in the system were necessary. Some significant changes have now been mandated and more changes will likely be made during the 1980s. In the next chapter we will begin to explore the links between government regulation of financial markets and this problem of inflation.

REGULATION OF OTHER THRIFT INSTITUTIONS

Financial intermediaries which principally serve to make loans to and accept deposits from consumers are known as thrift institutions. One of the most important types of thrift institutions is the savings and loan. But other thrift institutions include mutual savings banks (MSBs), credit unions (CUs), and, to a certain extent, finance companies. Each of these three intermediaries serves a somewhat different purpose and each is regulated in a different way.

The Role of Other Thrift Institutions in the Economy

Of the three intermediaries which we refer to as other thrift institutions, the mutual savings bank is most like the savings and loan. MSBs exist almost exclusively in New England and New York, and in those states they serve essentially the same purpose that savings and loans serve throughout the rest of the country; that is, they extend mortgage loans. Unlike credit unions and finance companies, they are not heavily involved in financing a wide variety of consumer purchases. They are therefore not quite the shopping center for consumer financing that we will find characterizes the other two thrift institutions. At the end of 1977 mutual savings banks as a whole invested approximately 65 percent of their assets in mortgages. The second largest component of the asset side of their balance sheet is represented by corporate bonds, which comprise about 15 percent of their assets. On the liability side of their balance sheets, mutual savings banks look very much like savings and loans. They are authorized to attract savings and time deposits like commercial banks and savings and loans and they are subject to the same interest-rate ceilings as commercial banks. In the late 1970s their ratio of highly liquid savings deposits as opposed to time deposits with fixed maturities was about 2 to 1.

In recent years credit unions have emerged as the institutions which provide a real shopping list of consumer financing. Essentially, they provide installment credit to consumers. Their overall position in this market was described in Chapter Twelve and the total volume of their installment lending during the 1970s was shown in Table 12-3. This table shows that credit unions are the third largest source of consumer installment financing. Table 18-1 documents the wide variety of purposes for which these consumer loans are used. The table shows that the most important single purpose for credit union loans is to finance automobiles. But beyond that single category, the loans are highly diversified.

Though credit unions make a wide variety of different types of consumer loans, they do almost nothing else. On the whole, the balance sheets of credit unions are probably the most concentrated, on both the asset and liability sides, of all the thrift institutions. On the asset side, credit unions invest exclusively in consumer loans. Unlike mutual savings banks, they do not invest significantly in such things as corporate bonds. Moreover, they generally hold only a small portion of their assets in highly liquid form such as U.S. Treasury bills. Credit unions have not made first-mortgage loans, principally due to regulatory restrictions which, until recently, have limited the maximum maturity for loans which they can offer to 10 years. This has effectively kept them out of the first-mortgage business. Many credit unions have been willing to make second-mortgage loans and home-improvement loans, which generally can be written with maturities of 10 years or less. On the liability side, credit unions have obtained their funds almost exclusively from what are called shares. Shares are essentially like savings deposits in that they have no stated maturity and may be withdrawn upon notice. They have also been subject to interest-rate restrictions on share accounts, as have most other types of thrift institutions. Unlike other thrifts, during most of the 1970s this was virtually the only type of deposit account which credit unions were able to offer. Recent changes in regulations have altered this situation and we will examine these shortly.

Credit unions are generally small institutions which are owned by the depositors; that is, they are mutual organizations. The average credit union in 1978 had total assets of about $3 million, while the average commercial bank was more than three times this size. For about 80 percent of these credit unions the bond of association which provides the basis for the institution is a common employer or the members of a union. The mutual form of organization is a common form of ownership for most thrift institutions. Virtually

TABLE 18-1

Purposes for Loans from Credit Unions

| PURPOSE AND SECURITY | NUMBER OF LOANS | AMOUNT OF LOANS | | PERCENTAGE DISTRIBUTION | |
		TOTAL ($ THOUSANDS)	AVERAGE SIZE	NUMBER OF LOANS	AMOUNT OF LOANS
Total	12,119,245	$23,007,403	$1,898	—	—
Not distributed	12,076,522	22,913,684	1,897	—	—
Distributed	42,723	93,719	2,194	100.0	100.0
Purpose of Loans					
Durable goods, total	16,136	43,043	2,668	37.8	45.9
Automobiles					
New	4,869	20,574	4,226	11.4	22.0
Used	5,318	12,491	2,349	12.4	13.3
Furniture, home furnishings, and household appliances	2,927	3,868	1,321	6.9	4.1
Boats, mobile homes	944	3,224	3,415	2.2	3.4
Other	2,078	2,886	1,389	4.9	3.1
Personal, household, and family expenses, total	19,682	30,522	1,550	46.1	32.6
Nondurable goods	1,512	1,985	1,313	3.5	2.1
Vacations	2,073	2,693	1,299	4.9	2.9
Education	634	1,219	1,923	1.5	1.3
Medical, dental, and funeral expenses	1,424	2,234	1,569	3.3	2.4
Taxes	965	1,641	1,701	2.3	1.8
Insurance	798	1,228	1,539	1.9	1.3
Debt consolidation	3,446	6,567	1,903	8.1	7.0
Other	8,830	12,955	1,467	20.7	13.8
Repair and modernization (Residential)	5,149	11,166	2,169	12.1	11.9
Real estate, total	958	6,432	6,713	2.2	6.9
Farm	201	1,245	6,194	.5	1.3
Nonfarm	757	5,187	6,852	1.8	5.5
Business	798	2,556	3,203	1.9	2.7

Source: *Annual Report of the National Credit Union Administration*, 1977, p. 7.

all credit unions and MSBs, plus a sizable percentage of savings and loans, are mutual associations. In the savings and loan industry, there has been a significant movement away from the mutual form of organization and toward equity ownership. Most observers agree that the equity form of organization provides greater flexibility and efficiency for the savings and loan than does the mutual organization. But whether there will ever be significant changes in ownership structure of credit unions and MSBs is questionable.

The final type of thrift institution is the finance company. Finance companies include all the leftover types of institutions which cannot be fit easily into one of the other principal categories of institutions. There are essentially three types of finance companies which extend loans to consumers. The first type is the finance company which is tied to a particular retailer or manufacturer. For example, GMAC is the finance company affiliated with General Motors. GMAC finances automobiles, but it also engages in a variety of other financing activities not dealing with consumer loans (see Chapter Thirteen for a discussion of corporate financing through finance companies). The second type of finance company is tied to a commercial bank and exists to circumvent government regulations, particularly those regarding branching. For example, Citicorp operates a nationwide chain of finance companies under the name of Person to Person. It is widely believed that this business is motivated at least in part to position Citicorp in the event that nationwide branching is ever permitted. The final type of finance company is an independent company which accepts deposits from consumers or uses bank loans to fund consumer as well as business loans or leases. The key to these institutions is that, unlike commercial banks and thrifts, they are essentially unregulated. They can accept deposits and pay rates above regulation ceilings. They are also uninsured at the federal level and are not subject to the controls that apply to banks and other thrifts.

Finance companies are the second most important source of consumer installment credit, after commercial banks and before credit unions. But in the middle of the 1970s finance companies had a little more than half of their total loans extended to businesses rather than to consumers. Unlike mutual savings banks and credit unions, finance companies do not derive most of their funds from deposits. Most of their funds come from bank loans, commercial paper, and other nondeposit liabilities distributed in the market. In 1975 deposit liabilities represented only about 2 percent of all funds acquired by finance companies. Finance companies are therefore not thrifts in the same sense as credit unions and mutual savings banks. For, while they extend a large volume of loans to consumers and compete directly with MSBs and credit unions for consumer loans, they have not been an important direct conduit for consumer savings.

Regulating the Other Thrifts

As indicated earlier, there is no separate federal regulatory agency for mutual savings banks. Much of the regulation of these institutions is conducted on a state level. The majority of MSBs are insured, however, by the FSLIC and these institutions have to observe the same deposit ceilings as do commercial banks. The individual state regulatory agencies closely supervise the assets which MSBs are allowed to hold as investments.

Credit unions, on the other hand, have their own federal regulatory agency, the National Credit Union Administration (NCUA). The NCUA came into existence in 1970 when Congress passed the National Credit Union Act. Prior to that time credit unions were regulated by the Department of Health, Education, and Welfare. The NCUA now provides most of the same functions that other regulators perform for commercial banks or savings and loans, including provision of insurance, inspection, and control of risk.

Credit unions have been severely restricted as to the types of loans and investments which they can extend and the types of deposits they can offer. They have been restricted to making consumer loans and investing in government securities. In a few states credit unions have been allowed to invest in high-grade corporate bonds. Until 1977 federal regulations limiting the maximum maturity of credit union loans kept them out of the market for residential mortgages. But amendments to the National Credit Union Act passed in 1977 have liberalized this restriction so that they may now hold first-mortgage loans with 30-year maturities.

Unlike the other intermediaries subject to federal regulations, credit unions have been subject to restrictions on the maximum interest rate they can charge on loans as well as deposits. Until the late 1970s, the maximum rate was 12 percent. This rate became unreasonably low during the interest-rate peak of the late 1970s, so the regulators raised the ceiling. Whether this kind of restriction will be a binding constraint on credit unions in the 1980s is difficult to determine. Federal regulators also restricted credit unions to offer passbook-type share drafts during much of the 1970s. Once other financial intermediaries began to offer money market certificates, this constraint threatened to place credit unions in a difficult situation. Therefore, in the late 1970s they were given expanded powers to offer variable-rate savings accounts.

One of the most controversial forms of regulation imposed upon these institutions, as well as upon savings and loans and commercial banks, is the system of ceilings on deposit interest rates. We have already seen that one of the main consequences of these ceilings is the process of disintermediation which has caused so much difficulty for the savings and loan industry. But deposit ceilings can cause harmful disruptions even for institutions which are not constrained to place their assets in fixed-rate mortgages, as MSBs and CUs are not. Deposit ceilings cause interest rates on deposit accounts to be below competitive levels in times when market interest rates are at their peak. This can lead to a gain for the owners of depository institutions if the rate of interest they can earn on their asset goes up with market interest rates and if it is difficult for at least some savers to switch out of deposit accounts subject to ceilings. The relevant questions regarding these distortions are: What is the magnitude of the excess profit created by deposit ceilings? What are the uses to which these excess profits are put?

While it is difficult to acquire precise answers to these questions for the nation as a whole and for each of the different types of depository institutions, some interesting evidence is available. One study which covered the impact of deposit rate ceilings on MSBs in Massachusetts from 1970 to 1975 was conducted by Robert Taggart.[1] Taggart concluded that by 1975 deposit ceilings had reduced interest rates on deposit accounts by 125 basis points or 1.25 percentage points, resulting in a loss to depositors in Massachusetts MSBs of over half a billion dollars. Much of this gain was dissipated by these MSBs in an attempt to attract new customers. In order to attract customers, these MSBs generated excess expenses amounting to roughly 40 percent of this total loss. A sizable portion of this expense was used to establish new branches and other facilities which would provide convenience to customers. In effect, when deposit institutions are prohibited from competing with prices, they compete by spending funds on convenience, advertising, and other services. These other services are generally a less efficient means of attracting customers and therefore amount to a penalty imposed upon consumers.

The tax advantages available to MSBs are essentially the same as those open to savings and loans. These mutual organizations must pay taxes on the income earned after fixed interest payments to depositors, and a nonmutual association must pay taxes on profits after interest expenses. However, credit unions do receive special tax treatment. They have been classified as nonprofit organizations and are therefore exempt from federal income taxes. As a result, credit unions distribute all their revenues, after expenses, to their members in proportion to the volume of business the members have with the credit union. This tax advantage has become increasingly controversial as credit unions have become a more significant part of the market for consumer financing. The tax advantage gives credit unions a competitive advantage in this market which is not enjoyed by other institutions providing consumer financing. It seems inevitable, if credit unions continue to grow as they have in recent years, that this tax advantage will be reduced.

Probably the most important regulatory change affecting both credit unions and MSBs during the 1970s involves what are called NOW accounts and share drafts. NOW (negotiated order of withdrawal) accounts and share drafts are essentially checking accounts which earn interest. By developing and securing permission to offer these accounts, credit unions and MSBs began to compete directly with commercial banks for demand deposits. Moreover, they could offer interest payments on their equivalent of demand deposits and commercial banks were prohibited from doing so. They were, therefore, in a position to compete very effectively. NOW accounts first came into existence in 1972 when the Massachusetts Supreme Court held that Massachusetts state law did not prohibit state chartered mutual savings banks from offering savings accounts from which checks or drafts could be written. An MSB in New Hampshire immediately recognized that there was no distinction between the laws in the two states and began offering NOW accounts shortly after the Massachusetts decision. Congress became concerned that these might spread nationwide and therefore passed a law which

---

[1] See Robert A. Taggart, "Effects of Deposit Rate Ceilings: The Evidence from Massachusetts Savings Banks," *Journal of Money, Credit and Banking* (May 1978), pp. 139–157.

prevented NOW accounts in all states except Massachusetts and New Hampshire. In 1976 the law was amended to permit NOW accounts in all New England states and share drafts, which are essentially the same thing, were authorized for credit unions. At that time the interest rate on share drafts was still restricted to a maximum of 7 percent. With the enactment of these laws, New England became the location of an experiment to see how effectively a system which permitted interest-bearing checking accounts at savings institutions could work.

The conclusion has been that the system works rather well. And this experiment has led to a more permanent nationwide change. The change is embodied in the Depository Institutions Deregulation Act of 1980 which authorizes nationwide NOW accounts. This legislation takes a major step toward more uniform financial institutions. Essentially it stipulates that all depository institutions will be able to compete for deposits that are as transferable as bank-offered demand deposits and that earn a competitive interest rate. Whether the 1980s will be a time of more legislation which will lead us closer to a world of "unisex financial institutions" remains to be seen.

PENSION FUNDS AND THEIR REGULATION

The financial institutions which we have discussed thus far in this chapter are all *depository* financial intermediaries. This means they offer some combination of demand, savings, and time deposit accounts. It is depository institutions which have been most heavily regulated in the United States, essentially to avoid the instability and prospect of failure which plagued the banking industry during the nineteenth and early twentieth centuries. However, in the contemporary U.S. economy, other financial intermediaries are also quite important. The principal other intermediaries are pension funds and insurance companies. We will examine the regulatory system for these institutions next.

The Characteristics of Pension Funds

Pension funds became an increasingly important element in financial markets in the 1960s and 1970s. Their presence has been particularly noticeable in the equity markets, where they have become the largest single investor. They have not become major participants in the municipal-bond market because the earnings of the funds are not taxable when they are earned. Instead, the individual's share is taxable when it is received as income after retirement.

One does not have to look back too far in history to find a time when pension funds were a very small part of financial markets. Most people simply did not contract with specialists to manage investments for their retirement and employers did not offer retirement programs as a benefit for employees. People provided for their retirement through their own personally managed investments, depended on their children, and after the 1930s, relied to some extent on Social Security. But in the post-World War II era in the United States, pensions became a more common part of the average employment contract, and as a result the industry which managed pension funds grew.

Managing a pension fund and ensuring that the commitment to provide pensions is honored is not a simple business. The pension fund manager is an agent who is entrusted with considerable responsibility. For most individuals who intend to collect on their pensions, it would be an exceedingly difficult task to monitor the activities of a pension fund manager to be sure that the job was performed honestly and efficiently. In most instances, the manager is responsible to the individual's employer or union as well, but the interests of these entities may not perfectly coincide with those of the employee. There exists, therefore, a potential for abuse, or the problem of agency which is item 3 on our checklist at the beginning of the chapter. It is because of both this potential and the perception of actual abuse when pension funds were unregulated, that pension funds are now subject to fairly extensive regulations.

There are four basic characteristics of any pension fund or pension program. They are the extent to which benefits are *vested*, the extent to which the pension plan is *funded*, the nature of *insurance*, and the type of *commitment* in the pension plan. We will discuss each of these in turn.

An individual's pension program is said to be vested when his or her right to the pension commitment is not conditional upon a continuing relationship with a particular employer. For example, a pension may be said to be vested after 5 years. This means that while the total volume of pension benefits may accumulate from the initial time of employment, the employee cannot actually claim those pension funds unless he or she is employed for 5 years. If, for example, the employee is fired or moves to another job after 4 years, then pension benefits are forfeit. However, if he or she retires after 20 years, then pension benefits accrue for all 20 years. From the standpoint of a company providing pension benefits, this means that its pension liability is not necessarily based on everyone currently employed. Rather, it is based on everyone who is expected to be vested. If a company employs 10,000 workers, but none ever stays longer than 4 years and pensions are vested at 5 years, then it has no real pension liability.

The extent to which a pension liability is funded is the extent to which funds have been invested and, after earning an assumed rate of return, will be available to pay the promised pension. It is best to illustrate this with an example. Suppose a company has 100 employees, all of whom are expected to retire 30 years from now. Suppose its pension commitment to each of those employees is to have $100,000 available for each of them on the day of their retirement. Also suppose that this company can invest funds today which will earn 8 percent interest for 30 years. The amount of funds it will have to invest today in order to have $100,000 30 years from now, at an 8 percent annual interest rate, is $9,938 per employee. If the employer has invested $9,938 for each employee, then the pension program is fully funded. If, however, the employer has set aside only half of the $9,938, then the pension program is only half funded. Many companies and governments pay their pension commitments largely out of their current earnings and hence have pension programs with very low funding. This works fine as long as the company continues to generate sufficient profits to pay current pension commitments. But profits may deteriorate when there remain many years of outstanding pension liabilities. Hence, the advantage of funding. One well-known largely unfunded pension program is the Social Security program of the United States government.

One option open to a pension fund is to purchase insurance. Under this arrangement the employer, or whatever party is arranging the pension, contracts with an insurance company to provide pension benefits and pays an annual premium for the insurance. Such insured pension programs are almost always highly funded so that the risk in the arrangement is reduced. The insurance company in these instances is acting as trustee, adding its own security or reputation to that of the party arranging the pension. Noninsured pension funds are also often managed by trustees. The trust departments of commercial banks often fulfill this role.

Finally, pension funds vary according to the type of commitment which is made to the recipient of the pension. Some pension funds promise a fixed payment, say $1,000 per month for life. These may even include escalator clauses such that the monthly payment varies with the rate of inflation. In this instance the benefit accruing to an individual recipient may be greater or less than he or she pays in, depending on longevity. In other cases, the pension may hinge on the performance of the pension fund as an investment. That is, the pension an individual receives may depend upon the value of the individual's share of the pension fund at retirement.

Regulation of Pension Funds: ERISA

Throughout most of the post-World War II period in the United States, pension funds were almost completely unregulated. But in 1974 the U.S. Congress passed and President Ford signed the Employee Retirement Income Security Act (ERISA). ERISA constitutes a comprehensive regulatory system for private and government pension funds. It came into existence in response to public pressure upon the federal government to halt perceived abuses of private pension funds operating in the United States.

The real or alleged abuses which led to this pension reform legislation fall into three main categories: highly restrictive requirements for vesting, mismanagement of pension fund investments, and failure to fund vested benefits. One of the things which caught public attention prior to the enactment of ERISA was the public disclosure of restrictions on vesting which could be found in many private pension funds. Cases were uncovered where vesting took place after 25 years of continued service to a particular company, yet employees were laid off after 24 years. In another case, continued service meant service within a single division of a company. Workers who moved within a company therefore failed to have their benefits vested. These kinds of stories were particularly effective in attracting public attention. However, reliable data on total vesting across the country also caused considerable concern. A survey conducted by the Department of Health, Education, and Welfare in 1972 revealed that only half of the full-time employees of private industry participated in pension or profit-sharing plans. In addition, only a third of those had vested benefits.

The public debate about pension funds also focused concern on the potential for excessive risk-taking on the part of pension fund managers. In most pension funds the commitment regarding the pension to be paid did not depend on the performance of the pension fund investment. As a result, the pension fund beneficiaries stood to gain nothing from superior performance on the part of the fund. Any such gains would accrue to the managers of the fund. However, poor performance would threaten the commitment to beneficiaries. Hence, while pension fund beneficiaries bore a substantial amount of risk, they did not share in any gains. This created an incentive for pension fund managers to take large gambles.

The third significant perceived abuse involved low levels of funding for vested pension funds. An unfunded pension program depends entirely on the continued profitability of the company providing the pension benefits. A funded pension program has additional security. The security of a funded plan hinges on the performance of the invested assets as well as on the future performance of the company. As a result, increased funding leads to increased security for the pension fund beneficiary. However, it is more expensive for the sponsor of the pension fund. Prior to the enactment of ERISA, many pension funds had very low funding levels, which tended to increase the instances in which beneficiaries lost their pension benefits.

The restrictions on pension funds included in ERISA are designed to place minimum requirements on vesting, funding, and to control risk taking by fund managers. First of all, ERISA establishes minimum requirements on eligibility for pension benefits. It requires that no employee older than 25 years or with more than 1 year of service with a company, or who was hired more than 5 years before normal retirement age, may be denied the right to participate in a pension plan. The minimum requirement for vesting set by ERISA involves three options which a plan may utilize. They are:

1 Ten-year vesting: 100 percent vesting after 10 years of service
2 Graded vesting: 25 percent vesting after 5 years of service, then increasing by 5 percent per year to 50 percent vesting after 10 years of service; thereafter increasing by 10 percent a year to 100 percent vesting 5 years later
3 Rule of 45: 50 percent vesting when a participant's age and years of

service add up to 45; then increasing by 10 percent a year to 100 percent vesting 5 years later[2]

In addition the legislation imposes other restrictions which attempt to close loopholes limiting access to pension fund benefits.

The law also imposes requirements on funding vested pensions. Essentially it stipulates that the pension benefits earned by an employee during a given year must be funded during that year. In addition it sets minimum standards for assessing the current funding necessary to assure a given benefit level at some time in the future. Finally, it specifies penalties for companies which fail to adequately fund their pension plans.

With regard to the management of the pension fund itself, the law establishes legal responsibility on the part of the management for managing the fund in a "prudent" manner. It also establishes some restrictions on allowable investments, particularly on real estate, and it establishes requirements on disclosure which assure public access to the records of the fund's financial transactions.

ERISA has also created a government insurance program for pension beneficiaries. This insurance is provided by the Pension Benefit Guarantee Corporation, located within the U.S. Department of Labor. The purpose of this insurance is to guarantee pension benefits in the event that an individual pension fund terminates without adequate funding for the existing vested beneficiaries.

ERISA is designed to deal with the same kinds of problems which have led to regulation of other financial institutions. The manager of a pension fund is an agent who is supposed to serve the best interests of the pension fund beneficiaries, but this agent has conflicting interests, particularly if the agent is also the employer of the beneficiary. Moreover, if the beneficiaries are generally less sophisticated than the employer with regard to the financial transactions involved, then employers will have an incentive to write contracts which attempt to take advantage of their relative sophistication. Finally, if each beneficiary has only a small stake in the pension fund as a whole, it may be too costly for him or her to adequately supervise the activities of the pension fund managers. All of these problems are the same kinds of problems which arise in other segments of the financial markets and which have led to either disclosure regulation or direct insurance and control of risk.

INSURANCE COMPANIES AND THEIR REGULATION

The system for regulation of insurance companies is much less elaborate than the regulatory systems which govern other financial intermediaries. In

[2] This is extracted from Jack L. Treynor, Patrick J. Regan, and William W. Priest, Jr., *The Financial Reality of Pension Funding Under ERISA*, Copyright Dow Jones-Irwin, Homewood, Ill., 1976, p. 98. Reprinted by permission of Dow-Jones Irwin. In addition, the preceding discussion of ERISA draws heavily on this source.

this section we will explore how insurance companies are regulated and why the differences in regulation are so great.

Life Insurance Companies

Life insurance companies not only provide a service to the consumers who purchase insurance policies but they also serve an important function in capital markets. During most of the 1970s they were the largest single purchaser of corporate bonds and one of the largest purchasers of commercial mortgages. Their role in the bond market and the nature of their investment decisions are discussed in Chapter Thirteen. In addition, Figure 13-10 in that chapter documents the magnitude of their net acquisitions of corporate bonds throughout the 1970s.

The key to the life insurance business lies in the predictability of death rates for the population as a whole. Life insurance companies can estimate with great precision the proportion of the population which will die each year. That precision even extends to the ability to estimate the proportion of various subgroups of the population, such as age-groups, that will die. But it is exceedingly difficult for anyone to accurately predict the deaths of single individuals. Therein lies the benefit of insurance. If an insurance company insures enough individuals, its risks approach those of the population as a whole, whereas our individual death remains unpredictable. We are therefore willing to pay a price to be insured, which makes insurance profitable.

But life insurance companies have traditionally provided more than just life insurance. They have also served as a vehicle for savings for contingencies other than death. This is accomplished through whole life policies which include a savings as well as an insurance plan. The importance of these whole life policies has been declining in recent years as individuals have exhibited a preference for term insurance. This is strictly life insurance without any savings plan incorporated into the policy.

The nature of the risk which is insured by life insurance companies has meant that the life insurance business is not highly volatile. There is relatively little variability in the need for life insurers to pay benefits. As a result, life insurance companies have had a natural tendency to choose relatively stable investments. The stability of the industry has meant that there has been little perceived risk of market failure and, hence, relatively little need for regulation. Compared to commercial banks, life insurance companies are neither as potentially volatile, nor do they play as central a role in the operation of the entire economy. As a result, there is virtually no regulatory system for life insurance companies at the federal level.

Life insurance companies are regulated in the states in which they are located. Most of this regulation is directed at the problem of agency and takes the form of insuring that the investments which are undertaken are not unduly risky or that they are "prudent." Most states restrict life insurance companies from investing heavily in equities in order to limit risk. They also review the prices charged by life insurance companies for policies. But the stability of the industry generally implies that these restrictions create little difficulty.

Property and Casualty Insurance Companies

Property and casualty insurance companies provide protection against damage done to person or property from crime, negligence, accidents, or acts of nature. This is a distinctly different business from life insurance, both with respect to the types of investments which property and casualty insurance companies make and with respect to the inherent risk of the events which the insurance protects against. As discussed in Chapter Fourteen, property and casualty insurance companies invest heavily in municipal bonds as a result of the way they are taxed. In the late 1970s roughly half of their total assets were committed to municipal bonds.

The volatility of this business arises from what is called in the industry the "underwriting cycle." The *underwriting cycle* refers to the "boom and bust" cycle in profits from underwriting insurance. What this means is that in bad years the property and casualty insurers experience rather large losses on insurance alone. This occurs when premium income is significantly less than the claims for casualty losses. In these years the industry survives because of the profits it earns on its investments. In years when the insurance claims are more modest, the industry as a whole is more profitable. Moreover, the companies actively compete with prices and service to attract insurance customers and use the premium income attracted in profitable years as a source of funds to invest. This is illustrated in Table 18-2, which shows, for the years 1960–1973, the premium income, underwriting profit, and profit as a percent of premium income earned by fire and casualty companies that were organized as equity rather than mutual companies. The table shows that the average profit over this period was negative.

Property and casualty insurance companies face a somewhat unusual combination of regulatory schemes designed to deal with agency problems and avoid market failure. All of the regulation of this industry, like the life insurance industry, is at the state level. To varying degrees, each of the state regulatory agencies enforces restrictions on the types of investments in which the insurance companies are allowed to engage. They maintain requirements that the companies hold reserves to insure their solvency in the event of significant losses from either investments or casualty claims. In addition, they regulate the prices which the insurance companies are allowed to charge. This system combines some of the forms of regulation which we have learned are applied to almost all financial intermediaries, but it also incorporates regulation of prices and rates of return, which is common in the public utilities industry. As a result, this industry probably has one of the most unique regulatory systems in the country.

The property and casualty insurance industry does not look at all like the typical regulated monopoly. There are a large number of firms which vary considerably in size. Moreover, the industry is not particularly concen-

TABLE 18-2

Profits from Underwriting for Fire and Casualty Insurance Companies from 1960 to 1973

	(1) NET PREMIUMS	(2) UNDERWRITING PROFIT	(3) (2) AS % OF (1)
1973	30.03	.225	.75
1972	27.60	.915	3.32
1971	24.84	.679	2.73
1970	22.43	−.154	−.69
1969	19.97	−.396	−1.98
1968	17.83	.201	1.13
1967	16.35	.10	.06
1966	15.20	.103	.68
1965	13.80	−.425	−3.08
1964	12.65	−.348	−2.75
1963	11.88	−.219	−1.84
1962	11.59	.003	.02
1961	10.79	.030	.28
1960	10.53	.066	.62
			Average −.05

Source: R. D. Hill, "Profit Regulation in Property and Liability Insurance," *Bell Journal of Economics* (Spring 1979), p. 175. Data extracted from *Best's Aggregates and Averages*. Reprinted by permission.

trated, meaning that the largest firms do not control a large portion of all the business in the industry. Unlike the typical regulated monopoly, regulation here is aimed more at setting minimum rather than maximum prices. The justification for this is the belief that if competition were completely uninhibited, it would ultimately lead the industry into large-scale bankruptcies, which in turn would mean large numbers of defaults on insurance contracts. The most prevalent type of regulatory scheme across the country involves state rating bureaus setting minimum rates which are approved by each state's insurance commission. Under the McCarran-Ferguson Act of 1945, these price-fixing arrangements have been exempted from the antitrust laws. Of all the regulatory systems for different industries which operate in the United States, the regulatory system for property and casualty insurance companies has probably received the least outside scrutiny. With the exception of recent controversies surrounding no-fault insurance, insurance regulation has not been highly controversial and has not attracted widespread public attention.

SUMMARY

In the last four chapters we have outlined the essential ingredients of a rather complicated regulatory system for financial markets and institutions.

This regulatory system is the outgrowth of a long process of trying to reduce instability and eliminate the potential for conflicts of interest in financial markets as well as of a desire to promote certain social interests, particularly housing. To a large extent this regulatory system has been successful. Since the early 1930s we have not experienced banking panics, as were common in the nineteenth century. Moreover, the public is largely protected from the fraudulent practices which received so much publicity after the stock market crash of 1929.

Yet despite its successes, the regulatory system has been under intense pressure during the 1970s and that pressure is not likely to let up during most of the 1980s, despite the changes mandated in the reform legislation of 1980. This regulatory system worked most efficiently during the years when the United States experienced prosperity and low inflation rates. With the advent of significant inflation, the weaknesses in the system have become more apparent. The regulatory system has protected, if not spawned, a diverse set of financial institutions with narrow purposes and constituencies. If these institutions are confined to relatively narrow financing roles, they are unable to diversify risk to the same degree that commercial banks are. Hence, they need protection. This protection, particularly the system of interest-rate ceilings on deposit accounts, has become harder to maintain as inflation has increased. Furthermore, the system of government insurance and control of risk which was originally applied to commercial banks, because they were the institutions which managed the payments mechanism, has also been afforded to almost all financial intermediaries. Simultaneously, if not as a direct result, financial intermediaries have become a middleman in almost every financial transaction in the economy. The result of all this has been a tremendous shift of risk from the private participant in the market to the government. Moreover, many of the decisions and the methods of conducting business which we observe in the market are motivated by a desire to avoid regulations to the maximum extent possible. This behavior ranges from the establishment of bank holding companies to the practice of competing for depositors' funds with toasters and other gifts because competition with interest payments has been prohibited.

During the 1950s and 1960s, as some of the nontraditional financial institutions grew in size and importance, the potential flaws in the regulatory system received little attention. Disintermediation was not yet a really significant problem and, while there was competition for government protection among various segments of the financial industry, the underlying problems were not as severe. But by the late 1970s the situation had significantly changed. Savings and loans were demanding increased assistance to protect them from the dilemma posed by disintermediation. Yet they opposed undoing the system of rate regulation and the margin given them over commercial banks in competing for savings and time deposits. On the other hand, commercial bankers were attempting to defend their exclusive territory of demand deposits from encroachment from the thrift institutions with NOW accounts and from the brokerage and mutual fund industry with money market funds. The bankers, however, were split among themselves on the desirability of interstate branching, the large money-center banks advocating that it must be allowed and the smaller banks seeking to avoid it. At the same time, the commercial bankers sought avenues into the brokerage and investment banking business. Throughout this period the dealer and auction markets in the United States were changing rapidly due both to tremendous technological change affecting the exchange process and to regulatory changes which increased competition within these markets, particularly the New York Stock Exchange.

All of these forces represent increasing pressure for a fundamental change in the regulatory system. By and large, they do not promise a change away from the system of deposit insurance and control of risk in the principal financial intermediaries. Moreover, they do not portend a substantial relaxation of the regulations designed to limit problems of agency or conflicts of interest. In fact, in this area, the 1970s witnessed significant increases in regulation of this kind, particularly regarding pension funds. Instead, most of the pressure is directed at the fragmentation of the financial markets, which the regulatory system seems to promote. The pressure is for increased competition among intermediaries and less protection of special-purpose institutions, such as savings and loans. This unisex financial institutions movement may be the most important regulatory issue of the 1980s.

QUESTIONS TO IMPROVE UNDERSTANDING

1 Commercial banks are insured in order to avoid the social cost of large-scale bank failures, as occurred in the 1930s. This system of insurance has been extended to most other depository intermediaries which do not function exactly like commercial banks. Is this extension completely justified? What criteria can be used to evaluate how far the government should go in insuring against failure?

2 Discuss the essential features of the regulatory system for savings and loans which are distinct from the regulatory system for commercial banks.

3 Why have the regulators been unable to deal successfully with the problem of disintermediation and still preserve savings and loans as institutions which invest almost exclusively in long-term fixed-rate mortgage contracts? What role does inflation play in causing these difficulties?

4 Compare the basic purposes served by MSBs, credit unions, and finance companies. Outline the basic structure of regulation for each. Can you explain why they are different?

5 Deposit institutions engage in a variety of different types of behavior to circumvent regulatory restrictions. One example of regulation which causes much evasive behavior is deposit ceilings. How do deposit institutions try to evade these regulations and what impact does this have on consumers?

6 Explain what a mutual organization is and how it works. How are mutuals taxed? What special tax advantage is given to credit unions?

7   Explain what a NOW account is. Why are NOW accounts an important point of contention between commercial banks and thrift institutions?

8   What is the difference between a funded and a vested pension fund? Why is a company's pension liability dependent upon vested pension benefits?

9   How does ERISA effect funding and vesting of pension benefits? What are some of the major types of abuses which ERISA is designed to prohibit?

10 What is so unique about the regulatory system for property and casualty insurance companies? How does this regulatory system compare to that typically used for a natural monopoly?

11 It has been argued that a central feature of the regulatory system for financial intermediaries is to shift risk from depositors to other parties. Sum up the various ways in which this risk shifting takes place. Why is reform of this regulatory system so difficult to accomplish?

REFERENCES

Bedford, Margaret E.: "Federal Taxation of Financial Institutions," *Monthly Review*, Federal Reserve Bank of Kansas City (June 1976), pp. 3–15.

Flannery, Mark J.: "Credit Unions as Consumer Lenders in the United States," *New England Economic Review*, Federal Reserve Bank of Boston (July–August 1974), pp. 3–12.

Hill, R. D.: "Profit Regulation in Property Liability Insurance," *Bell Journal of Economics* (Spring 1979), pp. 172–191.

Jaffee, Dwight: "What to Do About Savings and Loan Associations," *Journal of Money, Credit and Banking* (November 1974), pp. 537–549.

Kane, Edward: "Short-Changing the Small Saver," *Journal of Money Credit and Banking* (November 1970), pp. 513–522.

————: "Good Intentions and Unintended Evil: The Case Against Selective Credit Allocation," *Journal of Money, Credit and Banking* (February 1977), pp. 55–69.

Kidwell, David, and Richard L. Peterson: "A Close Look at Credit Unions," *Bankers Magazine*, vol. 161 (January–February 1978), pp. 71–80.

Pierce, James L.: "The Fine Study," *Journal of Money, Credit and Banking* (November 1977), pp. 605–618.

Rose, Peter S., and Donald R. Frazer: *Financial Institutions*, Business Publications Inc., Dallas, Tex., 1980.

Taggart, Robert A.: "Effects of Deposit Rate Ceilings: The Evidence from Massachusetts Savings Banks," *Journal of Money, Credit and Banking* (May 1978), pp. 139–157.

Treynor, Jack L.: "The Principles of Corporate Pension Finance," *Journal of Finance* (May 1977), pp. 627–638.

————, Patrick J. Regan, and William W. Priest, Jr.: *The Financial Reality of Pension Funding Under ERISA*, Dow Jones-Irwin, Homewood, Ill., 1976.

Report of the National Credit Union Administration, Washington, D.C., June 1978.

Chapter Nineteen

FRACTIONAL RESERVE BANKING
AND GOVERNMENT REGULATION
OF THE MONEY SUPPLY

This chapter provides a transition. The transition is between a discussion of the problems of regulating financial markets and institutions, which has been the subject of the last four chapters, and the explanation of the links between financial markets and the aggregate economy, which is the subject of Part Five of this book. The specific topic addressed in this chapter is how the Federal Reserve System regulates the supply of money in the economy.

In a very narrow sense the Federal Reserve's basic purpose is to regulate commercial banks. But, in reality, the Federal Reserve influences the well-being of the entire economy through its control of the supply of money. In this chapter we will focus on how the Federal Reserve exercises control over the money supply and we will try to come to grips with how a fractional reserve system of depository institutions operates. In the final part of this book we will examine the links between the Federal Reserve and the aggregate economy.

This chapter is organized as follows. We will start by considering the alternative ways that the supply of money may be defined. Then we will examine the mechanics of how the Federal Reserve can control the supply of money. Finally, we will examine the central issues about how monetary policy ought to be conducted.

ALTERNATIVE DEFINITIONS OF MONEY

The Function of Money

Before we examine the structure of the Federal Reserve System and how it controls the supply of money, it is helpful to have a reasonably precise definition of what constitutes money. We need to understand what the criteria are for defining money, historically what has served as money, and the problems involved in agreeing upon what should be categorized as money today.

To see how to define money it is necessary to understand the function which money serves in an economy. Money is an asset which serves as a *unit of account* and *medium of exchange*. We will begin by examining money's role as a unit of account. To say that money serves as the unit of account means that the prices of all goods and services are denominated in money (e.g., in dollars in the United States). In this sense money is simply a measuring device like inches, pounds, or litres. Moreover, the fact that we denominate the price of everything in money greatly simplifies the process of doing business. The alternative would be to state the price of every good in terms of every other good, that is, the price of lamb chops in terms of Toyota Coronas. This would make it exceedingly difficult to carry out everyday transactions, as this would essentially be a barter economy.

In our contemporary economy money also serves the purpose of a *medium of exchange*. This means that people hold balances of an asset called money which they exchange for goods and services they buy and sell. Hence, money is a commodity itself, not merely the unit of measurement in an accounting system. In the world we live in it is difficult to imagine conducting business transactions without exchanging money. Regardless of what we purchase or sell we are willing to accept money in exchange because we know it will be readily acceptable throughout the economy. As a result, we choose those items to use as money which minimize our costs of executing transactions. For example, we would find it difficult to use cows as money. The difficulties might not be overwhelming if we wanted to purchase something that cost exactly one cow. Then we would merely have to worry about transporting, feeding, and cleaning up after the cow. But suppose we wanted to purchase something that cost half a cow. Then we would have to worry about butchering and preserving the meat. If we started using cows for money, we would eventually wind up exchanging frozen meat. In effect, hamburger would drive out cows as a medium of exchange. Similarly, if some other asset were viewed as presenting lower costs of transacting, it would come to replace hamburger as a medium of exchange. The implication of this is that an economy will naturally evolve to using those assets for a medium of exchange which involve the lowest cost of transacting. These assets are characterized as being the most liquid assets in the economy.

There is yet another requirement for an asset to function successfully as money, though it is not exactly a function of money. The requirement is that the supply of the asset be sufficiently independent of the events in the rest of the economy that the value of the asset cannot be easily altered by participants in the economy. To see why this is important it is best to examine a few of the commodities that have historically been used as money. In the United States one of the first commodities to be used as money was tobacco. The reasons are not hard to understand. It was a valuable commodity which was produced throughout the mid-Atlantic colonies. But unlike cows, it was highly divisible and could be exchanged with low transaction costs. The ultimate problem with tobacco as a money was that there was a tremendous incentive for everyone to increase production so as to increase their stock of money. Hence the supply of tobacco money was not independently determined.

The need for an independent supply of money has historically dictated that money be based on some precious commodity, such as gold or silver. The advantage of these commodities is that they are supplied by nature and cannot be produced like tobacco. At one time gold and silver were directly exchanged as money. But because of the costs of actually making transactions in gold and silver, it has long been more efficient to use coins or, more recently, paper to represent the medium of exchange. The success of such substitutes has historically depended upon whether the institutions issuing them were perceived as trustworthy so that the currency could always be redeemed in gold.

As discussed in Chapter Seventeen, in this century the United States abandoned the commitment to link money to any precious commodity. The shortcoming of a system where the supply of money is directly tied to a precious commodity is that the supply of money might well grow at a very slow (fast) rate while the economy grows at a very fast (slow) rate. The result, as will be explained in some detail in Part Five of this book, would then be deflation (inflation). Such a deflation is precisely what occurred during much of the latter half of the nineteenth century in the United States. The alternative to a commodity-based money is that the supply and the determination of what serves as money be subject to the regulations imposed by the government, or, in the United States today, the Federal Reserve System.

What Constitutes Money Today?

It is not an easy task to define money in our contemporary economy. The problem is that there are now many assets which are close to meeting the requirements for money described above. To see what serves as money today we can start with the assets which most clearly fit our concept of money. The first asset which is generally recognized as money is cash or currency. This includes the paper notes and metal coins issued by the Federal Reserve and the Treasury in denominations from as small as a penny to as large as $1,000. The second asset which is generally understood to be money is demand deposits at commercial banks. These are the balances in checking accounts held by individuals and corporations throughout the country. These are thought of as money because they are universally accepted as a medium of exchange. Moreover, as a result of the regulatory system discussed in Chapter Seventeen, these assets cannot be discounted and must be exchanged at their face value. It is certainly true that checks drawn on demand deposit balances are not always accepted without some guarantee of payment. But this does not mean that the demand deposits themselves do not function as money. What it does mean is that a check itself does not guarantee that the demand deposit exists. Hence additional proof or insurance that the demand deposit exists and that the check will be paid upon demand is often required in order to purchase a commodity or service with a claim on a demand deposit. If the reliability of payment of deposits were seriously enough impaired, then they would cease to function as money. But in the United States today these are generally accepted as money or the medium of exchange. Figure 19-1 shows the magnitude of cash in the hands of the public and demand deposits in the United States from 1972 to 1979. It also shows the sum of cash and demand deposits. This is referred to as M_{1a}. Figure 19-1 indicates that the money supply as measured by M_{1a} has been growing, though at varying rates, throughout this historical period.

There has been a long-standing debate about whether the money supply should also include time and savings deposits at commercial banks. Some argue that people substitute back and forth between these assets so closely that it is unreasonable to exclude them from the definition of the money supply. When these are included in the money supply, along with cash and demand deposits, the money supply is referred to as M_2. It is evident from Figure 19-2 than M_2 has generally grown at a faster rate than has M_{1a}.

In recent years there has been growing dissatisfaction with using either M_{1a} or M_2 as acceptable definitions of the money supply. The reason for this is that a number of close substitutes for demand deposits have evolved. This is only one aspect of the various pressures for change in the financial institutions industry which were discussed in the last four chapters. One of the recent substitutes for demand deposits has been money market mutual funds. A money market mutual fund functions like a demand deposit in that checks can be written on the account. But unlike a demand deposit, they pay a market-determined interest rate. The interest rate is determined by the earnings of the fund and the balances of the fund are invested in Treasury securities. The popularity of money market mutual funds is evident in Figure 17-3 in Chapter Seventeen, which shows the tremendous growth in the volume of these funds during the late 1970s. Other substitutes have also

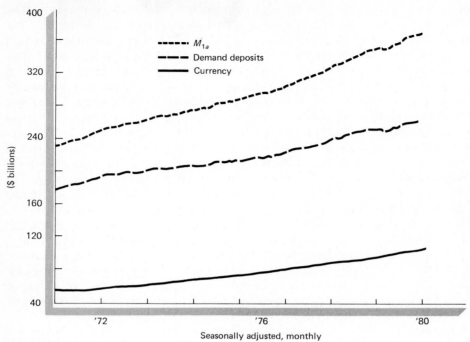

FIGURE 19-1
M_{1a}. Demand deposits and currency, 1972–1979. Source: *Federal Reserve Chart Book.*

emerged to compete with demand deposits. These include share drafts offered by credit unions, which are essentially demand deposits which pay
interest, and similar types of accounts called NOW (Negotiated Order of
Withdrawal) accounts offered by savings and loans.

The growth of these close substitutes for demand deposits has caused
the Federal Reserve to reconsider the proper definition of the supply of
money. In February 1980 the Federal Reserve started publishing data for an
expanded definition of the supply of money M_{1b}, which includes most of
these substitutes, though not money market mutual funds. Hence, there is
now a measure of the money supply available for almost any definition of
money one wants to choose. Table 19-1 presents definitions of the measures
of the money supply discussed here, and related monetary aggregates, and
Figure 19-2 shows the recent rates of growth in some of these variables. It is
evident from this figure that as more assets are included in the definition of
money, the supply of money becomes larger. But it is not at all clear which is
the best definition.

There is yet another possibility for defining the money supply which, in
comparison to M_{1a} and M_{1b}, involves less rather than more aggregation. This
alternative definition of money is called the *monetary base* or *high-powered*

money. The monetary base (B) consists of cash in the hands of the public and reserves held by commercial banks which are members of the Federal Reserve System. Reserves include deposits held with the Federal Reserve by commercial banks and cash held in the vaults of commercial banks.[1] The recent behavior of the base is also shown in Figure 19-2. As will become evident as this chapter proceeds, the base is called high-powered money because more aggregate measures of the money supply, such as M_{1a}, M_{1b}, and M_2, are multiples of the base. Therefore, if the base expands, M_{1a} will expand by a multiple of the expansion in the base. The difference between the base and the M_1's is totally accounted for by the difference between reserves and demand deposits as both the base and the M_1's include cash held by the public. The idea that the base represents money hinges on the argument that when transactions are made using demand deposits, the asset which banks exchange is reserves. As a result this "high-powered" money really underlies all other transactions. As long as there is a clearly definable, unique set of assets which individuals and corporations use as a medium of exchange, then the base is a less attractive definition of money. But in today's financial environment, with a multitude of special types of liquid assets which are close substitutes for demand deposits, the concept of a distinct money other than the base is becoming more nebulous.

[1] It is important to note that as the changes in reserve requirements specified in the Monetary Control Act of 1980 are gradually phased in, these definitions will change. Reserves will then be held by all depository institutions, not just *member* banks. But this change will take place over an 8-year period.

FIGURE 19-2

Levels of the monetary aggregates: 1970–1979. Source: *Federal Reserve Bulletin,* various issues.

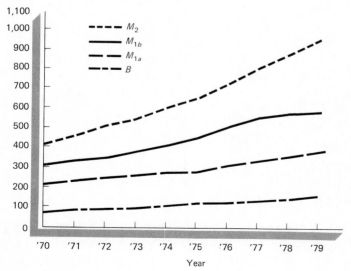

TABLE 19-1

Definitions of Monetary Aggregates

SYMBOL	DEFINITIONS
C	Cash, including currency and coins, in the hands of the public.
R	Reserves—includes deposits with Federal Reserve Banks plus cash in vaults.
B	Monetary Base $= C + R$.
D	Demand deposits—checking account balances.
M_{1a}	Narrow definition of the money supply $= D + C$.
M_{1b}	Modified definition of M_{1a}—includes M_{1a} plus NOW accounts, automatic transfer accounts, credit union share drafts, and demand deposits at MSBs.
M_2	M_{1a} + time deposits at commercial banks.

The ambiguity regarding the appropriate measure of money may not be alleviated as the changes in the nature of regulation of financial institutions specified in the Financial Institutions Deregulation Act of 1980 are phased in. The act has far-reaching consequences and extends the Federal Reserve's authority to impose reserves beyond commercial banks, to all depository institutions offering demand- or transaction-type accounts. As a result, the Federal Reserve may be able to develop direct control over all of the components of M_{1b}, but it is also possible that new substitutes for these accounts may arise and the problem of adequately defining as well as controlling money will be exacerbated. In the meantime, one must pick some definition of the money supply to work with, and the most logical choice at this juncture seems to be M_{1b}. M_{1b} is the best measure of what actually serves as money, but as an explanation of how the Federal Reserve actually controls the supply of money, M_{1b} has its drawbacks. The most important drawback is that the mechanisms which allow the Federal Reserve to exercise control over the accounts offered by nonbank institutions will only gradually be phased in during the 1980s. This process will include the application of reserve requirements to the various deposits in M_{1b} and elimination of such requirements on most time and savings deposits. Until that phase-in is more complete, it will be difficult to spell out exactly how M_{1b} is linked to the base. As a result, we will explain how M_{1a} has traditionally been influenced by the base. In time, as the new regulations become effective, a similar but not identical relationship will come to apply to the relationship between M_{1b} and the base. Now that we understand what money is, we need to examine how its supply is regulated by the federal government. The government agency which is responsible for this control is the Federal Reserve System (Fed). We will examine the basic structure of the Fed next.

THE OPERATION OF THE FEDERAL RESERVE AND CONTROL OF THE MONETARY BASE

The Organization of Power Within the Federal Reserve

The Federal Reserve is an unusual government agency in many respects, but its most unusual characteristic is its apparent autonomy from both the executive and legislative branches of the government. Its autonomy comes both from the way it is organized and from its budgetary independence. The Federal Reserve is controlled by a seven-member Board of Governors. Each member of the Board is appointed for a 14-year term with one term expiring every 2 years. Appointments of Board members are made by the President with the consent of Congress and, due to retirements, are often made more frequently than the 2-year interval. One of the seven members of the Board serves as its Chairman. The Chairman is selected by the President for a 4-year term. Unlike almost every other agency in the federal government, the Federal Reserve does not have to go to Congress for a budget. The Fed is self-supporting and, in fact, returns billions of dollars to the Treasury each year from the profits it earns on its portfolio of government securities (see Chapter Twenty-two for a more detailed treatment of these profits).

But the formal independence of the Federal Reserve may overstate the reality of the matter, for the Federal Reserve's independence persists only with the consent of Congress and the President. There is always the possibility that the Federal Reserve Act will be modified to further alter the accountability of the Federal Reserve. Many have argued that this implicit threat has always been sufficient to compel the Federal Reserve to conduct monetary policy in a way that serves the interests of the President or of Congress.[2]

The organizational structure and distribution of power within the Federal Reserve System is the result of a number of compromises made over the life of the System. When the System was first created, the offices of the Board were located in Washington, but the country was divided into 12 districts with a Federal Reserve bank in each district. Considerable power was allocated to the district banks. Specifically, they had the power to grant loans and set the terms for those loans to individual commercial banks in each district and to buy and sell United States government securities on their own accounts. In the 1930s this power was consolidated in Washington under the direction of a committee which maintained representation from the district banks. This committee, known as the Federal Open Market Committee (FOMC) remains the single most important decision-making body within the Federal Reserve System. It is composed of the seven members of the Board of Governors, plus the President of the Federal Reserve Bank of New York,

---

[2] See Raymond E. Lombra, "Reflections on Burns's Reflections," *Journal of Money, Credit and Banking* (February 1980), pp. 94–105, for a discussion of the political aspects of the conduct of monetary policy during the time Arthur Burns was Chairman of the Board.

plus, on a rotating basis, four of the other eleven district bank presidents. It is the FOMC which has the real responsibility for determining monetary policy.

The power of the FOMC results from its control of what are called open market operations. Open market operations involve the purchase or sale of U.S. Treasury securities by the Federal Reserve. This is the principal tool by which the Federal Reserve determines the money supply. The FOMC meets once a month in Washington, and on special occasions when necessary to decide on the future course of monetary policy. The FOMC meetings are held in secret, but as of 1980, edited minutes of the meeting are published in the *Federal Reserve Bulletin* with approximately a month's delay.[3]

The Chairman of the Board of Governors has historically been an immensely powerful figure within the system, though not always within the rest of the government. This is certainly not inherent in the system itself, as the Chairman has little formal power. Within both the Board and the Open Market Committee the Chairman has only one vote, just like other members. He does not affect the tenure of the other members of the Board, though he does have some control over their personal budgets and perquisites. The power that the Chairman has historically commanded has been largely a result of the personality and political skills of the individuals who have occupied the job.

An interesting example of the importance of the individual to this job is provided by Arthur Burns, who served as Chairman from 1970 to 1977. Arthur Burns was appointed to the Chairman's job by President Richard Nixon after he had already established one of the most successful careers in the economics profession in this century. Arthur Burns's career spanned nearly the entire twentieth century. He was a professor of economics at Columbia University in his early twenties. (He was even Milton Friedman's first economics professor.) He later became the Chairman of the Council of Economic Advisors for President Dwight Eisenhower. During these years he developed a close relationship with then Vice President Richard Nixon.[4] At the end of the Eisenhower administration, he became head of the National Bureau of Economic Research, the most widely known private economic research organization in the United States. Because of Burns's distinguished career prior to becoming Chairman of the Board of Governors, and because of the political and economic skill he had acquired during this career, he became an extremely powerful if not dominating force within the Federal Reserve. Probably more so than at any other time, the reality of the power of

[3] In the mid 1970s a suit was brought against the Federal Reserve Board by a law student at George Washington University which claimed that the secrecy surrounding the FOMC meetings violated federal law regarding public access to government meetings. This court case has raised the question of whether the FOMC should immediately announce its policy decisions and a transcript of its deliberations rather than release a highly edited statement with substantial delay. At the time this is written this issue has not been resolved.

[4] See William Safire, *Before the Fall*, Doubleday, New York, 1975, for an interesting description of the relationship between Richard Nixon and Arthur Burns and for an account of Burns's role in the Nixon administration.

the Fed was a matter of the personal power of the Chairman. The decision-making process within the Fed could not then and will probably not in the future be properly understood without recognizing this potential power of the Chairman.

Open Market Operations and Control of the Monetary Base

Over the approximately 70 years it has been in business, the Federal Reserve has acquired a rather large portfolio of U.S. Treasury securities. As of September 1979 the Fed owned $115 billion worth of Treasury securities, which represented approximately 14 percent of the total stock of such securities outstanding. This means that at that time the Fed owned 14 percent of the total national debt. The Fed doesn't buy such securities purely in order to make a profit. Instead, it is principally through the purchase of such securities that the Federal Reserve supplies reserves to the banking system. It is the Federal Open Market Committee which sets the guidelines for the purchase and sale of such securities and its operating arm, the Open Market Desk at the Federal Reserve Bank of New York, which actually conducts the transactions. These transactions are referred to as open market operations.

The basic mechanics of open market operations are relatively simple. When the Open Market Desk, under the direction of the FOMC, decides that Treasury securities should be purchased it calls up any of a number of dealers in such securities. The Fed maintains a list of commercial firms, usually large brokerage houses or banks, which continually make a market in Treasury securities and for any given transaction it will choose some dealer on this list. The Federal Reserve then agrees to buy a certain volume of securities at the going price, say $10,000,000 worth of securities. The Federal Reserve Bank of New York then issues a check to the securities dealer for $10,000,000 and the Federal Reserve receives title to the securities. If the securities dealer is not a commercial bank, then that dealer has the check from the Federal Reserve Bank of New York deposited in its bank. The deposit balances of the dealer are increased by $10,000,000 and the deposits which that commercial bank holds with the Federal Reserve Bank of New York are increased by $10,000,000. This represents a net increase in the reserves of the banking system, for there is no offsetting decline in the deposits of any other bank. The net impact of this is illustrated in the following hypothetical balance sheet. The demand deposits of the commercial bank in question, which are a liability on its accounts, are increased by $10,000,000. Offsetting this is a comparable increase in reserves in the form of deposits with the Fed. Hence, this bank and the banking system now have $10,000,000 in *new reserves which did not previously exist at all.*

BALANCE SHEET OF COMMERCIAL BANK

ASSETS	LIABILITIES AND NET WORTH
Reserves = +$10,000,000	Demand deposits = +$10,000,000

When open market operations take place, the public as a whole merely exchanges one type of asset for another. That is, when the Federal Reserve buys securities the public exchanges Treasury securities for demand deposits. But as a consequence of this exchange the banking system acquires new reserves. This is because reserves are the deposits of commercial banks with the Federal Reserve. The unique and relevant characteristic of reserves is that they constrain the total supply of deposits which the commercial banking system can make available to the public. If the required ratio of reserves to deposits is, say, 20 percent, and the total stock of reserves is, say, $20 billion, then the maximum amount of deposits which can be issued by the banking system is $100 billion (20 percent of $100 billion is $20 billion). Therefore, when new reserves are created the banking system can let deposits expand. On the other hand, if the Federal Reserve withdraws reserves through open market sales of securities, the banking system must limit deposits to a smaller volume than it did previously. To see the links between reserves and the total volume of deposits more clearly, we must examine what is called the "multiple expansion process."

DETERMINANTS OF THE MONEY SUPPLY

The Multiple Expansion Process

In order to examine the links between reserves and M_{1a} we will begin with a simple example of a banking system where there is no cash and only one type of deposit, demand deposits. We will also assume that all banks are members of the Federal Reserve and that all these banks always try to hold exactly the amount of reserves which are required. The required ratio of reserves to demand deposits will be represented by v, and it will be assumed to be equal to 20 percent. We want to examine the impact on the total supply of demand deposits of an increase in reserves through an open market purchase of, say, $10,000. In this simple example, where we assume there is no cash, this increase in reserves is equivalent to the increase in the base. (Recall that the base is equal to cash plus reserves.)

Suppose that the initial purchase of Treasury securities by the Open Market Desk of the Federal Reserve Bank of New York is from a securities dealer named Jones & Henry. Also suppose that Jones & Henry has its demand deposit account with First Bank. When the transaction is made between Jones & Henry and the Federal Reserve Bank of New York, Jones & Henry has the payment made by the New York Fed credited to its demand deposit account at First Bank. Therefore, the demand deposit balances of First Bank increase by $10,000 and its reserves with the Federal Reserve Bank of New York increase by an equal amount. The hypothetical balance sheet for First Bank before this transaction is shown on the next page.

BALANCE SHEET OF FIRST BANK BEFORE OPEN MARKET PURCHASE

ASSETS		LIABILITIES	
Reserves	200,000	Deposits	1,000,000
Loans	800,000		

Before the Open Market purchase the actual reserves maintained by First Bank were exactly equal to the reserves required by the Fed, that is, 20 percent of its demand deposits. After the transaction the balance sheet looks as follows:

BALANCE SHEET OF FIRST BANK AFTER OPEN MARKET PURCHASE

ASSETS		LIABILITIES	
Reserves	210,000	Deposits	1,010,000
Loans	800,000		

Now First Bank has $8,000 in reserves above what the Fed requires which can profitably be used to fund new loans.

Suppose that First Bank extends a new loan to someone who wants to purchase a new car. The new car purchaser receives a check for $8,000 from First Bank and presents it to the new car dealer. The new car dealer then deposits the check in his or her bank, say Second Bank. The accounts of First Bank will be altered so that loans are increased by $8,000 and reserves are decreased by the same amount:

BALANCE SHEET OF FIRST BANK AFTER EXTENSION OF NEW LOAN

ASSETS		LIABILITIES	
Reserves	202,000	Deposits	1,010,000
Loans	808,000		

Similarly, the books of Second Bank will show an increase in reserves of $8,000 and an increase in deposits of the same amount. Suppose Second Bank has exactly the required amount of reserves, 20 percent of deposits, before this transaction, as shown below:

BALANCE SHEET OF SECOND BANK BEFORE AUTOMOBILE PURCHASE

ASSETS		LIABILITIES	
Reserves	120,000	Deposits	600,000
Loans	480,000		

Once the new car has been purchased, the $8,000 additions to reserves and deposits will be reflected as follows:

BALANCE SHEET OF SECOND BANK AFTER THE AUTOMOBILE PURCHASE

ASSETS		LIABILITIES	
Reserves	128,000	Deposits	608,000
Loans	480,000		

Second Bank is now in the same position First was when it received the initial $10,000 increase in reserves in that it has excess reserves that it did not previously have. The magnitude of the excess reserves is smaller than for First; they now represent 80 percent of $8,000, or $6,400. Second Bank may now extend a new loan and generate new deposits of $6,400 for some other bank and still meet its reserve requirements exactly. Another bank will then receive $6,400 in new reserves and 80 percent of that will be in excess of that which is required. This process will continue virtually indefinitely until all the reserves held in the system become required.

As these reserves are distributed throughout the banking system and new loans are created, the total stock of deposits continually increases. Initially, when the Open Market Desk purchased Treasury securities from Jones & Henry, demand deposits increased by $10,000. Then, with the loan made by First Bank they increased another $8,000, and with the loan by Second, $6,400. As more loans are made, demand deposits will continue to increase by $5,120, then $4,096, etc. This multiple expansion process will lead to a total increase in demand deposits which can be represented as follows:

$$\Delta D = \Delta B + (1 - v)\Delta B + (1 - v)^2 \Delta B + (1 - v)^3 \Delta B \\ + (1 - v)^4 \Delta B + \cdots \tag{19-1}$$

where ΔD represents the total change in deposits and ΔB represents the initial change in the base. In this example, where the reserve requirement is 20 percent and the initial increase in reserves or the base is $10,000, this can be expressed

$$D = 10,000 + .8 \times 10,000 + .8^2 \times 10,000 + .8^3 \times 10,000 + \cdots \tag{19-2}$$

Because Eq. (19-1) is a convergent series (this means that the terms get smaller and smaller and converge, in this case, on zero), it is possible to rewrite it in a much simpler form, which makes it relatively easy to calculate the total increase in deposits. The simpler expression is[5]

$$\Delta D = \frac{1}{v} \Delta B \tag{19-3}$$

---

[5] Equation (19-3) can be derived as follows: Eq. (19-1) indicates that

$$\Delta D = \Delta B + (1 - v)\Delta B + (1 - v)^2 \Delta B + (1 - v)^3 \Delta B + \cdots \tag{19-1}$$

Multiplying both sides of Eq. (19-1) by $(1 - v)$ yields

$$(1 - v)\Delta D = (1 - v)\Delta B + (1 - v)^2 \Delta B + (1 - v)^3 \Delta B + \cdots \tag{19-1c}$$

In this example this means that the total increase in deposits is five times the initial increase in reserves, or $50,000 = (1/0.2) 10,000.

The idea behind this multiple expansion process is that reserves place a constraint on the total volume of deposits which banks can issue. As a result, as the volume of reserves goes up or down, the volume of deposits which the system as a whole can support increases or decreases by a multiple of that amount. But the idea that the magnitude of the multiple expansion in deposits is equal to $1/v$ hinges on the assumption that all banks will increase deposits to the maximum extent they can and that there are no other leakages from the system. However, there definitely are leakages from this system in the real world and we will consider those next.

Leakages from the Multiple Expansion Process

There are three principal types of leakages from this multiple expansion process which tend to reduce the magnitude of the ultimate expansion of deposits. These are leakages into cash, excess reserves, and time deposits. We will briefly analyze the effects of each type of so-called leakage.

First, the multiple expansion process as described above assumes that people never choose to hold a portion of their new deposits in cash. Yet if people choose to convert part of each round of increase in deposits into cash, then the expansion of the money supply will tend to be smaller than it otherwise would. The reason is that each time people choose to hold cash rather than demand deposits, the reserves of the banking system decrease and with this goes a decrease in the stock of deposits which the reduced volume of reserves can support. Increases in the public's cash holdings entail decreases in reserves because the total stock of reserves is composed of cash held in bank vaults and deposits with the Fed. As a result, when the public exchanges demand deposits for cash, reserves decline and so must the total supply of money. We can summarize the effect of a leakage into cash with a modified form of Eq. (19-3). To derive this equation we first need to decompose the change in the base (ΔB) into its component parts, a change in reserves (ΔR) and a change in cash held by the public (ΔC):

$$\Delta B = \Delta C + \Delta R \tag{19-4}$$

But we know that the actual change in reserves will be equal to the required

---

Subtracting Eq. (19-1a) from (19-1) yields

$$\Delta D - (1 - v)\Delta D = \Delta B$$

This can be simplified to read

$$\Delta D \cdot v = \Delta B$$

or

$$\Delta D = \frac{1}{v} \cdot \Delta B$$

reserve ratio v times the ultimate change in deposits, ΔD. In addition, if we postulate that the change in cash holdings will be some fraction c of the change in deposits, then by substituting these expressions in Eq. (19-4), we have

$$\Delta B = v\Delta D + c\Delta D \qquad (19\text{-}5)$$

This can be further simplified to read

$$\Delta B = (v + c)\Delta D \qquad (19\text{-}6)$$

Next we can divide both sides by the sum of the required-reserve ratio and the cash-demand deposit ratio $(v + c)$, and we have an expression for the increase in deposits which is similar to Eq. (19-3):

$$\Delta D = \frac{1}{(v + c)}\Delta B \qquad (19\text{-}7)$$

The important difference is that the total expansion in deposits is now smaller than it was before c was introduced. If c is equal to 0.05, then in the example above deposits will expand by a multiple of 4 $(1/(.20 + .05) = 1/(.25))$ rather than 5.

Another type of leakage takes place because banks choose to hold some excess reserves. In effect, some banks choose to hold more reserves than required as a cushion against a future deficiency. The incentive for doing this is that banks will incur a penalty if they run short of reserves; hence, there is an incentive to avoid this penalty. The nature and magnitude of this penalty depends upon the method the bank uses to cover its shortage of reserves. A bank which experiences a reserve deficiency has essentially three options. First, it can sell an interest-bearing asset. The cost in this case is the forgone yield on this asset. Second, it can borrow from the Federal Reserve. In this case, the cost includes the interest rate which must be paid to the Fed, known as the discount rate, plus the prospect that this increased borrowing may lead to closer supervision of the bank's activities. Repeated borrowing often leads to such increased attention, or at least there is a general belief that this is the case. Third, the bank can borrow from the Federal Funds Market. In this instance, the cost is the yield which must be paid to obtain Federal Funds.

We represent the desired level of excess reserves as some proportion of total demand deposits. If we define e as the ratio of excess reserves to demand deposits, then the expansion process can be modified to incorporate excess reserves as follows:

$$\Delta D = \frac{1}{(v + e)}\Delta B \qquad (19\text{-}8)$$

Again, as in Eq. (19-7) where we examined the effect of a leakage into cash, the result of this leakage is that the multiple expansion process leads to a smaller volume of deposits than would be the case if banks held no excess reserves. If banks tend to hold, say, 1 percent of deposits in excess on average (and in the late 1970s e was 1 percent or less), then this would mean that the magnitude of the multiple expansion in the example above would fall from 5 to $1/0.21 = 4.76$.

The final leakage is from demand deposits into time deposits. If individuals choose to convert some portion of new demand deposits into time deposits, this obviously means that demand deposits will not increase as much as they otherwise would. It does not necessarily mean that reserves will be changed, however, if reserves are required for time as well as demand deposits. As long as time and demand deposits have the same magnitude of reserve requirements, then reserves will be unaffected by this substitution. Assuming that the reserve requirements are the same, the increase in both demand and time deposits resulting from an initial change in the base can be expressed just like Eq. (19-3):

$$\Delta D + \Delta T = \left(\frac{1}{v}\right)\Delta B \tag{19-9}$$

where ΔT equals the change in time deposits chosen by the public. Then, if we know the proportion which time deposits represent of the total we can compute ΔD. For example, if 60 percent of new deposits go into time deposits, then the multiple increase in demand deposits will be only 40 percent of $1/v$. If $1/v = 5$, then the magnitude of the multiple increase will be $(1 - 0.6) \times 5 = 2$. If reserve requirements are lower on time deposits than on demand deposits, then the shift to time deposits will not lead to as large a decline in the multiple expansion as described immediately above. In effect, this is like reducing the value of v. In the limit if reserve requirements on time deposits were zero, they would not constitute a leakage at all.

A Model of the Money Supply Process

It is now possible to explain the connections between the level of the money supply and the level of the monetary base. We know that as the base is increased through alteration in reserves, deposits will increase by a larger amount. We also know that there are some leakages into cash, excess reserves, and time deposits. To summarize all of these relationships we will examine what is called the money supply multiplier. Actually the expressions derived in the last few pages are simplified versions of this money supply multiplier and would apply if some leakages did not exist. For example, when there are no leakages at all, then the money supply multiplier is simply $1/v$ and the money supply can be expressed as

$$M_{1a} = \frac{1}{v} B \qquad (19\text{-}10)$$

But we want to determine the multiplier when all the leakages we considered above are taken into account.

We can derive this multiplier from the definitions of both the money supply and the base. The multiplier is simply the factor which must be multiplied by the base in order to obtain the money supply. If we represent the multiplier by m, then it can be expressed as

$$m = \frac{M_{1a}}{B} \qquad (19\text{-}11)$$

We know that M_{1a} is equal to cash in the hands of the public C plus demand deposits D, and we know that the base is equal to cash in the hands of the public plus reserves R. Substituting these into the expression for m yields

$$m = \frac{C + D}{C + R} \qquad (19\text{-}12)$$

We can also express reserves as a function of the required and excess reserve ratios, v and e, and the stock of demand and time deposits, D and T:

$$R = (v + e)(D + T) \qquad (19\text{-}13)$$

This implies that reserve requirements are the same for both types of deposits and that banks hold a fraction e of both types of deposits in reserve in addition to those reserves which are required. When this is substituted for R in Eq. (19-12), the money supply multiplier can be rewritten as

$$m = \frac{C + D}{C + (v + e)(D + T)} \qquad (19\text{-}14)$$

Finally, in order to express every term in the money supply multiplier as a proportion of demand deposits, we can divide the numerator and denominator of Eq. (19-14) by D. This yields

$$m = \frac{c + 1}{c + (v + e)(1 + t)} \qquad (19\text{-}15)$$

where $t = T/D$.

Equation (19-15) shows that the money supply multiplier is dependent upon four ratios: v, e, t, c. We can abbreviate this by expressing the money supply multiplier as $m(v, e, t, c)$, where the parentheses mean that m is a function of $v, e, t,$ and c, not that m is multiplied by $v, e, t,$ and c. Moreover, only one of these ratios v is directly controlled by the Federal Reserve. The rest are determined by the public. If people choose to hold more cash or time deposits relative to demand deposits, or if banks choose to hold more excess reserves relative to demand deposits, then this will cause the money supply multiplier to change. Moreover, the relationship between all four of these ratios and the money supply multiplier is negative, such that as any of these ratios goes up (down) the money supply multiplier goes down (up).

We can summarize this relationship between the base and the money supply with what we will call the money supply function, which simply says that the money supply represented by M_{1a}, is determined by the product of the base and the money supplier multiplier, where the money supply multiplier is, in turn, dependent upon the four ratios v, e, t, c:

$$M_{1a} = B \cdot m(v, e, t, c) \tag{19-16}$$

HOW SHOULD MONETARY POLICY BE CONDUCTED?

Equation (19-16) explains how the money supply is determined in a simple concise algebraic relationship. However, the actual task of controlling the money supply is not as simple as just plugging numbers into this equation. In spite of the fact that there is little disagreement that this is the way to explain what determines the money supply, there is much less agreement as to whether this provides a useful guideline to actually controlling the money supply. To see the reasons for this disagreement we must consider how monetary policy has been and might be conducted.

The Evolution of Federal Reserve Policy

As we learned in Chapter Seventeen, the Federal Reserve System was created in 1913 as a response to the panic of 1907. The principal powers given to the Federal Reserve when it was originally created were the ability to extend loans to member commercial banks, the ability to buy and sell government securities, and the power to compel member banks to hold reserves. As it has turned out, probably the most important result of the Federal Reserve Act was that a central bank was created and empowered to control the supply of money through its control of bank reserves. Yet at the outset, the Federal Reserve's perception of its purpose was not to control the supply of money. Instead, it was to provide what has been referred to as an "elastic currency." This means that it was designed to prevent liquidity crises like those which plagued the U.S. banking system before the Fed was created. It was not wholly successful, however, as the largest of these crises occurred after the Fed had been in operation for some 16 years.

The idea of ensuring an elastic currency essentially meant that money and credit would be available to provide for the needs of trade and commerce. This is known as the "real bills doctrine."[6] The essence of the real bills doctrine incorporated two principles. The first was that as the economy expanded, the Federal Reserve's function was to ensure that enough money and credit were available so as not to hamper that expansion. The second was that the Fed was to discipline bankers so they did not engage in or finance what was judged excessive speculation. If the economy contracted, then money and credit should contract with it. The real bills doctrine essentially meant that the Federal Reserve should assume a passive role as far as the money supply itself was concerned. In this view the money supply, or its rate of growth, was a by-product of economic events. This view implied that the Federal Reserve should allow the money supply to pursue whatever course the economy dictated. As long as the Federal Reserve made loans and reserves available to banks to guarantee their liquidity, then it was fulfilling its principal purpose.

Today many, but not all, economists argue that the Fed should control the money supply so that it does not expand and contract with the economy. Rather than allowing money to be a by-product, they argue that control of the money supply should be the principal objective of the Fed. In order to appreciate how the Fed operates today and why it has met such vehement criticism in recent years, it is important to understand the gradual evolution of the Fed's principal objective from one of insurance of liquidity to the point where it at least makes the public pronouncement that it seeks to control the money supply.

The debate about the real bills doctrine dates back to the first few decades the System was in existence. In the early years of the Federal Reserve System, prior to the Great Depression of 1929, there was a struggle for power between the Board of Governors of the System, located in Washington, and the 12 regional Federal Reserve Banks spread throughout the country. This power struggle at least partly reflected a difference of opinion as to exactly what the purpose of the System was. By and large, most of the district bank presidents believed that the Federal Reserve was to function as a banker's bank. They espoused the real bills doctrine. But throughout those years they were often dominated by the forceful president of the New York Federal Reserve Bank, Benjamin Strong. The New York bank was originally and remains the most important bank in the System. In part this is because New York has long been the financial center of the country, but it is also because the New York bank dealt directly with foreign banks and governments. Benjamin Strong argued that the Fed should not be entirely passive, but should use its powers to buy and sell government securities in order to influence reserves in a countercyclical manner. Strong died in 1928 and the view that the Fed should be a passive entity concerned with the stability of interest rates again became the dominant belief within the System as the country approached the Great Contraction of 1929.

[6] See Robert Craig West, *Banking Reform and the Federal Reserve, 1863–1923*, Cornell University Press, Ithaca, N.Y., 1974, for an extensive discussion of the real bills doctrine and its role in the development of the Federal Reserve System.

Contemporary critics of the Federal Reserve, particularly Milton Friedman, have argued that this passive policy, if not responsible for the Depression itself, was a principal contributing factor to its depth and longevity. Between 1929 and 1933 the supply of money in the United States declined by approximately one-third. While clearly concerned with the Depression itself, the Federal Reserve evidenced little direct concern for the behavior of the money supply or of other aggregate measures of credit in the economy. The Board members simply did not perceive it to be their responsibility to try to influence these variables.[7] Their view was aptly summarized by Governor Norris of the Philadelphia Federal Reserve Bank in September of 1930 when the system was considering a proposal to undertake actions to influence reserves in a countercyclical manner. The proposal was voted down by the Governors of the individual banks and Governor Norris expressed their view:

> We have always believed that the proper function of the System was well expressed in the phrase used in the Tenth Annual Report of the Federal Reserve Board (1923)—"The Federal Reserve supplies the needed additions to credit in times of business expansion and takes up the slack in times of business recession." We have therefore necessarily found ourselves out of harmony with the policy recently followed of supplying unneeded additions to credit in a time of business recession, which is the exact antithesis of the rule above stated.[8]

In his memoirs Herbert Hoover wrote rather disparagingly of this dominant view within the Federal Reserve System, one also held by the then Secretary of the Treasury, Andrew Mellon:

> [These people] felt that government must keep its hands off and let the slump liquidate itself. Mr. Mellon had only one formula: "Liquidate labor, liquidate stocks, liquidate the farmers, liquidate real estate." He insisted that, when the people get an inflation brainstorm, the only way to get it out of their blood is to let it collapse. He held that even a panic was not altogether a bad thing. He said, "It will purge the rottenness out of the system. High costs of living and high living will come down. People will work harder, live a more moral life. Values will be adjusted, and enterprising people will pick up the wrecks from less competent people."[9]

This debate about whether monetary policy should be essentially passive and seek to provide liquidity for the system, or whether monetary policy should be directed toward ensuring stable growth in the supply of money persists to this day. While today it would be difficult to find serious individuals who condone allowing the money supply to drop precipitously as it did in the early 1930s, there is little consensus, short of this, about what the

---

[7] See Jane W. D'Arista, "Federal Reserve Structure and the Development of Monetary Policy: 1915–1935," Staff Report of the Subcommittee on Domestic Finance, Committee on Banking and Currency, House of Representatives, December 1971, for an extensive account of the views of the Board and the debate within the Board at this time.

[8] Ibid., p. 128.

[9] *The Great Depression, 1929–41, The Memoirs of Herbert Hoover*, The Macmillan Company, New York, 1952, p. 30. Reprinted by permission.

Federal Reserve should seek to do with the supply of money. To see this more clearly it is enlightening to contrast these events of nearly a half a century ago with the very recent evolution of monetary policy.

From the end of World War II until a few years ago the Federal Reserve aimed monetary policy at short-term interest rates. When it wanted monetary policy to be tight it set out to raise short-term interest rates. On the other hand, when it wanted monetary policy to be loose it set out to lower short-term interest rates. Moreover, it was always concerned with preserving "orderly conditions" in financial markets. This means that it has always been concerned that interest rates not be too volatile. This method of doing business began to face serious criticism in the mid-1960s. The principal objection was that by concentrating on interest rates, control of the money supply was sacrificed, and the critics argued that the real test of whether monetary policy was tight or loose was whether the money supply was growing at a fast or a slow rate.

In the early 1970s the Federal Reserve began to respond to this criticism by concerning itself more directly with rates of growth in the money supply. And in 1975, for the first time in its history, the Federal Reserve agreed to report targets for the future rate of growth in the supply of money to Congress on a quarterly basis, and to be accountable for meeting those targets. This agreement is known as House Concurrent Resolution 133. Though by this time there was a general agreement that the Federal Reserve should seek to control the supply of money, there was no agreement that the Fed should totally abandon attempts to closely control short-term interest rates. The Fed continued to use the federal funds rate (see Chapter Ten for a description of the federal funds market) as its direct target for monetary policy. The policy therefore became one of trying to control the long-run growth of the supply of money by controlling the federal funds rate in the short run.

On October 6, 1979, in the wake of growing pressure on financial markets, the Federal Reserve formally abandoned the policy of trying to tightly control the federal funds rate. It announced that it would try to directly control reserves, and through reserves, the supply of money. And, within a fairly wide range, it would allow the market to set the federal funds rate on a week-by-week basis. While there has been considerable disagreement about how much of the change is really cosmetic as opposed to substantive, this has probably been the most dramatic alteration in the stated purpose of monetary policy in the history of the Federal Reserve System. In spite of the significance of this event, the debate about the proper conduct of monetary policy has not ceased and probably never will.

The Contemporary Debate About the Conduct of Monetary Policy

The contemporary debate about monetary policy focuses on what should be the proper rate of growth in the supply of money and how the supply should be controlled. In the last part of this book we will concentrate on the importance of the rate of growth in the money supply in controlling the economy as a whole. At this point we will focus on the controversy surrounding the alternative ways in which the Federal Reserve could seek to control the money supply.

One view of how to control the money supply is to use the analysis of the link between the monetary base and the money supply developed earlier in this chapter. From this view the Federal Reserve would conduct open market operations in a manner that leads to a desired change in the supply of money by altering the base at a certain rate based on an estimate of what the money supply multiplier will be. The problem with this is that if the multiplier changes, then this will alter the change in the base that is needed to achieve a desired rate of change in the supply of money. As long as the money supply multiplier remains constant, then if the Fed wants the money supply to change by, say, 6 percent it has to increase the base by 6 percent. Therefore, the Fed has to try to estimate what the multiplier is likely to be and then try to change the base by an amount which leads to the desired increase in the supply of money. The problem of forecasting the money supply multiplier is not a simple one. The volatility of the multiplier is illustrated in Figure 19-3 where the multiplier is plotted for the period from 1970 to 1979. As a result of this volatility and other problems involved in directly controlling reserves, the Fed can never precisely control the supply of money. So the question is: Can the Fed achieve control of the money supply within some reasonable margin of error?

FIGURE 19-3

Money supply multiplier (m_{1a}/B). Source: *Federal Reserve Bulletin*, various issues.

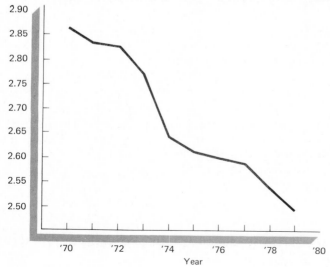

Throughout its history the Federal Reserve has been reluctant to try to control the money supply in the manner described above. The Federal Reserve has long had two basic objections to the suggestion that it should try to directly control reserves.[10] The first, and probably least serious in the long run, is that it is difficult to forecast the multiplier and to know what reserves and the money supply really are from week to week. Hence, there are real practical difficulties involved in trying to directly control reserves in the very short run. Critics of the Fed have argued that many of these difficulties are ones that the Fed has created for itself and that such difficulties should not stand in the way of proper long-run control of the supply of money. The second objection is that by attempting to strictly control reserves the Fed will sacrifice control over short-term interest rates and this will cause serious problems in financial markets. The critics respond that it is generally impossible to control both interest rates and reserves simultaneously; therefore, if the Fed really seeks to control interest rates, it loses control of the supply of money.

To see what is involved in this argument about interest rates it is important to briefly examine how the Fed has operated in recent years. For some time the Federal Reserve has conducted its policy by trying to control the interest rate on federal funds.[11] The way it has done this is by standing ready to conduct open market operations—that is, buying or selling Treasury securities which increase or decrease reserves—and thereby directly affect the supply of federal funds and consequently the federal funds rate. If the Open Market Desk at the Federal Reserve Bank of New York observed that the federal funds rate started to rise above the target set by the Open Market Committee, then it would buy securities or supply reserves to the market in order to drive the funds rate back down. In this way the Fed has tried to keep the funds rate very close to its stated target or within a target range. It has always been difficult to directly measure how successful this policy has been because when it becomes difficult to maintain a given target rate it is always possible to change the target. And because the Fed chose its federal funds target based on a long-run range for growth in the supply of money, it was always possible to try to justify a change in the target. In any event, the target was never explicitly stated ahead of time; rather, the target always had to be inferred from watching to see what interest rate the Fed tried to maintain.

But the result of this method of operation is that reserves will increase or decrease by whatever amount is necessary to achieve the desired control of the federal funds rate. Depending upon how the federal funds rate target is chosen, this may lead to large increases or decreases in the supply of money. Indeed, the central criticism of Federal Reserve policy in recent years is that it has allowed the money supply to grow at a high rate when the economy is in a boom and has permitted its growth rate to decline when the economy is

---

[10] For a detailed statement and defense of the Fed's position on this issue, see Alan Holmes, "Operational Constraints on the Stabilization of Money Supply Growth," in *Controlling the Monetary Aggregates*, Federal Reserve Bank of Boston, June 1979, pp. 65–77.

[11] For a critical review of the Fed's conduct of monetary policy in recent years, see William Poole, "Burnesian Monetary Policy: Eight Years of Progress?" *Journal of Finance*, May 1979, pp. 473–484.

in a recession. The critics contend that if the Federal Reserve would follow a policy of more direct control of reserves, rather than interest rates, it would avoid this problem.

On October 6, 1979, the Federal Reserve announced that it would shift its emphasis in exactly this direction. It would permit the federal funds rate to fluctuate within a much wider band and it would concentrate on more direct control of reserves. This did not mean that the Fed would totally abandon any attempt to limit the fluctuation in the federal funds rate; rather, the emphasis would be more on reserves. The initial consequences, at least for the federal funds market, were relatively dramatic. Figure 19-4 shows a graph of the behavior of the funds rate from July to December 1979. The figure shows that the funds rate increased until October 1979, but that it wasn't particularly volatile. Volatility is indicated by the vertical lines on the graph, which measure the highest and lowest daily average rates. However, beginning in October the funds rate increased dramatically and became more volatile. It remains too early to tell whether or not there has been a significant and long-term change in policy, or whether monetary policy will gradually return to the old mode of conduct.

SUMMARY

In this chapter we completed our examination of how the government regulates financial markets. Specifically, we focused on how the Federal Reserve regulates the supply of money in the economy. We began by exploring the

FIGURE 19-4
Level and volatility of the federal funds rate. This figure shows the weekly average and range of daily rates on federal funds during the weeks before and after October 6, 1979.

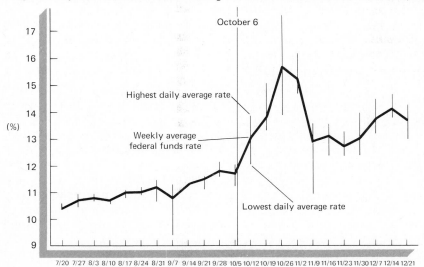

different ways that money can be defined. Then we examined the way money is created in a fractional reserve banking system. Finally, we introduced the controversial issue of how monetary policy ought to be conducted in the U.S. economy. This chapter serves as a transition into the material in Part Five of this book, which deals with how financial markets influence the level of economic activity in the economy.

We discovered that in the U.S. economy of the 1980s it is not obvious how money should be defined. Money serves as a medium of exchange and unit of account. In addition, in order for any asset to function successfully as money the quantity of it must be independently determined. This means that we cannot use some commodity as money which can easily be reproduced. For centuries this condition was met by using a precious metal as money. But money in today's economy is not linked to any such commodity. Instead, we use currency supplied by the government and deposit accounts at financial institutions as money. The difficulty involved in choosing a working definition of money today is that there are a number of different types of deposit accounts which come close to satisfying our requirements for money. These include demand deposits at commercial banks and similar accounts at other institutions. The best available measure of all of these accounts is referred to as M_{1b}.

To understand how the total volume of money is determined in the economy we examined how the Federal Reserve exercises control over the money supply. The Federal Open Market Committee is the most important decision-making entity in the Federal Reserve System because it decides on the volume of open market operations. Open market operations refer to the purchases and sales of Treasury securities by the Federal Reserve. We learned that when the Federal Reserve purchases (sells) securities it increases (decreases) the volume of reserves in the banking system. This constitutes an increase in the monetary base which is equal to the sum of reserves and currency in the economy.

Next we learned that it is the total volume of reserves which places a constraint on the total volume of deposits in the system or on the supply of money. Because reserves must be held at a fixed percentage of deposits, any increase or decrease in the volume of reserves increases or decreases the volume of deposits which financial intermediaries can support. As a result, whenever reserves increase, there is a multiple expansion in the volume of total deposits and therefore in the supply of money. We learned that the magnitude of this expansion is determined by four variables: the required reserve ratio, the desired excess reserve ratio, the ratio of time deposits to demand deposits, and the ratio of cash to demand deposits. These variables determine what we call the money supply multiplier, and the money supply can be expressed as a product of the monetary base and this money supply multiplier. This relationship between the monetary base and the money supply shows how actions taken by the Federal Reserve influence the total supply of money.

An understanding of the multiple expansion process and the relationship between the base and the multiplier does not necessarily convey an understanding of how the Federal Reserve actually goes about influencing the supply of money; therefore, we also examined the procedure used by the Federal Reserve to conduct monetary policy and the ongoing debate about how the Federal Reserve should conduct policy. We found that throughout most of its history the Fed has concentrated on controlling short-term interest rates rather than the supply of money.

During this time it sought to drive interest rates down in order to make monetary policy easy and drive interest rates up in order to tighten up on monetary policy. Only during the 1970s did the Fed publicly announce that it would seek to control the supply of money. Moreover, the principal procedure for accomplishing this objective was still to seek to control short-term interest rates and through those rates, seek control of the supply of money. It did this by choosing a target level of a particular short-term interest rate (the federal funds rate) and supplying the amount of reserves necessary to meet that target. This leads to control of the money supply only when there is a clear relationship between the funds rate and the money supply. As we will discover in the final chapters of the book, this dispute about whether monetary policy should focus on interest rates or on the supply of money is an important element in the disagreement between so-called monetarists and Keynesians about how financial markets and monetary policy influence the economy. We turn to that topic next.

QUESTIONS TO IMPROVE UNDERSTANDING

1 Explain the real bills doctrine. Why is the real bills doctrine inconsistent with the objective of directly controlling the supply of money?
2 What was House Concurrent Resolution 133 and what was its significance? What change occurred in monetary policy in October 1979 and what was its significance?
3 Discuss the functions which money serves and the requirements it must meet. Why did tobacco not survive as a form of money while gold did?
4 What serves as money in the contemporary U.S. economy? Why did it become necessary to change the definition of money in the late 1970s?
5 What is the Open Market Committee and what is its purpose? Why has it been described as the most important decision-making body within the Federal Reserve System?
6 Some argue that the Federal Reserve is virtually an arm of the executive branch of government and others argue it is virtually independent. Evaluate the merits of each position.
7 Suppose there are no leakages in the multiple expansion process. Why is the multiplier then equal to $1/v$?
8 Suppose the Federal Reserve Bank of New York sells $100 million worth of Treasury securities. Trace the impact of this transaction through the banking system if reserve requirements are 15 percent.

9 Suppose that we know that $v = .06$, $e = .005$, $c = .4$, and $t = 2$. What will be the value of the money supply multiplier?

10 Suppose that the Federal Reserve wants the money supply to grow at 8 percent per year and it expects the multiplier to be constant at the value in question 9. What rate of growth in the base does it need to reach the goal of 8 percent growth in the supply of money? What would be needed if the multiplier fell to 2.1?

11 Why do you think the money supply multiplier is difficult to forecast?

12 How does the Federal Reserve operate if it uses an interest-rate target, specifically, the federal funds rate?

REFERENCES

D'Arista, Jane W.: "Federal Reserve Structure and the Development of Monetary Policy: 1915–1935," Staff Report of the Subcommittee on Domestic Finance, Committee on Banking and Currency, House of Representatives, December 1971.

Holmes, Alan: "Operational Constraints on the Stabilization of Money Supply Growth," Controlling the Monetary Aggregates, Federal Reserve Bank of Boston (June 1979), pp. 65–77.

Lombra, Raymond E.: "Reflections on Burns's Reflections," Journal of Money, Credit and Banking (February 1980), pp. 94–105.

Poole, William: "Burnesian Monetary Policy: Eight Years of Progress?" Journal of Finance (May 1979), pp. 473–484.

Safire, William: Before the Fall, Doubleday, New York, 1975.

West, Robert Craig: Banking Reform and the Federal Reserve, 1863–1923, Cornell University Press, Ithaca, N.Y., 1974.

FINANCIAL MARKETS
AND THE
AGGREGATE ECONOMY

Part Five explains the links between the financial markets and the rest of the economy. In particular, Part Five focuses on the question of how monetary policy influences the financial markets and, in turn, the rest of the economy. This is an issue upon which there is little consensus and it is one of the most important ongoing debates in economics. The purpose of Part Five is to spell out the essential features of the two major positions in this debate. One side has been given the label monetarist because those who advocate the monetarist view believe that monetary policy is an, if not the most, important determinant of changes in the level of nominal income in the economy. Those who advocate the other side, labeled Keynesian after the famous British economist John Maynard Keynes, are more skeptical about the central role of monetary policy in the economy. The first two chapters of Part Five explain the essential features of each view or school of thought. Chapter Twenty focuses on the monetarist view. It explains the theory advocated by the monetarists of how monetary policy influences the level of nominal income in the economy. It also examines the empirical evidence offered by monetarists to support their position and it examines the conclusions which monetarists draw about how monetary policy should be conducted. Chapter

Twenty-one examines the same issues from the Keynesian vantage point. First it explains the Keynesian theory of how financial markets influence the economy and the empirical evidence consistent with their view. It then analyzes the Keynesian view of how monetary policy should be conducted. The final chapter of Part Five focuses on the problem of inflation. It explores the monetarist and Keynesian views of the causes and the possible cures for inflation, and it explores how inflation has influenced financial markets.

Chapter Twenty

HOW FINANCIAL MARKETS
AFFECT THE ECONOMY:
THE MONETARIST APPROACH

In the next three chapters we will explore the links between financial markets and the rest of the economy. Economists tend to refer to the rest of the economy as the "real" side or the "real" sector, as opposed to the financial side or the financial sector. Our principal objective is to understand how the financial markets influence important variables in the real sector of the economy, particularly prices and the level of income.

There are two competing views about the nature of the links between the real sector and financial markets. One view we will label Keynesian and the other monetarist. The central purpose of this chapter and the next is to compare and contrast these two points of view. This chapter deals with the monetarist view and the next with the Keynesian. It is something of an oversimplification to say that there are only two distinct and well-defined views of the links between financial markets and the economy. More realistically, there are a large number of different points of view with only shades of difference between them. But there are two distinct poles in this spectrum of views and it is useful to organize the discussion which follows around these two poles. The very existence of a diversity of views means that in the next few chapters we will not develop a single accepted account of how financial markets affect the economy. Rather these chapters synthesize an ongoing debate about how the system works.

A PERSPECTIVE ON THE MONETARIST–KEYNESIAN DEBATE

Of the two polar views in this debate, the monetarist view is certainly the oldest. Some have even characterized it as "old-time religion." This view is associated with a long tradition of economics taught at the University of Chicago during both the twentieth and the latter part of the nineteenth century. But there is both an old monetarist view, which was popular prior to the Great Depression of the 1930s, and a new or more modern reincarnation of this view, which gained popularity in the 1960s and 1970s. The reason for the decline and subsequent rise in popularity of monetarism is really the advent of Keynesianism during and after the Depression. With the onset and persistence of the Depression many people came to the conclusion that the old-time religion was bankrupt and that a new explanation of aggregate economic behavior was needed. That gap was filled by John Maynard Keynes with the publication in 1936 of his classic book, *The General Theory of Employment, Interest, and Money*. Keynes's views subsequently became the basis for a whole generation of economic thought. But as the economic conditions in the United States and the world changed from those which characterized the 1930s and 1940s to those of the late 1960s and the 1970s, a serious challenge was presented to the advocates of the Keynesian view. A new form of the old monetarism arose. These new monetarist economists, spearheaded by Milton Friedman at the University of Chicago, argue that the Keynesian analysis is seriously flawed. They allege that the Keynesian view assigns an insignificant role to financial markets in general and monetary policy in particular, in determining the course of aggregate economic events. By contrast, the new monetarists make financial markets and monetary policy the centerpiece of their analysis of aggregate economic behavior.

Monetary policy is definitely not the only ingredient in financial markets which might be important for the real economy. For example, in Part Four it was argued that the regulatory structure that is imposed on the savings and loan and banking industries may have a significant effect on the level of real activity in the economy. Yet historically, monetary policy has been the object of the most extensive and vehement debates regarding financial markets and the real economy. The question is how monetary policy determines the underlying conditions in financial markets.

As the development in the next few chapters proceeds, it will be useful to think of monetarists and Keynesians as being at odds over three basic questions. Each of these questions pertains to the role of money and the effectiveness of monetary policy in a market economy. These questions are:

How does monetary policy affect the real economy?

How strong is the effect of monetary policy on the economy?

How should monetary policy be conducted?

These three questions underlie the discussion of the monetarist–Keynesian debate which follows.

In order to develop a reasonably precise statement of the monetarist and Keynesian views we will need to employ a fair amount of algebra. This will be necessary to explain the relationships between important variables in the economy. To minimize confusion regarding the symbols used in these equations, Table 20-1 contains a list of most of the symbols used and their definitions. This table can be found near the end of this chapter. The table contains all the symbols used in Chapters Twenty, Twenty-one, and Twenty-two.

THE DEMAND FOR REAL MONEY BALANCES

The concept of the demand for money is a relevant part of both the monetarist and Keynesian views of how the economy works. However, the demand for money is the centerpiece of the monetarist view of the economy, while in the Keynesian analysis it is only one of a number of equally important relationships in the economy. Therefore, the logical starting point for a description of the monetarist camp is with the demand for money. Once we understand the determinants of the demand for money, we can examine how the demand for money fits into the monetarist framework and we can acquire an understanding of why it is of such special importance.

It is actually the demand for real money balances, rather than simply the demand for money, which is the critical element in the monetarist analysis. The distinction is that when we refer to money, without qualification, we generally mean the nominal stock of money or money balances, without adjustment for inflation. By real money balances we mean the stock of money adjusted for the level of inflation. Using M_1 (either M_{1a} or M_{1b}) as our definition of money, the total nominal stock of money balances in the economy is simply M_1. But total real money balances are M_1/P, where P represents the aggregate price level.

To see how we measure real money balances let's take M_{1b} as our measure of nominal money balances and the consumer price index as our measure of the price level. The consumer price level is measured as an index relative to some point in time. For example, the consumer price index in October 1979 was 225.5, with a base of 100 in 1967. This means that during the interval from 1967 to October 1979 consumer prices increased by 125.5 percent. M_{1b} was equal to 383.9 during October 1979. Real money balances were therefore, 170.2 (383.9/2.255). This means that the money supply in October 1979 was equal to 170.2 expressed in 1967 dollars. It should be apparent that the absolute amount of the real money supply is not particularly meaningful. The usefulness is in the ability to compare real numbers for two time periods when they are expressed in prices defined at the same point in time.

To understand the demand for money is to understand why economic agents—that is, individuals and corporations—hold their wealth in money rather than other forms. In Chapter Two the forms of wealth available in the economy were divided into five broad categories: money, bonds, equities, physical capital, and human capital. Therefore, the choice facing each economic agent is a choice of how to allocate resources across these various forms of wealth. The factors which determine this choice are not fundamentally different from those which determine the demand for any commodity that one might consume. We think of the demand for any commodity as being determined by the level of income, the price of that commodity relative to the prices of other goods which may be complements or substitutes, and finally the tastes of individuals. Similar factors determine the demand for money.

Specifying the Demand for Money

To specify the demand for money is to identify the variables which influence people's desire to hold money and to define the nature of their impact on the demand for money. We will represent this relationship between money demand (M^d) and its determinants with a demand for money function. If we let X represent the set of variables which measure wealth and the relative rates of return on money and other forms of wealth, then we can express a demand function for nominal money balances as follows:

$$M^d = f(X) \tag{20-1}$$

The task at hand is to carefully specify the variables contained in X. We will identify three types of variables which influence the demand for real money balances. They are wealth or permanent income, the rates of return on alternatives to money, and the expected rate of inflation. We will discuss each of these in turn, beginning with wealth.

The first and possibly most important variable is the level of wealth, W. The basic decision involved in choosing a level of money is how to allocate wealth across various types of assets. As a result, the principal constraint on an individual's or the economy's decision as to how much money to hold is the level of wealth. However, as discussed in the early chapters of this book, it is relatively impractical to try to measure the total stock of wealth for the society as a whole, as there are some components of wealth which do not have readily defined market values. This is particularly true of human capital. But we know that wealth is simply a capitalized income stream. Hence we can use income as a proxy for wealth, if we find it easier to actually measure income.

In order to make use of income as a proxy for wealth we cannot simply substitute the level of nominal income, measured at a particular point in time, for the level of wealth of the economy at that time. The reason is that wealth is the discounted value of expected future income, and measured income in any one period may well be above or below the expected level of long-run future income. Instead, we substitute what is called permanent income. The concept of permanent income was made popular by Milton Friedman as a basis for explaining aggregate consumption of all commodities, as well as the demand for money.[1] Friedman's concept of permanent income is that it is the level of long-run income that people expect they will average in the future. Because it is the expected value of future income levels, it is thought to be permanent. We will represent permanent income with the symbol Y'. The difficulties involved in measuring permanent income are discussed below.

The next important determinant of the money demand function is the relative rate of return on alternatives to money as ways of holding wealth. By relative rate of return we mean the return on some other asset, such as equities, relative to the return on money. The difficulty inherent in specifying these relative rates of return is that we cannot directly observe the rate of return on money. In the United States the government has long fixed the explicit nominal rate of return on money at zero by prohibiting the payment of interest on demand deposits. But this by no means implies that the actual return on money is zero. In fact, if people received no benefit or return from holding money, they would not hold it. Instead, the return on money is by and large a service flow. That is, the maintenance of money balances eases the cost of buying and selling goods and services or executing transactions. If we had to convert some kind of bond or equity into the medium of exchange, money, every time a purchase of goods or services was to be made, we would incur substantial costs of transacting. These include the costs imposed by the market of actually selling the security as well as the cost of expending our own time and effort on making the transaction. To be sure, as technology has become more sophisticated, many of these costs have been reduced. But as long as such costs of transacting exist, money will yield a service flow and we will hold positive balances of it. Unfortunately, practical problems of measuring this return on money still remain. To circumvent these problems it is generally assumed that the value of the services which money provides remains constant, or at least, is independent of changes in yields on other forms of wealth.[2]

The other aspect of relative return is the expected rate of return on other forms of wealth. We might set out to specify and measure each of the rates of

---

[1] See Milton Friedman, *A Theory of the Consumption Function*, Princeton University Press, Princeton, N.J., 1957.

[2] On the other hand, one might assume that the return on money fluctuates with the returns on some other assets in the market. The implications of this alternative assumption have been explored by Benjamin Klein, "Competitive Interest Payments on Bank Deposits and the Long-run Demand for Money," *American Economic Review*, 64 (December 1974), pp. 931–949.

return on distinct assets for inclusion in the money demand function. But we know that the rate of return on human capital is difficult if not impossible to measure. So we avoid specifically including it.[3] The other important items are the expected rate of return on equities, r_e, and the expected rate of return on bonds, r_b. As either of these rates of return is perceived to increase, the opportunity cost of holding money increases and the demand for money declines.

The final element affecting the return on money is the rate of inflation. Inflation penalizes those who hold their wealth in money, for the value of money holdings declines directly with the rate of inflation. Moreover, people's expectations of the future rate of inflation influence the rate of return they anticipate from holding money. Therefore, it is the *expected* rate of inflation, which we will symbolize $(1/P)$ $(\Delta P^e/\Delta t)$, which is normally included in the money demand function. As the expected rate of inflation increases, the demand for money decreases.

So we can summarize the money demand function as follows:

$$M^d = f\left(\overset{+}{Y}', \frac{1}{P}\frac{\overline{\Delta P^e}}{\Delta t}, \overline{r}_e, \overline{r}_b\right) \tag{20-2}$$

The positive or negative sign over each variable influencing money demand indicates whether money demand increases $(+)$ or decreases $(-)$ as the variable in question increases.

Real Versus Nominal Money Demand

Recall that our purpose is to define the demand for *real* money balances. So far we have the demand for nominal money balances. To move from nominal to real demand we can start by trying to simplify Eq. (20-2). Moreover, the first simplification we can introduce also helps to clarify a potential ambiguity about Eq. (20-2). The ambiguity is whether the appropriate rates of returns for equities and bonds are real or nominal returns. If the rates of return are nominal, then the explicit introduction of the expected rate of inflation is unnecessary, because the market's estimate of the expected inflation rate is contained in the nominal interest rate. So if we include nominal interest rates in the demand function, this incorporates a measure of expected inflation. This also handles the difficult problem of measuring the expected inflation rate. The best available measure is the one provided by the

---

[3] Milton Friedman and others have argued that one way to incorporate human capital into the money demand function is to include a variable in the function which is defined as the ratio of human to nonhuman wealth. Friedman points out that, because human wealth cannot be sold as capital, as the ratio of human to nonhuman wealth increases, people's wealth becomes less liquid. He argues that in order to offset this illiquidity they will hold more of their wealth in money than they otherwise would. As a result, as the ratio of human to nonhuman wealth increases, the demand for money is supposed to increase. Friedman argues that this is useful in explaining long-term changes in the demand for money. See Milton Friedman, "The Quantity Theory of Money: A Restatement," in Milton Friedman (ed.), *Studies in the Quantity Theory of Money*, University of Chicago Press, Chicago, 1956.

market and included in the nominal interest rate. Henceforth, the interest rates in the money demand function should be thought of as nominal rates.

Another simplification which is often used in dealing with money demand is to collapse the rates of return on bonds and equities into a single interest rate. The only substantial justification for this is that there may not be enough differences in the returns on these types of wealth to justify dealing with them separately. And in long-run equilibrium this should be true. Therefore, if we represent the nominal interest rate as r, the simplified money demand function can be written:

$$M^d = f(Y', r) \qquad (20\text{-}3)$$

Now we will distinguish between the demand for money in real and in nominal terms. In Eqs. (20-2) and (20-3) money demand is measured in nominal rather than real dollars. This means it is not adjusted for inflation. The conversion from nominal money demand to real money demand should involve no change in the determinants of the demand function. The same functional relationship should hold with nominal changed to real money and income. This presumes that people do not alter their behavior in any significant way if the unit of measurement in which their transactions take place is altered. For example, suppose that we double the number of dollars required to make every purchase and simultaneously double the level of income of all people in the economy. The effect should be to double the demand for money. An increase of a smaller or lesser amount would constitute a substantive change in behavior. Yet the only change which has taken place is a change in the unit of measurement. When people's money demand can be expressed in this way they are said to be free of "money illusion."

If we want to see the impact of a change in the price level on money demand, we could divide the level of nominal permanent income Y' by the price level P. The resulting income variable is now real permanent income, which we will label y'. Assuming that this increases money demand by the same proportional amount it reduces Y', then we should simultaneously multiply the money demand function by P in order to offset the effect of dividing Y' by P. Hence, we should be able to write the money demand function as follows, for any value of P:

$$M^d = Pf(y', r) \qquad (20\text{-}4)$$

Alternatively, we can move the P which multiplies the function to the left-hand side of the equation:

$$\frac{M^d}{P} = f(y', r) \qquad (20\text{-}5)$$

This says that the demand for real money balances depends on permanent income, in real terms, and the nominal interest rate, according to a function which is independent of changes in P.

We can illustrate this money demand function with a diagram as in Figure 20-1. The vertical axis in the figure measures the nominal interest rate r, while the horizontal axis measures the nominal quantity of money demanded. The relationship between these variables is illustrated by the slopes of lines labeled $M^d{}_1$ and $M^d{}_2$. These lines are drawn for two distinct values of y': y'_1 and y'_2. Because increases in permanent income increase the demand for money, higher values of y' correspond to lines drawn further to the right. For example, line $M^d{}_2$ represents the quantity of money demanded at different levels of the nominal interest rate if permanent income is y'_2.

Thus far we have learned that the demand for money is dependent on three basic factors, the level of permanent income, the expected rate of inflation, and the real rates of return on alternative assets. We have also learned the distinctions between real and nominal money balances and how the demand for real money balances differs from the demand for nominal money balances. Now that we see what the demand for money is and what determines it we need to explore how the demand for money is used by the monetarists. To do this we will examine the modern quantity theory. As we will soon discover, the central concept of the modern quantity theory is velocity and velocity is simply another way of looking at the demand for money. Hence, the demand for money serves as the foundation for the modern quantity theory.

THE MODERN QUANTITY THEORY

Prior to the popularity of Keynesian theory, monetarists were not known as monetarists. This is a label which has been applied in more recent years. The intellectual precursors of modern monetarists are known as quantity theorists. In order to highlight the intellectual bloodline, the theory advo-

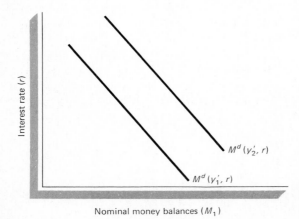

Interest rate (r)

$M^d(y'_2, r)$

$M^d(y'_1, r)$

Nominal money balances (M_1)

FIGURE 20-1
The demand for nominal money balances. The slope of the two money-demand curves shows that money demand is negatively related to the interest rate. The shift in the curve from M^d_1 to M^d_2 illustrates that money demand is positively related to permanent income.

cated by contemporary monetarists is often labeled the modern quantity theory. In some respects the similarities between the modern and original quantity theorists are more in form than substance. The form of both versions of the quantity theory can be summarized in a simple equation:

$$MV \equiv Py \qquad (20\text{-}6)$$

where y is real income, V is the velocity of money, and M and P are defined as above. In fact, this question is an identity, which means it is true by definition. We use the symbol $\equiv$ for an identity. The attractiveness of this identity lies in its simplicity and in the interpretation and usefulness of the concept of velocity. The original quantity theorists had one interpretation of velocity and the modern quantity theorists have quite another. To understand the arguments of the contemporary monetarists we must understand their concept of velocity.

The Concept of Velocity and the Modern Quantity Theory

The essential idea behind the modern quantity theory can be expressed without reference to the concept of velocity. But because the concept of velocity has long been such an integral part of the monetarist position, it is important to understand velocity and the way in which it is used by monetarists. First, we will develop their argument, without reference to velocity.

The monetarists argue that, within some limits, the Federal Reserve can make the money supply whatever it wants. Hence, we treat the money supply as determined independently of the rest of the economy. In addition, the monetarists argue that the money demand function described above is a very stable and predictable relationship. Monetarists contend that equilibrium in the economy can be represented by an equilibrium between the quantity of money supplied and the quantity of money demanded. This equilibrium condition can be represented as follows:

$$M^s = M^d = f(Y', r) \qquad (20\text{-}7)$$

Suppose that the level of nominal permanent income and the interest rate are such that this equilibrium condition is satisfied. This means that at the existing level of income and interest rates, people are willing to hold the quantity of money supplied by the Federal Reserve. Now suppose the Federal Reserve disturbs this equilibrium by increasing the supply of money so that

$$M^s > M^d \qquad (20\text{-}8)$$

The monetarists argue that people do not passively accept these excess money balances, unless something determining money demand changes to restore equilibrium. If the money demand function is stable, which is to say that people do not willingly accept new money balances without some substantive inducement to hold them, then either nominal income or interest rates must change to bring about a new equilibrium. Furthermore, the monetarists generally argue that the variable which does, in fact, change to bring about the new equilibrium is the level of nominal permanent income. They argue that the effect of interest-rate changes on money demand is generally so small as to be inconsequential.

This monetarist explanation of the effect of money on income is usually made using velocity and Eq. (20-6). To see how the argument can be recast in this form, we need to alter Eq. (20-6) slightly by dividing through by M so that we have velocity on the left-hand side:

$$V = \frac{Py}{M} \qquad (20\text{-}9)$$

Now, we can define velocity in two ways, just as we can approach the quantity of money in two ways: the quantity supplied and the quantity demanded. First, we will examine desired velocity, V^d. Typically, when monetarists refer to velocity, they are referring to desired velocity, for they argue that velocity is simply an alternative way of stating the demand for money. Hence, desired velocity is simply the public's desired ratio of nominal income to nominal money balances:

$$V^d = \frac{Py}{M^d} = \frac{Py}{f(y', r)} \qquad (20\text{-}10)$$

However, just as there can be a disequilibrium between the quantity of money supplied and the quantity of money demanded, there can be a difference between desired and actual velocity. Actual velocity, V^a, is the actual ratio of nominal income to nominal money balances:

$$V^a = \frac{Py}{M^s} \qquad (20\text{-}11)$$

But in equilibrium, when the public's demand for money is equal to the quantity of money supplied, actual velocity must equal desired velocity:

$$V^a = V^d \qquad (20\text{-}12)$$

We can summarize this equilibrium relationship by interpreting the M and V in the original Eq. (20-6) as the quantity of money supplied and the equilibrium desired level of velocity, respectively:

$$M^s V^d = Py \qquad (20\text{-}13)$$

The logic conveyed by this equation is as follows. Suppose the money supply is increased. In order to maintain equilibrium, either velocity must decline or nominal income must increase. If it is nominal income which changes to bring about an increase in the demand for money, then the right-hand side of Eq. (20-13) will adjust in the new equilibrium. But if people respond passively to changes in the money supply, such that income does not have to change for the demand for money to change, then a decrease in velocity may absorb the entire money supply increase.

Diagramatically we can represent the monetarist interpretation of a change in the money supply as inevitably leading to a change in nominal income:

$$\uparrow M^s\, V^d = \uparrow Py$$

Conversely, a money supply change might simply be absorbed by a change in velocity:

$$\uparrow M^s \downarrow V^d = Py$$

This could happen if either the money demand function itself changes as the supply of money changes, or if interest rates decline and that decline causes no change in income. The first possibility is usually characterized as a situation where money demand, and hence velocity, is unstable.

It is important to contrast the concept of velocity contained in the modern quantity theory with the earlier concept of velocity espoused by economists in the early part of this century. At that time, Eq. (20-6) was known as the "equation of exchange." The concept conveyed by the equation of exchange can best be summarized by stating the equation in words. The equation says that the total quantity of money in circulation, multiplied by the number of times it turns over or changes hands, is equal to the average price level of all transactions, multiplied by the number of transactions. The concept of velocity employed then, of a rate of turnover, is vastly different from the concept of velocity contained in the modern quantity theory. In its more modern reincarnation, velocity represents the equilibrium ratio of nominal income to desired nominal money balances. It is in no way related to a rate of turnover. Moreover, the original quantity theorists argued that velocity, interpreted as the rate at which money turned over, was approximately constant. Hence, an increase in the supply of money necessarily led to an increase in nominal income. But contemporary monetarists do not argue that velocity is constant. Rather, they argue that money demand, and hence velocity, is a stable and predictable function. And their theory depends upon the validity of this proposition. If velocity is unstable or unpredictable, then the relationship between the money supply and income is unstable and unpredictable. We will examine this proposition next.

Is Velocity Stable and Predictable?

The monetarists contend that they can provide a perfectly adequate explanation of the behavior of velocity, while the Keynesians disagree. One reason for this argument is a fundamental disagreement about the relevant time horizon over which velocity must be predicted. Keynesians perceive a role for activist policies on the part of the government which try to smooth or reduce *short-run* fluctuations in the level of nominal income. As a result, they believe that if velocity is to be a useful concept, we must be able to satisfactorily explain the monthly and quarterly changes in velocity. For without such predictability, it would be difficult to try to influence nominal income by exerting direct control over the money supply; the connection between the two would simply be too unstable. On the other hand, monetarists perceive the role of the government in general, and the Federal Reserve in particular, as contributing to long-run stability by *not* manipulating the rate of growth in the money supply in the short run. They believe that attempts to manipulate the money supply in the short run create instability rather than stability. (More will be said about these policy differences at the end of the chapter.) As a result, they are much less concerned with explaining short-run changes in velocity. Instead, they focus on long-run trends in velocity.

To see more specifically what is involved in explaining velocity, it is useful to examine Figure 20-2. This figure shows the behavior of velocity

FIGURE 20-2

Velocity in the United States (based on M_{1a}). The shaded areas in the figure show the periods of recession which occurred prior to 1978. A recession is defined as a period of two consecutive quarters of decline in gross national product.

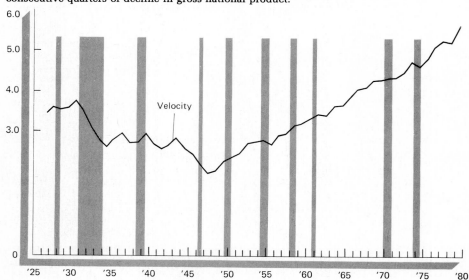

from 1925 to 1979. The figure shows that velocity has tended to increase over this time period, but that it has also had a *procyclical pattern*; that is, it has tended to rise and fall with the level of income. A procyclical pattern is evident by noticing that velocity tends to fall during or near the shaded time intervals in the figure. The shaded areas represent periods of recession.

There appears to be a relatively simple explanation for the tendency for velocity to increase over recent years. The long-run increase in velocity can be attributed to increased efficiency in the process of carrying out transactions. This has led to a decreased demand for money, relative to income. Since the late 1940s, a number of financial assets have developed which are viewed as substitutes for money, for example, credit union shares and money market mutual funds. Moreover, the speed and efficiency with which the payments mechanism works has increased. As a result, the cost of transacting has declined and with it, the need for money balances. This has been particularly noticeable in very recent years as the technology for efficient cash management has blossomed. It seems likely that this trend will continue and even accelerate.

The procyclical pattern in velocity can be explained in two ways. One explanation, advanced by Milton Friedman,[4] relies on the fluctuations of permanent income relative to nominal income, in any given period. Because permanent income represents expected future long-run income, it changes less, in any given period, than does nominal income. Only if the change in nominal income were perceived to be permanent would permanent income change by the same amount. But most changes in nominal income are perceived to be transitory, so that only part of the change is reflected in permanent income. If part of this perceived change in permanent income is allocated to money balances, then the change in money must be less than the change in permanent income, which, in turn, must be less than the change in measured nominal income. This means that when nominal income changes, the numerator in Eq. (20-9) will be altered by a greater amount than will the denominator; therefore, velocity will tend to rise and fall with income.

An alternative explanation for the procyclical behavior of velocity relies on the observation that interest rates move procyclically. Because the quantity of money demanded is negatively related to the level of interest rates, an increase in interest rates will lead to a decline in desired money balances.[5] This will tend to diminish the growth in the demand for money caused by an increase in income, and velocity will move procyclically.

It seems difficult, if not impossible, to provide a definitive answer as to which explanation is correct. But the reliance of the latter explanation on the behavior of nominal interest rates is much more consistent with the Keynesian than the monetarist view. Interest rates do not have a very explicit role in the monetarist framework, but they are a critical part of the arguments

---

[4] Ibid.
[5] See Henry A. Latane, "Income Velocity and Interest Rates: A Pragmatic Approach," *Review of Economics and Statistics*, XLII (November 1960), pp. 445–449.

offered by the Keynesians. The significance of this dispute will be emphasized in the next chapter.

CAUSE AND EFFECT IN THE MONETARIST THEORY: THE PORTFOLIO ADJUSTMENT PROCESS

An important criticism of the modern quantity theory, as it has been articulated thus far, is that it still leaves the mechanism by which money supply changes are transmitted to changes in nominal income unspecified. Even if we understand the behavior of velocity, we are still left with a "black box," as far as any detailed explanation of cause and effect is concerned. How is it that the level of nominal income increases in response to the injection by the Federal Reserve of excess money balances? Here we will sketch the answer which the monetarists as well as some of their Keynesian critics have provided to try to fill in the gap.

The Portfolio-Adjustment Process

The monetarists' view of how changes in the supply of money are transmitted to changes in income can be characterized as a process of portfolio adjustment. Monetarists argue that economic agents have clear preferences as to how to spread their wealth over the various forms in which it may be held. As a result, they approach the demand for money as a question of how much wealth should be held in the form of money rather than bonds, equities, physical capital, or human capital. If the Federal Reserve creates a disequilibrium between desired and actual money balances, then individuals who acquire excess balances through transactions will seek to shift these balances into other forms of wealth. By so doing they increase the demand for these other forms of wealth.

Milton Friedman and Anna Schwartz have provided a lucid explanation of what is meant by this portfolio-adjustment process. In a paper published in the early 1960s they argued:

> It seems plausible that both nonbank and bank holders of redundant balances will turn first to securities comparable to those they have sold, say, fixed-interest coupon, low risk obligations. But as they seek to purchase these they will tend to bid up the prices of those issues. Hence they, and also other holders not involved in the initial central bank open-market transactions, will look farther afield: the banks, to their loans; the nonbank holders, to other categories of securities—higher-risk fixed-coupon obligations, equities, real property, and so forth. As the process continues, the initial impacts are diffused in several respects: first, the range of assets affected widens; second, potential creators of assets now more in demand are induced to react to the better terms on which they can be sold, including business enterprises wishing to engage in capital expansion, house builders or prospective homeowners, consumers—who are potential purchasers

of durable consumer goods—and so on and on; third, the initially redundant money balances concentrated in the hands of those first affected by the open-market purchases become spread throughout the economy. As the prices of financial assets are bid up, they become expensive relative to nonfinancial assets, so there is an incentive for individuals and enterprises to seek to bring their actual portfolios into accord with desired portfolios by acquiring nonfinancial assets. This, in turn, tends to make existing nonfinancial assets expensive relative to newly constructed nonfinancial assets. At the same time, the general rise in the price level of nonfinancial assets tends to raise wealth relative to income, and to make the direct acquisition of current services cheaper relative to the purchase of sources of services. These effects raise demand curves for current productive services, both for producing new capital goods and for purchasing current services. The monetary stimulus is, in this way, spread from the financial markets to the markets for goods and services.[6]

An alternative way to describe the process they have in mind begins by defining a new variable which we will label q.[7] We define the variable q as the ratio of the price of an asset relative to its reproduction cost. The ratio q is designed to measure the pressure of demand for an asset, relative to the cost of reproducing it. For example, suppose the prices of houses in a particular locale are bid up above the cost of building new houses. This increase in q will encourage builders to increase the production of new houses and, as they do so, the cost of building houses will increase. This will continue until the price of new houses rises to match the going prices of existing houses. We can think of q as representing the amount of excess demand for an asset. If q is greater than 1, then there is an excess demand for the asset and production of the asset will increase. If q is equal to 1, then the market is in equilibrium with no excess demand and no incentive to increase or decrease production. Finally, if q is less than 1, then production will be curtailed and assets will depreciate until q rises to equal 1.

The relevance of q is that it can be thought of as the true indicator of the effect of the money supply on nominal income in the economy. If the Federal Reserve creates a disequilibrium by increasing the supply of money over the amount demanded, then people will attempt to adjust their portfolios out of money into other assets. As they do so, they will bid up the prices of these assets and raise the level of q for a variety of assets across the economy. And q will remain high until nominal income increases enough to create a new equilibrium between money supply and money demand.

While q has tremendous value as a theoretical representation of the state of monetary policy, its practical value is limited because we do not directly observe the value of q. Data are not collected on the value of q and it is not a variable which can easily be computed. Economists have made attempts to

---

[6] Milton Friedman and Anna Schwartz, "Money and Business Cycles," *Review of Economics and Statistics,* supplement, February 1963, pp. 60–61. Reprinted with permission of North Holland Publishing Company.
[7] See James Tobin, "A General Equilibrium Approach to Monetary Theory," *Journal of Money, Credit and Banking,* I (November 1969), pp. 15–27, for the original development of q.

estimate the aggregate value of q for the U.S. economy on an historical basis. Figure 20-3 contains such an estimate constructed by the Council of Economic Advisers for the period 1960 to 1979.[8] While this is useful for aggregate historical analysis, it is of limited value for measuring the condition and effect of monetary policy.

But, regardless of the practical difficulties with measuring q, it is important to recognize its role in the portfolio adjustment process which underlies the monetarist view of the economy. The essence of their argument is that people have stable notions of how they want to allocate their wealth across different types of assets. Any external force which compels them to alter this allocation will create a reaction which attempts to undo that forced reallocation. In the case of a change in the money supply, the market provides a mechanism by which a new desired allocation can be achieved. As economic agents try to undo what the Federal Reserve has done, they bid up prices of assets and, hence, q. If the economy has additional capacity, this leads to increased production and the cost of new goods rises until q falls to 1. A necessary part of that adjustment is a change in nominal income. Next, we will try to assess the timing and size of this effect.

[8] See *The Economic Report of the President*, U.S. Government Printing Office, 1980.

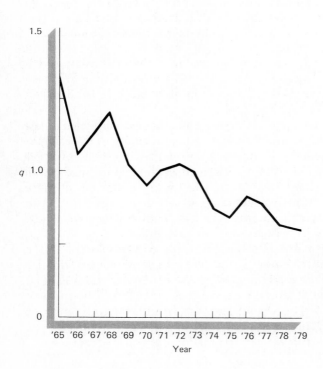

FIGURE 20-3
The market value of corporate assets relative to replacement cost (q), 1965–1979. This figure shows that q has been declining during most of this period.
Source: *Economic Report of the President*, 1980.

Testing the Monetarist View

A number of economists have tried to devise empirical tests of whether or not the monetarist view is a reasonably accurate description of the way the economy works. One approach to such testing is to try to statistically identify the relationship between changes in the supply of money and changes in the level of nominal income. Another approach is to conduct detailed analyses of the historical episodes which have been characterized by quite different patterns of growth in the money supply. Milton Friedman has been closely associated with this second approach. In his classic book, coauthored with Anna Schwartz, *A Monetary History of the United States, 1867–1960,* Friedman studied the details of each episode in nearly 100 years of U.S. monetary history.

The fundamental tasks in both types of tests are to determine whether there is a strong association between changes in the supply of money and nominal income and to determine whether it is changes in money which cause the changes in income, rather than the reverse. Friedman and Schwartz's summary of their evidence on these points is particularly lucid:

> In our view, the most convincing evidence supporting the idea that money plays an important independent part is not statistical evidence but evidence of a rather different kind—that garnered from study of the historical circumstances underlying the changes that occurred in the stock of money. This evidence is much more clear cut for major movements (in income) than for minor. Major movements in U.S. history include the deep depressions used here to distinguish deep from mild depression cycles in our classification of historical reference cycles; the substantial inflations which have occurred primarily during wartime; and a few long-continued movements in one direction, such as the generally rising level of money income and prices from 1896 to 1913. With respect to these events, the historical record justifies two important generalizations.
>
> 1. There is a one-to-one relation between monetary changes and changes in money income and prices. Changes in money income and prices have, in every case, been accompanied by a change in the rate of growth of the money stock, in the same direction and of appreciable magnitude, and there are no comparable disturbances in the rate of growth of the money stock unaccompanied by changes in money income and prices.
>
> 2. The changes in the stock of money cannot consistently be explained by the contemporary changes in money income and prices. The changes in the stock of money can generally be attributed to specific historical circumstances that are not in turn attributable to contemporary changes in money income and prices. Hence, if the consistent relation between money and income is not pure coincidence, it must reflect an influence running from money to business.[9]

Few if any historical studies exist which rival Friedman and Schwartz's work in scope or depth. Yet the relevance of their conclusions for contem-

[9] Milton Friedman and Anna Schwartz, op. cit., p. 50.

porary economic conditions is continually challenged and debated. Aside from questions about important changes in the historical circumstances, the central question has been whether the statistical evidence drawn from relatively recent data supports the conclusions drawn by Friedman and Schwartz.

One method for statistically identifying the relationship between nominal income and the supply of money has been made popular by economists at the Federal Reserve Bank of St. Louis.[10] The St. Louis model, as it has become known, attempts to statistically explain the changes in nominal income based on past changes in the money supply or the monetary base. The critics of such methods offer at least two substantial arguments. The first is that while such estimates may be valuable as a simple forecasting device, they still represent essentially a black box as far as providing an explanation or test of how monetary changes affect the economy. The second is that the apparent relationship between money and income may be more a reflection of a causal effect of income on the money supply, rather than the reverse. Such disputes are not currently and may never be satisfactorily resolved.

Rational Expectations and the Monetarist View

Some people have carried the idea of tracing the effect of changes in the money supply to an illogical conclusion. One example of this has been the attempt to forecast changes in security prices with past changes in the money supply. Some of those who have tried this have constructed statistical models which attempt to explain the change in an index of stock prices such as the Dow Jones Industrial Average or the New York Stock Exchange Index.[11] The idea behind this is that if the money supply grows at a high rate for a sustained period, it should cause prices on equities to be bid up, as the portfolio-adjustment process suggests.

The difficulty with this procedure is that it runs counter to the efficient markets hypothesis. As explained in Chapter 6, the semistrong form of the efficient markets hypothesis maintains that all publicly available information about the future values of equity securities will be incorporated in the current prices of those equity securities. Publicly available money supply information fits this description quite well. When the current money supply change is announced by the Federal Reserve, any information contained in that change is immediately used by the market to alter prices at that point. Therefore, the current change in equity prices cannot be related to past changes in the money supply in any meaningful way, for those past changes represent old information which has already been incorporated in equity prices. What can influence current equity prices is any new information

[10] See Leonall Anderson and Jerry Jordan, "Monetary and Fiscal Actions: A Test of Their Relative Importance in Economic Stabilization," *Review*, Federal Reserve Bank of St. Louis, 50 (November 1968), pp. 11–24.
[11] See Michael S. Rozeff, "Money and Stock Prices; Market Efficiency and the Lag in Effect of Monetary Policy," *Journal of Financial Economics*, 1 (September 1974), pp. 245–302, for a summary and critique of such models.

about the future course of monetary policy which is contained in the current change in the money supply. For example, if the market expects the Federal Reserve to restrain the growth of the money supply, and yet a large rate of growth is announced for the current week, then this may cause the market to revise its expectations and equity prices will respond accordingly.

The efficient markets argument is often given another name when it is applied to the market's reaction to changes in the money supply or changes in other policies of the government. That name is "rational expectations." There is no fundamental distinction between the hypothesis that expectations are rational and the hypothesis that markets are efficient. Regardless of the name applied, the hypothesis asserts that markets make efficient use of information. Another way of stating this, and a way which is often associated with the rational expectations label, is that people do not make systematic mistakes, or that in the long run they behave as if they understand how the economy works. For if people efficiently use available information, and this in fact leads to *systematic* underestimates of some important economic variable, then the systematic over- or underestimate will itself become relevant information which can be used to correct the market's estimates. Any alternative explanation of a market's long-run behavior relies on a belief in systematic mistakes.

The implication of the rational expectations argument can be synthesized with the maxim: You can't fool all the people all the time. The market sets the prices of assets based on what it expects will be the returns to those assets in the future. As a part of this process the market forms an expectation of the future course of action of the Federal Reserve in determining the supply of money. In the short run the Federal Reserve can fool the market, and thereby change asset prices. But in the long run the market will gradually learn from the Federal Reserve's behavior.

THE MONETARIST PRESCRIPTION FOR THE CONDUCT OF MONETARY POLICY

The rational expectations argument draws a distinction between the short-run and long-run effects of monetary policy. This emphasis on the long run as opposed to the short run is probably the single most important difference between monetarist and Keynesian views of how monetary policy should be conducted. It is also intertwined with the disagreement between the two groups about whether monetary policy should be directed at controlling interest rates or the supply of money.

As we shall discover in the next chapter, the Keynesian view of monetary policy is that actions of the Federal Reserve influence interest rates and interest rates affect the real side of the economy. The actual quantity of money supplied is incidental to the Keynesian view. On the other hand, the money supply is central to the monetarist view of the relationship between the financial and real sides of the economy. It is not so much that monetarists think interest rates are irrelevant. They would largely agree with the analysis of the pricing of assets and the determination of the interest rates presented in the first two parts of this book. It is just that they perceive an important long-run role for the money supply as a determinant of fluctuations in the level of nominal income and they believe that the direct effect of monetary policy on interest rates cited by the Keynesians is a short-run or transitory effect.

The monetarist view of how monetary policy should be conducted in practice follows directly from their theory of how the money supply influences income. They argue that the money supply should be controlled directly by the Federal Reserve. Moreover, they argue that interest rates should be left free to fluctuate to whatever extent the market dictates. They believe that any attempt by the Federal Reserve to achieve short-run control over interest rates inherently sacrifices long-run control over growth in the quantity of money.

The monetarists also argue that monetary policy should be conducted according to what is called a *money supply rule*. To see what this means we need to return to the basic equation of the modern quantity theory stated in Eq. (20-6):

$$MV \equiv Py \qquad (20\text{-}6)$$

In order to use this equation to talk about the conduct of monetary policy, we need to restate this equation in terms of the rate of change in each variable. If we let Δ stand for the change in a variable so that, for example, $\Delta M/M$ means the rate of change in the money supply from one period to the next, then Eq. (20-6) can be rewritten as follows:

$$\frac{\Delta M}{M} + \frac{\Delta V}{V} = \frac{\Delta P}{P} + \frac{\Delta y}{y} \qquad (20\text{-}14)$$

This means that the rate of change in the money supply plus the rate of change in velocity must equal the rate of inflation plus the rate of change in nominal income.

The question the monetarists ask of this equation is: What should be the appropriate rate of growth in the money supply? To answer this question we will alter the equation somewhat by moving velocity to the right-hand side:

$$\frac{\Delta M}{M} = \frac{\Delta P}{P} + \frac{\Delta y}{y} - \frac{\Delta V}{V} \qquad (20\text{-}15)$$

In order to determine the rate of growth in the money supply we have to specify the values for the variables on the right-hand side of the equation. The logic in choosing these variables is the following. From historical evidence we observe that velocity has a tendency to grow at a certain percent, say 1 percent. We observe from long-run historical evidence that real income tends to grow at a certain percent, say 3 percent. Therefore, if we expect that the long-run patterns of growth in velocity and real income will be the same in the future, then we can fill these in on the right-hand side of the equation. Given these future growth rates for velocity and real income, if we want the future inflation rate to be zero, then the rate of growth in the supply of money must be 2 percent:

$$2\% = 0\% + 3\% - 1\%$$

The assumption which underlies this conclusion is that changes in the growth of velocity and real income are not influenced by monetary policy in the long run. Rather, the influence of monetary policy is largely on the rate of inflation. Hence, we can extract our estimates of the growth of velocity and income from the historical evidence, and then we can choose the rate of growth in the money supply that will generate the desired rate of inflation. Presumably, this desired rate of inflation is zero.

Despite the fact that this argument is relatively simple, the difficulties involved in estimating the actual future growth rates in velocity and real income may not be. Arguments over the proper values of these estimates have persisted for some time, and it will never be possible to know these values with certainty. But monetarists argue that, even with imprecision about the exact rate of growth in the money supply which is best, a fixed rule is better than no rule at all.

One reason they take this position is that when a money supply rule is not followed, as it almost never has been, they believe monetary policy tends to contribute to instability in the economy rather than reduce it. In testimony before the Senate Committee on Banking, Housing and Urban Affairs, Professor Carl Christ summarized this argument exceedingly well:

The Federal Reserve's actions in pursuit of business cycle stability have been like the action of passengers on a ship who become worried about a temporary roll of the ship to starboard, and run to the port side of the ship in an effort to stabilize it. Slowly the ship responds to the extra weight on its port side, and recovers from its roll to starboard, but then the motion continues and the ship rolls to the port side. The passengers now worry about the roll to port, and run to the starboard side in an effort to stabilize the ship once more. The ship responds slowly to the extra weight on its starboard side, straightens up, and then rolls to starboard again, perhaps more than before. Of course, the passengers are only making things worse by their action. The proper thing for them to do is to run neither to the right nor to the left, but to position themselves so that their center of gravity is in the center of the ship, so that they do not aggravate and perpetuate its rolling motion. The analogy is an apt one. We know that an increase in the rate of growth of the money stock stimulates the economy after a delay of something like 6 to 18 months, and that a decrease in the rate of growth of the money stock depresses the economy, again after a lag of about 6 to 18 months. Since presently available methods cannot accurately and reliably predict the timing and severity of a recession 6 to 18 months ahead, the Federal Reserve cannot use monetary policy effectively to prevent recessions that arise from nonmonetary causes. If the Federal Reserve tries to do so, it will too often not recognize that a recession is coming until too late to take action against it. If the Federal Reserve waits to increase the rate of growth of the money supply until it is sure there is a recession (as in February, 1975), there is a grave risk that by the time the effects of that increase come to fruition, there will be no further need to combat recession, and indeed by that time the problem is likely to be inflation. That is why so many economists have urged that the Federal Reserve increase the money stock at a slow steady rate of three or four percent a year, come what may. It would avoid the "too much, too late" kind of mistake that the Federal Reserve has been making for thirty years and more.[12]

A second reason for advocating a money supply rule relates to the circumstances which govern modern monetary arrangements, compared with those which existed earlier in this century and throughout history. Until the middle of this century, the United States was on a gold standard. This meant that the government promised to convert dollars to gold at a prespecified conversion rate. In other words, the government's money was backed by

[12] See Carl Christ, *A First Report on the Conduct of Monetary Policy,* testimony before the Committee on Banking, Housing and Urban Affairs, United States Senate, June 6, 1975, p. 10.

TABLE 20-1

Symbols Used in Part Five

SYMBOL	DEFINITION
M^d	Money demand
M^s	Money supply
W	Wealth in the economy
Y'	Nominal permanent income
y'	Real permanent income
r	Nominal interest rate
$\dfrac{1}{P}\dfrac{\Delta P^e}{\Delta t}$	Expected rate of inflation
P	The level of prices
V	Velocity
V^a	Actual velocity
V^d	Desired velocity
y	Real income
r_s	Short-term interest rate
r_L	Long-term interest rate
B	Monetary base
m	Money supply multiplier
S	Aggregate saving
I	Aggregate investment

gold and as a consequence, the supply of money was determined by the supply of gold. The disadvantages of a system where the ability of the government to alter the supply of money is constrained by the supply of gold is that the economy may grow faster than the gold supply, resulting in deflation. The advantage of such a system is that the government is unable to increase the money supply at a rate which produces high inflation, unless the supply of gold expands to permit it. The government's natural temptation to resort to inflationary increases in the supply of money to support deficit spending is limited by the available supply of gold.

The discipline forced on the government by a gold standard is arbitrary; that is, changes in the supply of gold may be unrelated to a given country's rate of economic growth. Hence, essentially by chance there may be either inflation or deflation. It is for this reason that the gold standard was eventually abandoned. Yet the monetarists seek a mechanism that replaces the discipline of the gold standard, one that eliminates the government's temptation to inflate. They argue that the money supply rule does this and that it has the further advantage of being less arbitrary. The growth rate which the rule recommends is the one believed to be consistent with the rate of growth the economy would sustain with zero inflation.

SUMMARY

In this chapter we explored the monetarist view of how financial markets influence the rest of the economy. Our analysis of the monetarist position proceeded in three basic stages. First, we examined the modern quantity theory. This is the principal monetarist theory of the links between monetary policy and the economy. Second, we looked behind the modern quantity theory to try to acquire a better understanding of the cause and effect relationship envisioned by the monetarists. We found that the argument that is at the root of the modern quantity theory is that a change in the supply of money begins a process of portfolio adjustment which leads to a change in the level of income. Finally, we examined the monetarist prescription for how monetary policy should be conducted—the idea of a money supply rule.

Our examination of the modern quantity theory started with the demand for money. The idea behind the demand for money is that there is a stable and predictable relationship between the quantity of money people choose to hold and other important variables in the economy. We found that the demand for money is principally dependent upon the level of permanent income and the nominal interest rate. We also found that it was important to distinguish between nominal and real money balances. The demand for real money balances is dependent on real permanent income in the same way that the demand for nominal money balances is dependent upon nominal permanent income.

Next we examined the basic tenets of the modern quantity theory. The modern quantity theory starts with the assumption that within some limits the Federal Reserve can make the quantity of money whatever it chooses. If the Federal Reserve increases the supply of money, then it creates an imbalance between the quantity of money people want to hold and the quantity of money in the economy. We found that velocity in the modern quantity theory is merely another way of expressing the demand for money—velocity is simply the desired ratio of nominal money balances to nominal income. Once this change has occurred, something must adjust to create a new equilibrium so that $MV = Py$. The monetarists argue that it is not velocity which adjusts, but the level of nominal income. The key to this argument is the demand for money, for if money demand is unstable or unpredictable, then changes in the money supply or money may well be offset by changes in velocity or money demand. Hence, the monetarist position rests on their concept of the demand for money.

The modern quantity theory has been popular and useful because of its simplicity. But its simplicity has also generated a substantial amount of criticism. One of the criticisms is that there is no explanation of how changes in the supply of money actually are transmitted into changes in income. The explanation which has evolved to fill in this gap is referred to as the portfolio-adjustment process. The portfolio-adjustment process describes the way people adjust their portfolios in response to an increase or decrease in the supply of money. The monetarists contend that the portfolio-adjustment process involves virtually all types of wealth. This means that people do not adjust simply from money into other short-term assets. Instead, they adjust into all kinds of assets. In this way, prices of all assets respond to the changes in the supply of money. In turn, as prices are bid up there is increased incentive to produce new assets, and income rises. We will find in the next chapter that this explanation of how the economy responds to changes in the supply of money is quite different from the one offered by the Keynesians. At that time we will be able to contrast the two points of view.

Next, we briefly examined the alternative ways that the monetarist view has been tested. There are essentially two procedures for such testing. One is to devise statistical tests using data from the actual experience of a given economy. The question at issue is whether significant changes in the level of nominal income can be statistically related to changes in the supply of money. There is a well-established statistical relationship between changes in nominal income and changes in the supply of money. But there is a continuing debate between monetarists and Keynesians as to whether money causes changes in income or income causes changes in money. Another procedure for testing involves analysis of historical episodes when the supply of money experienced a significant change. Milton Friedman and Anna Schwartz analyzed an approximate 100-year period beginning in the 1860s in the United States and concluded that changes in the supply of money do have a significant and independent impact on the level of income. But there is considerable debate about how relevant their conclusions are for our contemporary economy.

Finally, we examined the argument that monetary policy should be determined by a money supply rule. The basic idea behind a money supply rule is that there is a rate of growth in the money supply which, if maintained in the long run, would lead to a zero rate of inflation. The monetarists contend that the Federal Reserve should be constrained to permit the money supply to grow at that rate. The principal reason for making this a rule is that it would eliminate the temptation to finance federal government deficits by increasing the money supply at an excessive rate. In this way, a money supply rule provides the same external constraint as the gold standard provided in earlier times.

Probably the most important single feature of the monetarist view is their emphasis on the long run. The equilibrium between money supply and money demand which they describe is an equilibrium which may take several years to work out. Similarly, their prescription for monetary policy argues that in the long run a money supply rule will lead to low inflation rates. They believe that it is too difficult to attempt to try to use government policy to offset more short-term fluctuations in the economy. Historically, the Keynesians have disagreed. They have sought a better understanding of the short-term relationships which link monetary policy with the economy. And they have been interested in attempting to smooth out the short-term fluctuations in the economy. We will examine their view in the next chapter.

QUESTIONS TO IMPROVE UNDERSTANDING

1   Explain the basic determinants of the demand for money. Why is money demand affected by permanent rather than current income?
2   What is the difference between nominal and real money balances and between nominal and real money demand? What is money illusion? How would the money demand function be affected if the economy suffered from money illusion?
3   Explain the basic logic of the modern quantity theory. How does the modern quantity theory differ from its predecessor?
4   Why do monetarists say that velocity is simply the demand for money? Why is it important to their theory that velocity be a stable and predictable function? How do the monetarists account for the procyclical pattern in velocity?
5   What is "q" and what is its significance to the monetarist view?
6   The modern quantity theory is sometimes criticized as being essentially a "black box" in that it provides little explanation of cause and effect. If you were to make this criticism, how would you present and defend it?
7   Essentially two kinds of evidence have been offered by monetarists to support their view. One kind is historical and the other statistical. Milton Friedman has argued that the historical evidence is very persuasive. Briefly summarize the

historical evidence. Why do you think he finds it so appealing? How might you criticize this type of evidence?

8 The monetarists argue that monetary policy should be guided by a money supply rule. What is their rule and how does it follow from the modern quantity theory?

9 Some people say that the monetarists would like us to return to the days of the gold standard. In what ways is the monetarists' money supply rule like a gold standard? In what ways does it differ?

10 What do you find most and least appealing about the monetarist position?

REFERENCES

Anderson, Leonall, and Jerry Jordan: "Monetary and Fiscal Actions: A Test of Their Relative Importance in Economic Stabilization," *Review*, Federal Reserve Bank of St. Louis, 50 (November 1968), pp. 11–24.

Christ, Carl: *A First Report on the Conduct of Monetary Policy*, testimony before the Committee on Banking, Housing and Urban Affairs, United States Senate, June 6, 1975, p. 10.

The Economic Report of the President, U.S. Government Printing Office, 1980.

Friedman, Milton: *A Theory of the Consumption Function*, Princeton University Press, Princeton, N.J., 1957.

————: "The Quantity Theory of Money: A Restatement," in Milton Friedman (ed.), *Studies in the Quantity Theory of Money*, University of Chicago Press, Chicago, 1956.

————, and Anna Schwartz: "Money and Business Cycles," in Milton Friedman (ed.), *The Optimum Quantity of Money and Other Essays*, University of Chicago Press, Chicago, 1969, pp. 230–231.

———— and ————: *A Monetary History of the United States 1867–1960*, Princeton University Press, Princeton, N.J., 1963.

Klein, Benjamin: "Competitive Interest Payments on Bank Deposits and the Long-run Demand for Money," *American Economic Review*, 64 (December 1974), pp. 931–949.

Latane, Henry A.: "Income Velocity and Interest Rates: A Pragmatic Approach," *Review of Economics and Statistics*, XLII (November 1960), pp. 445–449.

Rozeff, Michael S.: "Money and Stock Prices; Market Efficiency and the Lag in Effect of Monetary Policy," *Journal of Financial Economics*, 1 (September 1974), pp. 245–302.

Tobin, James: "A General Equilibrium Approach to Monetary Theory," *Journal of Money, Credit and Banking*, I (November 1969), pp. 15–27.

Chapter Twenty-One

HOW FINANCIAL DECISIONS
AFFECT THE ECONOMY:
THE KEYNESIAN APPROACH

This chapter deals with the Keynesian view of how financial markets influence the economy. As in the previous chapter, our primary concern will be with the effect of monetary policy on financial markets and on the real side of the economy. The Keynesian view of this subject will be presented here as if there were a single well-defined alternative to the monetarist position described in the previous chapter. For the sake of exposition it is almost essential to proceed as if this were true. But there is probably less uniformity and greater divergence of opinion among those who are Keynesian in orientation than among those who associate with the monetarist viewpoint.

The Keynesian view is called the cost-of-credit approach because, unlike the monetarists who emphasize the modern quantity theory, the Keynesians emphasize the impact of monetary policy on the cost of credit in the economy. The cost of credit is measured by market interest rates; therefore, the Keynesian view focuses on the effect of monetary policy on interest rates and the effect of interest rates on investment and income. Furthermore, as a rule, Keynesians argue that monetary policy has a weaker effect on the economy than the monetarists claim, at least when monetary policy is expansionary. Keynesians argue that an expansionary monetary policy is not strong enough to bring an economy out of a recession or a depression, but on the other hand, a contractionary monetary policy may well be strong enough to cause a recession. Finally, Keynesians and monetarists disagree about what constitutes, or at least the appropriate way to measure, expansionary or contractionary monetary policy and, therefore, what the proper conduct of monetary policy should be. In this chapter we will examine the Keynesian view and contrast is with the monetarist alternative. In addition to describing the Keynesian view and comparing it with the monetarist, this chapter synthesizes a number of ideas which have been presented throughout this book. It draws heavily on the determinants of real and nominal interest rates and the concept of segmentation presented in Part Two. It also draws heavily on the money supply process explained in Chapter Nineteen.

AN OVERVIEW

The essence of the Keynesian argument is represented in Figure 21-1. This figure summarizes the chain of events which the cost-of-credit view argues is set in motion by an increase in the supply of money, M_1 (M_{1a} or M_{1b}). This chain of events can be summarized as follows: A money supply increase leads to a decrease in the short-term interest rate (r_s). This in turn leads to a decrease in the long-term interest rate (r_L). These changes in interest rates represent a decrease in the cost of credit which is used to finance investments. The decline in the cost of credit leads to increased investment spending (I). Total income, or gross national product, is composed of two basic components, investment and consumption; therefore, as firms and individuals decide to increase investment, income or GNP also increases.

The description of the Keynesian view which is presented in this chapter is organized around the sequence of events pictured in Figure 21-1. We will examine each link shown in the figure in order to develop a complete understanding of how Keynesians perceive that monetary policy influences the real side of the economy. It should be kept in mind throughout that Keynesians are skeptical about the effectiveness of monetary policy. They argue that if monetary policy is going to be effective, this is how it would work, but they are always questioning whether something will interfere with the effect of monetary policy. Hence, late in this chapter we will pinpoint ways in which this chain of logic may break down.

There is really a more fundamental issue than any of those mentioned above which differentiates monetarists and Keynesians. This issue pertains to the underlying philosophical differences between the two positions. While we will spend little time directly dealing with this underlying issue, it

$$\uparrow M_1 \longrightarrow \downarrow r_s \longrightarrow \downarrow r_L \longrightarrow \uparrow I \longrightarrow \uparrow Y$$

FIGURE 21-1
The chain of logic in the Keynesian or cost-of-credit approach to the impact of monetary policy on income.

is important to be aware of it from the outset. Monetarists believe that a competitive economy is fundamentally stable. This means that a competitive economy does not generate its own cycles of recession and boom and it is not inherently doomed to experience periodic deep depressions. To monetarists the proper role of government is to facilitate the operation of an exchange economy, but not to control the economy or to try to make it more stable. As discussed in the previous chapter, monetarists believe that a monetary policy which is not governed by a simple rule creates additional instability. In contrast, Keynesians believe that, at times, the economy may be unstable. They argue that this instability calls for various forms of government intervention in the market. With respect to monetary policy, it calls for an activist or countercyclical policy. This means that monetary policy should be adjusted to offset the fluctuations in the economy. It seems virtually impossible that this basic philosophical difference about the nature of a competitive economy will ever be resolved. There will always be disagreement on this issue, but some of the other points which separate monetarists and Keynesians are subject to more precise analytical treatment and to empirical testing. This chapter seeks to identify these points and discuss the relevant empirical evidence.

Throughout this chapter we will examine the Keynesian view of the effect of monetary policy on the real side of the economy. The discussion will focus on the impact of an increase in the rate of growth of the money supply in order to explain the Keynesian view. But the argument could just as well be presented for decreases in the rate of growth of the money supply. We will stick with increases just to make the explanation consistent throughout. Moreover, throughout much of the chapter we will be interested in the short-run effects of monetary policy. The Keynesian emphasis on the short-run grows, in part, out of their philosophical position that government policy needs to be used to influence the stability of the economy. As we concentrate on the short run, we will hold the expected rate of change in prices constant during much of the discussion. We will be interested in examining the effect of monetary policy on interest rates when the expected rate of inflation remains unchanged. This means that we are really focusing on the effects of monetary policy on *real* interest rates, for the difference between nominal and real rates is simply the expected rate of inflation. During the discussion of the Keynesian view which follows, we will actually use nominal interest rates rather than real rates, but with the expected rate of inflation constant, any change in the nominal rate must represent an equal change in the real rate.

THE SHORT-TERM IMPACT OF MONETARY POLICY ON INTEREST RATES: THE LIQUIDITY EFFECT

In this section of this chapter we will examine the first two links in the chain of logic represented in Figure 21-1. We want to see how monetary policy affects interest rates in the short run. Then later in the chapter we can trace the impact of the change in interest rates on investment and income. This short-run effect of monetary policy on interest rates is called the liquidity effect. When we are finished with the chapter we will find that it is the first of three effects of monetary policy on interest rates. In tracing the liquidity effect we will hold the level of income constant. This means that we want to see how monetary policy influences interest rates in order to see how a change in interest rates ultimately changes the level of income. Therefore, in order to trace out the causal relationship we need to keep income constant at the outset.

Monetary Policy and the Short-term Interest Rate: Equilibrium Between Money Supply and Money Demand

One way to examine the effect of monetary policy on interest rates is to start with the money supply and money demand analyses presented in earlier chapters. In Chapter Nineteen we learned that we could represent the money supply process with a money supply function. That money supply function indicated that the quantity of money supplied is determined by the product of the monetary base (B) and the money supply multiplier (m):

$$M^s = Bm$$

In turn, the money supply multiplier is determined by four ratios: the required-reserve ratio, the ratio of desired excess reserves to demand deposits, the ratio of time deposits to demand deposits, and the ratio of cash to demand deposits (v, e, t, c).

Similarly, in Chapter Twenty we developed a money demand function. The simplest version of this money demand function indicates that the nominal quantity of money demanded is dependent on the level of permanent income and the nominal interest rate. We represented this equation as follows:

$$M^d = F(Y', r)$$

We can see directly from the money demand function that money demand is dependent upon the interest rate. Moreover, we know that the relationship is negative, so, as the interest rate increases, the quantity of money demanded decreases.

On the other hand, it is not obvious from the money supply equation how nominal interest rates affect the quantity of money supplied. To determine this relationship we must examine the effect of changes in nominal interest rates on the monetary base and the money supply multiplier. The base will increase with nominal interest rates because, with the discount rate charged by the Fed unchanged, higher nominal interest rates will encourage banks to borrow more from the Federal Reserve, leading to an increase in reserves and the base. Similarly, a higher nominal interest rate will encourage banks to lower their excess reserves, which will lead to an increase in the money supply multiplier and the money supply. We therefore conclude that the quantity of money supplied is positively affected by the level of the nominal interest rate.

We can represent the relationships between the nominal interest rate and the quantities of money supplied and demanded in a diagram like Figure 21-2. The vertical axis in the figure measures the nominal interest rate, while the horizontal axis measures the quantity of money. The downward-sloping curve represents the money demand function. The upward-sloping curve represents the money supply function. This diagram shows how the equilibrium interest rate is determined at the point of intersection between the supply-and-demand curves for money. The figure illustrates that, for a given level of permanent income, there is a unique interest rate which equates the quantity of money demanded with the quantity of money supplied.

Figure 21-2 can be used to illustrate the Keynesian view of the effect of changes in monetary policy on the interest rate, holding the level of income constant. We know from Chapter Nineteen that there are a number of things the Federal Reserve can alter in order to influence the money supply. But the principal tool of the Federal Reserve is its open market operations, and this tool directly affects the level of reserves and the monetary base. A purchase of securities in the market by the Federal Reserve leads to an increase in reserves and the base, and this shifts the money supply function to the right, which increases M^s to $M^s{}'$, as shown in Figure 21-3. In order for a new equilibrium to be achieved so that the quantity of money demanded is equal to the new larger supply of money in the economy, something in the system has to change. If we hold income constant and the quantity of money demanded is negatively related to the level of the interest rate, then the interest

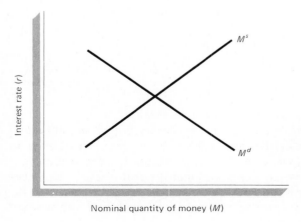

FIGURE 21-2
Equilibrium between money supply and money demand. The figure shows that there is a unique interest rate at which money supply is equal to money demand.

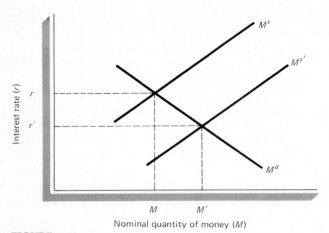

FIGURE 21-3
Effect of an increase in the base on interest rates. As the base increases, the money-supply curve shifts to the right causing interest rates to decline.

rate will fall until a new equilibrium is achieved. The new and lower equilibrium level of the interest rate is represented as r' in Figure 21-3. Only at the lower interest rate is the quantity of money supplied equal to the quantity demanded.

This tendency for an increase in the money supply to lead to a decrease in interest rates is often referred to as the "liquidity effect" of money on interest rates. This liquidity effect is the immediate and short-run effect of changes in the money supply on interest rates. Monetarists and Keynesians do not disagree about the basic logic of the liquidity effect, but they do disagree about its significance. Keynesians argue that if monetary policy influences the real economy, it starts with the liquidity effect. They argue that an expansionary monetary policy decreases interest rates. In fact, they often judge whether monetary policy is expansionary or contractionary by whether interest rates are high or low. Monetarists argue that the liquidity effect is generally very short-lived, and therefore reject the conclusion that an expansionary monetary policy leads to decreasing interest rates.

The Money Supply and the Loanable-Funds Market

You might get the impression from the above discussion that the sole function of the rate of interest is to influence the money supply-and-demand functions. But we know that the interest rate serves a much broader role in the economy. Chapter Seven was devoted to explaining the determinants of the real interest rate. That chapter explained that the real interest rate is the price which allocates resources across time and, in equilibrium, it is the price which equilibrates both desired saving and investment and desired lending and borrowing. We should be able to relate the analysis of money supply and money demand to the analysis presented in Chapter Seven of the determinants of the real interest rate. To do so we need to examine the effect of changes in the supply of money on the market for borrowing and lending or the loanable-funds market.

To see how the money supply can be incorporated into the loanable-funds market we need to return to the definitions of the supply and demand for loanable funds presented in Chapter Seven. In the loanable-funds market we treat the supply of money as a component of the supply of loanable funds or as a source of lending. This means that increases in the volume of money in the economy represent increases in borrowing and lending. As the quantity of money supplied is increased, this represents new lending in the economy as a whole. Hence, we can think of this as shifting the curve showing the total amount of lending at each level of the real interest rate to the right. This shift is illustrated in Figure 21-4. The supply curve for loanable funds labeled S indicates the supply of funds in the market or the total desired amount of lending at each level of the real interest rate. A part of this desired lending is based on a given level of the money supply, say M. If the Federal Reserve increases the money supply to a higher level, say M ', this will cause the supply curve to shift to the right. This, in turn, will cause a decrease in the level of the real rate of interest. The new equilibrium is reached where the desired level of lending is equal to the desired level of borrowing, represented by the curve labeled D at r '.

The equilibrium rate of interest in the loanable funds market is the same as that which creates an equilibrium between money supply and money demand. The distinction between the analyses is that in the money supply-

FIGURE 21-4

The effect of an increase in the money supply on the loanable funds market. An increase in the base causes the supply of loanable funds (lending) to increase, which leads to a reduction in interest rates.

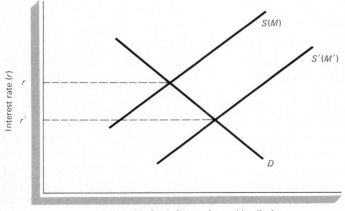

Loanable funds (borrowing and lending)

and-demand analysis we are implicitly assuming that other factors which affect desired borrowing and lending remain unchanged, while when we examine loanable funds we are simply not according money supply and money demand any special significance. But it is important to recognize that a crucial factor is held constant in each analysis. With both approaches the equilibrium interest rate is determined with the level of nominal income held constant. That is, we assume that the interest rate adjusts to form an equilibrium without any change in the level of income. This assumption makes the analysis only a partial equilibrium. To understand the relationship between financial markets and the real economy we must examine how changes in the interest rate lead to changes in the level of nominal income. In order to do so it is important to recognize, as explained in Chapter Seven, that when desired borrowing and lending are in equilibrium, then aggregate saving and aggregate investment must also be in equilibrium. By turning to an analysis of saving and investment we will be able to complete the link between financial markets and the real economy. We will do this shortly.

Which Short-term Interest Rate?

The discussion so far has been devoted to explaining the short-run effect of monetary policy on the short-term interest rate which is emphasized by the Keynesians. But even if one understands the logic involved in the explanation, it is sometimes difficult to pin down exactly what interest rate or rates we are talking about in the real world. It is therefore important to relate this discussion to the actual conduct of monetary policy and the observed behavior of short-term interest rates.

There are a vast number of short-term interest rates, each one applying to a particular type of security or debt contract. Some of these securities were described in Part Three when we examined the money market. Generally, when we speak of *the* short-term interest rate we mean all of these rates, because we think of a common interest rate which underlies them all. The factors which are unique to each security account for all the differences between these rates.

Despite the generality of the concept of the short-term interest rate, the federal funds rate is of paramount practical importance both because it has long been the focus of monetary policy and because it represents one of the shortest term rates generally available in the market. The federal funds rate is the rate paid for loans which generally have a maturity of one day and which are made between financial institutions. When the Federal Reserve engages in open market operations, it directly affects this interest rate. Expansionary open market operations immediately increase the supply of federal funds and drive down the federal funds rate. Rates on financial contracts with longer maturities are closely linked to the federal funds rate. The process of substitution between alternative financial contracts, if there is a profitable opportunity to do so, ensures this. If there are only limited barriers to substitution between financial instruments, then the federal funds rate cannot be driven down and held there without the rates on other financial instruments following a similar course. So, as the Federal Reserve puts pressure directly on the federal funds rate, this pressure soon affects other short-term rates as well, such as Treasury bill rates, commercial paper rates, and even prime interest rates. Only if the markets for these other securities are segmented, such that little substitution takes place between markets, would the interest rates in these markets move in diverse directions.

The logic underlying the Keynesian view is that changes in monetary policy set in motion changes in the costs of borrowing and lending. In the case of an expansionary monetary policy, increases in the money supply lead to decreases, first in the federal funds rate, and shortly thereafter to decreases in other short-term interest rates. These rates represent the cost of all forms of short-term borrowing. As these costs decline, short-term borrowing becomes more attractive and more borrowing takes place. But most income in any economy results from long-term rather than short-term investments; therefore, we need to understand how Keynesians argue that the changes in short-term interest rates are transmitted into changes in long-term interest rates. We will examine this argument next.

Monetary Policy and the Cost of Capital

The next link in the Keynesian chain of logic running from a change in the supply of money to a change in the level of income involves what is called the cost of capital. The cost of capital is simply the cost of funds or capital which are used to finance long-term investments. The Keynesian argument is that an increase in the supply of money decreases short-term interest rates, which in turn leads to a decline in the cost of capital. We therefore need to examine the link running from short-term interest rates to the cost of capital. An important aspect of the cost of capital which is often given extensive treatment in the field of corporate finance pertains to the cost of issuing different types of securities, such as debt and equity. We will not deal with this topic here. Instead, we will presume that there is a common interest rate underlying the cost of all types of securities which a corporation might issue and we will focus on the connection between this long-term rate and the short-term rates discussed above. This means that we must again examine the term structure of interest rates; the link between short-term and long-term interest rates.

Three theories of the term structure were discussed in Chapter Nine. The unbiased expectations theory argues that long-term interest rates are equal to the geometric average of the market's expectation of future short-term rates [as stated in Eqs. (9-1) and (9-8)]. On the other hand, the segmentation theory argues that each maturity represents a separate market, and the interest rate prevailing for that maturity is the rate that equates desired borrowing with desired lending at that maturity. In the segmentation theory, long-term rates are unrelated to the market's expectations of future short-term rates. The preferred habitat theory blends the two theories and implies that long-term rates represent the sum of the market's expectation of future short-term rates and a premium which market participants demand as compensation for investing with a maturity longer or shorter than they prefer.

These theories have different implications regarding the Federal Reserve's ability to influence the cost of capital. First, consider the segmentation theory. If each maturity represents a distinct market, then actions taken by the Federal Reserve which influence short-term interest rates will have no effect on long-term rates and the cost of capital. Long-term rates will be determined solely by the demand and supply for long-term funds. Only if the Federal Reserve directly entered the long-term market would it have any effect on the long-term interest rate.

On the other hand, if the unbiased expectations theory is correct, then changes in expected future short-term interest rates would directly affect current long-term interest rates. As a result, actions of the Federal Reserve which affect only today's short-term interest rate will have no effect on the cost of capital. In order for the Federal Reserve to affect the cost of capital, the change in the short-term interest rate must be perceived as a long-term change. It must be perceived as permanent. If the market expects that a change in short-term rates will be reversed some months hence, then the effect on long-term rates will be slight. Because the long-term rate represents an average of a long period of expected short-term rates, a change in expectations for even a year or two will have only a limited effect. This does not mean that even relatively short-lived, high, short-term rates will have no effect on the economy, but the effect on long-term interest rates will be limited.

Essentially the same argument applies if the preferred habitat theory is correct. But the argument becomes less and less relevant as the liquidity premiums become larger. If liquidity premiums exist but are relatively small, then long-term rates are largely determined by expectations of future short-term rates, and changes in these expectations will be the principal determinants of changes in the long-term rates. As liquidity premiums become larger, however, they begin to dominate the effect of expectations. If expectations become totally irrelevant, then we return to the segmentation theory where monetary policy can affect long-term rates only if the Federal Reserve directly buys and sells long-term securities. The bottom line is that if liquidity premiums are significant determinants of long-term rates and if they change through time, then the link between short-term and long-term rates is not very well defined.

The idea that long-term rates are, at least in part, reflections of the market's expectations of future short-term rates, suggests that short-term rates ought to be more volatile than long-term rates. For, while short-term rates may go up or down, only if the market expects that these rates will go up (or down) and stay there, will the long-term rate change by a comparable amount. This prediction about the relative volatility of rates has been confirmed by historical experience. For example, Figure 21-5 shows the yield curves which existed near the interest-rate peak of the 1974 recession and approximately 9 months later in 1975, when rates had fallen considerably. The figure illustrates that short-term rates changed by quite large amounts, relative to long-term rates. This type of pattern has been common to all business cycles in contemporary U.S. history. Moreover, this pattern emphasizes the point that it is more difficult for the Federal Reserve to alter long-term rates than short-term rates, because long-term rates reflect the market's expectations about the Federal Reserve's actions over an extended period.

Given that the Federal Reserve can alter the short-term and to a lesser extent the long-term interest rate, the next question becomes: How do these changes in interest rates affect real investment decisions? We will examine this part of the Keynesian argument next.

FIGURE 21-5

Yield curves for Treasury securities near the peak and trough of the 1974–1975 recession.

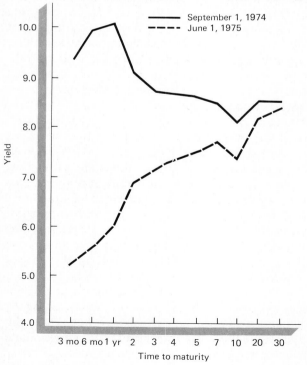

THE EQUILIBRIUM REAL INTEREST RATE AND THE LEVEL OF INCOME

The basic idea behind the Keynesian view of the effect of monetary policy is that the Federal Reserve can alter the cost of capital throughout the economy, and as the cost of capital falls, investments which were previously unprofitable become profitable. This increased investment then leads to a higher level of income in the economy. To fully appreciate this part of the Keynesian argument we need to examine the logic behind this proposition and we need to see how a new equilibrium is achieved with a higher level of income as a result of an increase in the supply of money by the Federal Reserve.

The Cost of Capital and Investment Demand

This part of the story begins with what is called the *investment-demand schedule*. The investment-demand schedule simply shows the desired level of investment for an individual company or for an entire economy as a function of the cost of capital. To explain the investment-demand schedule for a particular company we need to utilize the concept of net present value developed in Chapter Three. We learned in Chapter Three that an invest-ment project can be viewed as profitable if it has a positive net present value when future cash flows are discounted at the appropriate discount rate. At any given point, an individual company is likely to be considering a number of investment projects. How many of these projects may be viewed as profit-able depends upon the cost of capital which is used to determine their net present value. If the cost of capital falls, then more projects will have posi-tive net present values and more investment will be undertaken. As a result, we can conclude that as the cost of capital falls, the desired level of invest-ment increases. An example of this relationship is presented in Table 21-1. The table shows that XYZ Company is considering five separate invest-ments. The investments are listed across the top of the table from most profitable to least profitable. The rows of the table show the net present value of each investment at different levels of the cost of capital. The table shows that at a cost of capital of 20 percent, only the first project is profitable, but if the cost of capital falls to 5 percent, then all five projects are profitable. The results of this table are summarized in Figure 21-6. This figure shows the level of desired investment by firm XYZ at different levels of the cost of capital. We refer to this as the investment-demand schedule for the firm.

Just as we can represent the investment-demand schedule facing an individual firm, we can represent the investment opportunities facing an economy with a similar schedule. To do so we merely aggregate the investment-demand schedules of all the individual firms into an aggregate investment demand schedule for the economy. There is no real difference between the two schedules, except that when we aggregate we can eliminate

TABLE 21-1

Investment Demand for XYZ Company

COST OF CAPITAL (%)	NET PRESENT VALUE OF INVESTMENT PROJECTS ($ millions)				
	1	2	3	4	5
25	−0.5	−0.8	−1.1	−2.6	−3.1
20	0.3	−0.3	−0.5	−1.9	−2.2
15	1.4	1.1	0.3	−0.6	−1.5
10	2.1	1.7	1.2	0.2	−0.6
5	3.2	2.4	1.8	1.2	0.3
	INVESTMENT REQUIRED FOR EACH PROJECT ($ million)				
	27	30	15	26	18

the lumpiness of the schedule for an individual firm. For a single firm the schedule jumps from one level of investment to another in a discontinuous manner. When we aggregate these individual schedules, we derive a much smoother curve as represented in Figure 21-7. As in the case of the individual firm, this curve slopes downward. Two curves are drawn in Figure 21-7, corresponding to two levels of nominal income, Y_1, and Y_2, where Y_2 is greater than Y_1.

To see why increases in income or GNP cause this curve to shift to the right it is necessary to examine the net present value (NPV) of an investment

FIGURE 21-6

Desired investment for XYZ Company at different levels of the cost of capital. This figure illustrates the investment spending undertaken by XYZ Company shown in Table 21-1.

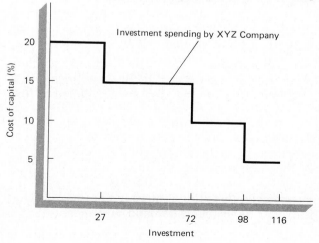

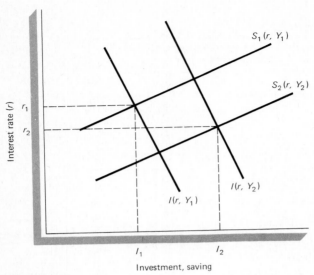

FIGURE 21-7
Investment demand- and saving-schedules for the economy. The figure illustrates how an
increase in nominal income shifts both curves to the right and leads to a lower interest rate.

project a little more carefully. We can define the net present value for an
investment project which is expected to generate a cash flow of A_t in period t
for N periods as

$$\text{NPV} = -I + \sum_{t=1}^{N} \frac{A_t}{(1+r)^t}$$

where I is the initial investment required in the project and r is the cost of
capital. If we take the future cash flows as given, then we know that as the
cost of capital falls, the net present value of the project will increase. When
net present value becomes positive, the investment is worth undertaking.
This is what is illustrated in Figure 21-6. But we can also take the cost of
capital as given and ask what happens to net present value if the estimated
future cash flows, the A_t's, increase. The answer is that the net present value
of the project will increase. Now we can identify the impact of increases in
the level of income or GNP on the investment-demand schedule for the
economy. It is generally believed that as income goes up, estimates made of
the future cash flows on investment projects throughout the economy go up
as well. In effect, this says that investors become more optimistic about
future cash flows as income or GNP rises. We can represent this effect by
shifting the investment-demand schedule to the right, as in Figure 21-7. This
says that at a given cost of capital, investment demand will increase with
increases in income.

Equilibrium Investment and Saving

The question we want to address with this investment-demand schedule is: What happens to the aggregate level of investment and the level of nominal income as the interest rate which equilibrates desired borrowing and lending declines? We know that the interest rate determined in financial markets declines as the money supply increases. We have already interpreted the interest rate determined in financial markets as the cost of capital, or the cost of obtaining funds to finance investment projects. We know that as the cost of capital falls, investment projects which were previously unprofitable become profitable. These projects are the ones which have a positive net present value at the new lower cost of capital.

As this additional investment takes place the level of nominal income in the economy will increase as well, because nominal income is equal to the sum of investment and consumption. In order to understand the final equilibrium which the economy reaches we must take into account the consequences of this increase in the level of income. To do so we should recall from Chapter Seven that for the economy as a whole to be in equilibrium, desired investment must equal desired saving. When actual borrowing is equal to actual lending, then actual saving must equal actual investment, and for this equality to represent an equilibrium, the interest rate and the level of income must adjust so that actual saving and investment are the same as desired saving and investment.

We can complete this analysis of the equilibrium in the economy if we introduce one additional schedule into Figure 21-7. This schedule shows the relationship between desired saving in the economy and the levels of income and the interest rate. The real rate of interest exerts a positive influence on saving, such that as the real interest rate increases so does the amount of saving. Similarly, the level of income has a positive effect on saving, such that aggregate saving increases with the level of nominal income. These relationships are presented by the upward-sloping curves in Figure 21-7. Each curve represents the amount of saving generated in the economy at different interest rates and for a given level of income. For example, S_1 shows the relationship between saving and the interest rate if income is equal to Y_1. As the level of income increases to Y_2 the saving curve shifts to the right to S_2.

In order to describe the equilibrium reached by the economy as a whole, we need to use these investment and saving curves to trace the level of income and the interest rate which results as investment increases. We know that as the interest rate which brings about an equilibrium in the financial markets falls, the cost of capital decreases and investment spending increases. The increased income generated by this additional investment shifts both the investment and saving curves to the right, as illustrated in Figure 21-7. As these curves shift to the right, the interest rate which equilibrates desired investment and desired saving, falls. This process continues until a new equilibrium level of income and rate of interest are reached, say at r_2 and Y_2. At this new equilibrium, the real interest rate will be lower and the level of income higher than they were prior to the initial increase in the money supply. For this conclusion to be assured, it is necessary to note an assumption which is implicit in Figure 21-7. This figure is drawn under the assumption that a change in income has a larger effect on desired saving than it has on desired investment. As a result, for a given increase in income, the S curve shifts farther to the right than does the I curve. This implies that the equilibrium interest rate falls as the level of income increases. This is generally thought to be an accurate assumption, so we won't worry about other possible outcomes.

There is one additional point about this equilibrium which needs to be mentioned. The initial effect of an increase in the money supply is to decrease the interest rate. This decline in the interest rate on financial contracts leads to a general reduction in the cost of capital, which stimulates investment spending and raises income. Generally, this increase in income feeds back on the financial markets so that the initial decrease in the interest rate is moderated. This can be illustrated using money supply and money demand curves as in Figure 21-8. The initial equilibrium which prevailed before the Federal Reserve increased the money supply is shown in Figure 21-8 as the intersection of M^s_1 and M^d_1 at an interest rate of r_1. Then the Federal Reserve increased the monetary base so that the money supply curve shifted to the right to M^s_2 and the interest rates fell to r'_1. As investment and income begin to rise, the increase in income causes the money demand curve to shift to the right to M^d_2. The new equilibrium occurs at an interest rate of r_2, where M^s_2 and M^d_2 intersect. Moreover, this is the same interest rate which equilibrates desired investment and saving, as shown in Figure 21-7. This moderating effect of income on interest rates due to the shift in the money demand function is called the *income effect* on interest rates.

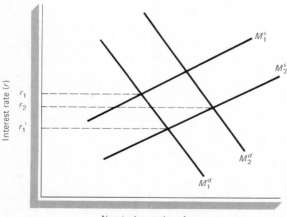

FIGURE 21-8
The liquidity and income effects of money on interest rates. The figure illustrates that the initial liquidity effect of an increase in the money supply is to reduce interest rates from r_1 to r'_1. The income effect moderates this decline and the interest rate settles at r_2.

Figures 21-7 and 21-8 illustrate that when the economy has adjusted to the increase in the money supply initiated by the Federal Reserve, the interest rate and the level of income, investment, and saving have all changed. Moreover, from the Keynesian vantage point, the principal force behind this change is an alteration in the cost of credit. There has been no reference to any concept of portfolio adjustment or of substitution between different forms of wealth, a notion that was central to the monetarist view. Instead, a change in monetary policy creates a divergence between the cost of capital or credit and the rate of return on productive investments. This gap is closed by acquisition of additional credit and the expansion of investment until the rates of return on financial contracts and on real investments are brought into equilibrium.

A SYNTHESIS OF THE DIFFERENCES BETWEEN THE KEYNESIAN AND MONETARIST VIEWS

One of the most important differences between monetarists and Keynesians is that they have different explanations for how the system works. Monetarists emphasize the portfolio-adjustment process and Keynesians, the cost-of-credit approach. But economists in general are awfully hard to pin down and this particular part of that discipline is certainly no exception. So it shouldn't be surprising that there is at least one group of so-called Keynesians which does not quarrel with the idea of a portfolio-adjustment process, but provides a different interpretation of its outcome from that offered by monetarists.[1] It is therefore exceptionally important to develop a synthesis of the differences between monetarist and Keynesian views which both contrasts these two explanations of how the economy is affected by the Federal Reserve and highlights the conflicting implications for the conduct of monetary policy. Part of this synthesis will be presented in the next chapter, which deals with inflation, but the bulk of it is presented in the next few pages.

There are two important points of contention between monetarist and Keynesian schools of thought regarding the links between financial markets and the real side of the economy. The first regards the extent of segmentation in markets; the second, the relative importance of the underlying determinants of the nominal interest rate and the proper role of interest rates in the conduct of monetary policy. Both of these differences derive from the monetarist emphasis on the long run and the Keynesian emphasis on the short run. We will analyze the two points of difference in turn.

---

[1] This school of thought has been centered around James Tobin of Yale University. Tobin is responsible for developing the concept of q introduced in Chapter Twenty. The explanation of how monetary policy influences the economy as offered by Tobin involves a process of portfolio adjustment. But the conclusions which Tobin usually draws from this framework are often quite at odds with those in the monetarist camp.

Segmentation and the Monetarist–Keynesian Controversy

Keynesians have been critical of monetary policy as a reliable tool for influencing the economy because they believe that the causal chain identified at the beginning of this chapter may break down. They don't deny that the Federal Reserve can influence the money supply. They do, however, argue that the response to the money supply change may dissipate without ever causing any significant change in nominal income. The argument has traditionally been made using the cost-of-credit approach, but it can easily be made within the portfolio-adjustment framework as well. The essence of the argument is that markets are sufficiently segmented from one another that changes which initially impact one market may never be transmitted to other markets. In effect, the argument is that markets can act as buffers which absorb changes in costs, rather than as efficient transmitters of those changes from one segment of the economy to another. To see more specifically what this entails, we will examine how the chains in the cost-of-credit approach might break down and then examine a similar argument in the context of the portfolio-adjustment process.

We will examine three arguments which can be viewed as various types of segmentation. They affect the first three links in the chain of logic which defines the cost-of-credit approach, and are illustrated in Figure 21-9.

LIQUIDITY TRAP   A long-standing proposition is that the Federal Reserve may occasionally be unable to compel short-term interest rates to decline, because the market becomes dominated by "bear speculators." Bear speculators are individuals who believe that interest rates have a floor below which they will not go, or that prices of short-term financial assets have a ceiling above which they will not go. If the Federal Reserve tries to buy short-term assets from such people, as the price reaches this ceiling, they are willing to almost completely convert into cash in order to avoid the capital losses which surely will come when prices fall and rates rise. As a result, it is argued that the Federal Reserve reaches the point where it can increase the money supply almost indefinitely without being able to force interest rates below that floor. The implication is that the chain of logic in the cost-of-credit approach breaks down at the first link and the actions of the Federal Reserve on the money supply become segmented from the rest of the financial markets. It can be argued that liquidity traps have existed at various points in history, but it is exceptionally difficult to produce definitive empir-

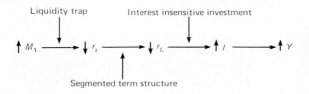

FIGURE 21-9

This figure illustrates the three principal ways the chain of logic in the cost-of-credit approach can break down.

ical evidence on this point. It seems true that if the market were dominated by bear speculators who were unwilling to change their minds as the Federal Reserve continued to force interest rates down to their perceived floor, then a liquidity trap could exist. Yet the question seems to be whether the Federal Reserve has the power and wherewithal to compel the market to change its mind in the event such a situation arises. This question is open to debate.

SEGMENTED TERM STRUCTURE   Another possibility is that the Federal Reserve may be able to alter short-term interest rates, but that this may have no effect on long-term interest rates. This problem arises if the term structure of interest rates is determined by the segmentation theory. If each maturity is a distinct, segmented market, then changes in the short-term rate will only affect short-term investment decisions. In order to influence the cost of capital for all investments, the Federal Reserve would have to intervene directly in each market. It can be argued, however, that because the Federal Reserve's principal operations deal with short-term debt, it is inherently less capable of influencing long-term rates.

INTEREST-INSENSITIVE INVESTMENT   The third way the chain of logic may break down occurs if investment decisions are insensitive to changes in the cost of capital. Keynesians often argue that business executives make investment decisions based on "animal spirits" and, hence, do not respond readily to changes in the cost of capital which might result from changes in the money supply. This argument is based on the idea that the estimates of returns from investment projects fluctuate much more than does the cost of capital used to determine the net present value of these projects. This means that decisions on investments will be dominated by changes in investors' expectations rather than changes in the cost of capital. As a result, Keynesians argue that while the Federal Reserve could influence investment decisions by altering the cost of capital, this effect is not likely to be very important. If this argument is correct, then the financial markets are largely segmented from the markets for real investment.

The segmentation argument is also of critical importance within the portfolio-adjustment process advocated by monetarists. The degree of segmentation determines how broad or extensive the portfolio-adjustment process will be. For example, suppose that money balances and Treasury bills are perceived to be close substitutes but are thought to be segmented from the rest of the financial markets. Then, if the Federal Reserve increases the supply of money, investors may attempt to shift out of money into Treasury bills. By so doing they may bid up the price of Treasury bills until there is a new equilibrium between the two assets. If this is the extent of the portfolio-adjustment process, however, then the effect of monetary policy on the real side of the economy will be very weak. Keynesians tend to believe that segmentation is an important part of real-world financial markets. They argue that while this segmentation should be dissipated in the long run, we simply cannot wait for the long run. Hence, the substitution process will often be cut short and monetary policy ineffective or unreliable. Monetarists are more interested in the long run and believe that segmentation, if it exists at all, is a highly transitory barrier to substitution across markets. Hence they believe that monetary policy has a strong effect on the real side of the economy.

Real and Nominal Interest Rates Revisited

Early in this chapter the assumption was made that the expected rate of inflation would remain constant. This meant that whenever we examined factors causing changes in nominal interest rates, we were really looking at changes in the real rate. This assumption is a critical point in the monetarist–Keynesian controversy. Both sides agree that the assumption is strictly inappropriate, but they differ about the relative importance of changes in inflationary expectations and changes in the real rate in determining changes in nominal interest rates. Monetarists argue, as did Fisher in the early part of this century, that the real interest rate is essentially constant and that most observed changes in nominal interest rates can be attributed to inflationary expectations. Keynesians, on the other hand, place less emphasis on inflationary expectations.

To understand the substance of the disagreement it is best to summarize the two effects of money supply changes on interest rates which were identified in this chapter, and add to these a third effect called the price anticipations effect, or the premium for anticipated inflation. The three effects are the following.

1   *Liquidity Effect*: The initial decrease in interest rates by an increase in the money supply
2   *Income Effect*: The tendency for the initial interest-rate decrease to be moderated by the effect of increased income on money demand
3   *Price Anticipations Effect*: The increase in nominal interest rates which results as money supply changes cause the market to expect higher rates of inflation

The Keynesian school of thought concentrates on the first two effects of monetary policy on interest rates, and generally gives the third effect short shrift. The monetarists generally argue that the third effect is almost the entire story. This is virtually what Fisher argued many years ago. The monetarists contend that monetary policy works through the portfolio-adjustment process. Then, because they perceive monetary policy to have a strong influence in determining prices and income, they argue that high rates of change in the money supply generate expectations of inflation. These expectations of inflation increase nominal interest rates. It is largely through this response of interest rates to inflation expectations that nominal interest rates actually enter the monetarist view of the Federal Reserve and the economy. Furthermore, the monetarists would argue that markets are efficient in incorporating information about future inflation rates. This means that nominal interest rates rapidly and efficiently respond to high rates of growth in the money supply by incorporating the expected inflation rate that the money supply growth implies. Monetarists are led by this logic to the conclusion that increases in the money supply tend to increase, rather than decrease, observed interest rates.

Keynesians acknowledge each of the three effects on interest rates listed above, but are reluctant to accept the monetarist argument that the price anticipations effect dominates. Instead, they maintain that the first two effects are empirically significant. As a result, they conclude that in the short run, money supply increases cause interest rates to decline. In the long run, if the high rate of growth in the money supply causes inflation, then the inflation expectation will cause rates to go up. However, Keynesians believe that the cause and effect relationship between money and inflation is not so clear to the market, and consequently an increase in the money supply does not cause an immediate increase in inflationary expectations. They conclude that it is still fruitful to judge monetary policy, at least in part, by its effect on interest rates. Moreover, they conclude that there is an important role for a countercyclical monetary policy, guided by interest rates. This means that the Federal Reserve should press interest rates upward at the peak of a business expansion and force interest rates down to stimulate investment when the economy is lagging. Monetarists reject both the attempt to use monetary policy in a countercyclical manner and the idea that monetary policy is tight when interest rates are high and loose when they are low.

It should be apparent that differences about the causes and effects of inflation are a central part of the monetarist–Keynesian dispute. We will turn to this topic in the next chapter.

SUMMARY

In this chapter we examined the Keynesians' view of how monetary policy influences the economy and then we contrasted the monetarist and Keynesian positions. The Keynesian view hinges on what we have called the cost-of-credit approach. This approach focuses on the effect of monetary policy on the cost of credit in the economy. The Keynesian argument can be summarized as follows. An increase in the supply of money reduces short-term interest rates. This decline in short-term interest rates leads to a decline in long-term interest rates. This amounts to a reduction in the cost of capital which determines the profitability of investments throughout the economy. At a lower cost of capital more investments are undertaken and this means an increase in income. Most of this chapter was devoted to explaining each step in this chain of logic.

The Keynesian analysis begins with the demand and supply for money, just as does the modern quantity theory, but the Keynesians emphasize the impact of a change in the supply of money on interest rates. Specifically, they say that an increase (decrease) in the money supply will cause interest rates to fall (rise). This is the liquidity effect of money on interest rates. The initial decline in interest rates is largely limited to short-term rates because open market operations deal with short-term rates, but a continuing increase in the rate of growth in the money supply should have an impact on long-term interest rates as well. This first portion of the Keynesian chain of logic emphasizes the effect of Federal Reserve policy on interest rates where interest rates represent the cost of credit.

The next step in the chain of logic traces the impact of changes in the cost of credit on investment decisions. The relationship between the cost of credit and the volume of investment is embodied in the investment-demand schedule for the economy. The investment-demand schedule is constructed on the assumption that investment decisions are based on a net present value criterion. This means that all investment projects which have a positive net present value, at the available cost of capital, are undertaken. If the cost of capital falls, then more investment projects will become profitable and investment spending will increase, which in turn leads to an increase in the level of income. As a result, the decrease in interest rates which the Federal Reserve set in motion leads to an increase in income because it makes it cheaper to obtain funds for investment. We traced the increase in income back to see its effect on interest rates and found that the increase in income caused the money demand curve to shift to the right. This moderated the initial decline in interest rates. This secondary effect on interest rates is called the income effect. In the final equilibrium which results when both effects are accounted for, desired saving is equal to desired investment at a lower interest rate and higher level of income.

In the latter part of the chapter we synthesized some of the essential differences between the monetarists and the Keynesians. We noted that most of the substantive disagreements both about how the system works and how monetary policy should be conducted have their roots in the philosophical differences between the two schools of thought. The monetarists are concerned with the long-run equilibrium performance of the economy. They believe that in the long run a competitive economy is stable and they attribute many of the difficulties in the contemporary performance of the economy to government interference. The Keynesians, on the other hand, generally are concerned with short-run as well as long-run problems. They tend to believe that a competitive economy may need government intervention in order to remain stable. The more specific differences in the links between financial markets and the economy can be broken down into three central issues: the extent of segmentation of markets, the important determinants of nominal interest rates, and the proper procedure for conducting monetary policy.

The Keynesians believe that there are a number of factors which may cause the chain of logic developed throughout this chapter to break down. Each of these possible difficulties leads to segmentation between markets. One possibility is that the Federal Reserve may be unable to bring interest rates down when it wants to because of a belief in the market that rates have hit their floor. Another is that long-term interest rates may be segmented from short-term interest rates. A third is that investment decisions may not be very sensitive to changes in the cost of capital. Monetarists argue that none of these aspects of segmentation is very significant in the long run.

Keynesians emphasize the liquidity and income effects of changes in the money supply on interest rates; monetarists argue that these are transitory effects. Instead, they emphasize that high rates of growth in the supply of money create an expectation of inflation and that higher expected inflation rates mean higher interest rates. Therefore, they conclude that increases in the supply of money lead to higher, not lower, interest rates.

Finally, monetarists and Keynesians disagree about how monetary policy should be conducted. Keynesians judge monetary policy by its impact on interest rates, and monetarists reject this. Monetarists believe that the only appropriate measure of whether monetary policy is tight or loose is the rate of growth in the supply of money. Furthermore, Keynesians reject the money supply rule proposed by the monetarists and emphasize that the Federal Reserve must be able to exercise discretion in deciding how it will influence both interest rates and the growth in the money supply. The monetarists contend that this discretion has led to inflation. The reason why is developed in the next chapter.

QUESTIONS TO IMPROVE UNDERSTANDING

1 Explain the basic difference(s) between the "cost-of-credit" and "portfolio-adjustment" approaches in explaining the links between monetary policy and the real economy.

2 Suppose the Federal Reserve uses open market operations to sell securities. Explain the liquidity effect on interest rates that this action will have.

3 What short-term interest rate(s) is (are) first affected by open market operations? Describe how other short-term interest rates respond to this initial change.

4 How do open market operations influence the cost of capital? How is this related to the term structure of interest rates?

5 What is the investment-demand schedule for the economy? How is it related to individual firm's assessments of the net present value of projects they have under consideration?

6 Suppose the economy is in equilibrium such that desired saving is equal to desired investment, as illustrated in Figure 21-7. Next suppose some external event causes the level of income to decline. How would this affect saving and investment and the real interest rate? Could the Federal Reserve offset this change in the real interest rate? How? Do you think it would be very effective?

You may want to answer this question both before and after you read Chapter Twenty-two.

7 Suppose the Federal Reserve increases the supply of money. This will have an initial effect which tends to reduce interest rates. But this initial effect will be moderated somewhat as income changes. Explain and illustrate these two effects.

8 Explain how different views about the extent of segmentation in markets separate monetarists and Keynesians.

9 What is the price anticipations effect on interest rates? How do Keynesians and monetarists differ on the practical significance of this effect?

10 It has been emphasized that monetarists are concerned with the long run and Keynesians with the short run. Can you summarize how this basic difference in points of view leads to more specific differences in their explanations of how monetary policy influences the economy?

REFERENCES

Hicks, J. R.: "Mr. Keynes and the 'Classics'; A Suggested Interpretation," *Econometrica*, 5 (1937), pp. 147–159.

Friedman, Milton: "Factors Affecting the Level of Interest Rates," in Donald Jacobs and Richard Pratt (eds.), *Savings and Residential Financing*, U.S. Savings and Loan League, 1968.

Modigliani, Franco, Robert Rasche, and J. Phillip Cooper: "Central Bank Policy, the Money Supply and the Short-Term Rate of Interest," *Journal of Money, Credit and Banking* (May 1970), pp. 166–218.

Smith, W. L.: "A Graphical Exposition of the Complete Keynesian System," *Southern Economic Journal* (October 1956), pp. 115–125.

Tobin, James: "A General Equilibrium Approach to Monetary Theory," *Journal of Money, Credit and Banking* (February 1969), pp. 14–29.

Chapter Twenty-Two

MONETARY POLICY,
FINANCIAL MARKETS,
AND INFLATION

This chapter deals with one of the most important forces impinging on the economies of the United States and the rest of the world in the 1980s: inflation. The rate of inflation in the United States and in some other Western democracies has skyrocketed in the last decade. In the late 1950s and early 1960s Americans became adjusted to a rate of inflation which was negligible; prices were almost completely stable. But starting in the late 1960s the rate of inflation in the United States began to increase, gradually at first, and then dramatically in the late 1970s. The pattern of growth in the rate of inflation is documented in Figure 22-1, where the rate of change in the consumer price index is shown for the period beginning in 1953 and ending in 1979. The figure shows that the largest percentage increase in the consumer price index occurred in the last year of this 27-year period. The pattern shown by this figure is not encouraging. The prospect that the rate of inflation might continue to climb as it has in the past decade has become an issue of great national concern.

In this chapter we will explore both the principal causes of inflation and some of its effects. We will also evaluate some of the competing explanations of the causes of inflation. Moreover, we will discover how financial markets

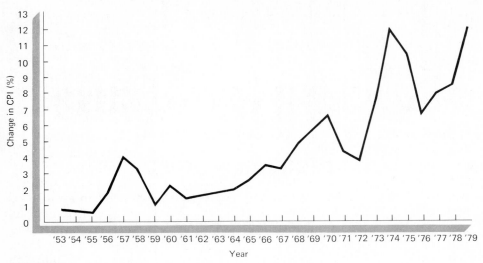

FIGURE 22-1

Annual rate of change in the consumer price index, 1953–1979. Source: *Annual Report of the President 1980.*

as well as individuals and companies, depending on the types of financial instruments they have bought and sold, are affected by inflation.

The causes of inflation are hotly debated throughout our society. This debate is one of the most important ingredients in our political campaigns. Various segments of our society perceive the causes of inflation differently. Moreover, academic economists are widely divided about the causes of inflation. One school of thought contends that it is a consequence of excessive growth in the money supply; another says that it is a result of a wage-price spiral, or more recently, an oil-price spiral; others claim it is big business or monopolies which cause it. The arguments on each side have been stated and restated many times and yet it seems that few people are persuaded by these arguments. The basic arguments will be presented again here. But in addition it will be argued that it is futile to try to decide which is correct. The more relevant issue is: How can inflation be stopped? When this question is addressed it becomes more apparent why different groups in society believe in different theories of inflation. For the real problem is that someone has to pay the price of bringing the rate of inflation down. So each group contends that some other part of society should pay that price and they defend that theory of inflation which is consistent with their self-interest. The value of understanding the various theories of inflation is that it helps us understand where the costs of curbing inflation will fall.

But before we take up the debate over the cause and cure for inflation, we will examine the effects of inflation. First, we will examine the wealth redistributions that inflation can cause. Then we will come to understand that inflation is a kind of tax. It taxes our holdings of money and other financial claims which decline in value as inflation increases. Finally, we will examine how corporate equity and debt securities have been affected by inflation.

WEALTH REDISTRIBUTIONS DUE TO INFLATION

The effects of inflation have been dealt with at various junctures throughout this book. The first substantive chapter, Chapter Two, described the kinds of redistributions of wealth which inflation has created at different times in history. For example, the apparently unanticipated deflation which occurred in the United States during the late nineteenth century led to an alleged redistribution of wealth from farmers to their creditors. This spawned the populist movement which culminated in 1896 with the presidential campaign of William Jennings Bryan on a platform of coinage of silver. More recently, in the 1970s, there was an apparently unanticipated inflation which led to wealth transfers from creditors to debtors. Chapter Eight pointed out that observed interest rates on debt contracts can be viewed as the sum of the real interest rate and a premium equal to the expected rate of inflation. At this point we want to explore, somewhat more systematically, how both anticipated and unanticipated inflation can lead to wealth redistributions. First, we will consider the effect of unanticipated inflation on standard debt contracts. Then we will examine how even anticipated inflation can create a wealth redistribution which is really a form of taxation.

Wealth Redistribution Created by Unanticipated Inflation

We already know from Chapter Eight that the purchasers of debt securities demand a premium to compensate them for the expected rate of inflation. But we have not yet specifically examined the impact on the balance sheets of lenders and borrowers of actual rates of inflation which are higher or lower than anticipated. We will do so now.

To keep the discussion as simple as possible, we will assume that there are only two types of assets available to everyone in the economy. We normally think of these two types of assets as debt and equity securities. But now they will be referred to as monetary and real assets, respectively. This does not mean that the two classification schemes are completely interchangeable. Debt and equity securities have some characteristics which do not easily fit into the monetary-real classification. But the purpose here is to examine the effect of inflation, and the distinction between monetary and real assets suits this purpose rather well. The significance of these new labels is that debt is a claim on a future payment which is fixed in money terms, while equities, now called real assets, are not titles to fixed money payments.

A money claim is a contractual agreement for one party, the debtor, to pay another party, the creditor, a prespecified dollar amount at some time in the future. Money claims include money itself, savings deposits, short-term debt instruments, such as Treasury bills, and long-term bonds, such as mortgages. On the other hand, real assets involve no claim to a prespecified dollar payment. Instead, they are generally residual claims to the income accruing to an asset after all monetary claimants have been paid.

We want to investigate what happens to money creditors and money debtors if there are unanticipated changes in the inflation rate. The difference between a money creditor and a debtor is simply a matter of whether an individual has borrowed more than was lent or has greater monetary liabilities than assets. If lending exceeds borrowing, the person is a money creditor; whereas if borrowing exceeds lending, he or she is a money debtor. Table 22-1 shows an example of a money creditor and a money debtor. The money debtor has borrowed $20,000 to add to his initial equity of $10,000 and has invested $20,000 in real assets and $10,000 in money assets. By comparison, the money creditor has equity of $20,000 and has borrowed only $10,000 in order to invest $20,000 in money assets and $10,000 in real assets. The money creditor and debtor in this table are representative of all the money creditors and debtors in the economy in that the money debts of one are exactly equal to the money assets of the other. Therefore, in this table we see an example of the kind of redistribution of wealth which takes place as the inflation rate deviates from that which is anticipated.

In the example presented in Table 22-1, both market participants expect that the rate of inflation will be 100 percent. Furthermore, to keep the algebra simple, it is assumed that the real interest rate is zero. The table then shows the changes in the balance sheets of both individuals if the actual inflation rate turns out to be 50, 100, and 150 percent. It is important to recognize that the nominal value of money debts and money assets will be unaffected by the actual inflation rate. For example, the net money debtor contracts for $20,000 worth of debt at the beginning of the period and, with 100 percent expected inflation, agrees to repay $40,000, regardless of the actual inflation rate. But the real *return* on such contracts fluctuates with the actual inflation rate in that the $40,000 payment will be less costly if the inflation rate has been 150 percent rather than 50 percent. On the other hand, the value of real assets rises perfectly with the inflation rate, and hence, their real value is fixed.

The fundamental point which this table illustrates is that money debtors do well when the market underestimates the rate of inflation, while money creditors do well when the market overestimates the rate of inflation. Moreover, the gain of the money debtors is the loss of the money creditors. That is, unanticipated inflation, whether higher or lower than anticipated, redistributes wealth. It does not lead to a net change in wealth of all participants in the market.

To see that this is true, first examine what happens to the money debtor. If the inflation rate is exactly that which was anticipated, 100 percent, then

TABLE 22-1

Balance Sheets of Money Debtors and Creditors (100% Anticipated Inflation)

	BEFORE INFLATION	AFTER 50% INFLATION	AFTER ANTIC- IPATED 100% INFLATION	AFTER 150% INFLATION
		NET MONEY DEBTOR		
Money assets	10,000	20,000	20,000	20,000
Real assets	20,000	30,000	40,000	50,000
Total assets	30,000	50,000	60,000	70,000
Money debts	20,000	40,000	40,000	40,000
Equity	10,000	10,000	20,000	30,000
Total	30,000	50,000	60,000	70,000
% Increase in equity		0%	100%	200%
% Change in real value of equity		−33%*	0.0%	20%
		NET MONEY CREDITOR		
Money assets	20,000	40,000	40,000	40,000
Real assets	10,000	15,000	20,000	25,000
Total assets	30,000	55,000	60,000	65,000
Money debts	10,000	20,000	20,000	20,000
Equity	20,000	35,000	40,000	45,000
Total	30,000	55,000	60,000	65,000
% Increase in equity		75%	100%	125%
% Change in real value of equity		17%	0	−10%

* This is computed as follows:

$$1 - \frac{\text{Nominal Value of Equity in period 2}}{(1 + \text{inflation rate}) \times \text{Nominal value of equity in Period 1}} = 1 - \frac{10,000}{15,000}$$

there is no gain or loss on financial contracts in money terms. Therefore, the value of the money debtor's equity increases at the same rate as inflation. If the market overestimates the rate of inflation by 50 percent, then the money debtor loses $10,000 on net money debts, but also gains $10,000 on real assets, so the nominal value of his or her equity remains unchanged, though the real value of this equity has declined by one-third. On the other hand, if the market underestimates the rate of inflation, he or she gains $30,000 on real assets and still only loses a nominal value of $10,000 on net money debts. Therefore, the nominal value of his or her equity increases by 200 percent, which makes the real value of that equity 20 percent greater than it was before.

The pattern of gains and losses from unanticipated inflation is exactly the opposite for the money creditor. Again, he or she experiences no real gain or loss if the actual inflation rate is equal to the expected inflation rate, but if the market overestimates the rate of inflation, then there is a gain in real terms; that is, a net gain on money assets of $10,000 and a gain on real assets of $5,000. As a result, the nominal value of equity increases 75 percent, which means that its real value rises by 17 percent. If the market underestimates the rate of inflation, then the nominal gain on net money assets is still $10,000, but this now implies a smaller real gain. In fact, the real value of equity now declines by 10 percent.

The example illustrates that for the economy as a whole, where the net borrowing of all monetary debtors equals the net lending of all monetary creditors, the effect of unanticipated inflation is to transfer wealth. In this example, the money debtor paid the money creditor a net of $10,000, regardless of the rate of inflation. This was a good deal for the debtor if the inflation rate was above the expected rate, but it was a bad deal if the actual rate was lower than expected. It is important to recognize that neither party would expect to profit from this, ex ante, given that they had the same information and expectations. Only if a market participant has superior information relative to the market, can he or she *expect* to profit from inflation.

Inflation as a Tax

There is another kind of wealth redistribution created by inflation, and this one is a little bit more devious. Moreover, inflation does not even have to be unanticipated for this redistribution to take place. The basic idea behind this kind of redistribution is that people who hold money during inflations lose and the entity issuing the money, the government, wins. In this situation individuals who hold money are net money creditors, with respect to that asset, and the government is a net money debtor. Moreover, as far as government-issued money is concerned, the nominal interest rate is fixed at zero, so any inflation at all, anticipated or not, leads to a wealth transfer from holders of money balances to the government. This, in effect, is a kind of tax imposed on money. Moreover, it is a devious tax, because most people do not perceive that they are paying it. And the tax is not small.

The nature of this tax is easiest to understand if we temporarily imagine that the only type of money in the system is government-issued cash. This means that we will imagine there are no demand deposits. An important characteristic of government-issued cash is that it earns no interest; its nominal return is fixed at zero. Hence money balances will decline in value by the amount of inflation, whether it is anticipated or not. For example, suppose an individual has wealth of $100,000 and holds 5 percent, or $5,000, in money. To keep the example simple we will imagine that this individual is neither a money creditor nor debtor in the sense that we examined above, so that the rest of his or her wealth is invested in real assets. Now suppose that there is 10 percent inflation. The nominal value of the person's real assets goes up by 10 percent, but the nominal value of his or her money balances remain unchanged. This person has therefore lost 10 percent, or $500, in real terms on his or her money balances. This is a tax imposed upon him or her equal to 10 percent of their money balances.

It should be apparent that there is a wealth transfer here, but it may not be obvious who gains and how that gain occurs. The idea that this is a tax relies on the link between the monetary policy of the government and the rate of inflation. By printing more money than people want to hold, at a given level of income, and issuing it to the public, particularly in our simple example with no demand deposits, the government determines the inflation rate. The government will create inflation if it distributes new money instead of either taxing or borrowing from the public. The production of more money and the generation of inflation become a substitute for more direct methods of taxation.

The inflation tax has been used by governments for centuries. Most of this time the supply of money was virtually equal to the government-supplied stock of cash so that the process was almost as simple as the description above. Most of the historical instances when an inflation tax has been used to a large extent were cases where government expenditures were increased to fight a war. In ancient times the method used to impose the inflation tax was to reduce the gold or silver content of coins. More recently, such as in the Civil War in the United States, the government simply printed whatever amount of paper money was needed to finance the war, and labeled this currency greenbacks.

During the twentieth century the mechanism for imposing an inflation tax has become much more complicated. The reason for the added complication is the growth of the commercial banking industry and the prevalence of demand deposit money as well as government-issued currency. The tax still operates in the same manner regarding government-issued currency, but it does not work the same way with demand deposits. Instead, in a fractional-reserve banking system like the one described in Chapter Nineteen, the government directly taxes commercial banks which hold reserves with the government. The inflation tax is on reserves and government-issued cash rather than directly on the entire money supply. In a system which has only government-issued currency, monetary policy is determined by how much of that currency is distributed to the public. But with a fractional-reserve banking system, monetary policy is determined by the amount of currency plus the quantity of reserves supplied to the public. With reserve requirements unchanged, the quantity of reserves is determined by the government's purchase or sale of government securities through open market operations. If the Federal Reserve purchases Treasury securities and increases reserves, it means that the government is obligated to impose lower direct taxes or borrow less from the public than it would otherwise have to do. In effect, the increase in reserves becomes a substitute for borrowing or other forms of taxation. Moreover, the reserves supplied to the banking system bear no interest, just as government-issued currency bears no interest. To the extent that this increase in reserves puts upward pressure on the price level, it imposes a tax on the outstanding stock of reserves and government-issued currency. If the banking industry is perfectly competitive, then the banks will pass on this tax to their customers who use demand deposits. As a result, holders of government-issued currency bear the full brunt of the inflation tax, while the tax on reserves is passed on to the customers of commercial banks.

It is possible to develop a fairly precise estimate of the magnitude of the inflation tax in the United States by examining the sources of financing for the U.S. Treasury. One such source is the profit which is earned by the Federal Reserve System and returned to the Treasury at the end of each fiscal year. The Federal Reserve earns its profits largely through the returns on its portfolio of government securities. It has acquired these securities as it has increased the total reserves in the banking system over the past 7 decades in which it has been in operation. From the standpoint of the Treasury the securities held by the Federal Reserve represent securities it did not have to sell to the public. The public has been compelled to hold additional money balances rather than additional Treasury securities. The important difference is that these money balances do not earn an explicit rate of interest, whereas the Treasury securities do. By selling these securities to the Federal Reserve, the Treasury avoids having to pay that interest, because those interest payments, net of Federal Reserve expenses, are returned to the Treasury. The Federal Reserve's profit is the inflation tax.

The magnitude of these profits in recent years is shown in Table 22-2. When the inflation rate was relatively low by historical standards, this tax was low. For example, the table shows that the tax was only $1.6 billion in 1965, or 1.4 percent of the revenues from the personal income tax in that year. But by 1976 the tax rose to $8.0 billion, which is approximately half the revenues from all excise taxes collected that year and is greater than all the funds used for revenue sharing during 1976. If the inflation rate continues to climb, so will the interest rate on Treasury securities, and with it the magnitude of the inflation tax.

Common Stock as an Inflation Hedge

One way investors try to deal with inflation is to place their wealth in assets with rates of return which rise and fall with the actual inflation rate. In the simplified world presented in Table 22-1, these assets are all lumped under the heading of real assets. If an investor had no money debts and had all his or her wealth invested in real assets, then this would represent a perfect inflation hedge, for the real value of this investor's wealth would remain unchanged as the inflation rate fluctuates. In the late 1970s investors tried to do exactly this. They invested heavily in many commodities which they believed would increase in value with inflation. Moreover, many of these

TABLE 22-2

The Magnitude of the Inflation Tax and Other United States Government Revenues: 1965–1979 ($ billions)

YEAR	TOTAL GOVERNMENT RECEIPTS	PERSONAL INCOME TAXES	EARNINGS OF THE FEDERAL RESERVE SYSTEM DEPOSITED WITH THE TREASURY
1965	116.8	48.8	1.6
1966	130.9	55.4	1.9
1967	149.6	61.5	2.1
1968	153.7	68.7	2.5
1969	187.8	87.2	2.9
1970	193.7	90.4	3.5
1971	188.4	86.2	3.9
1972	208.6	94.7	3.6
1973	232.2	103.2	3.9
1974	264.9	119.0	5.4
1975	281.0	122.4	6.7
1976	300.0	131.6	8.0
1977	356.9	156.7	6.5
1978	402.0	181.0	7.4
1979	465.9	217.8	9.2

Source: *Federal Reserve Bulletin*, various issues.

* Also includes other miscellaneous receipts which are a very small portion of the total.

assets did in fact increase in value. But one type of asset, which was traditionally thought of as a good inflation hedge, did not. That asset is common stock or equity claims on companies. Common stocks have generally been thought to be a good inflation hedge because they are the residual claim to all earnings after money debtors have been paid. Hence, if there is unanticipated inflation, it should work to the benefit of equityholders over debtholders. But in recent years it hasn't worked that way. The returns on equities have been quite low. Table 22-3 shows how low these returns have been, compared to returns on other investments, such as Treasury bills, real estate, and human capital. For example, during the 1971–1975 period the NYSE provided only a 1.6 percent nominal return while the inflation rate was 7.1 percent and Treasury bills earned approximately 6 percent.

There are at least three possible explanations for this recent behavior of the prices of common stocks. One is the argument that corporate taxes increase with inflation so that inflation leads to a decline in after-tax returns. The second is that investors are systematically undervaluing equity securities. The third is that inflation causes investors' expectations of future earnings to decline. We will review each of these arguments in the next few pages.

Consider the tax argument first. The proponents of this argument contend that corporate taxes increase with inflation due to two peculiarities about the way taxable income is computed. First, income includes paper

TABLE 22-3

Average Annualized Nominal Returns on Assets (%) and Inflation Rates (% Change in CPI)

VARIABLE INFLATION	1/53– 12/57 1.3	1/58– 12/62 1.3	1/63– 12/67 2.2	1/68– 7/71 5.1	8/71– 12/75 7.1
Treasury bills					
1 month	1.9	2.2	3.7	5.5	5.7
2 month	2.1	2.7	4.0	5.9	6.0
3 month	2.3	3.0	4.1	6.1	6.4
Real Estate*					
r_1	1.0	0.6	1.7	5.9	6.2
Labor Income†					
h_1	2.2	3.4	5.2	4.7	6.1
Common stocks‡					
NYSE index	12.3	12.8	12.5	3.0	1.6

Source: Eugene F. Fama and William G. Schwert, "Asset Returns and Inflation," *Journal of Financial Economics*, 5 (1977), p. 123.
* Computed from the home purchase price component of the CPI.
† Computed from changes in labor income.
‡ Based on a value-weighted index of NYSE securities.

profits on inventories; that is, increases in the value of inventories due to inflation which will never actually be realized by the company in question. Second, income includes depreciation which is calculated on the basis of the original cost of the asset, rather than the replacement cost. Both of these factors tend to overstate reported corporate profits for tax purposes. This leads to higher levels of taxes than would otherwise be the case, which in turn, reduces the real returns on the total capital of corporations. But there is a potentially offsetting effect which tends to counter these tendencies for taxes to rise with inflation. That effect is the increased tax deduction of interest expense as expected inflation drives up nominal interest rates. Higher nominal interest rates mean larger tax deductions for interest expense, which tend to reduce the total tax bill as a proportion of total profits. Some have argued that these two effects are largely offsetting, so that total after-tax corporate profits, adjusted for inventory, profits, and depreciation on a replacement cost basis, plus interest expense, have been driven neither up nor down in recent years.[1] If total corporate profits including interest have not significantly declined, then one might question whether the prices of equities are, in some sense, too low.

It is possible that investors have been making an error in valuing equities, such that their assessment of value is too low, based on any "rational" analysis. Such an argument is generally very distasteful to economists because it is based on the notion that the market is slow to learn or is

[1] See Franco Modigliani and Richard A. Cohn, "Inflation, Rational Valuation and the Market," *Financial Analysts Journal* (March/April 1979), pp. 24–44.

relatively inefficient. But the argument has nonetheless been taken seriously by at least one economist with a considerable reputation. One of the "errors" that it has been alleged that the market may be making is to capitalize profits by an inappropriate discount rate.[2]

To understand the nature of this error we need to examine a very simple model of the value of an asset. Suppose that the market expects the underlying stream of *real* earnings accruing to an asset to remain the same during each future period. We will represent this constant expected *real* return per period as $\overline{X}$. Also suppose the market expects the future *nominal* earnings of the asset to grow at an expected inflation rate, p. If this revenue stream were expected to go on indefinitely, then the value of the asset could be approximated as

$$V = \frac{\overline{X}}{r_N - p} = \sum_{t=1}^{\infty} \frac{\overline{X}(1 + p)^t}{(1 + r_N)^t} \tag{22-1}$$

where r_N represents the nominal interest rate. Equation (22-1) illustrates that the appropriate discount rate for the *nominal* stream of earnings accruing to the asset is the nominal interest rate, but the appropriate discount rate for *real* earnings is the *real* rate.

It has been argued that the market is confused about the differences between real and nominal earnings in valuing corporate equities. The alleged mistake is that the market incorrectly capitalizes reported accounting earnings at the *nominal* interest rate, when they should be discounted at the real interest rate. This would lead to an undervaluation of equity securities. The alleged reason for this is that inflation alters the meaning of reported accounting profits, after taxes and interest. During inflation, these reported earnings no longer represent the true earnings of the equity owners of the firm, for inflation constantly shifts the value of the firm between debt- and equityholders. For example, if the *nominal* amount of debt financing in a company is left unchanged during a period of inflation, then the *real* amount must be declining. In such a situation the accounting returns to equity no longer represent the true nominal returns to equity. If the market does not understand this, then it may inaccurately value equity securities in general. The implication of this argument is that when the market discovers its error it will revalue equities and the stock market will experience an appreciable increase. That the market would virtually never discover such an error seems highly implausible.

The difficulty with arguments such as this one is that it is virtually impossible to distinguish between this undervaluation argument and the alternative hypothesis that investors' expectations of future returns have declined. To see what this means we need to reconsider Eq. (22-1). The undervaluation argument took expected future real returns $\overline{X}$ as given. But

[2] Ibid.

suppose that inflation affects the market's expectation of future real returns. This effect might be due to a belief that inflation will lead to wage and price controls, which will hurt corporate profitability, or to the belief that attempts to use monetary policy to halt inflation will cause a recession which will hurt corporate profitability. Either reason suggests that inflation leads to corrective actions by the government which reduce future real profits. If inflation is perceived to be serious enough, then this may cause a substantial decrease in $\overline{X}$, and with it, the value of equity securities. This argument seems to be a powerful alternative to the proposition that the market has undervalued equities.

This final explanation for the poor recent performance of equity securities emphasizes the market's reaction to the long-run consequences of inflation. This hypothesis contends that inflation does not lead simply to a redistribution of wealth as discussed here. Rather it suggests that inflation will itself influence real income, if left unchecked. It also implies that actions which are usually taken to try to control inflation also take their toll in real income. To understand why this may be true, we need to examine the causes and possible cures for inflation.

WHY DO WE HAVE INFLATION?

In this part of the chapter we will examine the two most popular theories of the causes of inflation. We will call them the monetary explanation for inflation, and the cost-push explanation. The discussion of both of these explanations of inflation will not be directed at the particular episode of inflation which the United States has experienced in the 1970s and 1980s. Rather, this section focuses on the logic of each competing theory. After each theory is presented, the recent inflation in the United States will be examined.

The Monetary Explanation of Inflation

Milton Friedman has argued that: "Inflation is always and everywhere a monetary phenomenon." What he means by this is that virtually every significant inflation in history was accompanied by an unusually high rate of growth in the supply of money. Throughout most of history this was a consequence either of changes in the supply of gold, usually occurring in wartime, or decisions to debase the currency by reducing its backing with gold. For example, during the Middle Ages in Europe, nearly a century of relative price stability came to an end as gold and silver from the Spanish colonies in the New World began to flow into Europe. During the next century, prices rose several times.[3] But the relationship between money and prices is probably most evident in the cases of extremely high inflation, or

---

[3] See E. H. Phelps Brown and Sheila V. Hopkins, "Seven Centuries of the Prices of Consumables Compared with Builder's Wage Rates," *Econometrica* (November 1956), pp. 296–314.

hyperinflation, as, for example, occurred in Germany during the 1920s. In that case, in the period of a few years the price level increased more than 300 percent per month and the money supply at a slightly lower rate.[4] It is also true that money supply expansions accompanied every major period of inflation in the United States and that prolonged periods of deflation, such as occurred in the mid-nineteenth century in the United States, were accompanied by declines in the supply of money.

While there is little disagreement about the historical record itself, there is considerable disagreement about the proper interpretation of that record. Some argue, as does Milton Friedman, that the high rate of growth of the money supply is the single most important cause of inflation. Others argue that high money supply growth is an inevitable product of an inflationary economy, but that the root cause of the inflation lies elsewhere.[5]

The rationale for Friedman's conclusion about money and inflation lies in the modern quantity theory, which was presented in Chapter Twenty. We know from that chapter that the monetarists believe that an increase in the money supply causes an increase in nominal income, Py. What we do not know is how that change in nominal income may be divided between a change in prices P and a change in real income y. The monetarists do not provide any really substantive answer for this question. Instead they point out that at any given point in time, with the existing level of technology and size of the labor force, there is a maximum level of real income or a maximum rate of growth in real income that the economy can sustain. As the actual level of real income or the growth rate of real income approaches the maximum, then increases in the supply of money intensify the pressure for prices to rise. In order to simplify this concept, economists have developed a notion of the full-employment level (or rate of growth) of income. This is the level (or rate of growth) of income at which everyone who wants to work is employed. At this income, unemployment is only what is called "frictional," where those unemployed are between jobs or are unable to work. The monetarist explanation of inflation is that if the money supply increases at a rate faster than the rate of growth in real income at full employment, less the long-run growth rate in velocity, then this will cause inflation.

This relationship can be expressed with the equations developed in Chapter Twenty. The basic equation of the modern quantity theory was expressed in a convenient form in Eq. (20-14):

$$\frac{\Delta M}{M} + \frac{\Delta V}{V} = \frac{\Delta P}{P} + \frac{\Delta y}{y} \tag{22-2}$$

This equation indicates that with a given change in velocity, once the level rate of growth in real income reaches its maximum at full employment,

[4] See Phillip Cagan, "The Monetary Dynamics of Hyperinflation," in Milton Friedman (ed.), *Studies in the Quantity Theory of Money*, University of Chicago Press, Chicago, 1956.
[5] See James Tobin, "Inflation and Unemployment," *American Economic Review*, March 1972, pp. 1–18.

additional increases in the rate of growth in the money supply are directly translated into changes in prices. The same idea was illustrated in Chapter Twenty with an example where velocity is increasing at 1 percent per year and real income is growing at 3 percent per year. This means that prices would increase at a rate 2 percent lower than the rate of increase in the supply of money. If the money supply grew at 10 percent, then the inflation rate would be 8 percent.

It must be recognized that the monetarists are usually interested in the long-run behavior of the economy. In the short run the rate of inflation can be quite volatile, and even the most vehement monetarists would not claim that this relationship holds. But they believe that inflation is really a very long-run problem. There are no good quick fixes or solutions. Hence, though the link between the money supply and inflation may look tenuous in any given quarter or year, they insist that Eq. (22-2) expresses the important long-run relationship.

The Cost-Push Explanation of Inflation

A popular alternative explanation of inflation relies on the pressure on wages of increasing costs. Specifically, the cost-push argument states that an initial increase in costs, usually in the form of wage increases, leads to a spiral of price increases which in turn calls for further cost increases. It is these continuing rounds of cost and price increases that are alleged to create inflation. There is no doubt that an increase in wages or other costs, such as the cost of energy, will lead to an increase in prices. The question at issue is whether such an initial increase in wages will lead to a perpetual sequence of increases in prices. If it can, then a cost increase can lead to inflation. But if it cannot, then a cost increase will lead to a single price increase and that will be the end of it. In other words, a cost increase can cause a *one-time* increase in prices but not continuing price increases. And it is continuing price increases that we think of as inflation.

To analyze the cost-push explanation for inflation we will utilize a simple model of the market for labor. Our purpose is to examine what happens when the wage demands of labor increase due to the imposition of some minimum price for labor, presumably through a labor union. But it is important to recognize that labor merely serves as an example. The example might just as easily be oil or some other commodity. Moreover, the only reason for attributing the cost increase to a union or other organized decision-making group is that we want to concentrate on the effect of a conscious decision to try to increase costs, as opposed to some natural cost increase due to, say, the decreased supply of some raw material.

The labor market is represented by the supply-and-demand curves drawn in Figure 22-2. The vertical axis of the figure measures the nominal wage rate w and the horizontal axis measures the quantity of labor demanded and supplied L. We will assume that the demand for labor is depen-

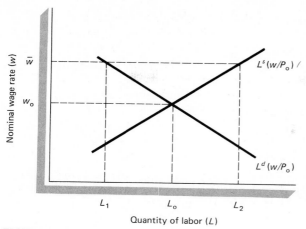

FIGURE 22-2

Supply and demand for labor and the equilibrium wage rate. The figure shows that the equilibrium w_0 is less than the wage demanded by a union $\overline{w}$.

dent on the real cost to firms of using labor which is the real wage rate w/P, and is represented as $L^d(w/P_0)$ for price level P_0. We will also assume that the labor-supply curve is dependent upon the real wage rate, so that more labor will be supplied as real wages increase. This means that the positions of both curves are determined by the price level. Now suppose that labor unions which represent some portion of the work force insist that the nominal wage paid to them must not be less than some amount, say $\overline{w}$. In other words, the union demands a contract wage of $\overline{w}$ and the workers accept nothing less. This means that the labor-supply curve becomes horizontal at this nominal wage or that the original labor-supply curve shown in Figure 22-2 is altered to conform to this contract wage. The implication is that some workers will now receive a wage which is higher than they would otherwise be willing to accept for the work they supply.

Suppose the economy was initially in equilibrium with full employment prior to the imposition of the union contract wage. This equilibrium is represented by the intersection of the supply-and-demand curve at a nominal wage rate of w_0 and an employment level of L_0. At this equilibrium there is no unemployment. Now the union announces the new minimum wage, which means that the new effective labor-supply curve begins at $\overline{w}$ and is horizontal until it intersects the old upward-sloped labor-supply curve. But with this higher nominal wage rate, employers demand fewer workers and more workers seek to be employed. The gap between the quantity of labor supplied at $\overline{w}$ and the quantity of labor demanded is $L_2 - L_1$. This represents the magnitude of unemployment which has been created.

The decrease in employment created by this increase in the nominal wage rate means that companies will have to curtail production and the supply of goods and services will fall. Moreover, as production levels are cut, the aggregate prices of goods and services will be bid up. This means that inflation, as well as unemployment, will develop. We can think of this inflation as happening in either of two ways. We can imagine that firms cut production levels and goods become more scarce. As this happens excess demand develops and prices are bid up. Alternatively, we can imagine that as firms see the higher cost of labor, they respond by relying on labor less intensely and passing on as much of the cost increase as possible in the form of prices. In either case, the result is the simultaneous occurrence of both inflation and unemployment. The effect of the price increase on the labor market is illustrated in Figure 22-3. As the aggregate price level increases from P_0 to P_1, the labor-supply curve shifts to the left and the labor-demand curve shifts to the right. The result is that unemployment is diminished by the increase in prices, from $L_2 - L_1$ to $L_4 - L_3$, but it is not totally eliminated. As long as this particular labor market represents the cost of the sole factor used to produce all goods and services, then the price increase which is precipitated must be less than the initial wage increase of w to $\overline{w}$, for that wage increase caused firms to substitute into other, now less expensive, factors of production. An across-the-board increase in costs for all factors would lead to a commensurate increase in prices. Therefore, unemployment emerges and prices are at a higher level than before the imposition of the minimum union wage.

It is important to see that in the long run this is a self-defeating process. The only way the union in this example generates a higher real wage for its members is to decrease the demand for their services. The price paid for the higher real wage is the unemployment created. Moreover, if the union perceives that the price increase has thwarted its goals—that is, if it expects its

FIGURE 22-3
The response to a wage demand of $\overline{w}$. This figure illustrates the effect on prices and unemployment if wage demands exceed the equilibrium level. The first response is unemployment, measured by $L_2 - L_1$. Then, if the wage increase is validated prices will rise until there is a new equilibrium with the original level of employment L_0.

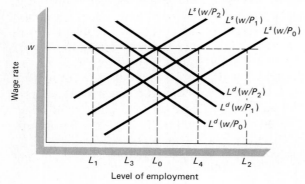

initial nominal wage increase to be the same as its ultimate real wage increase—then it may seek to raise nominal wages yet again. But the result of further increases will be more unemployment. It is in this sense that it is argued that the cost-push explanation of inflation is faulty. Cost increases cannot lead to *continuous* price increases, and inflation is usually thought of as continuous increases in prices.

This does not mean, however, that cost-push inflation doesn't happen. What it does mean is that cost-push can't be the entire story. The rest of the story involves the participation of the government. Since the end of World War II, the United States government has accepted the responsibility for trying to promote full employment. In fact, this goal was recorded in law in the Employment Act of 1946. What this has meant is that the government has used its monetary and fiscal powers to try to stimulate the economy when unemployment has developed.

To see how this will affect the situation described in our labor market example we need to examine Figure 22-3. When unemployment develops, as it has in this example, the Federal Reserve can try to eliminate that unemployment by increasing the rate of growth of the money supply. When the economy is underemployed, this increases both the price level and the level of real income. As the price level is bid up, the labor-supply curve shifts further to the left and the labor-demand curve further to the right. This lowers real wages and reduces unemployment until the price level reaches P_2 and a new equilibrium is attained. At this level of prices, unemployment has been eliminated and real wage rates are back to their original level. When this happens the government is said to have *validated* the original wage increase. The labor union is back to where it was originally and may be encouraged to start all over again. If it does, and if the government validates the next wage increase, this process can lead to inflation. But it is important to recognize that inflation develops only because the government validates the wage increase instigated by the union and the union tries again.

The incentive to engage in this kind of process depends upon the willingness or ability of the party which is setting a ceiling price to tolerate unemployment of its resources. In the case of labor unions, it seems implausible that this incentive would be very strong, for widespread unemployment would lead to the disintegration of the union. In the case of some natural resources, such as oil, the incentive might seem to be stronger.[6]

---

[6] A third possible argument is that monopolies cause inflation. This argument is simply incorrect. If a particular product were sold by a monopolist, it would have a higher price than if it were sold in a perfectly competitive industry. This is the conclusion of the basic microeconomic analysis of the pricing of products under monopoly as opposed to perfect competition. But there is nothing in our theory of monopoly pricing which indicates that monopolies will have an incentive to increase prices in circumstances where perfectly competitive firms would not. The only way monopoly power leads to inflation is when an industry initially becomes monopolized. In that instance, the price of the product in the industry will rise from the perfectly competitive level to the monopoly price. But in order for this to account for inflation, it is necessary for monopoly power to continually increase. It seems implausible that this can be a principal cause of inflation over the long term.

The Elusive "True" Cause of Inflation

It should be apparent that the "true" cause of inflation is exceedingly elusive. For inflation, as we see it today in Western democracies, is not the result of a single independent process. Instead, inflation is a consequence of various groups, in the United States and throughout the world, attempting to accumulate a larger share of the available wealth. These quarrels over how to divide the national income are manifestations of deeper underlying social problems in the society, but they are reflected in the form of upward pressure on costs. Where possible, these costs are passed on in the form of higher prices.

But the rub is the phrase, "where possible." The government's management of its debt and of its monetary policy determines what is possible. If the Federal Reserve chooses to strictly control the rate of growth of the money supply, then cost-price pressure will lead to unemployment. In this way the Federal Reserve can force the economy to bear the consequences of the increased costs. But the Federal Reserve can also expand the supply of money in order to offset the rising level of unemployment and thereby validate the original cost increase. It is only with this complicity between groups in the society demanding larger incomes and the government validating their demands, that persistent price increases or inflation, is generated. Who, then, is responsible for this inflation? Some argue that it is the Federal Reserve or the government, and others argue that it is the cost-push process or, more fundamentally, a breakdown in the social contract in the society.

The real debate is not about where to pin the blame for inflation, for the search for a true single cause of inflation is inherently elusive. Instead, the real debate is about the least costly way to bring the rate of inflation down. The monetarists assert that the only real way to control inflation is through the supply of money. The counter-argument is that monetary restraint which is sufficient to halt inflation will lead to a recession or even depression and this is too large a price to pay. Instead, it is argued that inflation will only be halted if the social pressures which lead to the cost-push spiral are reduced or eliminated. Monetarists are very skeptical that this can ever be successfully accomplished.

Can Inflation be Stopped with Monetary Policy?

On the surface, the monetarist cure for inflation looks relatively simple and painless. In its simplest form the modern quantity theory suggests that we can make the rate of inflation whatever we want by simply adjusting the rate of growth in the money supply. The implication for economic policy would seem to be that if the rate of growth in the money supply and the rate of inflation get out of hand, the Federal Reserve must curtail the rate of growth of the money supply. But, historically, when this has been attempted the result has been to lead the economy into a recession which increases the rate of unemployment, yet achieves little decrease in the rate of inflation. The resulting economic situation has come to be known as "stagflation": the simultaneous occurrence of both high rates of inflation and unemployment. It is possible to identify the episodes in the last 20 years when this stagflation has taken place by inspecting Figure 22-4. This figure shows the combinations of unemployment and inflation experienced in the United States since 1960. Throughout most of the 1960s the figure shows a pattern of increasing inflation and decreasing unemployment. But in 1970 that pattern was broken. 1970 was a recession year, brought on, in part, by a reduction in the rate of growth of the money supply. However, it is evident from Figure 22-4 that the recession did not appreciably decrease the inflation rate. Instead, it resulted in an increase in the rate of unemployment. The inflation rate declined somewhat in 1971 and 1972, though the unemployment rate did not. But the inflation rate returned to the 1970 level in 1973. Again, in 1974 a number of events combined with a tighter monetary policy to bring on the 1974 recession. But this attempt by the Federal Reserve to curtail inflation was foiled as both inflation and unemployment increased and the United States experienced unprecedented stagflation.

Part of the reason for the 1974 episode of stagflation was the unprecedented increases in the price of natural resources, particularly oil. But in addition to the problems caused for the economy by increasing energy prices

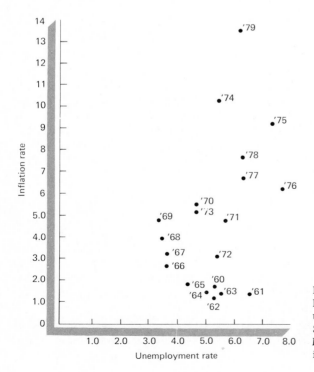

FIGURE 22-4
Rates of inflation and unemployment in the United States, 1960–1979. Source: *Federal Reserve Bulletin*, various issues.

problems were created by trying to slow inflation with monetary policy. To see the difficulties involved it is useful to utilize the modern quantity theory to construct a diagram which relates the rate of growth in the money supply to the tradeoff between inflation and unemployment. We can write the basic equation for the modern quantity theory as follows [see Eq. (22-2)]:

$$\frac{\Delta P}{P} = \frac{\Delta M}{M} + \frac{\Delta V}{V} - \frac{\Delta y}{y} \tag{22-3}$$

We can think of this as a linear equation between the rate of change in prices $\Delta P/P$ and the rate of change in real income $\Delta Y/Y$, where the intercept in the equation is defined by the rate of growth in the money supply plus the rate of growth in velocity, $(\Delta M/M) + (\Delta V/V)$, and the slope is equal to -1. This relationship is illustrated in Figure 22-5, where the vertical axis measures the inflation rate and the horizontal axis measures the rate of change in real income. Three curves with a slope of -1 are drawn in the figure, corresponding to three distinct rates of growth in the money supply, 4, 6, and 10 percent. In addition, each curve is drawn on the assumption that velocity grows at 1 percent. Curve BB' represents the possible combinations of inflation and growth in real income if the growth in the money supply is 6 percent, while curve AA' illustrates the possible combinations if the money supply grows at 10 percent.

The modern quantity theory normally assumes that the economy is in long-run equilibrium at a rate of growth in real income which requires full

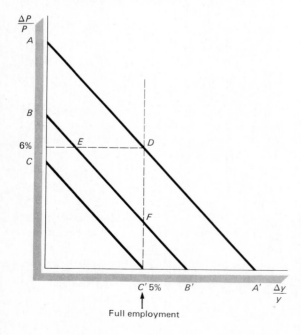

FIGURE 22-5
The tradeoff between inflation and real economic growth. Each diagonal line shows the combinations of inflation and growth in real income consistent with a particular rate of growth in the money supply.

employment. As an example, full-employment growth is assumed to be 5 percent and is designated by the dashed vertical line originating at C'. To illustrate this equilibrium, suppose the money supply is growing at 10 percent per year. Then the long-run equilibrium would be at point D, which implies 5 percent growth in real income and 6 percent inflation (6% = 10% + 1% − 5%). Now suppose the Federal Reserve reduces the growth rate in the money supply to 6 percent from 10 percent, so that there is a shift from curve AA' to curve BB'. If this had no effect on real income and took its toll entirely in inflation, then the economy would move directly from point D to a new equilibrium at point F, but this is not what happens. Instead, the economy moves toward point E rather than point F. This means that there is little decline in inflation, but unemployment develops as the rate of growth in real income declines.

It is not too difficult to identify the reason for this response. When firms experience a short-run decrease in demand for their products, whether created by a tight monetary policy or by some other cause, their immediate response is to cut production levels rather than alter their price structure. Firms prefer to cut production to match lower sales and pass on increasing costs rather than to alter their profit margins. This behavior will not necessarily persist if the decline in demand is perceived to be long term rather than relatively transitory. But in the early stages of a recession it is not apparent how long the decline in demand may persist. And the result is that inflation and unemployment occur simultaneously.

The monetarists conclude that if the rate of growth in the money supply is decreased and held down, then the economy will eventually adjust to a new equilibrium with lower inflation. For example, in Figure 22-5 if money supply growth were lowered to 4 percent, the long-run equilibrium would be at C', with zero inflation and full employment. But the Keynesian counterargument is that this eventually may take too long and be too costly. It was Keynes himself who quipped: "In the long run, we are all dead."

Figure 22-5 characterizes one of the most serious dilemnas facing Western economies. If the government continues to validate demands for higher wages and other cost increases with an expansionary monetary policy, then inflation will continue. But if the government tries to reduce inflation with a contraction in the rate of growth in the money supply, the resulting adjustment process is both long and painful. The only thing about this process that seems certain is that the higher the rate of inflation, the more difficult and costly will be the process of bringing it back down. It is not an understatement to conclude that the fate of the market economy hangs in the balance.

SUMMARY

In this chapter we learned about inflation—how it affects people who hold financial assets, how it is created, and how it might be stopped. The basic effects of inflation are something that most people in the United States now understand all too well. The first thing that was emphasized is that it is important to understand that inflation creates transfers of wealth. More precisely, it is *unanticipated* inflation which creates wealth transfers. We learned early in this book that interest rates on financial contracts include a premium to compensate lenders for the inflation which they expect. Hence, if actual inflation is always equal to that which is expected, then there will be no redistributions of wealth as a result of inflation. However, if inflation exceeds the expectation of lenders, then they will lose on their financial contracts and borrowers will gain, and if inflation is less than expected, then lenders will gain at the expense of borrowers. The nature of these wealth redistributions was illustrated in this chapter through an example which showed how net monetary creditors and net monetary debtors fare as inflation is over- and underestimated.

It is an overstatement to say that all wealth redistributions created by inflation require that the inflation be unanticipated. For inflation leads to wealth redistribution from the public to the government regardless of whether it is anticipated. We call this the inflation tax. We learned that the inflation tax occurs because the government restricts the interest earned on balances of cash and on reserves held by financial intermediaries. As the rate of inflation increases, the public loses and the government gains because the interest which the government does not have to pay increases. This increase acts as an alternative source of revenue for the government and is therefore called an inflation tax.

We also examined the impact of inflation on the rate of return on equity securities. Equities have historically been viewed as a viable inflation hedge because they are claims on the residual earnings of corporations after monetary creditors have been paid. Hence, it was thought that equityholders should benefit from unexpected inflation. However, it did not work that way during the 1960s and 1970s. We examined a selection of arguments as to why the return on equities has been so low. One argument is that investors have been discounting future real earnings at nominal interest rates. The argument is that this has led to equity prices which are too low, based on "rational" valuation of future returns. But we also learned that an alternative argument is that the market has lowered its estimate of expected future earnings because it believes that continued inflation will hurt corporate profitability. Unfortunately, it is difficult to find convincing tests which can distinguish between these two hypotheses.

Next we turned our attention to an examination of the causes of inflation. There are essentially two competing explanations of inflation. The monetarists argue that inflation is a result of an excessive rate of growth in the supply of money. The Keynesians argue that inflation is essentially a result of a cost-price spiral. It was emphasized that a cost-price spiral cannot lead to continuing price increases unless it is validated by government policy. If a validation does not occur through, say, an increase in the supply of money, then cost increases will lead to unemployment rather than inflation.

In the United States in recent years the government has opted for validation through high rates of growth in the supply of money to prevent unemployment. As a result, it was emphasized that it seems futile to argue about the true cause of inflation. The relevant questions are how inflation can be reduced and what will be the cost of reducing it. These are exceptionally difficult questions to answer.

QUESTIONS TO IMPROVE UNDERSTANDING

1 Explain the difference between anticipated and unanticipated inflation. How does unanticipated inflation create wealth transfers? Give an example.

2 What is the inflation tax? Why has the inflation tax increased in the United States in recent years? What reform of financial market regulation would be necessary to eliminate the inflation tax?

3 Some people have argued that common stocks are undervalued because inflation has caused the market to make errors in its pricing. Explain the nature of the error that may be involved. What do you think of this argument?

4 What other reasons can you think of why common stocks have had such poor returns as inflation has increased? What other assets do you think make good hedges against inflation?

5 Explain why Milton Friedman has often said, "Inflation is always and everywhere a monetary phenomenon."

6 What is the cost-push explanation for inflation? Trace the impact of a change in the cost of a good such as oil on the aggregate price level and on the use of that good.

7 What is "validation" of a cost-push inflation? Suppose that no validation occurred? What would happen to the cost-push inflation?

8 What is stagflation? Explain why stagflation occurs when the Federal Reserve seeks to curtail inflation by cutting the rate of growth in the supply of money. Can you see a way out of the problem created by stagflation?

REFERENCES

Brown, E. H. Phelps, and Sheila V. Hopkins: "Seven Centuries of the Prices of Consumables Compared with Builder's Wage Rates," *Econometrica* (November 1956), pp. 296–314.

Cagan, Phillip: "The Monetary Dynamics of Hyperinflation," in Milton Friedman (ed.), *Studies in the Quantity Theory of Money*, University of Chicago Press, Chicago, 1956.

Fama, Eugene F., and William G. Schwert: "Asset Returns and Inflation," *Journal of Financial Economics*, 5 (1977), pp. 114–146.

Friedman, Milton: "The Role of Monetary Policy," *American Economic Review*, 58 (March 1968), pp. 1–17.

Modigliani, Franco, and Richard A. Cohn: "Inflation, Rational Valuation and the Market," *Financial Analysts Journal* (March/April 1979), pp. 24–44.

Tobin, James: "Inflation and Unemployment," *American Economic Review* (March 1972), pp. 1–18.

Chapter Twenty-Three

CONCLUSION

The last 22 chapters have covered a lot of territory. As you have gone through these chapters it may have been easier to grasp the details about how financial markets work than to identify and place in perspective the important issues. There are two important questions which we should be able to answer regarding all of this material. They are: What are the most important things we have learned? What are the most important things we do not yet understand? This final chapter presents some concise answers to these questions. But it should be apparent that these answers are very subjective. The answers in this chapter are my answers to these questions. Now that you have almost finished this book, you should be in a position to provide some answers of your own. After all, if the last 22 chapters have made one thing clear, it is that there are few aspects of financial markets on which all observers agree.

In order to keep the topical structure of this book in perspective, in this last chapter we will proceed through each of the five parts of the book. For each part we will examine two important things we have learned and two important unanswered questions.

PART ONE: THE VALUE OF ASSETS

What We Have Learned

HOW TIME AND UNCERTAINTY DETERMINE VALUE   We learned as early as Chapter Two that an asset is essentially a claim on a future stream of income. And in almost all cases the magnitude of that future stream of income is not known with certainty. As long as people demand to be paid a price to forgo consumption—and that price is the rate of interest—then the time distribution of future income will influence the value of the asset to which that income will accrue. The exact relationship between the time distribution of income and value is the topic of present value. The value of an asset is the present value of the future income stream when discounted by the appropriate interest rate. This is the first of the two important forces which determine value. The second is uncertainty. We found in Chapters Four and Five that we can develop specific measures of the uncertainty that surrounds future income. We also found that we can represent the way individuals make investment decisions as a tradeoff between the expected return of an asset and the risk of that asset. The question of how to make this tradeoff is one of personal preference. We also learned that the risk borne by any individual depends upon the portfolio of assets which that individual holds. This is because diversification reduces the risk of a portfolio of assets. As a result, the market value of any asset is based on its contribution to the risk of the portfolios of those individuals who hold it.

HOW MARKETS UTILIZE INFORMATION   The second important feature of financial markets which was emphasized in Part One was the way markets produce and aggregate information. In order for the value of any asset to be determined in a market, the participants in the market must have some information about the income stream which may accrue to that asset. In Chapter Six we learned that this information is produced and distributed to the market in a variety of ways. Sometimes information is directly distributed to the market and sometimes it is tied in with the provision of other valuable services, as in the case of financial intermediaries. All market participants form judgments of future returns based on the information they have available, and the market serves as a device which aggregates this information. In this way prices represent aggregates of individual judgments. Because there is competition for information which can be used to estimate future returns on assets, there is pressure for information to be produced and distributed efficiently. Markets where there is only a competitive return on producing and distributing information are called efficient markets.

Important Unanswered Questions

ARE WE MISSING SOMETHING IN OUR THEORY OF HOW RISKY ASSETS ARE PRICED? In Part One we explored how to analyze the risk and expected return of an asset and how to combine assets into portfolios. And we used this to explain a theory—known as the capital asset pricing model—of how the marketplace actually values risky securities. The theory is built upon some rather elaborate and even distasteful assumptions. In addition, the predictions which it generates do not conform with the observable world as nicely as we would like. The question is: What is missing from this theory? Is there simply an important piece of the real world which is left out of the theory? Is the theory really fundamentally untestable and, hence, not really a theory at all, as some have charged? Is there a practical better theory? We simply do not yet know.

HOW DOES THE MARKET FOR INFORMATION FUNCTION? We know that financial markets aggregate available information into the prices of assets. But we know very little about how this is done. The reason for this may be that we know very little about the market for information itself. We can observe around us that information is produced and distributed in a number of ways, ranging from the direct sale, as in *The Wall Street Journal*, to more complicated mechanisms, as in the case of financial intermediaries. But we do not know why each form of information distribution is used, how information itself is priced, how the decision to invest in information is made, and what the return on information may be. These are very important issues because the financial markets serve the purpose of bringing information together to determine prices. And we know much more about the assets themselves and the markets in which they are traded, than we do about the information which determines their price.

PART TWO: THE DETERMINANTS OF MARKET INTEREST RATES

What We Have Learned

HOW TIME PREFERENCES AND INVESTMENT OPPORTUNITIES DETERMINE THE REAL INTEREST RATE   Part Two explains how observed market interest rates, or nominal rates, are determined. The concept of the interest rate which underlies all these rates is the real interest rate. The real rate is the interest rate on a single-period risk-free financial contract where there is no inflation and there are no taxes. The starting point for understanding market interest rates is therefore to understand the determinants of the real rate. As a conceptual matter we have a fairly clear understanding of what determines the real interest rate. There are two ingredients which come together to influence this rate. The first is the set of real investment opportunities open to market participants. Real investments involve the production of some real capital goods which can be used to produce goods or services in the future. The second involves the attitudes of individuals in the economy toward present as opposed to future consumption. These two ingredients determine an equilibrium interest rate which represents the rate of return on real investments, the rate at which individuals prefer to trade current for future consumption, and the interest rate on financial contracts. When the market is in equilibrium, there is a single real interest rate which represents each of these three concepts. In long-run equilibrium this interest rate is believed to be fairly stable, as the rate of return on the economy's entire capital stock does not change quickly.

WHY NOMINAL RATES DIFFER FROM THE REAL INTEREST RATE   In Part Two we identified the most important factors which account for the level of observed nominal interest rates. All nominal rates can be thought of as the real rate plus premiums for special factors which distinguish the security in question. The important factors which determine these premiums are the following: (1) the expected rate of inflation, (2) the risk of the security, (3) the security's tax treatment, (4) the security's maturity, and (5) relative security supplies. In Part Two we learned what each of these factors means and how they affect the yields on securities. We also surveyed the empirical evidence on the relative importance of these factors in the determination of various nominal rates. In recent years probably the most obvious factor causing changes in nominal rates has been the expected rate of inflation. As inflation rates have increased and the expectation of high future rates has become established, nominal interest rates have increased accordingly. Similarly, it is relatively simple to see the effect of differential tax treatment of different securities by examining the differences in yields on comparable municipal and corporate bonds. The municipal bonds have consistently lower yields because they are free from federal income taxes. In the case of differences in maturity, or the term structure of interest rates, the differences in nominal yields are evident from inspections of yield curves at different points but the specific reasons for these differences are not so evident. While we can identify alternative explanations of the term structure, it is not as easy to establish which is correct.

Important Unanswered Questions

DO CHANGES IN INFLATION EXPECTATIONS OR THE REAL RATE EXPLAIN SHORT-TERM CHANGES IN OBSERVED NOMINAL RATES?   While we have a fairly clear understanding of the identity of the factors which determine nominal interest rates, we do not have as good an understanding of the relative importance of each of these factors in explaining specific changes in nominal rates. This is particularly important in explaining changes in short-term rates such as Treasury bill rates. For example, a reduction in Treasury bill rates, like that which occurred between March and June 1980, a period when 90-day bill rates fell from 14 to 7 percent, might be attributed to a reduction in the expected rate of inflation. But it also might be attributed to a change in the real interest rate. In all likelihood both the real rate of interest and the expected rate of inflation are changing simultaneously. And as they do, the nominal rate of interest changes accordingly. However, because we do not actually observe the ex ante real interest rate demanded by the market, it is exceedingly difficult to determine the actual cause of any particular change in nominal interest rates. We know that in long-run equilibrium, the real interest rate demanded on financial transactions must be the same as the real rate of return on the economy's capital stock. But this does not mean that for reasonable periods of time these two real rates do not diverge. During such periods the ex ante real rate demanded on financial contracts may fluctuate considerably and thereby cause changes in nominal rates. But we do not know how large changes in the real rate may be relative to changes in the expected rate of inflation.

HOW SIGNIFICANT ARE LIQUIDITY PREMIUMS IN THE TERM STRUCTURE?   A question which is very similar to the one which was just discussed pertains to the relationship between short- and long-term interest rates. We know that long-term interest rates are determined in part by the market's expectation of future short-term rates. But we also know that if market participants are averse to risk, then they will demand a premium to bear the risk of changes in future short-term rates—a liquidity premium. What we do not know is how important these liquidity premiums are in determining observed long-term rates, just as we do not know the relative importance of changes in the real rate and changes in inflation expectations in determining changes in short-term nominal rates. The underlying difficulty is that we do not directly observe liquidity premiums in the market just as we do not directly observe the ex ante real interest rate. The challenge is to devise some way to measure liquidity premiums so that we can see whether supply-and-demand pressures at each maturity have a significant impact on the term structure. In addition, it would be desirable to be able to measure and even predict this impact on a regular basis. As yet we can do this only very imperfectly.

PART THREE: FINANCIAL MARKETS AND INSTITUTIONS IN THE UNITED STATES

What We Have Learned

A TAXONOMY OF MARKETS   The most important thing we learned in Part Three is how to organize the maze of financial markets which we observe in the United States into a coherent classification system or taxonomy. Markets were divided into three basic types in Part Three according to the way the exchange of assets actually takes place. These three types of markets are referred to as auction, over-the-counter, and intermediated markets. We explored the features of each type of market, the reasons why each market is used, and examples of each type of market. The value of this kind of taxonomy is that, first, it allows us to make sense out of the complex financial world which we observe and, second, it shows us how a particular market is supposed to work so that we can evaluate the efficiency of markets which we see around us.

THE IMPORTANT FEATURES OF THE MARKETS SERVING THE THREE MAJOR SECTORS OF THE UNITED STATES ECONOMY   The second important thing we learned in Part Three is not any single theory or taxonomy. Instead, it is simply a familiarity with the institutional features of the financing of the major sectors of the United States economy—the consumer, business, and government sectors. There are no simple or concise lessons which can be synthesized from the portrait of these markets which was presented in Part Three, with one exception. Part Three emphasizes the diversity and richness of the American capital markets. It shows how a competitive financial system responds to the varied needs of a modern industrial economy. The immense number of distinct markets and types of securities which have evolved to serve specific needs underscores the value of a competitive system. It is the detail and the diversity itself which is the important thing we learned in Part Three.

Important Unanswered Questions

WILL TECHNOLOGICAL CHANGE SIGNIFICANTLY ALTER THE OPERATION OF FINANCIAL MARKETS IN THE 1980S?   Technological change has been so rapid during the twentieth century that new industries have been created and old ones have become obsolete almost before many of the participants realized what was happening. Those who understood the impact of technological change have often profited from it and those who did not have lost out. Technological change has also been a crucial determinant of the types of financial markets which have prospered in the United States. For much of the nineteenth century commercial banks comprised virtually the only significant type of financial market. It was not until the corporate form of organization began to prosper that auction markets like the New York Stock Exchange emerged to trade corporate securities. And as communication systems improved, over-the-counter markets grew to be strong competitors of the auction type of market. In the twentieth century, as the economy grew and expanded after the Great Depression of the 1930s, the problems of assessing the expected returns and risk for a wide variety of different securities became more complicated. This encouraged the growth of a set of financial intermediaries which specialized in these activities. Their growth was further augmented by a system of insurance and government control which shifted risk from the marketplace to the government. Two important changes have taken place in the 1970s which are causing financial markets to adapt again. The first is major technological progress in the system of communicating and processing information. This progress ranges from the evolution of low-cost minicomputers to the advent of telecommunications technology, which permits swift, low-cost transfer of information in an electronic form. These changes have altered the need for regional financial markets and institutions and have blurred the distinction between auction and over-the-counter markets. The second major element of technological change is the advent of high inflation rates, a change that certainly cannot be viewed as progress. This has fundamentally changed the nature of the risks that each securityholder and institution bears in every financial transaction. During the 1980s the institutions and markets will have to adapt to these changes. How extensive this adaptation will be and who will be the winners and losers remains an unresolved but fascinating question.

HOW WILL HOUSING FINANCE BE CHANGED IN THE 1980S? One of the most important practical problems facing financial markets in the early 1980s is how to reorganize the system for housing finance. We learned in Part Three that the market for home mortgages is one of the largest financial markets in the United States. And it is probably the one which has been most severely affected by inflation. With the advent of high and volatile interest rates, the long-term fixed-rate mortgage has become virtually obsolete. The only way it can be maintained is with some government subsidy or with a long-term decline in the rate of inflation. The question is what will replace it and how will the financial institutions which have long provided that mortgage—the savings and loans—be affected by this change?

PART FOUR: REGULATING FINANCIAL MARKETS AND INSTITUTIONS

What We Have Learned

THE RATIONALE FOR REGULATION OF FINANCIAL MARKETS Part Four explored the principal features of the regulatory system for financial markets. But it also attempted to explain *why* this regulatory system came into existence and to identify the problems which can arise in an unregulated market which can interfere with the operation of that market or cause it to fail altogether. There are two basic sources of the problems which can provide a logical or economic justification for regulation. The first pertains to the development of monopoly power and the second pertains to the function of financial markets as collectors and distributors of information. Much of our regulatory system is designed to limit monopolistic practices, particularly that part of our system which applies to auction and over-the-counter markets. But an important additional purpose is to regulate the distribution of information and the individuals and institutions which possess special information. This understanding of the economic rationale for regulation is exceptionally important for two reasons. First, it makes it possible to make sense out of the maze of regulations which currently exist. Second, it makes it possible to evaluate the merits of each component of that regulatory system. This is important because regulation is costly and it can be used to protect as well as eliminate vested interests. During the 1980s, as many of these regulations are reexamined, a clear understanding of these issues will be of tremendous importance.

HOW INFLATION HAS CHALLENGED THE VIABILITY OF THE REGULATORY SYSTEM FOR DEPOSITORY INTERMEDIARIES   The regulatory system which governs financial intermediaries which offer deposits was designed in large part as a response to the Great Depression of the 1930s. The system which emerged from the period imposed restrictions on the interest payments on deposit accounts. After World War II these restrictions came to be used as a device to protect the savings and loan industry and support the construction of housing. This protection meant that savings and loans as well as commercial banks would not have to compete for funds with interest payments and would therefore be immune from substantial risk of rate changes if they made commitments to long-term mortgages. This system of regulation had its difficulties throughout the 1960s and early 1970s, but it was able to function as long as inflation—and therefore market interest rates—were relatively low. However, once inflation and interest rates began to accelerate as they did in the late 1970s, this system of deposit ceilings became unworkable. Investors simply withdrew their funds from those deposit accounts which had regulated rates below prevailing market-determined interest rates. In the early 1980s this system is being phased out. How this will work remains to be determined.

Important Unanswered Questions

SHOULD WE STOP PROTECTING SPECIAL FINANCIAL INSTITUTIONS?   The regulatory system which emerged in the 1930s has led to a set of institutions which serve specialized purposes and clienteles. The important feature of this set of institutions is that they have not emerged and prospered in a competitive market environment. Instead, they have been protected by the government through the regulatory system. The important question which the prospect of deregulation poses is should these institutions continue to be protected or should more competition be allowed? If competition is encouraged through such devices as the elimination of restrictions on interstate branching of commercial banks and permission for savings and loans and credit unions to significantly diversify their investments and loans, then a vastly different intermediation industry may well result. This issue is likely to be extremely important during the 1980s.

HOW MUCH RESPONSIBILITY FOR REGULATING THE FLOW OF INFORMATION SHOULD BE GRANTED TO THE GOVERNMENT?   We learned in Part Four that financial markets can suffer from serious problems if information is not widely distributed throughout the market or if those who are entrusted with special information misuse it. During most of the twentieth century the trend has been toward increased regulation of the distribution of information and of financial institutions which make decisions for those who may be less well-informed. Yet many argue that the distribution and use of information is now overregulated. Much of the criticism of this aspect of regulation has been directed at disclosure laws. But the criticism also applies to regulation of investment companies and financial intermediaries. Those who defend the current extent of regulation of this kind are inclined to view the period before these regulations came into existence—prior to the 1930s—as a period which was unnecessarily unstable. That instability is attributed in part to the imperfections in the distribution of information and to the fear of market failure resulting from perceived conflicts of interest. The important question is whether it would be possible to substantially deregulate the distribution and use of information without creating real or perceived conflicts of interest.

PART FIVE: FINANCIAL MARKETS AND THE AGGREGATE ECONOMY

What We Have Learned

THE KEYNESIAN AND MONETARIST VIEWS OF THE LINK BETWEEN MONETARY POLICY AND THE REAL ECONOMY   Keynesians and monetarists have long disagreed about how monetary policy works and how it should be conducted. We see part of this debate played constantly in the popular and financial press where we can find quite lengthy discussions of the appropriate growth rates for monetary aggregates like M_1 and M_2. Yet it is difficult to understand the significance of these issues without an understanding of the underlying, more arcane debate about how the economy responds to monetary policy. Part Five was devoted to providing that explanation. It argued that the monetarist view can best be summarized with the phrase, "portfolio-adjustment approach." This view assumes that all market participants have a desired portfolio composition which includes some portion of total wealth in the form of money. When the central bank injects more money into the system than people choose to hold, they will not respond passively. Instead, they seek to shift out of money and, thereby, bid up the prices of other assets until income rises to a level where they are willing to hold the quantity of money supplied. The emphasis here is on the response of the economy to the quantity of money supplied rather than on the way the Federal Reserve may influence interest rates. On the other hand, the Keynesian view can be summarized with the phrase "cost-of-credit approach." This view assumes that the Federal Reserve's principal effect is on market interest rates and that the quantity of money is a by-product of this process. When the Federal Reserve pursues an expansionary policy it drives down market interest rates and makes credit cheaper. The Keynesians tend to believe that the portfolio-adjustment process of the monetarists may not be very far-reaching or effective. These two opposing views lead to quite different conclusions about how monetary policy should be conducted and about the role of monetary aggregates and interest rates in the economy. An understanding of these differences is central for an understanding of the economic policy debates which are now such an important ingredient in our political process.

HOW MONETARY POLICY AND INFLATION ARE RELATED   The natural extension of the debate between Keynesians and monetarists about the link between financial markets and the real economy is the debate about the "true" cause of inflation. Monetarists argue that inflation is caused by an excessive rate of growth in the supply of money. Keynesians argue that there are a number of other causes all growing out of deeper social problems in the society. Principal among these are escalating demands for higher wages or increases in the prices of natural resources which lead to higher prices. The monetarists counter that these changes cannot cause continually rising prices or a spiral of increasing costs and prices. Instead, such a spiral must be supported by an expansionary monetary policy. Hence, they conclude that the cause of inflation is still the excessive rate of increase in the supply of money. This debate is probably more revealing of the ways inflation may be stopped than of the "true" cause of inflation. The issues are who would bear the cost of bringing the rate of inflation down and what will be the cost if it is not brought down. The monetarist position is that there is no realistic alternative to using monetary policy to stop inflation and that the destruction of our market economy is the probable cost of inaction.

Important Unanswered Questions

CAN A DISCRETIONARY MONETARY POLICY CONTRIBUTE TO LONG-RUN STABILITY? The Keynesian view of monetary policy, and the one long practiced by the Federal Reserve, is that the Federal Reserve must have discretion to judge how much the money supply should increase or decrease, depending upon the current economic circumstances. The largely monetarist critics of the Federal Reserve have argued that such discretion has decreased not increased the long-run stability of the economy. They argue that discretion has led to a policy where the supply of money has tended to increase when the economy is expanding and decrease when it is contracting—the Fed has allowed the money supply to follow and exacerbate the fluctuations of the economy rather than offsetting those fluctuations. They argue instead that a monetary rule is needed which stipulates a particular rate of growth in the money supply. The task of the Federal Reserve would then be to see that the rule is followed. The unanswered question is whether a discretionary policy could ever be used to increase the stability of the economy. The monetarists argue that for this to be possible we would have to know *much* more about how the economy responds to monetary policy, particularly the timing of that response, than we are likely to know in the near future.

IS A MONETARY RULE FEASIBLE?   There is a legitimate question, however, whether a monetary rule is really feasible—not on an economic basis but on a political basis. A monetary rule demands that government limit its own ability to control monetary policy. The temptation to use monetary policy to finance government deficits has proved tremendous. The political barriers which stand in the way of closing that option for the future may be insurmountable. The question which is left is whether it would ever be politically feasible to adopt such a rule.

Appendix

PRESENT VALUE TABLES

Appendix Table 1 Discount factors: Present value of $1 to be received after t years $= 1/(1 + r)^t$

Interest rate per year

Number of years	1%	2%	3%	4%	5%	6%	7%	8%	9%	10%	11%	12%	13%	14%	15%
1	.990	.980	.971	.962	.952	.943	.935	.926	.917	.909	.901	.893	.885	.877	.870
2	.980	.961	.943	.925	.907	.890	.873	.857	.842	.826	.812	.797	.783	.769	.756
3	.971	.942	.915	.889	.864	.840	.816	.794	.772	.751	.731	.712	.693	.675	.658
4	.961	.924	.888	.855	.823	.792	.763	.735	.708	.683	.659	.636	.613	.592	.572
5	.951	.906	.863	.822	.784	.747	.713	.681	.650	.621	.593	.567	.543	.519	.497
6	.942	.888	.837	.790	.746	.705	.666	.630	.596	.564	.535	.507	.480	.456	.432
7	.933	.871	.813	.760	.711	.665	.623	.583	.547	.513	.482	.452	.425	.400	.376
8	.923	.853	.789	.731	.677	.627	.582	.540	.502	.467	.434	.404	.376	.351	.327
9	.914	.837	.766	.703	.645	.592	.544	.500	.460	.424	.391	.361	.333	.308	.284
10	.905	.820	.744	.676	.614	.558	.508	.463	.422	.386	.352	.322	.295	.270	.247
11	.896	.804	.722	.650	.585	.527	.475	.429	.388	.350	.317	.287	.261	.237	.215
12	.887	.788	.701	.625	.557	.497	.444	.397	.356	.319	.286	.257	.231	.208	.187
13	.879	.773	.681	.601	.530	.469	.415	.368	.326	.290	.258	.229	.204	.182	.163
14	.870	.758	.661	.577	.505	.442	.388	.340	.299	.263	.232	.205	.181	.160	.141
15	.861	.743	.642	.555	.481	.417	.362	.315	.275	.239	.209	.183	.160	.140	.123
16	.853	.728	.623	.534	.458	.394	.339	.292	.252	.218	.188	.163	.141	.123	.107
17	.844	.714	.605	.513	.436	.371	.317	.270	.231	.198	.170	.146	.125	.108	.093
18	.836	.700	.587	.494	.416	.350	.296	.250	.212	.180	.153	.130	.111	.095	.081
19	.828	.686	.570	.475	.396	.331	.277	.232	.194	.164	.138	.116	.098	.083	.070
20	.820	.673	.554	.456	.377	.312	.258	.215	.178	.149	.124	.104	.087	.073	.061
25	.780	.610	.478	.375	.295	.233	.184	.146	.116	.092	.074	.059	.047	.038	.030
30	.742	.552	.412	.308	.231	.174	.131	.099	.075	.057	.044	.033	.026	.020	.015

Interest rate per year

Number of years	16%	17%	18%	19%	20%	21%	22%	23%	24%	25%	26%	27%	28%	29%	30%
1	.862	.855	.847	.840	.833	.826	.820	.813	.806	.800	.794	.787	.781	.775	.769
2	.743	.731	.718	.706	.694	.683	.672	.661	.650	.640	.630	.620	.610	.601	.592
3	.641	.624	.609	.593	.579	.564	.551	.537	.524	.512	.500	.488	.477	.466	.455
4	.552	.534	.516	.499	.482	.467	.451	.437	.423	.410	.397	.384	.373	.361	.350
5	.476	.456	.437	.419	.402	.386	.370	.355	.341	.328	.315	.303	.291	.280	.269
6	.410	.390	.370	.352	.335	.319	.303	.289	.275	.262	.250	.238	.227	.217	.207
7	.354	.333	.314	.296	.279	.263	.249	.235	.222	.210	.198	.188	.178	.168	.159
8	.305	.285	.266	.249	.233	.218	.204	.191	.179	.168	.157	.148	.139	.130	.123
9	.263	.243	.225	.209	.194	.180	.167	.155	.144	.134	.125	.116	.108	.101	.094
10	.227	.208	.191	.176	.162	.149	.137	.126	.116	.107	.099	.092	.085	.078	.073
11	.195	.178	.162	.148	.135	.123	.112	.103	.094	.086	.079	.072	.066	.061	.056
12	.168	.152	.137	.124	.112	.102	.092	.083	.076	.069	.062	.057	.052	.047	.043
13	.145	.130	.116	.104	.093	.084	.075	.068	.061	.055	.050	.045	.040	.037	.033
14	.125	.111	.099	.088	.078	.069	.062	.055	.049	.044	.039	.035	.032	.028	.025
15	.108	.095	.084	.074	.065	.057	.051	.045	.040	.035	.031	.028	.025	.022	.020
16	.093	.081	.071	.062	.054	.047	.042	.036	.032	.028	.025	.022	.019	.017	.015
17	.080	.069	.060	.052	.045	.039	.034	.030	.026	.023	.020	.017	.015	.013	.012
18	.069	.059	.051	.044	.038	.032	.028	.024	.021	.018	.016	.014	.012	.010	.009
19	.060	.051	.043	.037	.031	.027	.023	.020	.017	.014	.012	.011	.009	.008	.007
20	.051	.043	.037	.031	.026	.022	.019	.016	.014	.012	.010	.008	.007	.006	.005
25	.024	.020	.016	.013	.010	.009	.007	.006	.005	.004	.003	.003	.002	.002	.001
30	.012	.009	.007	.005	.004	.003	.003	.002	.002	.001	.001	.001	.001	.000	.000

E.g.: If the interest rate is 10 percent per year, the present value of $1 received at the end of year 5 is $0.621.

Appendix Table 2   Future value of $1 by the end of t years $= (1 + r)^t$

Number of years	Interest rate per year														
	1%	2%	3%	4%	5%	6%	7%	8%	9%	10%	11%	12%	13%	14%	15%
1	1.010	1.020	1.030	1.040	1.050	1.060	1.070	1.080	1.090	1.100	1.110	1.120	1.130	1.140	1.150
2	1.020	1.040	1.061	1.082	1.102	1.124	1.145	1.166	1.188	1.210	1.232	1.254	1.277	1.300	1.323
3	1.030	1.061	1.093	1.125	1.158	1.191	1.225	1.260	1.295	1.331	1.368	1.405	1.443	1.482	1.521
4	1.041	1.082	1.126	1.170	1.216	1.262	1.311	1.360	1.412	1.464	1.518	1.574	1.630	1.689	1.749
5	1.051	1.104	1.159	1.217	1.276	1.338	1.403	1.469	1.539	1.611	1.685	1.762	1.842	1.925	2.011
6	1.062	1.126	1.194	1.265	1.340	1.419	1.501	1.587	1.677	1.772	1.870	1.974	2.082	2.195	2.313
7	1.072	1.149	1.230	1.316	1.407	1.504	1.606	1.714	1.828	1.949	2.076	2.211	2.353	2.502	2.660
8	1.083	1.172	1.267	1.369	1.477	1.594	1.718	1.851	1.993	2.144	2.305	2.476	2.658	2.853	3.059
9	1.094	1.195	1.305	1.423	1.551	1.689	1.838	1.999	2.172	2.358	2.558	2.773	3.004	3.252	3.518
10	1.105	1.219	1.344	1.480	1.629	1.791	1.967	2.159	2.367	2.594	2.839	3.106	3.395	3.707	4.046
11	1.116	1.243	1.384	1.539	1.710	1.898	2.105	2.332	2.580	2.853	3.152	3.479	3.836	4.226	4.652
12	1.127	1.268	1.426	1.601	1.796	2.012	2.252	2.518	2.813	3.138	3.498	3.896	4.335	4.818	5.350
13	1.138	1.294	1.469	1.665	1.886	2.133	2.410	2.720	3.066	3.452	3.883	4.363	4.898	5.492	6.153
14	1.149	1.319	1.513	1.732	1.980	2.261	2.579	2.937	3.342	3.797	4.310	4.887	5.535	6.261	7.076
15	1.161	1.346	1.558	1.801	2.079	2.397	2.759	3.172	3.642	4.177	4.785	5.474	6.254	7.138	8.137
16	1.173	1.373	1.605	1.873	2.183	2.540	2.952	3.426	3.970	4.595	5.311	6.130	7.067	8.137	9.358
17	1.184	1.400	1.653	1.948	2.292	2.693	3.159	3.700	4.328	5.054	5.895	6.866	7.986	9.276	10.76
18	1.196	1.428	1.702	2.026	2.407	2.854	3.380	3.996	4.717	5.560	6.544	7.690	9.024	10.58	12.38
19	1.208	1.457	1.754	2.107	2.527	3.026	3.617	4.316	5.142	6.116	7.263	8.613	10.20	12.06	14.23
20	1.220	1.486	1.806	2.191	2.653	3.207	3.870	4.661	5.604	6.727	8.062	9.646	11.52	13.74	16.37
25	1.282	1.641	2.094	2.666	3.386	4.292	5.427	6.848	8.623	10.83	13.59	17.00	21.23	26.46	32.92
30	1.348	1.811	2.427	3.243	4.322	5.743	7.612	10.06	13.27	17.45	22.89	29.96	39.12	50.95	66.21

Interest rate per year

Number of years	16%	17%	18%	19%	20%	21%	22%	23%	24%	25%	26%	27%	28%	29%	30%
1	1.160	1.170	1.180	1.190	1.200	1.210	1.220	1.230	1.240	1.250	1.260	1.270	1.280	1.290	1.300
2	1.346	1.369	1.392	1.416	1.440	1.464	1.488	1.513	1.538	1.563	1.588	1.613	1.638	1.664	1.690
3	1.561	1.602	1.643	1.685	1.728	1.772	1.816	1.861	1.907	1.953	2.000	2.048	2.097	2.147	2.197
4	1.811	1.874	1.939	2.005	2.074	2.144	2.215	2.289	2.364	2.441	2.520	2.601	2.684	2.769	2.856
5	2.100	2.192	2.288	2.386	2.488	2.594	2.703	2.815	2.932	3.052	3.176	3.304	3.436	3.572	3.713
6	2.436	2.565	2.700	2.840	2.986	3.138	3.297	3.463	3.635	3.815	4.002	4.196	4.398	4.608	4.827
7	2.826	3.001	3.185	3.379	3.583	3.797	4.023	4.259	4.508	4.768	5.042	5.329	5.629	5.945	6.275
8	3.278	3.511	3.759	4.021	4.300	4.595	4.908	5.239	5.590	5.960	6.353	6.768	7.206	7.669	8.157
9	3.803	4.108	4.435	4.785	5.160	5.560	5.987	6.444	6.931	7.451	8.005	8.595	9.223	9.893	10.60
10	4.411	4.807	5.234	5.695	6.192	6.728	7.305	7.926	8.594	9.313	10.09	10.92	11.81	12.76	13.79
11	5.117	5.624	6.176	6.777	7.430	8.140	8.912	9.749	10.66	11.64	12.71	13.86	15.11	16.46	17.92
12	5.936	6.580	7.288	8.064	8.916	9.850	10.87	11.99	13.21	14.55	16.01	17.61	19.34	21.24	23.30
13	6.886	7.699	8.599	9.596	10.70	11.92	13.26	14.75	16.39	18.19	20.18	22.36	24.76	27.39	30.29
14	7.988	9.007	10.15	11.42	12.84	14.42	16.18	18.14	20.32	22.74	25.42	28.40	31.69	35.34	39.37
15	9.266	10.54	11.97	13.59	15.41	17.45	19.74	22.31	25.20	28.42	32.03	36.06	40.56	45.59	51.19
16	10.75	12.33	14.13	16.17	18.49	21.11	24.09	27.45	31.24	35.53	40.36	45.80	51.92	58.81	66.54
17	12.47	14.43	16.67	19.24	22.19	25.55	29.38	33.76	38.74	44.41	50.85	58.17	66.46	75.86	86.50
18	14.46	16.88	19.67	22.90	26.62	30.91	35.85	41.52	48.04	55.51	64.07	73.87	85.07	97.86	112.5
19	16.78	19.75	23.21	27.25	31.95	37.40	43.74	51.07	59.57	69.39	80.73	93.81	108.9	126.2	146.2
20	19.46	23.11	27.39	32.43	38.34	45.26	53.36	62.82	73.86	86.74	101.7	119.1	139.4	162.9	190.0
25	40.87	50.66	62.67	77.39	95.40	117.4	144.2	176.9	216.5	264.7	323.0	393.6	478.9	581.8	705.6
30	85.85	111.1	143.4	184.7	237.4	304.5	389.8	497.9	634.8	807.8	1026	1301	1646	2078	2620

E.g.: If the interest rate is 10 percent per year, the investment of $1 today will be worth $1.611 at the end of year 5.

Appendix Table 3 Annuity table: Present value of $1 *per year* for each of *t* years $= 1/r - 1/[r(1 + r)^t]$

Interest rate per year

Number of years	1%	2%	3%	4%	5%	6%	7%	8%	9%	10%	11%	12%	13%	14%	15%
1	.990	.980	.971	.962	.952	.943	.935	.926	.917	.909	.901	.893	.885	.877	.870
2	1.970	1.942	1.913	1.886	1.859	1.833	1.808	1.783	1.759	1.736	1.713	1.690	1.668	1.647	1.626
3	2.941	2.884	2.829	2.775	2.723	2.673	2.624	2.577	2.531	2.487	2.444	2.402	2.361	2.322	2.283
4	3.902	3.808	3.717	3.630	3.546	3.465	3.387	3.312	3.240	3.170	3.102	3.037	2.974	2.914	2.855
5	4.853	4.713	4.580	4.452	4.329	4.212	4.100	3.993	3.890	3.791	3.696	3.605	3.517	3.433	3.352
6	5.795	5.601	5.417	5.242	5.076	4.917	4.767	4.623	4.486	4.355	4.231	4.111	3.998	3.889	3.784
7	6.728	6.472	6.230	6.002	5.786	5.582	5.389	5.206	5.033	4.868	4.712	4.564	4.423	4.288	4.160
8	7.652	7.325	7.020	6.733	6.463	6.210	5.971	5.747	5.535	5.335	5.146	4.968	4.799	4.639	4.487
9	8.566	8.162	7.786	7.435	7.108	6.802	6.515	6.247	5.995	5.759	5.537	5.328	5.132	4.946	4.772
10	9.471	8.983	8.530	8.111	7.722	7.360	7.024	6.710	6.418	6.145	5.889	5.650	5.426	5.216	5.019
11	10.37	9.787	9.253	8.760	8.306	7.887	7.499	7.139	6.805	6.495	6.207	5.938	5.687	5.453	5.234
12	11.26	10.58	9.954	9.385	8.863	8.384	7.943	7.536	7.161	6.814	6.492	6.194	5.918	5.660	5.421
13	12.13	11.35	10.63	9.986	9.394	8.853	8.358	7.904	7.487	7.103	6.750	6.424	6.122	5.842	5.583
14	13.00	12.11	11.30	10.56	9.899	9.295	8.745	8.244	7.786	7.367	6.982	6.628	6.302	6.002	5.724
15	13.87	12.85	11.94	11.12	10.38	9.712	9.108	8.559	8.061	7.606	7.191	6.811	6.462	6.142	5.847
16	14.72	13.58	12.56	11.65	10.84	10.11	9.447	8.851	8.313	7.824	7.379	6.974	6.604	6.265	5.954
17	15.56	14.29	13.17	12.17	11.27	10.48	9.763	9.122	8.544	8.022	7.549	7.120	6.729	6.373	6.047
18	16.40	14.99	13.75	12.66	11.69	10.83	10.06	9.372	8.756	8.201	7.702	7.250	6.840	6.467	6.128
19	17.23	15.68	14.32	13.13	12.09	11.16	10.34	9.604	8.950	8.365	7.839	7.366	6.938	6.550	6.198
20	18.05	16.35	14.88	13.59	12.46	11.47	10.59	9.818	9.129	8.514	7.963	7.469	7.025	6.623	6.259
25	22.02	19.52	17.41	15.62	14.09	12.78	11.65	10.67	9.823	9.077	8.422	7.843	7.330	6.873	6.464
30	25.81	22.40	19.60	17.29	15.37	13.76	12.41	11.26	10.27	9.427	8.694	8.055	7.496	7.003	6.566

Interest rate per year

Number of years	16%	17%	18%	19%	20%	21%	22%	23%	24%	25%	26%	27%	28%	29%	30%
1	.862	.855	.847	.840	.833	.826	.820	.813	.806	.800	.794	.787	.781	.775	.769
2	1.605	1.585	1.566	1.547	1.528	1.509	1.492	1.474	1.457	1.440	1.424	1.407	1.392	1.376	1.361
3	2.246	2.210	2.174	2.140	2.106	2.074	2.042	2.011	1.981	1.952	1.923	1.896	1.868	1.842	1.816
4	2.798	2.743	2.690	2.639	2.589	2.540	2.494	2.448	2.404	2.362	2.320	2.280	2.241	2.203	2.166
5	3.274	3.199	3.127	3.058	2.991	2.926	2.864	2.803	2.745	2.689	2.635	2.583	2.532	2.483	2.436
6	3.685	3.589	3.498	3.410	3.326	3.245	3.167	3.092	3.020	2.951	2.885	2.821	2.759	2.700	2.643
7	4.039	3.922	3.812	3.706	3.605	3.508	3.416	3.327	3.242	3.161	3.083	3.009	2.937	2.868	2.802
8	4.344	4.207	4.078	3.954	3.837	3.726	3.619	3.518	3.421	3.329	3.241	3.156	3.076	2.999	2.925
9	4.607	4.451	4.303	4.163	4.031	3.905	3.786	3.673	3.566	3.463	3.366	3.273	3.184	3.100	3.019
10	4.833	4.659	4.494	4.339	4.192	4.054	3.923	3.799	3.682	3.571	3.465	3.364	3.269	3.178	3.092
11	5.029	4.836	4.656	4.486	4.327	4.177	4.035	3.902	3.776	3.656	3.543	3.437	3.335	3.239	3.147
12	5.197	4.988	4.793	4.611	4.439	4.278	4.127	3.985	3.851	3.725	3.606	3.493	3.387	3.286	3.190
13	5.342	5.118	4.910	4.715	4.533	4.362	4.203	4.053	3.912	3.780	3.656	3.538	3.427	3.322	3.223
14	5.468	5.229	5.008	4.802	4.611	4.432	4.265	4.108	3.962	3.824	3.695	3.573	3.459	3.351	3.249
15	5.575	5.324	5.092	4.876	4.675	4.489	4.315	4.153	4.001	3.859	3.726	3.601	3.483	3.373	3.268
16	5.668	5.405	5.162	4.938	4.730	4.536	4.357	4.189	4.033	3.887	3.751	3.623	3.503	3.390	3.283
17	5.749	5.475	5.222	4.990	4.775	4.576	4.391	4.219	4.059	3.910	3.771	3.640	3.518	3.403	3.295
18	5.818	5.534	5.273	5.033	4.812	4.608	4.419	4.243	4.080	3.928	3.786	3.654	3.529	3.413	3.304
19	5.877	5.584	5.316	5.070	4.843	4.635	4.442	4.263	4.097	3.942	3.799	3.664	3.539	3.421	3.311
20	5.929	5.628	5.353	5.101	4.870	4.657	4.460	4.279	4.110	3.954	3.808	3.673	3.546	3.427	3.316
25	6.097	5.766	5.467	5.195	4.948	4.721	4.514	4.323	4.147	3.985	3.834	3.694	3.564	3.442	3.329
30	6.177	5.829	5.517	5.235	4.979	4.746	4.534	4.339	4.160	3.995	3.842	3.701	3.569	3.447	3.332

E.g.: If the interest rate is 10 percent per year, the present value of $1 received at the end of each of the next 5 years is $3.791.

INDEX